BUREAU OF INTERNATIONAL RESEARCH
HARVARD UNIVERSITY AND RADCLIFFE COLLEGE

THE BRITISH COMMONWEALTH
AT WAR

THE

British Commonwealth

AT WAR

EDITORS

William Yandell Elliott & H. Duncan Hall

CONTRIBUTORS

WILLIAM YANDELL ELLIOTT

H. DUNCAN HALL

HEINRICH BRÜNING

CLAIRE NIX

WILLIAM S. McCAULEY

ERIC ROLL

GWENDOLEN M. CARTER

B. S. KEIRSTEAD

FRED ALEXANDER

F. L. W. WOOD

LUCRETIA ILSLEY

Essay Index Reprint Series

BOOKS FOR LIBRARIES PRESS
FREEPORT, NEW YORK

D
760
.A x 1
E45
1971

INTERNATIONAL STANDARD BOOK NUMBER:
0-8369-2106-2

LIBRARY OF CONGRESS CATALOG CARD NUMBER:
70-134072

PRINTED IN THE UNITED STATES OF AMERICA

Preface

This book was planned by Professor William Yandell Elliott before the outbreak of the war, and a grant made available for it by the Bureau of International Research of Harvard University and Radcliffe College, shortly after the war began. Some of the chapters were in first draft by 1941, while difficulties of communication especially delayed others and compelled changes of outline. As Professor Elliott undertook heavy responsibilities in connection with the war in the Office of Production Management, the bulk of the editorial work from early in 1941 fell to Mr. H. Duncan Hall. In their present form all the chapters have been revised to include events through the spring of 1942, and there are some references to later events.

The book makes no pretence at covering the whole of the vast canvas indicated by its title. Though it presents a fairly detailed picture of the British Commonwealth of Nations, fully organized for total war and nearing the peak of its great strength at the moment when the United States came finally into the war, whole sections of the story have been perforce omitted. There is no military history in the book — only passing references here and there to the great episodes. There is no chapter on the diplomatic, political, and psychological war waged by the British Commonwealth. In order to reduce the bulk of the volume the material prepared on the colonial Empire has had to be omitted. This the editors particularly regret, because a book on *The British Commonwealth at War* is obviously incomplete without details of the great contributions of the colonial Empire in man power, money, and vital resources or the strategical importance of certain key points like Colombo, Gibraltar, Aden, and Malta. Dictates of space, and the neutrality of Eire, have also resulted in the omission of a long chapter on Ireland's constitutional, political, and economic situation.

There is some disproportion in the space allotted to the different parts of the Commonwealth. The emphasis put upon the English system of war administration and the more elaborate treatment of such problems as labor and finance in Great Britain are due to the much greater impor-

v

tance of the organization of the United Kingdom, not only to the war effort, but in so far as it illustrates the organization of a highly industrialized country for war. It therefore offers a useful basis of comparison not only with our problems in the United States but also with the methods by which similar problems have been handled in the other countries of the Commonwealth.

The central emphasis of the book is twofold: first, how the British Commonwealth, as a whole, worked as a political instrument and a mutual security system under the impact of the war, and the effect of the war on its political, psychological, and constitutional structure; and second, how the British democracies and India adapted or transformed their political, administrative, and economic systems to fight a total war. The book is a study of democracy in action not merely on a national but also an international scale, since it deals with a unique international democratic organization of states.

The preparation of the book has been beset by difficulties inseparable from any attempt to make an objective and authoritative study of so vast and complex an organization as the British Commonwealth under the stress of the war. Information has not always been easy to obtain. But the thanks of the editors are due to a number of people in official positions in various parts of the Empire, particularly in the British Embassy in Washington, the British Library of Information in New York, the legations of the British Dominions in Washington, the offices of the British and of the Dominion High Commissioners in Ottawa, and the official representatives of India in New York and Washington, for freely giving their time and supplying valuable information without which the book could not easily have been completed. War conditions increased the difficulties of preparing and publishing a book contributed to by collaborators dispersed throughout the English-speaking world. The embarrassing promptness of some of the collaborators in delivering their manuscripts, for which the editors were grateful, nevertheless, confronted them with the difficulty, which they have failed in some cases to overcome, of keeping the prompt chapters up to date while waiting for the late comers. Some material went astray for reasons unknown — enemy action, or "friendly" censor, or merely perhaps loss in the mails.

The editors have done their best to coordinate the different chapters, but, apart from some unavoidable cutting, the authors remain responsible for their contributions. The chapter on India has been left anonymous because, apart from the editors, a number of people supplied material for it. We are indebted to Miss Claire Nix and Miss Edith Haley for the great pains to which they have been put to hold the book together through various stages and for their efforts to see it into print.

W. Y. E.

H. D. H.

CONTENTS

THE BRITISH COMMONWEALTH
AT WAR

CHAPTER I

Introduction

by William Yandell Elliott

At the critical turning point in the war marked by the landing of Allied forces in Algeria and Morocco, after a cumulative series of disasters to the arms of the United Nations had shaken the faith of many as to its ultimate outcome, it is more than ever necessary to take stock of the war effort of the British Commonwealth of Nations.

Prompted by the shortages of tin and rubber that have already shown their effects, the dullest mind can have no doubt of the importance of the British Empire to the safety and defense of the United States. As shortages appear in many other essential war materials, this lesson will be driven home in unmistakable terms. The isolationists who asked, what interest had we in the fate of Britain's armies and Britain's Empire, who inquired why we should do battle for Singapore and the Dutch East Indies, why indeed we should not retire to our own shores and prepare ourselves against all comers, are now finding a brutal answer. Our own shores are not safe from attack; our continent is not self-sufficient for war.

The answer first was made plain in the shock of Pearl Harbor and the disaster to American arms by the sudden onslaught of Japan. It was brought home by the efforts of German submarines to blockade not only our own coasts but the Caribbean. Supplies from abroad that were essential to our war effort were suddenly threatened, and the very movement of gasoline and oil necessary to our whole economy in coastwise shipping has been tragically endangered.

Not only the manganese, chromite, tungsten, antimony, cobalt, and other minerals on which the war effort depends, but the supplies of the vital fibers, of many fats and oils, almost equally essential, are being seriously cut down by the loss of sea control in some vital areas of the war.

The civilian population has already begun to feel the pinch, not only in depleted supplies of sugar, coffee, and possibly other things that it has not been necessary or possible to ration, but in the inability to produce enough wool adequately to maintain civilian supplies of clothing. Bananas and cocoa have followed not far behind, with many other diminished imports that will cause dislocation and want.

These facts form an object lesson to all those who asked in the past, " Why defend American beyond its own shores? " Many of them who were prepared to defend South America as a duty to our own security in supply are learning with alarm that South America is not enough, and that its defense simply adds an insupportable burden if we are not to carry the war to the enemy; or if we were forced to fight alone on two ocean fronts, to say nothing of safeguarding the sea lanes in the far areas of the world from which some of the most necessary of our war supplies come.

Viewed in the simplest terms, the situation which has been critical and well-nigh desperate with the British fleet still in the picture would have been next to hopeless if the British Commonwealth had not been kept fighting. Our sheer self-interest in the preservation of England as the main front base of our own defense against Hitler has long been apparent to all who think at all. Even if England and her Empire were to go down today, we should have had those precious months, even years, of preparation without which we should have faced the fleets of Germany and her satellites, probably including Vichy, on the one flank and, who knows, perhaps the fleet of a Vichified England as well, and on the other the full weight of the Japanese onslaught.

The only answer that those who still criticize aid to Britain, Russia, China, the Dutch, and Australia can make to this analysis is that Japan would have been satisfied without attempting to smash us, and that Hitler would have permitted us to remain unarmed masters of the Western Hemisphere. It passes belief that men of good faith, now fully aware of the nature both of Hitler's and of Japan's ambitions, can ask to sacrifice the Allies who gave us precious time to arm, and who, if we can only ourselves support them adequately, can make victory possible. Are they of good faith who suggest this course?

Presumably, some of the revelations of the investigation into Mr. Viereck's activities in franking out German propaganda through both senators and representatives in our own Congress, *with their full knowledge* of the source of the material and of its objects, should teach us as a nation something of what we must do to protect our own sources of information, even official sources.

It is worth while commenting on some of the popular misconceptions fostered by those who did not need Mr. Viereck to prompt them after their line was taken, and they were committed to it. They seized on Churchill's remark, made in a mood of generous concession to the American Congress, that Pearl Harbor might not have been such a disaster had we not sacrificed planes to Britain and Russia. The plain fact, and it has been adequately attested by the report of the Roberts Commission, is that we had planes and ships entirely adequate to defend Pearl Harbor. The humiliating thing is that some of those planes and many of those ships were knocked out by a surprise that should never have been permitted, and that could not have been avoided by not sending planes to Britain or Russia. Indeed, it was the assumption, sedulously planted by isolationists, that we could not be attacked which led to the carelessness of the divided command at Hawaii. It was a state of mind which this country threw off with great reluctance. Mr. Churchill, in his broadcast made in the nadir of the depression that followed the loss of Singapore, said of the entry of the United States into the war, " That is what I have dreamed of, aimed at and worked for, and now it has come to pass." His language was of course seized upon by those who felt that our entry into the war was engineered by Great Britain. There is no question that Britain had desperately to depend on our full support and must have worked in exactly the way that Mr. Churchill described. On the other hand, the event that brought us into the war was not a further attack on Thailand or the Malay Peninsula or an overflow of Japanese forces towards Rangoon, but a carefully conceived blow at our own naval power. The war overflowed on us, as it was bound to do unless we conceded Japan control of the entire Pacific.

Japan, at least since the days of the Tanaka Memorial in 1927, and probably from the generation that followed the war with Russia, has understood the simple strategy of mastery. She could not accomplish her ends in the Pacific, and after that in South America and elsewhere, without crippling the United States. The Tanaka Memorial itself stated that Japan could not crush China without first crushing the United States. We had been given ample warning of her intention. Its realization was simply made more possible by the necessity we were under of meeting attack in the Atlantic as well.

The complexity of the strategy of a true world war, totally unlike the simple operations of the first so-called World War, staggers the minds of simple persons unused even to maps and totally free of any conception of the real struggle for world mastery that Germany and Japan have planned. Had we been more powerful, we might have driven a bargain with them, as Colonel Lindbergh and others suggested, and helped to divide the world with them, even joining in attacks on the weakened Empire of Britain and assisting in the destruction of Russia. But without the overwhelming strength that would have made such a bargain possible, regardless of its hideous moral implications, we had little to offer as an ally beyond the consent of impotence.

At this time the preservation of the British Empire in its main outlines and the restoration of a world in which the principles of the British Commonwealth can be extended to India more really than the governing class of England have previously been willing to consider become prime objectives in our war aims as well as our peace aims. It is not only that this great reserve of wealth and man power, if turned over to our enemies, would upset the future balance of the world so that our children's children would have to redress it if we were to be a free nation. The raw materials on which our industrial salvation desperately depends come in the main from areas that we must protect through the ability to protect not only South America, but South Africa and the Indian Ocean.

That is what makes the war effort of Australia and the war effort of South Africa, the war effort of New Zealand, the war effort of Canada, the dogged holding of the United Kingdom through slow starvation and imminent peril of invasion, essential to any American safety at the present time, and more than essential to any ultimate victory. In dark periods ahead, when disappointment may shake the stoutest hearts, it is essential never to forget that the will to victory must be fanned by our efforts and our help in those hearts that can aid us to victory. To maintain South Africa against wavering, to strengthen Australia as a future base to retake the Pacific, to join Canada in a mighty continental effort as one great North American war machine, these things are essential.

We must, it is clear, be able to maintain the supplies to ourselves on which the supplies to all others depend. Those ships that are carrying aid to the defense of others and to support offensives also bring back our supplies. Manganese for our steel mills, chromite, on which our whole war effort depends, mica, without which no plane flies, graphite, without which crucibles are at best reduced to a very low efficiency and must in many cases be completely altered, these depend upon control of the Indian Ocean. This is to say nothing of rubber and tin, the loss of which we are already beginning to count in terms of economic disloca- tion and the possible stagnation of our own domestic transportation system. The fibers for the ropes of our whole naval program, the fats and oils on which we depend for glycerine for explosives, as well as the molasses and other ingredients of ethyl alcohol for the same program, the nitrates and the copper of Chile as well as Bolivian tin, all these depend upon sea control. Japan could interdict us from South America and the Pacific with far greater success than Germany has had on our Atlantic coast if we did not make that move impossible by retaining bases past which Japan does not dare proceed and by denying her those bases without which her fleet cannot operate successfully in these waters.

It is of little use to bemoan the strategy that did not keep three hun- dred planes at Singapore as a minimum reserve, with the possibility of adding other hundreds within weeks rather than months. The planes that were then concentrated for American defense, had they been usable at Singapore, could have turned the whole tide of that operation, and could have provided the umbrella for the Prince of Wales and the Repulse, the loss of which so grievously upset the whole balance of naval power. Judgment has been entered on that chapter of omission. It was a tragic judgment, but its lesson was plain. We had to defend more adequately, and the British had to defend more adequately, the central areas of sea control. That is what the American people must understand in terms of the essential strategy of this war. To defend ourselves is to carry the war to the enemy and to prevent him from overrunning those island chains that give him the control which we have for long taken for granted. Freedom of the seas for war has not had really to be fought for by our nation since 1812.

Freedom of the seas, in short, means not a legal conception of ability to trade with neutrals or to enjoy without effort the large blessings of naval control; it means a desperate struggle now and henceforth to preserve that naval control against an alien balance of power brought to bear on our antiquated fleets, whittled down by years of pacifism and of isolationism.

Freedom of the seas, for that reason, means the maintenance of the British Commonwealth of Nations as our own front line. It means preserving, no matter what goes down, the essential areas, Australia, South Africa, if possible India, and at all cost the United Kingdom itself. The string of islands across the Indian Ocean, the Mauritius, Amirantes, and Seychelles Islands, the Maldive, and the Laccadive Islands would screen the Indian Ocean if we controlled Ceylon and Madagascar, even if the Indian frontier and the Andaman Islands should have gone down. To hold them is as essential as to hold Australia and New Zealand.

To whom shall we look for the protection of these areas? Not to ourselves alone; it is clear that we are unequal to the whole task. It is equally clear that the British and their dominions alone are unequal to the task. That was what Churchill's words in his Singapore speech really meant. Without the preservation of the huge man power of China and of Russia in the picture, we and the British together might not be equal to the task.

That is why an honest assessment of the war effort of the British Commonwealth, in order that we may judge our own responsibilities and what lies ahead of us to secure victory, is essential in the formulation of American strategy. That Empire as a world empire holds the key to world control. A study of its resources, of its politics, of the strategy of its defense, of its war production, is a vital element to every calculation we now must make to assure our own victory.

More than that, an understanding of this war effort and what it means will do more than any other single thing to allay the real anger and anguish that we as a people felt in seeing Singapore go down and in judging the British at fault.

In any unexpected reverse, the greatest problem is to keep Allies pulling together. The very human tendency is for each to blame the other. Both are to blame, but blame is of small use except as a spring board to profit by the lessons of defeat and turn them into victory. It is essential to maintain in the American people the courage that carried Washington through the darkest hours of the Revolution because of his unwavering faith in his cause. It is essential to call on the same courage that carried Lincoln through the Civil War. The backing that leadership will get will depend of course on the leadership itself. It is also essential in these times to provide those who must back the leader with the knowledge of what democracies elsewhere have been able to do and what we may expect of them. That is the object of this book.

It is a book hastily put together, partly out of date as it was being written, bound to be out of date before it is in print. It does not show as it might the failures of a complacent old Empire or of a smug ruling class that nurtured up its own destroyers. It does not analyze either the dry rot of easy habits of rule, or the courage that won the Battle of Britain. But it does give an idea of the scope of Britain's effort, of her weaknesses as well as her strength, of the administrative and political problems of the dominions as well as Britain, of her man power and her machine power.

It is interesting for an American to contrast Mr. Duncan Hall's emphasis on psychological factors and traditional institutions with Dr. Brüning's more analytical treatment of administrative problems. The book seems to me the more valuable for the contrast and the representation of different points of view. In this way it may stand a chance of being more than a tract for the times, such as books written under the compulsion of war emotions tend to be. At least it stands, by the contribution of it of the former German Chancellor, as a sign of hope for the international community of scholarship.

CHAPTER II

The British Commonwealth of Nations in War and Peace

by H. Duncan Hall

1. The Opening of the War Books

The closely guarded British War Book, wherein is set out in detail the whole complex procedure for the change-over from peace to war in Great Britain and the Empire, was taken from its safe and opened in Whitehall just before Munich, in September 1938. The similar War Books were opened at the same time in Ottawa, Canberra, Wellington, Pretoria, and Delhi. The " precautionary stage " telegram required by the War Book was dispatched to all parts of the British Empire warning them that war was likely to break out, thus enabling them to take their preliminary dispositions — such as ordering their naval vessels to their prearranged stations, manning coastal batteries, securing the safety of their shipping, looking after enemy shipping, controlling exchange. The actual " war telegram," announcing that war had broken out, was not sent then because of the postponement made possible by the Munich Conference.[1] But the War Books remained open. In some parts of the Empire they

---

[1] For the procedure in 1914 see Ernest Scott, *Australia during the War: Official History of Australia in the War of 1914–1918*, Vol. XI, p. 6 f.

were given a thorough revision in the light of the experience thus gained. When, twelve months later, the " war telegram " was finally dispatched from Whitehall to the dominions and to India and the colonies, the whole vast, international system of the British Empire and Commonwealth, composed of some sixty separate administrations, intermeshed as a single war machine.

To describe the legal and administrative processes involved in this act of " going to war " would require a large volume. The mere texts of the Orders-in-Council issued from London through the Colonial Office, and extending to all colonial dependencies the Emergency Powers (Defense) Act of August 1939, and the Local Defense Regulations issued in each colonial territory, covering the field of economic warfare as well as other essential measures of civil and military defense, would fill another. And the similar legislation, statutory orders, and regulations issued in the self-governing dominions and India would fill at least another stout volume. A study of these laws, orders, and regulations — issued everywhere in the scores of separate administrative capitals in the name of the common Crown — and of the actual carrying into effect of this legislation in the various countries and territories, would convey a better understanding of the real meaning of the British Empire than any study of mere constitutional theory. If the machinery, especially on the side of economic warfare, worked more smoothly and with greater speed than in 1914, it was due to several reasons: first, because the lessons learned and the precedents established in the First World War had not been forgotten; second, because of the experience gained in applying limited economic sanctions against Italy in 1935; and third, because of the chance to overhaul the machinery afforded by the false start of Munich.

But though the machinery geared in smoothly enough, was unity real or illusory? The answer is clear. When at the outset of the war Mr. Menzies, the Australian Prime Minister, spoke of this unity and of the spirit behind it, his words were typical of hundreds of declarations coming from all parts of the Empire except Eire: " We know," he said, " that the British nations throughout the world are at one. There is unity in the Empire ranks — one King, one flag, one cause. We stand with Britain." The dominions, it may be said, were free and adult nations; but what of the dependent colonies? As the Under-Secretary of State for the Colonies said in the House of Commons on November 20, 1940, " The outbreak of hostilities was the signal for a unanimous outburst of loyalty and support from all parts of the colonial Empire." [2] The free gifts given by every conceivable body in all of the colonies had reached in the first year of the war " the wonderful total " of £17,000,000. And, in addition, many millions had been expended by the various small communities on local defense. They gave the enemy no aid or comfort in Britain's darkest hours. Some were to fall because of weak links in the defenses of the oceanic Empire; but none by defection.

However it is looked at, this spontaneous solidarity stands out as a unique and remarkable fact. In 1917 General Smuts in a famous speech in London referred to the British Commonwealth of Nations as " the only League of Nations that has ever existed." The League of Nations born of the First World War did not survive twenty summers. But the British league weathered the tempest that destroyed the new League. When the League of Nations collapsed there fell with it a vast complex of still-born treaties, multilateral pacts, nonaggression treaties, and alliances built up by a generation of lawyers and statesmen at Geneva. But something else more fatal had happened: the very lifeblood of mutual trust and loyalty had frozen in the veins of international society.

War in the past has played a far greater part in moulding and reshaping the British Empire than is usually realized. The way in which this Second World War is reshaping the Empire-Commonwealth, how its political, constitutional, and technical machinery has stood the test, how the Commonwealth has actually functioned during the War, the real nature of its inner cohesion — this is the subject to be explored in the following pages.

The terms " Empire " and " Commonwealth " are used here more or less synonymously in accordance with the usage of official documents. Historically the term " Empire " was first applied to England to denote not domination but rather the independence and equal sovereignty of England; that is, its complete freedom from any external control like that of the Holy Roman Empire. This is its essential meaning in the famous Statute 24 of Henry VIII — before Britain had colonies — which declared, " This realme of England is an Empire." The term " Commonwealth " came to be used to denote the possession of internal liberty. It was because of the growth inside the old historical Empire of a group of autonomous self-governing states, " freely associated " with the Mother Country and each other, that the term " British Commonwealth " began to be current about the time of the First World War.

---

[2] *Journal of the Parliaments of the Empire*, Vol. XXI, p. 32.

The term "The British Commonwealth of Nations" was first used in an official document in the Anglo-Irish Treaty of December 6, 1921, and in the Irish Free State Constitution Act of the Imperial Parliament, 1922.

The relation of the British Empire and the British Commonwealth is most authoritatively indicated in the Report of the Inter-Imperial Relations Committee of the Imperial Conference of 1926.[3] The Committee's report deals with "one most important element" in the Empire which had now "reached its full development — we refer to the group of self-governing communities composed of Great Britain and the Dominions. . . . *They are autonomous Communities within the British Empire, equal in status, in no way subordinate one to another in any aspect of their domestic or external affairs, though united by a common allegiance to the Crown, and freely associated as members of the British Commonwealth of Nations.*"

To Nazi leaders, watching restlessly for signs of weakness in an opponent, this whole process of constitutional development which had turned an Empire into a Commonwealth of Nations, each member of which, in the words of the Balfour Report, "is now master of its destiny," was a clear sign of disintegration. When their own rearmament, their militarization of the Rhineland, and the taking over of Austria and the Sudetenland were met by appeasement, their judgment was confirmed. There is little doubt that Hitler invaded Poland in 1939 believing that neither England nor France would fight.

It is important to note that the policy of appeasement was not merely the policy of the Government of Neville Chamberlain. It was a policy shared in varying degrees by all the dominion cabinets and persisted in until the fall of Prague in March 1939. It was as near to being a common foreign policy of the whole British Commonwealth as any policy since 1919.

To those who desired the fall of the British Empire the signs seemed therefore propitious. It was not strange that in Berlin, Rome, and Tokyo, from 1937 onwards, there was incessant talk, some in the open and more underground, of the vast changes that were about to come in the frontiers, of the world and in the distribution of power as a result of the fall of the British Empire — changes more vast than those which followed upon the decline and fall of the Roman Empire.

---

[3] Cmd. 2768, 1926.

2. *The Commonwealth and the League*

Looked at from the outside nothing could have seemed more striking than the contrast between the British Commonwealth and the League of Nations. The former was gradually shedding its constitutional ties while the League was feverishly building a more and more intricate spider-web of contractual relations between its members. On one side stood the members of the Commonwealth busy removing all outworn bonds that might suggest any inequality of status and emphasizing the *freedom* of their association. This " freedom " included the absence of clearly defined commitments to come to each other's assistance or to submit disputes between themselves to any form of court or arbitral tribunal. On the other side stood the members of the League busy trying to strengthen their association by weaving between themselves an increasingly intricate pattern of treaties of mutual assistance and nonaggression. But the appearance was in fact very different from the reality. The British democracies, in shedding some of the legal structure of the old Empire, were clearing the decks for more effective action as a Commonwealth of " freely associated " nations; whilst at Geneva the growing mountain of paper was a sure sign of the malaise and weakness of the League. It was a modern instance of the endless weaving of legal formulae that went on in primitive intertribal assemblies, as in the Althing of mediaeval Iceland.[4] It was magic-thinking of the kind indulged in by primitive societies which sought, by the creation of magical formulae, to buttress up from the outside, as it were, their own lack of inner strength and cohesion.

The period in which the emphasis was laid by the British Dominions upon status, rather than upon their common interests and their obligations as members of the British Commonwealth, lasted for little more than fifteen years; it ended roughly in 1935, when the world began to be once more manifestly unsafe for small powers. The dominions which placed the most emphasis upon status were Canada, the most secure of all the dominions, and Eire and South Africa which, because some of their population had recently been at war with Britain, were under a deep psychological necessity to assert their independence. Australia and New Zealand, the most exposed to danger from war, the most British in the composition of their populations, the most free from memories of past friction with Britain, placed far less emphasis upon status and far

---

[4] See, for example, *The Burnt Njal Saga.*

more upon the sharing of mutual obligations with the other members of the Commonwealth and the making of contributions to the common defense. Neither Australia nor New Zealand had even taken the trouble to adopt the Statute of Westminster, so that legally the British Parliament could still pass laws extending to them — although, as the Statute itself states in its preamble, it would not be in accordance with " the established constitutional position " if the Parliament of the United Kingdom were to attempt to do so " otherwise than at the request and with the consent " of their governments.[4a]

Yet the continued existence of the legal power of the Imperial Parliament, unchanged by the Statute of Westminster, to legislate for any member state of the British Commonwealth, if it so requests, serves as a reminder of the underlying unity of the Empire.

Looked at from the inside, before the war, the Empire gave little of the appearance of imminent dissolution that seemed so clear to its enemies when they looked from the outside through veils of misunderstanding and wishful thinking. The pulling down of an old and out-of-date façade helped rather to reveal the solid lines of the structure. More was done in these years to rebuild what had been pulled down than was commonly realized. It was true that the rebuilding did not take the form of new contractual bonds. It consisted rather of the typically British expedients of conventions or understandings and new methods of consultation and cooperation.

There was considerable rebuilding of this sort in two directions after 1919. First, new and more effective machinery for the handling of foreign affairs was set up in the dominions, each of which created Departments of External Affairs.[5] In the second place, there was a great development in the free and rapid communication of information on foreign affairs between the parts of the Commonwealth, the setting up of an intra-Empire diplomatic system, and of closer liaison between the various defense departments. The danger of divergence in foreign policies was met in part by agreement upon new constitutional conventions of a positive character imposing the duty of consulting with one an-

---

[4a] In October 1942 the Government of Australia decided, because of practical difficulties in the drafting of legislation, to introduce a bill for the ratification of the statute.

[5] The first Department of External Affairs in any dominion was set up in Australia in 1901. It was dispersed in 1916 but reconstituted and attached to the Prime Minister's department in 1921. As is the practice in the other dominions, the Prime Minister usually held also the Portfolio of External Affairs. From 1934 the portfolio was held separately, and in 1935 a separate department was set up with two divisions, the Political Section and the International Cooperation Section. See *Annual Report of the Department of External Affairs*, Canberra, 1936. Appendix A.

other before taking action in foreign affairs and defense.[6]

The smooth functioning of the British Commonwealth on the eve of the war was due in no small measure to the fact that its statesmen had been for many years in frequent personal contact with each other at London, in Geneva, and elsewhere; that its leading officials in the departments dealing with foreign affairs and defense and economic matters had frequent personal contact with their opposite numbers. It was due also in a measure to the ceaseless work of the Empire Parliamentary Association, through its branches in all the Parliaments of the Empire, in bringing into close personal contact through conferences and by other means, a large number of the members of the Parliaments of the Empire. Because men knew one another, because they realized they had certain vital ideas and interests in common and acted upon the same unspoken fundamental assumptions, they were able to work together with a minimum of friction.[6a]

An explanation of the character of the British Commonwealth will not be found in any legal formulae or constitutional documents. The peoples of the Commonwealth are bound together by a multiplicity of institutional ties; but these are not gathered together in any logical or uniform system. Even a general concept like that of " equality of status " covers the utmost diversity of constitutional relationships. Each dominion with " dominion status " has its own peculiar relationship to Great Britain determined by many different factors drawn from its past history and present condition. One has adopted the Statute of Westminster, and another has not. One has special agreements regulating the utilization by the British navy of naval bases, another not — because it takes such use completely for granted. South Africa and Eire have their own Great Seal; Canada, Australia, and New Zealand use the Great Seal of the United Kingdom when they want to have issued by the King full powers to plenipotentiaries to negotiate and sign treaties. The governors of the Australian states are still able to act as agents of the British Government. The Governor-General on the other hand is no longer an agent or representative of the British Government, but (in the words of

[6] E.g., the decisions taken by the Imperial Conferences of 1923 and 1926 regarding prior notification or consultation in all negotiations affecting foreign relations. " Thus, no sooner had equality of status been recognized, and the right of each Dominion to formulate its own foreign policy been extended, by inference, indefinitely, than a convention was established to limit the exercise of that right in the interests of Commonwealth solidarity." *The British Empire*, Royal Institute of International Affairs, London, 1937, p. 218.

[6a] See *The Community of the Parliaments of the British Commonwealth* by H. Duncan Hall in the *American Political Science Review*, December 1942.

the Imperial Conference of 1926) the "representative of the Crown," acting in the role of a constitutional monarch.

With all this great diversity goes also a remarkable fluidity. There is fluidity in procedure and the working of institutions. The dominions in some capitals have their own diplomatic agents, but all of them including Eire use in many parts of the world the services of British diplomats and consular officials. It was even possible in November 1939 for a new member of the Australian Cabinet (who happened to be in Ottawa when selected) to be sworn in as an Australian Minister of the Crown by Lord Tweedsmuir, Governor-General of Canada, acting by request of Lord Gowrie, Governor-General of Australia. An Australian Prime Minister, Mr. Menzies, addressed the Canadian House of Commons from the floor of the House. The King on a visit to Canada in 1939 acted as King of Canada. "In person," he said on his return, "I presided over the Canadian Parliament at Ottawa, and assented to legislation; in person I received the credentials of the new Minister of Canada's great and friendly neighbor, the United States; in person I signed the Trade Treaty between the two countries."

There is the same fluidity in the matter of personnel. A Canadian becomes prime minister of Great Britain, and an ex-prime minister of Canada becomes a British peer. The Australian Minister in Washington, Mr. R. G. Casey, is suddenly appointed a member of the British War Cabinet and charged as Minister of State with the coordination of the Empire war effort in the Near and Middle East. Englishmen, Scotsmen, Welshmen, and Irishmen become prime ministers of the dominions. The late Prime Minister of New Zealand (Mr. Savage) was an Australian; the present Prime Minister (Mr. Fraser) was a Scotsman; and the Deputy Prime Minister (Mr. Nash) was an Englishman. Australians become British diplomats and command ships of the Royal Navy, and British naval officers serve in the Royal Australian Navy. In this diversity and fluidity — or as Winston Churchill put it " the glorious resilience and flexibility of our ancient institutions " — lies part of the secret of the strength of the Empire and its capacity to absorb shocks.

3. The Effect of the Failure of the League on Commonwealth Foreign Policy

At the last Imperial Conference to be held before the war, that of 1937, a cold wind was already blowing from Germany and there was less talk of status and autonomy than at any Imperial Conference held since 1918. Eire was absent. Prime ministers from the dominions were eager to point out that the great constitutional changes had not impaired the inner cohesion of the Commonwealth. The Australian Prime Minister, Mr. Lyons, said, " Despite the forebodings of some who saw in this development a threat to Imperial unity, never has the Empire been more united." And the British Prime Minister, Mr. Chamberlain, in his final speech, emphasized the " profoundly impressive " " solidarity of opinion " " on all big issues," despite the great diversity of the Empire.[7]

It was in this spirit that the whole range of foreign affairs was examined. Statements were made by each of the prime ministers of " the views of their respective governments." But " no attempt was made to formulate commitments which in any event could not be made effective until approved and confirmed by the respective Parliaments."

In this connection it is of interest to note that in 1937 for the first time in the history of the constitutional relations of the Empire, a Conference of Parliaments was held alongside and linked organically with the Conference of Governments. The conference of representatives of all parties in the Parliaments of the Empire was held shortly before the Imperial Conference of Governments. This interlinking was achieved by the arrangement made by the Empire Parliamentary Association, in calling the Parliamentary Conference, that the head of each parliamentary delegation should be a cabinet minister who was also a member of the subsequent Imperial Conference. It was thus possible to estimate in the Empire Parliamentary Conference the measure of unity likely to be attained by members of all parties in the various parliaments on any given question. If this expedient could have been adopted earlier in the postwar period, it might have enabled the prime ministers gathered in the Imperial conferences to coordinate more easily the foreign policies of their countries, and to agree upon a joint policy with the reasonable assurance that they would have their parliaments behind them.

But there was one great difficulty in coming to agreement on more than general principles in such Empire conferences. The common unifying principle on which the policies of each government and the general policy of the group, had been based — namely, the League of Nations — had been deliberately attacked by Japan, Italy, and Germany. As the Australian Prime Minister put it in 1937, " Of recent years the declared policy of the British Nations has been based on the League's

---

[7] *Summary of Proceedings,* Cmd. 5482, 1937, p. 53.

concept of permanent peace insured by the principles of conciliation, arbitration, and collective action. These principles constituted a focal point for a common Empire policy." It had not always been thus. Because of the use of the League made by Eire and South Africa to consolidate their independence, the League had seemed to many up to about 1930 to be an instrument of division rather than a unifying principle. But the great aggressions from 1931–37 made the League and its principles a rallying point for the Empire.

It was on the basis of these principles that the Empire had pursued a common policy in imposing sanctions upon Italy after the invasion of Abyssinia in 1935. Now that this basis had been shot away, through the failure of the nations to collaborate effectively by means of the League machinery to check Italy and to prevent the German remilitarization of the Rhineland, on what principles could the British Commonwealth fall back?

The Imperial Conference of 1937 gave no outward sign that it had discovered any. All that it could do was to state its " close agreement upon a number of general propositions," which amounted to a restatement of several of the general political and moral principles on which the Covenant of the League itself was founded. But in the discussions on defense, there was given the real answer to the attempt of the Axis powers to disintegrate the Empire by diplomatic and psychological war. The members of the British Commonwealth had their own inner mutual security system. The *outer rampart* of general collective security having been breached, the members of the British Commonwealth fell back upon the *middle rampart* — the mutual security system of the Commonwealth itself — and they began at the same time to strengthen the *inner ramparts* of national defense.

4. The Impact of the War upon the Commonwealth

I · HOW THE EMPIRE WENT TO WAR

The differing procedures adopted by the Dominions in entering the war throw some light on the nature of the British Commonwealth. Above all they illustrate the diversity which underlies such phrases as " dominion status." The procedures ran all the way from the separate and formal declaration of war on behalf of Canada, made by the King on the advice of his Canadian ministers, through the less formal procedures of Australia and New Zealand, to the extreme of complete neutrality in Eire. The Canadian procedure implied the doctrine of the divisibility of the Crown. The procedures of Australia and New Zealand were based on the conception of the unity of the Crown, and embodied the doctrine, " When the King is at war we are at war." In Canada and South Africa the procedure was adopted of securing a decision by Parliament; and only when Parliament had decided was the formal declaration of war issued.[8] In Australia and New Zealand, Parliament later approved unanimously the action already taken by the Government in declaring the existence of a state of war immediately upon the notification of Great Britain that she was at war with Germany.

It was not until September 10, 1939, seven days after Britain was at war with Germany, that a proclamation was issued in Ottawa declaring that " a state of war with the German Reich exists and has existed in our Dominion of Canada as from the tenth day of September, 1939." The procedure, as the Prime Minister outlined it to the House on the 11th, was intricate. Following the acceptance of an address from the Throne by the House on the 9th, the Cabinet had met and had decided, on the advice of the King's Privy Council of Canada, to forward a petition to the King with a view to the authorization by him of the issue of a proclamation declaring a state of war. The series of steps taken were: concurrence by the Privy Council; approval by the Governor-General; cabling of instructions to the High Commissioner in London; the submission of a petition to the King in London; his assent at 11:15 a.m. on September 10; and finally the publishing of the proclamation in Ottawa, an hour and ten minutes later, in a special edition of *The Canada Gazette*. There are many other details in the Canadian procedure which have to be taken into account in drawing any deductions from it in support of constitutional theories regarding the divisibility of the Crown or Dominion neutrality. Reference is made to some of these points in the discussion below regarding neutrality.

In Australia and New Zealand no separate proclamation of a state of war was issued by the King on behalf of these dominions. A few minutes after the British Prime Minister's broadcast announcement from London on September 3, 8 p.m. Australian time, that Britain was at war, the Australian ministers met in Melbourne, and approved a proclamation to be issued by the Executive Council declaring a state of war. Then the Australian Prime Minister at 9:15 p.m. broadcast to the Australian people a statement announcing that " Great Britain has declared war, and,

---

8 See Chapter X, on the South African declaration.

as a result, Australia is also at war." The proclamation appeared immediately afterwards in a special issue of the *Commonwealth Gazette*, No. 63, of September 3, 1939, and began with these words:

EXISTENCE OF WAR

PROCLAMATION

. . . I, the Governor General . . . acting with the advice of the Federal Executive Council, do hereby proclaim the existence of war.

This was, however, in the nature of an internal notification required under the Australian Defense Act, 1903–39. So far as New Zealand and Australia were concerned, the declaration of a state of war from an international point of view was an action taken at their request and on their behalf, by Great Britain as the leading state in the British Commonwealth of Nations. (Incidentally Great Britain had diplomatic representation in Berlin, which Australia and New Zealand had not.) The nature of this part of the procedure is shown by the telegram from the Government of New Zealand received in London on September 3.[9] The telegram refers to " the intimation just received that a state of war exists between the United Kingdom and Germany." It went on to associate His Majesty's Government in New Zealand with the British action with which they " entirely concur ":

The existence of a state of war with Germany has accordingly been proclaimed in New Zealand and H. M. New Zealand Government would be grateful if H. M. Government in the United Kingdom would take any steps that may be necessary to indicate to the German Government that H. M. Government in New Zealand associate themselves in this matter with the action taken by H. M. Government in the United Kingdom.

There was nothing doubtful about this procedure; it was clear-cut. It was based explicitly on the constitutional principle held firmly by most Australian and New Zealand statesmen and constitutional lawyers that " when the Empire (or the King) is at war, we are at war." Some at least of the leading statesmen and constitutional lawyers of Canada and South Africa have always adhered to the same constitutional principle. If there is division of opinion as to whether the " dominion status " of Canada and South Africa is actually in accordance with this constitu-

---

[9] *The Times*, London, September 4, 1939.

tional principle, there is no such division in Australia and New Zealand.[10]

Australia's declarations of war against Japan, Finland, Rumania, and Hungary were an important departure from former procedure. In these cases war was declared by the Governor-General under power specially assigned to him by the King to declare war against these four specifically mentioned countries. This power was issued by the King on the exclusive advice of the Australian Government.[11]

The case of South Africa is again different. Under the Status of the Union Act, 1934, the Governor-General of South Africa, acting on the advice of his South African ministers, is empowered to exercise the external prerogatives of the Crown, which include the proclamation of neutrality. The view held by some statesmen and lawyers in South Africa, especially General Hertzog, that this Act (together with the Royal Executive Functions and Seals Act, 1934,[12] the Statute of Westminster, 1931, and the Balfour Report, 1926) implied a right of secession and of neutrality, and gave a legal basis for the theory of the divisibility of the Crown, is not accepted by some other leading statesmen and lawyers, including some Afrikaners as well as British. For example, neither General Smuts, the present Prime Minister, nor Mr. Hofmeyer, Minister of Finance, has accepted these interpretations of the meaning of dominion status in South Africa. Mr. Hofmeyer in the debate on entry into the war declared that " he had, as a matter of constitutional theory, con-

---

10 For this reason such statements as " The legal divisibility of the Crown even on the issue of peace or war may now be taken as established," go too far. H. V. Hodson, " The British Empire," *Pamphlets on World Affairs*, No. 2, New York, 1939.

11 The Minister of External Affairs, Dr. H. V. Evatt, explained the procedure to Parliament on December 16 as follows: " As to the procedure adopted, there are three comments which should be made. First, it was important to avoid any legal controversy as to the power of the Governor-General to declare a state of war without specific authorization by His Majesty. . . . We therefore decided to make it abundantly clear that there was an unbroken chain of prerogative authority extending from the King himself to the Governor-General. For that purpose we prepared a special instrument, the terms of which were graciously accepted by His Majesty. . . . His Majesty assigned to His Excellency, the Governor-General, the power of declaring a state of war, first with Finland, Rumania, and Hungary, and second, a state of war with Japan. . . .

" Secondly, the procedure adopted was in accordance with the practice that, in all matters affecting Australia, both the King and his representative will act exclusively upon the advice of the Commonwealth Executive Council. The instrument will, in due course, be countersigned by the Prime Minister of the Commonwealth. United Kingdom Ministers took no part in the arrangements which were made directly with the palace authorities by our High Commissioner in London. Similarly, the actual proclamation of a state of war was made by his Excellency the Governor-General on the advice of his Executive Council.

" Thirdly, the history of the transactions illustrates the fact that separate action by the King's Governments in the United Kingdom and the selfgoverning Dominions is perfectly consistent with close cooperation in all matters affecting their common interests."

12 See Chapter X.

sistently taken the line that when any part of the British Commonwealth was at war, the rest of the Commonwealth was also automatically at war." [13] General Smuts has upheld the view that the Commonwealth is *de jure* a unit in war, though on August 25, 1938, just before Munich, he declared that South Africa would not automatically be at war as in 1914, though she could not stand aside in case of war. Apart from all constitutional theories, it was the policy of immediate participation in the war, as proposed by General Smuts, which the South African Parliament supported, and which it has continued to support more strongly as the war develops. On September 6, 1939, three days after the information was received from London that Great Britain was at war with Germany, the Governor-General of South Africa issued a proclamation of war between South Africa and Germany.

But, whatever these differences in constitutional theory, there was solidarity in action. Anyone who went from Ottawa to Pretoria and from Pretoria to Canberra and Wellington in the first fortnight of September 1939 and who studied the legislative and administrative steps being taken in connection with the war, would not have found in them, and certainly not in the executive action being taken by the King-in-Council or on the King's behalf by the Governor-General-in-Council, or in the legislation by the King-in-Parliament, much ground for suspecting that there were important differences in constitutional theory in different parts of the Empire.

II · THE MYTH OF DOMINION NEUTRALITY

The difficulty of theorizing about the constitutional relations between the members of the British Commonwealth is vividly illustrated when we look at the much discussed problem of dominion neutrality and the effect of the war upon it. In discussing this problem, Eire must be regarded as a special case from which valid inference cannot safely be drawn regarding the constitutional relations of the members of the British Commonwealth. The time has gone when Eire set the pace and provided the precedents for constitutional development in the Commonwealth. By her own action in the present war she has placed herself in a position which, from a legal point of view, she claims to be one of merely " external association " with the Commonwealth. She has placed herself in the position Arthur Griffith warned against in the Dail on December 19, 1921, of being " half in the Empire and half out." By her action in

---

[13] *J. P. E.,* Vol. XX, p. 980.

proclaiming neutrality when the existence of the whole Commonwealth and the freedom of each of its members is at stake, she has adopted a policy which, so long as it lasts, makes her membership of a different kind from that of any other member.

When the new Irish Constitution came into effect in 1937 Britain and the dominions let it be known that they did not regard the new Constitution as putting Eire outside the Commonwealth.[14] Eire began in this war with neutrality; we do not know where she will end. A war still in midstream which has witnessed strange transformations might yet have in store another less startling change — a declaration of war by the King on behalf of Eire. De Valera, indeed, may have envisaged such a possibility when, in accordance with what appeared to be the will of the people, he chose the part of neutrality in 1939 after discussing the matter with the British Government. He let it be understood at that time in London that " external association " meant that if Eire were at any time to go to war, it would do so through the King, the agent of Eire in formal relations with foreign powers, the " King of Ireland " as the new Coronation Oath of 1937 declared him to be — with no sign of opposition from de Valera. The character of the war and the part being played in it by the millions of Irishmen abroad — especially in Australia and the United States — may have its influence on the mother country of Eire in deciding her final policy. The Irish abroad, like many individuals in Eire itself, take their full share in waging the common war.

The question of dominion neutrality must be looked at against the general background of neutrality in international relations as affected by the present war. It is in relation to this new international climate that the problem of neutrality in the British Commonwealth and the meaning of the events of September 1939 must be discussed.[15]

" Neutrality," according to Oppenheim, " may be defined as *the attitude of impartiality adopted by third States towards belligerents and recognized by belligerents, such attitude creating rights and duties be-*

---

14 The statement issued by His Majesty's Government in the United Kingdom on December 30, 1937, read that " they were prepared to treat the new constitution as *not* effecting a fundamental alteration in the position of the Irish Free State, in future to be described under the new constitution as Eire or Ireland, as a member of the British Commonwealth of Nations. H. M. Government in the United Kingdom have ascertained that H. M. Governments in Canada, the Commonwealth of Australia, the Dominion of New Zealand and the Union of South Africa are also so prepared to treat the new constitution."

15 In this light it is meaningless to say, as a recent writer said, " The result of the procedure followed in September 1939 may be regarded as settling for all time the question of Dominion neutrality." H. McD. Clokie, " The British Dominions and Neutrality," *American Political Science Review*, August 1940.

tween the impartial States and the belligerents." [16] By any such definition neither Canada, South Africa, Australia, nor New Zealand were in
any sense, at any time, neutral.[17]

There remains the narrow question whether the procedure adopted
in Canada and South Africa, in entering the war, established for these
two countries a theoretical right of neutrality in relation to fellow members of the Commonwealth. A case can be made out for this theory; but
the procedure has received no authoritative interpretation in this sense
by any member of any Government or in any Parliament or Court in
the British Commonwealth. On the contrary, since 1938 the weight of
authoritative opinion has been thrown heavily against views of the kind
that were current in the earlier years after the last war. And as far as we
can look into the future of the British Commonwealth, it is improba-
ble that support will exist after this war for the idea that in theory or practice members of the British Commonwealth can be neutral in respect of
one another. For if the British Commonwealth is not an organization for
mutual security, if its members are not able to count on each other, at
least in time of dire crisis, what meaning and purpose can it have? It is
noteworthy that even in the one quarter where such an idea did receive
serious and powerful support — namely, from General Hertzog and the
five members of the South African Cabinet and sixty-seven members of
Parliament who supported him in the vote of September 5, 1939 — there
was a fundamental ambivalence. The resolution they supported simply
conjured away the war by a magic formula.[18] It was neither neutrality
nor anything else.

---

[16] Oppenheim, *International Law*, 1926, Vol. II, p. 475.

[17] The amendment moved by General Smuts on September 4, 1939, and approved by the
Union House, was that South Africa " should refuse to adopt an attitude of neutrality in this
conflict." On September 3 the Canadian Prime Minister sent a message to London pledging
whole-hearted support of Great Britain and caused a statement to be issued saying, " In the
event of the United Kingdom becoming engaged in war in the effort to resist aggression the
Government have unanimously decided, as soon as Parliament meets (September 7), to seek its
authority for effective cooperation by Canada at the side of Britain." *Bulletin of International
News*, September 9, 1939, p. 54.

[18] The full text reads as follows: " The existing relations between the Union of South
Africa and the various belligerent countries will, in so far as the Union is concerned, persist
unchanged as if no war is being waged. Upon the understanding, however, that the existing relations and obligations between the Union and Great Britain or any other member of the British
Commonwealth of Nations, in so far as such relations or obligations resulting from contractual
obligations relating to the naval base at Simonstown, or its membership in the League of Nations,
or in so far as such relations or obligations would result impliedly from the free association of the
Union with other members of the British Commonwealth of Nations, shall continue unimpaired
and shall be maintained by the Union, and no one shall be permitted to use Union territory for
the purpose of doing anything which may in any way impair the said relations or obligations."
J. P. E., Vol. XX, p. 969.

The discussions in the Canadian Parliament, in the debate of September 9 and in previous months of the same year, were especially noteworthy for declarations of policy, by Government and Opposition leaders in both Houses, which were more strongly against the theory and practice of neutrality, so far as Canada was concerned, than at any previous time since the First World War. On January 16, 1939, the Prime Minister, while reiterating the policy — to which he had for many years pledged himself — of consulting Parliament before Canada went to war, proceeded to quote the famous statement of Sir Wilfred Laurier, in the Canadian House of Commons in 1910: " If England is at war, we are at war and liable to attack. . . ." " This," Mr. Mackenzie King went on, " was a statement of Liberal policy then, . . . a statement of Liberal policy today, and as it will continue to be under the present Liberal administration." [19] The leaders of the Opposition at various times in both Houses were even more emphatic in the same sense. But perhaps the most noteworthy of the pronouncements on the subject were those made, in almost identical terms, on March 31 and September 9, 1939, by Mr. Lapointe, the French-Canadian jurist, Minister of Justice, and second in command in the Canadian Cabinet. The purpose of his statements on both occasions was to show the " insurmountable difficulties in the way of Canada being neutral from a practical point of view, and the almost insurmountable difficulties from a legal point of view." [20] On March 31 he had said that " the Statute of Westminster never purported to dissolve the bond between the nations of the Commonwealth. Indeed, it was intended to strengthen and maintain that bond, which is the principle of unity." [21] On September 9, Mr. Lapointe said: " It is impossible, practically, for Canada to be neutral in a big war in which England is engaged . . . we are using the diplomatic and consular functions of Great Britain throughout the world. Some of the most important sections of our criminal code are predicated on the absence of neutrality in the relations between Canada and Great Britain . . . our shipping legislation is predicated on our alliance with Great Britain. . . . If we had neutrality all Canadian ports would be closed to all armed vessels of Britain. . . . We would have to prevent enlistment on Canadian soil for the army or navy of Britain. . . . Canadians would have to fight British vessels, if they wanted to be neutral during a war. We would have to

[19] Canadian House of Commons, *Official Report of Debates*, 1939, Vol. I, p. 52.
[20] J. P. E.
[21] Canadian House of Commons, *Official Report of Debates*, 1939, Vol. III, pp. 65–66.

intern British sailors who came to seek refuge in any of Canada's ports. . . . We have contracts and agreements with Britain for the use of the dry docks at Halifax and Esquimalt. . . . Could Canadians in one section of the country compel other Canadians in other sections to remain neutral and to enforce such neutrality even against their own King . . . ? For the sake of unity we cannot be neutral in Canada." [22]

To sum up, in September 1939 neutrality was considered impossible in all parts of the British Commonwealth outside of Eire. Other reasons apart, it was impossible because each dominion recognized at once that its own existence was directly at stake in the war.

5. The Working of the Constitutional Bonds and the Machinery of Cooperation

We must turn now from this negative aspect to something positive, the actual working of the constitutional bonds and the machinery of cooperation under the stress of the war. This involves especially a consideration of the working of the Crown as an institution, the functioning of the diplomatic and conference machinery of the Empire, the conduct of foreign policy, and the machinery for the coordination of defense.

I · KING AND CROWN

The Crown is the keystone of the constitutional structure of the British Commonwealth of Nations — as of that of each of its constituent parts (with the partial exception of Eire), including the Indian Empire and the colonies. Each executive authority, whether the Cabinet in the United Kingdom, or a dominion cabinet, or the executive council in a colony, exercises its power directly or indirectly in the name of the Crown.[23] A cabinet minister anywhere in the Empire is a " Minister of the Crown." Executive acts are performed in the name of the King-in-Council, or on behalf of the King by the governor-general-in-council or the colonial governor-in-council. In each part of the Commonwealth the legislative power is more than Parliament; it is the King-in-Parliament. A law is enacted by the King, or his representative, " by and with the advice and consent " of the Houses of Parliament.

[22] *Ibid.*, Special War Session, p. 67.

[23] Compare the famous phrase of Sir Robert Borden in his Peace Conference Memorandum (*Canadian Parliament Papers*, 41 J., 1919), " The Crown is the supreme executive in the United Kingdom and in all the Dominions, but it acts on the advice of different Ministries within different constitutional units."

The far-reaching powers given to ministers of the Crown, under the wartime emergency legislation, by each Parliament — subject always to the retention of full power of public criticism by the Parliament — have increased the importance of the Crown as a unifying factor in the British Empire. But the Crown is more than an instrument of executive and legislative power. An even more important function is indicated in the words of the Statute of Westminster: " the Crown is the symbol of the free association of the members of the British Commonwealth of Nations." British subjects throughout the length and breadth of the Commonwealth and beyond it " are united by a common allegiance to the Crown." They are identified with one another, become members of one another psychologically, through the common symbol as well as the common person. Such a symbol might play a part as a unifying factor, though it were but the figure of a person who never existed, such as Uncle Sam. When the symbol is embodied in a real person, that person himself must inevitably play a part in the working of the institution.

The fact that, as perspective now shows, the abdication of King Edward VIII had no adverse effect upon the unity of the Empire, indicates the vitality of the institution of the monarchy irrespective of the personality of the King. After the first shock there was an upsurge of unity throughout the Commonwealth around the new King. The coronation ceremony was of great political and psychological importance in consolidating the Empire. For the first time in such a ceremony, all the peoples participated through the radio in what was in a sense a vast family rededication to the Empire and the higher purposes which it served in the world. The peoples gathered round the radio from the villages in the highlands of Scotland to the lonely sheep stations in the Never Never of Australia. The peoples heard the King reply firmly to the question put to him in the new coronation oath, which for the first time mentioned separately Canada, Australia, New Zealand, and South Africa.

Will you solemnly promise and swear to govern the peoples of Great Britain Ireland Canada Australia New Zealand and the Union of South Africa, of your Possessions and the other Territories to any of them belonging or pertaining, and of your Empire of India, according to their respective laws and customs? [24]

---

[24] Speaking of the new oath at the Imperial Conference of 1937, the Prime Minister of Canada said, " For the first time in this great ceremony it was recognized that the relationship between the King and his people of Canada is direct and immediate."

The direct relationship of the King to Canada was heightened by his visit with the Queen in June 1939. Of the political importance of this visit on the very eve of the war there is much evidence. Conventional words had a sudden poignant vivid reality when M. Lapointe, the French-Canadian statesman, said in the House on September 9: " Our King, Mr. Speaker, is at war and this Parliament is sitting to decide whether we shall make his cause our own." [25] Or when, in the Quebec elections in October 1939, which turned largely on the issue of complete participation in the war, he appealed " to the feeling of loyalty to the Crown on the part of French-Canadians generally, a feeling which was so markedly intensified by the Royal visit." [26]

When the war broke the King spoke over the microphone, directly to his people throughout the British Empire. " I send," he said, " to every household of my people this message spoken with the same depth of feeling for each one of you as if I were able to cross your threshold and speak to you myself." The peoples who listened were lifted out of themselves and united with an intensity that is perhaps unattainable by large groups of human beings except through their common identification with a chief. The spirit of hundreds of messages received in London in the early days of the war is typified in one from Lord Craigavon, Premier of Ulster: " Though Ulster be but a small link in the chain which encircles and binds the Empire, she is, by virtue of her strategical position and her hardy Northern stock, *a strong link — a link that will neither break nor bend before the King's enemies. We are King's men. We will be with you to the end."* [27]

II · IMPERIAL WAR CONFERENCE AND CABINET

While the King is the symbol of unity, it is the King's Ministers who carry on the work of government; and between the Ministers of the Crown in the different parts of the British Commonwealth there must be consultation and collaboration. The system of " consultative cooperation," whereby the British Commonwealth handles its common concerns and coordinates its common action in war and peace, includes many elements. But the element which by general consent would be placed first is the system of regular meetings between the cabinets, represented by

---

[25] Canadian House of Commons, *Official Report of Debates,* Special War Session, p. 65.
[26] *Round Table,* December 1939, p. 188.
[27] *National Review,* London, March 1940, p. 293.

the prime ministers or their deputies, in the Imperial Conference with its wartime variants of Imperial War Conference and Imperial War Cabinet.

The League of Nations was likewise a system of frequent conferences of governments, and it developed this procedure beyond the point it has attained in the British Commonwealth. This was the League's one strength: it had little or none of the many other elements that gave vitality and strength to the British Commonwealth. It is these other elements that have to be remembered when we try to account for the fact that the Empire could carry on without any Imperial Conference in the first two and a half years of the present war. This failure to use what appeared to be the chief political instrument of the British Commonwealth is all the more difficult to understand when we remember that the leaders of the Axis met in frequent conference, that the Supreme War Council met at intervals up to the collapse of France, and that even Roosevelt and Churchill met in the Atlantic Conference of August and at Washington at Christmas 1941, and that the Tripartite Conference of Great Britain, the U.S.A., and the U.S.S.R. met in Moscow in September 1941, with the German Army not far from the gates.

No adequate explanation is to be found in the fact that the prime ministers of the dominions had far greater tasks to handle in this war than in the last. This war is being organized and fought in widely separated regions — as a battle for the world. The dominions are no longer mere distant reservoirs of man power, but great arsenals of munitions and stores and centers of air power. And in addition to their armies stationed in Europe and the Near East, they have had to mount guard in some cases against the enemy on their frontiers.

These differences in the strategic situation, as well as factors like the independent status of the dominions, the new diplomatic system of the British Commonwealth, the daily meetings of the high commissioners with the Dominions Secretary, and new technical means of communication such as radio broadcasting and the airplane, make it difficult to draw a parallel between the First and Second World Wars. But in the first war there was a like initial delay — two and a half years — in the holding of an Imperial Conference. From 1914 to early in 1917 there were frequent visits to London of cabinet ministers, including most of the prime ministers. The Imperial War Conference met in the spring of 1917, and again in 1918. The first two sessions of the Imperial War Cabinet were held during these Imperial War Conferences; its third session began after the Armistice on November 20, 1918, and held twelve meetings before the end of the year and others in the first half of 1919.[28]

The Imperial War Cabinet and the Imperial War Conference were both meetings of Governments, the former being more directly concerned with the most urgent business of the war. Neither was an executive organ, despite the use of the somewhat misleading word *cabinet*. The Imperial War Cabinet was, as Sir Robert Borden, the Canadian Prime Minister, put it, " a Cabinet of Governments. Every Prime Minister who sits around that board is responsible to his own parliament and to his own people; the conclusions of the War Cabinet can only be carried out by the parliaments of the different nations of our Imperial Commonwealth." [29] As the Australian Prime Minister expressed it, " the government of the dominion . . . always remained in the dominion." [30]

But it is characteristic of the flexibility of British institutions that dominion prime ministers and ministers from time to time attended the British War Cabinet, so that there must have been days when the secretaries had to be careful to ascertain which of the two Cabinets they were recording, since there was little in the room, or the persons present, or the topics under discussion, which would distinguish one Cabinet from the other. From 1917 onwards, General Smuts sat continuously in the British War Cabinet and represented South Africa in the Imperial War Cabinet when in session. And, as the report of the British War Cabinet for 1918 indicates, after the close of the second session of the Imperial War Cabinet, " several meetings of the British War Cabinet were attended by such representatives of the Dominions as still remained in the United Kingdom." Indeed, as the terms of the invitation clearly showed, when the dominion prime ministers were summoned in December 1916 to come to a Conference in London, it was regarded as " a series of special and continuous meetings of the War Cabinet." [31]

As in substance there was little or no difference between Imperial (War) Cabinet and Imperial (War) Conference, it might have been expected that the use of the term Cabinet would not be objected to by the dominions after the war was over. But there were elements in the dominions which disliked and even feared the term *Cabinet* or *Council,* since under cover of it there might somehow creep in a power to make

[28] *Report of the War Cabinet,* 1918. Cmd. 325.
[29] *Ibid.*
[30] W. M. Hughes, *The Splendid Adventure,* quoted in Scott, *Official History of Australia in the War of 1914–1918,* Vol. XI, p. 756.
[31] *Round Table,* London, June 1917.

binding decisions. From the earliest days of the Imperial Conference there had been a persistent refusal on the part of the dominions to allow the Imperial Conference to develop into anything more than a periodical meeting of Governments. Anything in the nature of an Imperial council, any development likely to give the conference a more permanent character, was rejected out of hand. A permanent secretariat was rejected by the Conference of 1907. A suggestion by the Colonial Secretary of a standing committee of the Conference composed of the Colonial Secretary and the Dominion High Commissioners was rejected in 1911.[32] (It was destined to reappear again as a daily meeting of an entirely informal character held in the room of the Secretary of State for the Dominions during the great crises which preceded the present war and during the war itself.) There were undoubtedly some hopes in England that as a result of the experience of the war this objection on the part of the dominions might be overcome sufficiently to give the Imperial Conference somewhat greater authority and permanence. This hope was so definite that the British Prime Minister on May 17, 1917, told the House of Commons of the view taken by the members of the Imperial War Cabinet that " the holding of an annual Imperial Cabinet to discuss foreign affairs and other aspects of Imperial policy will become an accepted convention of the British Constitution." The same expectation can be traced in the phraseology used in the report of the British War Cabinet in 1918 in which " the establishment as a permanent institution of the Imperial Cabinet system " is mentioned, and also in the words of the official announcement in November 1920 of the summoning of the Imperial Conference of 1921 in which it was described as a " meeting on the lines of the Imperial War Cabinet meetings." Such phraseology was dropped from the official report of the Imperial Conference of 1921 in deference to the wishes of the dominions. It was characteristic that the " natural remedy for . . . giving the Imperial War Cabinet continuity by the presence in London of oversea Cabinet Ministers definitely nominated to represent the Prime Ministers in their absence," which was proclaimed in a resolution of the Imperial War Cabinet on July 30, 1918,[33] dropped completely out of sight and was never heard of again.

The same difficulties were manifest in the period from 1921 to 1941. The British Government was acutely aware of the deficiencies of the Imperial Conference system and its inability to provide for the " con-

[32] Cmd. 5741, 1911.
[33] Cmd. 325, 1918.

tinuous consultation in all important matters of common Imperial concern," which the Imperial War Conference had agreed in 1917 was essential. The Chanak incident in 1922, the difficulties in connection with the ratification of the Treaty of Lausanne in 1924, the inability to secure effective consultations on the Geneva Protocol, and the Locarno Treaties in 1924–25, were all illustrations of this deficiency. As the Prime Minister, Ramsay MacDonald, pointed out in his telegram to the Dominions on June 23, 1924, the "present system of consultation . . . has two main deficiencies. . . . It renders immediate action extremely difficult. . . . Conclusions reached at and between Imperial Conferences are liable to be reversed through changes of Government." [34] But the exchange of telegrams between the Governments led to no permanent results — not even the holding of more frequent Imperial Conferences, which was probably the most important method of meeting the deficiencies. An Australian proposal for a "permanent Imperial Secretariat" was never adopted. Mr. Mackenzie King, the Canadian Prime Minister, warned Mr. Ramsay MacDonald off dangerous ground by cabling, "We regard the Imperial Conference as Conference of Governments of which each is responsible to its own Parliament . . . and in no sense as Imperial Council determining the policy of the Empire as a whole." [35] It is characteristic of this discussion, and similar discussions on the same problem in later years, that the British Government saw the problem of coordinating the actions and policies of the Governments of the British Commonwealth with greater clarity and objectivity than the dominions.

In his opposition to the holding of an Imperial War Cabinet or Conference in the first two years of this war, the Canadian Prime Minister, Mr. Mackenzie King, tended to refer to it as if it would be a continuously meeting body, whereas the Imperial War Cabinet and Conference were never permanent bodies and held only occasional sessions. In his interview with the press on arrival in London in 1941 he justified his opposition to the meeting of an Imperial War Cabinet on the ground that "important decisions should not be made by one man but by a government as a whole." [36] But in fact the Imperial War Cabinet and Conference had not made decisions without reference to their constituent Governments. His opposition to such a cabinet or conference probably colored somewhat the remarkable tribute which he then proceeded to

[34] Cmd. 2301, 1925.
[35] Ibid.
[36] The Times, London, August 22, 1941.

pay to the existing system of communications and consultation between the Governments of the British Commonwealth. " A perfect continuous conference of Cabinets now exists," he said, " and there has never been a time when relations were closer between the Governments. Not a single point of difference has arisen on any essential subject since the outbreak of war." Six months before in the Canadian Parliament he had spoken of the existence of a " real but invisible Imperial Council made possible by these means of constant and instantaneous conference." This tribute was no doubt in a measure well founded. It was supported by the statement made by Mr. Malcolm MacDonald, British High Commissioner to Canada, in an interview with the Canadian press on May 20, 1941, that the system of intra-Empire communication between the heads of Governments in Britain, Canada, Australia, and South Africa had been speeded up so much that " it almost seems as though the four leaders were sitting around one table."

But in fact it was just this coping stone, the final meeting of the leaders round a table, that was missing. In all its lower ranges, in the matter of efficiently organized foreign offices and Empire diplomatic system, of military and naval liaison, of the exchange of information, the perfection of complete systems of intra-Empire air transport and cables and telephone, the structure of the Empire was far more solidly and efficiently organized than ever before in its history.

In the judgment of the British Government and of several of the dominion Governments, especially Australia, it was necessary for the effective conduct of the war and the formulation of war and peace aims to hold an Imperial War Cabinet or Conference, since no consultations by telephone or cable could substitute for the discussion round one table of the highly complex issues involved. The question of holding such a meeting was raised in the British House of Commons on September 21, 1939; and again on October 4, when Mr. Eden revealed that the Government had inquired whether the other Governments would be ready to send a cabinet minister to London for consultations. The result was the visit to London of cabinet ministers from each of the dominions for informal consultations in November and December 1939. This was followed by a number of visits by individual ministers from each of the dominions at intervals during 1940 and 1941. No less than seven Canadian ministers visited London prior to the visit of the Prime Minister; so that there has almost always been one Canadian minister in Britain since the early months of the war. The Australian Prime Minister,

Mr. Menzies, visited London in April and May 1941, followed some weeks later by the Prime Minister of New Zealand, whose visit overlapped with that of Mr. Mackenzie King in August 1941. Each of the prime ministers attended meetings of the British War Cabinet and Mr. Menzies attended also the Defense Committee of the Cabinet during the campaigns in the Balkans and Libya.[37]

A further serious effort was made, during the long visit to London of the Australian Prime Minister, to hold an Imperial War Conference. Mr. Churchill gave the House of Commons on June 24, 1941, the results of his inquiries. " As I have told the House," he said, " we very much desire such a Conference." Negative replies were received from Mr. Mackenzie King and General Smuts regretting their inability to attend a conference in the near future. For a short time in August the presence simultaneously in London of the Canadian and New Zealand Prime Ministers and of Lord Halifax, the British Ambassador to Washington, seemed to offer the possibility of convening an Imperial Conference. But the desire of the Australian Prime Minister to proceed to London, to represent Australia at the War Cabinet and in any conference, was thwarted by factions in the Australian Parliament, which brought about his resignation at the end of August. This situation illustrates a perpetual difficulty in the working of the Imperial Conference system, involving as it does the absence of a Prime Minister from the helm in his own Cabinet and Parliament, at times when such absence may be highly inconvenient.

There is a strong case for the holding of a small Conference of Parliaments parallel with an Imperial War Conference. Like the Conference held in 1937, it could be attended by a small representative delegation from each Parliament headed by a cabinet minister who would also sit in an Imperial War Conference of governments. It is of special importance that leaders of the opposition parties in the parliaments should also attend, as was the case in the Empire Parliamentary Conferences held in London in 1935 and 1937. The Parliamentary War Conference held in London in 1916 was of considerable importance from the point of view of forming and consolidating public opinion in the dominions, especially in Canada. A strong all-party delegation from the Canadian Parliament did visit London in October 1941 to confer with their col-

---

[37] The Canadian Air Minister also attended the War Cabinet early in August. It is of interest to note, as illustrating the elasticity of British constitutional procedure, that Mr. Harry L. Hopkins attended a meeting of the British War Cabinet on his arrival in London on July 17, 1941. M. Daladier, as French Prime Minister, was also present at the War Cabinet early in the war. General Smuts attended for five weeks late in 1942.

leagues at Westminster on war matters and to study the war effort of Great Britain and its relation to Canada. This was to be followed in December by similar delegations from Australia, New Zealand, and South Africa. The first two turned back; only the South Africans came. An effort was to have been made to bring these delegations together in a Parliamentary War Conference in England or in Canada. Out of this it was hoped would come a meeting between the leaders of the United States Congress and the British Parliament such as was proposed in May 1942.

The friction between Canberra and London between December 1941 and March 1942 [38] showed that the political machinery of the British Commonwealth was not functioning smoothly. Both the Australian and New Zealand Governments asked for the creation of an Imperial War Cabinet in London and an Inter-Allied Pacific War Council in Washington. These requests were put forward early in January and answered by Mr. Churchill in his speech in the House of Commons on January 27. "We have always," he said, "been ready to form an Imperial Cabinet containing the Prime Ministers of the four dominions." Unfortunately, he continued, it had not been possible for all of them to be present at one and the same time; but at every opportunity dominion prime ministers had sat in the British War Cabinet and the Defense Committee. In the last three months the Australian Government, he pointed out, had been represented on the War Cabinet by Sir Earle Page. The British Government had now agreed to the specific requests of the Australian and New Zealand Governments, that their accredited representatives should have the " right to be heard in the War Cabinet in the formulation and direction of policy "; [39] and similar facilities would be available to Canada and South Africa. The invitation was extended to India a little later. " The presence," Mr. Churchill continued, " at the Cabinet table of Dominion representatives who have no power to take a decision and can only report to the governments, evidently raises some problems, but none I trust which cannot be got over with goodwill here. It must not, however, be supposed that in all circumstances the presence of Dominion representatives for certain pur-

---

[38] See Chapter VIII, Part II.

[39] The Australian Minister of External Affairs stated in the House on February 25, 1942, that the Australian Advisory War Cabinet's interpretation that " the right to be heard in the United Kingdom War Cabinet ' in the formulation and direction of policy ' " carried with it " membership in the War Cabinet," was judged by Mr. Churchill as " not in accordance with constitutional practice."

poses in any way affects the collective responsibility of His Majesty's servants to the Crown and to Parliament."

As Canada and South Africa had not felt able to avail themselves of Mr. Churchill's offer, the Australian Government did not push the matter further. Their representative (Sir Earle Page) continued to attend meetings of the British War Cabinet and Defense Committee " whenever matters which were considered by the British Prime Minister to be of direct and immediate concern to Australia were under consideration." Sir Earle Page had " the right to be heard in the formulation and direction of policy," but had no power to commit his Government without referring back to it. His authority to speak for Australia was limited by the fact that he was not even a member of the Australian Cabinet. The essence of the Imperial War Cabinet of 1917–19, on the other hand, was that it brought together prime ministers or their deputies, that is those charged with the responsibility for leadership in their cabinets and parliaments, and able therefore in no small measure to commit their governments.

Pacific War Councils [40] have since been set up in London and Washington. That in Washington, both because of its membership and because it exists alongside the Anglo-American combined war machinery (the Combined Chiefs of Staff Group, the Munitions Assignments Board, the Combined Shipping Adjustment Board, and the Combined Raw Materials Board, the Combined Food Board, and the Combined Production and Resources Board), seemed destined to play a larger part than the London body, with which it maintained close liaison.

These parallel councils were in one sense anomalies, because they purported to deal with only a segment of an indivisible world war, for handling of which there was no general council of the United Nations, nor even an Imperial War Cabinet or Conference. The Combined Chiefs of Staffs Group which was the nearest thing to a war council on the plane of strategy, since it dealt with the war as a whole, was confined to strategy. It was not concerned with politics. Moreover, like the five other joint boards, it was purely Anglo-American in composition without representation of the U.S.S.R. or any other allied nation.[40a] The incompleteness and complexity of the Inter-Allied machinery was in part due to the geographical separation of the three great partners, and the

---

[40] See Chapter VIII, Part II.

[40a] A Canadian representative was included in the Combined Production and Resources Board in September 1942.

fact that two of them were on the periphery and separated from some or all of the war zones by immense distances.[41]

So far, then, the war has tested the Imperial Conference system and found it wanting. There have never been more contacts on the ministerial and official plane, and the communications system has never functioned as well as now. But the final coordination of the Conference has been lacking. The prime ministers of four of the dominions have individually attended odd meetings of the British War Cabinet. They have never conferred together as a group in conference, face to face. For their direct contacts with each other the prime ministers of the Empire have relied largely upon pentagonal telephone conversations from the five corners of the earth, when something more effective than the long-distance telephone was needed to defeat the unified strategy of the Axis. They have failed to achieve all the political, strategical, and psychological advantages offered by meetings of an Imperial Conference or Cabinet. Of these advantages not the least are those affecting morale. Such meetings of the leaders of the British Commonwealth of Nations furnish symbols

[41] The following extract from the ministerial statement by Dr. Evatt in the House at Canberra on February 25 illustrates the complexity of the machinery. Though the subsequent setting up of the parallel Pacific War Council in Washington might seem to add to the cumbersomeness of the procedure, as he described it, the close relation of the Council to the Combined Chiefs of Staffs Group was a compensating factor:

"A hypothetical case will illustrate the way in which this Pacific Council (London) fits into the general machinery. Let us assume that the Supreme Commander requires guidance or direction from the "higher authority" in relation to the supply of reinforcements or the like. The procedure is something like this: —

(a) The Supreme Commander in the Pacific telegraphs his question to a Combined Chiefs of Staff Committee which has been set up in Washington as the agency to represent the United States and United Kingdom Services. The Commander also telegraphs to the Chiefs of Staff Committee in London, which is a United Kingdom body.

(b) Both in London and in Washington, the telegrams are remitted to Joint Planning Staffs for examination.

(c) The Joint Planning Staffs submit reports to the Chiefs of Staff in London and the Chiefs of Staff Committee in Washington respectively, and the two staff authorities proceed to resolve any points of difference between them.

(d) When this has been done the British Chiefs of Staff submit a report to the Far Eastern (Pacific) War Council in London.

(e) Any differences of view between the members of the Council and the Chiefs of Staff are argued out in the Council.

(f) The agreed views of the Council are then telegraphed to the Chiefs of Staff Committee in Washington. If members of the Council differ the British Prime Minister is to "focus" the divergent views and communicate with Washington.

(g) If the Chiefs of Staff Committee in Washington accepts them, they are presented to the President who then issues the necessary executive order.

(h) If there is a difference of view between London and Washington, the President informs Mr. Churchill, who remits the matter to the Pacific War Council.

(i) Then, presumably, the whole matter returns to stage (e) and is thrashed out again."

of unity and determination. The leaders themselves are stimulated, and the sluggish and weak are fortified by the strong. The morale of the peoples is heightened. Fresh and more effective weapons for psychological war against the enemy are forged. By forgoing meetings of an Imperial War Conference or Cabinet, the dominions atrophy the central political institution of the British Commonwealth to which they have attached the greatest importance in the past. They deny their national status by throwing upon the British War Cabinet most of the responsibility for the higher political and strategic direction of the war. It is difficult to believe that such a situation can continue for long. The higher direction of the war effort of the British Commonwealth requires something in the nature of meetings at not too great intervals of an Imperial War Conference or Cabinet or Supreme War Council — the name matters little. And some such body is not less essential to coordinate the common efforts of the British democracies and India in the building up of a stable peace. The fault lies not so much with the system of the Imperial Conference itself, which despite all its difficulties can be worked. Provided command is maintained over the sea and the air above it — a condition threatened by Japan in the Pacific and the Indian Oceans in 1942 — conferences can be held at relatively short intervals without necessarily involving, even for the most distant parts of the Empire, more than several weeks' absence for the prime ministers or their deputies. In any case the right of any dominion prime minister who is able to visit London, to sit *ex-officio* — as a member by right without need of special invitation — in the War Cabinet, might be recognized.[42]

The main obstacles are to be found, when traced down to their roots, less in material factors than in mental attitudes. Even this brief record of the difficulties experienced by the British democracies in the last two generations, in bringing themselves to accept modest steps towards a more unified common direction of their foreign affairs and defense, should serve as a warning to those who have an easy optimism regarding the rate of progress which is possible towards world government.

III · COMMON EMPIRE FOREIGN POLICY

Broadly speaking, the effect of the war on the foreign policies of the members of the British Commonwealth has been to weave them together more than ever as strands in a single rope. When, in the interval between the two great wars, the strain at times slackened, the strands

---

[42] This suggestion was made by the *Times,* London, August 25, 1941.

might loosen and even fray out; but only to draw together when the strain increased in a crisis. It is not untrue to say that there existed a common, joint British Commonwealth of Nations foreign policy in the crises leading to this war, as there existed a single British Empire foreign policy before 1914.

The relative weakness of the dominions was increased by the rapid mechanization of war. They had enough sense of reality to know that there was no magic in their new equality of status with Great Britain which could make it possible to have the independence of policy which is the exclusive privilege of only the greatest of the Great Powers. They understood well enough the fundamental truth which they had " frankly recognized " in the Balfour Report of 1926; namely, that in the sphere of foreign affairs as in the sphere of defense, " the major share of the responsibility rests now, and must for some time continue to rest, with His Majesty's Government in Great Britain."

As that report pointed out, and subsequent developments have made still more clear, the special circumstances and geographical conditions of each country in the Commonwealth make it inevitable that there should be certain differences of approach and emphasis in the matter of foreign policy on the part of each government. If, in the words recently used by an Australian Prime Minister, Australia is a " principal " bearing " primary risks and primary responsibilities " in matters affecting the Pacific and the Far East, the same is true of England in relation to Europe, as Sir Austen Chamberlain pointed out in justification of the British policy expressed in the Locarno Treaties. It is true also of Canada in relation to the United States; but here there is no question of any primary risk, but only of an enviable security which has enabled Canada to profess a detachment to which the less secure dominions cannot hope to aspire.

Because of Australia's special interest in the Far East, the Australian Minister of External Affairs could on occasion talk of " the formulation and application of (Australia's) Far Eastern policy." [43] But the phrase meant little more than that her " Near North " is for Australia to a much greater degree than for any other dominion a region of special interest in the general field of common Empire foreign policy. This point was never for a moment forgotten at the five centers (namely, Canberra, London, Washington, Tokyo, Chungking) where Australian ministers and diplomats were shaping and carrying out Australia's

[43] Declaration in the Australian House of Representatives, November 28, 1940.

Far Eastern policy in the closest consultation with British ministers and diplomats. It was at the same time Australia which at the Imperial Conference of 1937 boldly used such phrases as " common Empire policy," " British Empire Foreign Policy," and " consistent and united Empire Policy." The only other dominion which could use such language was New Zealand.

Yet a broad general survey of the foreign policy of the British Commonwealth, in the interval between the two great wars, shows that the divergencies between Britain and the dominions were comparatively few and, in the long run, of no great importance. Such divisions as did occur arose largely from the discrepancies between the *theory of equal status* and the *reality of unequal stature*. In theory, the dominions had equal status with Great Britain; but in practice her enormously greater stature, as a Great Power with world interests, forced her into independent action and commitments without the dominions. The difference of stature led to some differences in matters of procedure such as representation at international conferences and the signing and ratification of treaties. The sensitiveness of the dominions in questions involving their status tended to give undue publicity to differences of this kind which were not really matters of substance.

From the end of the First World War and until about 1921 foreign policy was one and indivisible for all practical purposes. The report of the Imperial Conference of 1921 [44] has a number of phrases which reveal this conception of a unitary " foreign policy of the British Empire." In the Washington Arms Conference, 1921, and the treaties of Naval Limitation issuing from it, the naval forces of the members of the British Commonwealth of Nations were treated as a complete unity for international purposes, and all the members of the British Commonwealth signed and ratified as members of the group. Exactly the same procedure was followed in the subsequent treaties for the limitation and reduction of naval armament signed at London, April 22, 1930, and March 25, 1936 (except that Eire took part only in the 1930 treaty). There were a number of other instances of complete group action, such as the signing and ratification of the Paris Pact of 1928 and the accession in 1931 to the General Act of 1928. It is true that the principle of diplomatic unity had broken down badly at the time of the Chanak incident in 1922, but this was not followed by any serious consequences. The divergencies over the Lausanne Treaty of 1923 and the Locarno Treaties

---

[44] Cmd. 1474, 1921.

of 1925 were more apparent than real. In the case of the Locarno Treaties, Great Britain was able merely to keep the dominions informed but without full consultation in an Imperial Conference, although it tried to secure one. It had to enter into guarantees to which the dominions were not formally parties because, as Sir Austen Chamberlain put it in the House of Commons on November 18, 1925, " We live close to the Continent . . . we must make our decision." But the dominions were aware that they were likely to be involved in any ultimate consequences that might come from the Locarno Treaties.

Until the archives are thrown open, we can have no complete picture of the attitudes of the different dominions in matters of foreign policy prior to the present war. But from the information available, it is clear that, whereas Canada willingly received the information on foreign policy supplied by the Foreign Office, she preferred, and was even grateful, not to be " consulted "; she was very sparing in any expression of her own views, and in particular of saying expressly that she concurred with the views of the British Foreign Office; and she rarely put forward suggestions of her own. On the other hand Australia (and no doubt New Zealand, although the information published in her case is somewhat less full) repeatedly concurred in actions about to be taken by the British Government, and frequently gave her views when asked to do so. But it was only occasionally that she raised on her own initiative points for consideration by London and asked for an answer.

The procedure of endorsing the British Government's action used by Australia and New Zealand in connection with the declaration of war against Germany [45] was adopted on a number of important occasions by these dominions in the years immediately preceding the present war. For example, in connection with the signing of the Anglo-Italian agreement on November 16, 1938, and the recognition at the same time of the Italian conquest of Abyssinia, Mr. Neville Chamberlain announced the receipt of telegrams from the prime ministers of South Africa and Australia approving the intention to put the agreement into force. On the same day the Australian Prime Minister, Mr. Lyons, announced in the Australian House that " the Government has been in consultation with the Government of Great Britain and has expressed the opinion that the sooner the Agreement (with Italy) is concluded the better for the two countries immediately concerned and probably for the peace of

[45] See above, pp. 20–21.

the world." [46] The procedure here was parallel to that of the declaration of war in the sense that when the British Government informed the dominions that it intended to act, the Australian Cabinet indicated its concurrence and requested the British Government to associate Australia with the action taken. But on this occasion New Zealand refrained from concurrence. She never recognized the Italian conquest of Ethiopia, and now that Haile Selassie is back in Addis Ababa, events have caught up with her.

But the greatest occasion of a concerted foreign policy was at the outbreak of the war itself and in the events immediately preceding it. The false start at Munich was in a high degree an act of common foreign policy. Appeasement then was a policy to which all the Dominion Cabinets were as fully committed as Britain itself. [47] In the swiftly moving events following upon the German occupation of Czechoslovakia in March 1939, the dominion governments expressly or silently concurred at every point in the successive steps taken by the British Government, such as the momentous decision of the pact with Poland. The dominions had the fullest information regarding this treaty, although in form it was " an agreement of Mutual Assistance between the United Kingdom and Poland," and its obligations did not formally involve the dominions.

Although the British Government may not have possessed from a single dominion the formal assurance in advance that it would enter the war simultaneously with Great Britain, it knew by a thousand signs and indications that most if not all of the family of nations would act together, whatever the procedures might be, or the initial difficulties they might have to pass through in making their decisions. Mr. R. G. Casey, the Australian Minister at Washington, stated in a speech given on March 20, 1941, that: " Australia, on her own decision, declared herself in a state of war with Germany on the same day as Great Britain — and without any prior knowledge on Britain's part that we would do so — or even the slightest hint from Britain that we *should* do so." Nevertheless the British Prime Minister was able *before* the war, on September 1, 1939, to say to the House of Commons with complete confidence: " We shall enter (the war) with a clear conscience, with the support of

---

[46] *Parliamentary Debates,* Session 1937–38, p. 1110.

[47] E.g., the speech of the Australian Prime Minister in the House on September 28, 1938, in which he suggested that this policy had indeed been pressed by Australia upon the British Government.

the dominions and the British Empire, and with the moral approval of the greater part of the world." [48] To those who think of the British Commonwealth in terms of formal relationships and established procedures, this situation must remain an incomprehensible mystery. But it will offer no difficulty to those who realize that the key to an understanding of the British Commonwealth is the relationship of members of a family to one another.

During the war itself consultation, concurrence, and cooperation have been more complete than at any time since the war of 1914–18. The policy of the British Commonwealth of Nations, apart from Eire, has been one and indivisible. The veil was lifted for an instant by Mr. Churchill in his speech to the House of Commons on June 18, 1940, to reveal the working of the Empire machinery at the time of the fall of France and the evacuation of Dunkirk. It was the most critical moment in the history of the Empire. The speech showed Great Britain discussing whether it was possible to carry on, and then moving forward once more in the van of the British Commonwealth with " invincible resolve." " We have fully informed all the self-governing dominions and we have received from all Prime Ministers messages couched in the most moving terms, in which they endorse our decision and declare themselves ready to share our fortunes and persevere to the end." Gone with the winds of disaster were all delicate distinctions between information and consultation and endorsement!

In the offer as a free gift of naval bases in Newfoundland and Bermuda, and the exchange of other naval bases on the British Atlantic islands for fifty destroyers (August and September 1940), negotiations were conducted between Great Britain and the United States as principals, with Canada represented only by an observer. To safeguard her special position, and her right of acting as a principal in any further negotiations in relation to Newfoundland (which lies athwart her front door and is an integral part of her defense), a protocol to the bases agreement was drawn up at her instance.[49]

The Far East forms another chapter in this joint foreign policy. The closing and the opening of the Burma Road in the fall of 1940 revealed the United States in close consultation not only with Great Britain but also with other parts of the British Commonwealth most immediately

---

[48] *J. P. E.*, Vol. XX, p. 823.

[49] March 27, 1941. Cmd. 6259. See Grant Dexter in *Proceedings of the Fourth Conference on Canadian-American Affairs*, 1941.

concerned, such as Australia. The closing of the road was decided upon
" after full consultation with the (Australian) Commonwealth and the
other Dominion Governments." The decision to reopen it after October
18, 1940, " was taken with the full concurrence of the Commonwealth
Government and after close consultation with the United States Government whose interest in this area is closely allied to our own." [50] It is
indeed likely that when the full facts are known the foreign policies of
the United States and Great Britain in relation to the Far East will be
shown to have been, at least since the outbreak of the war, to all intents
and purposes first parallel and then joint. A number of illustrations of
such joint action could be given. They would cover the joint aid to
China, joint or parallel diplomatic or economic action against Japan,
and the planning of concerted defense measures. For several years a
joint policy towards Japan was followed, which President Roosevelt
defined as " keeping war out of the South Pacific for our own good,
for the good of the defense of Great Britain and the freedom of the
seas." [51] The freezing of all Japanese assets in all parts of the British Commonwealth and the United States which was announced on July 25, immediately after this remark by the President, was a signal illustration of
this joint foreign policy of the English-speaking peoples. As soon as
Britain was informed that the American action had been taken, a " parallel measure " was put into effect throughout the whole British Empire
including India, Burma, and the colonies. All commercial treaties between any part of the British Empire and Japan were simultaneously
denounced. It was a joint policy of economic sanctions against Japan.

The announcement on August 14 of the meeting of President Roosevelt and Winston Churchill and the text of the Atlantic Charter, together with the text of the joint Roosevelt-Churchill message to Stalin
made public the next day, indicated how far-reaching the joint policy
and action of Great Britain and the United States had become. Moreover, it indicated that in the stress of this great crisis, it had been found
necessary for Great Britain to enter into and carry through negotiations
of the utmost importance to the whole British Commonwealth, without it being possible for the dominions to participate directly. The dominion prime ministers had indeed been informed in advance of the Atlantic Conference, and they received the text of the declaration well in

[50] Sir Frederick Stewart, Minister of External Affairs in the Australian House, November 28,
1940, *Current Notes of the Ministry of External Affairs*, December 1, 1940.
[51] *New York Times*, July 24, 1941.

advance of its publication; but they were not invited to attend the meeting.[52]

The dominions had individually expressed their concurrence in the Atlantic Charter and the action following it. They were to give formal approval in the second meeting of the Council of Allied Governments in London on September 24 in St. James's Palace. The resolutions adopted by that Council, as on the occasion of its first meeting on June 12, 1941, constituted a joint act in a common British Empire foreign policy. It was an act, as Winston Churchill put it in his speech on June 12, of " the servants of the ancient British monarchy and the accredited representatives of the British dominions beyond the seas, of Canada, Australia, New Zealand and South Africa, of the Empire of India, of Burma and of our colonies in every quarter of the globe."

Here too something more than a joint Empire policy was involved. The common policy extended to all the Allies and to the U.S.S.R. But in relation to the U.S.S.R., as in relation to the United States, Great Britain was forced to take action with which the other nations of the British Commonwealth could not be formally associated. On occasion it was not even possible to consult them in advance. Mr. Churchill's important speech a few hours after Russia's entry into the war had to be delivered without the possibility of consultation with the dominions; and the Anglo-Soviet Pact signed on July 12, 1941, in Moscow was in form a pact between " His Majesty's Government in the United Kingdom " and the U.S.S.R. But as Winston Churchill announced to the House of Commons three days later, it was " a solemn agreement between the British and Russian Governments carrying with it the full assent of the British and Russian people and of the great dominions of the Crown for united action against a common foe."

More and more as Britain and America assumed the leadership of the United Nations, Britain found it necessary to take action with which the dominions were not formally associated, though rarely if ever without informing them of the action intended. The pattern which, therefore, emerges so far in the war is that of rings within rings. There is an inner ring of the common foreign policy of the British Commonwealth; a second, middle ring of common foreign policy of the English-speaking peoples grown still more definite with the entry of the United States into the war. A third, outer ring began to take shape in 1940 and 1941 in the

---

[52] The reason was not merely that the conference was a personal one, but that a wider conference would have made the necessary secrecy impossible.

group of Allied nations in London under British leadership; it widened with the entry of the U.S.S.R. into the war and came full circle when Japan's entry on the side of the Axis united the Far Eastern and the European wars into a single world war. Thus was born the United Nations.

IV · EMPIRE DIPLOMATIC SYSTEM

The war has seen a marked development of the system whereby the Governments of the British Commonwealth are represented in one another's capitals by high commissioners. The direct relations between ministers of the Crown in different parts of the Empire by means of personal visits and by telephone, telegram, and dispatch, are now supplemented by a well developed intra-Empire diplomatic system.

The conditions of war make it important that the contact between governments through diplomatic representatives should be closer and more speedy than in peace. The diplomatic representatives must be men of such standing and experience that they can act with the utmost speed in establishing direct contact between cabinet and cabinet and in getting things done with the least possible red tape. It is for this reason that London, in its relation with the dominions during the war, has changed over from career men (mainly high officials of the Dominions Office) as high commissioners to high commissioners of cabinet rank, who might even, in special cases, continue to hold their status of minister of the Crown in their new post. It was the same consideration which determined the action of the British Government in appointing Lord Halifax, a member of the War Cabinet, as Ambassador in Washington. Though Ambassador, he formally retains his rank as a member of the War Cabinet; and when he returned on a visit to England in August 1941 he resumed, as Mr. Churchill had indicated on his appointment, " his full functions and responsibilities as a Minister of the Crown." [53] In the same way, Mr. Malcolm MacDonald, who for nearly a decade had been Secretary of State for the dominions or colonies, was sent as High Commissioner to Ottawa, Sir Ronald Cross, formerly Minister of Shipping, to Canberra, and Lord Harlech (Mr. Ormsby-Gore), formerly Secretary of State for the Colonies, to Pretoria. The United Kingdom is also represented by high commissioners in Dublin and Wellington.

This tendency was carried further in 1941 by the stationing, in two important areas of regional defense, of ministers of cabinet rank, but

---

[53] Speech to the Pilgrims, January 9, 1941.

without portfolio, to represent and advise the War Cabinet, and to co-ordinate political, military, and economic arrangements in connection with the war. Mr. Duff-Cooper was sent to Singapore to improve co-ordination among British territories and civil and military authorities in the Far East. Captain Oliver Lyttelton was sent in a similar capacity to the Near East.[54] His successor, Mr. R. G. Casey, former Australian Federal Treasurer and Minister in Washington, was made on appoint-ment Minister of State with a seat in the British War Cabinet.

The same tendency to appoint Cabinet ministers to key positions is shown by the action of the Australian Government in sending to Wash-ington Mr. Casey, whose status was that of second in command in the Cabinet, and the sending by New Zealand to a similar post of its Dep-uty Prime Minister, Mr. Walter Nash. By a special act of the New Zea-land Parliament both Mr. Nash and Mr. Langstone, the New Zealand High Commissioner in Ottawa, retained their seats in the Cabinet.

While, from a formal point of view, the change-over to high commis-sioners of Cabinet rank may not be great, its practical importance is very considerable. As an official put it privately in Ottawa, Mr. Malcolm MacDonald can lift the receiver of the telephone without hesitation and talk directly with Mr. Mackenzie King and Mr. Winston Churchill; whereas a man whose career had been that of an official might think twice before taking any such step. But such arrangements are likely to be of a temporary character, not carried on beyond the period of the war, since men of Cabinet rank will probably wish to return again to their political careers. The war has brought about a considerable ex-pansion of the functions and the personnel of the High Commissioner's Office in Ottawa, necessitating the creation for the first time of a new post of Deputy High Commissioner.

These British high commissioners are appointed by the Dominions Office, and not, as ambassadors are, by the King on the advice of the For-eign Office. Their functions are of a quasi-diplomatic character; and in some cases, as in Ottawa, they have on their staffs officials seconded from the Foreign Office as well as the Dominions Office. The high commis-sioners, by whom the members of the British Commonwealth are rep-resented in one another's capitals, form a kind of private Empire diplo-matic system distinct from the diplomatic representatives of foreign powers. In the *Annual Report of the Canadian Secretary of State for*

---

[54] See below p. 72. Lord Swinton went to West Africa as Resident Minister in June 1942; and in December, Mr. Harold Macmillan to North Africa and Col. J. J. Llewellin to Washington — each as a Resident Minister of Cabinet rank.

External Affairs (1940) " the Representatives in Canada of Other Governments of His Majesty " are listed in one annex; while a separate annex is devoted to " Diplomatic Representatives in Canada," comprising the ministers of the United States, France, Japan, Belgium, and the Netherlands (to which are being added ministers for China, the Argentine, Brazil, and Chile). For the purpose of precedence, the high commissioners rank in relation to one another in the order in which their countries appear in the Statute of Westminster, 1931 (namely, United Kingdom, Dominion of Canada, Commonwealth of Australia, Dominion of New Zealand, Union of South Africa, Eire), and not in accordance with the date of formation of the office or of appointment of the individual. In Ottawa, as in London, high commissioners are exempt from the payment of customs and income taxes; they do not possess, however, the general legal immunities to which foreign diplomatic representatives are entitled.[55]

As regards the high commissioners of the dominions in London, the war has accentuated a change already marked in the prewar years. Whereas formerly they were mainly concerned with financial and trade matters, they now deal also with political issues, especially in relation to foreign affairs, the conduct of negotiations with the British Government, and defense. With the creation of the Pacific War Council on February 9, 1942, in which the dominions have been represented by their high commissioners, the political character of this office became marked.

The work of the dominion high commissioners in London has expanded in connection with defense and matters of an economic and financial character relating to the war. Their work has increased also as a result of the creation of separate dominion organizations to deal with dominion troops and air forces in England, and, in the case of Canada, the stationing in England of a representative (with staff) of the Department of Munitions and Supply. But this expansion is of less importance comparatively than in the First World War. This is partly because of the very frequent visits of Canadian Cabinet ministers to London and the transaction by them of the most important business connected with the war.[56] In this war, too, transactions involving Canada and the United Kingdom are being carried out in considerable measure in Ot-

---

[55] *The British Empire*, Royal Institute of International Affairs, p. 188. The accrediting of Mr. S. M. Bruce as Australian Minister to the Netherlands Government in London gives him a double status as member of both the Empire and the foreign diplomatic corps.

[56] The fact that 246 diplomatic bags were sent by Canada House in London to Ottawa during 1940, in comparison with 84 during 1939 illustrates the increase in the business of the high commissioners' offices. *Annual Report of the Canadian Secretary of State for External Affairs, 1940.*

tawa rather than in London. In Ottawa there is for this purpose almost the beginnings of a skeleton British Civil Service, with representatives from a number of government departments empowered with a greater autonomy and authority to make decisions than would normally be the case. This is true to a far greater degree in Washington, where there is a whole series of special missions and other agencies staffed by large numbers of British and dominion officials from a variety of government departments and empowered to make on-the-spot decisions of considerable importance. Close relations are maintained with the ministries in London by cables numbering several hundreds a day. Ministerial coordination and supervision are maintained to some extent through the British Supply Council presided over by the Resident Minister who with the Ambassador, Lord Halifax, exercises general jurisdiction over this organization. From the point of view of munitions and supply, Ottawa and Washington are playing a greater part than was the case in 1914-18; so also are Delhi, Canberra, Wellington, and Pretoria.

The closeness and the frequency of the contacts of the dominion high commissioners in London with members of the British Government, as well as with one another, have increased considerably during the war. It has been the custom during the war for the high commissioners of the dominions to meet together daily each afternoon with the Secretary of State for the Dominions, and in his room at the Dominions Office. The value of this development is that the Dominions Secretary, who since February 1942 has been a member of the War Cabinet, informs the Cabinet of any point arising in his discussions with the high commissioners pertinent to the matters under consideration by the Cabinet. But this is perhaps of less importance than the other purposes which these meetings serve. The Dominions Secretary also reports back to the high commissioners for transmission to their governments on the matters discussed and the decisions taken in the War Cabinet relating to the conduct of the war. He is able also to make known to the high commissioners the views of the British Government on any matter. These daily meetings are entirely informal and without minutes and secretaries.

How far these daily meetings of Dominions Secretary and high commissioners can fulfill some of the functions of an Imperial Conference depends on the standing of the high commissioners and their power to represent the views of their governments. Most of them are not at present men of Cabinet rank. Some can usually express only their personal views. Only one or two are able to speak habitually for their governments.

The functions and the importance of this new element in Commonwealth machinery fluctuate according to circumstances and are thus difficult to assess. They vary from time to time and from high commissioner to high commissioner. While the holding of daily meetings became a fixed practice during the war, it originated some years before the war. The practice appears to have begun about the time of Mr. Malcolm MacDonald's tenure of the Dominions Office. In all the international crises, as well as during the abdication crisis, daily meetings of the high commissioners were held in the Dominions Office; sometimes twice a day. During the Munich crisis long meetings were held beyond midnight. With the war, crises became continuous and the meetings became a matter of daily routine. Among the other wartime functions falling upon the offices of the high commissioners in London is participation in the Empire Clearing House set up in April 1942 to cooperate with the Combined Raw Materials Board in Washington.

The development of a system of high commissioners as between the dominions themselves is one of permanent importance which would have come in any case even without the stimulus of the war. South Africa sent an " Accredited Representative " to Ottawa in 1938. This was followed in 1939 by the appointment of a high commissioner from Eire. On September 11, 1939, a week after the outbreak of the war, the Prime Minister of Canada announced in the House of Commons the decision of the Government to appoint high commissioners in Australia, New Zealand, South Africa, and Eire. In welcoming this development on September 12 the spokesman of the Australian Government explained to Parliament that this was not merely a crisis measure but " a natural corollary in the present structure of the British Commonwealth to the exchange of High Commissioners between the Dominions and the United Kingdom." [57] Canada is as yet the only dominion which has completed its intra-Empire system of diplomatic representation, the others being represented only in London and Ottawa.

The announcement on July 21, 1941, by the India Office in London of an exchange of representatives between India and the United States " in the special circumstances of the war," together with the announcement some weeks previously of an agreement for the exchange of ministers between the United States and New Zealand, completed the chain of British Empire diplomatic representation at Washington. When this development began fifteen years ago with the appointment of a minister

[57] *J. P. E.*, Vol. XX, p. 941.

of the Irish Free State, followed by ministers of Canada and South Africa, the opinion was current in Washington that it would weaken the structure of the British Empire. The British Ambassador, in announcing to the Secretary of State of the United States the proposed arrangements for appointment of a minister of the Irish Free State in Washington, indicated that they " would not denote any departure from the principle of the diplomatic unity of the Empire." [58] This phrase, " diplomatic unity of the Empire," was qualified five years later in 1929 in a letter by the British Ambassador in Berlin to the German Minister of Foreign Affairs by the words, " that is to say the principle of consultative cooperation amongst all His Majesty's Representatives, as amongst His Majesty's Governments themselves, in matters of common concern." The British Ambassador then expressed the trust of His Majesty's Government in the Irish Free State that the establishment of an Irish legation would not only promote cordial relations between the Irish Free State and Germany " but also between Germany and the whole British Commonwealth of Nations." [59] These formulae have now become standard. The experience of nearly two decades has shown that the existence of dominion ministers at Washington has not impaired this principle. As Mr. Menzies has put it, the appointment of ministers in foreign capitals has been an addition to, and not a subtraction from, the diplomatic strength of Britain.

The interdependence of the countries of the Commonwealth has been strengthened rather than weakened by the close contacts with Washington due to the present war. The American Government has found it both convenient and necessary to deal with the British Commonwealth as a whole in many matters such as the allocation to different countries of material under the Lend-Lease Act. The British Commonwealth organization, which was built up for this purpose before American entry into the war, was the British Supply Council in North America; under it was the British Purchasing Commission, with subsidiary organizations, such as the Empire and Allied Requirements Committee on which were representatives of every country in the Empire.

This tendency for Britain to act on behalf of the dominions as leader of the British democracies in relation to the United States of America

[58] Letter of Sir Esmé Howard dated July 24, 1924; A. Lawrence Lowell and H. Duncan Hall, *The British Commonwealth of Nations,* World Peace Foundation, 1927.

[59] Letter of the British Ambassador in Berlin to the German Minister of Foreign Affairs, June 9, 1929, regarding the appointment of an Irish Minister. A. Berriedale Keith: *Speeches and Documents on the British Dominions, 1918-1931.*

was strongly emphasized by the setting-up of the Anglo-American war organization at Washington, and the parallel organization in London, in January 1942 as a result of the agreement between President Roosevelt and Mr. Churchill.[60] This organization, comprising the Combined Chiefs of Staffs Group, the Munitions Assignments Board, the Combined Shipping Adjustment Board, and the Combined Raw Materials Board, was Anglo-American; the dominions were not represented directly, though they had ready access to it through special liaison officers and representation on various committees. The Commonwealth Supply Council (incorporating the Empire Clearing House), composed of representatives of all Empire governments, was set up later in London to plan and coordinate certain aspects of Commonwealth production and requirements in cooperation with the Combined Boards in Washington.

Twenty years of participation in international affairs by the dominions has created something which did not exist in 1914, and which has added to the strength and cohesion of the British Commonwealth. It has built up in the dominions what formerly existed only in Britain, a body of men possessing a wide experience of the world outside their own countries, of cabinet ministers and ex-ministers, members of Parliament, diplomats and officials in the various government departments, and men holding responsible positions in commerce, journalism, and other fields. Their training ground has been partly in the international political and technical gatherings in Geneva under the League of Nations and International Labor Office, partly in international conferences held in London and elsewhere, partly in Imperial conferences, in conferences of Empire parliaments held under the auspices of the Empire Parliamentary Association in each of the capitals of the Empire, in intra-Imperial committees or conferences of a technical character and in the foreign services of each part of the Empire. Voluntary organizations for the scientific study of international affairs, such as the closely interconnected Institutes of International Affairs in each part of the Empire, have also played their part in this process.

V · EMPIRE COMMUNICATIONS AND EXCHANGE OF INFORMATION ON FOREIGN
    AFFAIRS

Despite the war, and the difficulty of communication involved in it, the stream of information, by cable and in documentary form, flowing out from Whitehall, continues during the war in greater volume

---

[60] Cmd. 6332, 1942. See above, pp. 37 and 50.

than ever. The extent of the documentation involved at moments of the greatest pressure was indicated by the Secretary of State for the Dominions, Mr. Malcolm MacDonald, on November 1, 1938, in the House of Commons. He gave the House information regarding the working of the system as laid down by Imperial Conferences, whereby "the Dominion Governments were kept constantly informed by telegraph of the information at the disposal of the United Kingdom Government as well as of the Government's policy regarding foreign affairs." The number of circular telegrams so sent to each of the Dominion Governments on foreign affairs since the beginning of 1938 (ten months) had been 398, of which some 150 were sent during the month of September alone.[61] As indicated above, this is more than an information service containing all the information available to the British Government, including the most secret. In dispatching a document the Foreign Office may ask whether the dominions have any views to express and, on occasion, whether they concur in an action which London proposes to take.

Since the building up of this system at the end of the First World War, the dominions have made available to the Foreign Office such information on foreign affairs as they had available from their own sources. They have also, though somewhat spasmodically, made such information available from time to time to each other. The interchange of high commissioners between Ottawa and the other Dominion capitals has begun to increase the exchange of information on foreign affairs between the governments.

This system of interchange of confidential state documents and information on foreign affairs is unique. There is no parallel to it anywhere in the field of international relations. It did not and could not exist between the members of the League of Nations. Only rarely and in a limited degree have allied nations been able to put all their cards in each other's hands. The system even goes beyond any confidential interchanges between a foreign office, like the State Department of the United States, and its ambassadors and ministers in foreign capitals. That this stream of documents should issue constantly from London to half a dozen capitals in the British Empire (with somewhat smaller streams passing in the reverse direction and between each two of these capitals), and that leakages of confidential documents or information should be exceedingly rare, is a remarkable tribute to the administrative efficiency

---

[61] *J. P. E.,* Vol. XX, p. 29.

and the quality of the personnel of the civil services and ministers of the Crown concerned. Such a system could not possibly exist in a society whose members did not have complete confidence in each other's good faith and good will. It could exist, therefore, only as between nations in an intimate family group such as the British Commonwealth.

After Dunkirk and the fall of Singapore, there was some interruption in the air-mail services, which now form one of the most important parts of the communications system of the British Commonwealth; (there were no such services in the First World War). These services still function regularly by commercial planes or bombers between all dominion capitals and London and cover many of the colonial territories in Asia and Africa. Indeed, there is now available, by means of the bombers being flown across the Atlantic and the return ferry service for pilots, a daily air-mail service which brings Ottawa as close to London for air-mail purposes as it is to Washington. And on both sides of the Atlantic full advantage is being taken of this service for the transport of state documents as well as ministers and officials on missions in connection with the war. The air-mail services available to some of the other dominions are less frequent than before the war, but adequate enough when supplemented by an extensive use of the cable and telephone. It is the fixed practice of the foreign offices of the British Commonwealth and their foreign services, for reasons of secrecy and security, to entrust diplomatic bags only to ships and planes of British and dominion registry. On occasion, however, official documents may be sent by other channels, e.g., American ships or clipper planes, entrusted to a " safe hand," i.e., a person, usually an official, carrying an official letter indicating that he is charged with responsibility for the delivery in person of state documents. For the same reason of secrecy, only a limited use is made of the telephone as a means of official communication between capitals of the British Commonwealth, or between them and their embassies or legations abroad. But on special occasions where the prime ministers have had to discuss matters of a complex and urgent character the telephone has been used freely and effectively.

All this serves to emphasize that the British is a maritime Empire. It came into being because Britain was a sea power. Its peculiar organization is in no small degree due to the fact of its being a maritime Empire; and safe communications by ships, by submarine, cable, and by air services using the same sea lanes as the ships use, and the same ports upon them, are vital to its continued existence.

The war has revealed some small difficulties in the organization of the existing machinery of cooperation which it should be comparatively easy to remedy. Even before the war, complaints were sometimes made that the machinery for the transmission of information from the Foreign Office to the external affairs departments and vice versa was too unwieldy, and that it occasioned frequent delay both in the transmission of information to the dominions and the transmission of dispatches from the departments of external affairs of the Dominions to the Foreign Office. These channels, at the London end, comprise the Dominions Information Department of the Foreign Office, and the Foreign Affairs Department of the Dominions Office, with subsidiary channels through the high commissioner of the dominion concerned and, in the case of Australia, through the liaison officer maintained in London by the Department of External Affairs. At the dominion end the inward communications go directly, except in the case of Australia, to the external affairs department. With the appointment of British high commissioners in the dominion capitals, there has developed a tendency, especially during the war, for London to use its high commissioners in the dominions as a channel for the transmission of documents or information, particularly those involving discussion, to the Prime Minister or the department of external affairs. In the case of Australia there is an additional complication due to the fact that the External Affairs Department is not administered by the Prime Minister, as in Canada, South Africa, and New Zealand, but as a separate ministry. Outgoing communications from Australia pass through the Prime Minister's Department to the Dominion's Office in London, and this additional complication has caused some criticism in Australia.

Apart from the purely official and departmental methods of communication which facilitate cooperation between the governments of the Empire in the conduct of foreign affairs, other steps towards unity of policy are the appearance of the Empire Parliamentary Association's quarterly foreign affairs report and the formation in each dominion parliament of an all-party study group on international affairs. Though groups of this character were established shortly before the war in the parliaments of the Australian Commonwealth, New Zealand, and the Union of South Africa, under the auspices of the Empire Parliamentary Association, it was not until the war had started and a further stimulus had been given to the study of external relations, that a similar group was formed in the Canadian Parliament at

Ottawa. These groups receive special information relating to the war and international affairs and they meet from time to time to hear confidential talks from experts specially qualified to deal with some aspect of foreign affairs. Both in helping forward the war effort and in providing machinery which will tend towards uniformity of action in dealing with international affairs and post-war problems, the groups may serve a most important purpose. The linking together of these groups by personal contact and conference, and through the Canadian group or the Parliament at Westminster, the forging of a link with the foreign affairs committees of the American Congress, are possible wartime developments.

While some of the sources of authoritative information, such as the reports previously sent by ambassadors or ministers from enemy countries or enemy-controlled countries, have now dried up, these have in some measure been replaced by reports gathered by the intelligence services. One new source of information is available which did not exist in any previous war, namely, the reports of the Monitoring Service of the British Broadcasting Corporation and the secret intelligence reports based upon the analysis by experts of the material received by the Monitoring Service. The purpose of these reports, which supplement the work of the ordinary intelligence service, is to work back from the words used as instruments of war by the Axis propaganda ministries and their satellites in occupied territory. In the matter of defense against the psychological war of the enemy and in the conduct of the counter-offensive, the dominions are necessarily dependent on Great Britain. Great Britain alone is in a position to maintain a central Empire staff in the radio war, and armies of listeners, translators, and central intelligence officers. The dominions have neither the resources nor the physical possibility of receiving in their territories one of the most essential parts of the total enemy propaganda, namely, that constituted by the long and medium wave broadcasts of the European stations, nor can they receive the Russian broadcasts other than short wave. A branch Monitoring and Broadcasting Service of the B.B.C. was, however, set up late in 1941 at Singapore, which received all broadcasts from Asiatic countries available in Singapore and itself broadcast in some sixteen languages.

Empire broadcasting as a means of informing and strengthening the public opinion on which the foreign policy of a democracy must rest, has played an extremely important part in this war. In the years immediately before the war, and during the war itself, the Empire Broadcasting Service of the British Broadcasting Corporation has increased enormously in importance. On an all-Empire hook-up the voices of the King and of political leaders reach into every household. Hundreds of thousands of short wave sets are tuned in daily all over the Empire to the B.B.C. short wave programs, particularly the news broadcasts. For example, these broadcasts are listened to by a very large portion of the English-speaking population of South Africa, particularly in their rebroadcast form over the South African stations. Three of the B.B.C. news bulletins and some of the talks in English are rebroadcast daily by South African stations. At the request of the Australian Broadcasting Commission, two of the B.B.C. news bulletins were rebroadcast daily by the Singapore station. The dominions themselves have been extending their short wave transmissions; Australia has set up a powerful station capable of transmissions throughout the world. Rebroadcasting facilities are also being developed in a number of the British colonies in the shape of medium wave transmissions.

We have traced here only part of the machinery of cooperation which knits together the Empire. There is, in a sense, far more than one Empire diplomatic system; there are many different systems of liaison. There is the system of military, air, and naval attachés of different parts of the Empire operating to maintain liaison for the defense services in London, Washington, and Ottawa. With the setting-up of the Pacific War Councils in London and Washington, and of the joint Anglo-American bodies to deal with strategy, shipping, supplies, the service liaison maintained by the dominions in London and Washington has been greatly extended by appointment of high-ranking officers to carry out these functions.

The importance of such liaisons between the principal departments dealing with external relations was emphasized by Sir Earle Page, Australian representative in the British War Cabinet, in a statement issued in London on January 14, 1942. The statement sums up the conclusions emerging from a close examination of the working of the system of Empire consultation. The chief defect in the machinery he found to be that consultations on the political or horizontal plane, i.e., between cabinet ministers, were not backed up by enough consultations on the vertical or administrative plane. Close and continuous contact between Government departments in London and the dominions " at a lower plane than the ministerial level and at a stage when foreign policy and strategy are still in a fluid form" is essential, he thought to insure effective consultations between the Prime Ministers or their deputies. The remedy he suggests is "a more active and complete system of liaison covering not only foreign policy (such as the Australian liaison officer attached to the Foreign Office) but also the three fighting services, as well as supply and economic relations." There was a great deal of consultation on the administrative plane between London and Washington from January 1942 onwards — probably more than within the Empire, owing to the large number of British officials stationed at Washington. Adequate consultation on this plane is essential as a permanent element in the peacetime machinery of the Empire as well as in Anglo-American relations.

There is growing also an important liaison between the councils of scientific and industrial research in different parts of the Empire and in the United States. For example, Great Britain has such a liaison officer attached to the National Research Council in Canada. In view of the importance of science from the point of view of the war, scientific missions have been dispatched by Great Britain and Australia to the United States, and American scientific missions have been sent to London. Moreover, there are the beginnings of a system of scientific attachés at the legations in certain of the capitals. In 1941, Canada sent a scientific attaché to Canada House in London, and an Australian scientific attaché was sent to the Legation in Washington.[62]

The machinery involved in the coordination of the production and distribution of the supplies required for the conduct of the war, and the coordination of the economic war now being waged on a common world front by each part of the Empire, would require a chapter of its own. How intricate is the problem of such coordination even within the limits of each part of the Empire is shown in some of the chapters which follow.

6. Coordinated Defense and Unity of Command

I · THE SYSTEM OF COORDINATED DEFENSE AND ITS WORKING

The British Commonwealth in normal times has no centralized defense system, no common navy, army, or air force, except in so far as

---

[62] Great Britain sent Dr. Darwin, Director of the National Physical Laboratory "as Director of a Central Intelligence Office working under the direction of the British Supply Council in North America to collaborate with United States research bodies." This mission is closely linked with Canada. The United States sent Dr. Conant, the President of Harvard University, to establish "a corresponding mission in Great Britain." Lord Hankey, 118 H. L. Deb., 5 s., c. 993.

the forces of the United Kingdom, and above all the Navy, are able to provide some measure of defense for the whole Empire. But, even in times of peace, the forces of the whole Empire are coordinated in such a way that, if the nations take a decision to make war together, these forces can intermesh smoothly and without friction, to form a common navy, a common air force, and a common army. In time of war, unified command of the armed forces in the field, including air and naval forces, is a matter of course. But even in time of war there is no centralized command or control with authority over all the land or air forces, or even of all the naval forces, of the British Empire. The unified command set up for the forces operating together in the field does not extend to those in the home bases, especially in the dominions. Even the forces of India and the dependent Empire, although under the supreme authority of Great Britain, cannot be considered as merely reinforcements of the British Army; but rather as localized systems of defense in a world-wide complex.

The basic principles of the defense systems of the various parts of the Empire are twofold: First, that each part shall provide in the first instance, as far as it is able to do so, for its own local defense; second, that its forces shall take part in the common defense of the British Commonwealth, when and to the extent its government and legislature so decide. The conception that the defense forces of one member should be available for the defense of the other parts of the Commonwealth is more highly developed in some places than in others. Only in the case of Great Britain is it taken completely for granted that the forces of the United Kingdom shall be available for the defense of the Empire as a whole.

The defense system of the British Empire consists therefore of a number of separately organized forces under the control of autonomous states; although there is a strong assumption that because of their family bond and common interests they will assist one another in time of need, they have not made express commitments in advance to render such assistance. Such a system necessitates a high degree of liaison and coordination if it is to work at all. The system worked out in the British Commonwealth, especially at the Imperial Defense Conferences of 1909 and 1911, of planning defense to ensure in advance such a high degree of coordination that the separate forces can be fitted instantly together and become parts of a homogeneous Imperial army and navy, is one of its most interesting and effective institutions. This system is in operation in all parts of the British Empire, except Eire, which decided not to train and equip its forces on the common lines. Under the Anglo-Egyptian Treaty of Alliance signed on August 26, 1936, the system was extended in part to Egypt.[63]

In time of peace the higher political liaison between the defense forces of the Empire is secured largely through the Imperial conferences, which devote a large part of their discussions to defense matters, and sometimes through special Imperial defense conferences. During the war there has been continuous consultation by telephone, cable, and visits by the responsible ministers, including the exchange of special missions.[63a] The Defense Committee of the British War Cabinet (the wartime form of the Committee of Imperial Defense), expanded from time to time to include visiting dominion ministers, has been the principal coordinating agency during the war. On the side of strategy and technique, liaison is maintained by constant consultations between the defense and supply ministries and the general staffs, especially at London.

In reporting to the House of Commons on the "astonishing story of comradeship in arms of the free citizens of the British Empire" in the African campaigns of this war, Lord Croft, Under-Secretary of State for War, said, "These campaigns had been truly Imperial, and troops of the Commonwealth of Australia, New Zealand, the Union of South Africa, Rhodesia, the African Colonies and the Sudan, along with the British troops and fine divisions from India had written great fresh chapters in British military history." [64]

Not the least part of the "astonishing story" was the fact that these units from the five ends of the earth, composed of different races and traditions, should have fitted instantly together and worked like a single well-oiled machine. No mere unity in the high command could have achieved such a result. Despite differences of external appearance in color, language, headdress, and uniform, each force had been trained with the idea that it was destined to form part of a single army. They had learned from the same army manuals. Their training and discipline had been on common lines. Their higher officers had been trained in the same higher staff colleges; they shared a common military doctrine and tradition, and many of them knew each other. As far as possible

---

[63] A letter attached to the treaty provides that "in view of the possible necessity of cooperative action between the British and Egyptian forces, the armament and equipment, land and air, of the Egyptian forces shall not differ in type from those of the British forces."

[63a] See above, pp. 47–55.

[64] *J. P. E.*, Vol. XXII, p. 185.

their equipment was on standard lines; the same rifles and machine guns and artillery, taking the same spare parts and the same ammunition. An Australian and a New Zealander, a Sikh, a South African, and a Scotch Highlander, could go to the same ammunition dump and find cartridges that fitted all the rifles and the machine guns and field artillery. The cartridges were the standard .303 — not the .300, with the little difference on the rim, taken by the standard American rifle. As these two cartridges are not interchangeable, American troops, fighting alongside of the Empire forces in Australia and elsewhere, have to be supplied from separate ammunition dumps.

The Committee of Imperial Defense. In the matter of its Imperial defense organization on the strategic and the technical side, the British Commonwealth was far from being planless and improvised. Even before 1914 there was a high degree of unified planning and uniformity of administrative practice in its defense system. On the naval side the British Admiralty planned for the defense of the Empire as a whole, its guiding principle being that of the strategic unity of the Empire on the basis of sea power. But it was the Committee of Imperial Defense which planned for all aspects of defense for the whole Empire. In this body the Empire possessed an efficient organization, typically British in its absence of a written constitution, and in its power to achieve far-reaching results with the minimum of formal machinery and an almost complete absence of publicity. It was the Committee of Imperial Defense which before 1914 planned with remarkable precision and incorporated in the War Book the action to be taken in the event of war. From time to time official reports and speeches have thrown some light upon its working. Lord Balfour and Lord Haldane referred to it in speeches in the House of Lords, in June 1926. They revealed that the chiefs of staff, who had already learned through their work in the committee to consult not merely from the point of view of their own departments but of " the common defense of the Empire," would now have this duty formally imposed upon them by the Warrant of their appointment. Lord Haldane, as one who had had almost a life-long contact with the Committee, not only on its political side, but also with its technical subcommittees,[65] gave some details of its working in relation to the dominions. The Committee, he pointed out, had purposely been kept purely advisory in character, subject only to the Prime

[65] At that time they numbered about thirty, and they have since been multiplied.

Minister, in order that the dominions should feel perfectly free to cooperate with it. Not being afraid of encroachment on their autonomy by an Imperial executive authority, they would be able to send their staff representatives to take part freely in the deliberations of the Committee when summoned to it. Since the war of 1914-18, representatives of Australia and New Zealand have frequently been present at the meetings of the Committee and have asked for and received advice on their defense problems. The other dominions, such as Canada, at least in recent years, refrained for political reasons from attending meetings of the Committee. But without being represented at its sessions the Defense Departments of both Canada and South Africa appear to have consulted freely with it. Here, as in the case of the higher political machinery of the Empire, the still lingering traces of political immaturity, from a psychological point of view, revealed in the attitude of the Dominions, had prevented the building up of an entirely adequate system of defense cooperation. During the present war, as at the beginning of the last war, the Committee of Imperial Defense has become the Defense Committee of the Cabinet.[66]

Unity in the Higher Command. An important element in the efficient coordination of Empire defense in time of peace has been supplied by the interchange of officers between the different defense forces and the common training provided by the Imperial Defense College. Before and during the war, officers from the three services of the United Kingdom have been attached to units in the dominions and vice versa. Part of the training of some Australian and New Zealand officers has been secured in the army in India. These interchanges have extended not only to the army but also to the navies and air force. The Imperial Defense College was set up in 1927. " Its purpose," in Lord Haldane's words in the speech referred to above, " was the training of the super-staffs, the higher elements of the staffs in the three Services," in the principles of Imperial strategy in their broadest aspects. The College has played an important part in the training of military, naval, and air officers from all the dominions (except Eire) and from India. Civilian officials, e.g., the Secretary of the Defense Department in Australia, have also passed through

---

[66] The Committee consists in normal peace times of the Prime Minister and persons summoned by him to the meetings. In practice, the ministers for the various defense departments and their principal advisors, the Chancellor of the Exchequer and the secretaries of State for Home Affairs, Foreign Affairs, the Dominions and Colonies, and India, are usually summoned to attend plenary sessions of the Committee.

the training of the College. The leaders of the armies of Great Britain and the dominions are thus largely men who have passed through the Imperial Defense College as instructors or students. For example, the two senior generals in the Canadian Army, Lieutenant-General Mc-Naughton and Major General Crerar, worked together in the Imperial Defense College with General Sir Archibald Wavell, Commander-in-Chief in India, Sir Alan Brooke, Commander of the Home Forces in England, with whom the Canadian Corps is serving, and General Sir John Dill, formerly Chief of the Imperial General Staff, later a member of the Combined Chiefs of Staffs Group in Washington. They were not only trained together, but came to form an inner group as experts in the new mechanized warfare, sharing identical strategical and tactical views. These are factors of incomparable importance from the point of view of the future campaigns of the war in the different areas in which the various Imperial Armies must operate.

The system of unity of command adopted in the present war in the different campaign areas is much the same as that adopted in the war of 1914–18. The system as it applied to the Australian forces in the different areas was summed up as follows by the Acting Prime Minister of Australia: [67]

> The General Officer Commanding Australian Imperial Force in Malaya commanded and administered all Australian Imperial Force units located in Malaya. Operational control was exercised by him, subject to the orders of the General Officer Commanding Malaya. The command and administration of the Australian Imperial Force, Middle East, was exercised by the General Officer Commanding, Australian Imperial Forces, Middle East, on the same basis. The Royal Australian Air Force units located at Singapore were under the operational control and direction of the Commander-in-Chief, Far East.

The situation appears to be in principle the same in respect of all the dominion military and air forces operating in Great Britain and in the other areas mentioned. As the Canadian Prime Minister explained to the men of the First Canadian Division on August 26, 1941, the retention of the Canadian troops in England was due solely to strategic reasons and not to any limitation imposed upon their use by the Canadian Government. " So far," he explained, " as the disposition of troops is concerned, the Canadian Government places no restriction

---

[67] *J. P. E.*, XXII, p. 268.

whatever upon any decision that may be made, other than that the Government itself shall have the opportunity of knowing what is contemplated and an opportunity of expressing its views." [68] This may be said to sum up the situation in respect of all the dominions. The principal difference between the situation in the present war and the First World War is the adherence, from the outset, as regards the military forces, and as far as practicable in respect of the air forces, to the principle of organizing dominion forces in their own separate divisions, army corps, and air squadrons.

It is not yet possible to judge how far this situation will be modified by the entrance of the United States into the war. In Australia supreme command over land and sea forces of the United Nations in the South Pacific was assumed by General MacArthur in mid-March with Lieutenant General George H. Brett of the United States Army in command of all air forces operating in Australia. A week later, Lieutenant General Sir Thomas Blamey (Australian) was appointed Commander in Chief of the United Nations land forces in Australia.

II · THE COMMON EMPIRE NAVY AND THE WORLD CHAIN OF NAVAL AND AIR BASES

The dominions have always steadfastly refused to accept the principle of a single Imperial navy, although none of them has maintained naval forces of sufficient strength to give them adequate naval defense without the assistance of the British Navy. The dominion ministers rejected an Admiralty memorandum circulated to the Imperial War Conference of 1918 proposing "a single navy at all times under a central naval authority." But they agreed, in a joint memorandum of reply, that the principles of coordination already being followed — namely, " the character of construction, armament and equipment, and the methods and principles of training, administration, and organization, should proceed upon the same lines in all the navies of the Empire." [69] These principles have been followed without deviation. The principle of unity of command in time of war had already been accepted in the Naval Agreement of 1911; and in accordance with this Agreement the ships of the Royal Australian Navy and of the New Zealand Division of the Royal Navy (now the Royal New Zealand Navy) were transferred to the control of the British Admiralty at the outbreak of the war. The same ap-

---

[68] *New York Times,* August 28, 1941.
[69] H. Duncan Hall, *The British Commonwealth of Nations,* 1920, p. 303.

pears to have been the case with the ships of the Royal Canadian Navy operating in the Atlantic convoys, in the Caribbean and in the convoying of Australian troops. In the case of Canada, as of Australia, some of the ships have continued to operate in the waters adjacent to their shores under the immediate control of the dominion naval authorities. Units of the South African naval force cooperated with the Royal Navy in the Mediterranean off the northern coast of Africa. The Royal Indian Navy has operated under Admiralty control from the outset of the war.

In the matter of naval forces, the principle of strategic unity has been more closely adhered to than in any other branch of defense. The Royal Navy itself has always been regarded by Great Britain, and also consciously or half-consciously by the dominions, as available for the defense of all parts of the British Empire in the seven seas. This was well expressed in the important speech of the First Lord of the Admiralty, Sir Samuel Hoare, in announcing the policy of building a navy able to operate in the Eastern as well as the Western Hemisphere. " The Empire was," he said, " an oceanic Empire with world-wide communications. . . . As it was the duty of the Navy to keep open the trade routes and communications of the Empire, it was essential that the Navy should be able to carry out their duty in both the Eastern and the Western Hemisphere." [70]

How close is the coordination between the Royal Navy and the Royal Australian Navy is shown by the following details: The Australian Navy operates in time of peace under the control of the Commonwealth Naval Board. The First Naval Member of the Board is a British naval officer selected in Britain after consultation between the two governments, to serve on the Board under the Australian Government. In matters of organization, promotion, training, etc., the Royal Australian Navy operates in accordance with the King's Regulations and Admiralty Instructions. It uses only the British naval manuals for tactical training. Some of its higher officers have always hitherto been senior British naval officers. At the outbreak of the war three of its six cruisers were commanded by British naval officers. Its adherence to a common doctrine is further facilitated by the training of its higher officers in the Royal Naval Staff College and the Imperial Defense College. The Royal Australian Naval College near Melbourne trains cadets who pass later through the naval torpedo, navigation, and signal schools at Greenwich

---

[70] *The Times*, London, December 3, 1937.

and Portsmouth in England.[71] Officers move freely back and forth between the Australian and the British Navies. Australian officers in the present war have commanded ships of the Royal Navy in the North Sea, and British officers command ships of the Australian Navy. Ships as well as officers are interchangeable. A British ship may become part of the Australian Navy on the Australian station and a ship of the Australian Navy may operate in the British Navy (in the Home Fleet or in the various stations, such as the Mediterranean, China, and the East Indies). When so serving in time of peace or war the Australian ship is under the command of the Commander-in-Chief of the station, subject to the general strategic control of the Admiralty. Two cruisers of the Australian Navy served thus with the Royal Navy in the Mediterranean during the sanctions crisis of 1935-36.

The principle of standardization and interchangeability of equipment is carried out in great detail. The uniforms are exactly the same except that Australian naval officers have the word " Australia " in addition to the " Royal Navy " on their buttons. Promotion in one navy carries with it corresponding rank in the other navy. But standards of pay are different — and the rum ration, traditional in the British Navy, is not apparently standard in the Australian Navy.

" The United States Navy," Mr. Churchill said on January 27, 1942, " is linked in the most intimate union with the Admiralty, both in the Atlantic and the Pacific. We shall plan our naval movements together literally as if we were one fleet." But the extreme difficulty of securing strategic and tactical coordination between the squadrons of different powers, never designed to operate as a single fleet, is shown in the disaster suffered by the United Nations in the Battle of Java Sea.

The World Chain of Naval and Air Bases. It has always been recognized, as witness many passages in the reports of Imperial Conferences, that defense of sea and air communications, and the bases necessary for this purpose, are peculiarly matters of common concern. The naval forces of this oceanic Empire could not carry out their functions of keeping the sea lanes open without a vast chain of major and minor naval bases encircling the globe — with links at points such as: Portsmouth, Belfast, Halifax, Esquimalt, Bermuda, the Falkland Islands,

---

[71] The ratings in the New Zealand Division of the Royal Navy (who are New Zealanders) receive their technical training as seamen, gunners, gun layers, gunners mates, at training establishments in Australia. Incidently, it may be noted here that the majority of the New Zealand army officers have been trained in the past at the Royal Military College at Duntroon, Australia.

Freetown, Gibraltar, Malta, Aden, Bombay, Trincomalee, Singapore, Hong Kong, Kilindini, Darwin, Albany, Melbourne, Sydney, Auckland, Suva. These give the Royal Navy an effectiveness in the exercise of sea power on a world-wide scale which could not be attained by the American Navy without similar bases, even if it were several times as large as the Royal Navy. The Atlantic Naval Bases Agreement, whereby the American Navy secured a fringe of protecting bases off its entire Atlantic coast, has a certain counterpart in agreements between different members of the British Commonwealth; for example, the agreement between Great Britain and South Africa regarding the maintenance of a British Naval Base at Simonstown, at the Cape of Good Hope, and the agreements with Canada for the use of the ports of Halifax and Esquimalt. By virtue of such agreements the British Commonwealth becomes in the matter of sea power to some extent an alliance with a certain contractual basis. The First Lord of the Admiralty informed Parliament on March 25, 1941, that a complete coordinated system for the repair of naval vessels in all the main seaports of the dominions, India, and the colonies, has been developed during the course of the present war. This world-wide chain of defensive bases and repair facilities has been greatly strengthened by the throwing open to the British Navy since 1941 of the repair facilities of all the main American ports.

The importance of having a chain of air bases with adequate fueling facilities, comparable to the naval bases of the Empire, was recognized in the Imperial Conference of 1926. Such chains of bases now exist, linking up the different parts of the Empire and following in part the principal shipping routes. During the war the airdromes and airports used by the Empire Air-Mail Services have been enlarged for military purposes and considerably increased in number. If victorious, the British Empire will emerge from the war with its system of sea and air communications — by land as well as by sea — vastly strengthened and far more important to its continued existence than ever before. For reasons of military necessity full details are not yet available regarding the important further developments which have taken place since 1938, and especially during the war, to make the Pacific south of the Equator an Empire air stronghold, particularly in the area between Northern Australia, New Guinea, Fiji, and New Zealand, and also to develop strategic air routes in the region of the Indian Ocean. When the United States entered the war these naval and air bases in all parts of the world and their repair facilities were thrown open to its armed forces.

The British Commonwealth Air Training Plan. The British Commonwealth Air Training Plan [72] is the outcome of intra-Imperial discussions which began in 1938. It is controlled by a sort of Commonwealth air cabinet composed of representatives of Canada, Great Britain, Australia, and New Zealand, acting either through their high commissioners in Canada or their air liaison officers, who link up with their own air councils or boards in different parts of the Empire. The plan consists of much more than the great organization in Canada. In its wider sense, it includes the preliminary training schools in Australia, New Zealand, and Great Britain in which the contingents receive their elementary training before passing through the central training schools in Canada. In addition to its participation in the plan, Australia trains large numbers of airmen outside the British Commonwealth Plan. South Africa has its own air training scheme, which since October 1940 has been training a certain number of British pilots. India also has its own air training organization. The former Australian Prime Minister, Mr. Menzies, justly said early in 1941 that the British Commonwealth Air Training Plan was the greatest piece of Empire cooperation yet evolved in the war.

Its importance is far greater than the mere output of pilots, observers, and air gunners. It is of profound significance to the Commonwealth from a political and psychological point of view. The psychological importance of the plan consists in the bringing together from the various parts of the Empire of an elite of young men, the few to whom, in Mr. Churchill's words, the many owe so much, and binding them to one another by the ties of common training, and the spirit of fellowship arising from their dedication to a common purpose. In the air force as in the navy there is a far closer intermingling than between the more separate units of the armies.

III · THE PROBLEM OF INDUSTRIAL STANDARDS

Behind the system of coordination of defense and uniformity of equipment lies the whole problem of industrial standards in the British Commonwealth. With the exception of Canada, which follows American standards, British engineering standards are generally observed throughout the British Commonwealth.[73] In view of the dependence of modern armies upon highly standardized equipment manufactured by mass

---

[72] See Chapter V.
[73] See *Report of the Imperial Conference on Standardization,* Cmd. 3716, 1930.

production, the problem of building up and maintaining common engineering standards between a group of countries cooperating in a common defense system is of vital importance.

The absence of such standardization between Britain and America, for example, affects the whole range of mechanized equipment from the bore of the guns to the component parts of armored vehicles, tanks, and airplanes. When war vessels of Britain or America enter each other's ports in any part of the world, they cannot use the ammunition stored there, since this is made to fit guns of different calibre and firing mechanism. Every British or Australian mechanic likely to be called on to service an American plane in England or Egypt or India or Australia has to provide himself with two kits of tools in the matter of wrenches, etc. — one to fit English standard nuts and bolts and another for American. The problem of getting grounded planes into the air by rushing the necessary spare parts to them is already one of considerable difficulty even for British planes. To provide the same service for American planes all over the world, far from the parent factories and without the special regional repair factories provided for the different types of British planes, is an extremely complex problem. The difficulty arising from lack of uniformity in engineering standards and designs has affected above all the manufacture of aircraft and tanks.

While in general the principle of uniformity of equipment has been maintained in the great mass of army equipment for the various Empire forces, it has broken down in some measure in the matter of aircraft and tank manufacture. The difficulty has been most serious in Canada, where factories had to be retooled in order to manufacture British planes such as the Hurricane in accordance with British designs and specifications. In order, however, to obtain full-scale mass production and to utilize in full the whole engineering resources of Canada, it has been found necessary to abandon the uniform Empire standards and to go over increasingly to American standards. Efforts are being made, however, by British and American experts to secure the greatest possible degree of standardization through the use of standard designs and interchangeable parts in airplanes, tanks, and other mechanized military equipment. The problem of conflicting standards is not, of course, one which is confined to the relations between American and British industries. It exists also in greater or lesser measure within British and American industry and even between their defense services; for example, between the American navy and the army. Only far-sighted and continuous effort will secure the degree of industrial standardization necessary to secure the colossal output of defense goods required during the war.

IV · THE NEW REGIONALISM IN DEFENSE AND SUPPLY

One of the most striking developments of the present war, which is without real parallel in the war of 1914-18, and which is likely to leave some permanent traces on the postwar structure of the British Empire, has been the development of a new regionalism in Empire defense. At first sight this seems paradoxical because it has come at a time when the mechanized war on land, at sea, and above all in the air, has given the Empire a greater strategical unity than ever before. But in fact it is nothing more than an extension of one of the basic principles of Empire defense — that the primary responsibility of each member (as of all states in all periods of history) is its own defense. The speed and range of modern weapons of war have made it necessary for whole regions comprising a number of states and territories to combine in regional mutual security systems. A regional organization of defense is also made necessary by the quantity and variety of raw materials and manufacturing skills required in modern war, which are beyond the capacity of single states however great.

The new regionalism in the British Commonwealth is an early symptom of the inevitable changes in the states system of the world involved in new technical developments. It is the certain forerunner of the grouping of many of the smaller and weaker states of the world into regional federations. The process may be seen at work in all parts of the world. The agreement between the governments of Poland, Czechoslovakia, Yugoslavia, and Greece announced at the International Labor Conference in November 1941, foreshadows a possible regional federation of all Eastern Europe between Germany and Russia. Canada and the United States, by the Ogdensburg Agreement and the Hyde Park Declaration [74] and other acts of long-term collaboration are deliberately building a permanent system of joint North American military and economic defense. The leasing by the United States from Britain of a whole chain of naval bases to form a protective screen from Newfoundland out as far as Bermuda and down as far as British Guiana, is but another aspect of North American continental regional defense. So is the similar protective screen developed from Kodiak Island through

---

[74] See Chapter V.

Hawaii to Samoa. The "Western Hemisphere" conception is that of a regional grouping of North and South America for defense and other common purposes.[75]

The Eastern Group Supply Council [76] at Delhi represents a different type of regional organization, with the coordination of war production in the British territories of the Eastern Hemisphere as its principal function. The corresponding military organization for the actual purchase and distribution of armaments and other military equipment — the Central Provision Office — supplies a far-flung series of local provision offices extending into Australasia, the Middle East, and Africa. The experience gained here, and in the similar large-scale planning of production and supply by combined boards in Washington and London, may be of significance in the solution of postwar economic problems.

Perhaps the most interesting and highly developed of such regional organizations is the Middle East Supply Centre at Cairo, which coordinates the non-military supplies with military requirements in the area including Egypt and the Sudan, Iraq and Persia, Palestine, Cyprus, Malta, Ethiopia, and the British East African Colonies and Mandated Territory. The Middle East Supply Centre was established during the summer of 1941 by Mr. Oliver Lyttelton, Minister of State in the British War Cabinet, and its first purpose was to facilitate shipping and transport.[76a] Mr. Lyttelton had been charged by the War Cabinet to concert "the measures necessary for the prosecution of the war in that theatre other than the conduct of military operations." His Middle East War Council included representatives of the commanders-in-chief, representatives of the governments of the various territories concerned, and representatives of various British embassies and legations in the region.

The importance of this regional political and supply organization was increased by the presence of American military missions in Cairo and Basra, the building of a great American supply base in Eritrea, and the development of trans-African supply routes by air and road from the Atlantic to the Red Sea. With the entry of the United States into the war the M. E. S. C. organization became combined Anglo-American, not

---

[75] Malaya, Burma, Australia, New Zealand, and the island groups in the Southern Pacific formed an obvious region for defense within the British Empire, and it had been expanded at the beginning of 1941 to include the Dutch East Indies and the Free French island possessions. See Chapter VIII.

[76] See Chapter XI.

[76a] The Supply Centre operates under the control of a small Executive Committee, and has its own secretariat, director, and secretary-general. Its functions, however, are those of supervision and coordination of civilian supply, production, etc., rather than direct administration.

only in respect of its central organs, but also of its local offices in certain territories.

Coordination between different regional areas from a political and strategical point of view is maintained through the War Cabinet in London, and by special missions.

Regionalism in defense does not necessarily imply regionalism in foreign policy. The very fact that in Britain, the Near and Middle East, and Southeastern Asia truly Imperial armies, comprising at least token forces of most parts of the British Empire, have been operating is an indication that behind the regional defense lies unity of foreign policy. The arrival at Hong Kong in mid-November 1941 of a Canadian force was accompanied by a significant declaration by the Canadian Prime Minister, strongly emphasizing this point: "Defense against aggression," he said, "actual or threatened, in any part of the world is today a part of the defense of every country which still enjoys freedom," and he went on to state that it was in accordance with this principle that Canada had joined the Imperial army defending the British Empire in the Far East.

7. The Foundations of the Empire — The Psychological Bonds and Governing Ideas

1 · "WHENCE COMES THE COHESION OF THE BRITISH EMPIRE?"

Whence comes the cohesion of the Brit. Emp.?
1. Patriotism. Loyalty. Custom.
2. Religion. Race. Pride in various manifestations. Habit. Language.
Mere law is the weakest of all bonds.

These words, jotted down by Lord Balfour a few weeks before his death, were revealed in a letter to the London *Times* on December 14, 1936. They form the theme on which this chapter must close, though it has been implicit in all that has been written above. But the emphasis of the chapter so far has been mainly upon institutions and the more concrete ideas and material relations. If the economic bonds, which are of the greatest importance, have been omitted it is mainly because they receive some attention in the other chapters of this book. We must turn now to the imponderables, the emotional forces and their accompanying ideas, which escape only too easily through the coarse meshes of the normal analysis with its emphasis upon certain formal or abstract categories. The British Commonwealth, whether in peace or war, can never be understood either by friend or enemy, or would-be impartial scientific observer, unless he has an understanding of these imponderables.

If this element is studied in the speeches of the leaders and statesmen of the British Commonwealth, it will be seen how largely it figures implicitly or explicitly in them. When King George VI tried at the London Guildhall to sum up his visit to Canada and the United States, he emphasized as his "first and deepest impression" that "even in this age of machines and mass production, the strength of human feeling is still the most potent of all the forces affecting world affairs." Mr. Churchill's speeches are full of understanding of this point. So also are the speeches of General Smuts — as when he said, in the Union Parliament in 1928, that the British Commonwealth was not held together like Empires in the past by law and sovereign authority: " Here," he said, " is an entirely new condition — no central force, but psychology, which is more powerful, the soul of a group of nations." Mr. Mackenzie King realized the importance of these imponderables when he explained in 1937 that the Imperial conference system worked easily because of " an antecedent and substantial measure of readiness to work towards common ends." It was indeed this basic psychological condition that alone made the machinery workable.

II · THE FAMILY BOND, ITS VALUE, AND CONSEQUENCES

The basic fact of the British Commonwealth is that it is a family of nations. The relations of its peoples to one another are those of the members of a family. This is not, as it is often taken to be, a mere analogy but a living reality. Only in this fact have we any key to the meaning of the words of the Official Historian describing Australia's response in 1914: " A warm, enthusiastic response to the magnetism of kinship thrilled the country as it had never been touched before in its most profound emotions." [77] Only in this fact is the real key to be found to the spontaneous and unpledged going together of the members of the British Commonwealth into war, or to those messages received by Winston Churchill from the Prime Ministers of all the dominions in the dark hours after Dunkirk — " messages couched in the most moving terms, in which they endorse our decision to go on and declare themselves ready to share our fortunes and persevere to the end."

[77] Scott, *Official History of Australia in the War of 1914–1918*, Vol. XI, p. 862.

In these phenomena there is something far more than the fact, better understood perhaps by political thinkers in earlier generations than in our own,[78] that the private family situation and the feelings, ideas, and traditions associated with it have a profound influence on the lives of men in the wider society of the State, influencing their relations as individuals to authority, and affecting their group loyalties and antagonisms and their political ideas and philosophy. In the British Commonwealth there is superimposed upon this normal situation characteristic of all societies, an additional factor — the family relation of the members of the Commonwealth to one another and the ideas and emotions appropriate to this relation. Each member nation of the family has its individuality due to many historical factors; but each has its own characteristic set of relations with, and emotional attitudes towards, the other members of its family of nations. This general set of emotional relations affects somewhat differently each citizen. His private family pattern may play a part in determining just where he fits into the general supernational family pattern — whether he exaggerates or underemphasizes a particular trend such as the independent status of his dominion in relation to the Mother Country, or the character and degree of loyalty of which his nature is capable.

It is easy to see how this family relation developed. The " great Dominions of the Crown " were not States built primarily by the conquest of subject peoples. English, Scotch, Welsh, Irish, settlers went to the new lands, taking with them from their homeland common ideas, traditions, ideals, and loyalties, all that makes up the character of a people, the cultural heritage of their mother countries.

Out of this common inheritance the dominions have developed their own individual societies. They have passed through a first phase of dependence on the Mother Country; their second phase was that of adolescence with its growing independence and self-reliance, its tendency to over self-assertion, its emphasis upon status and repudiation of the authority of the Mother Country, combined with an inability to accept the full responsibilities of autonomy. The third phase into which they now enter is characterized by an adult willingness and ability to accept responsibility, and unwillingness to remain dependent, combined with a reasonable acceptance of the family bonds without undue self-assertion or subservience. But if the Mother Country from which

---

[78] E.g., Sir Henry Maine, *Ancient Law*.

they sprang were to disappear, with all the loss of prestige involved for their common legal and political systems, the inner structure of each of the daughter societies would be profoundly affected.

It is only when we regard dominion nationalism in this light that we can understand its essential difference from nationalism of the normal type. At least in the wide sphere of the British Commonwealth nationalism is no selfish self-regarding thing. It is rather a nationalism like that of Britain itself, which, as it achieves the mental maturity that should go with adult stature, becomes increasingly aware of the need of subordinating itself freely to the requirements of life in the family of British nations.

Only when the history of the relations of Britain with the dominions is examined from this point of view (and such a history still has to be written) can the magnitude of the achievement of British statesmanship in building the new British Commonwealth of Nations be appreciated. The successful handling by Britain of this most difficult of all psychological transitions, after the initial disaster of 1776, demanded endless patience, a skill on the part of the much maligned Colonial Office, a degree of political maturity and wisdom in the successive British governments and parliaments, which have been rarely shown in history.[79]

Legal Consequences of the Family Bond. It is in this light only that we can measure aright the meaning and importance of legal conceptions such as the *inter se* doctrine. By this doctrine the family group of the British Commonwealth has established in some measure a private system of international law which refuses to recognize the relations between its members as being of the same character as the relations between normal states. For example, legal agreements between its members are not regarded as being in the nature of international treaties. In this light also must be considered the private system of commercial treaty relations involved in Imperial preference. These are regarded as lying outside the scope of most-favored-nation clauses in commercial treaties with foreign powers, because they are treated as private arrangements between members of an inner family circle. So also the private family arrangements regarding defense, which are implicit in the treaties

---

[79] It is characteristic that a Colonial Office Official, Sir Charles Lucas, in *Greater Rome and Greater Britain*, 1912, should have written one of the few essays on the " family analogy " in the British Commonwealth. See also W. Y. Elliott, *The New British Empire*, 1932, Chapter IV.

for limitation of naval armaments, and the private Empire diplomatic system.[79a] One can see this family conception actually working in the mind of an eminent constitutional lawyer, Sir John Latham, former Attorney General of the Commonwealth of Australia, now Chief Justice of the High Court of Australia. Speaking on the Statute of Westminster in the Australian Parliament on July 17, 1931, he said, " I regard the relations of the self-governing parts of the Empire, *inter se,* as corresponding closely in the political world to the relations of the members of a family in the personal world. I do not want the relations of myself and my children to be determined by rules written in a book, to which each of us must refer to discover who is right and who is wrong. I do not desire such things to be made rigid by legal rules and enactments." In this passage perfect expression is given to the psychological assumption on which the whole law is built and without a knowledge of which it cannot be understood.

III · THE FUNDAMENTAL ASSUMPTION OF MUTUAL AID

As an illustration of the basic political ideas which spring from this family bond we may take what might be called the conception of mutual security. The mutual security system of the British Commonwealth cannot be regarded as merely the outcome of the conception of a common interest in a system of collective security between independent states with which the League of Nations has made us familiar. A common interest may exist without people realizing it or being able to achieve it. The psychological bonds uniting the members of the League were too weak to enable this idea and the necessary political institutions to take root. It was an idea not yet able to command enough of the will and the instinctive emotional forces of the peoples to permit it to become a living reality.

The mutual security system of the British Commonwealth, on the other hand, has a solid psychological basis. It is no artificial creation, but the outgrowth of the family bonds uniting its members. Its roots lie deep back in the history of the Empire. It has behind it a long experience which has been embodied in a set of ideas and ethical principles,

---

[79a] The habit whereby the members of the British Commonwealth of Nations constitute " one family " when convenient, and independent sovereignties when equally convenient, has called forth protests from other countries, particularly as regards " *inter se* " exemptions from international covenants and from the most-favored-nation clause in commercial treaties. See my *New British Empire* and Robert Stewart, *Treaty Making Relations of the British Commonwealth of Nations.* W.Y.E.

such as the plain and simple principle that if you would command the loyal support of others, you must be loyal to them. It is the principle expressed by Charles James Fox in his letter to Talleyrand on March 26, 1806. In reply to the latter's inquiry as to a possible basis for peace, Fox pointed out that England " would not treat, still less conclude upon anything but in concert with her allies, especially the Emperor of Russia." " England," Fox wrote, " cannot neglect the interest of any of her Allies." [79b] If loyalty to your allies, how much more loyalty to the fellow members of your family of nations in the British Commonwealth! And it is striking that in September 1939 in the supreme hour when the dominion governments had to take their decisions, it was this simple principle of ethics that stood out in their minds.

Those who expressed this feeling most clearly in September 1939 were leaders like General Smuts and Colonel Reitz in South Africa and M. Lapointe, the French-Canadian leader; and by expressing it they showed how fully they had entered into the British Commonwealth as members of the common family. " I think that we should do our duty," said General Smuts to his Parliament; " we should do the proper thing and align ourselves with our friends, and we should ward off and prevent those dangers which are almost sure to overtake this country in the future, if we now isolate ourselves and have afterwards to face our ordeal alone." As M. Lapointe before the outbreak of the war put it, " If Canada has to rely on allies . . . those allies will have to rely on Canada." It was the certainty on the part of the dominions that in the event of war Great Britain would come unhesitatingly to their assistance, that made the great difference between the British Commonwealth and all other international associations like the League of Nations or groupings based upon multilateral or bilateral treaties of mutual assistance. Only certainty can breed certainty. Without it there can be no collective security, and it is a plant of slow growth.

IV · COMMON CITIZENSHIP AND COMMONWEALTH LOYALTY

The Prime Minister of Canada in his tribute at the Imperial Conference of 1937 to King George V said, " His conception of the Empire was always proclaimed in terms of the loyalties of the home and the affections of family life." And the speeches of leading statesmen in the Empire have been full of this same conception. The tributes of loyalty made by all the Imperial Conferences to His Majesty the King have

[79b] Papers relative to the Discussion with France in the Year 1806, London, 1807, No. 5.

been no mere empty formulae, but have expressed the inner reality of the British Commonwealth. The prayer of the Imperial Conference in 1937 that " Your Majesties may long be spared to strengthen the ties of affection and loyalty which unite all the peoples of the British Commonwealth under the Crown," as indeed all previous " loyal resolutions " from 1887 onward, expressed the family ties binding the peoples of the Commonwealth through the symbol of the Crown " as Head of this great family of peoples." The Imperial Conference was itself a gathering of the heads of the family, and the majority of Imperial Conferences have been associated with great events in the life of the Sovereign — such as the Golden Jubilee of 1887, the Diamond Jubilee of 1897, the Coronation of 1911, the Jubilee of 1935, and the Coronation of 1937.

Out of the spreading from the center by migration without breach of family ties, and with the continuance unbroken of the allegiance to the common Crown, there has come the most significant of all the institutions of the British Commonwealth; namely, common citizenship, the " common status " of " British Subject " as distinguished from the " particular (national) status." [80] The psychological importance of this institution of " common citizenship " as the basis and the symbol of the supernational loyalty and patriotism uniting British subjects all over the Commonwealth to each other, and particularly to the United Kingdom, cannot be overemphasized. This wider loyalty varies in degree and character with individuals. For whole groups of peoples, such as the French-Canadians and the Dutch South Africans, it exists in a lesser degree, or it may be even replaced in the case of some groups and individuals by antagonism towards the Commonwealth. Yet it must always be remembered that the British Commonwealth is a family of affiliated peoples almost as much as it is of kindred peoples.

The " common citizenship," and the feeling of a common patriotism extending out to the whole family of nations, remains the most important single factor to be taken into account in explaining, in Lord Balfour's phrase, " the cohesion of the British Empire." If there had been a breach of continuity of allegiance, a breaking of the family tie, with the profound psychological disturbances which may accompany such a change, the British Commonwealth as described here could never have existed. British, Canadians, Australians, New Zealanders, South Afri-

---

[80] Report of the Imperial Conference, 1937. Eire has legislated to eliminate the " common status," so far as its nationals are concerned, substituting for it what may be called a reciprocal citizenship.

cans, even Indians from British India, and most of the sixty millions of colored peoples in the colonial Empire, are not in law aliens to one another. They are fellow citizens in a vast supernational family of kindred and affiliated peoples.

It is inevitable that the picture of a highly complex situation boldly sketched in this last section should be oversimplified and overidealized. It has been objected that the British Commonwealth, because of its lack of a more centralized organization, failed to foresee and to arm itself in time against the aggression of the Axis powers. But this surely was the common failure of many democracies, whatever their form of organization. And it is not clear that if the British Commonwealth had had a federal organization it would have shown greater foresight or resolution in advance, or have met the crisis when it actually arose with less internal friction. " In this war the British Commonwealth has functioned as a unitary state almost as smoothly as if we had been provinces in a federation." These are the words in which high officials from Britain, Canada, and Australia summed up to the writer their judgment on the working of the machinery of the British Commonwealth during the war. Yet it is not clear that this loose type of organization will continue to be entirely adequate, or that it would be effective between states not bound by the strong psychological bonds that unite the members of the Commonwealth to one another.

It is in these bonds that the secret of the British Commonwealth lies. Its greatest leaders from Edmund Burke to Winston Churchill have understood. In one of his prophetic speeches five months before the war began the latter said:

" Some foreigners mock at the British Empire because there are no parchment bonds or hard steel shackles which compel its united action. But there are other forces far more compulsive to which the whole fabric spontaneously responds. These deep tides are flowing now. They sweep away in their flow differences of class and party. They override the vast ocean spaces which separate the Dominions of the King."

CHAPTER III

The British War
Administration

PART ONE
WARTIME ADMINISTRATION
IN GERMANY AND
GREAT BRITAIN[1]

by Heinrich Brüning

1. The General Problem of War Administration

A comparison of wartime administration in different countries, especially in Great Britain and any of the larger continental European countries, will always be a difficult task. The problems of different countries
in regard to raw materials, production, supply, and rationing varied
greatly even before the use of such enormous quantities of military
equipment and munitions as are required by modern warfare. Wherever

---

[1] In asking Dr. Heinrich Brüning, Littauer Professor of Government in the Graduate School
of Public Administration, Harvard University, to contribute to the present volume I have imposed
very heavily on his friendship. The following chapter is his current revision of a lecture comparing the organization of war controls of industry in Germany and Great Britain, which originally
formed the basis of discussion in a seminar that he and I conducted together at Harvard, and
which he has now kindly placed at my disposal. The chart of British administrative organization
which accompanies it is based on work done by members of the same seminar, particularly by
Miss Nix, who acted as secretary of the seminar — W.Y.E.

adequate supplies of food stuffs, feeding stuffs, and industrial raw materials were home-produced, or where their regular importation was unhindered, and where there was abundant man power and industrial capacity, problems of rationing, allocation, or priorities were practically non-existent. All that was necessary was clear and farsighted strategic planning combined with the right timing of orders for supply by the defense forces, and the close coordination of the military operations and supply of all the defense forces under one supreme command. All these are problems which have arisen in earlier wars.

At the beginning of the First World War almost all the belligerents expected it to be of the same character. They entered hostilities without any idea of, or preparation for, a long war, which exhibited before its close all the main characteristics of total war. Every country began with the administrative machinery, the methods of strategic planning, and the organization of supply to which it had been accustomed for more than half a century. The separate defense forces ordered their own ammunition and arms, uniforms, and food supplies through their separate and long established procurement offices. In some countries it was, however, realized very soon that the indiscriminate mobilization of miners and farm hands was threatening future fuel and food supplies. The blockaded countries were forced to recognize, too, that their available supplies of food and of agricultural requirements, as well as of industrial raw materials, were insufficient for a war of longer than twelve months.

Without some control of the market in these countries prices would have risen enormously, and hoarding would have produced widespread discontent and led to the disappearance of certain essential goods. Rationing, the fixing of maximum prices, and the control and requisitioning of raw materials were unavoidable. New industrial capacity had also to be found in addition to existing ammunition and arms plants, and skilled workmen who had been mobilized had soon to be released from the army for work in essential war industries. Plants of little or no importance for military supply had to be converted to war production or closed down, and their workmen took the places of the skilled men released from the army. As more firms changed over to war production and by various methods of organization more skilled labor was made available, step by step, without any comprehensive plan, an increasing number of raw materials were controlled directly, and their utilization by particular manufacturers determined in advance.

During the first half of the last war hardly any government tackled these problems with foresight or a full understanding of their magnitude. The control of various commodities and the organization of supply were improvised and somewhat haphazard. In some countries special, semi-independent organizations were formed outside the direct control of the government or the defense forces. Individual merchants and manufacturers competed with one another for raw materials and semi-finished goods. What was worse was that in almost every country the army and navy placed orders in competition with one another, without regard to cost or to whether the raw materials and man power available in a given period would permit their fulfillment. Without complete control and allocation of materials the distinguishing of certain orders as urgent and the issuing of various forms of priority certificates defeated their own purpose. They led only too easily to the creation of bottlenecks of every kind and prevented the full and steady employment of available capacity and man power, especially when priority orders were placed not directly by government departments but through interested agents and intermediate contractors.

There were severe drawbacks in basing production primarily on priority certificates. Certificates were issued in excess of the raw materials and semi-finished products available in a given period. It frequently happened that a manufacturer was able to secure with priority certificates all but one or more of the materials he required when, because of a temporary scarcity, he was without any possibility of obtaining the rest. This was doubly disastrous for the war effort, since the raw materials and semi-finished goods he had already acquired were wasted. Under the crude priority system, half of the necessary materials for a given type of armament might lie unused in one firm, and the other half in another, the materials, capacity, and labor of the two firms thus having no part in the productive process.

The situation was aggravated by the fact that until late in the war there was not in any country a sufficiently close relation between the planning of military operations and the estimation of the future supply requirements of the defense forces. For this the continual strategic miscalculations and tactical surprises of the last war were largely responsible. It was not of first importance to the Allies, whose relatively free disposal of the raw materials of the world was limited only by the shipping tonnage available to them; but the position of the blockaded powers was very different.

Their very limited supply of raw materials threatened to diminish in proportion to the enormous consumption of ammunition and increasing demands of mechanized warfare. In Germany it was soon discovered that military requirements had to be adapted not so much to productive capacity as to the supply of raw materials available. To exaggerate, one can say that the strategy of the Central Powers, especially during the second half of the war, when the employment of industrial capacity had reached an optimum, was dictated by the limited supply of raw materials. For the Allies, on the other hand, the amount of raw materials imported at any given time could be planned in accordance with strategic decisions.

In fact, of course, the Central Powers succeeded in spite of the blockade in importing considerable amounts of raw materials throughout the war. But the army and navy were forced, nevertheless, to coordinate their demands and to submit definite plans for fixed periods in advance. This was originally due to the efforts of the civilian administration and of a number of industrialists who did not share the optimistic views of some military and naval leaders about armament requirements and the possibilities of supply, and who succeeded in persuading the War Ministry that plans should be made as if for a war of unlimited duration. Civilian consumption had to be restricted and adapted to a bare minimum, and the production of civilian goods was concentrated in factories that could not be readily converted to war production.

Once that had been accomplished, and in the expectation that the war would last for at least three years after 1915, a formula was worked out to give the possible supply of any commodity for any period. This formula was:

$$D \text{ (supply for a number of months)} = \frac{M \text{ (supply on hand)}}{V \text{ (monthly consumption)} - Z \text{ (monthly production and import)}}.$$

The use of this formula for different materials made it possible to state when the demands of the defense forces were submitted exactly how far they could be satisfied and what would be left for civilian consumption. The production program for three years was divided into six-month periods, and the supplies of raw materials available in each month calculated. The program had to be so coordinated and the allocation of supplies to different firms so organized that each firm would have all the different raw materials it required at any time.

In the face of sudden changes in the military situation, changes had to be made in the plan of production, as they did with the Allies also. In Germany there was a certain rigidity, whatever changes occurred, due to the strict limitation of supplies. This meant of course that the strategic planning of the Central Powers was restricted by the conditions of long range planning of production to a degree that more than offset their strategic advantage of operating on interior lines of communication.

This was a reversal of Germany's position in the only two wars of the preceding hundred years in which all her military forces had been mobilized. The War of 1866 was somewhat like a civil war, and lasted seven weeks. The only real foreign war, in 1870, lasted only seven months, and was carried out on a basis of careful planning, coordination, and synchronization of supply with strategy in advance by the regular procurement branch of the Army. The outbreak of war in 1914, on the contrary, followed an increase in the size of the Army to which the organization of supply had not yet been fully adapted, so that all the trained man power available could not be put to use in the first six months of the war.

For two years before the outbreak of war in fact, the General Staff were so much preoccupied with reorganization and with fear of war against the combined forces of Russia, France, and Great Britain that General Moltke, in contrast to Admiral von Tirpitz, supported von Bethmann-Hollweg in his endeavors to reach an understanding with Great Britain. The Chancellor went so far as to reject urgent demands by the General Staff for increased economic preparedness, which he feared might endanger peaceful relations with England. The same difficulty of combining preparedness with appeasement was experienced in Great Britain before the present war.

All these experiences of the First World War formed the background of much discussion and the basis of critical studies in Germany after 1932. The results were embodied in the Four Years' Plan, in which the whole organization of military supply was built up behind a screen of other purposes, and in decrees issued at the outbreak of the Second World War providing for the coordination of strategic and economic planning, the civilian administration, and the various agencies of industry, agriculture, and the Nazi Party. Similarly in Great Britain many years before the outbreak of the present war the Committee of Imperial Defense prepared a plan and a skeleton organization for the mobilization of the economic resources of the Empire. This too was based on the experience of the last war and on plans adopted but not yet carried fully into effect when the breakdown of the Central Powers occurred in 1918.

It is therefore wrong to suppose that the chief of the Imperial General Staff and the able officers and civil servants collaborating in the Committee of Imperial Defense did not take into consideration with regard to organization in wartime the full impact of the danger of war with the Axis and Japan. It would be more correct to say that they were filled with apprehensions similar to those of the German General Staff and a few top ranking civil servants before 1914. They were handicapped, as the German General Staff was before 1914, by the fact that the Government did not fully appreciate the gravity of the situation and that too many people in influential positions were unwilling for defense preparations to be consolidated in peacetime.[1a] Plans for preemptive purchasing of a number of essential commodities such as, for example, metal alloys, which were proposed in 1937, would very likely if they had been adopted have rendered impossible the whole subsequent policy of the Nazis. When leading officials of a country that has been victorious in one war continue to occupy the same positions in a second, they are strongly inclined to rely on exactly the same methods which formerly proved successful, an average human reaction which has invited calamity throughout history.

There can be no doubt, however, that some of the major problems of modern total war were studied by the Committee of Imperial Defense and preparations made to meet them in the years immediately preceding the present war. This is true especially of the tentative organization of administration and supply on a regional basis in case communications should be interrupted by air attack. The coordination of certain aspects of civil administration, military organization, and supply was also considered, and before the outbreak of war certain outstanding civil servants were placed in political or administrative positions in which their experience and gifts could be brought to bear on these problems of organization in case of war.

Both Great Britain and Germany had learned that one of the most important conditions of victory would be the successful coordination of strategic planning, supply, and civil administration which was lack-

<hr>

[1a] Cf. the summary in the leading article, "Conduct of Foreign Policy," The Times, London, January 4, 1943.

ing in the last war. That is the problem to be discussed in this paper. It resolves itself into two related questions: how do the German and the English systems provide for general coordination of the war effort at the top? and how do they provide for coordination in detail at the regional and local levels? This of course involves the relations between political authorities, administrative officers, the defense forces, and associations of industry, trade, and agriculture at every stage of development. Special attention will be paid to the functions of the civil service, which are very different in Great Britain and Germany, but which in both countries have undergone essential modifications during the last war and the present one.

During the last war the executive functions of the German civil service with regard to supply were different from, and to some extent less important than, what they had been in earlier wars. The development of military and semi-independent organizations for the control and distribution of different commodities pushed the civil service somewhat into the background. With the exception of certain very able and farsighted men in top positions, some of whom became leading figures in the semi-independent war agencies created *ad hoc,* the civil service was not prepared to assume the tremendous burden of organization which resulted from the technical revolution of the last war. Only the top ranks of the civil service were concerned with these new problems, and its regional and local officers were affected, at most, indirectly. In the creation of agencies outside the civil service for the particular problems of the war there was little difference between practice in Germany and other Continental countries and in England.

Industrialists and business men occupied leading public positions in every country during the last war, because the methods and training of the regular civil service were not appropriate to the control and detailed allocation of particular commodities. Neither was there in any country a sufficient number of army and navy officers trained for such tasks, although both the British and the German navies occupied exceptional positions in this respect. In Germany the position of all the armed forces with regard to the organization of production has been greatly changed in the present war.

The Treaty of Versailles, like any knock-out peace imposed upon a virile nation, had unexpected consequences here and in other respects. Because of the compulsory reduction of the total number of officers in the German Army to 10,000, several hundred able young staff officers had to find some other livelihood. Thus they studied economics or science and technology at the universities, or entered business firms and there learned the details of organization and production as they could not have done in any other way. These people were later available for the administration of the Four Years' Plan. In industry they had risen in twenty years to top positions, where they combined with their earlier general staff or other military training wide experience of a particular business. There is a parallel in England in the case of former high officials of the Admiralty who now hold leading positions in industry.

Although in the course of the war there have been further parallels in the evolution of the British and the German administrative systems, there are essential differences between them resulting from historical causes. It must be emphasized from the beginning that a totalitarian form of government does not in itself make for easier and better planning or a higher degree of efficiency in administration, and that the functioning of the wartime administration in Germany to date has been largely due to the long established traditions of the Army and the civil service. That a democracy, under a federal form of government, is capable of the simplest and most efficient organization is demonstrated by the example of Switzerland, even though she has certain particular advantages of tradition and geography.

Hardly any other country combines decentralized administration with the highest degree of military preparedness in peacetime so successfully. The Swiss army organization has always received the highest tribute from the German General Staff; it was the model after which General Groener and other leading officers tried to organize the German Army on a purely defensive basis before their removal from power. The central government at Berne works largely through the agency of industrial associations and the cantonal governments. Thus it is kept in contact with reality and with the people, and escapes the great danger of over-centralized administration — blueprint thinking, with the habit of referring every question to some central office by correspondence, a method which stultifies imagination and initiative.

It is crucial for any country at war to avoid this danger, which is common, if one examines the facts, to all forms of government. What is most important is the supreme coordination of the main lines of policy, strategy, and supply. It is only the manner in which this is achieved that varies with the form of government and with the character, imagination, and driving force of leading figures in a country. What is next in importance is a system of administration in which execution in detail is decentralized, either through associations of industry, commerce, and agriculture, or regionally and locally, and in which flexibility, which is so essential in total war, is ensured. Regional administration cannot be successful without definite planning and the close coordination of every phase of the war effort at the center. The necessary harmony and firmness of will at the center depends, correspondingly, on coordination at the regional level of the execution by different branches of the administration of decisions reached at the top.

Above all it is necessary for the responsibilities of every branch and every member of the administration to be clearly defined in such a way as to prevent their interference in tasks that are not theirs. Those bearing final responsibility at the top must have some guarantee, which will not preclude the free adaptation of general instructions to varying circumstances by subordinate officials, that the different branches of the war organization are in gear at every level. Only so will they be free to plan ahead and to meet unforeseeable problems quickly and positively.

Clear cut responsibility is easier to achieve on paper than in fact, especially in a total war affecting every branch of production. It presupposes great self-restraint, not least on the part of those in central positions. This should not be confused with exclusive departmentalism; it is very dangerous for any official to ignore the relation of his own definitely prescribed functions to others'. Neither does a precise delimitation of his responsibilities relieve any one of the task of anticipating his possible duties under suddenly changed strategic conditions. Without such self-restraint and consideration of future contingencies, a man of great push and pull whose job is to speed up the production of a particular weapon may succeed only at the expense of other, equally essential types of production. This has happened more than once in several of the belligerent countries.

What the results of a sharp definition of functions will be depends largely on the balance struck between the enumeration of specific tasks and reliance on the discretion of executive officers. Constructive initiative should not be curbed, but neither can irresponsibility be tolerated. Too informal a method of procedure, especially at the level of supreme coordination, may end in muddling in spite of a clear distribution of authority on paper. The establishment of the essential conditions of successful administration, in wartime particularly, requires men of great administrative experience. It is in fact only through experience that the right combination of centralization in planning and decentralization in execution can be recognized. Experience without evenness of temperament is of course worthless, and in this respect the demands of war are more exacting than those of peace, since war administration involves a combination of the various methods of different professional types.

For the problems arising in every stage of total war to be solved promptly and efficiently, there must be close cooperation between political leaders, army and navy officers, the civil service, and business men and technicians, as well as a clear demarkation of their functions. The patriotism felt in wartime is sometimes expected to make cooperation spontaneous, and certainly it makes it much easier. The mentality and the methods of these different types, as well as their attitudes toward any given question, are nevertheless very different. Differences of experience and lifelong routine necessarily produce differences of outlook. One of the most difficult problems of wartime administration is the amalgamation, as far as that is possible, of these different and sometimes antagonistic conceptions.

There is no formula for its solution. Unless it is solved, however, the best-made plans are irrelevant. This is the lesson of the defeat of France. The law drafted by the French General Staff for the mobilization of the entire nation in case of war and adopted by Parliament in 1938 was unquestionably comprehensive, thorough, and systematic. It had little beneficial effect either when war occurred or in the prewar period. For want of vision and energy, and, even more, for want of close cooperation among political leaders, the defense forces, the bureaucracy, and business, much irretrievable time for arms production was lost, and the elaborate organization created meanwhile lacked the right spirit for the best combination of the different talents required.

Men who have spent their lives in politics always tend to choose the alternative that promises to excite least opposition at the moment. As they are accustomed to registering the slightest oscillations of public opinion, they are inclined to support measures that will produce the most favorable immediate emotional reaction. In wartime, if not in peacetime as well, this is a very dangerous method. The experience of history is certainly that farsighted and constructive measures are for the most part contrary to current tendencies, and therefore initially unpopular. If this were not the case, the successful accomplishments of the greatest political leaders would not have been attended by so much suffering and pain. These men, while accepting unpopularity, vitriolic abuse, and slander, neglected no opportunity to further those policies which alone could bring about lasting results.

Civil servants as a class, in many European countries, are trained too much to carry out instructions by a routine based upon regulations and precedents. They cannot approach their problems like a business man buying and selling on the open market in the particular interests of a single firm. They must establish uniform procedures of general applicability. In contracting for urgently needed supplies they cannot offer a premium for quick delivery without having some legal basis for it, or without some assurance that it will not create a precedent upsetting the oldest traditions of public expenditure. " Business looks forward, law looks backward," E. M. H. Lloyd writes in his admirable book *Experiments in State Control*.[2] With regard to business, the statement is, of course, intended only in the sense of this particular antithesis.

Even civil servants, like those employed by the German state railways, who enjoy great freedom of initiative are not safe from the risk of a routine conduct of business in accordance with established rules. Thus in long years of service, especially if it is in the same department of one ministry, they may easily lose what native imagination they possess. Seeing that constructive efforts are often frustrated by the expression of popular reactions in parliament or by over-cautious and unimaginative cabinet ministers, they learn to be slow in suggestion and to attend strictly to their explicit duties. Where they are a closed group, recruited on the basis of examination and promoted in accordance with seniority, they may, in addition, be unfit for tasks of economic organization which require firmness of purpose and flexibility in execution, as well as practical business experience.

When, as in wartime, the civil service assumes business functions, business men must assume the role of civil servants and accustom themselves to semi-governmental procedure. They bring with them to the tasks of war administration many qualities not ordinarily found among public servants. If they have risen to the top of great business concerns by merit, they have learned the technique of administration and the division of responsibility at different levels in detail. They calculate exactly the effect of any decision down to the lowest level of any branch of a firm. Civil servants share this advantage only in countries where they are frequently transferred between central administrative departments and the subordinate regional and local administration.

---

[2] *Experiments in State Control at the War Office and the Ministry of Food*, Oxford, 1924.

Business men are able to select the best man for a particular job without reference to general budgetary provisions or fixed rules of promotion. A man who fails to do well can be readily and easily exchanged. Successful business men must have vivid imagination as well as the genius and courage to make momentous decisions. Without being accustomed to take great risks they would not have attained leadership. They are not bound as civil servants are by precedent. They may learn, too, to establish definite responsibility for different agents in the execution of a decision once taken. They have often great technical experience or know what experts can give quick and accurate advice in technical matters. Finally, they may know how to deal informally with their staffs without sacrificing fixed responsibility and efficiency, although this has not been so in all cases during the last war or the present one. These are a few of the factors that make their services indispensable in wartime.

They suffer, on the other hand, from the handicap of unfamiliarity with politics, or rather, with parliamentary methods and political criticism. They may feel hampered, too, by the formalities of bureaucratic organization. Lack of military experience may put them at a disadvantage in their dealings with the defense forces. They may be unable, as they were in many European countries in the last war, to accustom themselves to the abruptness and icy objectivity with which general staff officers may change their supply specifications with changed military conditions, perhaps upsetting carefully planned and organized production just at its peak.

Business men in war administration may also suffer from too narrow a conception of their functions. Placing the orders of one large firm in a normal market is essentially different from the organization of production for total war. The possible implications of every step for the economy as a whole and for later adaptation to changed military conditions must be taken into consideration. This can be done only if those occupying top positions in the organization of production are initiated into strategic plans and conditions and have natural gifts sufficient to grasp their full importance. Another handicap for the business man who accepts a coordinating administrative position may be his tendency to concentrate on the aspect of any problem that is most familiar to him, leaving other considerations to the attention of specialists. When this is the case there will not be the uniform coordination of effort in every phase of production which, as the experience of the last and the present wars shows, officers trained in general staff duties can, with few exceptions, achieve. The real problem of the business man and the civil servant in war administration is that in making decisions that must determine future military supplies they run the risk of being blamed at some time for influencing strategy adversely. The natural desire to avoid such responsibility is a very important factor in organization. When the coordination of strategy and supply is substituted for unified direction, the chiefs of staff or commander-in-chief on the one hand and those civilians who are responsible for military supplies on the other almost inevitably find themselves concerned in one another's functions.

It has been very popular from time to time, in England especially, but also in other European countries, for journalists and politicians to abuse the "brass hats." This attitude is generally ill-founded. There are brass hats in every army, but their prominence may be due to the fact that in peacetime budgetary considerations have left little opportunity for quick promotion in the army, or for able young men, especially those whose intelligence and character would predestine them for careers in the military or naval staffs, to enter the armed forces. The right training of officers for staff work stimulates not only the qualities required for strategic planning or for a quartermaster's work, but also those required for general administrative functions in total war. It is in fact the question of training which is decisive. Good military training, while it includes the precise execution of orders, also makes for quick and bold decision. It should instill that calmness and courage in the face of unexpected difficulty which is essential to the unravelling of a confused situation.

Frequent transfers between the general staff and line commands provide the same opportunities to discover how plans and decisions made at the top are worked out in practice as are enjoyed by civil servants who are transferred between the central departments and the regional administration, and usually by business leaders. Whatever experience staff officers in the army and navy may gain of branches of the service in which they have not specialized enlarges their vision and reduces the danger of routine decisions. Any one who is forced from time to time to leave behind him most of what he has learned and to learn something different will gain in initiative and constructive imagination.

Staff officers who have studied problems of communication, executed great engineering projects as they have done in the United States, entered large engineering or business establishments, or carried out the organization of particular branches of public administration, bring to their war service experience and qualities which fit them to solve the problems of coordination in production not only at the top but also at the regional and local levels. Trained officers of the British Admiralty are to be found in peacetime in private naval construction firms and in the administration of dockyards and ports, and in wartime throughout industry. Such experience has been denied to the British Army, except for its procurement officers and the directors of the Royal Ordnance Factories.[3] For the rest, only the few army officers who held ranking positions in the colonial administration have had any general experience of administration. The lack of officers who combine general staff training with technical and industrial knowledge is a greater handicap in the present war than ever before, and is more dangerous, since Germany has, in consequence of the effects of the peace treaty already stated, a large number of such officers.

To sum up, one may say that in any country, whatever its political traditions or its available productive capacity, man power, and raw materials, there are two major problems of administrative organization for total war. The first is the coordination of strategic planning, supply, and civil administration at the top. The second is the coordination of production throughout the country. Only coordination at the regional and local levels will make the avoidance of bottlenecks possible as far as may be. Only if such coordination is efficient and assured can elaborate correspondence be eliminated. Bottlenecks occur not only in production but also in administration at the points where the burden of responsibility is greatest, and unless those who must make critical long-range decisions are freed of the burden of detail their vision will be obscured.

Closely related to these two problems is the organization of mass production in such a way as to secure the maximum flexibility consistent with volume. This, indeed, is the crux of modern war. Flexibility in design and volume of production are, as Captain Lyttelton has said, essentially opposed. The modern production engineer demands the manufacture of a given type as steadily as possible. This becomes more essential with every increase in the dilution of labor, as the employment of less skilled labor necessitates more elaborate tooling in order to simplify the manual actions to be performed. The most enormous output

---

[3] Great progress in the centralization of Army purchasing was made in Great Britain only during the second half of the nineteenth century.

secured by these means may, however, prove to be of no value in a military showdown. It is as true today as in the last war that the superiority of a particular tactic of offense or defense is only temporary. A type of airplane well adapted to tactical cooperation with large tank and motorized infantry masses may not prove to be of great value in large scale bombing, as was shown by the failure of the German attack on Great Britain in the months following Dunkirk.

The question is less vital to a country holding the strategic initiative than to its opponents. As soon as the Axis powers are forced, as the British Government has been several times, and as the United States Government has been, to adapt themselves suddenly to entirely changed conditions created by the initiative of their foes, the German organization may be seriously disturbed.

The changes made in the German supply organization in the spring of 1942 were probably occasioned not by the shortage of certain raw materials alone but by the continued absorption of German forces in Russia, the necessity of constructing new weapons of defense against threatened mass bombing, and the necessity of producing bombers comparable to the British and American in armor and striking power.

As war production approaches the maximum in all countries, the advantage of the possession of the strategic initiative may be reduced. The scope of strategic genius may be increasingly restricted, but strategic genius and tactical evolution will nevertheless continue to necessitate changes in the types of armament produced and in the organization of supply. The disturbing effect of such changes will be minimized where diplomacy and strategy are most closely combined, where the quickest advantage is taken of the results of technical observation of the performance of different weapons on the battlefield, and where the organization of supply is most flexible.

For Napoleon it was still possible to bring about the necessary coordination wholly in his own master mind. In the First World War, the only war for a century in which problems comparable to those that faced Napoleon arose, such coordination was not achieved in any country, and certainly it is doubtful whether any individual today can assume the role Napoleon performed for many years so successfully. The closer the coordination of the war effort at the top, and the greater the initiative permitted below, without danger to central executive control, the freer those who carry the burden of final decision will be to devote themselves to constructive planning and to the general direction of the gigantic war machinery. When maximum production is finally attained everywhere there will be an inevitable similarity between the administrative methods adopted in different countries, just as there was at the end of the last war. The wide variations of organization in different countries during the transitional period are largely explained by the beginning of preparation for war at different times and by differences in administrative tradition.

2. *The German System of War Administration*

I · THE TRADITIONS OF THE CIVIL SERVICE

Even in the greatest emergency of a total war, no government can create an administrative organization independently of the long established traditions of the country. Though this applies most directly to Great Britain, it is much more true of Nazi Germany than is generally realized. Napoleon could not have created the most perfectly centralized war organization the world had yet seen if it had not been for the complete centralization of the French administration under Richelieu and Mazarin. What he did was to revive their form of government, after the Revolution had destroyed all those traditional institutions which were least conformable to authoritarian military rule. There is one essential general aspect of this question. *The traditions of a country that owes its power to naval supremacy will differ in many ways from those of continental states.* Thus the role and the influence of the army and the civil service in normal times is much greater in almost every continental European country than in the Anglo-Saxon countries. In this respect there is no difference in principle between the German administration and the French. Since the beginning of the seventeenth century the political, military, and administrative evolution of these two countries has been determined by considerations which were all but unknown to England. Since this difference affects the present organization of the war effort in Germany and England as well as normal methods of administration, a few further comments may be in place.

The similarities of type among the administrations of different continental European countries are due in part to the fact that when a new and more efficient administration has been developed in one country principally for purposes of war, neighboring countries are forced to imitate it if they wish to survive. This was the case in many countries under the impact of the French military expansion in the seventeenth and eighteenth centuries. In most of them, including the greater part of Germany, there had for centuries been only a very loose central administration, the functions of administration remaining for the most part with the territories and towns. This changed as a result of the increasing predominance of a highly centralized administration in France during the one hundred fifty years preceding the Napoleonic era. The events of that period resembled today's. Then the success of the French administration in subordinating every other purpose to the expansionist policies of Richelieu and Mazarin compelled the countries chiefly threatened by them to imitate the French system. The military organization of old Prussia, of course, was dependent both on the French model and on an older, highly developed administrative system.

It was, however, the crushing expansion of the Napoleonic regime that led to the establishment nearly everywhere of centralized bureaucratic machinery especially adapted to the tasks of wartime. When Prussia was defeated in 1806 and forced into very much the position of Vichy France in 1940, farsighted patriots realized that Napoleon would be defeated only by the same kind of organization to which his success was largely due. The conception of the modern general staff appeared for the first time in Prussia, where it was combined, in the most critical period, with the French prefectural system and, contrary to the Napoleonic precedent, with a new and very democratic type of conscription. The subsequent development of a permanent general staff, culminating only under the elder Moltke, can be traced back in its essential lines to Napoleonic principles.

In peacetime the general staff had not only to plan the military operations required by any possible emergency, but also to plan the organization of supply in close connection with possible military operations. A form of civilian administration ensuring the organization of the civilian needs of the country in wartime and their coordination with military requirements was needed in addition. It cannot be doubted that the Napoleonic model of administration by *préfets* had great influence on the shaping of the civilian administration in Germany during the one hundred years between the Napoleonic Wars and the First World War, although the fact has been neglected for reasons of national pride. In Prussia, for example, and other German federal states a tendency to imitate the French prefectural system without regard for existing traditions prevailed in the years before the Allied victory over Napoleon. Attempts to effect a compromise between this system and older methods of administration have continued until the present war, in which the Napoleonic model has again, increasingly, prevailed.

The *federal tradition* has indeed been very strong throughout German history, and has demonstrated its power of survival again and again. Thus the decentralization of executive responsibility became a leading maxim of German administration. It had led to a combination of local self-government with devolution of the functions of the central government which was on the average, before the Nazis came into power, very happy. In this respect Germany differs greatly from both England and France.

In England after the Norman Conquest political power was far more centralized than in any other European country, and any tendency toward even limited regional autonomy was prevented. Neither was the delegation of the executive powers of the Crown for any large area to an officer responsible only to the central government, uniting in the hands of one man control over all the administrative problems of the region, fully accepted over any period of time. Because of the divergence in historical evolution, there are no precise and equivalent terms by which the fundamental differences in the methods of carrying out the policy of the central government on the Continent and in Great Britain can be expressed.

In France political and administrative centralization was established finally in the Napoleonic era. The existence of the *préfets* as agents of the central government did not imply any devolution of power to institutions of true regional self-government. The *préfet* in the Napoleonic conception was responsible only for the execution in his department of the instructions issued by the ministries in Paris, and the scope of representative government in the municipalities was as restricted as it was until the 1890's in England. In Germany, on the other hand, the vitality of politics and administration is strongest in the municipalities and the federal states. Every far-reaching increase of the power of the national government has been accepted grudgingly. It was only because of the experience of the two hundred years until the end of the Napoleonic Wars, in which Germany was the battlefield of foreign powers struggling for the domination of Europe, that the powers secured from the states by the national government in 1871, which, contrary to the popular impression abroad, were very slight, could be obtained.

Even under the Bismarckian constitution the importance of the federal states remained much greater in most branches of administration than that of the central government. In this respect Germany's constitutional and administrative problems resembled those of the United States, and the relation of the central government to the federal states was much the same. The central government could communicate with the self-governing municipalities or counties only indirectly through the administrations of the federal states, as the Swiss government does through the administrations of the cantons. The functions of the central government were about the same as those of the national executive in Washington during the same period; until 1920 even the right to impose and collect income taxes was reserved to the municipalities and the federal states. The powers of the Emperor were less than those of a president of the United States.[4]

Until 1919 there was no German cabinet. There were instead permanent secretaries in the different departments of the central government and a Chancellor, who was responsible for the whole policy of the government, but whose actual power ordinarily depended on the fact that he was also Prime Minister of Prussia. The Federal Council (*Bundesrat*), the members of which were appointed by the governments of the federal states, had much greater powers of control than has the Senate of the United States. The Chancellor had to obtain the approval of the Federal Council in advance for legislation introduced into the Reichstag. The larger federal states had their own armies and their own war ministers, though not separate general staffs. The only official access of the general staff to the Chancellor was through the Prussian war minister.

Within the federal states there was devolution of administrative power to provincial and district governors, whose functions were partly executive and partly those of control over self-governing provincial and local representative bodies.[5] The principle of this organization was to allow the greatest possible initiative to institutions of local self-government and to self-governing institutions of industry, trade, and agriculture, while ensuring general coordination by a single official in each district. To the stranger it seemed complicated, but it effectively com-

---

[4] The strength of his position depended on his constitutional powers in Prussia, the largest of the federal states.

[5] Prussia, which until 1938 comprised nearly two-thirds of the German population, was, and remains, divided into provinces and subdivided into districts. Some of the other federal states are no larger than Prussian provinces or administrative districts.

bined highly developed regional and local self-government with centralization at the top. It prevented the danger of over-centralization such as prevailed in France and prevented the rise of genuine local self-government there.

One of the greatest advantages of the German compromise was that every civil servant was trained to consider the *regional coordination of different branches of administration* as important as the work of the central departments. Civil servants in regional and local administration had to deal directly with people throughout the country in their daily lives, and not primarily with legislative provisions and statistical reports. They were expected to submit new problems as they arose to their superiors up to the central department, but they were left great freedom and discretion in carrying out the policy of the department in detail within the framework of existing legislation and administrative regulations. Under this system the social and industrial problems resulting from the rapid expansion of industry and the development of public utilities, almost all of which have been brought wholly or partly under the influence of government planning since the last decade before the First World War, were met, on the average, very constructively. The employment of technical experts as civil servants in the government-owned railways, mines, and forests, and the fact that cities elected men of professional training as mayors for terms of twelve years produced civil servants of broader vision, greater knowledge of general conditions, and greater initiative and adaptability than is possible under the narrower tradition of a civil service dominated by treasury officials with their exclusive emphasis on fiscal control.

Greater centralization and some curtailment of the powers of the federal states were necessitated by the problems arising from the last war and, even more, from the effects of the treaty of peace. In modern history at least, the accumulation of huge war debts generally leads to an increase in the power of the central government over the national resources and in its administrative functions, particularly in connection with taxation and unemployment, at the expense of the federal states. The Weimar Constitution created an opportunity for greatly increased centralization, without, however, providing any consistent redistribution of functions of national and state administration. Unfortunately, a tendency therefore prevailed for central ministries to set up separate agencies of their own throughout the country, thus destroying the established balance in regional administration. Much friction, duplication, and dissatisfaction was the outcome.[6] There were two undesirable consequences of particular importance, which impaired some of the best traditions of German administration.

Chiefs of the financial and the labor administration were appointed in each province with rank approximately equal to the provincial governor's, but dependent directly upon the central ministries. Thus there was no longer one man in each regional administrative unit responsible for the coordination of every aspect of administration within his area, as had been proved essential for efficient administration in the past. To have one such man who knows the different branches of administration as well as the people and the special conditions of his region greatly simplifies and facilitates the constructive solution of many problems. He must of course be endowed with vision, experience, and tact, and must have authority to make as many decisions as possible on the spot without reference to the central departments. Under such an arrangement, the responsibility of the central departments is normally limited to legislative planning and to issuing general instructions to the single responsible head of the entire administration of each region. Thus they are spared a voluminous correspondence about minor details and the impossible task of considering particular cases requiring immediate and flexible decision. Otherwise, the decision by central ministries of a multitude of individual cases not involving major questions of principle will be based only upon routine and precedent and will lead to the development of a purely legalistic method of administration. Members of the staff of a central ministry are always haunted in deciding questions in relation to special local conditions by the fear of creating a precedent that would be inappropriate to conditions in another part of the country.

The absence of a more systematic distribution of functions between the national and state administrations at the regional level, a problem which exists under every federal constitution, endangered another advantage of the older form of German administration — the exchange of civil servants among ministries, as well as between central ministries and the regional and local administration. A balance between centralization and decentralization, between planning and legislation and execu-

---

[6] Nevertheless, in grave situations in which the emergency powers of the president were invoked, the system was able, because of the traditions which remained alive in the civil service, to meet the greatest demands. A complete revision of the structure of prices, wages, and rents, for instance, was carried through in two months at the beginning of 1932 without the opening of any new administrative office or the appointment of any additional personnel. Cooperation between the central, state, and local administrations was perfectly satisfactory.

tion in detail is possible only when civil servants are frequently exchanged between the central, regional, and local administrations. Over a long period of time it became an established conviction in German administration that no one who had not held responsible positions in regional and local administration would ever do well in a central ministry. When young civil servants enter ministries without much experience and remain there permanently, they will become specialists and will in the long run offer routine objections to every constructive proposal. They will be unable to appreciate the effect of legislation and executive orders under different conditions in different parts of the country. Similarly, no one who remains always in the regional or local administration will appreciate the broader legislative problems of the central ministry. His outlook will be narrowed, and his reports and actions will hardly contribute to the constructive solution of national problems.

Thus an exchange of personnel between the different branches of administration is essential. After a high civil servant has assisted in the formulation of major legislation, nothing is better for him than to go into the regional administration. There he has time and opportunity to observe the detailed operation of the legislation. He comes into contact with individual citizens and with the actualities of life. Certainly he will return to the central ministry with a more practical conception and with fresh suggestions. Without such an exchange of personnel between the different levels of administration one of the main purposes of regional administration, the correction of abstract and theoretical tendencies by practical experience, will be frustrated.

When there is constant interchange of detailed practical experience and of central planning, the economic, political, and psychological reactions to legislation are transmitted from the bottom of the administration to the top as effectively as orders and instructions are transmitted from the top to the bottom, with mutual loyalty and understanding. This is parallel with the practice of the old German general staff. No officer was left on the staff for more than a few years without interruption. They were frequently transferred for a year or more to positions in the Army where they could test the plans they had formed and develop new ones on the basis of practical experience.

In both cases there is a further advantage incidental to the practice of transferring personnel. One of the greatest problems of administration is the wording of the instructions of central departments and of administrative orders for the execution of particular legislation. Such orders must be legally exact, but without stifling the initiative of the subordinate officer. The right combination of precise direction with a margin of discretion generally results only from actual experience in regional administration and consequent recognition of the necessity of adapting instructions to local conditions.

This has been, in essence, the ideal of the best civil servants and of political leaders in Germany in the past. An administration of this kind, if its members are capable, united in feeling, and zealous in their work and have learned to avoid publicity, may ensure some continuity of long range policy and, even under an extreme democratic constitution, may stabilize violent oscillations of public opinion. There is of course a latent danger that the bureaucracy may involve cabinet members in actions that are in the end detrimental to democracy. It is one of the major functions of parliament to prevent this by the presence of its best members in the cabinet.

There are other dangers. The German civil service, except for a relatively short period, was exclusive. That is to say, people without normal civil service training were unacceptable to it. Although the civil service itself was recruited from more or less all classes of the population, an able business man, for example, would not have felt at home in it or have been able to adjust himself to its procedure. This is one reason why, in the last war and the present war, so few industrialists have been able to assume functions of control over production and distribution inside the regular ministries. It is one explanation of the creation of semi-public institutions for the control of production, and for other purposes for which business or industrial experience is indispensable, in which business men can work in cooperation with the regular civil service without actually entering the ministries. This adjustment is much easier, as will be described later, under the British system of administration. Another handicap after the last war was that the regional organization of administration in the federal states was still too much influenced by methods developed when the problems of administration were very different, and when communication was not so easy as it is today. In the years 1930–32 the financial basis was laid down for a new integration of the whole administrative system, which could have been carried out in detail at the end of 1932.

These proposals were not, however, put into practice. The administration of justice and the police have been transferred from the federal states to the central government. The other administrative departments in the states have been subordinated to the corresponding ministries of the national government in Berlin. The state parliaments have been abolished, and the town councils have become little more than Nazi Party meetings under the leadership of the mayors. Otherwise, from the practical point of view of actual administration, the Nazis have left everything more or less as they found it. Certainly until the outbreak of war, and even now, the German administration, in comparison with the British, has not been so frictionless as is generally assumed. There is much unnecessary duplication of work in parallel organizations. Foreigners studying " new " organizations of industry, trade, and agriculture, often fail to realize that in the eight years of its absolute domination the Nazi Party has not achieved a constructive reorganization of the entire civil administration. This is of course the normal result of totalitarian government, unless the dictator is at once a military, political, and administrative genius. Revolutions are always prolific in abstract schemes of organization which fascinate the uninitiated onlooker by their apparent simplicity and by the ruthlessness of their imposition. Most of the innovations of the Nazis, the pseudo-corporative organization of agriculture for instance, are nothing but the amalgamation of existing private or public institutions, the organization of which was outwardly complicated but in fact exceedingly efficient. The continued working of these pseudo-corporative institutions, as well as many other organizations under Nazi supervision paralleling the regular civil service, is due only to people with a large experience and a great ethical tradition, who have, however, no powers of independent decision.

The coordination of the war effort suffers in many ways from overelaboration, resulting not, as in Great Britain, from the absence of any effective coordination at the regional level, but from the existence of too many parallel institutions. But one thing is certain — with the help of the Gestapo and other coercive Party organizations any plan once decided on is carried out ruthlessly in the smallest detail and in the most obscure community. Not only are legislation and regulations rigidly enforced in certain directions, but Nazi Party executives are also uninhibited by the law or decisions of the courts.

This is an enormous difference from the conditions of the last war. The German civil service and the courts were then all too reluctant to exercise their constitutional powers. Appreciating the difficulties with which every citizen was confronted, even the commanding generals in the corps areas made the least possible use of their rights of coercion.

The civil administration and the courts were so lenient in this respect that the number of minor violations tolerated had a cumulative effect and gradually undermined the authority of the law and the administration. Recent major administrative changes limiting the responsibility of the civil service may not be altogether unwelcome to it. The civil service, like the Army, perhaps, prefers to remain anonymous in the conduct of the war, leaving to the Nazi Party the onus of inflicting hardship and privation and even of failure.

From outside it cannot be seen how far the influence of the German Army and civil service has actually diminished in the past nine years. That they have had any influence in political questions since January 1938 is hardly possible. It is very important for any understanding of the situation in Germany to realize that there has been a constant struggle on the part of the Nazi Party to establish its own members in leading positions in the bureaucracy and to have the functions of general staff officers in the civil administration transferred to leading party members. Recent changes in this direction have resulted in a somewhat less consistent organization of production than existed during the first part of the war. To judge from newspaper reports, the power of the S.S. organization under Himmler's supreme command is now predominant in the whole police and civilian defense administration. Young Party members seem now to feel that they have learned enough of the tradition and technique of administration to replace experienced leading civil servants, contrary to the tendency which prevailed at the outbreak of war. Certain branches of industry have also been granted greater autonomy and self-government lately than they ever before enjoyed, in Imperial Germany, under the Weimar Republic, or under the Nazi regime.

Before the outbreak of war the consequences of substituting blueprint schemes for efficient private organizations and of the Nazi craving to duplicate established public institutions by party institutions of their own must have caused concern among military leaders and also among a few central figures in the Nazi Party. This is the reason for the promulgation at the outbreak of war of decrees scrapping many of the Nazi experiments in administration. The tendency of such decrees was to prevent any interference with the normal processes of public administration by Party leaders bearing no definite and open responsibility within the administration. The supervisory powers of the civil administration over the semi-public organizations of industry and agriculture were in addition transformed in most cases to specific executive powers. Within the administration, in the most influential positions especially, there had of course been many compromises with the ambitions of the Nazi Party. Party members in the Cabinet and in the positions of governors and presidents in the regional and federal administration hold final control in many respects.

II · THE CENTRAL DIRECTION OF THE WAR EFFORT

The form of coordination of every aspect of the war effort at the top and at the regional level adopted in August 1939, in which a few major changes were made later, clearly shows an effort to avoid irresponsible interference by Nazi Party agencies without reducing the Party's controlling influence and to prevent the conflicts of authority which contributed to Germany's defeat in the last war. During and before the last war the federal form of government imposed severe handicaps on the German war machinery.

The organization of supply at the beginning of the last war was the responsibility principally of the Prussian War Minister, and to a lesser extent of the war ministers of other large federal states. All of them received statements of military requirements from the Great General Staff at Imperial General Headquarters. It was soon found necessary to concentrate the functions of the war ministers of other states with regard to supply in the Prussian War Minister in Berlin, and this was accompanied by the establishment of a number of separate controls either under the authority of the Prussian War Minister or semi-independently.

There was much friction in the coordination of naval and strictly military demands, and between the Chancellor, who was responsible for foreign policy and all internal questions not of a purely military character, and the Chief of the General Staff there was even more. Until Hindenburg and Ludendorff came to the High Command in 1916 the Chief of the General Staff had not always sufficient authority to ensure that the procurement program of the Navy was not undertaken in competition with that of the Army. It was only in 1916, with the adoption of the so-called Hindenburg Program, that this problem of organization was temporarily solved. Final decisions in all cases of conflict were supposedly made by the Emperor on the advice of the Chancellor. This was constitutionally correct, and had been practical in the time of William I, when Germany had no Navy, and when no conflagration like that of 1914 could be foreseen. Except in the period before the last war, when he supported the Chancellor's objections to military preparations which might prove further obstacles to peaceful understanding in Europe, the Emperor's decision was only nominal.

At present Hitler actually enjoys the power which during the last war writers in foreign countries mistakenly attributed to the Emperor. He is Commander-in-Chief of all the defense forces; he must reconcile considerations of strategy and of foreign policy; he controls the various coercive institutions of the Nazi Party, including the *S.S.* and the Gestapo, which are under Himmler's executive direction. Beyond this, full responsibility for the coordination of the entire war effort was delegated by Hitler in August 1939 to a committee of the *Supreme Defense Council,* which had been established in peacetime under the chairmanship of Goering, who is also chairman of the special committee.

Hitler is represented on this executive committee in his capacity as Commander-in-Chief of all the defense forces by Field Marshal Keitel as Chief of Staff, and in his capacity as President and Chancellor of the Reich by the permanent directors of the President's Office and the Chancellery. Since Hitler has also assumed nominal command of the Army, the former commander, General Brauchitsch, who was originally a member of the Supreme Defense Council, has not been replaced. The only additional members of the committee are the Minister of the Interior, who is responsible for the whole civilian administration, and the Economic Commissioner-General, who is also Minister of Economics and President of the *Reichsbank.*

Neither the Foreign Minister nor the Minister of Food and Agriculture belongs to the executive committee of the Supreme Defense Council. The fact that the Minister of Finance is also excluded serves to illustrate the difference in character between the Defense Council and the present British War Cabinet. All this means that Goering has supreme executive authority for the coordination of the war effort outside foreign policy, strategy, and the activity of Nazi Party organizations. Goering's position is counter-balanced by that of Himmler, who, as has been said, receives instructions from Hitler directly. He is not a member of the executive committee of the Supreme Defense Council; his controlling powers, rather, are parallel to those of the Defense Council and independent of it.

Before sketching the main lines of organization down to the local level, it is important to emphasize certain essential characteristics of the administration in order to gain a better understanding of the British war administration by way of comparison. As chief of the *O.K.W.* (*Oberkommando der Wehrmacht,* High Command of all the Defense Forces) Field Marshal Keitel is effectively responsible for all the functions which Ludendorff performed only during certain periods of the last war, and then only *de facto,* not formally. He is at the same time Chief of Staff for all the defense forces and Minister of Defense. The Chiefs of Staff of the separate forces are subordinate to him, and he has a Deputy Chief of Staff, Colonel-General Jodl, with the special function of maintaining liaison between Hitler and the *O.K.W.* Thus Field Marshal Keitel is nominally responsible not only for the long-range strategic planning of the three defense forces, but also, as Minister of Defense, for the coordination of the supply of all three forces.

This, in combination with the fact that he and his staff are in close touch with every day's military events, is a very great advantage indeed. It guarantees coordination at the top, which, as we shall see, has not been achieved to the same extent in England. There can be no question that final decision as to the strategic plans of all the defense forces and the general allocation of supplies among them for at least two years ahead must rest with one man. He alone can at once issue the necessary instructions when a sudden reverse prevents the execution of prearranged plans and when expectations of success are disappointed. Officers of his staff decide not only changes in specifications but also the allocation of available industrial capacity and raw materials among the three defense forces in the light of strategic plans for more than a year ahead and corresponding tactical requirements.

For this purpose authority over armament production and over supply in general was concentrated at the outbreak of war in a twin department of the *Oberkommando der Wehrmacht,* the *Rüstungs- und Wehrwirtschaftsamt.* This was split up in the spring of 1942 into separate departments — the *Rüstungsamt* for technical specification and procurement, and the *Wehrwirtschaftsamt* for the coordination of all the economic factors in the conduct of the war. Both departments remained under the direction of the same general who had previously directed the united department. These two departments, as will be more fully described later, had even before the war their own regional staffs, which remain united as before under the authority of the commanding generals in the corps areas, and their inspectors in every important firm engaged in any way in the manufacture of armament.

Agricultural commodities are controlled in the Ministry of Food and

Agriculture, and other commodities by the Minister of Economics. The *Reichsstellen,* or controls, for different commodities in the Ministry of Economics were to a large extent directed until the beginning of 1942 by general staff officers, and the head of the coordinating materials department in the ministry was also a staff officer. In the Ministry of Transport general staff officers have until recently been responsible for the coordination of rail and motor traffic and for the organization and expansion of road haulage. Officers of the *Wehrwirtschaftsamt* may also attend the meetings of so-called *Hauptvereinigungen* which exist for every important agricultural commodity in the Ministry of Food and Agriculture. These last combine the functions of marketing organizations with the planning of the particular food products and feeding stuffs to be grown on every farm and the local enforcement of the program.

A large part of the production of armament and of the supply of raw materials for armament production is also controlled under the Four Years' Plan, which again includes in its organization officers of the *Rüstungsamt* and the *Wehrwirtschaftsamt* of the *O.K.W.* The office of the Price Commissioner, whose powers are dictatorial, is also included in the organization of the Four Years' Plan. Goering, as chairman of the executive committee of the Supreme Defense Council, as president of the organization of the Four Years' Plan, as chairman of the General Economic Council, and to a lesser extent as Air Minister, was originally responsible for the entire economic war effort, although until the spring of 1942 officers of the supply department of the *O.K.W.* exercised the actual direction.

The changes introduced, particularly in the control of certain materials and in the priority and allocation machinery, in March 1942 increase the difficulty of determining from outside the exact role of the *Economic Commissioner-General.* Since the beginning of 1940 he has been pushed somewhat into the background. He is primarily Goering's deputy-chairman of the *General Economic Council,* which is in effect a civil servants' coordinating committee. Its members are the permanent under-secretaries of the Ministries of Economics, Agriculture, Labor, Transportation, and the Interior, the National Forest Office, and the Four Years' Plan, the Reich Price Commissioner, a representative of the Nazi Party, and the general directing the *Rüstungsamt* and the *Wehrwirtschaftsamt.* The functions of the Economic Commissioner-General, apart from the direction of the *Reichsbank,* seem to consist in adjusting civilian consumption and foreign trade, through the commodity controls in the Ministry of Economics, to the requirements laid down by the supply departments of the *O.K.W.*

During the past year there has certainly been some diminution of the influence of general staff officers in the economy as a whole. The war administration is now less streamlined than before, and a graph illustrating the present organization would seem almost as complicated at the top as a chart of the British organization. The reorganization was necessitated by certain problems of production which had arisen in England before, and its result seems to have been to restrict the coordinating functions of the Economic Commissioner-General to those sections of the economy not directly concerned in the manufacture of armament and munitions.

The recent reorganization, which resembles in some respects the present organization in Great Britain, is best explained by a fact which is too often ignored. In the organization of production for total war there are parallel phases which occur in different countries at different times and different intervals. While Germany had an advantage over Great Britain in the construction of capacity for the mass production of armaments beginning in 1934, certain problems in the administration of the priority system and the more elaborate allocation of supplies which became acute in Great Britain immediately after the Battle of France arose in Germany more than a year later, after the Russian campaign of 1941.

The first, tentative period of rearmament began in Germany late in 1934. It entailed some control over production and the supply of labor, but it consisted primarily in the creation of new capacity for the mass production of tools and gauges, munitions, guns, and airplanes. It also included the further rapid expansion of synthetic oil and rubber capacity and the mining of low-grade ores.[7] This phase occupied three years. The program was not in every respect successful. The first mass production of airplanes in Germany, begun in 1936, was a partial failure and most of the planes so produced had to be scrapped in 1938. Even the type of plane put into production in 1938 proved unsuitable, as has been mentioned, for attack on Great Britain. With four years of experimen-

---

[7] The substitution of low-grade for high-grade ores is possible only to a limited extent. The coke required for the production of a ton of pig iron from low-grade German ore is about two and one-half or three times the amount required with high-grade ore, a serious drawback, since German coke production and transportation facilities before the occupation of Belgium were insufficient.

tation and production since the Nazis had come into power, only one tank division had been equipped by the spring of 1937. It was only during that year that the plans of the three years before were put fully into execution. Until the occupation of Czechoslovakia,[8] however, their limited productive capacity and supplies of raw materials, with the exception of stocks of grain, rubber, and oil, acquired largely with foreign credits, did not permit the Nazis to run the risk of war in their foreign policy. The pace of the Nazi rearmament could not have been kept up through 1937 if it had not been for the Anglo-German clearing agreement of October 1934.

During this period a system of *commodity control* was evolved in the Ministry of Economics, not primarily for the purpose of armament production, but rather because of the lack of foreign exchange. The method was not very different from that introduced in other countries at the outbreak of war. Agricultural production and marketing had been similarly organized, not on a permanent basis but *ad hoc,* before the Nazis came into power.[9] The Nazi platform had included the reorganization of the German economy on a corporative basis and a promise to the farmers of complete autarchy. Their promises have been realized in blueprint schemes of organization, within which older and very efficient voluntary associations in agriculture, trade, and industry have continued to function.

Exceptions to this statement must be made for the agricultural marketing organizations (*Hauptvereinigungen*) and for organizations in the flour milling industry and for the manufacture of " *ersatz* " products, all of which seem to have been fairly effective. They provided the model for the semi-corporative institutions for the control of certain branches of industry introduced in the early spring of 1942. In general, however, it is true that legislation for the corporative organization of various trades was given practical effect only where the lack of foreign exchange

---

[8] At the beginning of 1939 Germany had five tank divisions. The German occupation of Czechoslovakia, which had a higher armament capacity in proportion to its population than any other country in the world, however, changed the balance of military power in forty-eight hours. Czechoslovakia's army was, in addition, one of the most modern in respect to mechanical equipment. With this captured equipment Germany was able to transform four light armored divisions into tank divisions, thus raising the number of German tank divisions available at the outbreak of the war to nine.

[9] By 1932 Germany was virtually self-sufficient in all essential agricultural products except fat. The effort of the Nazis to achieve complete autarchy has been a failure, and is partly responsible for present difficulties of food supply.

made some form of strict organization inevitable and where there were available people with great experience of voluntary industrial association for more or less similar purposes.

The early introduction of control over certain commodities in order, to repeat the fact again, to conserve foreign exchange was greatly facilitated by the existence in a number of industries of long established forms of organization which combined a legislative origin and a certain amount of government control with all the flexibility of private management.[10] Neither the functions nor the form of these organizations was essentially altered until the spring of 1942. Most private *cartels,* despite the contrary opinion sometimes expressed abroad, have also survived, although deprived of certain vital functions. The Nazis, in effect, revived the cartel policy introduced in 1931 and abandoned in July 1932. The compulsory cartels formed principally for the expansion of *ersatz* industries were a Nazi innovation, as was the use of private cartels by the Price Commissioner to keep prices at approximately the level established by the Fourth Major Decree of December 1931.[11]

Wages were in general frozen at about the level established by the same Decree. In order to hold them at this level while employment was rapidly increasing during the first phase of rearmament, regional *Treuhänder der Arbeit* (Labor Trustees) were appointed under a *Reichstreuhänder der Arbeit.* They exercised dictatorial powers over wages and hours, and severe restrictions were imposed on the movement of labor between plants and industries.

All this is to say that the lack of foreign exchange brought about an

---

[10] The coal syndicate, for example, was originally based upon voluntary agreements in the different coal producing areas, where production quotas were established for each mining firm. These regional syndicates were placed by later legislation under the final control of a coal commissioner, who was advised by representatives of mine owners, miners, and consumers. The potash industry was similarly organized under legislation so that overproduction was prevented and competition on the world market facilitated. The government not only controlled these industries from above but was also a member of the different syndicates, since, as in many other Continental countries, mines had been owned and operated by the government from time immemorial. This was especially true of the later development of the potash industry in Germany. The employment in government mines of civil servants with special technical training made practical as well as legal control of the syndicates possible.

[11] Because of the loss of the major part of Germany's reserve of gold and foreign exchange, which at its postwar height was insufficient to cover her short-term foreign indebtedness, prices, wages, rents, and the rate of interest were fixed by decree in December 1931. As a part of the burden of taxation was shifted at the same time from real property to sales taxes, the entire basis of economic life was revised. These drastic measures were made possible only by their synchronization. The Nazis later had only to freeze price relations as they found them. Since 1933 there has been only a slight rise in the price index. This is, of course, a statistical illusion, since the quality of many goods has seriously deteriorated, and the real cost of living has risen considerably.

organization of scarcity such as nations normally accept only in war-time. Before the mass production of armament began in Germany control of production, prices, and wages had reached a degree to which many belligerent nations were unwilling to submit even during the first phase of the war itself. Neither this control alone nor any old or new form of voluntary or compulsory organization could have made it possible for the Nazis to wage war for more than a year, since it could not overcome the actual dearth of important raw materials, especially iron ore, resulting from Germany's loss of territory after the last war. The occupation of Norway, however, ensured a regular supply of high-grade iron ore from Sweden throughout the year. The armistice with France similarly ensured supplies of other types of iron ore and of various other essential materials.

In attempting to apply the legislation of 1934 for the corporative reorganization of the whole economy, the Nazis were confronted with the same difficulties as the Weimar Republic in attempting to implement existing provisions of the Constitution, which had been influenced by the Soviet Revolution. These earlier constitutional provisions were bound to fail, since their tendency was to replace voluntary industrial associations which solved the particular problems with which they were concerned exceedingly well according to the flexible principles of private management by institutions the functions of which would be rigidly defined by legislation. That would have meant depriving existing employers' and employees' associations of all vitality, and the subjection of very different industries to a uniform scheme of organization. There will always be conflicts of interest between industries for mass production, for which a national form of organization is preferable, if they can be brought within any organization, and smaller industries, to which a regional form of organization is better adapted. In this respect there has been even less approach to a balanced organization during the past ten years than under previous Governments which pursued a more cautious policy of non-interference.

The picture of economic organization in Nazi Germany is thus very complicated for an outsider. There is almost universal conflict between ideological blueprint forms of organization and others which have grown out of practical problems of production. This must have caused great toil and trouble to general staff officers and to old civil servants, particularly in connection with the utilization of all available industrial capacity to meet the requirements of the prolonged Russian campaign.

In Great Britain the more efficient utilization of existing capacity became a necessity even before the completion of plant expansion for the mass production of armament. In Germany, on the other hand, production in the period between the Battle of France and the Russian campaign was characterized by a rather loose dispersal of orders throughout industry in Germany and the occupied territories. Subcontracting reached a maximum in the summer of 1941. The increased demand for tanks, guns, and munitions in 1941 could no longer be met by the further dispersal of contracts. In addition, bottlenecks had occurred because the bureaucratic methods employed by the *Reichsstellen* in dealing with larger firms contracting directly with the *Rüstungsamt* were not appropriate in dealing with smaller firms. The amount of clerical work involved in the centralized control of materials for a great number of small firms threatened to become a serious hindrance to the full utilization of capacity and prompt delivery on contracts.

This explains why in the spring of 1942 new controls were organized and a newly appointed *Minister of Armament and Munitions* was entrusted with the control, standardization, and rationalization of armament production with the aim of concentrating production and man power in plants operating under the most favorable conditions of equipment and organization, transport facilities, and safety from bombing attack. He was charged in addition with the technical improvement of the design and manufacture of weapons and the oversight of armament priorities. Subsequently he has assumed the practical management of the Four Years' Plan. His full title is now *Generalbevollmächtigter für Rüstungsaufgaben und Beauftragter für den Vierjahresplan* (Commissioner-General for Armament and Executor of the Four Years' Plan). The appointment to such a position of an architect and engineer, not a staff officer, who had been responsible for important construction work before and during the war, indicates the preponderant importance at this stage of the war of purely technical aspects of production from the design of weapons to the rationalization and concentration of war industry. This new organization was intended to concentrate the executive control of armament production in the hands of one man who was acquainted with technical problems in the different stages of production, the same purpose for which, at almost the same time, Mr. Lyttelton was appointed Minister of Production in Great Britain.

The appointment of a Minister of Armament and Munitions seemed at first to introduce into the otherwise streamlined organization of supply in Germany an element of complication suggestive of the division of responsibility in Great Britain among the Deputy Chief of the Imperial General Staff, the Minister of Production, and the Admiralty and Ministries of Supply and Aircraft Production. As his powers became known, however, it was made apparent that by superseding in some respects the military elements that formerly exercised exclusive control of war production he was able to unite in his own hands all technical and administrative decisions affecting armament production without sacrificing the existing organizations of the *O.K.W.* and the Economic Commissioner-General. The former departments of the *O.K.W.* are closely meshed with the new ministry. The functions of the *Rüstungsamt* of the *O.K.W.* remain unchanged, but the *Rüstungsamt* itself is incorporated in the Ministry of Armament and Munitions. The same general remains chief of the *Rüstungsamt* and also chief of the *Wehrwirtschaftsamt,* which is directly subordinate to the *O.K.W.*

There can be no doubt that in the final phase of total war less efficient plants must be eliminated from production. The speed of production in different firms must be at least sufficiently uniform to ensure that the delivery of particular supplies essential to the opening of a new campaign will not be delayed by a few firms which may represent only a small fraction of total production. This is the sphere of the Minister of Armament and Munitions. His responsibility does not end with technical standardization of the design of weapons and their component parts, but includes the rationalization of every stage of manufacture to secure the maximum output.

It is for this reason that the *Rüstungsamt,* while remaining under the orders of the *O.K.W.,* has been transferred to the Ministry of Armament and Munitions. The *Rüstungsamt* places its own contracts as before, and the execution of contracts is inspected by its own regional and local officers, whose position in the regional administration has, however, as will be seen later, been somewhat changed since the establishment of the new ministry. Probably these officers receive more definite and more practical instructions in their dealings with the managers of armament plants because of the new relation of the *Rüstungsamt* to the Ministry of Armament and Munitions. An order by the Minister of Armament and Munitions for the increased supply of scrap suggests one of the reasons for the reorganization. Before and during the war the *Rüstungsamt* had accumulated enormous reserves of component parts of weapons and vehicles, which have been rendered obsolete by changes in design and are to be scrapped. Orders for newly standardized component parts are evidently to be placed by the Ministry of Armament and Munitions rather than the *Rüstungsamt* itself, and the minister will be responsible for their timing in such a way that reserves can be built up without the waste of production formerly entailed.

At the same time that the *Rüstungsamt* was incorporated in the Ministry of Armament and Munitions so-called *Hauptausschüsse* (Main Committees) for the major armament industries were established in the ministry, for the standardization of articles of mass production and rationalization of industry, and *Ringe,* technical committees covering all engineering production, for the standardization of component parts. This indicates clearly the principal function of the new minister. He is responsible for the best technical provision to meet the total requirements of the *Rüstungsamt* and for bringing designers and engineers into the closest possible contact with the *O.K.W.* in the statement of specifications. The same designers and engineers are concerned with the increase of output by the technical improvement of individual plants. Under the *Hauptausschüsse* there are special committees for specific problems, such as the design and production of tanks, in which officers with actual experience in battle of the use of the weapon in question meet with designers and engineers. For questions concerning both one or more of the committees of the *Hauptausschüsse* and one of the technical *Ringe,* a common expert chairman is appointed.

Here too the principle of ensuring coordination through the assumption by one individual of several closely related functions has been followed in each industry. In the iron and steel industry, for example, one man is chairman of the *Hauptausschuss* for iron and steel in the Ministry of Armament and Munitions, head of the iron and steel control in the Ministry of Economics, in which allocations of iron and steel are made for firms not working on armament orders, and leader of the new *Reichsvereinigung*[12] for iron and steel production, including the mining of iron ore, trade in iron and steel and scrap, and the supply of coal and coke for blast furnaces. He is appointed leader of the *Reichsvereinigung* by Goering; as chairman of the *Hauptausschuss* he is responsible to the Minister of Armament and Munitions; for the functions

---

[12] It is hard to know whether to call these institutions cooperative associations or corporations, as their legal character is dangerously vague.

remaining to the iron and steel control in the Ministry of Economics he is responsible to the Economic Commissioner-General. He is in addition a member of the Armament Council in the Ministry of Armament and Munitions, consisting of six high-ranking officers representing the three defense forces and nine industrialists. While the Ministry of Armament and Munitions was established with a view to the rationalization of all industry, its primary concern is with articles employed in warfare or, like railway engines, essential to the maintenance of war production. The Minister of Economics, or Economic Commissioner-General, is responsible for the production of articles, like textiles and shoes, both for military use and for civilian consumption and export.

This division of responsibility at the cabinet level, alien to the German tradition, is the consequence of a radical change from a form of control based on raw materials to one based on the major branches of industry, or rather on pre-Nazi associations, both private and statutory. With the vitality of all natural growth, they have survived the Nazi blueprint era either on a national or regional, a vertical or horizontal basis. These associations have now become executive public authorities. They are responsible in varying degree for planning, market regulation, and the allocation of materials within their industries and, in conjunction with the committees for their industries in the Ministry of Armament and Munitions, for increasing production by rationalization.

That explains the new term *Lenkungsbereich* (managerial control), which has replaced the former *Reichsstelle* (the English " control "). The directors of every *Lenkungsbereich* are leading members of the industries concerned, and they have been given control over related materials required in a single industry, such as iron and non-ferrous metals, with the aim of reducing the total number of central controls. It is a realistic adaptation to specific difficulties of supply, to established private organizations, and to the need for a system of control geared into the Ministry of Armament and Munitions. It is an essentially sound devolution of responsibility for the synchronized allocation of all the materials any firm requires, and also for ensuring the best use of the man power and materials available, to unbureaucratic private organizations with full executive authority.

When plans for the requirements of the *O.K.W.*, based on the strategic forecast, and for those of the civilian population have been agreed to in detail for a year or more in advance by the Minister of Armament and Munitions and the Minister of Economics, the director of each

Lenkungsbereich receives a branch plan for his industry together with block allocations (*Globalkontingente*) of the necessary materials. He has then to determine corresponding plans and reallocations for the different groups or cartels in his industry. They in turn are responsible not only for well timed allocations of materials to individual firms but also for the saving of material and labor by improved methods of production.[13] With the supervision of the Price Commissioner under the Four

---

[13] Under the *Reichsstellen* materials were sometimes allocated on the basis of quotas fixed in the period of rearmament before the war. A new method of allocation has been introduced in the industries for which *Reichsvereinigungen* have been established. Allocations of non-ferrous metals and iron and steel, for example, are now made in four main groups; these include contracts for standardized component parts placed by the Ministry of Armament and Munitions, contracts placed by the *Rüstungsamt*, production for the machine tool industry, and all other production, divided into a number of different categories, for which allocations are made through the non-ferrous metals control in the Ministry of Economics.

The Ministry of Armament and Munitions, the *Rüstungsamt*, the machine tool industry, and the non-ferrous metals control keep statistical accounts, like bank deposit accounts, with the *Rüstungskontor GmbH* (limited liability company with relatively low capitalization), an agency of the Ministry of Armament and Munitions, which serves as a clearing house for the amounts of materials consumed in any quarter of the year. The *Rüstungskontor* has also for prime contractors in each classification statistical accounts which presumably show the extent to which their capacity is being utilized and the size of their inventories at any given moment.

In placing a contract any government department issues with it a voucher for the allocation of the necessary materials. This voucher the prime contractor must present for validation to the *Rüstungskontor GmbH*. The *Rüstungskontor* is thus enabled not only to keep the total of orders placed in any category within the total amount of materials allowed for it, but also to control the timing of individual contracts in accordance with a general quarterly and yearly schedule of production and to prevent any department from getting out of line with the national program. It can at the same time prevent the placing of contracts with any manufacturer in excess of his capacity and can guarantee the availability of all the different materials required for the completion of any given order.

When the *Rüstungskontor* has approved a contract, it returns to the prime contractor a second, "transfer" voucher. This he delivers with his orders for semi-finished materials to his subcontractors, who must secure their own raw materials. The control of contracts in relation to capacity and to the amount of materials available in this second stage is not the concern of the *Rüstungskontor*, but of the new *Reichsvereinigungen*. Thus the transfer voucher must in turn be submitted for validation to the *Reichsvereinigung*. By this system the allocation of raw materials to individual firms in accordance with their capacity and with the total amount of raw materials available in any quarter is separated in most cases from the central control of production as a whole, which does not usually extend beyond prime contractors. It was discovered in the last war that between business practices and government accounting methods there is often a gulf which can be bridged only by a more or less independent institution combining essential characteristics of both. The *Rüstungskontor* represents such an attempt to reconcile bureaucratic control and efficient management.

Years before the war private *Auftragsbörsen* (contract exchanges) were organized on a regional basis under the control of the long established public offices (*Ausgleichsstellen*) that provided for the participation of small contractors and artisans in government work. The purpose of the new *Auftragsbörsen* was to bring representatives of the great armament firms into contact with smaller manufacturers. Plans and specifications were exhibited so that smaller manufacturers could see how their tools and labor force could be best employed. These regional exchanges continue to function, and in October 1942 the first nation-wide *Auftragsbörse* was held for two weeks in Berlin by the Ministry of Armament and Munitions. Firms were invited to attend by the

Years' Plan, they also control prices. The principal model has been the organization of the paper industry since the outbreak of war. Cartels which had survived only as blanket cartels to be revived in peacetime have been dissolved, and the functions of active cartels now include the executive direction of their members' particular operations. Thus the manufacturer no longer applies for his materials to several central controls, but simply to his private industrial association or cartel or to the regional commissioner of the *Lenkungsbereich*. Form-filling and the necessity of writing, telephoning, and travelling to Berlin have been minimized, and the personnel of the central controls has been cut in half.

In certain industries for which materials remain under the control of the Ministry of Economics this system is still in its introductory stages and has not been fully developed. In a second group of industries the direction of each *Lenkungsbereich* lies outside the Ministry of Economics in the hands of a leading industrialist. In the machine industry, for example, a former president of the long established association of machine manufacturers, in close contact with technical committees in the Ministry of Armament and Munitions, has full responsibility for allocations of materials, combined with executive authority over the rationalization and concentration of production, through subordinate associations for different branches of the industry.

A third and most important stage of development has been reached by the six corporative *Reichsvereinigungen* for iron and steel, coal, shoe manufacture, and different textile fibres. The *Reichsvereinigungen* for iron and steel and coal have evolved from semi-public, pre-Nazi organizations. Except for the fact that capital in the industries has not changed hands, they resemble the old I. G. Farben Combine in the chemical industry and the Soviet industrial trusts. Individual firms must follow the instructions given by directors of the *Reichsvereinigung* in accordance with plans formed in the *Hauptausschuss* of the industry in the Ministry of Armament and Munitions. They are told what to produce and how, and the price is fixed on the basis of the production costs of the best equipped plants. Where differences in cost are too great for this, group

---

Hauptausschüsse in the ministry and by the ministry's regional armament committees, and the requirements of the new system of standardization were emphasized. Products were grouped so that firms in the same category with bottlenecks either in labor or in tools could exchange orders among themselves. The principle is the same as that of the district capacity exchanges in Great Britain, with the difference that in Germany the organization has been expanded to a national scale.

prices are fixed for manufacturers of the same products under approximately the same conditions of cost.[14] The clerical labor involved in cost accounting separate contracts with individual firms is thus eliminated. Plants unable to produce on this basis are closed down or scrapped. The *Reichsvereinigungen* are responsible not only for the maximum utilization of capacity, materials, and labor and for the synchronization of deliveries by their member firms, but also for the definition of market areas with a view to the national saving of transportation. In this they have the benefit of the accumulated experience of private industrial associations, syndicates, or cartels.

III · THE REGIONAL COORDINATION OF THE WAR EFFORT

The coordination of every aspect of the war effort at the regional level was based until late summer 1942 mainly on the conditions of the last war. The principal regional divisions of the country for the wartime functions of administration were the eighteen *corps areas,* not the federal states or the provinces. In the last war commanding generals were appointed in these areas immediately after mobilization, with political powers similar to those provided for in case of war in most European countries. For the purpose of coordination their staffs included industrialists, agriculturalists, and journalists, all for the most part in their capacity as reserve officers. Under certain conditions the commanding generals also exercised control over the civil administration in order to prevent friction between the regular administration and the military organization in the corps areas.

As the war continued, and especially after 1916 when economic problems became increasingly complex, there was much criticism of the activities of the commanding generals in the corps areas. It became clear that while in a shorter war they might have accomplished the task of coordinating the entire war effort successfully, they had not all training or imagination enough to control the civil administration over a long period of time without seriously impairing its initiative. In the present war the corps area commanders have consequently held no political powers. Their responsibility has been limited to military questions, which include the organization of supply.

The *Rüstungsamt* and the *Wehrwirtschaftsamt* of the O.K.W. had

---

[14] The result has been a reduction in prices in the industries immediately concerned and in the prices of products in which these materials are used. Steady maximum production has also made possible the reduction of certain other cartellized prices.

until the summer of 1942 their own regional departments under the control of the commanding generals in every corps area. Their function was to coordinate the different factors in production and to keep the actual progress of production in gear at the regional level with central plans for production. These departments and the *Rüstungs-* and *Wehrwirtschaftsinspektoren* under them had to keep in close contact with the regional and local civil administration. In fact, the regional *Wehrwirtschaftsämter* established in every corps area in the period of rearmament and modelled on those of the last war were transformed into executive bodies (*Bezirkswirtschaftsämter*) comprising representatives of every government and Party institution connected with war economics and meeting under the chairmanship of provincial or state governors. The executive functions of regional officers of the *Rüstungsamt* and *Wehrwirtschaftsamt* were concerned only with war production. Inspectors of the three defense forces in every corps area were responsible for the discovery of new capacity for armament production, for remedying technical deficiencies in production, and for reporting labor shortages to the chief labor officers of the region.

Thus from the *O.K.W.* and the Supreme Defense Council down to the local level of administration and in individual plants the military element predominated in the organization of supply. The full importance of the military personnel has not been evident, however, to the general public, and it does not imply any influence in political questions or executive responsibility for the regional coordination of the different branches of civil administration with the military administration.

For the latter purpose, special *defense commissioners* were appointed at the outbreak of war in each corps area as controlling agents of the Supreme Defense Council. They have been drawn increasingly from among Nazi Party leaders, until by the end of 1942 all Party *Gauleiter* had become defense commissioners.[14a] They are in close regular contact with the generals commanding the corps areas. Each defense commissioner is advised by a board comprising the governors of the federal states or provinces[14b] wholly or partly included in his corps area, the local Party leaders, the district presidents (permanent heads of the civil administration in their areas), the chief of the regional organiza-

---

14a Thus there are now 42 commissioners instead of the original 17. Whenever the boundaries of the *Gaue*, which are identical with the old Parliamentary constituencies, do not coincide with those of the corps area, one of the commissioners in the area is made responsible for the others and is stationed in the town in which the corps area headquarters are situated.

14b In some cases the governor of the federal state and the *Gauleiter* are identical.

tion of labor supply, and the *Treuhänder der Arbeit,* who fixes wages and hours of work for the region.

The defense commissioner is responsible for the regional coordination of military, administrative, and Party institutions in the total war effort of his region. He must keep every branch of the civil administration, including public and semi-public organizations for production and distribution, the military organization, and the organs of the Nazi Party working together in each corps area. The necessary administrative duties of the defense commissioners are discharged not through separate regional defense offices but through the established offices of provincial governors in Prussia and officials of comparable rank in the other federal states and, in the territories annexed since the autumn of 1938, of *Gauleiter.*

Since provincial and state governors for the most part serve as the regional officers of the Economic Commissioner-General and are also from an administrative point of view agents of the General Economic Council, all executive functions outside the military organization and the Nazi Party are concentrated in their hands under the supervision of the defense commissioners. This salient fact must be emphasized in any accurate picture of the regional organization. It means that in spite of the introduction of regional defense commissioners traditional administrative organization and accumulated experience have been preserved in wartime. The defense commissioners, although all routine correspondence between military and civilian authorities must pass through their hands, have no staffs of their own. They use the permanent staffs of provincial and state governors.[14c]

Thus all communications between the Supreme Defense Council and its members, and likewise the General Economic Council and its members, and the civil administration in the country at large pass exclusively through the hands of experienced permanent officials. Apart from the *S.S.* and Gestapo and, more recently, the civilian defense organization, all of which are under Himmler's direct control, only the courts, the customs and revenue offices, the state railway offices, and the six new corporative industrial organizations controlled by the Ministry of Armament and Munitions have any direct communication with central ministries. This represents a major simplification of the work of the central

---

[14c] Under the administrative jurisdiction of the Minister of the Interior.

ministries, and it enormously facilitates coordination at the regional level as well as among the different central ministries.

Any remnants of self-government either in municipal institutions or in semi-public chambers of commerce and industry disappeared at the outbreak of war. Every such organization has become an executive instrument of the provincial governor and a cog in the war machine. The provincial or state governor, in his capacity as regional economic commissioner, can issue instructions to every public and private economic organization. That is to say, through the provincial governor the Minister of Economics, the Minister for Food and Agriculture, or the chief of the Forest Service can dissolve or amalgamate or subordinate to the regular civil administration any of the organizations, either long established or newly introduced by the Nazis, under his partial supervision and control.

In each province or comparable administrative area the governor has, in addition to the provincial economic office (*Bezirkswirtschaftsamt*), which developed from the regional *Wehrwirtschaftsamt* of the *O.K.W.*, a provincial office for food and agriculture (*Landesernährungsamt*) and another for forestry and timber products. The corporative oganizations of agriculture are subordinate to these offices and act as their agents. Below the provincial food and economic offices there are offices in every county and town. The food offices are responsible both for local production and for distribution. The economic offices coordinate production within their areas, with the special function of increasing capacity. Prices not fixed by the central Price Commissioner or in the corporative organizations of industry are controlled by these offices.

During 1942 private chambers of commerce, industry, and handicrafts have been combined to a large extent in *Gauwirtschaftskammern*. This is one step toward the still unrealized Nazi ideal of making the *Gau* the general administrative unit, as some are for labor supply and wage regulation. It represents an achievement for the Party, followed up as it has been by further inroads into the civil administration. It is a reversal of the tendency at the outbreak of war to scrap Party organizations paralleling the normal administration, though with the help of the Gestapo the Party has always been able to control individual members of the civil service and the Army. At present the prevailing tendency is for Party functionaries to succeed to key posts in the administration.

The new *Gauwirtschaftskammern* coordinate every aspect of production in small industrial units, in which there is not, as there is in the new *Reichsvereinigungen,* immediate contact with the Ministry of Armament and Munitions. Their task is to speed up rationalization outside the six new industrial organizations, and, since they are also political bodies, it is to be supposed that the power of the Party is behind them. They are not yet, however, organs of the Party. Their areas correspond to those of the labor administration and of the *Treuhänder der Arbeit.* The chairmen of the new chambers, who must be active industrialists, are appointed by the district Party leaders; they have authority to dissolve existing chambers of commerce and industry whenever they consider it necessary in order to save personnel or for closer coordination.

The organization of the supply of labor has until recently followed the outlines established before the Nazis came into power. The boundaries of the regional administration of employment exchanges and of all other questions of employment, including public work creation, were never identical with those of the provinces, but were determined rather by economic conditions. The same principles were applied in defining the jurisdiction of the regional arbitrators of wage and hour disputes, who have been succeeded under the Nazi regime by the *Treuhänder der Arbeit.* The central allocation of labor supply has recently been transferred from the high civil servant whose responsibility it had been for fourteen years to a prominent Nazi Party district leader. One of his first tasks was to work out new wage scales to replace established piece rates.[15]

The German transport system has hardly been changed by the Nazis. For many decades the railways and canals have been owned by the state and administered under a very flexible system of decentralization. Until 1919 there was a general staff officer in every regional office of the state railways, and this arrangement was reintroduced by the Nazis.

---

[15] The purpose of the new rates is to induce highly skilled workers to give up work that, with new tooling, can be performed by unskilled or semi-skilled workers. The former system of piece rates has been revised on the basis of " value units " of work. The least skilled process has a value of six units, while in mining, for example, the performance of the most highly skilled work has a value of forty-seven. White collar work is valued at from thirteen to seventy-five units, according to the different processes involved. The new rates mean that the output of skilled workmen may be increased without abnormal increases in their wages and in the cost of production. Imported labor from occupied countries, on the other hand, may be more strictly controlled from the point of view of efficiency, and among foreign workers the discrepancy between the least and most highly valued processes of white collar work may be reduced.

The government had obtained power to coordinate the railway system and road traffic, in order to prevent ruinous competition by an economic allocation of freight to the railways and to motor carriers, in 1931. For more than forty years regional syndicates and cartels had limited transportation costs in their industries by placing orders for all standardized products with the supplier nearest the particular purchaser, and this system is apparently now being extended. The utter neglect of the railways in favor of road transportation by the Nazis has, however, made it necessary to establish a more comprehensive organization. During the past winter a number of local freight officers for the different means of transport were appointed, with functions like those of the regional and local officers appointed in Great Britain by the Ministry of Transport and by the different supply ministries at the outbreak of war.

The pattern of regional organization drawn above underwent a further change in the late summer of 1942 when the Minister of Armament and Munitions formed regional armament committees in every corps area. These committees included the regional armament inspectors of the *O.K.W.* and representatives of the regional defense commissioners, the regional economic offices, the *Hauptauschüsse* and *Ringe* in the Ministry of Armament and Munitions, and of the *Gauwirtschaftskammern* (District Economic Chambers) of the area. It is not clear from reports published abroad whether the regional organization of the *Rüstungsamt* has been replaced, or whether it has expanded into the new armament committees, as the regional organization of the *Wehrwirtschaftsamt* of the *O.K.W.* was expanded in the first phase of the war into the provincial economic offices.

The new organization represents a great extension of the power of the Minister of Armament and Munitions at the expense of the Ministry of Economics, the Economic Commissioner-General, the employment exchanges, and, possibly, the military supply department. The armament committees must equate the demands for man power by the armed forces and by industry on a regional basis. It is also intended to introduce a regional control of individual plants that will eliminate all direct contact between manufacturers and central government departments and thus reduce bureaucratic work. The armament committees may be described as a combination of the separate British man power boards and regional production boards, given real executive responsibility and brought into close contact at the regional level with the administration of economic questions and with the military administration.

This very brief survey of the German wartime administration reveals several characteristics. The most important, although somewhat modified by the establishment of the Ministry of Armament and Munitions and its regional committees, has been the consistent military coordination of the entire war effort. The problem of the coordination and synchronization of strategy and supply has been solved as efficiently as the interference of Party leaders permits. As far as General Keitel has Hitler's approval, he is responsible for steering the whole war machine. As chief of the *Oberkommando der Wehrmacht* he determines the main lines of strategy and supply for a year or more in advance once Hitler has decided the largest questions of military and foreign policy. The functions of the Supreme Defense Council are, as has already been pointed out, in all likelihood limited to coordination as among the defense forces, the organizations of the Nazi Party, and the civil administration.

It is true that the coordinating influence of general staff officers in regional administration has been reduced. Nevertheless, the fact that the supply department of the *O.K.W.* has remained since its incorporation in the Ministry of Armament and Munitions under the single direction of the same general who controls the economic planning department of the *O.K.W.* and the fact that general staff officers remain in control of certain essential war commodities in the Ministry of Economics and continue to occupy, although to a lesser extent than formerly, both executive and advisory positions throughout the transport system show that the organization of the *O.K.W.* has at least remained intact.

It may be assumed that the regional coordination of every aspect of the war effort, although nominally the responsibility of the regional defense and regional economic commissioners and also, with regard to production, of the armament committees of the Ministry of Armament and Munitions is still largely dominated by the staffs of the commanding generals in the corps areas. They are undoubtedly informed by the *O.K.W.* of the general lines of strategy and of supply requirements many months in advance. The *O.K.W.*, on the other hand, can get direct, reliable, and detailed reports on the functioning of the supply organization, the production and distribution of food, the work of the civil administration, and the actions of Nazi Party agencies at any time from the staffs of corps area headquarters, the armament inspectors in particular plants or districts, and the regional liaison officers of its economic planning department. Through the corps area headquarters the urgency of various demands made by the military program is impressed on the local institutions of the civil administration and the Nazi Party.

This line of military authority converges in the offices of the regional defense commissioners, which are also the offices of state or provincial governors, with lines running from the Supreme Defense Council, the General Economic Council, the Economic Commissioner-General, and the Ministries of Economics and Agriculture. Thus the traditional concentration of responsibility for the entire administration of a large area in one man has been maintained. As far as the civil administration is concerned the function of the defense commissioner is not one of coordination merely. He has the power of decision over all questions that affect only his region. Thus the central ministries are spared a daily inundation of correspondence and the impossible task of considering innumerable particular cases. The commissioners report to the Supreme Defense Council and to its individual members and may make suggestions concerning any phase of the war effort. They may also request the fuller interpretation of legislation or executive orders.[15a]

Certainly in the *O.K.W.* and its regional organization everything appears to have been done to provide a constructive balance between centralization and devolution, between long range planning and flexible execution, without sacrificing clear responsibility or coordination. Final judgment is, of course, better reserved even in this respect until the system has been tested under other conditions than the generally favorable ones resulting from the fact that the Axis until the autumn of 1942 held the strategic initiative.

Whatever the present influence of the Army and civil service may be either centrally or at the regional level, the German administration is still characterized by concentration of responsibility for major decisions and devolution of authority over execution in detail. The system as such is certainly very well conceived. In spite of the increasing political control exercised, secretly or openly, by the Gestapo and other Nazi Party agencies, and admitting the possibility that some general staff officers

---

[15a] The Supreme Defense Council may appoint a special defense commissioner with overriding powers for any corps area.

may not be equipped for their tremendous responsibilities, it is impossible to deny the great advantages of the organization.

How far this system actually results in coordination at every level in the face of the ambition of every Nazi Party leader to duplicate the functions of existing institutions and the consequent plethora of parallel organizations can hardly be judged from outside. Neither can the effect that the constant threat of intervention by the Gestapo must have on the nerves of those who are doing constructive work. Certainly this threat must paralyze that free and spontaneous initiative which was shown in Great Britain after Dunkirk to be so important in unforeseen emergencies.

In any comparison between the German administration and others, three points should be remembered. First, because of the suppression of public criticism in Germany, failures are not registered outside. Secondly, Germany's long possession of the strategic initiative made the organization of supply much simpler than it can be in a country constantly on the defensive, particularly if in such a country circumstances make it inadvisable to reveal the full extent of military reverses. In the latter case frequent, sudden changes of plan for which no explanation can be offered create a general sense of frustration. Thirdly, changes in the organization of supply correspond to different phases of war production, which do not occur simultaneously in different belligerent countries. Much criticism of wartime administration in Great Britain and the United States is attributable to a failure to appreciate this difference in time periods.

It may be said, finally, that the German wartime administration is characterized by planning from the top down to every municipality and firm and by the greatest possible delegation of responsibility for execution in detail to decentralized administrative institutions either of the Army, the civil administration, organizations of industry and agriculture, or the Nazi Party. The practical obstacles that will always arise to the realization of preconceived plans could not, indeed, be overcome if it were not for the existence of a large number of civil servants trained in the close coordination of different branches of administration at the regional level. Without such coordination central planning will lack the necessary flexibility in application. This is the chronic problem of German administration. It is characteristic of the German mind to crave abstract perfection. Before the Nazis came into power their blueprint schemes of organization won great popularity. In nearly every case these schemes have gone awry in practice, like every previous attempt to introduce an artificial consistency into the system of administration. The tendency of the British mind is just the opposite, and " planning " finds little favor. Administrative organization is evolved gradually by induction and by trial and error. Every ministry, and perhaps each department of a ministry, expands its own activities as the occasion arises without concern for the functioning of the administration as a whole if the departmental chief is able to accomplish his immediate object. In comparing wartime administration in Great Britain and Germany it is important to bear this temperamental difference in mind.

3. The British System of War Administration

I · ADMINISTRATIVE TRADITION AND THE REGIONAL PROBLEM

In the preceding discussion two main lines of the present German war administration have been emphasized. General Headquarters (the *Oberkommando der Wehrmacht*) is finally responsible for strategy and supply. It controls the entire war effort directly or indirectly through its departments for general production planning and procurement, through their regional and local officers, and through the commanding generals in the corps areas. Thus the *O.K.W.* combines functions which in the last war General Headquarters performed only uncertainly and irregularly. The Army has, on the other hand, lost all influence in questions of internal and international politics in comparison with its position in the last war. This is the natural result of an expansionist, totalitarian form of government. The civil service has similarly lost all political influence, although it has been able to save certain administrative methods and traditions. The Army and the civil service may occasionally be able to prevent a disastrous political decision if they are warned of it in time, but they cannot look for support to Parliament or to public opinion, and key positions in the civil administration are almost all in the hands of Nazi Party members.

In England, despite the inclusive emergency powers voted to the Government in May 1940,[16] the Prime Minister remains accountable to Parliament for the general lines of policy, and each minister remains accountable for the policy of his department. How far Parliament can actually control the policy of the Prime Minister in time of war is doubtful. The Prime Minister and his small War Cabinet must sometimes

[16] See Appendix I.

take decisions of the gravest consequence in a few hours; Parliament may later call attention to, but can hardly correct, the results. It can, however, control the administration of each department of state as long as the minister remains unconditionally responsible to Parliament for the policy of his department and the actions, or inaction, of all its employees in Whitehall and in the country at large. This is the mainstay of British Parliamentary government.

It is also the major reason for the difficulty of regional coordination even now, when in spite of the absence of any established tradition the paramount importance of such coordination is universally admitted. The heads of departments are individually responsible for the execution of every decision of the War Cabinet. Thus the machinery of each department extends down to the local level and into individual firms. Even for executive functions that are similar or overlapping this principle is maintained, so that, to take an example, in an emergency the Ministry of Food may operate canteens for a particular locality, while the Ministry of Labor operates canteens for the factories in that locality.

Since a more detailed description of the British wartime administration, analogous to the preceding description of the German administration, is given elsewhere,[16a] the discussion here will be concentrated on the problem of coordination among the executive departments in the central government and in the country at large and on the influence of the civil service and the defense forces and its compatibility with the responsibility of the Prime Minister and the ministerial heads of departments. The role of *the civil service* in England, which was already very large in the last war, has greatly increased since then, and the range of its functions has been widely extended. Although there has been a sharp distinction between British and Continental tradition in this respect ever since many of the older traditions of Continental administration were broken under the impact of Napoleonic totalitarianism, more recent changes in the importance and the functions of the civil service in England and on the Continent have, despite temporary variations, followed somewhat parallel lines.

The influence of the German civil service declined during the last war and in the years immediately following. During the years between 1923 and 1925, when the disastrous effects of the extreme inflation and of stabilization at too high a rate of exchange made themselves fully felt, the civil service and the Army acquired a preponderance of actual

[16a] See Chapter III, Part II, p. 179.

power, which decreased again during the three outwardly prosperous years before 1929. In 1931 and 1932 the likelihood was that the relations of the civil service to the cabinet and to parliament would evolve in the same direction in Germany and in Great Britain. Everywhere in Europe in fact the influence of the civil service, although parliaments opposed it and attempted to obscure it, increased during the '30's. The case will be the same in any grave and prolonged financial and economic crisis. This is why one should expect the importance of the permanent civil service everywhere in the world to increase in the face of complicated problems of reconstruction in the postwar period. In many countries a new equilibrium may have to be established between the civil service, the cabinet, and parliament. A reverse tendency may be looked for only when the world enters a period of prosperity based on internal and international freedom of trade and enterprise.

There are many reasons for the growth of the influence of the civil service in periods of structural economic crisis. Emergency legislation, whatever its constitutional basis, often changes the character of law. Whenever measures have to be taken hurriedly and frequently legislation is bound to assume increasingly the form of decrees or executive orders; this has been more or less the case everywhere. The fact itself is evidence that the problems of legislation had become too complex, and changed too abruptly, for the normal parliamentary technique to be appropriate. Parliaments have striven to maintain their rights of criticism and ultimate control. For the rest they have had in many countries to accept their inability to compete with the accumulated experience, the routine, and the possibilities of long-range planning enjoyed by civil servants who may have devoted the imagination and effort of a lifetime to the solution of a particular problem.

In the light of the experience of all Europe in the interval between the two wars, it can be said without exaggeration that whatever the form of government the bureaucracy has provided a major element of stability. In the last analysis the bureaucracy alone has been in a position to guarantee some continuity in periods of emergency. Under a weak government it may enjoy great powers of initiative and exercise real, if not open, leadership; under a strong government it is restricted to executing orders and instructions. When the policy of a particular cabinet or prime minister seems dangerous, the bureaucracy may find means of indicating that it is not to be identified with the policy of the government, thus preparing the way for its own ascendancy to effective leadership when the government falls without its help. Trained in an old tradition, the bureaucracy is a permanent "brain trust," and not the servant of one government alone or of an unbalanced parliamentary majority. Thus whatever changes in personnel it may undergo, it survives as a body. It gradually accumulates a detailed knowledge of facts and personalities, as well as of the law, which gives its members enormous weight behind the scenes.

This is especially true everywhere of treasury officials. In any ministry, however, civil servants can support or handicap a policy by eliminating, in the first case, or introducing, in the second, a multitude of factual and legal objections. A minister may be generously supplied with information or starved out by the bureaucracy. No newcomer in office can do without its help, especially if he has been shifted frequently in different cabinets from one department to another.

A continuous merry-go-round of cabinet ministers such as occurred in France necessarily increases the power of the civil service in practice, without producing any constructive result. Constant changes in legislation and ambition on the part of a government to associate its regime with as many paragraphs in the statute book as possible, most pronounced in a totalitarian system, will greatly enhance the importance of the civil service. Even in a democratic state like France legislation gradually assumed in normal times, just as in emergencies, the character of administrative decrees, and the authority of Parliament consequently suffered. Most nations naturally fear such an evolution. There are outbursts in almost every parliament from time to time, after the event, against the influence of the civil service. For this the parliament itself is frequently to blame, since the preponderance of actual power in the civil service often results from an attempt to accomplish through frequent legislation functions which should be purely administrative.

It would be wrong to suppose that these are the only reasons for the power of the bureaucracy, or that its influence is always the same, or that it does not meet with strong resistance. The influence that the bureaucracy enjoys is ultimately due to the skill, the routine, and the endurance found in all institutions of long-established tradition. The bureaucracy in Germany, after periods of sterility in which it was the object of bitter criticism, has recovered its influence again and again by finding the will and vigor to reform itself, and has vied with Parliament in discovering administrative abuses and eliminating unnecessary duplication of effort and confusion. It was prepared to adopt efficient new methods of administration from private business and from the municipalities. It constantly measured popular reactions and responded to them by issuing administrative orders or by preparing legislation to be introduced to Parliament before the different political parties, conscious of the same reactions, had decided how to respond to them. In its best periods it was not directed by Parliamentary criticism but rather took the initiative in the passage by Parliament of measures that were sound for the country as a whole but not to begin with popular politically.

All this may be said, too, of the *English civil service* in the last war and again in the economic crisis in the early '30's. Until then the economic and administrative problems of Great Britain had been much simpler than those of almost any other European country. With a stable currency, more or less free trade, and the absence of state ownership and operation of transportation facilities, mines, or forests, government interference in the economy was largely limited to financial control. The civil service was not required to exercise any initiative except in the preparation of legislation in response to Parliamentary pressure. The policy of non-interference was easily compatible with extreme centralization of power, first in the Crown and later in Parliament. Fiscal and judicial control were all that was required for the enforcement of acts of Parliament. The experience of patronage in the seventeenth and eighteenth centuries also created suspicion of any activity by government officers.

Thus in English administration, contrary to Continental administrative practice, there has been until recently *no intermediate executive institution between the central government and the local authorities.* There are separate health officers, employment officers, factory inspectors, inland revenue and customs collectors of course, and officers of the departments of the Admiralty concerned with the royal dockyards, naval construction, engineering, ordnance, etc. The War Office has maintained ordnance factories and permanent depots for the regular and territorial armies in peacetime. There has, however, been no specific executive institution between the county councils or municipalities and the central administration. The county councils have only limited executive functions, which are defined by Parliamentary legislation.

There has been no office like that of the German provincial or district governor or, to take a somewhat different example, the French *préfet,* all of whom have general executive powers in their administrative areas.

In the absence of any such intermediate institution between Whitehall and the municipalities, changing conceptions of the government's role in economic planning and, more especially, the direct intervention of the government in economic life in wartime have led to the over-elaboration of the machinery of each of the central executive departments both at the top and in its subordinate branches.

There are other reasons for the rising influence of the civil service. The experience of the past fifteen years has shown that the increasing selection of members of Parliament by party machines rather than by the electorate has not served to improve the quality of Parliamentary representation. The fact that ranking members of the present Cabinet, with influence second only to the Prime Minister's, have been drawn from the civil service is indicative of the growing importance of the purely administrative functions of government and of administrative training. Whatever the future evolution may be, however, the tradition that has characterized relations between the civil service, the Government, and Parliament in England since the disappearance of the system of patronage is still very strong.

Why is it that, except for a few smaller countries, it is only in the Anglo-Saxon countries that this conception of the restricted role of the civil service in relation to parliament and the Government survives so strongly? It cannot be assumed that it is only because their love of an easy-going life of individual freedom is more pronounced than that of other nations. Except in wars and grave emergencies, a free and unregulated existence is most satisfactory to human nature everywhere. The Anglo-Saxon countries are conspicuous, however, for the performance of many tasks of a purely administrative character not by an effectively organized professional administration under the control of cabinet ministers, but by special commissions and committees and by semi-judicial institutions.

The explanation may be that extreme individualism and a loosely organized administration is possible in a country that has not suffered from foreign invasion for many generations and even appears from its geographic position to be immune. It is fair to state that in the long run *the nature of administration in peacetime,* and consequently the manner in which the requirements of war are met, *generally depends upon the probability of foreign invasion.* Great Britain has been able to rely in safety through four hundred years on her sea frontiers.

Alertness, naval preparedness, and the prompt adaptation of strategic plans to changes in the balance of naval power are all that is required for her security in normal times. This leads, rightly, to the control of peacetime armament in accordance with the demands of naval supremacy and the tactical development of sea warfare. It leads further to the independent organization of naval supply and to priority for naval contracts over those of the other defense forces. For the same reason, the views of the Admiralty usually tip the scales in considerations of British foreign policy. Great Britain's position has been changed by air armament and technical progress in the range, speed, and carrying capacity of airplanes. Even when the necessity of quick, simultaneous armament in the air and on the sea was recognized in 1937, however, priority was maintained for the orders placed independently by the Admiralty.

The peacetime role of the army in a country with sea frontiers is necessarily a minor one. In Great Britain the strength of the Army is generally reduced immediately after the conclusion of peace to what is required for skeleton forces in India and the Colonies, the protection of the lifelines of the British Empire, and the staffing of ordnance depots. Parliament cannot be induced to support a large army, or even a skeleton organization that could be rapidly expanded in case of war. As far as regards supply, the Army is the Cinderella of the defense forces in peacetime and during the first phase of a war.

As long as the Navy is able and ready to meet any threat of attack, military and civilian administration can remain loosely organized. Thus Parliament and the Cabinet will appear at least to direct the whole policy of the country, without the existence of a large civil service either at the top or at a subordinate, regional level, and without much planning ahead. Legislation is executed under the supervision of government inspectors by municipalities, and to a more limited extent by county councils or special commissions created *ad hoc*. Certain changes made in this picture by the administrative provisions for social security do not alter it essentially.

There is little incentive in such a situation, while the navy or air force can guarantee the flow of necessary imports, to the planning of armament production in peacetime. Any urgent arrangements can be made by cabinet ministers and their staffs on the one side and private associations in industry, trade, and agriculture on the other. In such an administrative system the permanent civil service is confined for the most part to the central ministries, and its methods conform to the pattern of treasury control. Political control over administration remains to parliament, and legal control, to the regular courts.

The condition of countries with open land frontiers is, and always will be, quite different. The necessity for a central direction of every branch of the administration in strict accordance with a general policy increases in proportion to the "openness" of the frontiers. In eastern Europe, where there are vast plains, and where rivers often fail to provide a natural barrier against attack, the tendency towards centralization is greatest. Military requirements, as a result either of long-established tradition or of repeated experience, have generally had an important influence on the normal method of administration. There are exceptions to this rule. In France, for example, Revolutionary and Napoleonic totalitarianism was at least as much responsible as considerations of military necessity for the centralization of the administration. The two factors combined to make the Napoleonic prefectural system the prototype of extremely centralized bureaucracy.

Such long range economic planning as was attempted in many countries after the last war can hardly succeed without a permanent body of experienced civil servants and without coordination at the regional level of most of the functions of administration. Otherwise an executive officer of one department may be ignorant of activities corresponding to his own by agents of other departments, or even of other divisions of his own department, in the same district. With one man responsible for the coordination of the activities of different departments within his region, instructions are passed down to the lowest ranks of the administration easily and quickly, and with some guarantee that they will be carried out as originally intended. Through such an official the central authorities will also discover whether a general instruction is impracticable, and why, more directly than through scattered agents of every branch of administration in each region. Members of an intermediate regional administration trained in peacetime in such duties of coordination as have already been described can contribute their knowledge of the population, of industrialists, farmers, and traders, to the solution of problems of military supply in wartime. In an era of total warfare this thorough knowledge of local conditions is especially important.

The absence of a regional administration of the Continental type in Great Britain has been a serious and admitted drawback in this war. It is extremely difficult for higher civil servants in Whitehall to ascertain how Government policy operates in detail in the country at large. Human reactions to executive directions will always make themselves felt more slowly than under the Continental system of administration. This means a waste of time, material, labor, and, even more, of human energy and imagination. Deficiencies are discovered by the ministries for the most part by accident, through the medium of Parliamentary criticism or of the enormous number of visits to the ministries made daily by industrialists and by labor and farm leaders. The physical capacity of the higher civil servants' is inevitably overtaxed, and this leads to the loss of their freshness, initiative, and imagination.

In wartime it means, too, that collaboration at the top between the civil service and the defense forces, in so far as it is dependent on a clear appreciation of conditions in the country, is defective. It is extremely difficult to form a picture of a nation's war effort from the correspondence of the separate departments of every ministry with municipalities, county councils, special local committees, and trade associations. Problems in the allocation of man power and industrial capacity can hardly be solved by this method. Since the Admiralty has had its own organization for the supervision of individual plants, and the Air Ministry has adopted a similar organization, there has been much friction and wasted effort both at the top and at the regional and local levels.

The British supply system and the whole organization of production was perhaps too much influenced in the first phase of the war by the system of raw material control developed during the last war. At that time people with business experience in a particular trade were appointed government purchasing agents. Little interference from central ministries was required, and wide discretion could be left to subordinate officers. In most cases ministers and high permanent officials were concerned only with decisions of major importance and with the enforcement of certain indispensable regulations ensuring uniformity of practice or preventing injustice and corruption.

Once leading officials in a ministry have secured a legal basis for action, they must formulate regulations to be observed uniformly. If their application in detail can be left without risk to subordinates with business experience, as is the case in the control of particular commodities, the higher officers have then to intervene only when a breakdown threatens and when new problems of general concern arise. In the solution of intricate questions of industrial capacity and man power which occur in each new phase of war production, and which vary in every part of the country and concern different ministries, this easy method is hardly applicable. This is especially so in the case of small firms not represented in any influential trade association. There the questions to be decided include the best possible use of their capacity, the advisability of their closing down, whether to withdraw their labor supplies or to increase them, and, finally, what raw materials and semi-finished products they may acquire, and when. Such problems can be solved only on the spot by officials whose instructions are broad enough to leave them a margin of freedom in deciding each case quickly on its merits, and who do not have to stop half-way because of a conflict of jurisdiction.

Such instructions must be formulated with a view to their application under widely varying circumstances. They must state what may and may not, rather than what should, be done. Good administration is an art very difficult to acquire. Breadth of vision and legal exactness in the central ministries must be combined with adaptability to special needs at the regional and local levels. This problem was solved by the German civil service in its best periods by the constant interchange of personnel between the different levels of administration.

Even such a tradition and training may prove inadequate without regular coordination between different departments at the regional level. If such coordination is lacking, and if the regional and local officers of different departments are not all imbued with similar principles, it may well happen that the constructive efforts of the regional officers of one department are frustrated by rigid insistence on precedent in another. This danger is increased when the experience of regional and local officials is limited to a single department, or when, as is the case with the British Admiralty in relation to the other supply departments, the regional organization of one department enjoys an established routine while the organization of other departments has been hastily expanded. Between regional officers with great experience of administration in one department and inexperienced or unimaginative officers in other departments there is bound to be friction and delay. The distinct and independent regional organizations of each ministry and each department within a ministry may be appropriately compared to threads strung in a loom without a shuttle.

At this point in the discussion it will have become clear why in every region one man of vision and experience and legal knowledge enough to reconcile the conflicting conceptions and methods of different departments is required to exercise over the officers of every department in his region the control exercised at the top by the central offices of each department separately. He can avoid duplication and delay and the establishment of overlapping agencies. Only the existence of regional officials responsible for the coordination of every phase of the war effort within their areas and with power to make quick decisions on the spot can prevent the national administration from becoming topheavy. It will spare the heads of departments in the central ministries the burden of enormous correspondence and constant committee meetings, which forces them to neglect their proper functions of general planning and control, however admirably fitted for them by training and experience they may be.

This is a great disadvantage of the British war administration in comparison with the German, in which all correspondence between regional officers and the Supreme Defense Council, the Economic Commissioner-General, or the central departments is handled by the permanent staffs of provincial and state governors. Such highly trained officials can unravel complications or decide special cases and so spare officials in the central departments as much time as possible for planning and general direction. The position of the *regional defense commissioners* in the twelve areas into which Great Britain has been divided for purposes of defense may seem analogous to that of the German defense commissioners; it was indeed hoped that the regional defense commissioners might perform the same function of coordination.

That would have meant that they assumed full responsibility in their regions for every part of the war effort outside the control of the Army, Navy, and Air Force. It would have meant, too, that any central department could obtain from the regional commissioners at any time a complete statement of the practical effect of its orders. By meeting from time to time with the principal ministerial committees of the Cabinet, the regional commissioners could have gained some insight into the most urgent problems of production and of interdepartmental cooperation, which can never be achieved by correspondence. In fact, however, the executive powers of the regional defense commissioners have been limited for the most part to the hypothetical cases of invasion or the interruption of communications with London by bombing attacks.

Without any responsible coordination at the regional level, each ministry has created its own more or less independent regional organization. There is not regular contact between the regional officials of all the departments and the regional defense commissioners, not to mention the absence of any jurisdiction by the regional defense commissioners over the officers of different departments. Nor have the regional officers of the various departments within the same region much contact with one another. Wherever there is coordination in any particular respect, as in the *area supply boards,* the officers of each department retain the right to refer any decision back to their own ministry. This of course entails renewed consultation among the different departments concerned at the top if corresponding instructions are to be issued to the different regional officers. The consequence is an enormous duplication of labor and loss of time both at the regional level and, where it is more important, at the top.

It appears, furthermore, that when regional coordination of the different departments concerned with production was first attempted through the area supply boards, the chairmen were retired naval officers and civil servants. That is to say, each of them had behind him very likely the training of a lifetime in a single branch of administration, which did not help him to understand the often very different methods of other services. Civil servants are for the most part exchanged between ministries only after they have reached the top positions of undersecretary or principal. Short of that, they become specialists in a particular routine. The great disadvantage of this training for any interdepartmental coordination is that civil servants in the lower ranks have no opportunity to acquire an understanding of the implications of one ministry's policies for the work of other ministries.

In local administrative agencies like the employment exchanges under the Ministry of Labor there will be a large number of officials who are acquainted only with the limited problems of their own offices and have no comprehensive knowledge of national issues. Thus they gradually forget the reasons for which their own branch of administration was originally established. There were many complaints, for example, at the beginning of the war that the officers of the employment exchanges had come during the prolonged economic crisis to confine their activities to the payment of the dole and no longer concerned themselves with the organization of the labor market or the causes of unemployment in different localities. From this one must conclude that the regional officers (divisional controllers) who existed, by exception from the practice of most other departments, in the Ministry of Labor failed to inspire the subordinate local officers with any constructive purpose. The particular functions and training of the divisional controllers of the Ministry of Labor during the prewar period are not clear, however, to the outsider.

In judging the whole present need for regional organization in the British civil service, one should remember that the evolution away from strict Treasury control toward greater initiative in civil service training has been comparatively recent and rather slow. Great Britain has had at her disposal in the last war and at present not only highly trained and farsighted Treasury officials, who have few equals in Europe, but also ranking civil servants with varied experience in responsible positions in different executive departments and in the colonies. It is on civil servants of this type that the main burden of coordination of the war effort at the top and at the regional level has fallen. Even the outsider sees that the tasks of Sir John Anderson, who rose in the home civil service to an Indian governorship before entering the House of Commons and the Cabinet, of the present War Secretary, who also held a responsible position in India before he became under-secretary of the War Office, and of many permanent under-secretaries and directors of divisions within ministries demand the highest personal qualifications. It is mainly because men of exceptional qualifications were available that the administration was kept in gear in the confusion of the suddenly changed strategic situation resulting from the defeat in France.

The existence of a limited number of such first class civil servants of very wide experience does not by itself completely alter long-standing traditions of the civil service determined by the form and incidence of *Treasury control*. Treasury control, for historical reasons and because of certain characteristics of the British Parliamentary system, is the most significant element of British administration. This is true to some extent in other countries as well, since the influence of every parliament originated with, and in the final analysis depends upon, the right to vote revenue and appropriations. Nowhere else, however, has this fact remained so plainly evident or received so much formal expression as in England, and nowhere else has the treasury exercised such strict control over local government through the administration of grants-in-aid.

The Chancellor of the Exchequer has played a predominant role in the Cabinet and in Parliament. Even the Prime Minister holds office as the nominal First Lord of the Treasury. The character and functioning of the entire civil service is largely decided by the Treasury's traditional control over expenditure and revenue. Since the office of head of the civil service was created it has been held by the permanent under-secretary of the Treasury. One can say without oversimplification that the traditional functions of Treasury officials have been the most important influence on the character and mentality of the civil service. This has been largely due, of course, to the principle of government non-interference in economic life except by fiscal control.

In many other European countries, although the influence of the treasury remained predominant in administration, other conceptions as well have evolved during the centuries in which the state has owned and managed mines and forests. Such tasks require special training in addition to normal civil service training. The whole outlook of civil servants so employed came to differ widely from that of treasury officials, who exercise a restrictive control over administration by checking expenditure. They were concerned rather with increasing the revenue of state owned properties or services by improved management. This entailed the combination of two different types of administration and made a restricted departmental outlook impossible.

Wherever the standards of the civil service were high, regional and local officers were expected to display initiative and creative imagination as well as a sense of definite responsibility. There were experts on all questions available in the civil service for important positions in the central ministries or elsewhere in the country whenever new problems of administration arose. They had the advantage of not having spent their lives in central offices, remote from realities and from the people whose conduct formed the object of legislation, and they were frequently exchanged between departments. Civil servants trained in the old treasury style, or those who have spent their lives in one department, rising slowly by seniority, cannot have the same knowledge of varying local conditions or the same adaptability.

Civil servants of the type developed in England under the system of Treasury control while it was the first ambition of the Chancellor of the Exchequer to present a budget without increased taxation, or even perhaps with a reduction of the income tax, are of course no longer to be found in the top ranks. Since the last war, and especially since 1931, the scope and the personal breadth of vision of leading officials in the British Treasury have been unrivalled, on the average, in most other countries. They cannot be blamed for the present difficulties arising from older traditions and methods of training in the civil service.

The indisputable fact is that for treasury control of expenditure, which is one of the vital functions of administration everywhere, men of a particular type, indifferent to the glamour of novel proposals for spending money, are needed. Unless they are hard and skeptical in this respect they will fail in their duty. The consequence, however, is in many cases an unimaginative rigidity. Elaborate formality on the part of the treasury may entail greater eventual expenditure than the ready acceptance of measures the original cost of which is apparently high. None of this matters if there is a balance in the administrative service as a whole between progressive and enterprising civil servants in other branches of the administration and more cautious, in the lower ranks possibly even pedantic, civil servants in the treasury. The danger lies in training an entire civil service on the model of the latter type and in confining the activity of the civil service exclusively to central departments.

Thus such outbursts against the civil service as occurred in the House of Lords in February and March 1941 and in the press overshoot the mark. In this case it is only natural that equally bitter criticism should since have been directed against politicians as a class. The shortcomings of the wartime administration in the first phase of the war should in fact be attributed to the British political system as a whole, which, with its very agreeable traditions and particularities, works so smoothly in normal times.[16b]

It is easy to understand why, when strict departmental traditions still survive in the older generation, efforts to coordinate even the placing of orders for armament by the different supply departments at the regional level have not been wholly successful. The very great reluctance of English business to accept any bureaucratic interference has deprived the civil service of much experience of economic problems. This is one reason why, for example, in the summer of 1942 prominent in-

---

16b The problem has been stated very well in a discussion of the *Sixteenth Report* of the House of Commons Select Committee on National Expenditure in *The Economist* of November 7, 1942. There a demand is made for a redistribution of responsibility among civil servants as a preliminary to the more logical distribution of functions among departments recommended by the Haldane Committee in 1918. " On the one hand, civil servants, even in key positions, are not encouraged or even expected to make decisions on their own responsibility, without a frustrating process of reference back, discussion, argument, self-justification, and self-protection. On the other hand, the existing rigid system of recruitment, appointment, grading and promotion frequently makes it impossible for the right men to be placed in the right positions." The author adds that " the entry of temporary civil servants from the outside world of business, scholarship, and the professions has shown what can be done to fit men to jobs, even with the existing inhibitions and frustrations." In the German administration much of the same criticism, which would formerly have been unjustified, may now be made of certain branches of the civil service which have been deprived under the centralized Nazi system of their old willingness to accept grave responsibility and to exercise initiative of their own.

dustrialists instead of civil servants were appointed regional controllers for the new Ministry of Production.

This is not symptomatic of a *malaise* peculiar to Great Britain. The administrative functions of individual industrialists and of corporative organizations in certain industries have been extended in Germany, too, as stated above, at the expense of the established administration. The use of a similar form of corporative organization for the self-government of whole industries in England has been widely discussed during 1942. To appreciate the whole problem of British administration, one must realize that the tradition confining the civil service almost exclusively to Whitehall is very strong, and that the regional officers who have been appointed by various departments have had little assistance in evolving some means of coordinating their efforts with those of the representatives of other departments in the same regions. They proceed in accordance with the emergency motto " Il faut se débrouiller."

It would be quite wrong to suppose that this method results in chaos. It merely fails to produce the maximum result possible when it may be most necessary. It does assure the Admiralty, where regional and local officers of long standing know the specific problems of shipbuilding and naval supply, of its maximum share of the industrial capacity and skilled labor of the country. Any department under a minister as indifferent to the inhibitions imposed by the necessity of general coordination as Lord Beaverbrook may likewise succeed in getting its share, but probably only at the sacrifice of steady production for all the defense forces and the adjustment of the whole production of the country to long-range strategic plans. With pulling and hauling between ministries, the task of coordination and mediation falling to the top civil servants becomes necessarily harder.

Suspicion of any intermediate administrative institution between the local authorities, which, it must always be remembered, have never enjoyed as much " home rule " as municipalities in pre-Nazi Germany or in the United States, and Whitehall is deeply rooted in the British nation. Hence any discussion of the possibility of making the office of regional defense commissioner permanent, and entrusting such regional commissioners with a large degree of responsibility in peacetime as a counterweight to over-centralization, has subsided. The Minister of Home Security, under whom the regional defense commissioners hold office, has said that if the regional commissioners were given executive powers over the different branches of administration at the regional level, the opposition of local authorities would be such that they would find no cooperation. The establishment of a permanent responsible regional organization and the development of a large civil service in the country would, it is true, entail some alteration of the British political system.

The results of this instinctive opposition to any effective regional institution for coordinating the independent activities of the regional officials of various ministries as they appear in the initial slowness with which plans decided on by the Cabinet are carried out is often overlooked. The inductive method, which is applied within each ministry as well as in interdepartmental coordination, takes time. Eventually of course the machinery of each department is improved, suitable positions are found for capable men, and, which is even more important, definite responsibility is established. Individual cooperation among the officers of different departments may then result in as effective coordination as is secured in Germany by the concentration of authority in each region, but the British system in comparison with the German is exposed to the disadvantage of a time lag.

An organization established by the method of trial and error, while it will not be systematic, will be practical and will be free from the dangers of conformity to an artificial pattern which exist at present in Germany. It may be surmised that the recent organization of *Gauwirtschaftskammern,* for example, was not due to necessity but rather to the Nazi hobby of streamlining everything on paper. Since the *Gaue,* while they are more or less identical with the regions of the labor administration, do not correspond to the corps areas or to the regional divisions of the provincial economic offices, further reorganization will be necessary before the various subdivisions of administration can be made to present an appearance of perfect congruity. There is the risk that in this process great experience and very valuable traditions may be sacrificed to political ambition and superficial uniformity.

The contrary is true of the British system. In the Ministry of Food, for example, rationing to consumers is based on county and municipal committees, which are grouped in regions corresponding to the civil defense regions. For more general purposes of distribution, however, the country is divided into eight areas, determined by purely practical considerations of transport, and local groups of wholesalers are forbidden to deal with retailers outside their areas. For the purchase of particular commodities from producers and their distribution to wholesalers, again, the various controls in the ministry have their own area divisions, which correspond to the centers of supply. This solution is very complicated on paper, but to all appearances very satisfactory in practice.

The adjustment of the supply of labor to present and future industrial capacity is of course much more difficult. The employment exchanges, which had, as has already been mentioned, atrophied with respect to certain of their functions, have been adapted to the present emergency in so far as they receive instructions locally from man power officers and from special labor supply officers for the industries to which Essential Work Orders have been applied, and regionally from the regional controllers of the Ministry of Labor. As far as can be judged, the somewhat casual system of consultation between labor supply officers introduced in the summer of 1940 has been replaced by closer coordination within smaller districts of the work of man power officers, who control military recruiting as well as the transfer of labor, and who receive instructions from the regional controllers of the ministry. The latter must have some knowledge of general problems of production and of the plans agreed on centrally by the supply ministries.

Responsibility for the coordination of the work of regional officers of the different supply departments now rests with the regional controllers of the Ministry of Production, who are, as has already been mentioned, not civil servants but business men and industrialists. The problem resulting from the existence of an independent and long established supply organization in the Admiralty has not of course been solved. Neither have the regional controllers of the Ministry of Production any executive authority over the representatives of other departments. In shipbuilding, where the functions of the Admiralty are definitely preponderant, the employment and release of labor and the allocation of capacity and materials as between naval and merchant shipbuilding and repairs are under direct Admiralty control.

II · CABINET RESPONSIBILITY AND COORDINATION

These few instances may perhaps convey an impression of the working of the British system. There can be no doubt that the maximum utilization of capacity is attained more slowly than under the German system. It is also true that the British system may be more flexible in emergencies. The method of proceeding at the regional level by trial and error may, however, entail great difficulties unless there is comprehensive planning in the Cabinet and close coordination among the executive departments in all military and supply problems. In the present German system, in which the best possible arrangements are made for such planning at the center, deficiencies at the regional level, where they exist, are less dangerous than in England. The commanders of the corps areas with their supply departments (*Rüstungsämter*) and the defense commissioners, whose staffs have a long training in regional coordination, can find the easiest way out of any difficulty. It is doubtful whether the regional controllers of the British Ministry of Production, business men familiar for the most part with one type of production, can be similarly efficient, especially since they have no executive powers. It is also doubtful whether the best British regional defense commissioners could assume the role of their German counterparts even if the Government desired it, since the British civil service has no tradition in the coordination of the functions of different departments at the regional level. The fact that a special regional commissioner for the supervision of communications in the London area was appointed in 1940 in addition to the existing defense commissioner and his deputies is evidence of this.

Had the British defense commissioners the function of coordinating every aspect of the war effort in their regions, it would nevertheless be difficult for them to obtain definite instructions from the Government, since every minister is anxious, because of his responsibility to Parliament, to keep all executive power in his department in his own hands. This factor also affects the method of cooperation among Cabinet ministers and top civil servants in the central ministries.

One main consideration should dominate the organization of wartime administration at the top and at the regional level — a right balance between centralization in planning and supervision and flexibility in detailed execution and adaptation to new tasks or changed conditions. When organization is too rigid and planning too conventional there is a danger that in sudden emergencies or under the strain of unforeseen developments the whole machinery may break down. The farther executive centralization is carried, the more that danger increases. But if there is no definite prearranged relation between central and regional administration, many valuable months and years may be lost in wartime by muddling through.

In the first part of this war, time counted heavily, since Germany had been able to begin the mass production of armaments at the end of 1936. Modern techniques of mass production necessitate a comparatively long interval between the designing and testing of a weapon and capacity production. Thus any country entering a war with a three years' lead in armament production and capacity has a great initial advantage over an opponent that will reach capacity production only later.

These factors must be borne in mind in an analysis of *coordination of central departments* in Great Britain, since they have contributed to make the tasks of wartime administration much heavier. The immediate difficulties increased when war actually broke out; they increased threefold after the Battle of France. This explains to some extent why necessary measures were delayed, why Cabinet members were constantly shifted, and why the organization of the Cabinet and the administrative services has undergone such frequent drastic changes. Ministers or committees which seemed energetic and efficient in one phase of the war failed when confronted with different problems of unexpected magnitude in the next. The methods and the personnel of committees that had developed a satisfactory routine after initial experimentation suddenly proved useless. Committees appointed for a particular purpose survived after having lost their original functions. Excellent team work achieved over long periods of regular collaboration and personal acquaintance failed in the face of novel and complex problems demanding greater imagination and physical vitality.

Whether or not advantage is taken of a nation's gifts of improvisation will depend on the constructive imagination of its political leaders and civil servants. The inventiveness of any nation varies from generation to generation. It is usually heightened after defeat. Whether or not political and military leaders and civil servants of imagination and initiative are available, however, the wartime problems of precise definition of responsibility and coordination of the main lines of foreign policy, strategy, and supply are the same.

There must be a small *war cabinet* or defense council to support and to control the prime minister's policy. Such a cabinet must be responsible for the general lines of strategy and of economic organization, and for the coordination of the whole administration as well as for the solution of specific problems as they arise. It cannot consider details, but it must make definite plans. It must be composed of people capable of quick decision, each of whom exercises direct supervision over a certain branch of administration. It must have team spirit. The *prime minister* should be freed as much as possible from the burden of detail. When particular cases that have acquired major importance are brought to his attention he must dispose of them decisively. He cannot indulge in procrastination by paper compromises that have no practical result. His mind must be kept fresh to anticipate the requirements of the immediate and the more distant future. All this means that he must have great experience, knowledge, imagination, courage, and strength.

He must exercise initiative in the general conduct of the war, and must also have the gift of putting the right man in the right place. He must refrain from occupying himself with everyone's business. His task is to keep his eyes and ears open, to inspire and direct the efforts of his colleagues, parliament, and the public. He must avoid the excitement of popular emotion by continual sensations, and he must express burning passion as well as serene calm and balance of mind. Such a figure cannot be found in every nation at every major crisis. Nor will he be able if he is in power to discover at once the collaborators he needs.

In the latter respect the British Prime Minister's difficulties are greater than any which exist in totalitarian states or in the United States. The President of the United States is restricted in his appointments only by the necessity in some cases of obtaining senatorial approval, which is assured in any grave emergency. He can appoint able and experienced men to direct the most important war agencies and assure them of a comparatively long tenure of office, which is one of the essential conditions of constructive leadership. They need not be members of his Cabinet, which therefore does not become so large that it is necessary to form a super-Cabinet, as is the case in England. When the President wishes to do so, he will have relatively little difficulty in conferring on one man full responsibility for the control of production, prices, and labor in relation to the war effort and in defining his functions as broadly as he chooses. He can decide whether to make the Cabinet the highest coordinating authority by including such a man in it, or whether to become himself the final arbiter by establishing independent agencies outside the regular departments. He may confine himself to acting as the impartial chairman of the Cabinet, or may hold Cabinet meetings only rarely, deciding the main lines of policy himself in consultation with individual Cabinet members or the heads of special agencies, or even with personal advisers.

Constitutionally the President of the United States could create a simpler, more sharply defined, and more centralized organization at the top than exists in Germany. He might, of course, encounter opposition in Congress if he attempted to put any military officer in the same dominating position that Marshal Keitel and his staff occupy under Hitler. Congressional control over legislation is much more active than Parliamentary control in England. At the beginning of a war, however, when popular emotion is strong enough to prevent any Congressional opposition, the President will have no difficulty in securing full powers. As enthusiasm subsides, he may of course have to meet greater resistance. In England, on the other hand, Parliament has been increasingly prepared as the country's danger has increased to confer any power desired on the Government, wisely confining itself to the function of constructive criticism.

Even with his present enormous powers, the British Prime Minister labors under difficulties which do not exist to any comparable extent in the United States. They result from the complexity of the interests of the world-wide British Empire, from deeply ingrained constitutional traditions, and, finally, from the necessity of maintaining a balance of power between the members of a coalition Government. In an empire scattered over all the earth the number and complexity of the questions involved in the efficient coordination of strategy and foreign policy, the timing of military action, the seizure of favorable strategic opportunities in spite of the possible consequences for foreign policy, and the coordination of the plans of the three defense forces is obviously overwhelming. The dominions of the British Commonwealth are bound only in a loose federal union by common allegiance to the Crown, and identity of interest in one part of the world does not necessarily imply identity of interest elsewhere. Strategic opportunities may be neglected in one theatre because to take advantage of them would involve political complications in another. Great Britain in fact enjoys complete freedom of strategic movement only after the entire world is arrayed in two or more opposing camps, and the complete and effective participation of all the dominions is assured.

The effect of existing British constitutional and political traditions in conditions like the present is to burden the Prime Minister, whose role in normal times is that of the chairman of a committee, with such a number of particular vital decisions that it is extremely difficult for him to find the necessary freedom for the planning and initiation of general lines of policy. His problems of organization arise in part from the fact that the head of every executive department in the British Government must be a member of the House of Commons or the House of Lords. For historical reasons, and because of a largely traditional division of functions which has little relation to the specific problems of this war, the Government includes more than twenty-five ministers of Cabinet rank. Each minister is responsible to Parliament for all the executive functions of his department, and this has led, as has been mentioned, to duplication and overlapping in administration in the country at large. The essential problem of coordination among departments in Whitehall and their officers in different parts of the country has thus assumed such proportions that it obscures the definite ministerial responsibility upon which the whole system of British Parliamentary government rests.

One manifestation of this is the rank growth of interdepartmental committees. Another is the formation of a super-Cabinet and super-ministries, though without any clear distinction between executive and coordinating functions and so without achieving the essential purpose of such super-groupings. A successful combination of closely related executive functions in a single ministry has been achieved only in the case of the Ministry of War Transport. Between the Ministries of Agriculture and Food, for example, there is cooperation but not unified direction, with little regular contact between their agencies in the country at large. None of the attempts made thus far to solve the problems of coordination of supply and of the strategy of the three defense forces, and thus to relieve the Prime Minister of very exacting duties, seems to have been wholly successful, although great progress has been made during 1942.

The difficulties inherent in long established traditions have been increased by the necessity of securing a balance of power in the Ministry and in the War Cabinet among the different Parliamentary parties in the coalition Government. *Government by coalition* in wartime has several drawbacks. The influence of very able ministers over their own parties is weakened by the absence of any active opposition to consolidate support within the Government for necessary measures. The lack of an official opposition for the expression of dissatisfaction in a long and disappointing war results also in the election of independent, non-party candidates who may upset established Parliamentary practice. By far the most important weakness, however, is that the Prime Minister is not free to select ministers for the departments in which they are most likely to be successful. Members of Parliament of long political experience have had to be appointed to positions in the Government for which administrative talents and experience should have been the only qualification. Others have been given sinecure Cabinet offices with nominal functions of general coordination. In fact the full burden of coordination of civil and of military affairs rests on a former civil servant holding political office and a general without executive powers performing the function of liaison between the Prime Minister and the service and supply departments, although it may be assumed that during 1942 the Minister of Production has acquired an increasing share of responsibility.

To anticipate a problem about which more must be said later, it is clear that a successful ministry of production must have executive responsibility for general economic planning, for supply for all the defense forces and the synchronization of production with strategy, and for the distribution of labor. That such responsibility has not been established is due not only to constitutional considerations, but also to the fact that very likely no one has seemed ready to assume these functions of supreme executive control, that if someone did the two major coalition parties would hardly agree to submit all these questions to his decision, and that there is no administrative organization for the coordinated execution of the instructions of such a ministry in the country at large.

The alternative to appointing ministers on the basis of their importance in their own parties rather than of their personal capacities is the appointment as ministers of civil servants, business men, industrialists, and trade unionists who are not members of Parliament and for whom seats in the House of Commons must be found or peerages created. By this means important offices have been increasingly neutralized from the political point of view. The War Office and the Ministries of Food, Production, Supply, War Transport, and Labor are now, and the Ministry of Works and Buildings and the Board of Trade have been, in the hands of men who entered the Government either before or immediately after having become members of Parliament for the express purpose of taking administrative office. Thus the constitutional position has been saved, and the civil service and the defense forces seem still to be subordinate to ministers who are members of and responsible to Parliament. This is, however, the outward constitutional aspect; it forms a legal screen for the actual preponderance of the defense forces and the civil service in planning and administration. Much misunderstanding of the British wartime administration and much exaggerated criticism of its coordination may be attributed to the existence of this screen, which also complicates any outline of executive functions.

Either under a coalition government or under a one-party government the gradual replacement of ministers who are not up to the jobs to which they have been assigned and for which they may have no inclination by other members of Parliament or by outsiders is a long and tedious process. Every British Prime Minister in the past has had to make ministerial appointments from among the members of his party in Parliament with a view to strengthening his hold over the party as a whole. He must consider prestige established and rewards earned in opposition. Members of Parliament who have been most conspicuous in criticism of a previous government and are consequently popular in the country may not be by any means the best people for important administrative offices. They may be devoid of creative imagination, energy, initiative, or administrative genius. Their efforts may be concentrated in Parliamentary or public brilliance. They may aspire to political longevity and therefore oppose beneficial but controversial measures, without hesitating at the same time to create differences in Parliament and the country if that promises to advance them on the ladder leading to the position of Chancellor of the Exchequer or even Prime Minister. The problem is not, of course, peculiar to Great Britain.

None of this mattered when the power of England was uncontested and her wealth expanding, and when even major political errors could be repaired without the loss of too much power and prestige. That was the ideal period for political leaders who were brilliantly gifted for parliamentary debate but amateurs in administration and therefore happy to refer any difficult question to the judiciary, to a special commission, or to some legalistic expert in the Cabinet. It passed during the last war. England's difficulties have been largely due to her return for some time between the last war and the present one to that easy-going and certainly most agreeable system. The most farsighted and energetic members of Parliament were pushed into the background lest they should spoil the picture of modest but steady progress.

Years ago it became evident that this method was unsatisfactory. Unprecedented tasks in organization and administration had to be performed in a very short time in 1931–32, and again after the need for rapid rearmament was recognized in 1936. Under the fire of Parliamentary criticism Cabinets were continually reshuffled. The Prime Minister was not free, however, any more than the present Prime Minister is, to choose the best men for the most exacting tasks. That was made the more difficult by the fact that the British Parliament, in contrast to many other European Parliaments, is very moderate in its criticism of ministers and is prepared to condone the blunders of anyone who openly confesses his mistakes or omissions. In the long run this is certainly a great advantage for the dignity of Parliamentary traditions, but for a Prime Minister of great imagination and initiative who is also loyal to the members of his old team, the difficulty of transferring Cabinet ministers who don't do well is not lessened by the very humane attitude of Parliament.

Thus the Prime Minister must always try to compensate for the deficiencies of particular Cabinet ministers by matching them with permanent under-secretaries who possess just the qualities they themselves lack. This is one of his most anxious tasks, and the eventual coordination of the war effort may depend upon his success. It requires enormous patience, tact, and keen judgment of personal qualities and temperaments. Problems will certainly arise on the civil service side as well; there is none too large a selection of civil servants eligible for under-secretaryships in any country.

Men with creative imagination, initiative, and willingness to undertake grave responsibility are not normally of a type also willing to remain in the background, patiently performing an enormous amount of daily work, drafting legislation and watching over its passage, without being able to determine at any point the manner in which the minister will carry it through the Cabinet committees, the Cabinet, and, finally, Parliament. The civil servant's only possibility of action is to prepare the ground for a constructive policy privately among his colleagues. Except for the " Chief Advisers " of the Government, who were appointed for the first time during the crisis of 1931, civil servants do not normally participate in Cabinet meetings. It may be assumed that even the chief advisers attended Cabinet meetings only occasionally. Their position in the administration is, in addition, somewhat anomalous, and many permanent under-secretaries may very well have taken exception to it.

The fact that Mr. Lloyd George when he was Prime Minister during the last war waived the traditional exclusion of everyone outside the Cabinet from Cabinet meetings was a great step toward bringing the views of ranking civil servants directly before the Prime Minister and Cabinet.[17] The methods of the War Cabinet were influenced, as every

---

[17] In other European governments in which civil servants have frequently been invited to attend formal Cabinet meetings, persons who did not belong either to the military or the civil

administrative institution in Great Britain has been, by the model of court procedure. Thus the War Cabinet reserved the right to call in at any time departmental chiefs, either ministers or civil servants, and outside experts, each of whom was expected to give his opinion frankly when asked for it, even if it differed from that of his superior or superiors.

The appearance of complexity and rigidity presented by the chart of the British administration at the back of this book may be misleading, since a long established informality of procedure makes the dependence there indicated of almost every department on the decisions of others non-existent in practice. There are certain dangers in this agreeable informality, especially when critical decisions have to be taken quickly. Although the *Cabinet Secretariat* circulates a record of decisions taken in Cabinet meetings to the different departments, there is no regular control over the execution of these decisions by individual ministers. In Germany, on the other hand, and similarly in many other Continental countries, the permanent secretary of the Chancellery has always been responsible for the exact application of Cabinet decisions by the departments affected.[18] This is of course a reflection of the position of the German Chancellor under the Bismarckian constitution, which, in spite of the changes made by the Weimar Constitution, was partially revived in practice later.

Where no established tradition governs the precise formulation of Cabinet decisions and the control of their execution, an additional bur-

---

service have nevertheless been rigidly excluded. Where parliamentary under-secretaries are not appointed to the executive departments from among the members of Parliament, the influence of the permanent under-secretaries is of course much more evident to the public. In Germany, for example, although the permanent secretaries of departments did not normally attend Cabinet meetings, they could do so either at the request or with the permission of the Chancellor. They could also at the Chancellor's request meet as often as and in whatever manner he decided either among themselves or with their respective ministers. There was, however, an established routine for such meetings. Flexibility and immediate access to the greatest knowledge and experience available were combined with clear-cut responsibility, the Chancellor having always the initiative in the establishment of such committees and final responsibility for their decisions. The Parliamentary duties of Cabinet members were lightened, in comparison with the British system, by the fact that higher civil servants could also answer questions in Parliament and could participate in debates whenever their ministers so instructed them, or when they were appointed by the government as commissioners for the discussion of a particular bill. This of course increased the influence of the civil service without increasing its formal responsibility. Higher civil servants, however, participated regularly and openly in much of the work of preparation and coordination which they perform only informally and in private in Great Britain.

[18] The decisions of the Supreme Defense Council are now communicated directly to the generals commanding the corps areas as well as to the defense commissioners, so that their full and accurate application is doubly guaranteed.

den is thrown on ranking civil servants. They frequently have to agree among themselves as to general lines of policy as well as on more specific questions. This partly explains the *duplication of ministerial committees by committees of civil servants*. Another reason is the amalgamation at the outbreak of war of the established interdepartmental organization of the *Committee of Imperial Defense* with other committees of the Cabinet. The existence of the Committee of Imperial Defense made it very easy in peacetime to bring Cabinet ministers, high civil servants, and military officers around the same table to develop common lines of action and a team spirit which could come fully into play at the outbreak of war. The fact that the first permanent secretary of the Cabinet, Lord Hankey, also one of the ablest public servants Great Britain has had, was for a generation secretary of the Committee of Imperial Defense as well was undoubtedly a very important factor in its success.

At first glance the transition from the work of preparation in the Committee of Imperial Defense to the organization of the first War Cabinet seems to have been well conceived and easily effected. It was facilitated by Mr. Chamberlain's use long before the outbreak of war of an *"inner Cabinet."* The Chancellor of the Exchequer became chairman of the Economic Policy Committee, which dealt with the most general economic questions, while three other major coordination committees concerned primarily with civilian questions have retained the form they had at the outbreak of war until today. The great problem of the coordination of strategy and supply, on which most subsequent criticism and change has centered, appeared to have been solved by the appointment of Lord Chatfield as chairman both of the Military Coordination Committee and the Ministerial Priority Committee.

The combination of responsibility for strategic planning, the actual conduct of the war, and the general allocation of man power, materials, and industrial capacity was in itself very farsighted. Lord Chatfield's position was as close an approximation to Marshal Keitel's as there has yet been in Great Britain, and probably as close as the traditions of English politics permit. The Prime Minister apparently considered his own functions to be those of a committee chairman and general coordinator, leaving him time for a certain minimum of initiative in policy and for participation in the relatively frequent meetings of the House of Commons during that period. Whether even a Prime Minister of a different type from Mr. Chamberlain would have found the calm and the freedom from daily business which is essential for the leader of a vast Empire in modern total war by a more precise delegation of executive responsibility may be doubted.

This organization might have been successful if the war had continued as Mr. Chamberlain seemed before the Battle of France to expect, and if there had been more men with imagination and driving force in leading positions. The first favorable impression, however, must be largely discounted on closer examination. To place the supreme coordination of all economic questions, with the exception of priorities in armament production and the allocation of materials, under the Chancellor of the Exchequer, was a concession to the traditional control of the Treasury over the whole administration which could not, with all respect to the abilities of high civil servants in the Treasury, be called constructive in view of the scale of the economic problems which were to be met.

Lord Chatfield's resignation as Minister for the Coordination of Defense in April 1940 on the ground that the tasks for which he was appointed before the war had been assumed by the Prime Minister and War Cabinet is also symptomatic. Possibly the War Office and the Air Ministry objected to the general determination of questions of priority by an Admiral of the Fleet. Perhaps, again, the Admiralty preferred after the occupation of Norway that the First Lord of the Admiralty, bearing full constitutional responsibility for naval policy, should preside over the two ministerial committees concerned with military operations and supply in order to ensure the cooperation of the three forces and their intelligence services in future; or perhaps difficulties occurred over the failure of any action to prevent the German occupation of Norway. Possibly, too, it had become clear that the task of coordination was one for a dynamic personality enjoying great political prestige. In succeeding Lord Chatfield as chairman of the Military Coordination and Ministerial Priority Committees Mr. Churchill, while remaining First Lord of the Admiralty, became in effect minister of defense in preparation for his succession to the premiership.

It is true that a small War Cabinet consisting of strong personalities could have assumed the functions performed by the Minister for the Coordination of Defense, and that this would have been a logical concentration of responsibility. The reasons given for Lord Chatfield's resignation, however, in connection with subsequent discussion in the press, indicated that although there had been a formal transition from the organization of the Committee of Imperial Defense to wartime administration, there was no clear realization of the fact that methods which had been appropriate for prewar planning and for the first stage of mobilization were no longer suitable for the actual direction of operations after war had begun. Moreover, the arrangement by which Mr. Churchill as Prime Minister became also Minister of Defense, responsible for the coordination of strategic planning and of supply in accordance with it, was suited to his dynamic temperament and to the situation immediately resulting from the defeat in France.

Mr. Churchill's intention was very likely to achieve the same highly concentrated direction of the main lines of policy, strategy, and the war economy which has been achieved, to date at least, in Germany in the present war. His position, however, created the impression that he was trying to accomplish still more than this, under constitutional traditions which permitted him to do even less. The difference between the central direction of the war in England and in Germany is that Hitler is finally responsible only for the most general coordination of strategy, foreign policy, and the pressure exercised in various directions by institutions of the Nazi Party. More than that is beyond the power of any man in a war of the magnitude of the present one.

In Germany formal responsibility for the coordination of military operations and the organization of supply rests, as has been emphasized before, with Marshal Keitel as chief of the *O.K.W.* His are functions which can be fully assumed only after the outbreak of war, but for them to be performed effectively there must be some practical experience of coordination under a single executive authority. No one without long military training in positions of definite responsibility will be able to establish an ascendancy over the three defense services. The danger of entrusting responsibility for coordination to a civilian is of course that he will be swayed by his own temperamental inclinations or by some strategic predilection or, on the other hand, act as an impartial arbiter, which means that he will form no plan except by compromise. In Germany consultation among the heads of the three forces before a final decision is reached does not end in a compromise of their separate views,[18a] a risk inseparable from the making of final decisions in committee.

The German system has been designed to avoid the difficulties which have beset the British Government, and which beset the German Gov-

---

[18a] Although the necessity of compromise with Hitler's personal views must be remembered.

ernment during the last war. Then the problem was to coordinate effectively the constitutional and traditional functions of the Emperor, largely nominal though they were, and those of the chiefs of staff of the Army and Navy, the war minister, and the Chancellor, who was responsible for everything except purely strategic decisions. At present the organization of the *Oberkommando der Wehrmacht* extends, as has been mentioned, into the regional and local administration and into individual factories. The *O.K.W.* has no real decision in foreign policy, and it can be assumed that in other connections there is friction between the organizations of the *Wehrmacht* and those of the Nazi Party. Except for broad strategic decisions dependent on foreign policy, however, Hitler's authority is nominal. That is why he has given increasing coercive powers to Himmler's organizations and has appointed a figure like Keitel to accept the military consequences of his foreign policy.

For any outsider to decide how well-founded much of the criticism of Mr. Churchill's conduct of business may be is very risky. His obvious difficulties may very well have arisen much more from the intrinsic nature of British administration and politics than from the personality of the Prime Minister. Here again the position is very different from that in the United States. The President of the United States is, under the Constitution, the Commander-in-Chief of the Army and Navy, and also, in practice, the final coordinator of the civil administration. This is the role Mr. Churchill may have tried to emulate.

In Great Britain there is *no Commander-in-Chief* of the three armed forces; the Imperial General Staff is in fact an Army staff only. Final decisions, before they are endorsed by the War Cabinet must therefore be reached by the three chiefs of staff together. The Prime Minister, and in some cases the War Cabinet, may have to decide, as Lord Hankey has pointed out, between conflicting proposals and demands by the three chiefs of staff. The Prime Minister's burden would be greatly relieved, and he would escape a very large part of the most earnest criticism directed against him, if there existed a chief of the joint staff of the three forces or a single commander-in-chief. Actual responsibility for military operations would then rest with the chief of staff, and the responsibility of the Prime Minister and the War Cabinet would be largely formal. Such a situation would, however, be contrary to all British tradition. It is also doubtful whether it would have been tenable without a particularly happy selection of the chief of staff, or, in any case, as long as Great

Britain remained on the strategic defensive without the possibility of a general strategic initiative.

The problem of selecting a suitable commander-in-chief or chief of staff for the three defense forces is especially complex in England, where the role of the Admiralty is traditionally preponderant. In peacetime the Navy provides the nerve system of the British Empire, and the Army figures only in wartime. A chief of the joint staff would have to have been, like General Wavell, in independent command of a campaign and to have made on the spot under very critical conditions decisions affecting the combined action of the three defense forces. In any government the position of political leaders refusing to support a plan of operations agreed on by the three forces and presented by a supreme chief of staff would become very precarious.[19]

There is, of course, no ideal solution of the relationship of political and military leaders. In wartime one sees a cloud of melancholy over political leaders who must accept responsibility for decisions that are not their own in purely strategic questions. The same cloud hangs over military leaders who are bound by political decisions to undertake or to abandon military operations against their professional judgment. Throughout history nations have owed the achievement of their aims more to the existence of political and military leaders who have shared the same qualities of vision, stability of purpose, and loyalty without unduly interfering in one another's spheres of action than to either military strength and skill or political genius alone.

One thing may be said with certainty about the *supreme coordination of British strategy.* Although the Prime Minister's burden is alleviated to a certain extent by the fact that the former secretary of the Committee of Imperial Defense, Major-General Ismay, serves as his personal chief of staff and attends the meetings of the Chiefs of Staff Committee, his total responsibilities are nevertheless greater than can be borne with complete success by any man. If the functions performed by General Ismay were to be assumed by a military leader with definite and open responsibility for strategic decisions, the Prime Minister would in fact be able to exercise a much more effective direction of the essential coordination of strategy and supply than at present. Such a solution the British na-

---

[19] Germany's defeat in the last war is of course an illustration of the possible consequences of such a situation. The Chancellor was constantly threatened by the resignation of the extremely popular nominal Chief-of-Staff, Hindenburg, and his First Quartermaster-General, Ludendorff. Although the Chancellor kept a liaison officer at General Headquarters, he was frequently forced to accept decisions effectively taken without his knowledge.

tion has not yet been prepared to accept. The decision of military questions by military experts to the extent that it was possible until 1942 in Germany would indeed affect the relation of the British Government to Parliament, and would be incompatible with the direct responsibility to Parliament of the three defense ministers and the Prime Minister.

There are two other aspects of the problem of supreme coordination which require some comment. First, the tasks of an officer serving as *permanent military secretary to the Cabinet,* or in some other capacity preparing the ground for intimate understanding between the statesmen who are finally responsible for policy and the chiefs of staff of the defense forces, are very delicate and trying. Whether he makes any contribution to victory or not will depend on his military vision and judgment, his tact, self-effacement, and loyalty. He holds no formal responsibility or executive authority, but his actual influence may be enormous. To bring about agreement between soldiers and politicians in military questions may not always be his most difficult problem. It may be harder for him to reconcile temperamental differences, between sanguineness on the one side and on the other inflexible detachment from emotional considerations such as results only from a lifelong discipline in rejecting comforting illusions as well as depressing doubt. In extreme emergencies everything depends on constant self-control and the ability to overcome misgivings, which paralyze initiative.

Such an intermediary between the defense forces and the Government must also expect military experts to dismiss the strategic conceptions of other people as dilettantism. On the other hand, an amateur of genius and decision may have great military vision without having a grasp, which is indispensable, of what General Wavell has called the " logistics " of warfare. The results of action decided on by a man of this type in opposition to the professional advice of military leaders may of course be disastrous. Briand's determination in confronting Marshal Joffre with a choice between holding Verdun to the last man and resigning his command and Clemenceau's action in 1917 in restoring the morale of the French Army are rare exceptions to the many cases of failure due to the intervention of civilians in strategy. President Lincoln's attitude of unwavering support for the commanding general is usually the safer course.

These considerations are more relevant to the eventual outcome of a war than almost any others. Yet texts of constitutional theory and administrative practice seldom mention them. Neither do they express any realization of the increasing isolation of statesmen who in critical periods must make vital decisions every hour, perhaps for years, in the face of conflicting advice. This psychological factor makes the delegation of definite responsibility for the general coordination of each group of closely related aspects of administration to a few individuals all the more desirable.

The Prime Minister should ideally have the assistance of a chief of the joint staff of the defense forces, of a super-minister for the complex organization of industrial production, labor supply, supplies of raw materials, and price control, and of another super-minister for agricultural production and food supplies. They should be able to issue directions which would be put into effect by existing departmental machinery down to the regional and local levels of administration, but they should themselves have no administrative responsibilities. Only so can they enjoy the necessary serenity and freedom to formulate the general principles of policy and to supervise their application. They are the people who, with the Chancellor of the Exchequer, if he is not unimaginative, the Foreign Secretary, and another minister responsible for home affairs, should constitute the War Cabinet. The Prime Minister could then, except in sudden emergencies, reasonably hope for success in his double task of acting as final arbiter in case of conflict and at the same time directing the enormous war machine.

Until the present, however, there has been no one in England to perform the functions of Marshal Keitel, nor is there any single directive power comparable to the influence of the *Oberkommando der Wehrmacht,* which pervades every level of the German administration. The executive authority of the present British *Minister of Production* is limited, and he can at best anticipate such differences among the production departments as the Production Executive had formerly to mediate after they arose. The *Joint Production Staff* under the chairmanship of the Minister of Production is composed of representatives of the armed forces and executive officers of the supply departments. The Minister of Production has no more executive authority over its members than his regional officers have over the officers of the supply departments in the consultative area supply boards over which they preside. The *Minister of Production* is a member of the War Cabinet, but if he is invited to attend the meetings of the Defense Committee of the Cabinet only from time to time, as was the Minister of Supply during 1940, his chances of success will be limited, and he may end only as the chairman of another of the succession of coordinating committees. The minister must have vision enough to foresee future bottlenecks in production and energy enough to prevent their occurrence, and he must also be fully initiated into the strategic situation and plans of future operations. Only so will he be able to instill into the supply departments an appreciation of future requirements and their implications for present production. He must, further, have the means of ascertaining how far his intentions are given effect by the different departments. Certainly the personal achievements of the present minister since taking office have been great.[19a]

The position of the *Treasury,* since it has been divorced from questions of supply, leaves little to be desired, and is certainly very different from what it was at the beginning of the war, when Sir John Simon presided over the Economic Policy Committee of the Cabinet. The presence of the Chancellor of the Exchequer in the War Cabinet and of Treasury officials in every interdepartmental coordinating committee ensures the observance of the financial policy to which the Chancellor of the Exchequer is committed. This policy is also decided in close consultation with a small permanent advisory committee of the leading financial experts of the country.

In general, however, *interdepartmental liaison* and the substitution of consultation for clear direction is still a predominant characteristic of the wartime administration. A major cause for this is the average quality of the ministers appointed in accordance with the demands of the coalition form of government and the members of Parliament selected by the party machines. The story of the transformations of the British Government in the past two years is largely the history of men appointed in order to preserve a balance of power in the Cabinet to positions for which they were not suited, instead of to positions in which their political prestige and experience might perhaps have served them well. " The War Cabinet was called or forced into existence," as has been written in a leading article in the London *Times,* " by the very need which is negatively expressed and exemplified in the multitude of committees." [20]

Certain *standing committees,* like the interdepartmental priority committee for the allocation of raw materials, have to all appearances arrived at perfectly satisfactory solutions, or at least at the definition of an intelligible policy. Coordination in execution in this respect is assured

---

[19a] Some changes in the organization of the Ministry of Production at the end of 1942 closely approximate the organization of the German Ministry of Armament and Munitions. But here again the tendency in Great Britain, as English critics have pointed out, has been rather to a better coordination among departments than to a clarification of executive responsibility.

[20] July 22, 1942.

by the issue of all specific allocations through the Ministry of Supply, where a record can be kept of the total consumption of materials for the purposes of different government departments. In the control of raw materials the British system is as efficient as the German system and in many ways simpler, a fact which is of course partly explained by the comparative ease with which imported commodities can be controlled as they enter the country and the absence in Britain of many of the complications of *ersatz* production.

There is no doubt that a number of *standing committees* could be dispensed with if the War Cabinet itself consisted of ministers with authority over groups of related executive departments, able to plan ahead and to issue definite instructions so that the heads of particular departments, and more especially the civil service, could see their own places in the general plan and could be held to account for the performance of specific functions. In an editorial entitled, " The Inner Cabinet," the *Times* [20a] has described this aspect of the problem as follows:

". . . The Ministries of Defense, Production, Food, Fuel, and War Transport all broadly exemplify a right functional principle of arrangement. . . . The advantages of a basic regrouping of the functions of central government are many and impressive. There would be an immediate gain in efficiency by making clearer the lines of authority, and by concentrating responsibility. It is a common complaint that on many matters requiring administrative decision the variety of departments to be consulted and the numbers of ministers whose responsibility is affected combine to make delay and timidity characteristic qualities of official action. . . . The present division of work between departments is not based on a conscious specialization of function but is mainly the product of historical development and political manoeuvre. . . . It cannot be too firmly emphasized that all the major administrative experiments of the war in this field have been applications of the method first suggested by the Haldane committee (in 1918), and that these experiments have been most successful when a genuine reallocation has taken place and reform has not stopped short at a token combination of offices."

There is interdepartmental consultation among the responsible heads of departments and civil servants about particular problems in the administration of every country. That is not the same thing as the institution of standing committees to which questions too various for *ad hoc* bodies are regularly referred. Such a system is fatal to individual responsibility and to constructive policy, since the chair-

[20a] January 4, 1943.

man of a committee is only too readily inclined to decide in favor of the majority opinion or to take a mean of the opinions expressed. Committees are too often the graves of enterprise and of good will. In any administration general direction must come first, and the detailed application of clearly enunciated principles and the coordination of closely related aspects of administration in committees must be only supplementary. It is not to be expected of human nature that effective direction will ever result from the dilution of individual responsibility and its transference to a collective body. In wartime the use of consultative committees should be limited to the arrangement of such details as are left in any case to high-ranking civil servants. To quote the *Times* again, " The fault lies not so much with the natural propensities of the civil service as with defects in its political leaders." [21]

Immediately below, or parallel to, the War Cabinet there are two supreme coordinating committees, the *Defense Committee* under the chairmanship of the Prime Minister and the *Coordinating Committee for Home Affairs* under the chairmanship of the Lord President of the Council.[21a] The present efficient coordination of every aspect of the national effort not directly concerned with military operations or supply in the latter committee could hardly have been achieved if it had not been for the presence in Parliament and the Government of this very able and experienced former civil servant. The Defense Committee is concerned both with military operations and supply; it receives reports from the Chiefs of Staff Committee in the former connection and the Joint Production Staff in the latter. Despite the efforts that have been made during 1942 to bring the technical design of weapons and the organization of production into closer relation with the particular requirements of the fighting forces, no fully satisfactory solution of the problem of the coordination of strategy and supply has been achieved.

The number of standing ministerial committees that have been formed and dissolved in England in the past three years contrasted with the continuity of certain interdepartmental committees of civil servants, shows where the difficulty has lain. It is, of course, not healthy for people to owe positions of great responsibility in such a grave emergency to political influence, and to rely in actual decisions on their experienced permanent staffs, while permanent officials have no opportunity to

---

[21] July 22, 1942.

[21a] This does not prevent the members of the Defense Committee from meeting, sometimes with other ministers, for special purposes in groups like the U-Boat Committee, of which the Prime Minister is chairman.

make suggestions or offer warnings directly to the War Cabinet without being expressly invited to do so. It may be taken for granted, therefore, that it is because of a high team spirit among the top officials of different departments that the system works. In certain branches of the war administration there is no doubt that a stabilization admitting of only minor improvements has been achieved.

As every belligerent country approaches capacity production, changes of policy and the adaptation of production to suddenly changed circumstances, especially under conditions of mass production, become more and more difficult. The organization of production may become very effective after maximum productivity is reached, but with every vital tactical change there will be an interval while production is shifted during which no strategic action can be undertaken. In this respect, especially, the present war has given rise to problems which are entirely new. The complexity of mass production is such that flexibility in changing over to new types of weapons may become more decisive than total output, or than strategic genius. It is here that the best routine elaborated in any department may fail. For this reason some form of regional organization to free local initiative from the restrictions of centralized bureaucratic control and to increase flexibility in the performance of any program is more urgent now than ever before.

There are two facts to be stressed in any final judgment of different systems of war administration. For many of the technical problems resulting from the peculiar character of modern warfare there is no perfect solution. This point the critics of any government frequently overlook. The recent administrative reorganization in Germany shows that no system, however well conceived in advance, will survive throughout a war of the technical character of the present one without undergoing radical and sudden alterations.

Critics of the statesmen who must bear the full responsibility for the conduct of the war also overlook the fact that a parliament by granting emergency powers to the Government and supporting, sometimes grudgingly, the policy of the head of the Government does not by this assure the success of his policy. Particularly if the prime minister is supported by a coalition of political parties because of his personal prestige, he will face something of the eternal Cromwellian problem of the absence of any strong opposition.[22] A man with a clear appreciation of present and fu-

---

[22] *The Economist,* July 11, 1942, p. 33. Cf. Lord Beaverbrook's speech in the House of Lords, February 9, 1943.

ture needs, who understands the organizational problems of administration in wartime and knows how to delegate definite responsibility in such a way as to ensure conformity with the main lines of his policy and flexibility in detail, and is not deflected from his purpose by the influence of his own emotions, can get whatever he wants from a parliament. Popular feeling and constructive criticism may no longer have their normal influence on the prime minister's policy if there is not the force of a strong opposition behind the criticism and advice offered. If the prime minister is a dominant figure he can secure himself against opposition by including the leading members of all parties in his cabinet. Nevertheless, he will bear the same responsibility as a dictator in a totalitarian government, without being able to override traditional constitutional obstacles to the fulfillment of his aims. Thus the British Prime Minister is not free either to appoint ministers or to define their functions without regard to political considerations. Although the responsibility of every minister to Parliament for the policy of his department relieves the Prime Minister of legal responsibility for the supervision of the entire administration, the extent of his actual responsibility increases correspondingly with the relaxation of Parliamentary control over the Government's policy. Criticism which fails to take into account this concentration of actual power and responsibility for which there is no suitable provision in the traditional constitutional system is often misdirected against individuals.

There is another thing which any critic of the British administration should in fairness recognize. There are two main types of administration. In many countries, in Germany especially, the Government and the civil service are expected to lead the nation in exercising foresight and constructive initiative. Up to a certain point it is very advantageous for members of the Government to have considered every possible emergency in advance and to have prepared practical measures to meet them. This may easily result, however, in rigidity and over-organization. The individual citizen becomes inclined to look for miracles from the government, and he loses self-confidence, resourcefulness, and the faculty of positive criticism. He fails to realize that his reliance on the wisdom of the Government implies increasing interference by the state in his personal affairs and daily life, and this he resents when it occurs. This is especially so, of course, when he is deprived of every opportunity of criticism, as under a totalitarian government.

The British Government, on the contrary, ordinarily waits upon public opinion, considering only the most urgent necessities of the hour. To this tempo the civil service has been forced to adapt itself. The haphazard trend of British politics has largely preserved the traditional constitutional balance among different institutions, but it has often brought the country to the brink of catastrophe in great emergencies. Even in normal times it has resulted in a refusal to tackle crucial economic and social problems. The leisurely atmosphere established throughout the country under the British political system is so highly valued that its consequences for national and, often, international security are overlooked. This system does, on the other hand, preserve a spirit of moderation and compromise in politics, and it protects the freshness of men's nerves. Citizens are more capable of improvisation in extreme emergencies, and can bring better support to the policy of the Government where the grinding of the administrative machinery is not always heard. In such an atmosphere the effects of a series of unexpected defeats are more easily overcome. The final test of any political and administrative system is whether it encourages and provides ample scope for individual initiative in a national effort firmly directed from above under well defined executive responsibility, and this final test can be made only after unforeseen reversals of the military position. In war it is the immediate positive reaction to the unexpected that is decisive.

PART TWO

THE ORGANIZATION OF SUPPLY IN GREAT BRITAIN

by Claire Nix

1. Preparation and Precedent

Several main considerations underlay the defense policy of the British Empire after the First World War. The disarmament of Germany, the consequences of the revolution in Russia, and the building up of a Continental military system including France, the nations of the Little Entente, and, more loosely, Poland resulted in French hegemony in Europe. For the British Government it was undesirable that this hegemony should result in such a consolidation of power that England's position would become insecure in the event of a threat to her Empire in another part of the world. Thus the complete elimination of Germany as a military factor by France and her allies, and likewise the disturbance of any economic and political stability in Germany by demands for reparations on the one hand and the agitation of the Third International on the other, had to be prevented.

The fact that Japan, by her alliance with England and her participation in the war against the Central Powers, had enormously improved her strategic position in the Pacific, and had emerged from the war with large reserves of capital and industrial capacity became a leading consideration of British naval policy. The cancellation of the Japanese alliance was an expression of the uncertainty of the Admiralty and the Foreign Office about the future in the Pacific, in China, and in India. Whether the dominions would again support England to the same extent as in the First World War was also long in doubt. The industrial capacity of the United States could be taken into account, but it was again doubtful whether the United States would be prepared to join in a struggle in which the safety of the British Empire might be involved. People in England who saw clearly ahead were undoubtedly alarmed for the future in case of a major conflict and undoubtedly watched Japanese policy with increasing suspicion after the occupation of Manchukuo.

Throughout these years desire to reduce the burden of public expenditure had dictated a policy of disarmament. The total defense expenditures of Great Britain were reduced by almost four-fifths between 1919–20 and 1922–23, and remained at approximately the same level from 1923 to 1936. The fixing of an international ratio for naval rearmament was designed both to prevent a naval race like that which preceded the First World War, and in which it would have been difficult for Great Britain to maintain supremacy over the United States and Japan, and also to prevent the formation of French and Italian fleets which might together become a threat to Great Britain. England had to prevent the preponderance of any group of countries with which she might possibly find herself in opposition. Until 1931 her policy consisted in cautiously balancing potential blocks of power, without any distinct tendency and without positive support of general disarmament.

The idea that England must by any means avoid the employment of such large forces as in the last war in any future Continental struggle prevailed over a long period; the Army was considered chiefly in relation to the defense of the dominions and colonies. From 1927 a very enlightened belief in the future of mechanized warfare, which the British Army inaugurated in 1917, was common, and the importance of air warfare was also appreciated. The proportion of total defense expenditure devoted to the Air Force was doubled between 1923 and 1930. In the design of tanks and airplanes Great Britain led every other country. No definite conception of their combined use developed, although the possibility was clearly envisaged while Field Marshal Lord Milne was Chief of Staff.

The Manchukuo crisis found Great Britain totally unprepared. Nor did it result in any close coordination between the policies of Great Britain and the United States. It was more than doubtful then whether a strong line would be followed by strong action on the part of the United States. At the same time that the economic crisis necessitated the reduction of Army expenditure, in 1932 and '33, the Committee of Imperial Defense began to study the questions of production and organization in case of war with Japan, which might produce a regrouping of powers. There was no idea at that time, or even during 1933 and the greater part of 1934, of the possibility of a rapid German rearmament.

The lack of many essential industrial materials within the German frontiers of 1919 made any threat from that quarter unlikely. Not even the military occupation of the demilitarized zone of the Rhineland by the Nazis in 1936 was seen to alter the situation essentially, since an agreement on naval rearmament had just been reached between Great Britain and the Nazis. Action then by Great Britain, had it been contemplated, would have been hampered by the position in the Mediterranean created by the Italian campaign in Ethiopia. A consciousness of growing danger existed, but it was hoped that the League of Nations could be mobilized, and that the threat of sanctions would be enough to prevent the expansion of any European power. Within the British Cabinet there was no accepted policy towards Italy, nor any willingness to come to a definite understanding with France about a policy to be pursued in the Mediterranean. This would in any case have been difficult with continual changes of government in France. Until 1937 the pace of German rearmament was not considered alarming. The certainty that Germany was far behind in beginning her rearmament and that she could be deprived of essential materials by a naval blockade supported the conviction that immediate action was unnecessary. Neither was there much desire for action in other governments in countries which were either still suffering from the effects of the financial and economic crisis or just beginning to recover.[23]

These facts help to explain Great Britain's difficulties in the organization of production and supply after the beginning of British rearmament in 1936. The problem of preparation for a total war was not considered in its entirety. Certain plans made in the Committee of Imperial Defense for the Empire, in the first place, could be put into effect only when events ensured the participation of the different dominions, and remained in large part on paper. In Great Britain defense expenditures in 1936, '37, and '38 amounted altogether to £1,250,000,000. The manufacture of ammunition was begun early, even railway repair shops being used for the purpose. Careful consideration was given to the immunization of new plants against bombing attacks; they were constructed partly underground and located chiefly in Lancashire, South Wales, and in the region of the Bristol Channel. By the fall of 1939 there were thirteen government ordnance factories in operation and three under construction. In the summer of 1942 there were forty-two.

Until the winter of 1938–39, however, government expenditure for new plant was devoted almost exclusively to the creation of capacity for aircraft manufacture. Great progress was made in the development of airplane types, but the actual increase of production corresponded only to the rate of training of pilots permitted by different supplementary budgets. Much of the capacity planned in the three years before the war came into production only at the end of 1939. In addition to the financing of new plant by the Air Ministry, most conspicuously in the construction of " shadow " factories for airplane manufacture in conjunction with automobile plants, manufacturers were offered special

---

[23] These statements concerning British foreign policy are made for their relevance to the organization of supply, and are necessarily much simplified from the political point of view. As the policy of the editors has been to allow perfect freedom of expression of opinion to each contributor, they are to be taken only as personal judgments. Attention should certainly be invited, however, to the attitude of the British Government of this period toward the Spanish War. Note should also be taken of the now pretty well documented Tory error of unwillingness to understand the inevitable association between Fascism and military expansion. It was a widely shared delusion that peace could be kept in such a world. — W. Y. E.

depreciation allowances in taxation and in government contracts for new additions to plant and were guaranteed the capital cost of expanded capacity for airplane production still unused after a given period of time. The storage of reserves of a limited number of commodities such as wheat, fats, whale oil, petroleum, and fertilizers was undertaken in the year before the war [24] on a modest scale and consequently with little disturbance of the markets. At the outbreak of war in 1939 ordinary reserves of rubber and tin had been depleted by the exchange of these two materials for United States cotton. The very large stocks of cotton goods held in England in consequence were for the most part destroyed in the bombing of 1940. The dispersal of large firms engaged in aircraft and tank manufacture into a number of small, in some cases duplicate, plants, which was undertaken in 1940, was designed not only to ensure continuous production in spite of enemy bombing but also to protect supplies of materials by scattering them.

The prewar phase of rearmament was in general characterized by hesitation to undertake full production and to organize the whole economy for the manufacture of armament in peacetime. Certainly fear of the dislocation of production and the consequences for the recovery of English trade which might result from a full dress rearmament, if war were after all avoided predominated. There was government planning of potential capacity, not of actual production.

This was in part a natural consequence of the purely consultative character of the *Committee of Imperial Defense*. Although 95 percent of the recommendations of the specialized interdepartmental subcommittees of the Committee of Imperial Defense may be of a detailed or technical nature requiring only the executive sanction of the particular departments concerned, the guiding principle of the committee's composition has been the reservation of all decisions of " policy " to the Cabinet as a whole. The principle of Cabinet responsibility is of course the explanation of the customary establishment of more or less informal standing or temporary committees of ministers and civil servants to consider problems affecting several departments or on special issues. It is also the objection offered to every proposal to concentrate authority over strategic planning, for example, or the organization of production, in any one minister whose decisions would to some extent determine the functioning of other departments. When executive action on a very large scale is required, joint Cabinet responsibility, while greatly increasing

---

[24] By the Board of Trade under the Essential Commodities Reserves Act, 1938.

the importance of the Prime Minister's position, also necessitates an elaborate organization of consultation between departments.

When the Committee of Imperial Defense was established in 1904 the Prime Minister was made its chairman so that its relation to the Cabinet should be as close as possible. Such an advisory committee has the advantage of flexibility of membership, ministers, civil servants, and private persons being equally eligible to participate in its meetings.[25] Before the last war its procedure was in one respect more formal than that of the Cabinet, as a small staff of Army and Navy officers kept a permanent record of the discussions of the committee and its subcommittees and regularly informed the departments concerned of conclusions reached. The committee was absorbed by the Cabinet, meeting as a War Committee or War Council of ministers, at the beginning of the last war, and the small staff of the committee became the Cabinet Secretariat.

Mr. Lloyd George broke the Asquith coalition Government in 1916 with the demand that a committee of three ministers be made responsible for the military conduct of the war, Mr. Asquith proposing in reply a second, corresponding, ministerial committee for "national organization." The *War Cabinet* as organized at the beginning of 1917 consisted only of Mr. Lloyd George as Prime Minister, three ministers without portfolio, and the Chancellor of the Exchequer, who was also leader of the House of Commons. Two more ministers without portfolio were added in the course of the war. War Cabinet committees including ministers who were not War Cabinet members, civil servants, and others were appointed for special questions and also for such general problems as "man power policy" and "demobilization," and were frequently superseded by other committees of slightly different personnel. People of all sorts appeared before the War Cabinet itself, which disposed of conflicting claims very much like a bench of judges.

The Cabinet resumed its normal form at the end of 1919, retaining from the period of the war only its permanent secretariat, which remained more or less identical with the secretariat of the Committee of

[25] In 1939 meetings of the main Committee of Imperial Defense were attended by any of the following: the Prime Minister, the Minister for the Coordination of Defense, the Chancellor of the Exchequer, the Home Secretary, the Lord Privy Seal, the Secretaries of State for Foreign Affairs, Dominion Affairs, Colonies, and India and Burma, the First Lord of the Admiralty, the Secretaries of State for War and Air, the Chiefs of Naval Staff, of the Imperial General Staff, and of Air Staff, the Permanent Secretary to the Treasury, and the Secretary to the Cabinet. Major-General H. L. Ismay, *The Machinery of the Committee of Imperial Defense,* in The Journal of the Royal United Service Institution, Vol. LXXXIV, No. 534, May 1939.

Imperial Defense. The reporting of Cabinet committee and subcommittee meetings by this secretariat, combined with the fact that Treasury officials attend all committee and subcommittee meetings, and that all proposals for legislation are examined before being submitted to the Cabinet in the Home Affairs Committee, which includes the law officers, provides some coordination of the extensive committee organization.

The subcommittees of the Committee of Imperial Defense itself before the present war fell into five main groups for strategy and planning, organization for war (including civil defense), man power, supply, and technical experiment and research.[26] The most important of the first group was of course the committee of the three chiefs of staff for the Navy, the Army, and the Air Force, with subordinate joint staff committees, which very largely retain their prewar organization. In the second group the Principal Supply Officers Committee dealt with industrial capacity and raw materials in time of war. Actual contracts were and are, however, placed separately by the contracts divisions of the supply ministries. The heads of these divisions meet under the chairmanship, since 1940, of a Treasury official in the *Contracts Coordination Committee,* where forms of contracts are standardized.[26a]

The duty of presiding over the Committee of Imperial Defense in the Prime Minister's absence was allotted in March 1936 to a newly created *Minister for the Coordination of Defense,* who also met with the chiefs of staff and presided over the Principal Supply Officers Committee. The minister's department consisted of two secretaries and

---

[26] Ismay, *op. cit.*

[26a] The Treasury has no responsibility for rates of profit allowed in contracts placed by the different ministries. Two separate branches of the Contracts Coordinating Committee are concerned with works contracts and with other contracts for more general purposes. To avoid delay in Treasury approval of particular contracts after the introduction of a program of rearmament in 1936, a Treasury Inter-Service Committee including officers of the three services was empowered to approve expenditure in advance of formal Treasury approval and to report total defense expenditure.

The commonest form of government contract has become the "fixed price" contract, with a specific price agreed to in advance, usually on the basis of investigation by accountants belonging to the government department concerned, of the cost of production of the same article under similar circumstances. For urgent work of which there is little previous experience the "cost plus" contract, under which the manufacturer receives the actual cost of production, whatever it may be, plus an agreed percentage as profit, is still employed. "Maximum price" and "target price" contracts have been devised to supply the incentive to reduction of cost of production which is lacking in the "cost plus" contract. Under the "target price" contract the manufacturer is penalized for exceeding the estimated cost of production and receives a premium when actual cost is less than the estimate.

clerical assistance.[27] Sir Thomas Inskip (Lord Caldecote), the first Minister for the Coordination of Defense, described his office as that of liaison between the chiefs of staff and the Cabinet and Parliament. His coordinating functions were extended to include civil defense after the appointment of Sir John Anderson as Lord Privy Seal with special responsibility for civil defense in November 1938. In February 1939 the former First Sea Lord, Admiral of the Fleet Lord Chatfield, himself became Minister for the Coordination of Defense. That he was primarily concerned with strategic coordination is evidenced by the fact that Mr. W. S. Morrison, then Chancellor of the Duchy of Lancaster, became his associate, acting as chairman of the Supply Officers Committee, as well as answering for the coordination of defense in the House of Commons.

At the outbreak of war Mr. Chamberlain's Cabinet was reduced, as a *War Cabinet,* to nine members, four of whom had no particular departmental responsibilities. The Minister for the Coordination of Defense became chairman of a *Committee on Military Coordination,* to which the defense ministers and the chiefs of staff belonged, and to which the organization of the Chiefs of Staff Committee was subordinate, and also of a *Ministerial Priority Committee,* to which the interdepartmental supply organization was subordinated. The other major committees of the Cabinet for war purposes were the *Civil Defense Committee,* the *Food Policy Committee,* and the *Economic Policy Committee,* under the chairmanship of the Chancellor of the Exchequer. In subsequent reorganizations of the Cabinet in April and May 1940, October 1940, January 1941, May 1941, and January and February 1942 the Chancellor of the Exchequer has lost his dominating position, and the dual responsibility for the coordination of strategy and of supply which was initially united in Lord Chatfield has been divided and redistributed.

The overall organization of supply naturally followed the lines that had developed at the end of the last war. In all the planning of the Committee of Imperial Defense, however, the United States with its productive capacity remained an uncertain factor. The United States attitude of neutrality made it doubtful that American resources, without which those who were responsible for England's preparation realized that the defeat of the Central Powers in 1918 would have been impossible, would be available again. Great Britain had to rely on her own

[27] His budget was £7,789.

capacity and that of the dominions and colonies. This fact must affect any judgment of the British organization of production. If it had been sure that airplanes and tanks, for example, could have been provided immediately from the United States, much capacity in England could have been made available for other purposes, and the direction of English industry would have been somewhat different.

A second difference in the position in this war from that at the end of the last arises of course from the unexpected German victory over France, after which Great Britain remained more or less on the defense strategically, unable even to occupy the very large part of the German Army available for action in other theatres. Thus even with the best plans and most detailed organization of production the actual result would always have been inadequate to the needs of the moment until the United States, having entered the war, should reach optimum production.

At the beginning of the last war there was no idea in England, or any other of the belligerent countries, of the eventual consumption of munitions and equipment. It was only gradually, and especially so in England, that the necessity of organizing production on the basis of strategic plans prepared at least a year in advance was recognized. In the recruitment of man power for military purposes and for industry, in the distribution of raw materials, and in the conversion of industrial capacity to war production a wholly empirical extension of public control was accomplished by a constant increase of the executive powers of the central government.[28]

The transfer of labor to war industries and recruiting for the armed forces were divided between employment exchanges, which were incorporated in the *Ministry of Labor* in 1917, and successive directors of recruiting or national service. A Ministry of National Service, later combined with the Ministry of Labor, was established for military recruiting in 1917, when the question of man power, following the introduction of conscription in 1916, had become acute. The chief executive officer of the exchanges in the Ministry of Labor provided liaison by serving also as director of labor supply in the Ministry of National Service.

The reservation of individual workmen in essential occupations was originally put at the discretion of prime contractors for the Admiralty,

---

[28] Most measures of government control of the economy between 1914 and 1918 were effected by order-in-council under the Defense of the Realm Act of 1914, the Munitions of War Act of 1915, and on the basis of a theory of the royal prerogative which was invalidated by the House of Lords in 1920, when actions taken on this basis were indemnified by act of Parliament.

War Office, or Ministry of Munitions. It was later transferred to the labor department of the Ministry of Munitions and then to the skilled trade unions, being fixed early in 1917 with recruiting officers in the twelve areas into which the country was divided for the manufacture of munitions. Central and local committees on reservation, containing trade union representatives and officials of the government departments concerned with supply, were set up to advise these recruiting officers. Under the Munitions of War Act prohibiting strikes and lockouts in war production, an interdepartmental Committee on Production including officials of the supply departments and the Home Office [29] became the tribunal for the arbitration of wage disputes. Its awards were consistently made on the basis of the cost of living. For the practical application of its decisions the Committee was dependent on negotiations between employers and employees.

Great Britain's dependence on imports of all basic food stuffs and most industrial materials, while it necessitates the central control of supplies in a war emergency, also makes control comparatively easy to impose. In the last war prices of jute, hemp, leather, hides, shoes, wool, flax, woolen and linen textiles were fixed by the War Office as the largest or the exclusive buyer, and distribution was determined by the licensing of dealers. Sugar, cereals, meat, oils and fats, and dairy produce were brought gradually under the control first of the Board of Trade and then of the *Ministry of Food,* which came into existence in the summer of 1917 when imports had been drastically reduced by the submarine campaign. Iron and steel, other industrial metals, explosives, and, for a time, coal supplies were similarly controlled by the Ministry of Munitions. As the import of various other commodities was licensed by the Board of Trade, more than 90 percent of imports into Great Britain at the end of 1917 were controlled by five government departments.

The *Ministry of Munitions* was established in May 1915 to provide for the armaments requirements of the War Office or the Admiralty, but in fact assumed responsibility only for War Office contracts, the Admiralty retaining its separate procurement organization. In its final form the Ministry was organized in more than fifty departments for different types of armament, grouped in ten general directorates. For the supervision of munitions contracts, the country was divided into twelve Munitions Areas. Within these areas the Ministry relied primarily on the initiative of fifty district Boards of Management com-

---

[29] Which was responsible for the regulation of conditions of work.

posed of manufacturers, principally in the engineering industry. These boards not only distributed contracts among the engineering firms in their districts but also operated, on behalf of the Ministry, " national factories " in which local engineering capacity could be pooled. In the industries under War Office control, too, regional boards within the industries, including in some cases representatives of labor, decided the proportion of work on government orders, for export, and for civilian requirements in different firms and the amount of reserve stocks to be held.

The issue of priority certificates for government orders was centralized in the priority department of the Ministry of Munitions. It was supplemented by the, sometimes fully independent, allocation of materials by the agencies controlling particular commodities and by licensing. It was only with the shipping crisis of 1917 that any determination in advance of the total requirements of production became necessary and that the definition of different classes of contracts in order of urgency was attempted. Until the end of the war all production plans remained subject to overriding considerations of the amount of shipping tonnage available. General priority orders early in 1917 established three categories of work: the first including the manufacture of armaments on government contract, merchant shipbuilding, and work especially certified by the Ministry of Munitions or the Board of Trade; the second including necessary repairs and replacements, certified exports, and other work certified by government departments as " necessary to the efficient conduct of the war," or to the effect that the requisite materials were available; all remaining civilian work falling into the third. A further refinement of three degrees of urgency for prime government contracts was introduced a year later.

All the government departments concerned with production were represented from an early period of the war on an informal " priority committee " in the Ministry of Munitions. This committee's authority varied in different departments and was lowest in the Admiralty, where conflicting priority certificates were sometimes issued independently. A *War Priorities Committee of the Cabinet* was formed only at the end of 1917, and then in a manner characteristic of the War Cabinet's methods of improvisation. The organization of airplane manufacture, the allocation of available resources between the Royal Flying Corps and the Royal Naval Air Service, and the question of combined operations had been referred successively to two independent boards without executive functions. A committee of ministers appointed in the autumn of 1917 to consider the priority that should be allowed to airplane production reported after one meeting that the duty assigned to it could be performed only by a standing committee on priorities for all war production. Thus, with the approval of the War Cabinet, the War Priorities Committee came into being under the chairmanship of General Smuts. It comprised the First Lord of the Admiralty, the Secretary of State for War, the Minister of Munitions, the recently created Secretary of State, Royal Air Force, and the Minister of National Service. Since the committee's purpose was to mediate conflicting demands it worked through interdepartmental boards for every major commodity in short supply. These boards and, in addition, a business men's committee on priorities in civilian industry and a committee on general services, or utilities, were subordinate to an interdepartmental Joint Priority Board, which relieved the main committee of ministers and the duplicate committee of civil servants of all but final decisions of particular importance. Special sub-committees considered priorities for shipping tonnage, labor supply, and building construction.

This more comprehensive organization was imposed so late on an economy already over-taxed that its working until the unforeseen cessation of hostilities in 1918 hardly affords a basis for critical judgment. In his excellent survey of commodity controls in the last war E. M. H. Lloyd writes that the absence of "an Economic General Staff" continued to be felt until the end of the war.[30] The futility of establishing the relative importance of particular products without uniform control of the materials of production had at least been demonstrated, and at the beginning of the present war emphasis was consequently placed on the "allocation" of raw materials to the requirements of the different armed services.

2. Evolution Since 1939

Supplies of *essential materials* are monopolized under the Ministry of Supply,[31] the Ministry of Food,[32] the Ministry of Aircraft Produc-

---

[30] E. M. H. Lloyd, *Experiments in State Control at the War Office and the Ministry of Food,* Oxford, 1924.

[31] The Ministry of Supply controls: chrome ore, magnesite, wolfram; cotton; fertilizer; flax; iron and steel; iron and manganese ores; leather and tanning materials; molasses and industrial alcohol; non-ferrous metals; paper; silk and rayon; sulphur and pyrites; timber; wool; dyestuffs.

[32] The Ministry of Food controls: animal feeding stuffs; bacon and hams; butter and cheese;

tion,[33] and, since November 1940, the Ministry of Works and Buildings. The Admiralty (for merchant and naval shipbuilding and naval ordnance), the production departments of the Ministry of Supply (for the equipment and munitions of the Army), since May 1940 the Ministry of Aircraft Production, the War Office (for Army construction and provisions), the construction departments of the Ministry of Works and Buildings (for most other government construction), the Ministry of Home Security (for the civil defense requirements of local authorities), and the Board of Trade (for civilian industry) are the principal competitors for their use. The act which established the Ministry of Supply in July 1939 also conferred on the government full legal powers to demand priority for the completion of government contracts before others and when necessary to take temporary possession of firms. Power to require firms to accept government contracts was conferred at the end of May 1940.

Why a *Ministry of Supply* should not have been created earlier in the defense program is hard to say. The Government had not decided to prepare as if for war, and the production of much greater stores of armament seemed idle while there was a shortage of trained officers and men in the Army, especially in the mechanized forces. Without compulsory service the organization of production for armament in time of peace will always be considered doubtfully. The results of the recruitment of volunteers for the Army begun in 1936 were negligible. Under these conditions provisions for an eventual increase of production if war occurred were considered sufficient. Conscription was introduced only after the occupation of Prague, and the formation of the Ministry of Supply to meet the increased requirements of the Army immediately followed it.

The definition of the new ministry's functions as those previously discharged by the procurement branches of the War Office, and by the Board of Trade in acquiring stocks of commodities, disappointed those advocates of the appointment of a minister to direct the adjustment of all industry to the requirements of defense who had hoped to find in the Ministry of Supply a ministry of economic planning. To most of the Government a ministry of the latter sort must have seemed ultimately undesirable in its economic implications, immediately dan-

---

canned fish; canned fruit and vegetables; cereals; cocoa; condensed milk; dried fruits; imported eggs; meat and livestock; oils and fats; potatoes; sugar; tea; imported fresh fruit and vegetables.

[33] The Ministry of Aircraft Production controls: aluminum; bauxite; fabrication of aircraft materials.

gerous in the possible range of its errors, and certainly contrary to the prevailing "judicial" conception of administration. The Minister for the Coordination of Defense held that the relations with industry already established separately by the Admiralty and the Air Ministry could not be improved by establishing such a planning ministry, and when the issue arose again in 1940, as it continued to do until after Captain Lyttelton was made Minister of Production in the spring of 1942, the Prime Minister argued that the responsibility of the Chancellor of the Exchequer for the stability of the currency in fact extended over the entire economy, and that a minister charged with the direct supervision of production would inevitably infringe upon the authority of the Treasury.

Consequently in the Admiralty, where alone contracting firms were systematically supervised by regional and local officers in peacetime, a closed organization of production for naval requirements extending into individual plants, and including the control of shipbuilding labor, has been maintained. Had the course of the war been what was expected in 1939, with prolonged fighting in northern France, while the Admiralty enforced the blockade, transported troops across the Channel, or made preparations for invasion elsewhere on the Continent, all its demands might have been met under this arrangement. In the suddenly changed conditions of 1940, however, when the tanks, trucks, artillery, and even machine guns of the British Expeditionary Force were lost, and when all available capacity was required for the manufacture of pursuit planes, the independent activity of different ministries became an obstacle to the organization of existing capacity for maximum production.

The *controllers of commodities in the Ministry of Supply,* who were appointed at the outbreak of war, are, like the controllers in the Ministry of Food, members of the controlled trades. Some of their staffs, although now paid by the government in an effort to reduce the cost of control, originally received their salaries from the trade associations, to which the government paid a fee for this service. Many of the central offices of the controls are located in the trading centers, the wool control for example, in Bradford, and the cotton control in Manchester. The first task of the controls was to fix the prices of the materials in question. In this connection costs were initially determined by trade association accountants, the ministry undertaking no independent investigation of profits until the spring of 1941. Besides the raw material controls, there are in the Ministry of Supply production directorates for munitions, tanks and transport, equipment and stores, and tools.

The various controls distribute supplies to individual firms in accordance with the contracts they have undertaken. Orders by or, in the case of certain civilian manufacture, authorized by particular government departments are so designated through each stage of subcontracting. In the manufacturer's application to the controls for supplies all government orders enjoy, in principle, the same urgency,[34] since changing proportions of the total available supplies of the controlled materials are allocated in advance to the use of each of the departments, and the contracts placed by any department should not require for their completion more than the quota of materials allowed to the department. In this respect there are no varying degrees of priority among authorized contracts.[35] The *Priorities Department of the Ministry of Supply*, which issues the priority authorizations for all government contracts, is in a position to estimate the total consumption of every department.

There was no correspondingly strict allocation of plant capacity to different and conflicting requirements. That would have necessitated intimate contact by the contracting departments with varying local conditions, for which no administrative provision was made. This is not a handicap to the Ministry of Aircraft Production, for example, when dealing with a few large producers of aircraft frames. In various other aspects of munitions production, however, it has resulted in the overloading of many plants and the neglect of others equally well or better equipped. Its disadvantages are most apparent in competition between the departments for engineering facilities, which are widely scattered.

The particular allocation of materials to each department is agreed upon in an interdepartmental committee of civil servants from the departments concerned. This committee is one of five *priority committees* concerned with materials and production, man power, industrial capacity, works and buildings, and transport respectively. Officials of the Pri-

---

[34] The very slight proportions of controlled materials remaining in excess of allocations to government departments are licensed by the controls to individual applicants.

[35] There are, however, general supplementary priority directions. See below, p. 183. During 1940 the interdepartmental committee on works and buildings priority established definite classes of construction with graded claims on building labor, and particular construction projects were assigned to one or another of these classes, a reversion to the discredited priority system of the last war. The result was that by the time the Ministry of Works and Buildings was created at the end of 1940 work had been undertaken 30 percent to 40 percent in excess of total building capacity.

orities Department in the Ministry of Supply keep records of their discussions and maintain some contact between them. The Materials and Production Committee is a combination of two committees on materials and on production which existed in the first period of the war, and the Man Power Committee is likewise a combination of two earlier committees on labor and on the distribution of man power between production and the armed forces. The Industrial Capacity Committee came into existence in the summer of 1940. Subcommittees of the main priority committees, like the Allocation of Traffic Subcommittee and the Works Contracts Subcommittee, are responsible for more detailed coordination. The looseness of this interdepartmental organization and the importance of purely personal factors may be illustrated by the fact that the chairmanship of the Materials and Production Committee, which was originally held, quite logically, by the then Parliamentary secretary of the Ministry of Supply, remained with the same gentleman when he became Parliamentary secretary of the Ministry of Aircraft Production, and later of the Ministry of War Transport, and is now held by the Minister of Works and Buildings, who was formerly director of a department in the Ministry of Supply concerned with total supplies of raw materials.

By agreement between the supply departments a circular instruction to industry to give first, second, and third priority to the production of a few specified articles and to any work for the armed forces or the merchant marine that could by this means be completed within a given short period of time was issued [36] in the crisis of 1940. The strict application of these directions necessarily interrupted existing production schedules, and a revised general instruction issued in November 1941 contained a proviso that the three higher degrees of priority did not apply to " machine tools, plant, or materials." Certificates are, however, issued for particular articles which are to be added to or removed from the list of those receiving the higher ratings, and in these certificates it may be stipulated that the special priority shall include machine tools, plant, and materials.

The distribution of transport facilities in accordance with the urgency of the various claims upon them has been greatly facilitated by the unification of control over shipping and railway movements, motor transport, and canals in a single *Ministry of War Transport* since April

---

[36] By the Ministry of Supply on behalf of the Admiralty, War Office, Air Ministry, and Ministry of Aircraft Production.

1941. The interdepartmental Allocation of Traffic Subcommittee meets in the ministry with the heads of its different divisions. Rail traffic is directed, very much as in the last war, by a *Railway Executive Committee* which includes the managers of the large railway companies and the London Passenger Transport Board. Initial agreements between the ministry and the companies provided for a minimum revenue for the entire railway system to be guaranteed by the government and a maximum permitted revenue, but in 1941 the payment of fixed rentals by the government was substituted for the earlier agreements. Shipping owners, on the other hand, operate their own vessels, which have been requisitioned by the ministry, as well as vessels built since the beginning of the war on the ministry's account [37] in return for fixed commissions under the direction of the *Shipping Operations Control,* a more bureaucratic agency than the Railway Executive. Most of the staff of the shipping divisions of the Ministry of War Transport performed the same or similar duties in the Marine Department of the Board of Trade before the war and in the short lived Ministry of Shipping instituted after the outbreak of war.

Several thousand motor vehicles have been chartered by the Ministry of War Transport and employed in the carriage of goods for which government departments are responsible. A larger pool of privately operated vehicles has been organized in regional offices paralleling those of the official pool. With the increasing scarcity of motor fuel and rubber it has been the policy of the Ministry to transfer all the freight possible from road to rail carriage. This has necessitated compensation of road haulage operators if adequate numbers of vehicles were to be maintained. At the end of 1942 the Government made proposals in which all vehicles employed in long-distance freight carriage were brought under unified control in a scheme closely resembling the control of shipping, with the difference that the owners of transport vehicles accepted in the national pool receive standard payments based on their prewar earnings whether or not the vehicles are in current operation.

In the field of exports and purchases abroad a committee corresponding to the interdepartmental priority committees was formed under the chairmanship of the under-secretary of the Ministry of Economic Warfare, who had been Chief Economic Adviser to the Government since 1931, in the first months of the war. With the subsequent exten-

---

[37] Since May 1942 tonnage built on government account has been allocated to individual shipping owners in proportion to their losses for purchase after the war.

sion of the blockade to cut off the greater part of the European market, this committee has become known as a *committee on world surpluses,* and in 1941 the Minister Without Portfolio, who was then the minister concerned with general questions of postwar reconstruction, presided over it. The division of the Ministry of Economic Warfare concerned with international problems of postwar trade, and the under-secretary, were transferred to the Board of Trade when the Minister Without Portfolio left the Government early in 1942.

At the same time a newly appointed Paymaster General, who has since succeeded to the position of Minister Without Portfolio, but without becoming a member of the War Cabinet, was charged with the general consideration of " reconstruction." Responsibility for the physical aspects of planning was transferred at the beginning of 1942 from the Ministry of Health to the Ministry of Works and Buildings, which was retitled Ministry of Works and Planning. The publication of two major reports on rural and urban development during 1942 led to the establishment early in 1943 of an independent Ministry of Town and Country Planning, the precise functions of which must, of course, depend on the adoption of a definite policy by the Government.

There has been no formal coordination of the *price fixing* powers vested in different departments of the government, outside of two interdepartmental committees on agricultural and food prices. These include representatives of the Ministry of Labor, which is concerned with the cost of living of wage earners, the Ministry of Agriculture, the Departments of Agriculture for Scotland and Northern Ireland, and the Ministry of Food, the interests of the Ministries of Agriculture and Food being opposed as those of seller and buyer. Maximum prices for consumer goods are fixed, subject to review by a referee appointed by the Lord Chancellor, by the Board of Trade.[38] The Board acts in consultation with a representative, advisory Central Price Regulation Committee, which receives complaints of excessive prices on behalf both of the Board of Trade and the Ministry of Food.

The fixing of maximum prices for consumer goods was followed, at the same time that all imports were brought under a licensing system in June 1940, by the drastic *limitation of supplies.* This was at first effected by orders forbidding wholesalers to supply retailers with more than a given percentage of their purchases in the corresponding period of the previous year. The assumption made in fixing percentages was

[38] Under the Prices of Goods Act, 1939 and the Goods and Services (Price Control) Act, 1940.

that a reduction of turnover by 75 percent would not threaten the continued existence of the consumer goods industries. The compulsory concentration of consumer production in the most efficient, "nucleus" firms, to operate at capacity while other firms in the same industries were closed or continued to operate only as selling and distributing organizations, was introduced in March 1941.[39] Firms that are closed down receive compensation from a levy on the earnings of those remaining in operation, a species of rationalization with which the British shipbuilding industry was familiar before the war. So that the plant capacity released would actually be transferred to essential uses, the acquisition of new factory and storage space outside the engineering and munitions industries was licensed under a Controller of Factory and Storage Premises, who became responsible for the allocation of storage accommodation among the different government departments.

The direct rationing of clothing and footwear to consumers began in the summer of 1941. The "telescoping" of retail trade has been a corollary of the limitation of civilian supplies, but there has been no government support for the rationalization of distribution comparable to the concentration of consumer industries. A committee representing retail traders reported in the summer of 1942 that during the war the number of "very large" and "large" shops had increased by 4 percent, although individual shops within these groups had lost 25 to 30 percent of their space and personnel, while the number of "small" and "very small" shops had decreased by 11 percent and 19 percent respectively. The response of the Board of Trade has been to guarantee establishments falling into the "small" category new stock equal to fixed percentages of their total turnover in given periods earlier in the war and immediately before the war.

Separate measures of price fixing, preemptive purchasing abroad, labor regulation, and procurement obviously require some correlation, if only for the negative purpose of ensuring their conformity with the financial policy of the Treasury. The direction of the main lines of production in accordance with strategic necessity, by such decisions as those in May 1940 that airplanes were of first importance, in the summer of 1941 that tanks were, and in the spring of 1942 that shipbuilding should take precedence of everything else, also requires more inclusive authority than a consultative committee of civil servants can have. It is

---

[39] By July 1942, 250,000 workers and above 55,000,000 sq. feet of factory space had been released under schemes of concentration.

in these broad aspects of planning and decision that the organization of interdepartmental coordination has most often proved defective.

At the beginning of the war "economic policy" was decided in the Treasury. In addition to the ministerial committee on economic policy under the Chancellor of the Exchequer, an interdepartmental committee of civil servants met under the chairmanship of the late Lord Stamp,[40] who was appointed Economic Adviser to the War Cabinet. He worked in the Treasury with a staff of four economists (the Economic and Financial Survey). Questions arising in the work of the interdepartmental priority committees were referred for decision to the ministerial Priority Committee under the Minister for the Coordination of Defense. The latter office ceased to exist in April 1940,[41] and the First Lord of the Admiralty (Mr. Churchill) became chairman of the Priority Committee and of the ministerial Committee on Military Coordination.

After the formation of the Churchill Government in May 1940 the War Cabinet was reduced to six members,[42] excluding the service ministers, and the Prime Minister assumed also the title of *Minister of Defense*. When Mr. Churchill, while still First Lord of the Admiralty, assumed the chairmanship of the two principal ministerial coordinating committees, the secretary of the Committee of Imperial Defense, Lieutenant-General H. L. Ismay, became his principal private secretary. This position he has continued to hold, with the additional title of Chief of Staff to the Prime Minister and Minister of Defense. His position more or less corresponds to that of the Chief of Staff to the Commander-in-Chief in the United States, and he represents the Prime Minister in the Chiefs of Staff Committee. The "Ministry of Defense" consists solely of General Ismay's office and a "statistical department"[43] under Lord Cherwell as scientific adviser.

[40] The chairman of the London, Midlands, and Scottish Railway, he had also been chairman of the standing committee of the Economic Advisory Council responsible for reports to the Government.

[41] See above, Part I, p. 157.

[42] The Prime Minister, the Lord Privy Seal, the Foreign Secretary, the Lord President of the Council, the Minister Without Portfolio, and the Minister of Aircraft Production. The Cabinet was enlarged to eight members in October 1940 by the inclusion of the Chancellor of the Exchequer and the Minister of Labor. In subsequent reshufflings of the leaders of the Labor and Conservative Parties until the end of 1942 the posts of Minister of Aircraft Production, Minister Without Portfolio, and Lord Privy Seal were eliminated from the War Cabinet, and the posts of Minister of Production, Secretary of State for Dominion Affairs, and Home Secretary were included in it.

[43] Cf. 373 H. C. Deb. 5 s., col. 1275. Lord Cherwell at the end of 1942 entered the Government as Paymaster General, his functions remaining unchanged.

The Committee on Military Coordination became by the change of Government the *Defense Committee of the Cabinet,* and its jurisdiction was extended to include questions of supply. The ministerial Priority Committee was replaced, in an inferior position, by the so-called *Production Council* under the chairmanship of the Minister Without Portfolio (Mr. Greenwood), whose career in opposition had in no way prepared him for an executive role. He became at the same time chairman of a revised Economic Policy Committee which was designed as the long-range planning branch of the Production Council. The membership of these last two committees was flexible enough to include on occasion any member of the Government. The occasion, however, was seldom, as meetings were held only once or twice a month. The Chancellor of the Exchequer was promoted to a *" Supreme Coordinating Committee "* of four ministers over whom the Lord President of the Council, then the former Prime Minister, Mr. Chamberlain, presided. After Mr. Chamberlain was succeeded as Lord President of the Council by Sir John Anderson in October 1940, the Supreme Coordinating Committee became in fact the final authority short of the War Cabinet in home affairs, its position corresponding to that of the Defense Committee in military affairs.

An expansion of production was promised by the formation in January 1941 of ministerial Import and Production " Executives " under the chairmanship of the Ministers of Supply [44] and Labor respectively.[45] The Production Council, and with it the Economic Policy Committee, disappeared. Lord Stamp resigned as the Cabinet's economic adviser shortly thereafter, presumably finding no place for his advice. The imports of different departments from North America had been regulated as far as necessary during 1940 by an interdepartmental committee under the parliamentary secretary of the Ministry of Shipping. As they increased in importance a *North American Supply Committee* was constituted by the Ministers of Supply and Aircraft Production and the First Lord of the Admiralty. (The resulting organization may be clarified by the chart inserted at the back of this book.)

In addition to the Production and Import Executives there remained the Defense Committee of the Cabinet — including the Prime Minister

---

44 After June 1941, the President of the Board of Trade.

45 The Import Executive consisted of the Ministers of Supply, Food, War Transport, and Aircraft Production, the First Lord of the Admiralty, and the President of the Board of Trade. The Production Executive consisted of the Ministers of Labor, Supply, Aircraft Production, and Works and Buildings, the First Lord of the Admiralty, and the President of the Board of Trade.

as chairman, the Lord Privy Seal and leader of the House of Commons (Mr. Attlee), the Foreign Secretary, the three service ministers and the chiefs of staff, the Minister of Aircraft Production, and, from time to time, the Minister of Supply — which dealt with war production as well as with military operations. When Lord Beaverbrook, who, as Minister of Aircraft Production, had been a member of the War Cabinet, resigned in May 1941, the office of " Minister of State " was invented for him, and he was made deputy chairman of the Defense Committee for supply problems, the Lord Privy Seal becoming deputy chairman for military operations. This delegation of the Prime Minister's functions as Minister of Defense lasted only a few weeks, until Lord Beaverbrook became Minister of Supply. He was succeeded as Minister of State by Captain Lyttelton, who was dispatched immediately to Cairo, with the duty of organizing the supplies of the armies in the Near East.[46]

Consultation among departments in the Production Executive and the subordinate interdepartmental priority committees was duplicated in production boards in the *twelve regions* into which England, Scotland, and Wales are divided for purposes of civil defense.[47] The area of each of the five home commands of the Army corresponds to the areas of two or three of these regions. They were created by legislation in March 1939, when *regional defense commissioners* were appointed to exercise the full authority of the central government in the event that communications between any region and the central government should be destroyed by enemy action. Some precedent for the regional division existed in the munitions areas of the last war, in the normal organization of the employment exchanges into nine geographic divisions, and in the appointment of Admiralty inspectors of naval construction and engineering for particular areas, which varied with the location of the particular industries.

Officers of every important ministry except those concerned with external affairs, and of several departments of some ministries, have since been appointed in each of the civil defense regions or areas, although

---

[46] See Chapter II, p. 72.
[47] Scotland, Northern, Northeastern, North Midlands, Eastern, London, Southeastern, Southern, Southwestern, Midlands, Northwestern, and Wales. In the regional supply organization the London and Southeastern regions are combined, and Northern Ireland, which has its own civil defense organization, is included in the supply organization. The London and Southeastern regions are also combined in the organization of the Ministry of Labor, which does not include Northern Ireland. The indiscriminate use of the terms "area," "region," "division," and " district " for the same administrative unit has created some confusion.

their offices are not all established in the same town in any region.[48] Their powers vary widely from the direct executive authority of the regional controllers of labor or transport to the "liaison" between the central ministry and local agencies provided by the regional officers of the Ministry of Agriculture. Within the Ministry of Supply particularly, the regional officers of different departments have frequently ignored or opposed one another's endeavors. Authority over the different departmental representatives lies with the regional defense commissioners only in such emergencies as have not yet occurred.[49]

The immediate functions of the defense commissioners have been limited to supervising the civil defense measures of local authorities, the expenses of which are borne by the Home Office (since the beginning of the war, the Home Office and Ministry of Home Security), and the special aspects of air raid precautions for which the Ministry of Health is responsible. The distribution of *emergency services* illustrates very well the necessity for local and regional as well as central coordination of the work of different departments. The civil defense services proper, which are operated by local authorities, are subject to Home Office supervision, as are fire services, which were nationalized under a Fire Service Department of the Home Office in 1941. The Ministry of Health, however, supervises conditions in shelters and rest centers and first aid services. The Board of Education is responsible for the evacuation of school children, and the Ministry of Health, for the evacuation of others. County authorities are responsible for the reception of evacuated school children; and local authorities, for the reception of other evacuees.[50] The Ministry of Food operates canteens outside the factories, and the Ministry of Labor, canteens inside the factories. For the emergency repair of air raid damage, the Ministry of Works and Buildings maintains dumps of building materials at strategic points. Repairs to private dwellings under a certain maximum sum are licensed by local authorities, and repairs to factories are decided by local Emergency Reconstruction Panels including local manufacturers and local or regional

---

48 In the Northeastern region, for example, the offices of the regional defense commissioner, the regional controller of labor, and the regional representative of the Ministry of Works and Building are in Leeds and the area supply board in Sheffield. In Scotland the area supply board is located in Glasgow and the regional defense commissioner and labor controller in Edinburgh.

49 For this reason the relations between the regional defense commissioners and the regional officers of the different departments of the government have been indicated on the chart of British administration at the back of this book with broken lines.

50 Indeed, the Ministry of Food, through the reports of local rationing committees, maintains the only complete census of population movements.

officers of the different supply departments. The regional defense commissioner decides the allocation of the total supplies released for repairs as between dwelling and factory reconstruction.

A short rehearsal of the wartime functions of different ministries will be enough to suggest the number of agencies of the central government, many of them affecting the lives of the population directly, which come into contact at the regional level. The powers of the *Ministry of Agriculture* have been largely delegated with respect to the increase of production to *War Agricultural Executive Committees* appointed by the minister, in districts which do not coincide with local government areas, and through them to local War Agricultural Committees including representatives of every parish.[51] The most important growers of the typical products of the area meet in the district committees under the chairmanship of a land officer of the ministry. They can require land that is not under cultivation to be plowed up, take possession of and operate " substandard " farms, allow grants for drainage improvements on behalf of the ministry to individuals and to county catchment boards, and extend credit to farmers for improvements, and they operate or let agricultural and drainage machinery owned by the ministry.

These committees come under the general supervision of land commissioners in the Ministry of Agriculture and of the eleven regional liaison officers already mentioned. Since the Agricultural Research institutes in England are responsible not to the Ministry of Agriculture but to the Agricultural Research Committee of the Privy Council, the ministry has suffered from a lack of scientifically trained personnel, which is not felt in Scotland, where the executive officers of the Agricultural Executive Committees are all officials of the Scottish Agricultural Colleges. Roughly parallel county committees, all of which include members of the corresponding District War Agricultural Executive Committee, have been established, with local subcommittees of their own, for the direction of the additional agricultural labor mobilized in the Women's Land Army.

The separation of production and marketing in the Ministry of Agriculture and purchasing in the *Ministry of Food* is an obvious handicap to the development of a consistent program, the more particularly since most agricultural subsidies are now borne by the Ministry of Food. The food ministry is responsible not only for central purchasing and

---

[51] This subdivision does not exist in Scotland where there are forty Agricultural Executive Committees.

distribution but also for rationing under the two heads of food and feeding stuffs. Its organization for the *rationing of feeding stuffs* consists of twelve divisional committees of manufacturers of feeding stuffs, wholesalers, and farmers, with executive officers from the ministry, and county feeding stuffs committees representing both farmers and traders. Although the areas of the feeding stuffs committees do not correspond to those of the agricultural committees, their relations are necessarily close, and their membership is overlapping. For *food rationing* there are more than fifteen hundred local food committees representing traders, consumers, and the local authorities, with the town clerk usually serving as executive officer. Food control officers of the ministry in each of the civil defense areas deal with many of the unforeseen problems of distribution resulting from war conditions. Complaints of excessive food prices or violations of price fixing orders reach the ministry through seventeen local Price Regulation Committees, again representative of consumers, traders, and local authorities, appointed by the Board of Trade early in the war. Although these committees were not concerned originally with food prices, but with the prices of other consumers' goods, they received such frequent complaints of food prices that they were given the alternative title of Food Price Investigation Committees. This fortuitous arrangement has the advantage of ensuring the conformity of recommendations made by the Central Price Regulation Committee to the Board of Trade on the one hand and the Ministry of Food on the other.

The trades organized in the *commodity controls* of the Ministry of Food have their own area divisions. Under the meat and livestock control, for example, there are eight Area Wholesale Meat Supply Associations and a Meat Importers National Association with twelve branch offices. The most severe criticism of the ministry has been for its failure to correct extravagance in distribution. The existence of national marketing boards for products like bacon and milk has not always contributed to the reduction either of duplication of facilities or of the number of separate processes in distribution. The compulsory pooling [52] of certain commodities and the definition of fixed areas for the distribution of others at the beginning of the war entailed so much waste and inconvenience that they were quickly withdrawn, and it was only in the early summer of 1942 that considerations of transport and personnel led the ministry to attempt a similar and more successful restriction of

[52] Elimination of trade names and substitution of standard grades at uniform prices.

distribution. Retailers in eight areas into which the country is divided for this purpose must draw their supplies from wholesalers in the same area. In other products such as margarine, bread, cake and biscuit, bacon, sugar, sweets, and flour, which the retailer and, in the last case, the baker frequently obtain direct from the manufacturer, they are restricted to purchases regardless of brand from the firms nearest. At the same time the retail distribution of milk was restricted to standard grades to be supplied to assigned districts by dairy companies in proportion to their share in the total consumption of the locality. In this connection the Ministry of Food departed from its established method of control through representatives of the trade controlled to make General Sir Robert G. Finlayson partly responsible for the administration of the milk scheme.

The allocation of available transportation facilities in the *Ministry of War Transport* requires a more unified regional organization. Twelve regional transport commissioners are responsible for the supervision not only of the divisional transport officers of the ministry, who are concerned with road traffic, but also of the district officers of railway companies, the actual operation of which is otherwise little affected by a nominal government control, and of the local transport officers of the Ministries of Aircraft Production and Food, the Admiralty, and the Ministry of Supply, the latter acting also on behalf of the Ministry of Agriculture,[53] and for the provision of additional facilities to satisfy requirements arising from the transfer of labor or industry. The regional transport commissioners also control the rationing of gasoline by officers of the Petroleum Department of the Board of Trade. A large part of the motor vehicles originally operated by the Road Haulage Branch of the ministry were taken over from a pool for the transport of meat supplies established by the Ministry of Food; most of the others were employed in connection with the clearance of ports. The ministry's pool of trucks was organized in six large areas and fourteen smaller divisions, but since all long-distance haulage has come under government control the divisions have been brought into conformity with the twelve civil defense areas. Canals are similarly organized into six areas, in each of which a committee of canal owners, representatives of other forms of transportation, and transport officers of different government departments has authority to allocate particular traffic to the canals. The canal

[53] Partly for the reason that the Ministry of Supply is responsible for the distribution of fertilizers.

systems of the six regions are coordinated through an advisory Central Canal Committee of which the Parliamentary secretary of the Ministry of War Transport is chairman.

The greatest transportation problems in England in wartime arise, of course, from the fact that goods are delivered in large convoys which are directed by the Admiralty to the ports that seem safest from attack. The collection of cargoes for and the quick distribution of cargoes brought in by numbers of ships the departure and arrival of which cannot be made known in advance, as well as the actual unloading and turnaround of the ships, is the concern of the *Port and Transit Control* of the ministry. The head of this department belongs, with the directors of the liner, ship management, and short sea shipping divisions of the ministry and the controller of commercial shipping, to the Shipping Operations Control. The loading of ships abroad with a view to expediting the discharge of their cargoes in England is superintended by officers of the Ships Distribution (Diversion) Section of the ministry. Within each port executive committees composed of the naval officers in command of the ports, shipping and railway agents, motor transport operators, representatives of dock labor, of traders, and of the government importing departments have been formed more or less spontaneously. In certain most congested ports the Ministry of Transport is the employer of all dock labor.[54] Regional port directors for the Clyde areas, the northwestern English ports, the Bristol Channel ports, and the ports of the eastern coast have been appointed by the minister to concentrate the efforts of the port committees and to coordinate their work with that of the central controls.

The functions of regional representatives of the *Board of Trade* are apparently limited to assisting manufacturers in the export trade to obtain transportation and to advising them how best to secure from the Board authorization of applications for supplies and labor.[55] The Controller of Factory and Storage Premises in the Board of Trade has his

---

[54] See Chapter IV, Part II, p. 244.

[55] Manufacturers of the same or closely similar articles have formed " Export Groups " through which applications to the Board can be made. There is a central Industrial and Export Council of which the President of the Board of Trade is chairman, and the Secretary of the Department of Overseas Trade, vice-chairman, and which includes Parliamentary secretaries of the Ministries of Supply and Labor, representatives of the Treasury, the Ministry of Economic Warfare, and the Foreign Office, the controllers of wool, cotton, and factory and storage space, and representatives of industry, commerce, finance, and labor. While the Council, which dates from February 1940, has met on a monthly basis, it has had sub-committees which met more frequently, and a small executive committee in permanent session. The functions of the Council, in spite of its large official membership, are advisory.

own representatives in the twelve regions, who must work in cooperation with the twelve licensing offices for private building maintained by
the Ministry of Works and Buildings. With the transfer of the powers
of the Ministry of Transport over electricity supplies to the Board of
Trade late in 1941, a new division was formed for the administration of
gas and electricity, and eleven regional Fuel and Power Commissioners were appointed. These officers were transferred to the *Ministry of
Fuel, Light, and Power,* which also absorbed the Department of Mines
under the Board of Trade, upon its creation in June 1942. They will be
responsible for the rationing of fuel to consumers. Regional controllers
of the Ministry of Fuel in eight coal mining areas exercise the government's recently assumed powers over the operation of coal mines and are
responsible for the actual output of the mines in their regions.

The organization of the *Ministry of Labor* [56] is unique in the delegation of the authority of all the central departments of the ministry over
the activities of their local agents and inspectors to a single controller
in each of the defense regions. Within his region he is responsible for
recruiting, training, the transfer of labor to work of urgent importance,
conditions of work, and the welfare of working people. Labor supply
inspectors, whose task is to secure the maximum use of the minimum
labor, report (except for the industries under Essential Work Orders)
to man power officers, whose task is the allocation of available man
power as between industry and the armed forces, and the directors of
employment exchanges, to whom particular applications for labor are
made. The regional controllers of labor have thus been better able than
any other regional officers to recognize bottlenecks in production, and
so far as they are due to lack of labor to remedy them. While periodical
instructions are issued by the Ministry of Labor in agreement with the
supply departments as to the types of production, or even the particular
firms, to which special priority in labor supply is to be granted, the regional controllers themselves may give first preference to any firms in
their regions in which comparatively small numbers of workmen are
required or which seem to them for any reason to deserve exceptional
treatment.

Since the beginning of the war officers of the departments concerned
with production, transportation, and trade have met in *regional supply
boards.* These were originally headed by the representatives of the munitions department of the Ministry of Supply. The director of the depart-

---

[56] See Chapter IV, Part II, p. 241.

ment was a former engineer-in-chief of the Admiralty, and it may be supposed that his appointees, "engineer ex-admirals," had the advantage of familiarity with regional supply organization in the only department in which it normally existed. That their organization was ineffective in planning the fullest use of capacity or coordinating the orders of the different supply departments is due in the first place to the absence of any general responsibility for production in the Ministry of Supply and in the second place to the very limited authority of the regional officers of the departments, who were concerned for the most part with the "progressing" of orders placed by their departments centrally. Agreement among the representatives of the supply departments in any region as to the placing of particular contracts in that region by any one of their departments was sought for the first time in July 1942.

Advisory committees of representatives of employers and labor, appointed by the Minister of Supply, were attached to the first regional boards. In the reorganization of the government in the crisis of 1940 control of the boards was secured briefly by the Ministry of Labor, and then returned to the Ministry of Supply. Six representatives of industry and labor were, however, added to the membership of each board, and the chairmen and vice-chairmen were chosen from among them. It is doubtful whether in some regions the members appointed ever assembled before 1941.

The role of the boards remained advisory, not executive, and in that capacity they reported after the establishment of the Production Executive in 1941 to its Industrial Capacity Subcommittee, or, presumably, to the chairman of the committee, the Parliamentary secretary of the Ministry of Supply. By the middle of 1941 the area boards included officers of the Ministry of Supply and the raw materials department of the Ministry of Supply, the controller's department of the Admiralty,[57] the Ministry of Aircraft Production, the Ministry of War Transport, the Ministry of Labor, the Ministry of Works and Buildings, the Board of Trade, and the regional committees of the Machine Tool Control in the Ministry of Supply. Something of what they might have accomplished is illustrated by the success of capacity exchanges or clearing centers established principally in the London area, but also under some other boards, for the use of small manufacturers. The creation late in 1941 in the Ministry of Supply of a division of regional control to supervise the regional

[57] The Third Sea Lord, who is a member of the Board of Admiralty, is responsible for naval supply, and is called the Controller of the Admiralty.

and local activity of agents of different divisions of the ministry was also symptomatic of an increasing effort to make the best use of existing capacity. The necessity for a more coherent regional organization of war production and for the closer application of technical resources to the tactical requirements of the armed forces was recognized in the formation of the *Ministry of Production* in March 1942. This date roughly marks the end of the construction of new capacity for armament production, the conversion of existing capacity to armament production, the recruitment of additional labor for armament work, or the release of labor from non-essential work for armament production. The importation of raw materials was at the same time restricted by sinkings and by lack of shipping tonnage. The conditions of production were thus narrowed, and any further increase of output depended on the more efficient use of the factors already engaged.[57a] The beginning of a great expansion of capacity for armament production in the United States also made it possible for British production to be concentrated to a certain extent on articles better produced, for reasons of quality, technique, materials, or transport in England than in the United States.

The central organization of supply under the Ministry of Production bears more resemblance to the organization under the Minister for the Coordination of Defense in 1939 than to that of the Production Council in 1940 or the Import and Production Executives in 1941. The latter bodies have given way to a *Joint Production Staff* corresponding to the Chiefs of Staff Committee. Its members have more authority than civil servants ordinarily can, and more knowledge of specific problems than is ordinarily expected of ministers.

The administration of the service departments is distinguished from that of other ministries by the fact that all major departmental decisions are taken jointly in the Board of Admiralty, the Army Council, or the Air Council by the responsible minister and the service or civil service heads of the various divisions. In the Ministry of Supply, the *Supply Council,* and in the Ministry of Aircraft Production, the *Air Supply Board,* likewise include the heads of important departments of each ministry. Although they are much more informally constituted, they too are designed to prevent difficulties from arising in the direction of highly technical services by temporary civilian ministers. The chair-

---

[57a] Cf., for example, Mr. Oliver Lyttelton's address to the Institution of Production Engineers, London, October 23, 1942.

man of the Supply Council is appointed for the purpose of general co-ordination in the ministry and has no particular executive responsibilities. The Joint War Production Staff is thus composed of the Assistant Chiefs of the Imperial General and the Naval Staffs, the member of the Air Council concerned with supply, the chairman of the Supply Council in the Ministry of Supply, the member of the Board of Admiralty concerned with production, and the highest official of the Ministry of Aircraft Production, meeting under the chairmanship of the Minister of Production or his chief adviser.

The Joint Production Staff, like the Chiefs of Staff Committee, is executive. There are subordinate to it, as there are to the Chiefs of Staff Committee, joint planning groups of representatives from different departments. These groups are sometimes formed *ad hoc* and are concerned with the production of particular weapons, their members working under the direction of the Department of Programs and Planning, which has been transferred from the Ministry of Supply to the Ministry of Production. Others, under the chairmanship of the special industrial adviser of the Ministry of Production, are standing committees concerned with more general questions of production efficiency and economy of man power.

The analogous Joint Planning Staff and Joint Intelligence Subcommittee under the *Chiefs of Staff Committee* and the Vice-Chiefs of Staff Committee are permanent bodies, and their members constitute a " joint staff " in addition to the staffs of the three services. The Joint Planning Staff consists of the directors of plans of the three services, but its subsections [58] include besides officers of the three forces liaison officers from the Ministry of War Transport, the Ministry of Economic Warfare, and the Ministry of Home Security. The Joint Intelligence Subcommittee also includes officials of the Foreign Office and the Ministry of Economic Warfare, and the Ministry of Economic Warfare is represented in the intelligence section for operations.

Responsibility for the *design of weapons* remains with the Ministries of Supply and Aircraft Production, to which the departments of scientific research in the War Office and the Air Ministry were transferred when the separate production ministries were established, and with the production department of the Admiralty. There are departments

---

[58] Strategical Planning Section, Executive Planning Section, and Future Operational Planning.

of scientific research and development in the Admiralty, the Ministry of Supply, and the Ministry of Aircraft Production. There is also an independent Department of Scientific and Industrial Research under the supervision of the Lord President of the Council, which is responsible for the work of the National Physical Laboratory and of the national Scientific Advisory Council. The Prime Minister as Minister of Defense has his own scientific adviser. A Scientific Advisory Committee in the Ministry of Supply and an Aeronautical Research Committee in the Ministry of Aircraft Production include scientists who hold government offices. The Aeronautical Research Committee is in addition interdepartmental, including besides the director of research and development in the Ministry of Aircraft Production and the supervisor of the Royal Aeronautical Research Establishment the director of meteorological research in the Air Ministry and the director of scientific research in the Ministry of Supply.

The new appointment of a scientific adviser to the War Office in the spring of 1942 suggests in itself that collaboration between the service and production ministries in meeting particular requirements has left something to be desired. At the same time the post of Deputy Chief of the Imperial General Staff for organization and equipment was created, the D.C.I.G.S. becoming a member of the Supply Council in the Ministry of Supply. An advisory board comprising officers from the War Office and the Ministry of Supply had been established in 1940 for the design and production of tanks. To this has now been added a Weapon Development Committee under the D.C.I.G.S. The appointment of a deputy to the Chief of the Imperial General Staff was followed in August 1942 by the appointment of a Deputy First Sea Lord to direct the administrative work of the Naval Staff in relation to training and material, and later of a Fifth Sea Lord as Chief of Naval Air Equipment. In the Ministry of Aircraft Production a Chief Naval Representative, who is a naval captain, and a staff of naval officers supervise the supply of naval aircraft. The reporting of the tactical performance of different weapons to the production ministries by qualified officers in the field was not organized systematically before the summer of 1942 and was only occasional.

The *Minister of Production,* unlike the ministers of the several supply departments, is a member of the War Cabinet. His executive powers are limited to the allocation of raw materials and machine tools, and upon this his influence over the supply departments must depend. The allocation of labor and the allocation of capacity for shipbuilding and repairs, over which the Admiralty retains complete control, have been specifically exempted from his jurisdiction. Even the Machine Tool Control and the Raw Materials Department, which, in contrast to the individual controls, is concerned with total supplies rather than with distribution to particular plants, have remained as before in the Ministry of Supply, certain of their officers being included also on the staff of the Ministry of Production. The Machine Tool Controller, for example, is also the head of a department in the Ministry of Production which supervises the actual progress of the procurement programs of the different supply departments. There is an industrial division in the Ministry of Production for the correction of defects of organization in individual firms and the improvement of facilities for armament production. It acts mainly at the request of other supply departments, and an advisory panel of industrialists and trade unionists, the successor of the Production Executive's Central Joint Advisory Committee, is attached to it.

The existing purchasing organizations of the Ministry of Supply, the Ministry of Aircraft Production, and the Admiralty in the United States were not disturbed by the creation of the Ministry of Production. In November 1942, however, the post of Minister Resident in Washington for Supply, " responsible to " the Minister of Production was established. The minister appointed, who had been employed since 1939 in the Ministry of Supply, the Ministry of War Transport, and the Ministry of Aircraft Production, must superintend the work of the British staffs of the five combined American and British boards and of various special British missions. On the overall Combined Production and Resources Board, with offices in Washington and London, British interests are represented by the Ministry of Production alone. Under the Production and Resources Board it has been possible to establish a technical " Combined Committee " for the standardization of steel production in Great Britain and North America, the members of which severally represent two combined boards and departments of the United States, Canadian, and United Kingdom Governments. Here again the Ministry of Production represents the interests of the other supply ministries in Great Britain.

To the growing list of regional officers, regional representatives of the Ministry of Production, all successful company directors, have been added. The *regional controllers of production,* who have in fact no executive authority over the regional representatives of other departments, have become the chairmen of the area production boards. Each board as reconstituted contains besides the regional representatives of the Ministry of Production, the Admiralty, the Ministry of Supply, the Ministry of Aircraft Production, the Ministry of Labor, and the Board of Trade, three representatives of employers and three of employees appointed by the Minister of Production, one of whom is the vice-chairman of the board and a member of its executive committee. The technical directors of capacity clearing centers in smaller districts are also appointed now by the Ministry of Production. The function of the regional controllers of production, as of their ministry, is to coordinate the activities of the different production departments. Their success, since every departmental regional officer remains accountable to his own department and can appeal any decision to it, must ultimately depend on the degree of authority which the Ministry of Production establishes centrally, although any prestige which the regional controllers enjoy locally may contribute to the ministry's authority. Indeed their appointments seem to have been made with a view to that end. The vice-chairmen of the eleven regional boards meeting together constitute a National Production Advisory Council. The officials chiefly concerned with regional organization in the Ministry of Production, the Admiralty, the Ministries of Supply, Aircraft Production, and Labor, and the Controller of Machine Tools also meet regularly in the Ministry of Production.

The existence of the Ministry of Production has at least resulted in the better definition of the aims of the supply departments and a more practical organization of coordination. When the Minister of Production was appointed it was stated that his role in relation to the supply departments would resemble that of the Minister of Defense in relation to the armed services. The actual organization of the Ministry of Production has served, however, to emphasize the barrenness of the comparison. The Minister of Production cannot override the other production departments. He tries presumably to form an independent estimate of the demands that may be made on them and of their common resources and to focus effort where it is most necessary or will be most profitable. Here the analogy between the Ministry of Production and an ideal defense ministry ends. The aim of the production departments is to satisfy the requirements of the armed forces; for this the systematic coordination of effort and the fixing of definite responsibility are essential. In the exertion of military power, on the other hand, the planned selection of strategic objectives is of the first importance. Success will not follow from the most perfect coordination of separate efforts without central decision and direction.

In Great Britain this central decision rests with three interlocking committees: the committee of the three Chiefs of Staff, who have "an individual and collective responsibility for advising on defense policy as a whole," to which the Prime Minister and his deputy belong; the Defense Committee of the Cabinet, which includes the Chiefs of Staff, and of which the Prime Minister is chairman; and finally the War Cabinet, to which the Chiefs of Staff may have direct access. Although it may be assumed that domestic questions are sifted very finely through the supreme coordinating committee on home affairs before they reach the War Cabinet, it remains doubtful whether the direction of military operations by the War Cabinet can be more than general or sporadic. The critics of this organization, who include among other distinguished officers the secretary of the Committee of Imperial Defense for thirty years and the last Minister for the Coordination of Defense, claim that it leads not to coordinated strategic planning, but to compromise, which is the opposite. A Minister of Defense of great military experience who was not Prime Minister, and who bore full responsibility for strategic planning, would enjoy a greater freedom of appeal to the War Cabinet against the three Chiefs of Staff or any one of them than can the Prime Minister himself, who must appear in any difference of opinion as both advocate and judge.[58a]

In summing up this brief outline of the British war administration one generalization unavoidably presents itself. The range and the vital importance of the government's wartime functions have led to the replacement of parliamentarians in most critical positions in the administration by experts, that is, by former civil servants and men of experience in private enterprise or organization. The Lord President of the Council and chairman of the supreme coordinating committee for home affairs and the Secretary of State for War are former civil servants. The Ministers of Production, Supply, Food, War Transport, and the former Minister of Aircraft Production are all business men. The Minister of Labor was a leading trade union executive. The great administrative problem before them is to avoid duplication between departments and between the regional and central levels of administration and to substi-

[58a] Cf. especially the debates in the House of Lords April 15, May 5, and May 20, 1942.

tute clear direction for consultation. The solution under rapidly changing conditions cannot be easy.[59]

---

[59] Some few remarks must be made in explanation of the chart of British wartime administration attached at the back of this book. Any schematic arrangement of an administration in
which executive authority is strictly departmentalized is difficult. It is necessary, however, to
give some impression of the interconnections of ministerial and civil servce committees. Since
the regional and local functions of each ministry are exercised separately, the number of lines
between ministries and local officers creates an exaggerated impression of complexity. The
Regional Defense Commissioners exercise a tentative control over the officers of other departments in the event of grave emergency, and their relations to the officers of other departments
in their regions have therefore been indicated by broken lines. The position of members of the
Ministry and of standing ministerial committees has been indicated by black boxes. The position
of standing committees of civil servants and of advisory committees has been indicated by broken
black boxes. Wherever possible executive authority has been indicated by solid connecting lines,
and a consultative relation by broken lines of connection. Different colors have been used to
connect the major ministerial committees with their subcommittees and with the departments
represented in them: black for home affairs; green for food policy; purple for the Import Executive; blue for the Production Executive; and red for defense and civil defense. These colors have
been carried through the organization of the departments most closely concerned in the work
of the committees, but other colors have been used to distinguish the departmental organization
of other ministries included in the same committees: brown for the Ministry of Labor under
the Production Executive; and orange for the Ministry of Transport under the Import Executive.
Below some of the ministers who are included in coordinating committees, such as the Lord
Privy Seal, the Minister Without Portfolio, and the Lord President of the Council there is of
course no departmental organization.

The arrangement of ministerial committees shown is roughly that from January 1941 to
February 1942. Since then successive changes have been made in the personnel of the War Cabinet. A Minister of Production has been appointed, and the Joint Production Staff under
him has replaced both the Import and the Production Executives. The Regional Production
Boards now report directly to the Ministry of Production. The chairmanship of the interdepartmental committee on world surpluses has since been transferred to the Board of Trade. The chart
also fails to include the independent Ministry of Fuel, Light, and Power created in June 1942,
and the Ministry of Town and Country Planning established in February 1943.

CHAPTER IV

The British War Economy

PART ONE
THE FINANCE OF BRITAIN'S WAR EFFORT

by William S. McCauley

1. Some Elementary Principles

The emphasis of mobilization economics on real resources of production quite properly relegates finance to a secondary position. But in democratic countries there is great danger that the problems of war finance may be pushed too far into the background of public consciousness. The objective of industrial mobilization for war is the devotion of as large a proportion of the national resources as possible to the production of weapons of war. It is not money that buys armaments, but men who, with the aid of machines, transform materials. The limits of the defense effort will be set by the availability of the real ingredients of production rather than by lack of money. Finance must, nevertheless, play an important role in the shifting of a large proportion of the nation's plant from the production of peacetime goods to the manufacture of armaments. This is especially true of capitalistic countries like Britain and the United States, where the absence in the early phases of the war effort of governmental machinery for the direct allocation of industrial capacity and the restriction of consumption has required greater reliance on financial policies to convert the economy to war production.

The objectives of mobilization finance should be threefold. The first objective, of course, is the provision of funds for defense expenditure. No government with a modern banking system at its disposal need fear a shortage of purchasing power over productive resources. Money can be created; and the danger of war finance is that reliance will be placed too largely on the creation of new funds instead of the transfer of money already in the hands of the public.

The second objective is for finance to become an adjunct of armament policy in facilitating the transfer of manufacturing plant from civilian to military production. This entails prohibitive taxation of the sale of non-essential goods not subject to direct governmental control.

The third and most important aim of armament finance is to preserve economic stability by imposing on the public the sacrifices required for the *large-scale* output of armaments. This necessity for public sacrifice is too little understood in countries accustomed to the existence of idle men and unused plant. It is true that in a capitalist economy which seldom operates at more than 80 percent of capacity initial expenditure on armaments may employ otherwise idle resources, so that no sacrifice in the standard of living is required. But as armament expenditure absorbs an increasing proportion of the national income full capacity is reached, and abundance and waste are superseded by scarcity and economy. At this point the consumption of civilians decreases as the consumption of the government increases. If the economy is not to be disrupted by a competitive scramble for goods, by sharply rising prices, and by social conflict, financial policy must be combined with price, wage, and rationing policy to reduce the consumption of civilians in order that the consumption of the government may continue to grow.

The three general methods of transferring purchasing power from citizens to the government are taxation, borrowing, and currency inflation. Taxation is, of course, the most desirable, as it leaves no heritage of debt. It is, however, impossible to increase revenue from modern tax systems as quickly as expenditure increases. The sharpest limitation on drastic increases in taxation is their effect on the business community. Sudden changes in the tax structure may upset specific calculations so that a downward spiral is the result. Until the economy reaches full capacity, small increases in taxation are wiser.

Because of this, and because of the magnitude of modern war expenditure, governments resort to large-scale borrowing from the public and the banks. Borrowing has many advantages. There need be no time lag before receipts are realized. People generally prefer making loans to paying taxes, however similar the economic effect in diverting purchasing power may be. A defense bond represents wealth, while a tax receipt does not. The possession of fixed-price government securities becomes less attractive when prices are rising, but this disadvantage can be overcome by strict control of the capital market to discourage investment in other securities.

The amount that can be borrowed is limited, however, to the genuine gross savings of the community, plus whatever can be raised from the savings of other nations. The replacement of depreciated plant can be suspended, and private investment at home or abroad forbidden. The amount of new savings can be increased by various controls that restrict consumption, such as price-fixing, rationing, and limitation of output. If foreign loans cannot be floated, existing foreign assets can be exchanged for foreign savings. But even with the adoption of measures to increase new savings and to realize past savings (by the sale of foreign assets), the sum the government can hope to raise by borrowing is definitely limited.

In an economy where wages, costs, prices, and production are not rigidly controlled by the government, there is no alternative to a resort to inflation when the Treasury's outlay exceeds its income from taxes and loans. Inflation is here defined as the restriction of civilian consumption by means of increased prices due to the creation and expenditure of new money by the government when the economy is near full capacity. It must be emphasized that borrowing in itself does not necessarily produce inflation, for if amounts loaned to the government would otherwise have been spent by the public, there is no net addition to the income of the economy. It is evident that when the government contributes more to the national income in expenditure than it withdraws in taxes and loans there will be an increase in the quantity of money while the quantity of actual resources remains fixed, or is reduced. In this case purchases by the government are in competition with those by the public, and prices rise, thereby diminishing the purchasing power of money. Wages and other costs rise subsequently, providing additional cause for further price rises in ascending plateaus of price-wage increases.

The fundamental problem of wartime finance is easily stated. As an economy approaches capacity, with employment of the unemployed, payment of overtime, and greater industrial activity, the total national income is increased. But as a growing proportion of production is devoted to armaments, the total supply of consumers' goods is reduced. Inflation is implicit in any situation in which total purchasing power is augmented while the amount of goods offered for sale is diminished.

To avoid inflation, the government must adopt one of two alternatives. Either the excess of private purchasing power over the amount of goods available for civilian consumption must be captured by the Treasury through taxation or borrowing, or a comprehensive control of prices and distribution must be imposed by the government. Otherwise, this surplus of purchasing power will be spent in pushing up prices, at the expense of economic stability and social justice.

2. British Defense Finance

On the basis of these general principles, we can turn to a study of the problems of British finance from the beginning of rearmament in 1936 until after the passage of the Lend-Lease Act in 1941. It is first necessary to understand the magnitude of Great Britain's transformation from a nation at peace to a fortress of war. As Chart I indicates, in 1935 the British spent for defense only 2.7 percent (£136.9 millions) of their national income; this percentage had risen just before the outbreak of war in 1939 to 13.4. But during the fiscal year 1941–42 domestic defense expenditure was expected to absorb at least 42 percent of the nation's domestic income.

The consequent reduction in the standard of living of the English people can be illustrated in another way. In 1935 forty-five million Britishers had more than £4,900 millions to spend on civil consumption and the upkeep and expansion of industrial plant. But in 1941 the public had £3,400 millions, 20 percent less. On the other hand, the domestic expenditure of the government had risen nearly five times from £776 millions to £3,700 millions.[1] Although this increased outlay was from a national income two-fifths larger (because of fuller employment and higher prices), a sizeable diversion of economic resources had also been undertaken.

To understand how this diversion was achieved, we must survey the financial policies of the Treasury. Any such survey falls naturally into

---

[1] See Chart I.

Chart I
British Budget Expenditure and Deficits 1935-1941
£ Millions

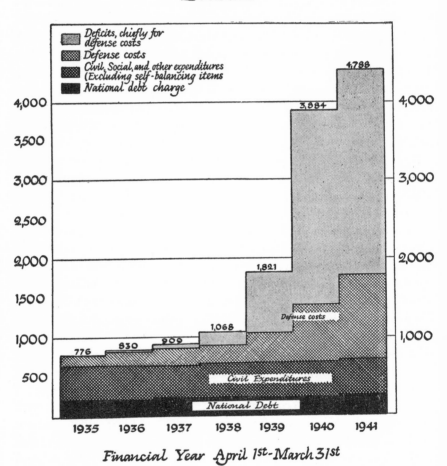

Financial Year April 1st-March 31st

two phases. The first is the stage of rearmament finance beginning in 1936 and lasting through the fiscal year 1938. The second is the period of war finance dating from the Budget of April 1939.

In the initial phase of British rearmament the dominant spirit was one of financial conservatism. In the middle '30's Britain was the only major country enjoying the orthodoxy of a balanced budget. While the United States, France, and Germany experienced large yearly deficits, the criteria of British finance were economy and retrenchment. This unique financial stability was the result of two favorable conditions. The first was internal economic recovery, producing larger revenues; the second was the conversion of the internal debt, reducing interest charges on the budget by one-third. The recovery Budgets of 1934 and 1935 included slight reductions in taxation and the restoration of expenditures that had been eliminated during the depression.

By 1936, when the British Government first markedly increased defense expenditure, it was apparent that the happy period of orthodoxy was drawing to a close. The Chancellor of the Exchequer, Neville Chamberlain, proposed to pay for the first year's rearmament without resort to borrowing, but he warned that to finance future defense outlays exclusively from taxation " would seriously cripple the industry of this country." [2] In 1937 the Government announced its plan of spending £1,500 millions on rearmament in the next five years. Parliament was asked for authority to borrow £400 millions of this amount. The same Government that had refused to increase the public debt by undertaking a productive program of public works at the depth of the depression was now compelled to borrow for rearmament at the peak of the business cycle. The Treasury was beset by a double sin: it was not only incurring deficits; it was incurring them at the wrong time.

To offset this double economic heresy, the provisions of the loan were curiously orthodox. It must be explained that the Government did not view the rearmament program as preparation for war. It was hoped that within five years the armed forces could be expanded and equipped, and that the costs of defense would then be limited to replacement and maintenance. Expenditure was expected to rise to a peak, perhaps in 1939, and to taper off when expansion was completed. The terms of the Defense Loan provided that borrowed funds would be devoted to the payment of the non-recurrent costs of rearmament; tax revenues would provide for

---

[2] 311 H. C. Deb., c. 54.

the recurrent costs of maintenance. The Treasury planned to repay the principal and interest of the loan after the five-year period of borrowing in thirty annual installments.

The Government's decision to increase the national debt to pay for rearmament was opposed by the Labor and Liberal Parties, but supported by financial and business opinion. The latter was reluctant to accept the heavy tax increases necessary for the full cost of rearmament to be met from current revenue. That does not mean that taxes were not raised during the years of rearmament; they were substantially. But in view of the strength of economic recovery in Great Britain the Government could have relied more on taxation than it did.

The British tax structure rests on two principal supports: (1) the personal income tax and (2) customs and excise taxes. Indirect duties on commodities like tea, tobacco, beer, and wine reach the low income groups which are not subject to direct taxation on earnings. Beginning in 1936 the standard rate of income tax was pushed higher year by year, and in 1938 it stood at 5s. 6d. This was a shilling above the 1935 rate and just under the record high of 6s. in 1919. The yield from income tax (including surtax) increased as a result of improved business conditions as well as heavier tax rates by £109.3 millions between 1935 and 1938.

Indirect levies were likewise increased; the tea duty was raised twice in 1936 and 1938, and in 1938 the tax on petroleum oil and alcohol was raised a penny a gallon. By 1938 customs and excise taxes were supplying £340.5 to the Treasury, £37 millions more than in 1935. But because of the greater reliance on income tax the proportion of total tax revenues derived from indirect commodity taxes fell from 48.7 percent in 1935 to 44.4 percent in 1938.

In the 1937 Budget the Chancellor of the Exchequer introduced a graduated tax on excess profits called the National Defense Contribution. The proposal satisfied no one. The Labor and Liberal Parties, who were the most frequent critics of " profiteering," opposed the tax because of its small estimated yield of only £25 millions *per annum*. Business interests in the Conservative Party feared, with some justification, that the tax would penalize prosperity, for it was to be levied on profits earned in excess of those earned in a standard period from 1933 to 1935.[3] Hostility to the tax was so acute that Mr. Chamberlain's first act upon

---

[3] An alternative method of profits valuation was permitted. It subjected to tax profits in excess of 6 percent of the assessed value of a company. 322 H. C. Deb., April 20, 1937, c. 1616.

becoming Prime Minister was to withdraw it and to substitute for it a flat levy on profits.[4]

As a result of tax revisions and of the growth of national income as business activity expanded, the budgetary revenue of 1938 was £927.3 millions, or nearly £149 millions above that of 1935. The Government expected defense costs in 1937 to amount to £278 millions and total budget costs to rise to £942 millions, of which £80 millions were to be met from loans. Actually, expenditures fell short of the estimate, and only £64.9 millions of Defense Loan were used. But in 1938 the political tension resulting from the Austrian and Czech crises in that year raised defense costs beyond expectations to £400 millions, out of a total budgetary expenditure of £1,068 millions. Of this, £128 millions were met from loans, which raised to £193 millions the amount of defense expenditure met by borrowing in two years.

To secure these funds the Government offered two series of Defense Loans to the public. In April 1937 an issue of £100 millions 2½ percent National Defense Bonds (redeemable 1944–48) was floated. This financial operation was poorly timed and was therefore not well received by the investment market. The loan was overpriced (issued at 99½) in comparison with the quotations of other gilt-edge securities, and in addition the City was profoundly disturbed by the National Defense Contribution Profits Tax announced just a few days before. Consequently an unusually large proportion of the loan was taken up by the public funds for later release to the market. A year later, in June 1938, a second issue of 3 percent National Defense Bonds (redeemable 1954–58) was opened for subscription. It was offered at 98 and, in contrast to the 1937 loan, was oversubscribed.

There is considerable evidence that the British Treasury geared the amount of its defense borrowing, and consequently the tempo of rearmament, to the surpluses accumulating yearly in the extra-budgetary funds. These public and semi-public funds generally received an excess of revenue from savings and pension payments over expenditure of about £75 millions in a moderately prosperous year, and this surplus was invested in government securities.[5] It was customary for the public

---

[4] This was a 5 percent levy on company profits, 4 percent on those of individuals and partnerships. It was to run for five years and was expected to produce 18 millions a year revenue.

[5] The extra-budgetary funds are administered by the National Debt Office and include: (1) the National Health Insurance Fund, (2) the Pensions Fund, (3) the Unemployment Insurance Fund, (4) the Post Office Savings Bank, (5) the Trustee Savings Bank, (6) miscellaneous sums managed by the National Debt Commissioners. For an analysis of the assets of these Funds, see N. F. Hall, " Some Technical Aspects of the Finance of Rearmament," *Economica*, May 1937.

funds to cooperate in the financial policy of the Treasury. The effect of this cooperation was to stabilize the gilt-edge securities market and to make the Treasury less dependent in the conduct of its financial operations on prevailing conditions in the investment market.

In 1937, when the Chancellor of the Exchequer, Neville Chamberlain, thought it possible to keep yearly deficits down to an average of £80 millions over the five years of "emergency" defense expenditure, the Treasury no doubt hoped to draw substantially on the revenues of these public funds in the flotation of public issues. A large part of the 1937 Defense Loan was, as we have seen, absorbed by these funds, but in the depression of 1938 these agencies were less able to take up government securities. This explains the more favorable terms of the 1938 Defense Loan. By 1939 the Government's borrowing operations would be so enormous that the extra-budgetary funds could make only a minor contribution to the flotation.

We can conclude that in the first period of rearmament financing through the fiscal year 1938–39 the financial position of the British Government was not unsatisfactory. It is true that the budget was unbalanced, but although the deficits were growing in size, they were not so large that they could not be financed without undue disturbance of the investment market. But in 1939 Britain experienced the first billion-pound Budget, and the trend of all segments of governmental expenditure was upward. As the national debt increased, the burden of interest charges became heavier. The costs of civil government, of social services, of subsidies were rising, and by 1939 the rapidly increasing expenditure for defense would dominate the whole British economy as well as the budget.

3. Wartime Finance

The year 1939 was the first year of war finance. The Government's efforts to arrive at stable estimates for expenditure were without success. British defense costs spiraled upward with each new threat of war, and finally with the fact of war. In February 1939 the Government stated that its outlay on defense in the fiscal year 1939–40 would be at least £580 millions. When Sir John Simon presented the Budget late in April the sum had risen to £630 millions. By late July Supplementary Estimates for the Defense Forces and the Ministry of Supply carried the figure to £749 millions. The outbreak of war added additional millions, and in the course of the fiscal year total expenditures reached £1,817 millions, of which £768 millions were borrowed.[6]

Large as this figure was in comparison with peacetime spending, it was less than half the amount the Government expended in 1940–41. Under the pressure of total war, one budget after another proved inadequate. Chancellors of the Exchequer tended to underestimate the costs of the conflict consistently. In April 1940, in the expectation of a war of stagnation, Sir John Simon presented his "Budget of Delusions," in which Britain's expenditure for 1940 was estimated at £2,667 millions, of which £2,000 millions were to be devoted to the war.

The idea that England could defeat Hitlerism by spending two-thirds of what the Nazis spent passed with the defeat of France.[7] Great Britain was then left alone to meet the financial burden of the war. After the formation of the Churchill Government in May 1940, the new Chancellor of the Exchequer, Sir Kingsley Wood, presented a second Budget in July 1940, which added another £800 millions to expenditure, raising war costs to £2,800 millions out of a total outlay of £3,467 millions. But by the end of the fiscal year 1940–41, actual expenditure amounted to £3,884 millions, of which about £3,200 millions were spent on the war.

The most notable aspect of these figures of expenditure is the relatively small proportion met from tax revenue, even after drastic increases in both direct and indirect taxation. The budgetary deficit for the fiscal year 1939–40 mounted from the £380 millions anticipated in February 1939 to £768 millions by the close of the year in April 1940. During the fiscal year ending March 31, 1941, the deficit reached the total of £2,475 millions, and during 1941–42, £2,702 millions. Revenue from taxes, which covered 87 percent of expenditure in 1938, furnished 36 percent of the Treasury's expenditure in 1940–41, 41 percent in 1941–42, and 50 percent in 1942–43.[7a]

The rising cost of the conflict to the British people can be more clearly illustrated perhaps by the following table, which shows the Government's *daily* expenditure and deficit during the war. The outlay on sup-

---

[6] On September 2, 1939, a Vote of Credit of £500 millions brought the estimated expenditure for 1939–40 to £1,933.3 millions, allowing for economies of £20 millions in the Civil Departments. Defense expenditure was to account for £1,249 millions of this. Actual outlay was £1,816.9 millions, which was £116.4 millions short of the estimate. This total does not include £4.2 millions outside the permanent debt charge.

[7] *The Economist* estimated that German war expenditure in 1940 was at the rate of about £3,000 millions *per annum*. May 4, 1940, p. 806.

[7a] When ordinary revenue reached a total of £2,819,850,783.

ply services, largely devoted to the war, rose from £3.9 millions a day in October 1939 to £11.8 millions in 1941 and £13.1 millions in 1942.

DAILY EXPENDITURES, REVENUES, AND DEFICITS [8]
(£ millions)

		Expenditure			
		Supply	Total	Revenue	Deficit
Oct.	1939	3.9	4.8	2.3	—2.5
Jan.	40	5.7	6.2	6.8	+ .6
Oct.	40	9.9	11.0	3.2	—7.8
Jan.	41	12.1	12.6	8.3	—4.3
Oct.	41	11.8	13.1	5.0	—8.0
Jan.	42	12.8	13.0	10.9	—2.1
Oct.	42	13.1	13.6	5.7	—7.9

The Treasury's increasing reliance on non-tax resources was exhausting Britain's holdings of foreign securities as well as driving the British economy into the disturbances of inflation. Since 1939 four budgets had been adopted, three of them wartime budgets, and all including heavy increases in tax schedules. The standard rate of income tax was raised from 5 shillings, 6 pence in 1938 to 8 shillings, 6 pence in July 1940. Surtaxes were sharply increased by about 25 percent, varying of course with the level of income, and estate duties were raised by 30 percent. Indirect taxes on beer, wines, alcoholic spirits, sugar, tobacco, matches, and entertainments were heavily increased. The tax on motor cars was raised from 15 shillings to 25 shillings per unit of horsepower. The charges for telephone, telegraph, and postal services were advanced in order that these state enterprises could contribute as tax collectors to the Treasury. In addition, two new taxes were introduced into the fiscal system: the Excess Profits Tax and the Purchase Tax.

Mr. Chamberlain had promised the House of Commons in the spring of 1939 that special steps would be taken to penalize profiteering resulting from the defense program. In June Sir John Simon introduced the Armaments Profit Duty, a 60 percent tax on the profits of armament firms holding defense contracts of over £200,000 in excess of profits earned by them in a standard period.[9] In the first emergency war budget of September 1939, the Armaments Profit Duty was succeeded by the Excess Profits Duty, which followed the same general principles,

---

[8] London and Cambridge Economic Service, *Bulletins.*

[9] This standard period was based on the more prosperous years 1935, 1936, and 1937, and the major objection made by business firms to the "depression standard" of the ill-fated National Defense Contribution profits tax of 1937 was thus avoided.

except that the new tax was levied on the profits of all firms. Although the rate was lifted to 100 percent after the formation of the Churchill Government, the yield in 1940 was only £96 millions.

The Excess Profits Duty was a revival of a tax employed in the First World War to divert the extraordinary profits of defense industries to the Treasury. But the Purchase Tax first announced in Sir John Simon's Financial Statement of April 1940 was an innovation in the British tax structure. This tax was levied not on retail sales, as is usually the case, but on wholesale transactions between a registered list of wholesalers and their retail dealers. As eventually modified by Sir Kingsley Wood, the Purchase Tax provided for a 33⅓ percent levy on luxury goods and a 16⅔ percent tax on more essential commodities. Food, drink, tobacco, and gasoline, which were already subject to heavy taxation, as well as children's clothing were exempt. As several months were required to compile a register of 40,000 traders and to overcome other administrative complexities, the tax did not become effective until the autumn of 1940. This accounts for its small yield of £26 millions during the year 1940–41. The yield for 1941–42, including £8 millions in arrears for the previous year, was £98 millions.

Even with the addition of these new duties and heavier rates for older taxes, the increased yield to the Treasury was dangerously inadequate. In the fiscal year 1940 the *increase* in government expenditures over 1938 was £2,816 millions, and the growth in tax revenue was scarcely one-sixth of this, or £476 millions. The return from the purchase tax could not be increased without imposing an inequitable burden on the consuming public and thereby raising the cost of living. Luxury taxes, if high, would so restrict consumption as to furnish little revenue, and if moderate, would fail to penalize non-essential industry. Excess Profits Duty could not be expected to produce more than £100 millions a year, unless price inflation multiplied industrial profits, and this the Government was anxious to avoid.

A fundamental shift in the British tax structure was required in order to provide a larger revenue and to avoid a continuing spiral of inflation. But this did not mean that the chief economic sacrifice could be borne by the rich alone. Even if all individual incomes above £2,000 a year had been confiscated by the Government, they would have amounted only to £60 millions a year. And, as J. M. Keynes demonstrated in his book *How to Pay for the War,* little more than £600 millions could be made available by the absorption of all individual income above £500 a year.[10]

The only substantial source of revenue would be a tax on the lower and middle income groups of the population, considerably increasing the contribution of the group with earnings of from £250 to £500 a year. It was to make some such sacrifice acceptable to this lower income group that Mr. Keynes devised his scheme for compulsory savings, or "deferred pay." Essentially, it was a plan by which increased taxation of small incomes in wartime would be compensated by postwar rebates to be financed from a capital levy. The Keynes savings plan was compulsory, but there was the prospect of future return. The virtues of the plan were that in wartime private consumption would be restricted and inflation thereby averted, while repayment in peacetime would stimulate purchasing power, thereby counteracting postwar deflation.

One other revenue proposal was frequently advocated, a tax on services. The expenditures of the English public on services of various kinds — transportation, lodging, domestic service — are largely neglected by the British tax structure. The Economist estimated that, after the exemption of essential professional services like medical treatment, a stiff turnover tax on services might yield about £150 millions a year.[11]

In the absence of any such fundamental revision of the tax structure, revenues were alarmingly insufficient.[12] In the two years of war finance from April 1939 to April 1941, the Government spent a total of £5,071 millions, of which only £2,458 millions were raised from taxation. This left a total deficit of £3,243 millions, 57 percent of the Government's outlay. The question immediately arises: how did the Treasury meet this enormous deficiency of revenue? The answer is that it did so by means of an increase in the National Debt, but that is only half the answer. It is not complete until we know two things: first, how did the Treasury conduct such gigantic borrowing operations; second, what were the available sources from which the funds were raised?

To answer the first question, a brief survey of the loan policy of the Treasury will suffice. It is apparent that the borrowing of £768 millions in 1939–40, and of £2,475 millions in 1940–41 called for a very different technique than was required for the smaller deficits of previous years. In the spring of 1939 Britain's economy was still suffering from the business recession of 1938, and any large issue of Defense Loan would have

---

[10] Keynes' income figures are, however, based on prewar rates of taxation.
[11] February 22, 1941, p. 235.
[12] See Chart I.

disturbed the investment market. In all probability the prices of gilt-edge securities would have fallen, and the rate of interest would have risen to the disadvantage of the Treasury.

It is generally admitted that as an economy approaches full employment the supply of savings increases, for company profits and the incomes of institutions are augmented in the larger national income. In addition, it must be emphasized that government expenditure financed from deficits ultimately creates the supply of savings to pay for itself. Payments made to contractors in time become wages, interest, and profits, and after percolating through the economy come to rest in the hands of persons or companies who do not spend their receipts immediately, who save. As these savings accumulate, the holders become anxious to invest them in profitable assets, and if no new investments are available, the funds will be shifted into gilt-edge securities. The prices of gilt-edge will rise, the rate of interest will fall, and an exceptionally favorable borrowing position will be created for the Exchequer. The Government can borrow funds in the form of long-term loans, which will be respent, resaved, and again lent to the Government.

Two conditions are essential to the success of such a plan. First, the Government must be able to meet preliminary expenditures until market conditions favor the issue of a public loan. This the Exchequer could do, by borrowing from the short-term money market through the issue of Treasury bills, while withholding public loans until savers were eager to invest in new government securities. The second essential condition was for the Exchequer to exercise control over the capital market, preventing opportunities for new investment and encouraging new savings to enter gilt-edge. When the banking system reached a position of high liquidity, new defense loans could be launched.

In April 1939 the amount of Treasury bills held by the public was about £150 millions below the level of previous years, and the banks were in need of additional short-term paper. The Treasury was in the fortunate position of being able to meet a large part of its deficit for 1939 at low interest by the sale of Treasury bills, which would in turn help to satisfy the appetite of the money market. By the end of the fiscal year 1939–40 the total amount of Treasury bills had risen to £1,427.7 millions, an increase of £535.3 millions over March 31, 1939.[18]

In November 1939 the Government sought to tap the savings of low

[18] The amount of Ways and Means Advances by public departments had increased by £33.6 millions from £27.9 millions on March 31, 1939 to £61.5 millions on March 31, 1940. The total Floating Debt was £1,489.2 millions on the latter date.

income groups by the issue of two small securities. One was a series of National Savings Certificates, carrying compound interest slightly in excess of 3 percent, offered in small lots at fifteen shillings each. The second was a 3 percent Defense Bond, purchasable in multiples of £5, with individual holdings limited to £1,000. But these were designed solely to interest the small investor, who was being urged by the National War Savings Campaign to lend to the Government, and produced only £122 millions in the fiscal year 1939.

Not until March 1940 did the Treasury consider gilt-edge prices sufficiently high for major long-term borrowing. Then a £300 millions issue of 3 percent War Loan, redeemable in nineteen and one-half years, was announced. This was oversubscribed, and was followed up on June 25, 1940, with the issue of 2½ percent National War Bonds (five to seven years) of unlimited amount. On January 2, 1941 a new issue of 3 percent Savings Bonds (1955–65) and a second series of 2½ percent National War Bonds were announced, followed in August 1941 by a third series of 2½ percent National War Bonds. Tax Reserve Certificates acceptable in payment of taxes due not less than two months nor more than two years from the date of purchase were issued in December 1941 at 1 percent interest. The amounts raised by these loans during the three financial years ending March 31, 1942, are shown in the following table.

GOVERNMENT WAR BORROWING, APRIL 1939–MARCH 1942[14]

(£ millions)

Increase in Long Term Debt	1939–40	1940–41	1941–42	1939–42
National Savings Certificates and 3% Defense Bonds	109	360	409	878
3% War Loan	98	202	3	303
2½% National War Bonds	...	592	724	1,316
3% Savings Bonds	...	89	577	666
3% National Defense Loan 1954–58 issued to National Debt Commissioners	...	75	45	120
Tax Reserve Certificates	...	...	192	192
Miscellaneous	2	36	9	47
Total	209	1,354	1,959	3,522
Increase in Floating Debt				
Treasury Bills	535	784	404	1,723
Ways and Means Advances	33	110	24	167
Treasury Deposits by banks	...	430	67	497
Total [14a]	568	1,324	495	2,387
Total Increase in Internal Debt	777	2,678	2,454	5,909

[14] Compiled from *The Economist*, annual national debt figures.

[14a] The total floating debt, to be distinguished from the total increase since 1939 given here, was £4,029,000,000 at the end of 1942.

Allowance must also be made for other borrowing operations of the Treasury such as the 1940 Conversion Loan and debt repayment to arrive at the net total of the actual deficit. The top limit of Defense Loans of £400 millions authorized in 1937 was raised to £800 millions in February 1939. In November 1939 the National Loans Bill permitted unlimited borrowing by the Treasury.

One of the most significant aspects of these figures is the abnormal dependence of the Treasury on short-term borrowing. Between March 31, 1939 and March 31, 1941 the Floating Debt increased by £1,896 millions to a total of £2,813.4 millions, and this expansion accounted for 55 percent of the Government's total borrowing during those two years. But nearly half of the additional Floating Debt in the hands of public funds and the exchange equalization fund, and nearly a fourth of the increase represented funds deposited by the banks with the Treasury, for which they received deposit receipts. This was a new development arising from the direct cooperation of the banking system with the Exchequer. Considering that nearly three-fourths of this expansion of the Floating Debt represented (1) Treasury bills in the hands of governmental agencies, (2) Ways and Means Advances by public departments, and (3) Treasury Deposit Receipts with the banks, the volume of bills " foisted on the banks " does not appear to have been excessive.

As a result of these combined long-term and short-term borrowing operations, Great Britain's gross National Debt stood at about £11,420 millions on March 31, 1941, and £14,070 millions on March 31, 1942. This was an increase of £6,369.6 millions above the postwar low point of March 31, 1935.

If the growing total of the debt was discouraging, there was some encouragement in the fact that the new loans were being raised at an average rate of interest of less than 2 percent, in contrast to the rate of 5 percent during World War I. This was due chiefly to the effective control of the capital market by the Treasury, the second essential condition of successful borrowing operations. All private investment not contributing directly to the war effort was in effect excluded.

In peacetime Treasury " influence " had been sufficient to insure the cooperation of investment houses, but after the outbreak of war formal machinery was set up. The existing Foreign Transactions Committee was called the Capital Issues Committee, and was asked to advise the Treasury on all applications for new investment issues. The Treasury's consent was required for all capital issues, with certain minor exceptions. Applications for foreign issues were required to show " urgent necessity and special circumstances," and proof was required that issues of domestic loans were " advisable in the national interest."

These regulations place the capital market at the service of the Treasury, and their effectiveness can be judged from the figures in the table below, which indicate that of £1,088.7 millions borrowed in 1940 only £17.9 millions were on private account. The expansion of plant required for increasing war production was financed almost entirely by the Government.

TOTAL BORROWING[15]
(INCLUDING "PERMISSION TO DEAL") NEW BASIS
(*Millions of pounds*)

Years	Govt.	Home Corpo- rations	Others	Total home	Empire	Foreign	Total issues
1936	60.2	82.1	306.1	448.4	33.8	1.2	493.9
1938	75.9	27.7	110.1	213.7	53.7	5.7	458.0
1939	36.8	12.1	66.2	115.1	25.5	2.2	142.8
1940	1070.8		16.6	1087.4	1.3		1088.7
1941	1497.5		8.0	1505.5	4.2	.1	1509.8
1942	1457.1		9.2	1466.3	.8	.1	1467.2

The second aspect of the problem, the origin of these borrowed funds, must now be considered. Apart from taxation, there are two general sources of revenue on which a government can draw — holdings of gold and foreign assets, and the gross savings of the nation.

It is evident that a government with command of the seas can convert its own gold reserves and the foreign securities or credits held by citizens of the nation into foreign exchange with which to pay for purchases abroad. But this conversion of capital assets is reflected in the items of the national debt. A private citizen receives cash or government bonds in return for the foreign securities he surrenders to the government. And in Great Britain when the exchange equalization fund sells its gold reserves to the Treasury it reinvests the proceeds of the sale in Treasury bills. British gold and foreign holdings at the beginning of the war could be expected, with favorable selling conditions, to produce at least a billion pounds of foreign exchange.[16]

But by far the more important source of funds to be diverted to gov-

[15] *The Economist,* January 6, 1940, p. 27; January 4, 1941, p. 16; January 3, 1942, p. 18; January 9, 1943, p. 52.

[16] For an analysis of British resources see Part III, Eric Roll, *Great Britain's Overseas Trade.*

ernment expenditure is represented by the gross savings of the nation. *Gross* savings may be defined for purposes of war finance as the part of the national income not spent in consumption. It comprises three elements: (1) replacement savings; (2) net new savings; (3) compulsory social savings. Replacement saving is the customary devotion of a part of current proceeds to the replacement of obsolete plant and the general maintenance of productive facilities. In a national crisis productive equipment may be allowed to deteriorate, and depreciation allowances can be diverted to the government. Net saving is the part of the annual national income normally available for investment in new business enterprise or new capital. By social savings are meant the surpluses of the health, old age, and unemployment insurance funds and other extra-budgetary funds, which are invariably invested in government obligations.

It was probable that in every year of full employment about £800 millions (on the basis of prewar prices) of gross savings would be available to take up Government loans. There are no official statistics to indicate prewar savings in prosperous years. Colin Clark estimates that in 1934 *net* savings were £461.4 millions.[17] This seems rather high for a year of moderate industrial activity, but it is likely that Britain's net savings from all sources would be between £450 and £500 millions in a year of high business activity.

To this £450 or £500 millions must be added another £400 millions of replacement savings. Not all replacement of course can be neglected even in time of war, but perhaps £300 millions of this could be diverted to government securities. The prewar savings of the extra-budgetary funds amounted, as mentioned above, to about £75 millions a year. This source might easily yield from £125 to £150 millions in wartime, as the result of decreased payments of unemployment insurance and the larger returns produced by a higher level of employment.

This brings the total real savings that might possibly be absorbed by government borrowing to between £700 and £900 millions.[18] This to-

---

[17] Colin Clark, *National Income and Outlay*, p. 190. J. M. Keynes, *op. cit.*, p. 22, considered £400 millions if anything, too low. In 1926 Mr. Coates told the Colwyn Committee that British net savings were about £500 millions a year, *Report of the Committee on National Debt and Taxation*, Cmd. 2800/1927, p. 17. *The Economist*, January 6, 1940, p. 22, gave total borrowing in 1936 as £493.9 millions. Investment issues are another expression of savings.

[18] Colin Clark, "The Determination of the Multiplier from National Income Statistics," *Economic Journal*, September 1939, estimates total investment, including depreciation allowances, at £760 millions for 1936 and £830 millions for 1937. *The Times*, February 22, 1939 gave larger figures for the same years: £877 millions and £893 millions.

tal could be considerably increased by sharp wartime reductions of personal consumption. Inflation, too, would increase the amount of savings as the money profits of industry were increased.

In April 1941 the Treasury published in a White Paper [19] an explanation of its financial operations during the first eighteen months of the war, and the practice of issuing an explanatory white paper when the budget is introduced now seems to be established. As the White Paper showed, government expenditure in the first twelve months of the war was £2,597 millions, and after the deduction of £1,148 millions tax revenue a deficit of £1,499 millions remained. This deficit was met in part by a draft on overseas assets of £542 millions, of which the prewar assets of the exchange equalization fund furnished £184 millions and overseas balances held in London and the sale of foreign securities the remaining £358 millions. This left a total of £907 millions to be financed from domestic resources out of gross savings, of which net savings (institutional and personal) produced £592 millions, replacement savings, £60 millions, and social savings (the extra-budgetary funds), £113 millions. Tax accruals accounted for £140 millions.

In the third six-month period of the war there was a striking increase of 60 percent in war expenditure, to an annual rate of £4,150 millions. Two significant and serious aspects of British deficit finance become apparent. The first is the rapid exhaustion of British overseas assets in the period after Dunkirk, and before the passage of the Lend-Lease Act. The draft on foreign resources in six months was £479 millions, of which £204 millions came from the Exchange Equalization Account. By March 1941 Britain had used up £1,021 millions of foreign assets, and the Treasury was scraping the bottom of its chest. By September 1, 1941, Britain's holdings of dollar assets had fallen to $1,527,-000,000.

Equally serious was the clear evidence of inflation in the figures for personal savings and draft on domestic capital assets, which had reached annual rates of £640 and £480 millions respectively. The voluntary savings campaign, in combination with rationing and price control of course increased the volume of personal savings, just as lack of men and materials for plant replacement increased replacement savings. But even allowing for these factors, it is unlikely that savings could have risen to such an extent without the inflationary creation of bank credit.

---

[19] *An Analysis of the Sources of War Finance* and *An Estimate of the National Income and Expenditure in 1939 and 1940.*

4. Wartime Inflation

There is no doubt that a proportion of British government borrowing has been financed by an expansion of bank credit. The inflationary technique of the last war has been used again. The table below clearly illustrates the extent to which the banking system has participated in the financing of the war.

CREATION OF CREDIT TO FINANCE DEFENSE EXPENDITURE[20]
(*nearest £ millions*)

	August 1939	August 1940	August 1941	August 1942	August 39–42
Bank Deposits	2,162	2,481	2,997	3,305	1,143
Treasury Deposits Receipts	...	26	469	634	634
Investments	570	682	935	1,082	512
Cash and Balances with Bank of England	224	273	316	351	127
Discounts	272	430	266	283	11
Loans and Advances	954	919	838	784	—170

The rise in bank deposits in the first year and a half of war indicates the extent to which bank credit was being expanded to help meet the budgetary deficits of the Government. Deducting a rough £20 millions to account for items in transit (bank checks, etc.), it can be stated safely that the creation of credit up to September 1940 amounted to at least £300 millions, and through February 1941, to £525 millions. The increase in Treasury deposits receipts and bank investments represents almost entirely funds placed at the disposal of the Treasury. But these increases do not reveal the full extent of the banks' support of armament finance. For the reduction in discounts and loans and advances was much less than would be expected from the curtailment of civil business and the drop in personal loans. A marked redistribution took place in loans and discounts, so that the bank credit extended to firms engaged on defense contracts and holders of Treasury bills was multiplied several times. Credit was being manufactured to pay for the war.

The effect of this additional credit was naturally to stimulate a rise in prices. Chart II on prices, wage rates, and bank deposits shows clearly the sharp rise in the cost-price structure after the outbreak of war, following a period of surprising stability in the years of rearmament. The volume of currency in circulation increased from £529,498,805 in Au-

---

[20] These figures are taken from the monthly averages given in *The Economist*. They apply only to the Clearing Banks, but the adjustments required to account for items in transit do not affect the general proportions.

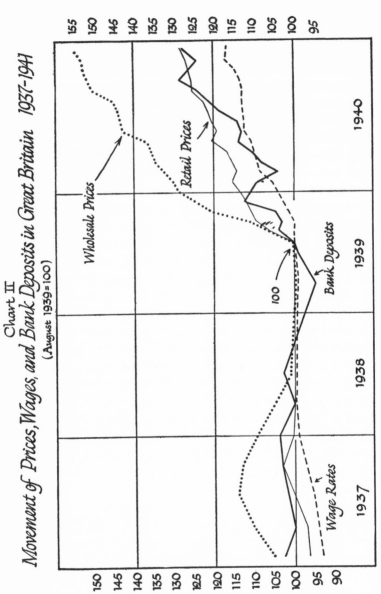

Chart II

Movement of Prices, Wages, and Bank Deposits in Great Britain 1937–1941

(August 1939 = 100)

Wholesale Prices, Board of Trade *General Index.* Wage Rates, London & Cambridge *Economic Service Index.*
Retail Prices, Ministry of Labour *Cost of Living Index.* Bank Deposits, *The Economist* Clearing Banks Monthly Averages.

gust 1939 to £667,257,551 in August 1941 and £830,016,655 in August 1942, or almost 60 percent in three years.

The first government borrowing for rearmament of £100 millions in 1937 may have been slightly deflationary in effect, as the budgetary deficit for the fiscal year was only £36 millions. But the effect of the deficit of £141 millions in 1938 was probably like that of a public works program. That the increase of defense expenditure through 1939 stimulated the exceedingly rapid recovery that characterized the months before the war is undeniable. In the spring of 1939 Britain's economy was approaching full employment, and there was imminent danger of inflation when war came.

After September 1939 the character of the British economy was divided. The armament industries showed the general symptoms of full employment, labor scarcity, rising wages, rising costs. Many non-essential fields of work, on the other hand, especially the luxury and white-collar trades, experienced falling demand with consequent unemployment and, in some cases, falling wages. But despite the existence of unemployment side by side with capacity output, the general movement of wages and of wholesale and retail prices was sharply upward. By February 1941, wholesale prices had risen 48.9 percent above those of August 1939, retail prices, 27.2 percent, and wage rates, 17.1 percent.[21]

These price increases can be divided roughly into two periods, from September 1939 through February 1940, and from then until the present. In the first period prices advanced rapidly; both wholesale and retail prices rose 10 percent in the first two months of the war. The causes of this were not primarily monetary. Since Britain imports most of her industrial raw materials, and the larger part of her food stuffs, the depreciation of the pound by 14 percent (from $4.68 to $4.03) at the beginning of the war, increased shipping charges, and higher cargo insurance premiums quickly affected the price level. This initial rise in living costs was followed by widespread wage increases, which in turn contributed to increased costs of production.[22] But the effect of these initial economic forces was largely exhausted by February 1940.

The continued, if slower, price spiral from the spring of 1940 on was largely due to the Government's financial policy, or lack of policy. Neither the Chamberlain nor the Churchill Governments had any compre-

---

[21] Subsidies paid by the Treasury to stabilize the retail prices of certain foods are estimated at more than £58 millions for 1940–41.

[22] The wage rates of many trade unions were linked to the Ministry of Labor's Cost of Living Index, so that wages and retail prices rose together.

hensive price-wage policy, and both encountered strong trade union opposition to the suggestion that wages be controlled. Excess Profits Tax of 100 percent and cost-plus contracts deprived plant managers of incentive to keep costs down, and wage demands were readily granted. In the armament industries workers' earnings increased twice as much as the rise in actual wage rates through the payment of overtime and bonuses.[23]

This increased income was not withdrawn from consumption through taxation or borrowing by the Government. Instead, the creation of bank credit to cover government expenditures added to the volume of consumer income competing for a reduced amount of goods. The rise in the price level through February 1941 was between 25 percent and 30 percent, and at least a third of this was the direct result of the use of bank credit to finance government deficits. If further maladjustment was to be avoided, heavier taxation, compulsory savings, extensive rationing, and more stable wage rates were essential.

The first two requirements were met in the Budget of April 1941, in which government expenditure for the fiscal year 1941–42 was estimated at £4,206.7 millions. Income tax was raised from 8 shillings, 6 pence a pound to 10 shillings. A system of compulsory savings ("deferred pay") was introduced; exemption allowances for income tax were lowered, and the additional income tax paid was to be credited to the taxpayer in the Post Office Savings Bank, to be repaid as savings after the war.[24] These two revisions of the income tax were expected to produce an additional £250 millions in a full year.

In June 1941 rationing was extended to all clothing. In July the Government expressed in a White Paper its opposition in principle to further wage increases. Sir Kingsley Wood had announced in his 1941 Budget speech that the Treasury intended to subsidize retail prices in order to hold the Cost of Living Index at 25 per cent or 30 percent above the prewar level, and it was hoped that this would offset claims for wage increases to protect the standard of living of the workers.

As a result of these measures the tempo of inflation was definitely retarded by the middle of 1941. There was evidence that the public was holding large sums of money idle and that the velocity of circulation of

---

[23] Between October 1938 and July 1940 earnings in the vehicle and aircraft industries increased by 58 percent, in the shipbuilding industry, by 51 percent, in the engineering trades, by 40 percent, London and Cambridge Economic Service's *Report on Current Economic Conditions, Memorandum No. 85,* February, 1941, p. 9.

[24] The provisions of the Excess Profits Tax were modified at the same time to permit one-fifth of the duty's being returned to the taxpayer as savings after the war.

money was falling. From June 1941 to September 1942 wholesale commodity prices rose only 5 percent, retail prices, 1 percent, and wage rates 9.5 percent.

In conclusion, it is necessary to evaluate British financial policy since 1936 on the basis of the three principles of defense stated in the beginning. First, it is evident that the British Treasury was able to provide funds with which to pay for armaments, but at the cost of exhausting Britain's assets of gold and foreign securities, and by the considerable creation of credit.

Secondly, British financial policy can be criticized for not having assisted, especially in the prewar period, in the shifting of the economy from civil to armament production. The facilities of the automotive industry should have been diverted to the aero-engine and aircraft industries, and the tax power could have been used to this end. The horsepower tax of 1939 did not serve this purpose; it penalized the use of cars and not their production. The Purchase Tax, with its high rates of $33\frac{1}{3}$ percent on luxuries, may have freed some economic resources for wartime uses, but it was too unselective to be of specific assistance. Moreover, it did not become effective until a year after the outbreak of war.

But the most important criticism of the Treasury must be for its failure to preserve the greatest possible economic stability in the country, the third objective of war finance. Chancellors of the Exchequer moralized repeatedly on the evils of inflation, but for the first year and a half of war the sacrifices necessary to avoid inflation were not imposed on the public in the form of taxation or compulsory loans. There are good reasons for not increasing taxes in a period of recession, like the first part of 1939, or in the middle of the fiscal year, when the war began, but by April 1940 the British public were willing to make heavier sacrifices than they were asked to bear. Since the costs of the war were constantly underestimated, tax revenues that were inadequate for estimated expenditure were disastrously so for actual expenditure. The Treasury's deliberate policy of indecision did not provide for the withdrawal of sufficient income from civilian consumption to prevent inflation. The British people, and especially the low income group, were forced to bear the burden of a greater rise in prices than the increase of non-monetary costs necessitated. The adoption of compulsory savings in 1941 marked what was in fact the first War Budget.

PART TWO

THE PROBLEM OF LABOR SUPPLY

by William S. McCauley

One of the major omissions of the Chamberlain Government was its failure to meet the problem of labor supply in a war economy. At the end of the First World War, approximately five million persons were engaged in the production of war materials for the armed forces. With the greater mechanization of modern armies and the growing complexity of industrial production, it was apparent by 1939 that eight million persons would be required in British war industry if Britain were to emerge victorious from the present war.

The transfer of such an enormous number from peacetime employment, or unemployment, to essential war work called for a great effort of national planning on the part of Britain's industry and labor under the leadership of the Government. Yet throughout the years of rearmament and war from 1936 into 1940, the National Government refused to assume the responsibility for creating and training the requisite labor supply and for distributing it in the armament industries as needed. As a result Britain experienced the phenomena of intense labor scarcity in key armament industries side by side with a number of unemployed exceeding one and one-half million. More than any other one factor, the shortage of skilled workers in vital armament industries impeded Britain's efforts to rearm.

1. The Years of Rearmament before the War

First of all we must examine the condition of the British labor market during the years of rearmament from mid-1936 to August 1939. During this period there was a chronic shortage of certain specialized types of

skilled labor. Private contractors engaged on armament work for the
Government reported their inability to secure sufficient welders, electricians, mechanics, lathe-turners, fitters, grinders, machine-setters, naval
and aircraft draftsmen, machine-tool craftsmen, and technicians for scientific and optical instruments.

A shortage of aircraft workers was the major bottleneck restricting
the expansion of the R.A.F. The 1939 Estimates of the Air Ministry
called for an expenditure on aircraft and engines of nearly £56,000,000
more than in 1938. But in August 1939, there were only 15,500 persons
listed as unemployed in the three fields of motor vehicles, cycles, and
aircraft, and their combined output — assuming they might all find
jobs — was estimated to be less than £11,000,000, only one-fifth of what
was required.[25]

Unprecedented demands for skilled craftsmen were made by the
armed forces as well as by civil industry. It is a characteristic of modern
defense forces that a large proportion of the men enlisted must have
some training as mechanics, welders, draftsmen, engineers, and electricians. The authorized strength of the British Army, Navy, and Air
Force increased more than 386,000 men between March 1935 and July
1939, and a large number of these (no statistics are available) were
skilled workers drawn from the civilian labor market.

Of course, the greatest demand for skilled labor came from civil industry, and during the four prewar years from 1935 to 1939 there was
a notable expansion in the total employment of the heavy industries
most affected by rearmament. In all fields related to the production of
armaments, the number of workers employed increased by 769,440 between July 1935 and July 1940. As would be expected, employment in
the aircraft industry showed the most sensational expansion, a growth
of 360 percent. Employment in explosives manufacture increased by
114 percent; in metal manufacture (including iron and steel), by 50
percent; in the manufacture of scientific instruments, by 38 percent; and
in the engineering industry, by 28 percent. There are no statistics available to show the increase in employment for defense work, but aside
from the aircraft industry, the larger part, probably two-thirds, of this
expansion was for civilian production.

During the first two years of rearmament, in 1936 and 1937, the

---

25 The 1935 Census of Production placed the gross output per worker in the motor vehicles,
cycles, and aircraft industries at £612 per year. Accounting for price increases, by 1939 this might
have been raised to £700 a year. *The Economist*, May 6, 1939, p. 297.

British economy was rising to new peaks of prosperity, and the requirements of civil industry were competing with defense work. The business recession, initiated in the fall of 1937, lasted through 1938 and
undoubtedly set free some trained workers in the engineering and automobile industries for employment in expanding defense work, somewhat relieving the scarcity of labor. But in the prewar months of 1939,
the situation in the labor market became serious again. The Government's prospective deficit of £511 millions in the financial year 1939-40
represented a total expenditure requiring the direct and indirect employment of 1,900,000 additional workers. Yet the total number of unemployed in April 1939 was only about 1,700,000. The establishment of
priority for defense work and the allocation of labor to the most urgent
production were essential if rearmament was not to be impeded.

Such measures, however, were not adopted. Both trade union leaders and politicians continued to explain away the fact of a labor shortage by referring to the large volume of unemployment in Britain. It is
true that throughout the 1930's the number of unemployed ranged from
one and one-half million to two million workers. But to assume that the
registered unemployed represented a reservoir of " labor " that could
be drawn upon to satisfy the needs of rearmament was to accept a statistical mirage for reality.

The Ministry of Labor's Register of Unemployed Persons is deceptive
for three reasons. In the first place it gives only a formal number of persons who may be out of jobs, but not in any real sense available for work.
In a normal month there are about 700,000 persons who are only passing between jobs, who are too old and infirm to work, or who have
had no working experience whatever. These people should be considered as unemployables instead of as available unemployed. If this 700,000
is deducted from the total of about 1,500,000 unemployed in the month
of May, 1939, less than 800,000 remains.

There is a second reason why even this residual figure brought little
comfort to defense contractors in search of employees, for the largest
part of Britain's unemployed were occupationally maladjusted for
armament work. In August 1939 there were nearly 450,000 unemployed
in the textile, coal mining, shipbuilding, and building and construction
industries, while at the same time there were only 58,000 workless in the
major armament and engineering trades. In Britain it is generally assumed that the point of effective full employment is reached when the
percentage of unemployment in an industry falls to 5 percent, for a

moderate labor reserve is necessary for employers' requirements to be met readily. Yet by August 1939, and in some cases throughout the years of rearmament, the percentage of unemployment in war industries was noticeably below 5 percent, while other industries had surpluses of 10 percent to 17 percent. Loom tenders, coal miners, and brick layers were not adaptable to work as aircraft fitters, engine mechanics, and draftsmen.

There was a third element of deception in the Ministry of Labor's figures, for even the small reserves of labor in the war industries were so maldistributed regionally as to be largely unavailable for defense work. The heaviest demands for armament workers were in the Midlands and the southern regions of Great Britain, and these were the sections of greatest labor scarcity with unemployment of 5 percent or less. The large surplus of idle workers was to be found in the depressed areas with declining export industries, in Wales, Scotland, Northern Ireland, and the north of England, where unemployment ranged from 11 percent to 19 percent. Within particular armament industries reserves of labor were as badly dispersed. In July 1939, *The Economist* found that for one prosperous armament industry unemployment in one administrative area was only 2 percent, while in a neighboring area it was 22.7 percent.[26]

Armchair economists forget when speaking of " full employment " that there is no such thing as demand for or supply of labor in general. Instead, there are demands for *specific* types of workers at particular points of employment. To utilize the hidden reserves of untrained or maldistributed labor, the British Government would have had to adopt a comprehensive man power program.

Such a program would have recognized that in modern war industrial man power is of equal importance with military man power, that the fighting forces are only the cutting edge of a highly synchronized industrial machine. First of all, the Government would have had to draft a plan of the future requirements in man power of both the armed forces and the defense industries. On the basis of such a program the Government should have arranged for cooperation between trade unions and employers to insure that adequate numbers of workmen would be available where needed. This would have entailed measures to absorb the unemployed in war work by intensified sub-contracting, the enlargement of the existing labor force by the admission of unskilled

---

[26] " Tapping Labour Resources," *The Economist,* July 22, 1939.

workers and unemployed women, an adequate training program to equip new workers for the simpler processes of war production, and a schedule of priorities for the use of labor where civilian employment was competitive with defense work.

These were the essential ingredients of a labor policy, but at no time in the years of rearmament from 1936 to 1939 did the British Government appear to recognize them. In the first place, the National Government rejected responsibility for the supply of labor required by the defense program. The Prime Minister said in March 1936, " As the defense scheme comes into being . . . problems will certainly arise with regard to the supply of the particular kinds of skilled labor which will be required . . . I regard these as essentially problems which should be faced and settled by the industries themselves." [27] This " hands off " attitude persisted through the first few months of the war.

The Government might plead that discussion between organized labor and organized management was the traditional method of settling internal questions in British industry, but as a result of the Government's refusal to accept full responsibility for the supply of labor, its meager efforts to transfer, dilute, and train workers were disastrously inadequate. We have seen that there were small surpluses of unemployed workers who might have been transferred to areas where labor was scarce. It is astonishing that the Ministry of Labor never made a survey of the registered unemployed to find what numbers might be experienced and available for armament work. Neither did the Government seek to overcome the natural immobility of labor by compensating workers for the cost of moving from one region to another.

Reliance was placed solely on the existing machinery of the Ministry of Labor's Employment Department with its 1,626 employment exchanges and offices scattered throughout the country. All unemployed persons registered at the exchanges, and employers reported all vacancies to them. This machinery had proved invaluable in the last war and could have played an important role in preparation for this one. But in the postwar years many employers had become prejudiced against the efficiency of the exchanges and preferred to find their own labor, while many exchanges found the payment of the dole their only function. Although the Ministry of Labor gave information on the availability of labor when requested, the employment exchanges were not fully

---

[27] 309 H. C. Deb. 5 s., col. 1840.

utilized, nor did they help to coordinate the letting of contracts by the service departments. Only about 30 percent of job vacancies were filled through the ministry's employment offices.

The Labor Department did provide allowances for the transfer each year of about 18,000–20,000 unemployed men from the distressed regions. Nothing was done, however, to expand this program to meet the specific needs of defense industry and the number of men so transferred actually decreased in 1938. The Government made some efforts, not conspicuously successful, to encourage the construction of munition plants in the depressed areas and to extend subcontracting. A number of Royal Ordnance Factories were built in the depressed regions, but the defense services did not exert sufficient pressure on private contractors to disperse their plants.

If the Government's efforts to facilitate the transfer of unemployed were ineffective, the measures taken for the dilution of labor by the admission of the unskilled were even more so. Conferences in April 1938 between the leaders of industry, labor, and the Government called for a " speed up " of armament production, and this was in effect a request for the engineering unions to dilute their ranks with unskilled workers. The two principal trade unions concerned in armament manufacture, the Confederation of Shipbuilding and Engineering Trades, and the Amalgamated Engineering Union insisted that the sacrifice of union standards implied by dilution should be accompanied by a Government pledge to restore the prevailing conditions at the expiration of the emergency. The unions pointed, in addition, to the regional reserves of unemployed engineers and shipbuilders and questioned the urgency of dilution at a time when unemployment was growing during the 1938 recession. The Chamberlain Government made no effort to meet these requests by the unions. No guarantee of the eventual restoration of union standards was given, and no steps were taken to absorb the surplus unemployed. Consequently, the trade unions refused the Government's request for dilution.

The unions' stubborn refusal to accept dilution may be condemned in the light of events. Nevertheless, the major responsibility must rest on the Ministry of Labor for failing to prepare a program to put the unemployed engineers to work and to guarantee the restoration of suspended trade union practices. Such a pledge of restoration was given by the Government in the Treasury Agreement of 1915 to secure the unions' consent to dilution in the First World War.

Among the unemployed there were thousands of workers who had little prospect of regular employment and with some training in the basic skills might have been rehabilitated for the armament industry. This would have required a scheme of labor training, both in government schools and in the factories; but the Government's training program was as timid as its action with regard to dilution. This was another case in which the Ministry of Labor had facilities at hand that might have been utilized to speed the rearmament program. In 1935 the Labor Ministry had established a few training centers in the depressed areas to rehabilitate the unemployed for work in some trade. Six-month courses were given in the basic elements of such crafts as plumbing, metal work, and draftsmanship. But throughout the years of rearmament this training was continued only as a minor social service for the submarginal worker. In 1939 the total capacity of the Ministry's fourteen training centers was only 8,739 persons. During the entire year of 1938 less than 14,000 men completed courses, and only a portion of these were trained for work related to defense industry.

Neither did the Ministry of Labor take steps to develop a program to train apprentices in the factories. Each employer was left to meet his own needs although individual employers, not knowing the future scope of the Government's program, could not foresee the labor needs of industry as a whole, and business men were naturally reluctant to divert their limited supplies of machines and craftsmen to the task of instructing apprentices who when trained might find work elsewhere. The development of a training program in the factories and training centers was a task for the Government, and this task, during the years of rearmament, was not undertaken.

Neither did the Government establish a system of labor priorities whereby skilled workers engaged in civilian work might have been shifted to more important defense work. The chief limitation on the expansion of the aircraft industry was the scarcity of trained workers, but even here, where priority was most urgent, the Government refused to call in engineering labor engaged on other work. The Air Ministry explained this inaction by stating in 1937 that:

> If you were to pick skilled men from other engineering industries, and draft them into the aircraft industry, it would cause a tremendous dislocation in the general engineering industry.[28]

---

[28] 321 H. C. Deb. 5 s., cols. 1774–5.

The policy of "business as usual" was never better stated. It over-looked the fact that in defense economics the shortage of available re-sources necessitates some planned readjustment of civilian production unless the defense program itself is to suffer from maladjustment.

2. The War — Phase I

With the outbreak of war in September 1939 positive action on the part of the Government was more urgent, for the dimensions of the labor problem were more vast. The general objective of British wartime labor policy, easily stated, but difficult of attainment, was to increase produc-tion with about one-half the number of *men* employed in peacetime. First of all, perhaps 5,000,000 men must be withdrawn from industry for the three fighting services, the merchant marine, and civil defense. Sec-ond, given the greater technical requirements of mechanized forces, it was probable that before victory could be won at least 10,000,000 persons must be employed in the armament industries, compared to the 5,000,-000 so engaged in the last war.[29] Third, Britain's export trade had to be maintained and, if possible, augmented in order to obtain the foreign exchange with which to pay for essential imports. Hence this gigantic transfer of 15,000,000 people to war purposes had to be made largely at the expense of Great Britain's domestic standard of living without im-pairing the health of the population as a whole.

To replace men drawn into the armed forces and to provide the labor required by expanding war industries, millions of idle persons had to be brought into active employment. There were three chief sources of man power to be drawn upon, (1) the unemployed, (2) nonworking women, and (3) white-collar employees engaged in the nonessential service trades. As for the unemployed, it was conceivable that a training and transfer program might cut the total number of workless persons from the 1,500,000 of October 1939 to about 500,000. The large number of nonworking women, however, represented the greatest single re-source of new labor. It was estimated that in Britain there were from three to four million unoccupied women (widows, wives, etc.) who might be brought into industry and the professions, to release men for fighting service or the more strenuous types of war work. In the First World War over 1,660,000 women found employment and at least twice

---

[29] *The Economist,* February 3, 1940, p. 189.

as many would probably be called into war work in this conflict. Finally, in the white-collar services there were at least 10,000,000 persons, about half the employed population of Britain, and from 2,000,000 to 4,000,000 of them could be shifted into war work by the restriction of their opportunities for civil employment.

These three sources together could provide the eight to ten million additional armament workers who would be needed in British industry by the end of the war. Of course, the transfer of such a large number of persons would take years, but the program could be carried out in phases, with perhaps two million people a year being brought into war production.

Unfortunately, for the first eight months of the war the Chamberlain Cabinet failed to formulate any program for the distribution of man power between the fighting front and the home front in such a way as to create the strongest possible army with the greatest possible equipment. With the exception of the calling-up of men for the armed forces, which was systematically carried out, the Government's efforts (1) to stabilize the labor market, (2) to expand the labor force by dilution, (3) to transfer and (4) to train workers, were insufficient in scope and ineffective in execution. Its one creditable performance was the mobilization of military man power. Immediately on the declaration of war on September 3, 1939, the National Service (Armed Forces) Act, 1939, was enacted. This superseded the Military Training Act of May to 1939, by which conscription had been introduced, and extended liability for compulsory military service to all men between 18 and 41 years of age. The calling-up proceeded smoothly, and by May 9, 1940, approximately 4,500,000 men had been asked by the Ministry of Labor and National Service to register, and 1,500,000 of them had joined the Army.

Early in 1939 the Schedule of Reserved Occupations had been established to prevent the enlistment in the Regular Army of trained workers required in war industries, and in this it was partially successful. But the actual mobilization of industrial man power, on the other hand, was neglected. One of the most crucial requirements of British industry was for some stability in the labor market, which had become increasingly chaotic since early in 1939. The scarcity of engineering labor and the efforts of the defense services to speed output by offering cost-plus contracts encouraged employers to offer attractions to the skilled craftsmen of other contractors. Labor scouts were sent out; a system of auctioning trained workers between different firms developed. Workers in the machine tool industry, the pivotal defense industry and one long suffering from labor shortages, left their jobs to accept better paid work in aircraft factories.

To prevent competitive bidding, Parliament had passed the *Control of Employment Act* in September 1939. This statute empowered the Minister of Labor to issue special orders prohibiting employers from advertising for workers or hiring (and rehiring) them without the consent of the Ministry of Labor. For all practical purposes, however, the Control of Employment Act remained a dead letter. Since it was an enabling act, it became effective only when special orders applying its provisions to particular occupations were issued by the Minister of Labor, and during the first seven months of the war, despite the increase of labor turnover, Ernest Brown issued no orders. Then the first *Control of Employment (Advertisement) Order* in April 1940 was applied to the building and contracting industries.

Six days before the outbreak of war, on August 28, 1939, the Amalgamated Engineering Union reached an agreement with the Engineering Allied Employers' National Federation permitting the entrance of less skilled male labor into the engineering and aircraft industries. This agreement, however, did not permit large-scale dilution, for the admission of new workers was hedged with numerous restrictions protecting local union privileges. Local committees composed of trade union and employer representatives were established to approve applications for additional labor. A national joint committee was established to adjust the differences in case of disagreement by these local committees. In addition, provision was made for the return to "normal" union practices after the emergency, and a record was to be kept of all modifications of union standards.

Seven months of war elapsed before the Ministry of Labor decided in March 1940 to take a partial census of the number of workers employed in the three major armament industries of (1) engineering, (2) motor vehicles and aircraft, and (3) shipbuilding and repairing.[30] To frame a major transfer program, the Government should have known not only the number of persons already employed in the war trades, but,

---

[30] All employers in these fields were asked to make returns to the Ministry of Labor by April 10, 1940 (and henceforth quarterly) of the number of persons engaged on work for the Government and the export and domestic markets and of the relative number of skilled and unskilled men, women, and juveniles employed. *Ministry of Labour Gazette*, April 1940, p. 105. The data received was not made public.

chiefly, the number employed in other industries who might be shifted into war work.[31]

In spite of the Minister of Labor's announced intention to intensify the labor training program, there were only 7,000 men enrolled in the government training centers in April 1940, and they were pursuing five-to six-month courses. At this rate the training centers could turn out 15,000 semi-skilled workers a year. For the inadequacy of the British program to be appreciated, it should be compared with the labor training program in Nazi Germany, where 16,000 instructors in 200 training camps of the Labor Front were prepared to train over 1,000,000 workers a year for German industry.

Given the Chamberlain Government's failure to enlarge appreciably the supply of munition workers by dilution, transfer, and training, British industry had to work longer and harder for armament output to be speeded up. In Britain there is no general Wage-Hour Act limiting the hours of employment for all workers. Instead, agreements between trade unions and employers customarily limit weekly working hours for men to from 44 to 48 hours a week, depending on the trade. Only for women and juveniles are maximum working hours set by law, at 48 and 44 hours respectively. During the rearmament years, and especially after the beginning of the war, the engineering, shipbuilding, and construction trade unions frequently agreed to considerable overtime. The statutory restrictions on the employment of women and young people engaged on defense contracts were likewise relaxed by the Home Office [32] after the war broke out. At first the supply departments authorized their contractors to work up to sixty hours a week. Subsequently, all munition factories desiring to employ women overtime were required to gain the permission of the factory inspectors, and this permission was readily given.

It was estimated that in December 1939 overtime in the engineering

---

[31] It is true that on September 5, 1939, the National Registration Act was enacted which provided that the entire population of the United Kingdom must be enrolled on the National Register. The purpose of the law however was not principally to procure man power information but to provide the Government with population statistics (to supplement the 1931 census) in order to facilitate the administration of conscription, evacuation, and wartime insurance.

Plans were made before the war for a Central Register of " scientific, technical, professional, and higher administrative personnel," and a Supplementary Register was established in December 1939 for persons in the same general categories whose careers had been interrupted by the war, and who were not qualified for the Central Register. The Central and Supplementary Registers were merged in March 1942 in an Appointments Department of the Ministry of Labor.

[32] The Factory Acts were administered by the Home Office until June 1940, when the factory inspectorate was transferred to the Ministry of Labor.

industry averaged twelve hours a week for the country as a whole, and was as high as thirty hours a week in some factories. This general resort to overtime was bound to increase costs as well as to react unfavorably on the health of British workers and on the productivity per head of British industry. But in the absence of a much larger number of workers to divide the total work effort there was no prospect of reduced working hours. Instead, the disastrous days of Dunkirk directly ahead were to call for greater sacrifices and still longer hours.

One scheme devised by the Ministry of Labor deserves special comment, for it indicates the fruitful achievements that were possible when the Government formulated a positive plan and called upon industry and labor for full cooperation. This was the organization of mobile squads of stevedores to be shunted from one port to another to overcome the congestion of dock facilities resulting from the diversion of British shipping. Joint committees of employers' and dock workers' representatives were set up in every port. The Transport and General Workers' Union compiled lists of dockers willing to be transferred to other ports upon notification from these committees that additional labor was needed. These volunteers were guaranteed a traveling and a living allowance and a minimum daily wage for a limited time by the Ministry of Labor.

Information for an exact appraisal of the Chamberlain Government's labor policy in the first eight months of war is not available, for statistics of actual employment in British industries were no longer published after the outbreak of war. Figures of unemployment are, however, available, and some conclusions can be drawn on this basis. The number of unemployed in Great Britain and Northern Ireland in August 1939 was 1,295,000. The dislocation of foreign and domestic markets by the blockade, evacuation, and the blackout created some additional unemployment after the outbreak of war. But after eight months of war there were only 254,000 fewer unemployed than in August 1939. Even this reduction of unemployment was chiefly accounted for not by the armament industries, but by coal mining, textile manufacture, building and contracting, clothing manufacture, and transport. When allowance is made for the men called to military service after June 1939, total employment is found to have decreased by about 1,050,000 between June 1939 and April 1940.[33]

---

[33] This represents a net decrease in the productivity of the British economy of from 5½ to 8½ percent. Since many men called to the colors were not engaged in registered occupations, the actual reduction of industrial employment may have been as low as 5%.

It is apparent that the labor policies of the Chamberlain Government were disastrously inadequate to the needs of industry in total war. Demand for armament workers was concentrated in the Midlands and the north of England. There was at no time any sufficient program for the transfer of unemployed workers or workers employed in nonessential trades to the six key industries of engineering, vehicle and aircraft manufacture, metal manufacture, other metal industries, chemical manufacture, and shipbuilding. At no time in the first phase of the war did the British economy approach the full employment of its resources of labor. Trade union disputes persisted, and wages were allowed to rise as rapidly as the unions could push them up, thereby stimulating the upward spiral of costs and prices.

3. The War — Phase II

With the formation of the Churchill Cabinet in May 1940, Ernest Bevin, former secretary of the Transport and General Workers Union, and one of Britain's outstanding labor leaders, was appointed Minister of Labor. It is to his credit that the Ministry of Labor was converted from an impassive registry of economic statistics to a true ministry of labor supply. The new Minister had more to do than to repair the omissions of his predecessor, for the task of British industry was enormously enlarged by the defeat of France. A more efficient distribution of man power between military and industrial requirements was urgent. The Army was to be expanded by 1,500,000 men, and the manufacture of armaments was expected to absorb another 1,000,000 within a year. The (second) Emergency Powers Act of May 1940 [34] conferred new powers over property and services on the Government, and the Minister of Labor sought in a series of decrees issued under the Act to increase the output of the existing labor force, to stabilize the chaotic labor market, and to bring new workers into the armament factories.

The Chamberlain Government's use of the Control of Employment Act, 1939, had been negative; it restricted the future engagement of workers by employers. But Regulation 58A under the Emergency Powers Act of May 1940 empowered the Minister of Labor " to direct any person in the United Kingdom to perform such services . . . as may be specified." [35] This gave Ernest Bevin practically unlimited powers.

[34] See Appendix I.
[35] *Ministry of Labour Gazette,* June 1940, p. 156.

During the remaining months of 1940, however, the Government was reluctant to take recourse to these powers; Mr. Bevin was opposed to any form of industrial conscription for British workers. As a result many essential measures depending on compulsion were long delayed, especially the transfer of workers from other industries to war work.

There was no doubt good reason for this reluctance " to make a nation of industrial slaves." Before large sections of British workers could be transferred out of civil industry, it was necessary to devise adequate machinery to administer the task.

As a first step in administrative reorganization, a joint consultative committee, composed of fourteen members, labor and industry each having seven representatives, was appointed to discuss with the department such problems as the regulation of wages, the postponement of holidays, the prohibition of strikes, and arrangements for the health and welfare of the workers.[36] Next Mr. Bevin established under his own chairmanship an advisory Labor Supply Board consisting of four newly appointed Directors of Labor Supply, two chosen from industry and two from the trade unions.

The regional organization of labor supply was based on the existing employment exchanges, which act for all purposes directly under the authority of the eleven Divisional Controllers who are the principal representatives of the Ministry of Labor in their regions. A staff of several hundred labor supply inspectors reported to twenty-seven labor supply committees, composed of officials of the ministry, which were set up in the engineering centers. Advisory panels in particular industries, such as iron and steel and shipbuilding, were associated with the committees. The labor supply inspectors were empowered to enter any plant to investigate requests for additional workers, to supervise training facilities, and to ensure the most advantageous use of skilled labor. These first labor supply committees gave way a year later to forty-four Man Power Boards, which are also official in their composition, and which combine responsibility for recruitment for the armed forces and the provision of labor for essential work.

For the immediate future output could be increased only by calling on the existing force of workers to increase their total effort. In the

---

[36] It was in effect a smaller and more workable subcommittee drawn from the membership of the National Joint Advisory Council of thirty representatives. This Joint Council was appointed in October, 1939, by the Chamberlain Government, after consulting the British Employers Federation and the General Council of the Trades Union Congress. *Ministry of Labour Gazette*, August, 1940, page 203.

disastrous days of Flanders and Dunkirk England's survival was at stake, and on May 22, 1940, Herbert Morrison, the Minister of Supply, ordered all Royal Ordnance Factories and private firms engaged on defense contracts to work twenty-four hours a day seven days a week. All holidays, both public and personal, were cancelled or ordered postponed for the period of the crisis. In the armament, engineering, shipbuilding, and munitions industries labor responded to this appeal and worked twelve-hour shifts, seventy to eighty-four hours a week without interruptions.

After two months of such strenuous effort, however, there was growing evidence that British workers were suffering from nervous and physical strain. Absenteeism was common. Employees arrived late; women workers especially suffered from illness and fatigue. In late July the Ministry of Labor issued a bulletin, setting forth certain general principles which should govern overtime employment. There it was stated that maximum war production must be maintained and in fact increased, but that the strain on workers of the seventy-eighty-hour week " must be relieved by an immediate reduction of hours." [37] Although a shortage of available labor might prevent a shortening of the work week to the optimum hours, which experience indicated to be in the region of fifty-six hours a week, it was none the less urgent to limit working hours to an average of sixty hours a week until the training of additional labor would permit a further reduction. Furthermore, the Ministry of Labor intended to enforce again after August 1 the limitations on hours of women and young persons, as provided in the Factory Acts.

The shortage of labor in British armament industries prevented the general adoption of these recommendations. In the absence of compulsory rulings applying to any industry as a whole, which the Ministry of Labor refused to make, individual employers found it difficult to reduce hours. The supply departments were urging contractors to speed deliveries and were offering payment on a cost-plus basis. Moreover, workers were anxious to obtain high overtime wage rates, and if one employer restricted overtime, workers would drift away to more lucrative jobs. Consequently, long hours and Sunday work persisted in many defense industries throughout 1940 and 1941. In May 1941 labor fatigue and truancy were still disturbing factors in the armament industries. Re-

---

[37] Hours of Work and Maximum Output, July 25, 1940, Ministry of Labor and National Service, pp. 2–3.

medial measures were left to the officers of the Factory and Welfare Department established in the summer of 1940 to supervise the welfare of workers outside as well as within the factories.

It was sought to increase the output of industry by eliminating the loss of work days due to strikes as well as lengthening the working week. During the first phase of the war strikes had continued at about their prewar rate, 70 to 90 a month. Although many of these disputes occurred in the aircraft and engineering trades, none was sufficiently serious for the Chamberlain Government to risk alienating the uncertain support of the trade unions by prohibiting strikes. But Mr. Bevin could walk where his predecessor had feared to tread. In June the Consultative Committee, on which the labor unions were represented, unanimously recommended that during the war emergency " it is imperative that there should be no stoppage of work owing to trade disputes." [38] The Committee urged that existing arbitration boards and facilities for collective bargaining continue to be used in all industrial disputes, but that where no agreement could be reached disputes should be referred to an arbitration tribunal whose decisions would be binding. These recommendations were embodied in the *Conditions of Employment and National Arbitration Order* in July 1940. Strikes and lockouts were prohibited; and a five-man National Arbitration Tribunal was established. Union standards of employment were imposed upon all employers in an industry whether or not they recognized trade unions.

Strikes have, however, continued to occur about as frequently as before they were prohibited. In the prewar years, 1935–1939, the monthly average of strikes was 78, and in May 1940 there were 92. In the crisis month of June workers voluntarily suspended strikes, and the number of disputes dropped to 30, but in July, the month strikes were banned, the total began to mount until in October 1940 it reached 92, more than for any month of 1939. But the number of workers involved and the work days lost were much lower than in pre-Flanders months. Disputes affected smaller numbers of persons and were settled more rapidly.

These disputes arose principally from demands for wage increases. Employers were surprisingly willing to meet such demands, for the original 100 percent Excess Profits Tax and cost-plus contracts have diminished the incentive to keep costs down. As a result most strikes have

---

[38] *Ministry of Labour Gazette,* August, 1940, page 210.

been settled quickly, generally by direct negotiation between the unions and employers or through the machinery set up under the Industrial Courts Act of 1919. In the first year of its existence the National Arbitration Tribunal had granted 144 awards. Although the prohibition of strikes had not prevented strikes, as World War I experience had indicated would be the case, the statement of industrial policy, which the report of the Consultative Committee was in effect, was useful in focusing the attention of the workers on the necessity of avoiding work stoppages whenever possible.

Arrangements for shunting dock workers from one port to another were strengthened during the summer of 1940. In the four great shipping areas of Liverpool, London, Newcastle, and Edinburgh local committees were superseded by regional Port Labor Inspectors directly responsible to the Ministry of Labor. These inspectors were given broad supervisory powers over dock workers, who were required to register with, and could receive employment only through, the Port Labor Inspectors. A wider reorganization of the conditions of dock labor was introduced in the Merseyside, Manchester, and Preston areas in March 1941, and later in the Clydeside area. First, all dock workers in those areas were henceforth to be employed and paid directly by the Government — by the Minister of Transport — although they would continue to work for private employers, who would be registered and supervised by the Regional Port Directors of the Ministry of Transport. Second, all dock workers were guaranteed a minimum of forty-four hours of work a week at a minimum wage, with the prospect of considerable overtime employment. The scheme was voluntary, but all dockers accepting work under it were required to accept any engagement to which they might be assigned by the Port Labor Inspectors. Dockers' wages, plus a percentage to defray administrative expenses, were to be paid by the employers into a central fund from which the Minister of Transport would pay the dockers. The purpose of these changes was to " decasualize " dock labor by substituting steady pay for the intermittent employment characteristic of dock work. The Government's direct responsibility was increased in August 1941 by the formation of a National Dock Labor Corporation. The Corporation, under a board of directors of eight members, two appointed by the Minister of Labor as his representatives and three each nominated by the employers and unions concerned, was to promote, finance, and administer schemes of employment, and to arrange for the transfer of dockers from one port to another. These reforms in the conditions of dock work will in all probability be continued in peacetime.

All these measures to lengthen the work week, to provide for the health of the workers, to prevent loss of time by strikes, and to facilitate the transfer of shipbuilding and dock labor were aspects of a primary objective — to increase production by a better utilization of existing supplies of labor. The second general objective of labor policy was to bring some order into the labor market. Under the powers of Regulation 58A, the *Undertakings (Restriction of Engagement) Order* was issued in early June 1940. This provided that in the engineering or shipbuilding industries no employer could hire workers except through the local Employment Exchange or under an approved arrangement between employer and union organizations. Workers normally employed in coal mining or agriculture, forestry, or horticulture could not be engaged in any other industry except by special permission of the local Labor Office. In July national minimum wages for agricultural labor were raised by about 35 percent.

All these "poaching" regulations were intended to stop the movement of labor from the poorly paid agricultural and mining trades to more lucrative jobs and the uncontrolled movement of labor within armament industry. They were only partially effective. They were difficult to enforce and were frequently evaded by employers; they did not prevent individual workers from quitting one job and finding another; nor did they enforce work discipline in the plants.

Stronger and more direct measures were announced in March 1941 in the form of "Essential Work Orders." These apply only to particular industries and make the right of employers to discharge workers, and the right of workers to quit their jobs, subject to the permission of a national service officer and at least a week's notice. Special tribunals representing both labor and management have been established under independent chairmen to hear appeals from workers and employers against the decisions of service officers. In addition, the employer is required to guarantee basic weekly minimum wage rates. Conditions and terms of work must accord with the standards set for the industry by collective agreements, and the plant management must make satisfactory provision for the welfare of employees. These Orders effectively tie the worker to his job, while at the same time attempting to establish satisfactory wages and working conditions for the employees.

Essential Work Orders have been issued for the principal defense industries, shipbuilding and ship repairing, the merchant marine, coal mining, building and civil engineering, dock transport, chemicals and iron and steel. They have been criticized for removing the employer's sanction of discharge to enforce discipline and for the delay inherent in the appeal procedure. Nevertheless, they have served to stabilize the labor market and have curtailed mobility of labor and laxness of discipline.

The third major objective of the Government's labor policy was to increase the total number of workers engaged in armament production. The most immediate source of additional workers was, of course, the unemployed. Several means existed to bring them into industry. First, the Schedule of Reserved Occupations, which, within certain age limits, exempted persons from enlistment in the armed forces, was revised. As the schedule was originally drawn up, nearly 4,500,000 men — far too many — were included. The chief weakness of the plan was that men were exempted according to categories, electricians and shipbuilders, for instance, and not according to actual employment in vital war work.

Various minor revisions were made in the Schedule during the latter half of 1940, and in April 1941 a Revised Schedule of Reserved Occupations, which embodied two basic changes, was issued. The ages of reservation in many trades were raised by from 5 to 10 years, the changes to become effective in three successive two-month periods. The second change was the introduction of a category of " protected work " within the reserved occupations, with a lower reservation age for workers employed on work of special importance in the war effort. Firms included in five general classes of essential work were listed on a Register of Protected Establishments.

From July 1940 anyone refusing work of national importance was disqualified from receiving unemployment benefits. In areas and industries with heavy unemployment panels representing employers, employees, and the general public were set up to review the unemployment registers and attempt to place workers unemployed for more than a month in industry or civil defense work. In September 1940 all evacuated persons without jobs were asked to register at the employment exchanges in their new districts.

In addition, the Ministry of Labor took steps to mop up hidden reserves of labor in the armament industries. By mid-June 1940 the percentage of unemployed in all engineering industries was only 1.8 percent, in the production of motor vehicles and aircraft, 1.5 percent, in the chemical industry, only 2.5 percent. For this small margin an Industrial Registration Order, requiring the registration of all men over the age of twenty-one who were employed in certain engineering, armament, and heavy goods industries but not engaged entirely on government contracts, was issued. All men under sixty-five years of age who had worked in any of these specified fields for one year at any time since January 1929 were likewise asked to register. As a result of these orders, surprisingly large numbers of skilled workers not wholly employed in war work were made available. In the northwestern administrative area alone a reserve of 61,000 men was discovered. Many of these were qualified engineers retained on the payrolls of inactive firms which disliked losing their staff of trained personnel to other companies. The Ministry of Labor's inspectors frequently investigated such cases and ordered the transfer of men from one company to another.

Finally, the Government sought to bring into war production whatever trained men were available either in the armed forces or among the growing population of refugees resident in England. In the military interlude following the collapse of France, about 3,000 skilled mechanics were temporarily combed out of the British Army for munition work.[39] Some effort to utilize the special talents of European refugees in Britain was long overdue when the formation of an International Labor Force, designed to register and find employment for all anti-Fascist aliens was announced in August 1940.

All these measures were helpful in the short run, but they could at best furnish only a small part of the estimated demand of the war industries for two million additional workers. As explained above, the chief sources of new labor were nonworking women and persons employed in nonarmament industries. May 22, 1940, the unions principally concerned with the employment of women in the engineering industry had agreed with the Engineering and Allied Employers National Federation to relax the previous restrictions on even the temporary admission of women into the engineering fields. In general, women were to receive equal pay with men for equal work, but where they lacked experience for the job, they were to undergo several probationary stages, totalling thirty-two weeks, before they received equal pay. The opening late in 1940 and early in 1941 of newly completed Royal Ordnance Fac-

---

[39] Previously under Ernest Brown about 33,000 skilled men not required for technical work had been released by the War Office.

tories required hundreds of thousands of women and girls. In November 1940 the Prime Minister appealed for one million people to enter the munition factories voluntarily within the next nine months.

A vast expansion of the Government's labor training program was necessary to facilitate this transfer of workers. The Ministry of Labor's training scheme was accelerated to turn out 200,000 instead of 15,000 trainees a year. In addition, the technical schools and colleges of the country introduced shorter and more intensive courses for 50,000 a year. This acceleration of labor training was unfortunately restricted by the Government's reluctance to divert skilled technicians and machine tools from production to instruction. The greatest training ground of all was in the factories, but although industrial management did train workers for their own immediate needs, they were under constant pressure from the Supply Departments to use their facilities fully to increase production. An official plan for training in the factories, with compulsory quotas of trainees for each plant and payment of private industry for the service, might have given useful results. A voluntary scheme of in-factory training was notably unsuccessful. The Government's failure to adopt such a compulsory labor training program undoubtedly impaired its other efforts to expand the supply of workers available for employment.

Throughout 1940 there was little resort to the unlimited powers conferred on the Minister of Labor and no resort to industrial conscription of labor. But by January 1941 Britain had reached the point of full employment where further expansion of war production could be achieved only by the contraction of civil output. The number of wholly unemployed persons in Britain was only 521,000 in January 1941, and as most of these were in fact unemployable, it was doubtful if the figure would be reduced very rapidly. The planned compulsory transfer of large numbers of workers from nonessential trades could no longer be postponed. Both the restriction of civil industry and the conscription of industrial labor were necessary.

It is true that many of the Government's policies since the outbreak of war had been restrictive of civil business. The savings campaign, heavy income and purchase taxes, and rationing had all reduced private purchasing power. In addition the Board of Trade's *Limitation of Supplies Orders* of June and November 1940 had reduced the supplies of raw materials available to certain industries with a view to decreasing both consumption and employment. But none of these measures was directly coordinated with demand for labor in the armament industries. On the contrary, they produced conspicuous waste of labor. In general, the firms affected continued to operate at reduced, and usually inefficient, levels of output. Consequently, a disproportionately small number of workers were actually discharged from their positions. Neither was there any assurance that the persons thrown out of work would actually find their way into armament employment.

For these shortcomings to be overcome there had first to be an overall plan whereby the reduced output of civil industry would be concentrated in a few firms working at capacity while the remaining firms were closed down and their facilities and employees made available for the production of armaments. The equipment and especially the workers thus disemployed had then to be conscripted and allocated for war work.

The Churchill Government adopted this twofold policy early in 1941. In March the Board of Trade announced its scheme " to concentrate production in a reduced number of factories working full time." [40] The program of concentration applied to more than thirty consumer-goods industries — textiles, cotton, woolens, silk, hosiery, pottery, cycles, plastics, musical instruments, and a host of others. The Government encouraged the trade associations in the industries concerned to formulate voluntary schemes of the particular firms to be closed out, and wherever possible make arrangements for their compensation. The Government stated its intention of using compulsion if voluntary programs were not forthcoming. The surviving nucleus firms in industries were granted some protection. They would receive available government contracts, and their supplies of raw materials, labor, and plant would be safeguarded as far as the circumstances of the war permitted. It was estimated that from 500,000 to 700,000 workers would ultimately be released for transfer to war work.[40a]

So that the labor released should be absorbed in armament trades, Great Britain accepted industrial conscription. On March 16, 1941 the Minister of Labor declared that all men between the ages of forty-one and forty-five, and all women of twenty and twenty-one years of age, if not already in war employment must register for it by mid-April. Persons registering were subsequently to be interviewed, and after their capabilities had been determined they were to be directed to report for

---

[40] *Concentration of Production,* March 1941, Cmd. 6258.
[40a] For the actual result, see Chapter III, Part II, p. 186.

training and eventual employment in shipyards, engineering works, and armament plants. The facts that in total war a nation's man power is indivisible and that the organization of those who produce is as essential to victory as the organization of those who fight had been faced. After eighteen months of war, Britain had at last an integrated policy for the utilization of man power.

During 1941, as further munitions plants came into production and the armed forces expanded, the crisis of man power became increasingly acute. In December 1941 the Government acted to relieve the crisis by introducing the National Service (No. 2) Bill. This statute extended the age of men subject to armed service, supplanted the Schedule of Reserved Occupations, and made women subject to compulsory service for certain branches of defense work.

The age of men liable to military and civil defense was raised from 41 to 51, and lowered from 19 to 18½ years, thereby bringing 2,750,000 more men within conscription. The Government stated its intention of posting men over 40 years of age to sedentary work and permitting the release of younger men for combat work. The Schedule of Reserved Occupations, which established exemption by occupational age-blocs, was replaced by a system of individual deferment. Beginning on January 1, 1942 the age of reservation was to be raised by one-year steps at monthly intervals, exemption was to be granted only to persons actually engaged in work of national importance.

The most striking provision of the Act at the time, though its later more extensive application has been accepted without sensation, was that women likewise were subject to conscription. Married women, and mothers with children under 14 years of age were exempt for the time being, although they could be directed into industrial employment under previous orders. Women between the ages of 20–30 years were to be called up immediately and directed into the Women's Auxiliary Services, civil defense, or factory work. Britain was approaching full mobilization of her man power resources.

The concentration of nonessential industries provided an example for the subsequent, inevitable concentration of war work in the most efficient " production units," which was begun in the autumn of 1942. The corresponding reallocation of labor among firms already holding defense contracts became Great Britain's most acute industrial problem. The licensing of new undertakings was restricted, with the aim of checking the trend of labor into congested areas, and less essential enterprises were compulsorily transferred from certain centers of specialized work.

To conclude, it is evident that it was not until after the formation of the Churchill Cabinet and the appointment of Ernest Bevin as Minister of Labor that the British Government assumed responsibility for the supply of labor to the armament factories. Even then it was nine months before the adoption of any coherent man power policy involving the allocation of labor. Bevin's primary objective in the summer of 1940 was an immediate increase in the output of weapons. For this purpose, overtime was accepted as an effective short-run policy. It was not until the late summer of 1940 that much progress was made in putting unemployed to work, and not until early 1941 that the organized compulsory transfer of workers was accepted.

PART THREE

GREAT BRITAIN'S OVERSEAS TRADE

by Eric Roll

The problems of foreign trade in time of war form only a part of the wider question of the proper economic organization of a country's war effort. That, in its turn, is inseparable from the whole complex of military, diplomatic, political, and social considerations which have to be taken into account when a nation is to be mobilized for war. But foreign trade deserves separate treatment here for at least two reasons. The economic life of Great Britain has for centuries been built up on a basis of vast economic relations — commercial and financial — with the outside world. And there is not a single important aspect of the British war economy which can be discussed without at once raising problems of an international character. The second reason arises out of this: most of the major decisions on war policy have their foreign trade aspect. Just as the war itself cannot be analyzed except in terms of a prolonged process, Britain's wartime overseas trade must also be viewed against the background of its development in the years preceding the outbreak of war. This survey begins, therefore, with a brief sketch of the trends in Britain's international economic relations during the period between the First World War and the Second.

1. The Background

Britain suffered particularly heavily from the decline of world trade which followed the war of 1914–18. In 1924, when much of the immediate postwar disturbance had disappeared, the volume of Britain's imports was about 2.5 percent higher than in 1913; but exports were still only three-quarters of their prewar volume. But by 1929, the peak year of the postwar period, the volume of exports was still 17 percent below the 1913 figure, while imports, due largely to relatively low food prices, were about 18 percent higher than before the war. Exports formed a continually declining proportion of national output. From 30 percent in 1907, they fell to 25 percent in 1924 and to 21 percent in 1930.

The picture presented by merchandise trade is strengthened when the rest of Britain's international transactions are considered. For more than a century, Britain has had capital invested overseas. For nearly a century she has been receiving each year large sums as payment of interest and repayment of capital on those foreign investments. These sums, together with the large annual net income she draws from abroad for the services of her shipping, her banks, and other financial institutions, have enabled her to finance larger purchases of goods from abroad than would have been possible from the proceeds of her merchandise exports alone. Since 1857 Britain has had a continuous series of annual import surpluses. But these have been more than offset by the other items mentioned. And although adequate statistics are not available for the earlier period, it is fairly certain that in every year between 1857 and 1931 Great Britain has had a current surplus on her balance of international payments. This has been available for the purpose of adding to her foreign investments.

The balance of payments on current account in the postwar period shows a fairly definite trend, interrupted only during a short part of the period. From 1920 to 1925 the annual surplus on all current items shows a continuous decline: from £252 million in the former year to £9 million in the latter. The next three years show an upward movement, due to the diminution of the import surplus which was brought about by the expansion of exports in that period of stabilization. In 1929, the current surplus reached £138 million. But this improvement was short-lived: in the following year the surplus had again fallen to £28 million; and in 1931 a deficit appeared for the first time. This was of the substantial amount of £104 million. The restrictive measures adopted in that year caused the deficit to diminish to £51 million in 1932 and made the balance even in 1933. But since then there has been only one year, 1935, in which Britain has had a current surplus. In each of the two last years before the present war broke out, there has been a current deficit of about £55 million.

These figures seem to indicate the presence of a long process of deterioration in Britain's current international transactions. A similar trend is revealed in Britain's position as an international creditor. In 1913, British subscriptions to new overseas issues exceeded repayments to the United Kingdom on account of past loans by £243 million. In 1928, this difference was only £108 million. And since the depression there have been only two years in which the difference has been a positive quantity. Overseas capital issues in London have fluctuated between a high of £143 million in 1928 and a low of £20 million in 1935. Since 1931, they have been increasingly strictly controlled by the government, with the result that the average of the ten years 1930–39 was £39.4 million as compared with £116 million for the preceding decade.[41]

The crisis of 1931 and the lengthy depression which followed it led to the adoption of a number of now familiar defensive and palliative measures, including the abandonment by Great Britain of her century-old policy of free trade. It has been argued, with justice, that the long-run effects of the adoption by Britain, the greatest international commercial and financial center, of such measures of restrictive economic nationalism would be to aggravate the economic difficulties of the world and to contribute to the intensification of political friction. The immediate result of these measures, however, was to improve Britain's in-

---

[41] It is not possible to measure the decline of British investments abroad precisely, owing to the difficulties of collecting comprehensive data and of fluctuations in market values. One indication may be obtained by Sir Robert Kindersley's estimate of the nominal amount of quoted foreign securities held by British residents. This shows a decline from £3,438 million in 1929 to £3,292 million in 1938. Moreover, it would appear that repayment has affected the most easily realizable assets and has left the composition of the remaining total less favorable than it used to be.

254 THE BRITISH COMMONWEALTH AT WAR

ternational economic position by arresting for a time the long process of deterioration. We find, for example, that while the volume of world trade fell between 1929 and 1934 by 22.5 percent, Britain's share in it rose from 13.05 percent to 13.85 percent. Perhaps the most striking single indication of the measure in which Britain succeeded in turning her international transactions in her favor is to be found in the figures for the terms of trade.[42] Taking 1930 as 100, this index rose to 110.3 in 1931, 110.8 in 1932, and 115.2 in 1933. This improvement is somewhat compensated for by a diminution in the total volume of foreign trade in these years. But, on the other hand, the subsequent decline in the terms of trade — to 112.1 in 1934 and 109.4 in 1935 — is more than offset by a rise in the volume of trade. It is true that the following three years showed a fresh decline in the terms of trade. But in 1937, they were still above the 1930 figure (in 1938 there was another substantial improvement); and if the volume index is taken into account, the rise was continuous from 1932 onward.

This improvement, whatever its more remote significance and consequences, reflects essentially the drive towards bilateralism in British trade. The inevitable depression phenomenon of agricultural prices falling more rapidly than the prices of manufactured goods was one factor in Britain's favor. In a buyer's market for food and raw materials, Britain, as one of the world's chief buyers of these products, was able to obtain good terms. The depreciation of sterling did not counteract this favorable development, but strengthened it, since a large number of Britain's suppliers followed the pound. With the creation of the Sterling Area, which excluded Canada but included some countries not in the British Empire, Great Britain carved out a trading area in which all the strong factors of her economic position showed up to their full advantage and the weaknesses could be minimized. The Ottawa Agreements brought much of the Canadian trade into line; and similar arrangements could thereafter be attempted with the remainder of the non-sterling world.

Since this alignment of British foreign trade is of great importance in relation to wartime problems, it may be worth while to summarize its effect. The following table shows the changes in the distribution of

[42] This measurement, specifically designed to show changes in the gain derived by a country from each unit of its foreign trade, reveals an interesting movement in the years following the depression. The net terms of trade are given by the ratio of the average price of exports to the average price of imports. They are an index of the changes in the amount of imports that are obtained for each unit of exports.

British trade as between the British Empire and European and non-European foreign countries.

Area	Percent of total imports from		Percent of total exports to	
	1929	1938	1929	1938
British Empire	29.4	40.4	44.5	49.9
Non-European foreign countries	32.5	26.1	22.7	18.2
European foreign countries	38.1	33.5	32.8	31.9

This table may be supplemented by the following figures which illustrate the effects of the creation of the Sterling Area:

Area	Percent of total imports from		Percent of total exports to	
	1929	1938	1929	1938
11 non-British free exchange countries	40.9	33.5	25.5	24.2
12 countries in the Sterling Area	31.9	36.2	38.3	44.5
4 former "Gold Bloc" countries	12.8	8.6	10.9	8.5

The composition of Britain's trade did not change greatly during the period reviewed. The protectionist policy diminished somewhat the proportion of finished goods within the group of manufactured imports in favor of semi-finished products. The exigencies of rearmament and the laying-in of reserves of food and raw materials are also revealed in a proportionate rise of the relevant imports in the last two prewar years. The share of manufactured exports declined slightly in favor of raw materials (mainly coal), and an important decline occurred in the value of re-exports, reflecting the diminished importance of British *entrepôt* trade in a world in which she and her competitors were engaged on an energetic drive towards bilateralism.

It is important to keep in mind the changes in the geographical distribution of British trade in the years before the war, because these changes — and the strains and stresses which they either followed or preceded — were responsible for many problems of wartime policy. The measures which brought about the greater concentration of trade within the Empire and the Sterling Area were designed to counter the weakened economic position of Britain, and while not so definitely bilateral in intention as measures adopted by Germany, particularly towards her neighbors in southeastern Europe, they were also of a monopolistic character. As such, they of necessity produced some friction. Within the Empire itself complaints were not unknown, and many modifications of the original Ottawa Agreements had to be introduced.

South Africa, for example, claimed that her purchases from Britain had risen more than those of any other country in the world, while her sales to Britain had declined. India, on the other hand, was increasing her exports to Britain, but diminishing her imports, particularly in cotton manufactures, from Britain. For Canada and Australia the picture was somewhat similar: a rise in the proportion of exports to Britain unaccompanied by any rise in the proportion of imports from Britain.

Those countries, notably France, which for a time formed the Gold Bloc, sharply reduced the proportion of their trade with Britain.[43] Trade with Germany and Italy, the countries with which Britain was to be at war, had declined in the last prewar decade. In the latter case, it was about halved both for exports and imports percentages. The proportion of British imports from Germany declined more heavily than that of British exports to Germany, though less heavily than the proportion of re-exports. In the countries of southeastern Europe, in which German methods of bilateral trade and payments agreements were most energetically pursued, British trade declined less than is often thought. This was due less to any very determined British counteraction than to the fact that the proportion of trade which Britain did with those countries had always been very small. In addition, imports and exports of Czechoslovakia, Italy, and Austria, from and to southeastern Europe were more similar to those of Germany and were, therefore, more affected by the German drive than those of Britain.

As far as the rest of the world was concerned, the movement of British trade seems to have been closely related to the development of individual trade agreements. In the case of trade with the three Scandinavian countries and Finland, with which trade agreements were concluded in 1933, there has been a sharp rise in the proportions. The same is true of Poland and the Baltic states. In the trade with the United States there was until 1938 a heavy decline of imports from that country with a small decline in exports and a considerable decline in re-exports. But the short record of the trade agreement concluded between the United Kingdom and the United States in 1938 suggests that, but for the war, the experience of the other trade agreements might have been repeated. The South American proportions declined for exports but rose slightly for imports, the decline in the proportion of exports being

---

[43] This reduction was not markedly reversed after the abandonment by these countries of their former gold parity, thus possibly indicating the greater importance of trade agreements as against currency factors in influencing the direction of trade.

particularly marked in the case of Brazil and Chile, where both Germany and the United States were able to expand. With Argentina, Britain has traditionally very close financial and commercial ties. Here, recent trade and payments agreements succeeded in maintaining the percentage of British exports, but were unable to prevent a fall in the share of British imports. The effect of the trade agreement with Russia conformed to the general pattern. The general course of the percentage of imports from Russia was steady, but that of exports, and much more that of re-exports, was upward.

Thus the general picture is one of a fair measure of success in the adoption of new policies. It offsets to some extent the impression of long-run weakness presented by British trade in the whole postwar period.

2. The War Developments

I. The general problems of the organization of the economy of a capitalist state for the purpose of waging war have been analyzed and debated at length for the last few decades, and particularly during the last two years. It is neither possible nor desirable to recapitulate this discussion here. In its simplest and most abstract terms the general economic problem of war is one of securing the necessary supplies. The scale on which the problem of supply appears in wartime lifts it out of the domain of public finance — budgeting, taxation, etc. — and causes it to affect profoundly every aspect of the existing economic structure.

In the last war, the technique in all belligerent countries was essentially an indirect one, although as the war progressed more direct measures were increasingly applied. The agencies of government appeared in the market as buyers equipped with purchasing power raised in part through taxation but mainly through borrowing. Their greater monetary resources, combined with some direct measures designed to discourage the purchase and production of non-war goods, enabled these governmental agencies to " bid away " goods, and the resources needed to make these goods, from their peacetime uses. It was largely through such inflationary processes, placing the burden on the mass of consumers, that the essential shifting of production and the necessary industrial concentration were achieved. It was no doubt due to the still largely fluid and competitive relations between different sections of capitalist enterprise, and to the relations between them and labor, that these indirect means had to be used. And since in 1914 monopolization of industry and integration of leading sections of it with finance and the state were much more highly advanced in Germany than in Britain, measures of direct control were adopted there earlier and to a greater extent.

The roles of inflation and of direct control, which in 1914–18 was used only tardily and mainly as an adjunct to inflationary finance, have now been in a sense reversed. In the present war, the methods of finance and the use of the market mechanism very soon became only supplementary to direct intervention.

The evolution of measures of domestic regulation during the course of the war has been in the direction of steadily increasing control. To-day, the formal possibility exists of establishing completely centralized control of the whole economic activity of the United Kingdom. And to a large extent this possibility has become a reality. This is not the place to discuss the significance of these measures, but it must be remembered that however far-reaching they may be, they do not fundamentally alter the economic structure. Essentially, reliance is still placed on the operation of the capitalistic process. Even though the rights and powers of many sections of private enterprise have been restricted by the action of the state, private property, individual enterprise, the profit motive, and the working of the market mechanism are still basic. In the field of foreign trade to which we now turn, it has also been clear that the competition of divergent interests has by no means been wholly eliminated by the vast apparatus of control which has been created.

II. Before we enumerate the measures for the regulation of Britain's foreign transactions, it is useful to look again at the international economic position which Britain occupied at the outbreak of the war. That position was generally recognized to be a strong one in spite of intermittent difficulties. Britain's foreign trade in 1938 still formed in value over 26 percent of world trade. She was by far the most important carrying nation, possessing the world's largest mercantile marine (18 million tons, as against the second largest, 9 million tons). Above all, she was still the world's largest foreign investor, her holdings being estimated at well over £3,000,000,000.

Probably the best single factor to take for an estimate of available economic strength is the amount of British assets in the United States at the outbreak of war. These were estimated to have been as follows: [44]

---

[44] Federal Reserve Board *Bulletin*, January 1941.

(in $000,000)

Central Gold Reserves	$ Balances	Readily marketable securities at market value	Total
2,000	595	1,080	3,675
(1914:165)	(1914:2,600–3,800		2,765–3,965)

A number of other resources might be added to this table. For example, British direct and other not immediately marketable investments in the United States were estimated at $1,185,000,000; and Canadian assets amounting to over $1,500,000,000, two-thirds of which were easily realizable, could also be regarded as available to the British Empire for war purposes. The American assets of other British countries should also be taken into account. The substantial French assets, amounting to over $3,500,000,000, could, until the French collapse, be counted as part of the financial strength of the Allies. When it is remembered that Germany's dollar assets amounted to only about $255,000,000 [45] as compared with a 1914 total of perhaps $1,000,000,000, the financial power of Britain appears in its true proportions.

The measures which were taken in the field of international trade fall into three classes. There are first the simple corollaries of domestic measures for the centralization of economic control. There are measures which supplement and reinforce domestic policy directed to the husbanding of resources. And finally there are the measures of active economic warfare. It is not necessary to list all of the very numerous new measures which have been adopted since the outbreak of war, some in the form of new legislation, others as regulations under the defense emergency powers, but the most important ones may be mentioned. The following fall mainly into the first category. The *Currency (Defense) Act* authorizes the use of the Exchange Equalization Account for war purposes. The *Import, Export and Customs Powers (Defense) Act* gives the Board of Trade the power to prohibit or regulate the import and export of all goods. The *Ships and Aircraft (Transfer Restrictions) Act* gives powers over the transfer of ships and aircraft to the Board of Trade and the Secretary for Air. The *Import Duties (Emergency Provisions) Act* allows the Treasury to act as if the (now suspended) Import Duties Advisory Committee had made a recommendation.

In the class of active economic warfare, there is the *Trading with the*

[45] According to the estimate of the U. S. Department of Commerce.

Enemy Act which imposes severe penalties for carrying on transactions with, or for the benefit of, the enemy; and the declaration of the blockade of German-occupied areas. The *Trading with the Enemy Act* follows the principles adopted in the last war, but it has a wider application, and its stringency has been increased by subsequent orders. The blockade, while again based on old-established principles, is much more broadly conceived and more comprehensive than it has ever been before. Not only is the Ministry of Economic Warfare charged with supervising the execution of the original, almost all-inclusive prohibition of imports into Germany; since the latter part of November 1939 and the use by Germany of the magnetic mine in shipping lanes, German exports, too, fall under the prohibition which is enforced by the British Navy and its contraband control. An elaborate machinery has been set up for checking the imports and exports of neutral countries against their peacetime quantities and estimated current requirements so as to prevent any leakage in the blockade of the enemy by way of those neutral countries.

The purpose of economic warfare is to deprive the enemy of materials essential for the prosecution of the war. This is done either directly by stopping his imports, or indirectly by preventing him from exporting and so obtaining the funds with which to pay for imports. It will depend on the whole military and diplomatic situation whether such a physical blockade is sufficient to achieve this purpose. At the outbreak of the present war, the existence of a large number of neutrals made it clear that active economic warfare would involve more than the imposition of a blockade and the use of appropriate economic and military means for enforcing it. The British blockade was supplemented from the very beginning by a carefully planned program of trade agreements with neutrals for which the " dog in the manger " was the inspiration. In addition to assurances that British exports would not find their way to the enemy, the agreements provided for large purchases from neutrals in order to prevent their products from being sold to the enemy.

These agreements have been very numerous and have covered single transactions and trade in particular commodities as well as the entire volume of trade with an individual country. It is not possible to list them all here or to discuss their details, since the rapidly changing diplomatic and military situation has caused, and is causing, continual modifications in them. Indeed, some agreements have remained dead letters because they were overtaken by events. But a few individual trade negotiations and agreements may be mentioned to illustrate some of the above-mentioned principles of economic warfare. We shall see presently that a number of important additional considerations were involved in these trade agreements; and we shall also discuss some of the difficulties which Britain encountered in her efforts to push this trade policy.

Within the first eight months of war Britain had concluded agreements with, among others, Turkey, Rumania, Greece, Belgium, Luxemburg, Switzerland, Spain, Norway, Sweden, and a number of South American countries. Apart from provisions relating to foreign exchange and payments (which are discussed below), the general framework of these treaties is broadly similar. While no details have been made public, it is known that all included reference to specific commodities and the quantities in which these were to be exchanged between the parties. For example, the pact with Turkey, signed on February 3, 1940, provided for the sale by Britain of airplanes, machinery, cotton, and other war materials in exchange for Turkish supplies of raw materials, including tobacco and dried fruit. The treaty with Spain, concluded a few weeks later, was designed to enable Spain to obtain such products as coal and machinery from Britain as well as important supplies (including oil) from the Sterling Area, while Britain was to expand her imports from Spain particularly of iron ore, pyrites, and fruit. The agreement with Switzerland, signed towards the end of April, was an interesting example of joint action between Britain and France. Like the agreements with Luxemburg and Belgium, it was entered into by the Allies jointly and was regarded as indicative of the greater concessions which they could jointly offer, and the greater pressure which their cooperation could exert. This agreement, too, provides for the sale to Switzerland of certain raw materials and some finished goods required by Swiss industry in return for purchases of various manufactures. Both this treaty and that with Spain contained clauses assuring Britain that her exports would not be re-exported to Germany.

III. It is to be remembered that many of the problems which formed the subject of negotiations were not connected with the blockade. For one thing, as has already been pointed out, Britain tried for a considerable time to enlarge her export markets, particularly in South America. In addition, much negotiation has been made necessary by the severe limitations upon certain non-essential imports and the criticism which these have called forth from former suppliers. More complex are the kinds of prohibitions or restrictions resulting not so much from the drive to confine imports to goods essential for the prosecution of the war, or from regulation of trade for political reasons, as from the need to achieve the optimum use of existing foreign balances and of funds accruing from current exports. These particular prohibitions and restrictions must, therefore, be considered in relation to foreign exchange policy in general.

The control of foreign exchange dealings, which constitutes one of the most powerful single means of foreign trade regulation even in time of peace, has been used as a vital supplement to the measures of direct wartime intervention. Since such control is comprehensive, it illustrates the chief trade problems of war more clearly than any other instrument of policy. It is, therefore, worthwhile to trace the evolution of Britain's exchange policy in some detail.

The pound sterling had been under pressure since early in 1938. But from the end of 1938 until the end of August 1939 (and particularly from March to August 1939) the rate maintained comparative stability round a figure of $4.68 as the result of continuous intervention by the British Exchange Equalization Account and a consequent very heavy loss of gold and foreign exchange resources. The approach and outbreak of the present war caused a steep fall in sterling. The rate slipped to $4.12 on August 28 when the authorities abandoned their support. It recovered at the end of the month but fell again to $4.075 on September 5. On that day, exchange control was instituted and an official rate established.

The first phase of British wartime exchange control lasted until January 8, 1940. Its measures can be briefly summarized as follows. The immediate step taken by the monetary authorities was the establishment of an official foreign exchange market, maintained by the Bank of England and by authorized dealers, in which official buying and selling rates for sterling were fixed. These rates were $4.02 — $4.06 to begin with; were later narrowed to $4.02 — $4.04; and later still the range was further reduced to $4.02½ — $4.03½. A series of regulations were issued designed to bring the bulk of foreign exchange transactions within the official market. Residents in the United Kingdom were obliged to sell to the authorities any funds they possessed or afterwards acquired in ten specified currencies at the officially established rates; and they were not allowed to deal in these currencies outside the official market.[46] The purposes for which foreign exchange could be obtained from the authorities (imports, payments of past debts, travelling expenses, etc.) were carefully circumscribed and made subject to a stringent system of licensing. The regulations were designed to make capital exports by residents impossible. By an earlier order, holders of securities in the specified currencies were required to register their holdings with the authorities and power was taken to order the sale of these holdings to the authorities. This power was exercised on February 8, 1940, with respect to 60 securities; and on April 14, 1940, another 112 securities were added to the list.

Combined with the regulation of imports, the exchange control set up a series of priorities of import sources and gave a general preference to imports invoiced in sterling. In the first place, all imports were discouraged (except, of course, those vital materials of war which the government itself had to obtain from abroad). Next to the preference for United Kingdom goods stood that for products of the Empire (including Canada). In the trade with these countries, sterling was the currency used; and in any case, the Empire had also instituted exchange control which was closely coordinated with that of Britain. France figured next as a preferred source of imports. Indeed, while the alliance lasted, France was fast becoming an integral part of the economic system of the British Empire.[47]

The fourth place in the list of sources of imports under the scheme of trade and exchange control was occupied by countries with whom Britain had concluded special treaties, such as Sweden, Spain, Turkey, Rumania and countries in South America. These treaties regulated the disposal of sterling exchange which the countries concerned were acquiring through their exports to Britain. Some examples may be mentioned to illustrate the principles involved. The agreement with Spain provided in the first place for a loan. The British Government agreed to lend £1.5 million which, added to the £2 million of Spanish funds accumulated in Britain and immobilized in the clearing account since 1936, would be applied to liquidate one-half of the £7 million of past

---

[46] These specified currencies were: United States dollars, Netherlands guilders, Dutch East Indies guilders, Swiss francs, belgas, Canadian dollars, French francs, Swedish kroner, Norwegian kroner and Argentine pesos.

[47] Of this tendency, the currency agreement between Britain and France concluded in December 1939 was the most visible symptom. It pegged the exchange at 176.5 francs to the pound and postponed the transfer of any balance in the transactions between the two countries until after the war.

debts to Britain frozen in Spain. The British Government also agreed to lend a further sum of £2 million to finance fresh Spanish purchases in the Sterling Area. The payments agreement proper in this treaty stipulated that the service on the above loan (consisting of interest until 1942 and thereafter of repayment of principal in ten equal annual instalments) should be the first charge on the sterling proceeds of Spanish exports. Of the balance, 45 percent was to be applied to the purchase of goods and the payment of shipping freights in the United Kingdom. Another 45 percent was reserved for purchases from United Kingdom firms of goods from specified parts of the Sterling Area. The remaining 10 percent was available for such payments as insurance premiums and royalties.

The treaty with Norway was said to have consisted of an agreement for a pound for pound clearing, thus reserving all sterling proceeds of Norwegian exports for purchases in the Sterling Area. Such a provision would be impossible in the case of a country whose balance of payments with the whole Sterling Area was normally in that country's favor, unless recourse was had to the more extreme measures of the German technique of bilateralism. Britain recognized this difficulty in her agreement with Sweden. This treaty allowed Sweden the use of sterling balances for purchases in two specified non-sterling markets, Belgium and Brazil, whose balances of payments with Sweden were complementary to those with the countries in the Sterling Area. Such concession means the loss of some exchange, and Britain has naturally been anxious to avoid it wherever possible.

Canada, although a part of the Empire, stood only fifth on the list, because she lay within the dollar currency area. A modification in this situation was, however, introduced when the Canadian exchange regulations were amended so as to permit exports to countries in the Sterling Area to be invoiced in Canadian dollars or in sterling (the general rule being that all exports had to be invoiced in United States dollars or in freely convertible currencies). Moreover, the bulk of the trade with Canada has been the subject of special arrangements.

Sixth and last on the list were the countries with free currencies with which no special payments or clearing agreement had been concluded. Of these, by far the most important was the United States. Since the United States is also the most important source of supply for most of the essential war materials, notably airplanes, the British authorities have been particularly assiduous in their efforts to husband their American dollar resources. This has been done by administration of the general import licensing regulations, by special prohibitions and restrictions, as well as by the exercise of the exchange control. In addition, there has been an increasing tendency to concentrate all British trade with the United States (or, at any rate, all British purchases in the United States) in the hands of government agencies.

The subsequent development of the British exchange regulations can be seen in retrospect as a tightening up of the control through a gradual restriction of both the supply and demand of sterling outside the officially established channels. This development is most usefully discussed in connection with the conflicting views regarding the most effective exchange and trade policy in wartime. At this point, therefore, a brief summary of the main changes since January 1940 may suffice.

The original regulations were far from completely watertight. In the first place, a free market continued to exist for all currencies other than the ten specified ones. This, however, was comparatively unimportant. What was much more important was that supplies of, and demands for, sterling could arise and meet outside the official market. One part of the supply came from non-residents who held sterling balances at the outbreak of war and who, although they could not obtain foreign exchange from the authorities, could liquidate their holdings if they could find other non-residents willing to buy these sterling balances. This supply was replenished by the proceeds of those foreign exports to Britain which were invoiced in sterling — as most of them were, especially those from countries with weak currencies. The foreign exporter could liquidate his sterling by selling it to some other non-resident account. The demand for this supply of non-resident sterling balances came from all those who had commitments in sterling to meet. Since the bulk of British exports had normally been invoiced in sterling and nothing in the first phase of exchange control interfered with that practice, there was a continuous demand for sterling from foreign buyers of British goods. With a stream of offers coming from non-residents anxious to liquidate their sterling holdings, even at a rate lower than the official one (of which they could not take advantage), and a demand originating from importers of British goods, a market for sterling outside the official one arose. In this free market, the one in New York being the most important, sterling was quoted at a fluctuating and often very considerable discount, and through it much exchange was lost to the authorities.

The first step towards abolishing this free market was taken in an order which from January 8, 1940 made very much more difficult than before the transfer of sterling from resident to non-resident accounts. Ten specific kinds of permitted transactions were laid down, and authorized exchange dealers were required to satisfy themselves by documentary evidence that any application was covered by the list. This restriction of the supply was followed by an order on March 7, 1940, which greatly reduced the demand for free sterling. It was laid down that as from March 25, 1940, all British exports of whisky, furs, rubber, tin, jute, and diamonds had either to be invoiced in United States dollars or, if invoiced in sterling, the authorities had to be satisfied that the sterling had been obtained from official sources, i.e., at the official rate. Since the six commodities constituted an important part of the exports from the Sterling Area, particularly to the United States, this meant that the demand for free sterling was severely curtailed.

The next landmark was June 7, 1940, when simultaneously a new and drastic diminution of the supply and demand of free sterling was brought about. Sales of British securities by non-residents (a source of disposable non-resident sterling balances) were prohibited. At the same time, it was decreed that all British exports to the United States and Switzerland had to be paid for in United States dollars, Swiss francs or official sterling.

The scope of the free market was so greatly reduced by these means that on June 11, 1940, the British authorities felt justified in asking the New York foreign exchange market to cooperate with them in making the official rate universally applicable. By July 18, 1940, the negotiations to this end had been concluded, and a scheme was announced by which virtually all transactions involving payments between Britain and the United States were to be settled through registered accounts and at the official rate. As a coping stone to this finished building of exchange control, there was added on August 21, 1940, an order prohibiting the import into the United Kingdom of British bank notes. While this order was designed to prevent the Germans from benefitting from any British notes seized in the territories occupied by them, it also closed one of the few remaining small loopholes in the system of exchange control.

The fact that exchange control is now practically all-inclusive, makes a discussion of some of the problems of policy somewhat academic. Nevertheless, the issues raised in the course of the evolution of the control are not without their practical importance for the future and form an important part in the whole scheme of trade policy in wartime. To the general problems of this policy we must now turn.

3. The Problem of Policy

I. In this section an attempt is made to deal briefly with the broader issues of wartime trade policy in the light of the factual summary already given. The subject cannot be discussed here exhaustively; and even a short analysis of its chief points is difficult. Policy in wartime is surrounded by secrecy. Details of agreements actually concluded are seldom published; and little information is made available on the course of negotiations with other countries. Reasons for particular actions and measures have been given from time to time; but they have rarely been either simultaneous with action or fully exhaustive when they have been publicly stated. Such official reticence on foreign trade matters is only to be expected, since policy in the economic sphere is regarded as being no different in essence from military policy. But the commentator's function is, as a result, often little more than guesswork.

Again, the concrete conditions of the war have been changing very rapidly, particularly after the comparative calm of the first six or seven months; critical comments on policy as it appears to be at any moment, as well as proposals for new measures, have, therefore, become inappropriate almost as soon as they have been made. Finally, it must be remembered that there are no " pure " foreign trade problems; they are to be regarded as one aspect only of a complex of problems of which all the parts are intimately linked together.

There is much interplay between economic, military, and diplomatic considerations in determining policy. An obvious example is that of the blockade. It is clear that the military and naval possibilities will be the first to be taken into account. Thereafter two questions arise: How far has military effectiveness to be supplemented, and by what means? and to what extent do diplomatic and economic considerations make it advisable not to do everything that military power makes practicable? Even recondite connections, though they may sometimes be ignored by those who make policy, should not be overlooked by the student. It is well to remember that foreign trade is peculiarly fitted to be thought of in connection with the major issues of the war. The future of the domestic economic and social structure, the machinery of political control, the future of the colonies, the relations with the dominions, the whole complex of problems embraced by the term imperialism, no less than the narrower trade problems, as, for example, the future of sterling or London's financial position after the war, obtrude themselves strongly into any study of the appropriate technique of wartime foreign trade.

One of the most striking expressions of the intimate connection between different parts of war policy is to be found in the long *versus* short war debate. As will be shown below, the slow evolution of a 100 percent exchange control and the slowness with which foreign assets were apparently liquidated in the early stages of the war, are examples of policies which were in part influenced by a belief in a long war of slowly gathering momentum. A strong belief, on the other hand, that the war would be short and intensive should have led to the placing of all the emphasis on military factors. Existing reserves of food in Britain would then have been considered adequate and no question about securing a continuous stream of food from abroad would have arisen. The ultimate effects of the war upon the position of London as an international financial center or upon Britain's share of exports markets would not have weighed seriously in the determination of day-to-day trade policy. Probably, too, there would have been less incentive to respect meticulously the feelings of neutrals in the application of the blockade.

Nevertheless, some basic economic facts remain even when all allowance has been made for the close interdependence of all aspects of war policy. Apart from the necessities of the blockade, we may say that dependence upon foreign supplies of certain goods is the most important of these basic facts. The amount of food, of raw materials, and of manufactured war materials, such as airplanes and munitions, that has to be imported is not an unchangeable magnitude. It will depend in part upon certain objective conditions (shipping space, efficiency of the convoy system, damage to domestic industry resulting from bombing, etc.). But it will also be affected by policy; and this, in its turn, will be influenced both by expectations (for example, about the duration of the war) as well as by decisions on such points as what amount of consumers' goods production is to be maintained, to what extent food is to be imported for the purpose of building up reserves, or how quickly available foreign exchange is to be used up. However, given a number of definite objective conditions and decisions on matters of policy, there will be a determinate amount of foreign goods which will have to be imported. This determines foreign exchange needs, and so provides one part of the data upon which exchange and export and import policy are based. The other part of the data by the means of which policy will be determined is to be looked for in any desires that may exist to achieve certain more distant objectives as, for example, the safeguarding of foreign markets in the postwar future.

II.   It is unlikely that in practice the problem has always presented itself to those in power in quite this way. But for purposes of analysis, some such logical approach will be found a convenient method. The first expression of the trade problem would thus be financial. The questions to be asked would be: What funds are immediately available for foreign purchases? how can they best be mobilized? and at what rate, and in what manner, are they to be used up? We have already seen the data available for answering this question, that is, the actual amount of British-owned dollar assets. The liquid foreign balances of British nationals were acquired by the government, as we have seen, immediately after the outbreak of war; and the exchange control, even in its early incomplete form, channeled all foreign exchange newly acquired by residents into government uses. The compulsory sale to the government of foreign securities held by residents followed after a considerable interval. The first list of February 1940 was confined to minor issues that were not very actively dealt in; but the second list was much more comprehensive and important. The gradualness of the application of the government's powers in this field was designed to make the acquiescence of those affected more certain and to avoid friction in important respects. The initial purchase of minor and inactive securities, combined with declarations that " orderly selling " was the policy of the British authorities, was designed to reassure the New York market that it would not be upset by any hasty British action. The authorities also showed themselves anxious to act by agreement rather than decree in allowing alien residents to apply for exemptions from the order to sell foreign securities, and in exempting altogether certain American holders who were resident in Britain.

The question of the rate at which these foreign assets have been used is a separate one. It is not possible to state with complete precision what the pace of liquidation has been. On this point, a distinction must be drawn between the earlier part of the war when a somewhat lax exchange control coincided with the absence of extensive military operations and the later stage.[48] A particularly well-informed writer made an estimate in May 1940 of the British gold and foreign exchange loss during the first six months of the war. The method was to estimate the foreign exchange needs in terms of the excess of current imports from hard currency countries over exports productive of " good " foreign exchange, and to deduct from that the estimated gold and foreign exchange receipts (mainly from newly produced gold of the sterling Empire and liquidation of foreign holdings and cash balances). The result was an estimated loss of gold or foreign exchange reserves, during the first six months, of $250,000,000.

It was pointed out that, while such a depletion was small in itself, it was kept at a low level by so rapid a liquidation of assets that the British authorities were unlikely to allow it to proceed for long. In the light of this interpretation, the tightening-up of exchange control which set in with the order of March 7, 1940, and which was quickly completed, could be regarded as a means of husbanding foreign assets more carefully and of covering a larger part of the current exchange outflow by current exchange acquisitions. This may well represent a fairly accurate description of the attitude of the British authorities at that stage of the war. The loopholes left in the original exchange control machinery were substantial, and considerable criticism was voiced in Britain of the waste of exchange resources which the British authorities were permitting. In the United States criticism was directed mainly against the apparent reluctance of the British authorities to make full and immediate use of their foreign investments for purchases of war materials in the United States.

The official British answer was never publicly stated, but it can nevertheless be presumed to have been in some such terms as these. Britain had to try and preserve as much of her foreign investments as possible for the sake of the postwar future. Britain, it could be argued, would then be badly in need of foreign supplies of food, materials for reconstruction, and industrial raw materials, and she would need the income from these foreign investments to finance many of her imports from abroad.

By the early months of 1941 the picture of Britain's relative financial strength was greatly altered. The intensification of the war had brought

---

[48] It has, for example, been suggested that voluntary liquidation of American securities from British sources, prior to the execution of the Government's scheme, amounted to $95,000,000 during the first three months of the war. This gives an indication of the amount of foreign exchange reaching the authorities from one source.

about a considerable change in the extent of British foreign investments and in the official attitude concerning their liquidation. In January 1941 the Secretary of the Treasury of the United States presented to the House Committee on Foreign Affairs in the course of its hearings on the Lend-Lease Bill, a statement of Britain's financial position. According to official statements, the net amount which the Sterling Area had to meet in gold and dollars during the first sixteen months of the war was $3,281,000,000. Of this total, $965,000,000 was covered by gold newly mined or dishoarded in the area, leaving a net drain on resources held at the outbreak of war of $2,316,000,000. This represented about half the prewar total. Allowing for minor differences of estimation and for minimum reserves necessary for the maintenance of current business, it was found that between $1,700,000,000 and $1,800,000,000 remained available to cover an estimated minimum net debit balance for 1941 of $1,500,000,000.

There has been some controversy over these figures and over the obvious political implication which they hold. With that controversy we are not here concerned. But whatever view one may take of the true extent of financial resources remaining available to Britain for purchases in the United States, it must be clear that considerable resources have in fact already been used up. The rapidly rising cost of the war, the increasing need for American supplies, the greater difficulty of producing exports and of transporting them, are all tending to increase the absolute demand for, as well as its relation to the current supply of, dollars. The total picture of this change in the relative financial position of Britain and the United States is fortified by such partial details as the sale of British direct investments in the United States, which was initiated in March 1941 by the disposal of the British holdings in the American Viscose Corporation, valued at $100,000,000.

The question of the future disposal of what resources remain is also very controversial. Leaving aside the more obviously political arguments, there are still profound economic problems involved in the possibility of a complete exhaustion of Britain's foreign assets. This is not the proper place for a discussion of these problems, since they are essentially problems of the postwar future. One's view of them will depend on the kind of postwar world which one posits or desires. If the premise is that of a restoration of an international trading system based to a large extent on countries which maintain a system of capitalist enterprise, then the transfer of Britain's foreign investments to the United

States must raise a vast problem of readjustment of traditional American economic policy. It can be easily seen how difficult it would be to fit such facts as the traditional American protectionist policy and the small experience of (and, possibly, aversion to) foreign lending, to say nothing of the fairly constant export surplus and the small relative importance to the United States of her foreign trade, with a newly acquired position of being the world's largest foreign creditor.

III. The most economical use of foreign resources readily available as a capital fund is only one of the problems of international war finance. In the case of countries with negligible foreign assets this problem does not even arise. Equally important is the maximization of current foreign receipts and their most economical use. This is the problem of export trade and exchange policy. We have seen the steps by which a solution of this problem was in fact reached. A brief summary of conflicting theories of the matter may now be added.

Much of the early discussion of the British exchange control was concerned with pointing out deficiencies in the mechanism and the waste of foreign exchange which resulted. It could be argued that the policy of granting import licenses more readily when the imports were invoiced in sterling created a continuous supply of sterling for the free market. Since sterling could be freely transferred from one non-resident to another, there was, as one writer said, a " basic contradiction " between the desire to husband dollar resources (through exchange control) and the desire to preserve the international character of sterling (by putting a premium on the invoicing of imports in sterling). Of a similarly contradictory character, it was said, was the action of allowing sterling to depreciate after the institution of control. Before control is established, a fall in the value of the currency acts as a deterrent to the export of capital. Afterwards, the control itself should be effective enough to stop such exports, which, it was claimed, was not the case. Such criticism seems logical enough. But when it is remembered that the authorities had to keep more than one objective in view, the difficulty of the situation can be more clearly realized. A contradictory policy becomes, then, merely the expression of an essentially contradictory situation.

One alternative before the British Government at the outbreak of war was to institute a full-fledged system of trade and exchange control which would have been fairly similar to that existing in Germany.

This would have meant the blocking of all balances in Britain and the creation of a number of different pounds at widely differing rates. It would have necessitated an aggressive drive towards a comprehensive system of bilateral trade agreements, and all the political and economic friction with neutrals which that would have involved. It would have roused considerable antagonism in the United States, at any rate in the short run, while in the long run it might well have destroyed forever the international financial position of London.

It is not the purpose of this study to examine the question whether the authorities were wise, especially in view of the course which the war subsequently took, to have let the above-mentioned considerations weigh in the determination of policy. But it seems certain that these considerations were in fact taken into account. Any realistic study must recognize that the British Government could not be expected, at the outset of the war when the exact alignment of all the different forces was still quite obscure, to take irrevocable, "logical" decisions on such fundamental issues as the whole future of British world financial supremacy. It can be, and has been, argued that the conditions in which the present war arose were such that Britain had to recognize the economic supremacy of the United States. As a condition of winning the war against Germany, Britain had to resign herself to a loss of her predominant position in international finance. Whether that is a true analysis of world economic forces or not, it would be naïve to suppose that the British authorities would accept and act upon such an assumption at the outset, and at a time when the United States was still neutral.

An explanation of the incompleteness and slow development of exchange control can be given in some such terms as these. To allow a free market in sterling to develop was to effect a compromise between completely prohibiting the withdrawal of foreign balances (which would have been fatal to London's international status), and making foreign exchange freely available at the official rate to all those non-residents who wished to withdraw their funds (which would have been far too costly). By creating a supply of free sterling and not interfering with the demand for it from foreign buyers of British goods, a liquidation of the "hottest" foreign balances in London could be effected without benefit of the official rate. It must, moreover, be remembered that the Sterling Area, with the addition at that time of France and her Empire, was excluded from this mechanism owing to the existence of coordinated exchange control and the special agreement with France.

London remained, therefore, the international banker and international debtor as far as that area was concerned. In relation to the non-sterling world, London became a short-term creditor; and this division made for greater elasticity and technical financial strength.

It may be that it was not necessary to go so far as to increase the supply of free sterling by favoring sterling-invoiced imports. But here, too, the authorities' desire seems clearly to have been to delay doing anything that would undermine the international status of sterling until they were absolutely forced to do so. In any case, the whole policy was a transitional one designed mainly to gain time. It made it possible to conclude special arrangements with individual large holders of sterling, and to explore the possibility of additional clearing agreements with different countries. We have also seen that from an early stage measures designed to tighten the control and to reduce the scope of the free market were introduced.

To explain the initial actions of the authorities in this way is to emphasize the difficulty of the situation which confronted the British Government. It is not intended to deny either that the actions lacked consistency or that they involved a considerable cost. The most important of the undesirable results of temporization was its effect upon the domestic price structure. The toleration of a free market for sterling undoubtedly increased the influence which depreciation had on the internal economic situation. It greatly encouraged inflationary tendencies, and has even been regarded by some as the chief cause of inflationary developments. The correlation between the British-American wholesale prices ratios and the pound/dollar free rate of exchange in the early months of the war is certainly very striking. While it is not possible to ascribe precise weights to all the influences at work, depreciation played an important part in giving wholesale prices that upward impetus which by January 1941 had carried them to a level 47.4 percent above the average of 1938.

The later evolution of exchange control has been in the direction of that greater completeness which critics demanded. This is true not only of the mechanism of control itself, but of the general principles of trade policy. The purpose of exchange control is not only to husband gold and foreign exchange, but also to make the country's terms of trade (that is, the ratio between the cost of imports and the proceeds of exports) as favorable as possible. Many writers have suggested (partly under the influence of the long history of German exchange control) that this aim might be achieved by maintaining, or even raising, the external value of sterling. One commentator has suggested that the best value of sterling would be nearer $5 than $4.

The reasons for this argument were as follows. Assuming that because of war-induced shortages, diversion of resources, and physical and economic limitation of shipping space, exports could not be increased, or even maintained at their prewar level, it must follow that depreciation could not give British exports a competitive advantage. Assuming further that foreigners' demand schedule for British goods had remained unchanged, the most effective policy for cheapening essential imports and avoiding inflation would be to raise the value of sterling by rigorous rationing of imports and consumption.

An examination of the relative depreciation of sterling in different countries was used to show the increased cost of imports due to depreciation; while the geographical distribution of British exports demonstrated that foreign demand for British goods, so far from falling, was likely to rise. All these data could then be made to support the policy of raising the dollar value of sterling.

The weakness of this proposal lies in the fact that once the pound had been allowed to depreciate, it would have required more than strict import control and rationing of consumption to raise the rate again. It seems clear that the cost of appreciation in terms of gold, foreign exchange, and foreign assets would have been very considerable. It was, therefore, a question of deciding whether the loss of goods due to the use of gold and other assets for the purpose of raising the exchange rate would have been more than offset by the gain of imports arising from a high value pound. It is doubtful whether a case can be made out for answering this question in the affirmative, especially in view of the increasing tendency — due to the very exigencies of the war — for imports to be more and more the subject of special deals, and for the decisive influence of the sterling rates in this respect to disappear.

The argument which has just been examined has the merit that it emphasizes the fallacy of assuming too lightly that depreciation of sterling would greatly encourage British exports. Of greater significance, however, are those proposals which affect the whole system of wartime trade policy. These generally begin with a statement of the undesirable features of exchange depreciation. The conditions of production and transport in wartime, it is said, make depreciation ineffective as a means for balancing trade. Sharp depreciation, moreover, leads to domestic inflation and decreases the value of income from foreign assets, most of which, in Britain's case, are in sterling. Another disadvantage among the many that could be cited is that the indirect tax on imports which depreciation represents is particularly unjust at a time when only vital necessities are supposed to be imported.

It is further pointed out that the elasticity of the demand for British goods varies from one country to another; that, therefore, the maximization of the terms of trade demands a policy of discrimination. Such a policy can be best executed by means of an extensive system of clearing agreements in which the value of the pound is fixed at as high a level as is politically practicable. This would cheapen imports and increase the proceeds of those exports with regard to which Britain is in a more or less monopolistic position. It has been argued that this policy would even increase the demand for competitive British exports in spite of the high pound, since the clearing partners would be forced (as many of them were under the German system) to spend funds accruing to them through their exports to Britain on the purchase of British goods.

The chief objection to this argument is derived from wider political, rather than from purely economic considerations. In the first place it must be remembered that, as has been frequently pointed out, the British Government would be slow to do anything which meant an irrevocable departure from that foreign trade mechanism through which London exercised its dominant position. The analogy of the supposed (but often controverted) success of German bilateralism would hardly be sufficient, since the conditions in which Britain was placed were quite different from those which caused Germany to adopt her clearing agreements policy. Britain's international position, which made it impossible for her to profit from the repudiation of debts, the structure of trade within the Empire, the possibility of intra-Imperial friction, the effect of any given policy on the United States, these and many other points would influence the decisions of the British Government. In particular, it may be pointed out that too aggressive a drive towards bilateralism (for example, in South America) would hardly have been well received by the United States, whose State Department had for long been committed to the defense of the most-favored-nation clause. And the United States itself, which was rapidly becoming Britain's most important supplier, was unlikely to join in a clearing agreement of the type envisaged.

Nevertheless, British policy did evolve slowly and cautiously in the way advocated by the protagonists of bilateralism. The number and range of trade and clearing agreements increased; and the order of March 7, 1940, which took six quasi-monopolistic commodities out of the depreciated free sterling market, can be regarded as a partial substitute for a clearing agreement with the United States. It increased the proceeds of exchange from the export of an important range of commodities and preserved for a time whatever stimulating effects the depreciated rate may have had on the export of competitive goods. The raising of the sterling price of monopolistic commodities, such as tin, which also happen to be greatly in demand in wartime, was another means of achieving the results of the German type of clearing agreement without provoking undue opposition.

Thus, in its practical working-out, exchange policy illustrates once again the close connection between the technical-economic, and the economico-political problem of warfare. A more detailed study than the present would, therefore, have examined Britain's relations with neutral countries in the light of the attitude of these countries to all the economic and political issues raised by the war. Britain had, for example, not concluded a trade agreement with the Soviet Union when that country was attacked by Germany, although negotiations had been going on for a considerable time. In the case of the United States, on the other hand, the absence of a comprehensive special wartime trade agreement did not prevent close cooperation. There was undoubtedly some friction, in the early stages, on such matters as the censorship of mails, the blockading of German exports, the problem of the exchange, British trade policy in South America, and many others; though no detailed official statement on these has ever been issued. But the general course of the measures adopted by the United States even in the early stages was characterized first by acquiescence in most of the major lines of British policy, including particularly the blockade, and later by active cooperation on an ever increasing scale. This cooperation was exemplified by the shipping provisions of the Neutrality Act and the raising of the embargo on arms shipments. Without such a broad conception of neutrality, the task of British economic warfare would have been made considerably more difficult.

4. Lend-Lease and After

On March 11, 1941 the Congress of the United States passed an Act "Further to promote the defense of the United States, and for other purposes." Its effect was immediately to alter Britain's wartime trade and, perhaps, to affect profoundly her postwar international economic relations. On June 22, 1941 Germany attacked the Soviet Union. That country became Britain's ally; and some of Britain's most difficult problems of trade and economic warfare were at once removed. In addition, entirely new prospects were opened up for the future alignment of international trade. On December 7, 1941 Japan attacked Pearl Harbor. Shortly thereafter the United States formally became a belligerent and Britain's ally; and within a few months great strides were made in the setting up of joint machinery for coordinating the economic activities of the two countries. These three great landmarks in the development of the present war mark the road which has led towards an increasingly planned and controlled international economic life of the United Nations and more particularly Great Britain.

Nothing illustrates these developments more than the great change in Britain's export policy. During the year 1941, the tendencies operative from the very beginning of the war were much accelerated. At the beginning of the year, British exports were still being fostered by an export drive which was served by all the usual means of advertising, good-will missions and the like, especially in South America and especially in regard to traditional export commodities such as cotton textiles. " Buy British " and " Britain delivers the goods " were the slogans heard at that time. Exchange pressure was particularly great, and it buttressed with the argument of national welfare a deep-seated commercial interest.

Even at that time, however, the more far-sighted observers realized that the export drive was bound to come up against powerful wartime obstacles, and that it could not for long be relied on as a contribution to solving Britain's exchange problem. Man power shortages became more and more acute. Material shortages became more and more acute. And facilities, too, were soon so strained that a concentration of civilian output in a few plants, with a conversion of the suitable remaining ones to direct war production, became an established policy. Finally, shipping movements and productive changes in other countries also made it increasingly difficult to harmonize import needs with the export drive. Military developments and the decline in import capacity due to sinkings necessitated diversions of mercantile tonnage in accordance with basic raw material and food import requirements, thus frequently making nugatory the efforts to expand exports.

The exchange problem was, of course, aggravated by these developments, and it was clear that a vicious circle was created which somehow had to be broken. Lend-Lease was the solution. It opened up to Britain a vast import potential which was not tied to Britain's ability to supply dollars for her overseas purchases. It immediately relieved the exchange pressure and permitted that relaxation in Britain's export drive which was in any case called for by fundamental wartime supply problems.

Lend-Lease took "the dollar-sign" out of U. S.-British trade and transferred the problem of international exchange between the two countries onto an entirely different level. It did, of course, put in a different light the fundamental problem of the economic relations of the two countries, and it created a major problem of postwar settlement. But for the purpose of the successful prosecution of the war, at any rate, it did tear aside the monetary veil, and it thus meant a very considerable step in the direction of a general realization of the basic supply problems of war.

Lend-Lease had another, somewhat slower but even more direct effect on Britain's export policy. From the very beginning of operations under Lend-Lease, it became obvious that substantial political difficulties might be encountered if Britain's exports were not consciously re-directed in the light of the newly-created import reservoir which, in the first instance, at any rate, was being financed by the American taxpayer. The British Government was fully conscious of this problem and showed great anxiety to prevent any cause being given for accusations that Lend-Lease was being used as a convenient means for strengthening or enlarging British export markets. On September 10, 1941 the British Government issued a White Paper which contained a declaration of its export policy. According to this declaration, the British Government does not permit the use of Lend-Lease goods for the furtherance of private interests, but only for the prosecution of the war effort. The British Government declares that British exports are restricted to the irreducible minimum necessary to supply or obtain materials essential to the war effort. Finally, the British Government declares that subject to certain exceptions, due to the difficulty of physical segregation or to the need to supply Empire and Allied countries, Lend-Lease goods and goods in short supply in the United States, would not enter into Britain's export trade.

Nor were Britain's imports unaffected by the developments of the war and by the institution of Lend-Lease. The latter allowed the creation of more rational import programs based on the all-important supply and shipping considerations rather than on the, in wartime, meaningless availability of foreign exchange. In general, it meant a vast increase in imports from the United States. The great increase in food imports from the United States illustrates best perhaps the supremacy of the need for shipping economy over the more normal commercial factors in international trade. As for the concentration of imports on goods essential for the prosecution of the war, the more recent developments of the war have merely intensified a tendency which, happily, had been in existence from the very beginning. What few nonessential imports remained, were completely eliminated after the fall of France. Strategic developments have, of course, also resulted in considerable shifts in sources of supply. The war in the Pacific, in particular, has cut out many imports and has in many instances resulted in changes in the geographical distribution of trade.[49]

As might be expected, so great a change in the relations between the United States and Britain as that occasioned by Lend-Lease could not take place without some measure of friction. Criticism has existed on both sides. Frequently it was misinformed or political in the narrowest sense. But occasionally there was also some genuine fear that vested commercial interests or undue concern with their relative postwar position was interfering with the countries' pursuit of the most rational and effective war policy. It is easy to see how the question of British policy outlined in the White Paper might become the basis of charges by both sides that foreign trade was being manipulated in accordance with ulterior motives.

It would be foolish to shut one's eyes to the existence of such criticism, particularly since it is now a thing of the past. Since the entry of the United States into the war, a number of developments have occurred which have immeasurably strengthened the tendency for emphasizing direct supply considerations which was inaugurated by the Lend-Lease Act. In the first place, there has been a substantial conversion of U. S.

---

[49] It is not possible to give figures, since statistics of the changes here discussed are now, quite properly, secret.

industry to war production with a consequent decline in the possibility of holding or winning export markets. Secondly, imports are increasingly controlled by war necessities. Thirdly, and perhaps most important of all, shipping has become as much an overriding factor for the United States — and for the other United Nations — as it was for Great Britain. This again meant that commercial motives of trade had to fall into the background. It is hardly possible now for Britain and the United States to accuse each other of trying to get new markets. They have too good an appreciation of each other's supply and production problems. It is, for example, notorious that Britain's exports to South America have fallen considerably while her imports from South America have increased, with a consequent large increase in the sterling balances held by South American countries. Even if she wanted to, it would not be possible for the United States to exploit this situation, since on grounds both of scarcities of man power and materials and of shipping shortage, the United States must strictly limit the goods which she can make available to South America.

This increasing congruence of the trading interests and possibilities of the two countries is becoming crystallized in the various combined boards created in Washington. Shipping, raw materials, food, production and resources, no less than military planning, come now increasingly within the purview of joint British and American organizations. There is, moreover, an increasing liaison with other United Nations. And, no doubt, before very long an even more direct joint planning by the two countries of their foreign trade — in so far as it is still of a civilian and commercial character — will be achieved and economic warfare in the narrower sense will thus become a joint effort. The British navicert, and the American export licensing system are already fully coordinated.

One powerful inducement to this general coordination, which is also a symptom of the progress already made, is the increase in what is often popularly referred to as " Reverse Lend-Lease." The present aid rendered by Great Britain and the British Empire consists both of goods — particularly of food and other material for U. S. forces overseas — and of services. No public statements have been made of the exact value of this reciprocal aid, but indications have been given that it is very considerable indeed. A general awareness of this aid and of the increase in U. S. production facilities called forth by British war orders of over $3,000,000,000 placed in the United States prior to Lend-Lease helps to remove the last traces of friction which Lend-Lease may have created. Reciprocal aid, moreover, is a powerful new concept and instrument of international exchange.

The United States has now signed so-called " Master Agreements " with a number of countries receiving Lend-Lease aid. That with Great Britain was concluded early in 1942. It is couched in only general terms as regards the " consideration " which is to be rendered for the Lend-Lease aid received. It does, however, bind the signatories to a mutual observance after the war of trade policies designed to work for " the expansion, by appropriate international and domestic measures, of production, employment, and the exchange and consumption of goods, which are the material foundations of the liberty and welfare of all peoples." The two nations also agree " to remove discrimination from trade, to work for the reduction of trade barriers, and to seek generally the attainment of the purposes set out in the Atlantic Charter." [50]

In addition, the United States concluded agreements for reciprocal aid with the United Kingdom, Australia, New Zealand, and Fighting France. These agreements, together with the protocol aid obligations towards Russia undertaken by the United Kingdom and the United States and the Canadian gift of $1,000,000,000 to the United Kingdom for the purchase of Canadian produce, may be cited as a few other outstanding symptoms of the emergence of a more complex mutual aid system among the Allies. The transformation of the original one-way flow of Lend-Lease from the United States to the United Kingdom into a more general system of mutual aid among all the Allies and the establishment of combined boards between the United Kingdom and the United States encourage one to hope that the basis has been laid for a brighter postwar future.

---

[50] See Appendix II.

CHAPTER V

Political Developments in Canada

by Gwendolen M. Carter

1. Before the Outbreak

In the last decade, doubt was often expressed that Canada would participate if another European war broke out in which Great Britain was engaged. This doubt was based on the independence of action of the senior Dominion, on Canada's geographical security and its proximity to the United States, and on the fear known to exist that participation in another conflict would strain Canadian unity to the breaking point. It underestimated both the strength of the British tie and Canadian awareness of the menace implicit in Nazism. The consciousness of a direct challenge in September 1939 bound surface divisions into a new and closer unity and in time resolved Canada's most delicate external problem, its close relations with the British Commonwealth of Nations and the United States.

These close relations are evident in economic life, where Canada's adverse balance of trade with the United States, the greatest source of its imports, is customarily met through its favorable sterling balance; in defense, where its geographical position makes it a pivot in the two defense systems of the British Navy and the Monroe Doctrine; in political and cultural fields, where the proximity of the United States is balanced by the British Commonwealth relationship and the less tangible links of tradition and sentiment. They provide external security but force Canada, for the preservation of its separate existence and individuality, to maintain a careful balance in external relations and to guard its internal unity.

Although different economic interests and racial backgrounds among Canada's 11½ million people have been reflected in policy, there has been no controversy over the continuance of the British connection, which all groups have accepted.

In the formative period before World War I, however, the relationship was interpreted somewhat differently by the two major parties, the Liberal, which under the leadership of Sir Wilfred Laurier dominated Quebec Province, and the Conservative, with a nucleus of "imperially minded" Canadians. The Liberals, though accepting the responsibility of Canada to go to the assistance of Great Britain in any major conflict, emphasized freedom of action, with the corollary that Canada had no right to influence British policy. The Conservatives supported a more positive policy of contributing aid to Britain, which they coupled with a claim to be consulted on British external policy.

The outbreak of war in 1914 found the Conservatives in office, but the wholehearted support of Laurier and the Liberals was pledged for the conflict. Unfortunately tactless handling of French-Canadian recruiting, their smaller proportion of enlistments, and other sources of internal friction caused growing feeling between English- and French-speaking Canadians which culminated in a struggle in 1917 over conscription for overseas service. In the ensuing election, parties divided on racial lines, an English-speaking Government facing a French-speaking Opposition. In the months following only wise leadership on both sides prevented active trouble. The experience was to cast a heavy shadow over future Canadian policy. A deep suspicion of the Conservative Party's external policy lasted long in Quebec and in some western communities. Over and above this were fears never wholly dissipated in the postwar period: fear on the part of French Canada lest it should find itself again in isolation from the rest of the country, and fear of the permanent destruction of Canadian unity should such an issue again arise.

Despite the smallness of the Canadian military establishments in 1914, Canada raised an army of over 600,000 men. It also made itself a base of supply for munitions during World War I. This activity was largely the result of the efforts of the Imperial Munitions Board, an agency of the British Government set up in 1915, under whose direction

Canadian factories produced huge quantities of shells, some 3,000 airplanes, and a considerable number of ships. The sudden industrial expansion, which raised Canadian exports of manufactured goods to Great Britain from a value of $8,500,000 in 1913-14 to $339,000,000 in 1916-17, came at a moment when the Canadian economy could best respond to it. The opening of the prairies in the decade preceding World War I had concentrated Canadian activities on construction. The end of this period was in sight when the new military demands stimulated the transfer of Canadian resources to production. In the four years of the war Canada emerged as an industrial country.

The postwar reaction common to all belligerents was intensified in Canada by the memory of the conscription crisis. Canadian policy became marked by unwillingness to assume obligations which might imply participation in another conflict.

At the time of the Treaty of Lausanne it was maintained that there was a moral freedom of obligation under pacts which Canadian plenipotentiaries had not negotiated or signed. Parallel with efforts to avoid commitments were those to secure a more independent status; Canada led the movement which resulted in separate dominion membership in the League of Nations. By contrast, in the field of Anglo-American relations with which it is vitally concerned, Canada made one small but possibly decisive contribution through its opposition at the 1921 Imperial Conference to the renewal of the Anglo-Japanese Alliance which, it feared, might extend to Great Britain the tension existing between the United States and Japan. Through this opposition the way was paved for the British acceptance of the invitation to the Washington Conference, out of which evolved the new conception of relations in the Pacific area embodied in the Four-Power Treaty.

The course of events after the failure of the attempt to enforce collective security in 1936 shattered Canada's aloofness and led it " inevitably closer " to Great Britain and to the United States.

Collaboration was at first implicit rather than explicit. In the matter of form, Canada avoided commitments, especially in its relations with Great Britain. There was, for example, no attendance at the meetings of the Committee of Imperial Defense, a fact which inevitably complicated cooperation later on. In relation to the United States, responsibilities were immediate, for Canada like many other states had neglected its defenses in the postwar period. Further curtailment of defense expenditure during the depression left the country with virtually no formal means of protection. Even before President Roosevelt declared at Chautauqua in 1936, "We can defend ourselves, and we can defend our neighbourhood," the Canadian Government recognized the necessity of reorganizing Canada's defenses so that it might be able to assume its own responsibilities in continental defense.

The comprehensive plan adopted for this purpose placed priority upon the fortification of coastal areas, the Pacific being given precedence, indicated the Air Force as Canada's first line of defense and the Navy as the second, provided a reorganization of the non-permanent militia along more modern and realistic lines, and sponsored a small armament industry to make Canada more self-sufficient. The program was moderate in scope, but by September 1939 Canada, although by no means fully prepared, was in a better position to provide its own protection than on the eve of any previous war.

Despite the obvious emphasis on home defense, the program had not gone unchallenged by those groups which feared to be involved in British wars. Although the plans were introduced and carried through by the Liberal Ministry, some of this opposition came from Liberals. The election of 1935 had brought this party its greatest majority since Confederation, 180 seats out of 245 in the federal House of Commons. But its members included diverse elements, one-third sitting for French-speaking constituencies and others representing varied industrial and agricultural interests. Such a combination taxed even the powers of its veteran leader, the Right Honorable Mackenzie King, a skilled though cautious parliamentarian. His control of his party was made still more difficult by the personal antagonism of the Liberal Premier of Ontario, Mr. Hepburn, and by the success in 1936 in the Liberal stronghold of Quebec of a party supporting local nationalism and provincial rights, the *Union Nationale* under M. Duplessis, who threatened to work with Mr. Hepburn for the discomfiture of Mr. King. Even more outspoken was the opposition to the defense program voiced by members of the C.C.F. (Cooperative Commonwealth Federation) Party, a small but well-organized group pledged to a moderate socialist program aiming to unite farmers and the urban laboring class. In contrast, the few comments of the Conservative Party, which formed the official Opposition, although it was composed only of thirty-nine members, favored closer cooperation with British defense plans, particularly through building up the Navy.

The logic of events gradually developed a more unified opinion.

When President Roosevelt emphasized closer continental relations in the face of danger abroad, in a speech of August 18, 1938, at Queen's University, Kingston, Ontario, there was general approval throughout Canada. Agreement on joint responsibilities for continental defense prepared the way for other measures of Canadian-American collaboration. Negotiations were reopened over the St. Lawrence Waterway scheme, there was further investigation of possible routes for an Alaska Highway, an invitation to an Inter-American Travel Conference was accepted (the first time the Canadian Government had participated in such inter-American activity), and the Canadian tariff structure was substantially modified to facilitate the Anglo-American Trade Agreement of November 1938.

The Canadian Ministry cautiously avoided committing itself on European events in the period which culminated in the Czechoslovakian crisis in the fall of 1938, but this was, in part, because though it was aware of the dangers of the situation, the country at large was not. The occupation of Prague brought from Mr. King a forecast of particular importance in view of his customary reluctance to make specific statements, " If there were a prospect of an aggressor launching an attack on Britain with bombers raining death on London, I have no doubt what the decision of the Canadian people and Parliament would be. We would regard it as an act of aggression, menacing freedom in all parts of the British Commonwealth." The announcement of the German-Soviet Pact helped to convince most of French-speaking Canada of the need for a united front. In September 1939 there was general agreement that Canada itself must decide the part it should play in any war in which Great Britain was involved, that its contribution would be largely economic, and its military effort relatively small, that there should be no conscription for overseas service. Events were to modify considerably the last two of these points, but the general agreement at this time was in itself of the greatest importance.

On August 22, 1939, following news that the British Parliament had been summoned, Mr. King informed the leaders of the opposition parties of the seriousness of the situation and received from them expressions of the fullest support. The War Measures Act of 1914, which had never been repealed, was brought into operation, and a number of Orders-in-Council began the process of bringing Canada to a war footing. Parliament was called for September 7, and the Prime Minister announced that if the Government of the United Kingdom became involved in war in an effort to resist aggression, the Canadian Government would seek authority for effective cooperation by its side. Thus, when Great Britain declared war upon Germany on September 3, it was clear that Canada would soon come to its support.

2. The Early Stages of the War

The fulfillment of the pledge that Canada should participate in war only by action of its own Parliament delayed its formal entry but not its preparation for conflict.[1] Parliament met for formal consideration of active participation in the war on September 7. It was not yet clear what means would be taken to bring the country to a status of active belligerency, but on September 9 it was announced that acceptance of the Speech from the Throne would be regarded as approving immediate participation. On the same evening the address was adopted without a division. Immediately following adjournment, the Cabinet met and approved an Order-in-Council authorizing the Prime Minister to advise the King to approve the proclamation declaring a state of war. On Sunday morning, September 10, Canada was formally at war with Germany.

Canada was the only dominion which took this procedure in adopting active belligerency. The form was important for the unity and effectiveness of the Canadian effort, for it threw responsibility directly upon all members and parties within the House. At the same time it assured groups throughout the country that the Government did not intend to precipitate action on its own initiative. On the major issue of participation in war all parties agreed.

Over the type and extent of Canadian participation considerable divergence of opinion was expressed. Mr. King's own survey of Canada's probable major activities emphasized responsibility for the defense of Canada, Newfoundland, Labrador, and British and French territory in the Western Hemisphere. He foresaw overseas aid primarily through air personnel. But there was general acceptance by both Conservatives and Liberals that other direct military aid might be sent abroad. Emphasis was also laid in general on the voluntary character of contributions. M. Lapointe, Minister of Justice and Mr. King's chief French-Canadian lieutenant, made it clear that he and the other Cabinet members from Quebec made their support of the Government conditional

---

[1] See below, Chapter VII, p. 330.

on exclusion from the military program of conscription for overseas service.

Parliament was kept in session only long enough to pass the War Appropriations Bill of $100,000,000 for the prosecution of war activities, and taxation measures which indicated that the Government intended to follow a " pay-as-you-go " policy.[2] It was then adjourned indefinitely, to the disappointment of many of its members. The Government, however, with support pledged by the other parties, preferred to work through Orders-in-Council. In the succeeding weeks it laid the foundations for military and economic aid and developed administrative instruments for limiting the effect on the civilian population of war conditions.

The fact that Canada had not assumed active belligerency until after the calling of Parliament and the formal vote on the Address had been satisfying to most French-Canadian nationalists, while the interest of English Canadians in the same procedure brought a new sense of unity. But a dangerous threat to this growing understanding arose with the announcement on September 25 that the *Union Nationale* Premier of Quebec, M. Duplessis, was calling a general election, to secure a mandate to resist certain war measures. M. Lapointe and the other Federal Cabinet members from Quebec came to the support of the provincial Liberal Party, pointing out that they would treat the results as a vote of confidence in themselves and would resign if M. Duplessis were returned. Quebec was thus faced with the loss of its representation in the Federal Government if it supported M. Duplessis' program. Beyond this, the success of the Liberal Party, which was brought into office in Quebec at the election on October 25, was the expression of a general desire for the maintenance of Canadian unity.

As early as September 19 the public learned that an expeditionary force had been decided upon after consultation with the British Government. In addition it was planned to send as many trained aviators, doctors, engineers, and technicians as possible to be absorbed into British units. The Navy was ready when war began to take its part in the transatlantic convoy system, and on September 16 the first convoy sailed. Close collaboration led to Canadian and British warships being interchangeable as need demanded. In addition to this support there was the Air Force, which was seen from the beginning to be one of Canada's most important contributions to the allied war effort. The strate-

---

[2] See Chapter VI, pp. 310, 314.

gic situation of Canada for air training had already been recognized in an agreement announced in the spring of 1939, to give advanced flying training to fifty airmen a year from the United Kingdom. A plan of far wider scope for a great training center in Canada for airmen from the United Kingdom, Australia, and New Zealand, as well as from the Dominion, was proposed by the British Government and worked out in detail by technical missions sent to Canada by the other countries.

The British Commonwealth Air Training Plan, as agreed on in November and announced in December 1939, provided for the training in Canada of about 35,000 pilots, observers, and wireless-operator air gunners a year by the time the scheme reached its maximum proportions. About 20 percent of these were to come from the United Kingdom, Australia, and New Zealand for advanced training, while 80 percent of the personnel was to be recruited in Canada. The R.A.F. was to supply some of the training staff, but when the organization was in full operation most of the approximately 40,000 men required to man it were to be provided by Canada out of those first trained under the plan. Costs of the scheme were divided roughly in proportion to the number of men trained for each government. Most of the aircraft required were to be supplied by Great Britain as its contribution, although elementary trainers and certain other planes were to be built in Canada. Of the total cost, amounting, it was estimated, to $600,000,000 for the period of the agreement, to March 31, 1943, $350,000,000 was to be Canada's share.[3] In marked contrast to the practice during the First World War, when the Imperial Air Force undertook its own recruiting and training in Canada independently of the Dominion authority, the program was to be administered by the Canadian Government and to be under the control of the R.C.A.F. with the advice and assistance of a Supervisory Board nominated by the participating governments.[4]

The huge proportions of the plan made necessary vastly increased facilities for air training before it could come into full operation. When

---

[3] By May 1941 the cost estimate had risen to $824,000,000, of which Canada's share was $531,000,000, or more than its total revenue in a normal year. A new agreement extending the plan to March 31, 1945 was negotiated in May 1942. The cost from July 1942 through March 1945 is estimated at $1,500,000,000, of which Canada's share will be $750,000,000.

[4] The Supervisory Board is under the Chairmanship of the Minister of National Defense, and includes the Minister of Finance, the Minister of Transport, representatives of the Governments of the United Kingdom, Australia and New Zealand, the Deputy Minister for Air of the Department of National Defense, and the Chief of the Air Staff. Contact with the Canadian Government is maintained by the Board through its Chairman, and with the Royal Canadian Air Force through the Chief of the Air Staff.

fully organized the training was to be carried on in ninety-three schools which covered every aspect of air force work. Sixty new air fields were needed, and about twenty others had to be enlarged.

To indicate the scope of the task, it is necessary only to enumerate some of the special training demanded by the complex character of air operations. Adequate staffs for the flying schools necessitate highly skilled flying instructors and also officers of administration, equipment and accounting, wireless engineering, and armament, as well as operators, instructors, and armorers, each of whom requires special training in specially equipped schools. Provision had to be made for the training of mechanics to do the work of checking, overhauling, and repairing the aircraft used by the pilot pupils, while supplementary repair depots, equipment units, and schools for training motor-boat crewmen and aircraft inspectors had to be organized.

Recruits are assembled in manning depots where they receive two weeks' drill and a general introduction to air force work. The next stage is carried on in the initial training schools, where a course of five weeks is given in such subjects as air force law, mathematics, flight theory, mechanics, air armament, and physical training. After this the recruits are divided into three groups as pilots, observers, and wireless-operator air gunners.[5] In each branch extensive instruction in the special field is coupled with sufficient training in the others to make it possible to take over those duties in case of emergency.

Pilots begin in the elementary flying training schools with a seven weeks' course of instruction in the ground school and in the air. This is followed by ten weeks with intermediate and advanced training squadrons, flying service types of aircraft. Some of these schools concentrate on instruction in piloting fighter planes and others on training bomber pilots.[6] At this later stage, the Canadians are joined by the Australians, New Zealanders, and British, sent for advanced training under the plan after receiving elementary instruction in their own countries.

Observers, who chart the course of the plane and also aim the bombs on raids, spend fourteen weeks at an observers' school learning air nav-

---

5 Prospective pilots must be between 18 and 31, while observers and wireless-operator air gunners must be between 18 and 33. Pilots and observers must have passed junior matriculation (University entrance) or equivalent, and wireless-operator air gunners must have completed successfully two years of High School.

6 Originally, student pilots concluded with two weeks at a bombing and gunnery school for instruction in the use of machine guns and in bombing technique but this was later omitted. All the periods of training given are those in effect at the end of 1941 and represent some increase over the periods originally allowed.

igation, aerial photography and reconnaissance duties such as sketching, observation, and spotting enemy positions and concentrations, following this with six weeks at the bombing and gunnery school for special training in the use of bomb-sighting devices, as well as the handling of machine guns, and ending with four weeks in advanced air navigation. Wireless-operator air gunners, who maintain touch with home bases and handle the armament, begin their specialized training with twenty weeks in a wireless school, followed by four weeks in the bombing and gunnery school concentrated upon the use of machine guns and training in repairing them. After the completion of this training the three groups form an air crew pool, from which some are chosen as instructors and the rest assembled at embarkation depots. Once overseas, they receive operational training preparatory to active service.[7]

After the first enthusiasm, realization of the length of time required to bring the Air Training Plan under way soon brought criticism upon the Government for not having foreseen and begun to meet the need when the issue of training British pilots first arose. To this was added considerable criticism of the slowness of recruiting, inadequacies in the equipment of the soldiers, and above all the smallness of the orders coming to industry from abroad. While Canadian Government contracts from July 1, 1939, to March 31, 1940, totaled $176,000,000, the orders of the British Supply Board in Canada between October 20, 1939 and March 31, 1940, amounted only to $70,000,000 of which the major portion was not placed until the first quarter of 1940. Moreover, there was irritation at British slowness in releasing plans and patents, and at the difficulty of meeting apparently rigid specifications for which Canadian firms were not equipped. Impatience over the gap between the desire to give help and the opportunities being offered foreshadowed a vigorous indictment of the sins of omission and commission of the Liberal Ministry in the Parliamentary session, scheduled to open January 25, 1940. To the disapproval expressed in the statements of the federal Opposition leaders was added a vote of censure in the Ontario legislature on January 18, which was jointly sponsored by Mr. Hepburn, the Liberal Premier, and Colonel Drew, the Conservative opposition leader, and carried by a decisive majority of forty-four to ten. To the dismay of the Opposition leaders, Mr. King presently declared that this made it necessary to go to the country for a nation-wide vote of confidence. Despite protests at hav-

[7] Active service is undertaken in the R.A.F. or R.C.A.F. In May 1942 R.C.A.F. Headquarters overseas was given general supervision over R.C.A.F. personnel attached to the R.A.F.

ing to fight an election without having had a full discussion of the war effort, Mr. King, waiting only to defend his policy in general terms, decided upon a dissolution the evening of the day Parliament met.

The two months' campaign succeeding the sudden dissolution of Parliament centered about the extent of Canada's effort in the war. It was in the main a clear-cut battle between the two major parties, the Conservatives charging that more should have been done, particularly in preparation for the Air Training Plan, and Mr. King standing on the record of his Government and the unity it had commanded. The election on March 26 provided the somewhat unexpected result of a substantial increase to 53 percent of the popular vote for the Liberal Party as well as the retention of its overwhelming majority within the House. There was still impatience over the smallness of war orders from outside. But in the situation existing in March 1940 many groups felt it was neither wise nor necessary to ask Canada to increase its own war contribution. Beyond the satisfaction of at least a majority of the voters with what had been done was the feeling that the King Ministry provided the best possibility of preserving national unity through its hold upon the two great racial entities of the country and their support of its policies.

Events were beginning to move, however, in a direction which made the continuation of previous policies impossible. The occupation of Denmark and of Norway gave the military situation a new character. But from April on there was a growing appreciation in Canada of the need of Hemisphere defense and of extending increased aid abroad. The demands made upon British resources by the outcome of the Battles of Flanders and of France made it necessary to turn for as many additional supplies as possible to Canada. The pent-up impatience of a people which had found it difficult to understand why full use had not been made of its resources received a sudden outlet. This helps to explain the immediacy of the response to the new situation.

3. The Response to the German Westward Drive

The response of Canadian public opinion to the Norwegian campaign was in some respects more immediate than that in Britain. Satisfaction with the Government's program of limited participation was replaced in many quarters with demands for increased aid. To these, the attacks on Holland and Belgium gave a new intensity. On May 15 the German Army broke through the French lines, an ominous background for the first session of the dominion Parliament the following day. From the party point of view the Liberal Ministry, with the national election behind it and commanding 183 out of a total of 245 seats, appeared in a stronger position than in even the previous Parliament. The Conservative Party was numerically small, as was the C.C.F. Party, returned at its former strength of eight members, and the Social Credit group, reduced in numbers to eleven. The spur to action was not party activity but overseas events and national concern.

In an atmosphere of great tension, Mr. King announced to the House accelerated recruiting, with a full corps abroad as its eventual aim, and the organization of a veterans' home guard and reserve companies of veterans. The British Commonwealth Air Training Plan was to be speeded up with the aim of completing during 1940 the training establishments planned for construction in two years.

When this decision was taken the elementary training establishments were just coming into operation. The plan of using civilian flying facilities for this stage had been adopted from British experience. Each flying club throughout Canada was offered the sponsorship of a company to be incorporated with a capital of from $35,000 to $50,000 to operate an elementary flying school. The Government furnished the buildings and loaned aircraft, while the companies provided the management.[8]

Serious curtailment of the schedule was threatened by lack of advanced training planes, a large number of which had been expected from Great Britain but could not be sent. Full-scale elementary training was, however, continued and other aspects of the Plan accelerated in the hope that aircraft would eventually be forthcoming. The production of advanced trainer air frames that could take United States engines was begun in Canadian factories. A number of trainers intended originally for France were secured through the British Purchasing Commission in the United States, and some shipments from Britain were resumed in July, with the net result that there was no alteration of the form of the Training Plan and its pace was increased.

As the Battle of Flanders was lost and the withdrawal from Dunkirk

---

[8] For each four weeks period during which a group of seventy pupils was trained, the company received a fee of approximately $1400 to cover instruction, food and maintenance of the aircraft. In order to prevent excessive profits it was eventually decided that no company should be allowed to pay a dividend of more than 5 percent on the subscribed capital. The company's books are supervised and new arrangements are made about twice a year on the basis of the profits of the preceding period.

began, Canada extended all possible aid. The second R.C.A.F. contingent was sent abroad, arriving May 29. After the withdrawal from Dunkirk Canadian troops of the division already in England were landed in France, only to be immediately evacuated. Canadian destroyers were serving with the British Navy in United Kingdom waters. All available equipment was rushed overseas, including fighter planes in use by the R.C.A.F. Airplanes on order in Canada and in Great Britain were released for British use and bombers en route to Canada for use in the Air Training Plan were sent back to the United Kingdom. At the request of the British Government, Canadian troops were sent to the West Indies, to free British regular troops garrisoned there, and to Iceland.[9]

In no place did the separate French peace bring more potential complications than to Canada with its large French-speaking population. But under the leadership of Cardinal Villeneuve, M. Lapointe, and Premier Godbout of Quebec, the French-speaking elements threw their continued support behind the cause which they had adopted as their own.

Secure in this support, the Ministry assumed emergency powers to mobilize human and material resources for the defense of Canada under the new National Resources Mobilization Act. Stressing that the mobilization of man power would relate " solely and exclusively to the defense of Canada on our own soil and in our own territorial waters," [10] the Prime Minister repeated his pledge against conscription for overseas service at the same time that the Ministry of National Defense announced provision for compulsory military training. This training, largely because of the restricted training facilities available, was limited to one month. Subsequently the period of training was extended, but in any case, unlike the selective service plan later adopted in the United States, the measure was intended only to be supplementary to the main Canadian recruitment which is on a voluntary basis.

The seriousness of the issues faced in the new international situation stimulated demands for a national government to give united direction to a united effort and a war cabinet whose members would be free from departmental duties. Though the Prime Minister argued that the election returns had given a national mandate to the Liberal Party, he made tentative moves to satisfy these demands. Some well-known Con-

9 On June 10, 1940, Italy declared war on Britain and France, and the following day the King approved the proclamation declaring a state of war between Canada and Italy " as and from the tenth day of June.
10 House of Commons, *Official Report of Debates*, June 18, 1940.

servative business men who were not in Parliament were asked to take portfolios in the Government. Following their refusal, a limited number of the Liberal ministers were designated a War Committee,[11] and four of the leading figures of Opposition groups were offered associate membership in this body or, as an alternative, regular consultations with ministers. Leaders of the Conservative Party felt slighted, however, by the offers made to non-Parliamentary Conservatives and also considered that acceptance of either plan would hamper their freedom of action without giving them sufficient share in the formulation of policy. The leader of the C.C.F. Party also declined the proposals, and no further effort along these lines was made by the Prime Minister.

While Canada's defenses were being strengthened, as much as possible was spared for the overseas effort to which public opinion was almost wholly directed. Unknown to the public, however, discussions concerning Canada's place in the scheme of North American defense were being carried on in continuation of private conversations between President Roosevelt and Prime Minister King during the previous three and a half years. They were based on the cooperation between Canadians and Americans already evident in the Permanent International Joint Commission and the more recent plans for the Alaska Highway and the St. Lawrence Seaway. But they had far-reaching implications not only for Canadian-American relations but also for those between the United States and all parts of the British Commonwealth.

On August 18 announcement was made, during a meeting of the President and the Prime Minister at Ogdensburg, of an organization for joint defense which potentially brought Canada and the United States closer together than they had ever been before and made it virtually inevitable that such close relations should be permanent. The joint statement gave only the bare facts that a permanent joint board on defense, consisting of four or five members from each country, most of them from the services,[12] would be set up at once, to commence immediate studies relating to sea, land and air problems, including personnel and matériel and to consider " in the broad sense " the defense of the northern half of the Western Hemisphere. The Board's first report was made on October 4, and the public was told that a Boston-Halifax defense

---

[11] See below, Chapter VII, pp. 359–362.

[12] The Honorable Fiorello H. LaGuardia was made head of the United States section, and Colonel O. M. Biggar, C. C., of the Canadian section. Other members included representatives of the army, navy, and air services of both countries, and a secretary from both the Department of State and Department of External Affairs.

line of ships and airplanes was planned capable of meeting an invasion five hundred miles at sea.

The Permanent Joint Board on Defense is a consultative body, with no executive power. Its reports are confidential. It appears, however, that it considers the whole field of North American defense and that its advice has been followed closely. Though the full extent of its influence cannot be known, the significance of the first permanent defense board of its kind is undeniable.

The Ogdensburg Agreement was not an isolated move. Almost simultaneously Mr. Churchill announced the offer to the United States of ninety-nine-year leases for air and naval bases in Newfoundland and Bermuda. To this gift was added an agreement, announced September 3, whereby the right to acquire similar bases in the Bahamas, Jamaica, St. Lucia, Trinidad, Antigua, and British Guiana was acquired in consideration of the transfer to Great Britain of fifty over-age destroyers. Six of these destroyers became units of the Canadian Navy and were already commissioned by the end of September.

Behind the negotiations resulting in the offer of bases Canadian initiative may well lie. At least it is known that the offer of the Newfoundland base was made to the United States with Canada's special approval. Canadian troops had been garrisoning Newfoundland since the beginning of the war, but because of its limited sea power Canada needed further assistance in protecting that area. That responsibility was shared with the United States in an area so vital to Canadian defense was the best indication of the permanence of the defense relations signalized in the Ogdensburg Agreement.[13]

The consummation of the British-American arrangement gave a new perspective to the Ogdensburg Agreement. The fear that attention to the defense of Canada would detract from aid abroad gave way to a realization that they were part of a common problem and that the only question was one of proportion. The widening impact of war caused by the German drive to the west had demanded an intensification of effort in every sphere. The results could be measured not only in terms of men and matériel but also of planned cooperation on a scale unimagined before the great emergency was faced.

---

[13] Canada's special interest in Newfoundland was recognized in the Protocol added to the Bases Agreement, March 27, 1941 (Cmd. 6259).

4. Consolidation of Effort

For the year from June 1940 to June 1941, Canada was Great Britain's strongest ally and the one closest to it geographically. During this period, and indeed, throughout 1941, Canada held first place as an outside source of supply for British war needs, except in airplanes. Further aid in guarding the convoys of the North Atlantic was provided with Canadian naval expansion and the extension of American aid in this sphere. In September 1940 Canadian forces on active service at home and abroad amounted to nearly 200,000 men, of whom 161,000 were in the Army, 11,149 in the Navy, and 26,500 in the Air Force. In the next nine months unspectacular but steady development virtually doubled the size of the Navy, bringing the mobilized strength to more than 20,000 by July 1, 1941, and to over 200 vessels.

In air training a new development was the establishment, in the autumn of 1940, of R.A.F. air schools in Canada under the direction of the British Air Liaison Mission at Ottawa. They were later integrated with the larger training plan. The Commonwealth Air Training Plan was also expanding, and by July 1, 1941, all but 12 of its schools were in operation. For the first time, all available applicants were being accepted and installed in schools immediately after enlistment. It was planned to recruit 36,000 men in 1941, 7 to 10 percent of this number coming from the United States by midsummer. Training of other personnel was keeping pace, so that the twenty-five Canadian squadrons to join the R.A.F. in 1941 would be served by Canadian ground-crew and administrative staff.

In the dark days following Dunkirk, the Canadian division had been the most fully trained and equipped of the forces in England which might have had to meet invasion. It remained a matter of consistent policy to continue to send new Canadian units to Great Britain. On Christmas Eve 1940, the formation of a Canadian army corps overseas was announced, just a day before the eighth contingent reached the United Kingdom, and brought the Second Division to full strength. In the summer much of the Third Division joined them, and Canada's first tank brigade. By July, there were approximately 220,000 in the active Army, of whom about 100,000 were overseas.

The period of training under the compulsory military service program was extended from one month to four in February 1941. Before the first group under the four-month plan concluded their service, it was announced that all called up for training would be retained for the duration. About one-half of the trainees have volunteered for active service, and the rest are posted to home defense duties to relieve men of the active Army for overseas. Other relief was provided by the recruitment of a Canadian Women's Army Corps, parallel to Women's Auxiliary forces in the other branches, to take over such duties as those of drivers, cooks, clerks, and messengers. By July, the Reserve Army numbered about 170,000, approximately one-half of whom were on full-time duty.

In the field of supply, the elaborate plant extension construction program [14] begun after the fall of France was bearing results but at the same time confronting serious scarcities which threatened to limit it. Within the country there was a shortage of skilled labor, of some raw materials, and of machine tools. As Canada turned more and more to the United States to make up its deficiencies in matériel, another even more serious block threatened — an exhaustion of Canadian funds with which to continue purchases in the United States. Since December 1940 Canada had borne the full burden of expenditure in the United States both for components for its own individual war contribution and for those needed for British orders from Canada.

The Lend-Lease Act of March 12, 1941, solved the serious situation which had been caused by Great Britain's financial stringency. Canada, however, preferred not to accept Lend-Lease aid if some other way could be found to meet its problems. That way became known through a joint statement by President Roosevelt and Prime Minister King, made on April 20, known as the Hyde Park Declaration. Though little publicized, it had far-reaching implications. It extended to the field of supply the principle of joint planning to provide not only for Hemisphere defense but also for aid to Great Britain and " the other democracies."

To meet Canada's immediate need for exchange there was to be more extensive buying by the United States of Canadian raw materials and supplies. Canadian purchases from the United States for use in British war orders were to come under Lend-Lease. This provided considerable relief and the possibility of more nearly balancing exports and imports. In the long run it appeared that not all of Canada's deficit in the United States could be met by these means and that some movement of gold and disposal of assets would continue to be necessary. The great change in the situation, however, was the acceptance of the " economic interde-

[14] See Chapter VII, p. 337.

pendence of Canada and the United States as the foundation of the programme of war production in both countries." [15] This meant not only that subsequent problems would be met by joint action but that efforts would be made to prevent them from arising.

The general principle was accepted that each country was to provide the other " with the defense articles which it is best able to produce, and, above all, produce quickly." The increasing duplication in war materials being produced by the two countries was thus to be restrained and future expansion to be planned jointly. A Material Coordinating Commission was formed in April 1941 consisting of officials of the Office of Production Management and of members of Canada's Wartime Industry Control Board. Its special responsibilities were to collect and exchange information on raw material supplies in the United States and Canada, and to consider their maximum utilization. Wider still in scope were the Joint Economic Committees set up in June 1941 by the two countries to explore the possibility of a greater degree of economic cooperation in fields not already covered by other agencies. Their responsibilities were extended also to studying possibilities of reducing " the probable postwar dislocation " resulting from the changes the two economies were undergoing. A Joint War Production Committee established in November 1941 at the recommendation of the Joint Economic Committees now coordinates the war production of the two countries and authorizes the free movement of essential supplies. In the ensuing year diplomatic conversations led to an agreement on steps to establish freer trade between Canada and the United States and with other nations after the war.

The Hyde Park Declaration and the measures which followed it were logical extensions of the planned cooperation announced at Ogdensburg in August 1940. The interrelation of military matters and war production was clear. It was from members of the Joint Defense Board that the proposals for the Material Coordinating Committee and the Joint Economic Committees came. With their acceptance in implementation of the Hyde Park Declaration, collaboration in meeting the needs of Hemisphere defense was extended to the whole field of war production. Beyond this was the agreement that wartime cooperation should be continued for wider purposes in peacetime.

---

[15] Mr. King in the House of Commons, April 28, 1941.

5. The Impact of Widening War

The new widening of the war which added Russia, Japan, and the United States to the major powers engaged brought Canada from the periphery of the war to its center. Canada's declaration of war against Japan came a few hours before those of the United States and Great Britain. Closer on both Atlantic and Pacific coasts than the United States to the main Axis powers, Canada seriously faced for the first time the possibility of enemy attack. With the slack of its man power and its productive capacities already taken up, Canada became confronted with a new urgency by the conflicting demands of home activities and overseas aid.

The first great widening of conflict, the outbreak of the Russo-German war on June 22, 1941, raised special problems for Canada. It was not clear immediately that French Canada would be ready to accept the Soviet Union as an ally. The question lay largely in the attitude to be adopted by the Catholic hierarchy. But throughout the war, its influence had been placed on the side of national unity, and this attitude was to be maintained in the new crisis. Under its ecclesiastical and political leaders, French Canada, though maintaining its inherent dislike of Communism, agreed to cooperate with the rest of Canada and its allies in aiding Russia against their common enemy.

The Far Eastern war has turned much public attention to the protection of Canada's Pacific coast, which is virtually linked by Alaska and the Aleutian Islands to the Asiatic mainland. Fortunately, nature facilitates its defense, for along most of its six hundred miles of extent, mountains rise sheer out of the water making a natural barrier from 50 to 100 miles in width and rising to a height of 7,000 to 10,000 feet. Only two passages exist which might serve an invader from the sea, the Fraser Valley, through which Canada's two transcontinental railways run, and the more northerly Skeena Valley, where a trunk line terminates at Prince Rupert. Both areas, particularly that around Vancouver, are fortified and guarded by Canadian troops. Beyond its immediate territory, however, were responsibilities for the Alaska panhandle bordering northern British Columbia and the Yukon and for aiding communications between the State of Washington and Alaska. To serve both purposes, the Canadian Government, on the recommendation of the Permanent Joint Board on Defense, had already built a chain of air bases which, linked with existing Trans-Canada Airlines facilities, made pos-

sible the rapid transfer of fighter planes to Alaska as well as the maintenance of a coastal patrol. When the intensity of the Pacific conflict led
to a shortage of shipping with which to transport supplies to Alaska
and raised the danger of submarine attack, it was determined to build
a highway to Alaska linking the air bases. Although much of the road
goes through unbroken country, it was completed in November 1942.[16]

In British Columbia are centered practically all of Canada's Japanese, who number just under 25,000. Already in January 1941 a voluntary registration of Japanese had been conducted. In the first week after
Pearl Harbor, registration was made compulsory. In January 1942 special regulations limited their movements. In February, in a move parallel
to the Pacific coast arrangements in the United States, enemy aliens were
ordered to evacuate British Columbia west of the Cascade Range of
mountains by April 1.

The success of Japanese arms in the East and the menace of the Nazi
war machine in Europe faced Canadians in the spring of 1942 with two
great problems concerning the use of their resources. Both concerned
the distribution of Canadian man power. There were those, particularly,
but not exclusively, in Quebec, who felt that the new dangers accentuated the need for home defense. In contrast was the outspoken support of
the new Conservative leader, Mr. Arthur Meighen, for conscription for
overseas service.[17] The second division was between those who felt that
all available man power should be placed in the armed forces and those
who maintained that Canada's greatest contributions were in the field of
supply and that care should be taken to keep adequate personnel both
in industry and agriculture.

With his usual habit of compromise, Mr. King chose the middle way
in regard to both controversies. Home defense forces, particularly of the
R.C.A.F., are being strengthened. There is no slackening in the steady
voluntary recruitment which had brought the armed forces to 422,000 at
the end of 1941 (295,000 in the Army, 100,000 in the Air Force, and
27,000 in the Navy) and is expected to bring them to 600,000 by March
1943. But in the light of the new situation abroad, Mr. King asked to be
released by a nation-wide plebiscite on April 27 from the pledge not to
draft soldiers for overseas service.[18] Following the plebiscite Mr. King

---

[16] The expenses of construction are borne by the United States Government, and the road will
become part of the Canadian highway system after the war.

[17] Mr. Meighen was replaced as leader of what is now to be called the Progressive Conservative Party in December 1942 by Mr. John Bracken.

[18] The plebiscite resulted in a 64 percent vote in favor of releasing the Government from its

introduced a Government measure in the House of Commons to delete clause 3 of the National Resources Mobilization Act under which men called up for compulsory military service could not be sent overseas. In so doing, he declared that " we are obtaining men for overseas service at the present time as rapidly as we can train them." With the passing of the measure, the Government was empowered to institute conscription for overseas service when it was found necessary.

On the other issue of the distribution of man power between the armed services and the needs of industry and agriculture, Mr. King has also chosen a middle course. Compulsory military service for home defense has been extended to all men between the ages of twenty-one and forty, selection to be by lot. To increase the numbers available for service or for war industry, entry into a large number of occupations has been prohibited for men over seventeen and under forty-five years of age. The increasing needs of industry are to be met by bringing in women and older men. Employment in agriculture is to be more or less stabilized. Farmers' sons and agricultural laborers need not undertake compulsory military service if they are considered essential workers in agriculture. No man employed in agriculture may accept other service without permission except to enlist in the armed forces.

In its fourth year of war, Canada is reaching full utilization of its human and material resources. Its most spectacular contribution, the British Commonwealth Air Training Plan, is now associated with the American air training program through the Combined Committee on Air Training in North America.[19] All of Canada's own war contribution, and practically all of what it has supplied Great Britain, has been financed by Canadians. In 1942 a direct gift has been made to Great Britain of a billion dollars worth of munitions, raw materials, and food stuffs. In addition an interest-free loan of $700,000,000 has been extended for the duration of the war, and $295,000,000 worth of Dominion securities have been repatriated. Additional burdens are imposed by heavy buying in the United States, which continues to confront Canada with a deficit, which amounted to $142,000,000 in 1941. Canada's own war expenses for 1942 will exceed by far what it spent in the whole of World War I.

pledge not to impose conscription for overseas service. The civilian vote was 2,670,088 in the affirmative and 1,547,724 in the negative, while the military vote was 251,118 to 60,885. All provinces except Quebec had a majority for the affirmative.

[19] Set up in May 1942, following an Air Training Conference in Ottawa in which fourteen of the United Nations were represented.

Beyond all this, history may designate Canada's share in developing collaboration with the United States and in extending it to Great Britain as its most significant achievement. In so far as it has been, to quote Prime Minister Churchill in Ottawa in December 1941, " a potent magnet drawing together those in the new world and in the old," Canada has made a decisive contribution not only to the war but also for the future.

CHAPTER VI

Canada's Economic War Policy

by B. S. Keirstead

Introduction

The Canadian economy on which such heavy new demands and responsibilities have fallen was not organized for war, and from the military point of view it had certain obvious weaknesses. There were, however, elements of strength, sources of great potential power, once the transition to a war organization had been accomplished. Besides her great export surpluses of grain and other agricultural produce, Canada possessed both metallurgical and manufacturing industries of first-rate importance and was the fifth ranking commercial power in the world. Her metallurgical output includes coal, in which she has satisfied more than 50 percent of her requirements, iron and steel, now developed to the point of being nearly adequate to the support of her war industries, an annual oil production of 10,000,000 barrels, and nickel, aluminum, copper, zinc, silver, and gold,[1] in all of which she has large export surpluses. In addition she has the greatest per capita development of hydroelectric power in the world, which will be even higher when the St. Lawrence Waterways Project is executed. Canadian nickel mines produce 85 percent of the world output.

Canadian manufacturing, small compared with that of the United

---

[1] Annual gold production is $200,000,000.

States, has nevertheless replaced agriculture as the largest industrial source of income, and has put Canada among the first ten manufacturing countries in the world. With a gross peacetime value productivity of over $3,500,000,000 and a " value added " of more than $1,500,-000,000, Canadian manufacturing was equipped to make an important contribution to the war needs of the British Commonwealth. The internal organization of manufacturing industry, characterized by the large-scale firm, has made for the maximum strength in time of war. The concentration of ownership and the comparatively small number of firms to an industry, all of considerable size, a phenomenon no͟ without evil social implications in peacetime, has permitted the rapid organization and complete control of industry for war purposes. It has meant, further, that mass production methods were familiarly in use, and it has facilitated the rapid and most economic expansion of industrial plants in sectors already well served by reservoirs of hydroelectric power. We may notice also the advantages that accrue from close proximity to the United States. Many Canadian firms are branches of American business.[2] They have " entered into the fruits " of American labor in industrial research, scientific methods, and efficient management. Technically, Canadian business has been able to enjoy a similar order of superiority to that enjoyed by the United States. Moreover Canada is able readily to draw on the United States for supplies of precision instruments, and she is able partly to rely on the American engineering and chemical industries. This, however, cannot entirely be entered on the credit side.[3]

Finally one should mention the human qualities without which all natural wealth is not a real and active but merely a potential and passive asset. The Canadian population is a mixed one in which the British elements, amounting to about 50 percent, predominate. Then follow the French, about 30 percent, and people of other European stock, mainly German, Scandinavian, Italian, Polish, and Slav, about 20 percent. In general the population is of a high level of health, intelligence, and training. In morale, in labor skills, in productivity, it would rank very high compared with European peoples. But the depression years have left their mark. Canadian governments, dominion and provincial, with few exceptions, have been notorious for their indifference to social wel-

---

[2] Canada is normally the largest purchaser of the United States, and United States investments in Canada are larger than in any other country.
[3] See below, p. 322.

fare and there have been conditions of malnutrition, disease, and dire poverty, conditions which have been neglected as in few other advanced nations. It has taken the crisis of a dangerous war to illuminate the evils of social neglect.

Of the weaknesses of Canada as a military nation must first be set her complete lack of defense preparations. In 1938, her last peacetime year, her estimates for defense were $32,000,000, and in 1939 the ordinary budgetary defense provision was $34,000,000, sums which represented rather less than 1 percent of the total national incomes of those years. One may set this percentage against the German provision which in 1939 totalled 50 percent of the whole national income. Even in Britain 25 percent of the national income was devoted to war by the peacetime budget of 1939. Canada had few industries engaged in direct war production, and her basic industries were all engaged along peacetime channels. To maintain her small peacetime navy she had bases at Halifax and Esquimalt and a shipbuilding industry, which had little experience in the construction of war vessels. The Royal Canadian Air Force depended rather on British aircraft production than on the infant industry that was just being established in Canada. Her army of 4,000 men used weapons and equipment standardized throughout the British Empire and supplied mainly by Great Britain, although Canada did maintain the Dominion Arsenals.

Hence the Canadian economy started, so to speak, from scratch in the race of belligerents to maximize their war production. The changeover to a full war basis, difficult under any circumstances, was rendered all the more difficult for Canada by certain other weaknesses in her economic position. Canada's has always been an exposed economy; approximately 30 percent of her total net production is normally exported. Her chief industries are far more dependent than any important American industry on export markets. Many of these were shut off or reduced with the outbreak of war, either because they were in enemy territory or because of British rationing and the establishment of Admiralty shipping priorities. The immediate effect, particularly on the wheat-growing west, was one of extreme dislocation and market depression which served to increase the confusion attendant on the shift of industry to a war basis.

Further, the Canadian economy is a regional one. Manufacturing industry is concentrated in southeastern Ontario and western Quebec.

Also in Ontario and Quebec in the northern areas and about the Great Lakes are the metallurgical industries, based on the rich mineral deposits of the Laurentian shield. The prairies are agricultural, primarily dependent on the wheat economy and consequently desirous of good export markets and low prices on manufactured goods. British Columbia is a prosperous maritime economy with mining, forestry, specialized agriculture and horticulture, secondary manufactures, and a great Pacific trade. The Maritime Provinces on the Atlantic seaboard are comparatively poor with a diversified, not very abundant, agriculture, small-scale manufactures, some small share in the Atlantic trading, but primarily dependent on the forest and metallurgical industries and fishing.[4] These different economic regions with various and often conflicting interests have given rise to serious problems affecting the federal structure of Canada. It has always been difficult to find some compromise for the general opposition between a national policy directed towards the greatest economic efficiency conceived in pecuniary or production concepts and one directed towards national welfare conceived as a general level of well-being in the least well-favored as in the best-favored regions. In wartime this opposition takes the form of setting the greatest possible efficiency of industrial war effort against the needs and welfare of some of the nonindustrial regions.

Finally we must notice a noneconomic source of weakness which, though coming from without the field of economics, had direct consequences on Canadian economic development for war. Economic war planning must be integrated with general strategy. The economy must be geared to produce the supplies as and when they are strategically required. Now the Anglo-French grand strategy was defensive. The Allies meant to stand behind the natural sea defenses of Britain and the Maginot line of France, gradually weakening Germany by blockade, and in the meantime organizing and mobilizing their own industrial resources. They enjoyed at that time an overwhelming advantage in potential economic strength. This strategy gave Canada ample time to accomplish a slow transition to a war economy, avoiding the worst

---

4 The treatment in the text is necessarily oversimplified and compressed. Quebec Province has a peasant population dependent on mixed agriculture and parts of Ontario are well-known for horticulture, dairy farming, gardening, and mixed farming. In the western provinces of the prairies are found mining both of coal and metallic minerals and the oil industry of Turner Valley. The statement that metallurgical industries are concentrated in the central provinces must be qualified in the light of the gold, silver, copper, and zinc production of British Columbia and the iron and coal industry of Nova Scotia.

confusion of a revolutionary change-over. It also meant that the Canadian economy could be geared to the British, with standardized equipment and with British airplane engines, wartime tools, and engineering components. Canada could specialize in raw material production and in those lines of manufacturing, such as motor vehicles, in which she enjoyed advantages, while drawing on Britain for those goods in which the more mature industrial economy enjoyed a comparative advantage. When this strategical assumption was overturned by the German success against France, the whole economic plan had to be changed. England had need of all her own tools, armor steel, every item of equipment. Nothing could be spared for Canada, who had to improvise equipment for her own forces, revolutionize her industrial plans, and find either within her own boundaries or in the United States sources of supply for the equipment, tools, and so forth she had expected to get from England. Thus the military crisis led to some of the most difficult problems that Canada has had to face in preparing her economy for war.[5]

1. The First Phase (September 1939–May 1940)

It is, of course, essential in modern war that military and economic strategy be part of one " master plan " or " grand strategy." But the academic or newspaper critics who believe that an entire war can be set out, so to speak, in a blueprint and handed over as a whole to the military, naval, and economic architects to turn into reality, have failed to understand the essential nature of warfare. You are not, in war, operating on a passive substance which you can mould to your plans, not dealing, to change the metaphor, with a constant, or even with a variable whose mutations can be plotted or " projected " with certainty along some regular curve. The very essence of war is the resistance of the enemy, his ability to thwart your plans, divert your intentions, defeat and confound your schemes. The first test, therefore, of any " grand strategy," is elasticity; the decisive trial of the strategist, adaptability. It is true that military and economic planning must be part of a whole, that fiscal and monetary policy must serve supply, that supply and the proper allocation of the agents of production must be so organized that various supply departments do not bid against or thwart one another, and that all this economic planning must be directed to serving the military requirements so that decisive weight can be thrown against the enemy where he

---

[5] See Chapter VII, p. 337.

is weakest when he is least well prepared. But it is equally true that the military strategy must provide for alternatives, must be ready to modify the disposition of forces so as to frustrate the enemy's strokes, to counter-attack if the suitable moment comes. Thus the needs of the military are fluid, subject to change. It is essential that the economic program be such as to meet these fluid needs, and that supply departments be not so rigidly confined to a " master plan " as to be unable to meet *ad hoc* problems as and when they occur.

All this is especially relevant to Canada, because, as a minor power (in the early days of the war), she had but little part in making the master plan and had rather to accept the part therein assigned to her, which was to specialize in the production of those war goods in which she enjoyed a comparative advantage. In general Canada, under the original scheme, was relied upon to produce food stuffs, raw materials, and nonferrous metals. She undertook, as well, to provide for the establishment of the Air Training Plan, and Canadian manufacturing industry was to supply her own forces with clothing, various items of personal equipment, and certain small arms and ammunition. Her motor vehicle industry was called upon to supply both the Canadian and, in part, the British forces, and some explosives were made, and plant construction was started for the expansion of munitions and explosives supply.

Immediately following the declaration of war [6] Parliament was summoned in special session and voted the sum of $100,000,000 for national defense.[7] Certain additional taxes were imposed, notably a 20 percent surtax on all taxable income under the Income War Tax Act,[8] and an Excess Profits Tax,[9] and certain minor indirect taxes chiefly directed against luxury goods. On the whole the Government, however, decided not to impose heavy taxation at that stage. Canada had a large amount of unemployment and of under-employment both of men and of capital. Inasmuch as heavy taxation tends to have a regressive effect, the Govern-

---

[6] See Chapter V, p. 288.

[7] An Act for granting to His Majesty aid for National Defense and Security, September 11, 1939.

[8] An Act to amend the Income War Tax Act, September 12, 1939.

[9] The Excess Profits Tax Act, September 12, 1939; this Act provided for two schedules of rates at the option of the taxpayer. Schedule A was a graduated tax beginning at 10 percent of profits in excess of 50 percent and not exceeding 10 percent of the capital employed, and rising to 60 percent of profits and not exceeding 25 percent of capital. Schedule B imposed a straight levy of 50 percent on all " profits in excess of the average annual income of the taxpayer . . . for the four years 1936, 1937, 1938 and 1939. . . ."

ment proposed, until its spending program was under way, to stimulate employment and industrial expansion by short-term loans from the commercial banks.

This policy was followed with satisfactory results. Though there was the usual recession both in prices and employment immediately after the outbreak of war, and though there was considerable dislocation in agriculture, the commercial pick-up and industrial expansion followed at once. The Government borrowed $200,000,000 from the commercial banks on two-year notes at 2 percent, and the Bank of Canada's assets increased between August and November by $107,000,000 as a result of open market buying. This increase in reserves enabled the banks to increase their deposits by just over $300,000,000. The stimulus to business activity was reflected in all the indices of retail and wholesale turn-over, industrial production, and prices, though these indices showed a considerable sag in the early months of 1940. When, in the spring of that year, the Government floated a public loan of $200,000,000 and increased its own spending, there was a renewal of business expansion, which then continued throughout the year and was apparent in industries producing for civilian consumption as well as in the heavy and armaments industries.[10]

Apart from these no extraordinary powers were assumed by the Government for economic control. It was presumed that the monetary policy and government borrowings would stimulate enterprise and that government expenditures would direct labor and capital into war channels. The free price mechanism was relied upon to function as the agency through which public, like private, demand would gain effect.

2. The Crisis (May 1940 and After)

When the storm broke and the German armies marched through Holland, Belgium, and then accomplished in twenty-one days the complete defeat of the army which inherited the tradition of Jena and defended the principles of 1789, the whole ordering and marshaling of the strength of the British Empire was thrown into confusion. The invasion of England was imminent, and the military equipment of England was a mass of burning, charred, or broken metal strewed along the plains from Antwerp to Dunkirk.

That there was confusion is to be expected, that mistakes were made

---

[10] See Table I, p. 315.

may be presumed; yet when the ministers met the House of Commons during the critical days of May and June there was neither hysteria nor a sense of frustration. No attempt was made to formulate a new war plan on the grand lines of the old. Immediate *ad hoc* problems of supply had to be tackled as they arose. Gradually, however, as the immediate demands were satisfied, and as the summer passed without invasion, a new policy began to be formulated.

I · SUPPLY

The immediate problem was of supply. It is, perhaps, usual to look on this as a matter of production, and to regard as distinct questions, fiscal and monetary policy, labor policy, and capital allocation. There is a convenience in this method for it is almost essential to impose classifications to order and elucidate a complicated question. Nevertheless the problem of supply is a complex involving all economic relationships. It consists in obtaining labor and capital in the war industries in sufficient quantities to provide the required production. Where there are scarcities, the labor and capital must be apportioned so that the most urgent needs are first filled, and so that great accumulations of half-finished material, shells for instance, are not piled up waiting such components as fuses, the production of which waits on a supply of skilled labor that has been too rapidly consumed in the manufacture of steel for shell casings. Thus on examination the supply problem is seen to include the planning not simply of production within this or that industry, but the ordering, as between various branches, of the supply of capital and labor disposal. Thus war supply is only a special case of the general economic problem of allocating scarce means to manifold ends. The labor and capital must be found by training and transferring the unemployed or those employed on unnecessary peacetime pursuits. This means that production must be expanded to the limit of the national capacity and that civilian demand must be reduced, and reduced if possible without affecting the morale, health, or efficiency of the population. Involved is the whole question of war finance, of industrial and price controls, of rationing, and of monetary action. Thus, in reviewing the problem of supply and its treatment in Canada throughout the period of crisis after May in 1940 to midsummer, 1941, we must keep steadily in mind, even if we are obliged to pursue but one thread of thought at a time, that economic policy had ultimately to be conceived and developed as a whole.

First must come, though it has been often neglected, the continuation of the Canadian supply of raw materials. Canadian agriculture had to supply foods for an England deprived of Scandinavian and Dutch sources, and the wheat economy, with its European market depleted, had to yield place, at least in part, to the production of hogs, stock, and dairy produce. The shift from wheat could not be either immediate or in any proportion to the decline of the market, and, to save the prairies from utter destitution, the Government had, at considerable public expense, to undertake to store and to market millions of bushels of unsold wheat. Canadian copper, nickel, and aluminum production had to support, as they have adequately done, the war needs of the Empire, and gold production was increased to finance the purchase of United States supplies. Canadian steel had to make the war industries as self-sufficient as possible.[11]

Despite all difficulties, the Canadian industrial effort of 1940 was a considerable achievement. In the industries in which there existed, prior to the war, plant, experienced management, and skilled labor, fast schedules were set and exceeded. The British Army of the Nile was carried forward to crush Italian power in North Africa in Canadian built motor vehicles; its supply was maintained by Canadian trucks. The Canadian Active Army of four divisions with reinforcements and Corps troops and an even larger number of men in the Reserve Army were clothed and supplied by Canadian industry.[12]

During 1941 the military demands were further increased and it was made known that Canadian industry had developed to the point where it was possible to raise and equip armored divisions in Canada. Before the end of 1941 Canada had promised to send to England an armored brigade to act with the first and second divisions of the Canadian Army Corps now in England, and also to dispatch the third infantry division and a full armored division.[13] Keels for the first destroyers to be constructed in Canada were laid down in early summer, 1941.

In the industries in which there had been little if any previous Canadian experience, chiefly tanks and military aircraft, the difficulties were

---

[11] Steel production in 1940 and 1941 has been 43 and 77 percent above 1939.

[12] Canada also undertook to build weapons of the following categories: 40-mm. Bofors anti-aircraft guns; 3.7-inch anti-aircraft guns; 25-pounder guns and carriages; Colt-Browning aircraft machine guns; Colt-Browning tank machine guns; 6-pounder guns for tanks; 2-pounder anti-tank guns and carriages; 4-inch guns and mountings; 12-pounder guns and mountings; 4-inch naval guns; 6-inch naval guns; Lee-Enfield rifles.

[13] About 10,000 vehicles are required for an infantry division.

greater and deliveries were not always made on schedule. Some 3,000 tanks were ordered in Canada in 1940, but actual production was postponed until early in 1941. Airplane manufacture in Canada was for the most part concentrated on trainer aircraft, though some bombers and some Hurricane fighters were ordered for the Royal Air Force and a few flying boats for the Royal Canadian Air Force.[14]

In sum, the Canadian accomplishment in production may best be realized by comparing the advance in the production indices of 1940 over 1939 with the advance of 1930 over 1925. In twelve months under Government direction and the stimulus of war as much was accomplished as during five years of the greatest peacetime industrial expansion modern capitalism has experienced under the stimulus of private profit. But in 1940 the progress was made under conditions of a changeover in the type of product and of machine tools and the adaptation of labor skills that amounted to an industrial revolution.

II · FISCAL POLICY

The supply departments thus set out requirements and, in the main, fulfilled them by an enormous transition and expansion of Canadian industrial production. How were the labor and capital obtained and directed to carry out this war program? The Government, as we saw, stimulated industrial expansion by its fiscal and monetary policy in the early months of the war. It carried forward about $200,000,000 in cash from its long-term borrowings into the fiscal year of 1940 and thus maintained the slightly inflationary policy it had initiated. But in the June 1940 budget it was clear the Government meant to begin the fiscal restriction of consumers' demand. Wars must be paid for out of current income in the sense that the weapons and munitions of war have to come out of the current production of the nation. How they are paid for does not affect this basic truism. If the Government pays for them by taxing the public it simply takes away the amount of the tax from potential consumers or from potential investors who might otherwise invest in peacetime capital and it spends the proceeds in purchasing war goods or wartime capital equipment. Fewer consumers' goods or peacetime capital goods are bought and consequently the demand for labor and capital in the peacetime trades falls off, and the agents of production are directed into the war industries. A tax, levied according

---

[14] By the spring of 1942 over 300 airplanes were being turned out every month.

to ability to pay, imposes the sacrifices of consumers' satisfactions roughly according to ability to bear sacrifices.

A long-term loan may likewise impose certain sacrifices of consumers' goods. It is generally not subscribed from current income but from accumulated savings, although the average investor, if he reduces his accustomed liquid balance at the bank, is apt to curtail expenditure until he re-establishes it in whole or in part. Thus a loan may result in some restriction in consumers' demand, and to a greater extent in a restriction of demand for peacetime capital goods. But on the whole a loan is not effective, as a tax is, in imposing regular sacrifices of consumption. Also a loan means that though a sacrifice of at least potential satisfactions is made by the class with bank balances, this class obtains a claim on the community as a whole which must eventually be met. Hence it is a mistake to consider loans as an alternative to taxation. The ideal of war finance is to restrict consumers' demand and to increase production. Until the mystical limit of full employment is achieved, loans tap idle resources and give the Government spending power and the central bank lending power that can be used to increase production. Thus war finance must strike the right balance between taxing and borrowing, increasing the proportion to be carried by taxation as the economy approaches full employment.

TABLE I. DOMINION REVENUES AND EXPENDITURES, 1938-42 *
($000,000's)

	1938–39	1939–40	1940–41	1941–42 †
War Expenditures	72	207	795	1,414
Total Expenditures	552	680	1,249	1,893
Total Revenues	502	562	873	1,481
Deficit	51	119	377	413

* Canadian House of Commons, *Official Report of Debates*, Vol. LXXX, " Appendix to The Budget, 1942–43," p. 10.
† Estimated.

The Canadian budget for the fiscal year 1940–41,[15] which was introduced in June after the collapse of France, reflected in part the new role which Canada had then to play in the war. It forecast war expenditures of at least $700,000,000 with possibly another $150,000,000 required before the end of the year; $200,000,000 for the repatriation of Canadian securities held in England, thus providing England with Canadian dollar exchange; and ordinary government expenditures of

---
15 See Table I.

$448,000,000. To meet this total of expenditures of $1,500,000,000 the Government had in hand a cash balance of $200,000,000 carried forward from the previous fiscal year; and it proposed to raise by taxation $760,000,000; by war savings certificates (voluntary small-scale loans subscribed over a period of time with the same general effect as taxation of reducing consumers' demand) about $50,000,000; and the balance of about $500,000,000 by borrowing. Actually tax revenues were more elastic and expenditures were rather less than the budget forecast, so that something under $400,000,000 was all that was required from borrowing, an amount which was subscribed in one appeal to the public.

The new taxation was restrictive, although there was nevertheless a considerable expansion in the production and consumption of consumers' goods. The taxation of the 1940–41 budget must be regarded as having limited the expansion of consumption rather than as having imposed an actual curtailment. New direct income taxes amounting to $35,000,-000 from the new National Defense Contribution Tax and an increase of $58,000,000 in the personal income tax which resulted from a sharp increase in rates, and increased indirect taxation, most of which was transferred to the consumer, amounting in all to $86,000,000, confiscated for the state something less than a third of the total increase in the national income. The new Excess Profits Tax yielded $100,000,000, and this definitely restricted the ability of corporations to invest their profits in increased plant facilities for ordinary peacetime production.

The budget was designed to shift an increasingly large share of the productive resources of the country into war channels; but it was not a restrictive budget in the sense of imposing an actual reduction in the consumption of ordinary peacetime goods and services. It did, of course, reduce the consumption of certain classes, particularly those of middle and higher incomes, though it would be a serious error to suppose that any severe sacrifices were borne by the upper income groups. On the other hand previously unemployed and under-employed workers and their families were able to restore their scale of living to something like a minimum standard of health and comfort. The general expansion in the consumers' goods industries indicates one of the weaknesses of this method of relying on the price system for the necessary redistribution of productive resources in a war economy. It takes very heavy taxation and a long period of time before any considerable redistribution of resources occurs, particularly if general economic expansion is going on, and, further, there are certain obstacles to this redistribution which the price mechanism is by itself incapable of surmounting. These obstacles are the technical difficulties of adapting plant, the occupational immobility of labor, and the unwillingness of industrialists to make large investments in wartime plant without some guarantee against a dead loss on the investment when the war emergency is over.

These considerations led many Canadian observers, most of whom no doubt approved the Government's middle of the road budget, to hope that the budget would be followed by direct devices to overcome these obstacles, and that the Government would use some of the extraordinary powers over capital and labor which it had taken to itself under wartime legislation, powers which included the right to expropriate property, to direct an industry or, if the industry failed to accept direction, to take over the management for the duration of the war, to set and fix prices including wages, to establish priorities and ration the consumption of raw materials, and to mobilize labor for war work.[16] During 1940 the Government did make some progress in the direct approach to these problems, but that there was some disappointment was evident both from criticism in the House of Commons and in the newspaper and periodical press.

The military situation demanded with the utmost urgency the most rapid possible development of Canadian industry and expansion of Canadian munitions and war output. In wartime the price mechanism is not only slow to give effect to military demands, it cannot even properly reflect them in many instances, because with no competitive market there is no way of making economic valuations. If a decision is to be made between ten airplanes and ten tanks it is not an economic one but a strategic one, and strategic, not pecuniary, considerations must determine the allocation of steel as between the airplane and the tank industries. Similarly, who is to say that $1.25 a day represents a soldier's marginal productivity? Wage payments as between army and industry are certainly no guide for the proper distribution of man power, and the

---

[16] An Act respecting a Department of Munitions and Supply, September 12, 1939.

An Act to confer certain powers upon the Governor-in-Council for the mobilization of National Resources in the present war, June 21, 1940.

An Act to amend the Department of Munitions and Supply Act, June 14, 1940.

An Act to amend the Department of National Defense Act, July 8, 1940.

An Act respecting a Department of National War Services, July 12, 1940.

An Act respecting the payment of compensation for the taking of certain property for war purposes, August 1, 1940.

price system in the labor market ought not to be relied on as the method of drawing labor from peacetime to wartime employment. Exactly the same argument holds true with even greater force in the field of capital.

One looked, therefore, to the budget for the year 1941–42 for a more realistic conception of the needs of total war, and certainly few Canadians have complained that taxation was too light. The budget proposed to raise a total of $2,670,000,000 including the financing of British purchases in Canada, purchases which must of course come out of the Canadian real income for the present. Of this total, the Government proposed to raise $1,450,000,000 by taxation, about $200,000,000 from such government trust accounts as the Unemployment Insurance fund and from the sale of war savings certificates, and the balance of about $1,000,000,000 by borrowing. The increase in direct taxation was heavy and practically put a limit to any increase in spending from the new incomes created by the war, and it also provoked a sharp curtailment in the spending capacity of the middle and upper incomes. In terms of aggregate social income the effect was to produce a slight curtailment as over 1940 in the consumption of consumers' goods but to leave the level of consumption rather higher than in 1939. This means in effect that there were more incomes being earned than there were in peacetime and that in general the working class were able to improve their standard of living, particularly during the year 1940, but that this improvement was stabilized by the 1941 budget at the 1940 level.

Sacrifices have been made by the upper income groups who have had to reduce their level of consumption, nevertheless the upper income groups are still left with large spending surpluses. A man with an income of $20,000 a year may look upon the tax of $9,000 as very heavy, but actually a bachelor (for we are considering the tax on single persons) with a net income, after paying taxes, of $11,000 cannot be said to be undergoing privation. In a country with everything at stake in a total war it ought to be possible to set a maximum net income and if this were done at a level, say, of $5,000 there is no question but that a very considerable reduction amounting probably to $200,000,000 or $300,000,000 could be effected in consumers' spending on luxuries and comforts. In a siege economy in the third year of war this might have been possible, and there were some Canadians who felt that the Government could well have imposed these additional sacrifices and to this extent have increased its share of contributions to the Commonwealth war effort. However this may be, the 1941 budget definitely put an end to the expansion in the production of consumers' goods and it diverted to the supply of war needs nearly one-half of the national income.[17]

The Excess Profits Tax of 1940 was continued for the fiscal year 1941–42, though in a form somewhat amended to remove seeming injustices, and yielded $140,000,000, so that a very definite restriction was placed on new investment by private corporations. The tax levied a 75 percent rate on all profits in excess of the 1936–39 average plus a straight 18 percent corporation tax on gross profits or a 40 percent tax on all profits, whichever is higher. The Excess Profits Tax Act was amended however to provide for "hard" cases. This tax and the very heavy public borrowing[18] were certain to have the desired effect of curtailing private investment;[18a] but as the Minister of Finance himself said there will be required "also the careful limitation of our commercial and industrial investment to such plant and equipment as will aid in carrying on the war and as is necessary to the maintenance of essential services."[19] Thus the administration came at length to the admission that the price system even under the stimulus of stringent taxation was too slow and ineffective a mechanism for the direction and allocation of wartime investment. Mr. Ilsley announced that an Order-in-Council had been passed "making it necessary for any person or firm erecting or extending building structures for industrial and commercial use or installing machinery and equipment to apply for and obtain a license."[20] The responsibility for administration is vested under the Order-in-Council in the Director-General of Priorities under the Department of Munitions and Supply.[21]

The budget for 1942–43, which was not presented until June 1942 envisaged a total expenditure of $3,900,000,000, or about two-thirds of the national income. Revenues of $2,145,000,000 were anticipated on the basis of increased tax yields and refundable taxes, leaving $1,755,000,000 to be met by borrowing. It was estimated that about one-third of this figure would come from government cash balances, Unemployment In-

---

[17] There are some who have said that whereas America, even before she entered the war, had lent goods to Britain under Lend-Lease, Canada, her partner in the British Commonwealth, was making her pay cash for everything she received. This is not true. See below, p. 322.

[18] In the case of the first Victory Loan of 1941 a total of over $700,000,000 at a time when notice deposits were at a peak of $1,800,000,000.

[18a] Ordinarily gross investment, derived mainly from the profits of industry, is about $1,000,000,000 a year in Canada, of which some $300,000,000 represents new capital investment.

[19] Honorable J. L. Ilsley, budget speech, April 25, 1941, House of Commons, *Official Report of Debates*, unrevised edition, Vol. LXXIX, No. 60, p. 2550.

[20] *Ibid.*

[21] See Chapter VII, pp. 337, 340–342.

surance funds, and corporate investors, but "a very large balance should," according to the Minister of Finance, "be provided by individual purchases of War Savings Certificates and bonds."

In the new budget personal income taxes and the National Defense Tax were combined and made deductible at the source, and their incidence increased. There was an attempt to mitigate the severity of the new tax rates by making a portion of them refundable in the postwar period, with 2 percent accrued interest. This refundable tax has come to be known by common consent as " Forced Savings." The same principle was applied to the Excess Profits Tax, which was raised to 100 percent, 20 percent being refundable — a provision designed to afford protection in the form of increased reserves to industries, especially smaller industries, in the postwar period. Taxation on luxuries was intensified and extended, and was clearly intended less to increase revenue than to restrict consumption, thus affording a supplementary form of commodity rationing.

III · DIRECT CONTROL

The direct control over investment by means of a licensing system introduced in 1941 culminated a gradual development of regulatory powers. During the first phase of the war Canadian fiscal policy had been based on the assumption that the economic objective of maximum mobilization of resources for total war could be attained largely without the aid of direct restrictive controls over consumer behavior and without direct compulsory controls over industry. Such control was to be kept at a minimum, being regarded as inimical to Canadian industrial traditions and unnecessary so long as the economy remained considerably below full employment. 1941 was a period of transition at an ever accelerating rate from indirect to direct government restriction of consumers and compulsion of producers.

The Wartime Prices and Trade Board, set up at the beginning of the war, was designed to provide for the regular supply and stable price of consumers' necessities.[21a] It could not meet the problems of raw material rationing and capital priorities. In the early months of the war controllers under the Ministry of Supply were put directly in charge of steel,

---

[21a] In order to maintain ceiling prices and to prevent the drain of certain commodities to the United States, the Board has found it necessary, notably in the case of beef, to buy up output at American prices and distribute at the ceiling price in Canada, the American ceiling having proved elastic.

timber, oil, coal, and certain other basic metals. Their duties were to maintain an adequate supply and see that it was properly apportioned among war industries. For the most part they were able to achieve their results by informal methods, because on the whole industry was either glad to cooperate or was willing to do so rather than see the controllers forced to use the powers they possessed. General coordination and planning of their activities were provided by the Wartime Industries Supply Board, supplemented by the Wartime Requirements Board.[22]

Further the Government engaged directly in investment both on its own account and on account of the British Government. Fiscal policy made available to the Government a large share of the annual Canadian savings, thus reducing the ordinary demand for producers' goods and machinery. In place of this demand there is the vastly increased demand of the war industries for capital goods. But as in the United States, producers hesitated to embark on large construction to meet a war demand which will be of temporary nature and leave them at the war's end with an overexpanded plant. To meet this difficulty and provide for new fixed capital where needed the Government has allowed in some cases for the amortization of new plants by permitting contractors on war account to charge in their prices an amortization write-off calculated on a two- or four-year depreciation, an extravagant way of solving the problem. The Government in effect pays for new plant in its orders over two or four years, but in the end the plant belongs to the corporation. Another method is for the Government to build new plant, lease it to the industry, and retain ownership after the war. This gives the Government a direct interest in, and control over, war industry and promises interesting developments in the postwar period.[23]

IV · FOREIGN EXCHANGE

Another control over capital has been the control of foreign investment and foreign exchange. In the summer of 1940 the Foreign Exchange Control Board registered all Canadian-held securities in the United States, took over Canadian-owned American dollar balances, prohibited pleasure travel in the United States and, in December, under power of the Foreign Exchange Conservation Act,[24] prohibited certain types of imports. The obvious result was to cut off the consumers' im-

---

[22] See Chapter VII, pp. 340, 341.

[23] For more detailed description and recent figures, see Chapter VII, p. 337.

[24] The Foreign Exchange Conservation Act, December 1940.

ports from the United States, setting free exchange for the purchase of war goods and machinery. There may be far more important long-run results. Canada is ceasing to be in England's debt as her own government acquires ownership of bonds and stocks of her industries formerly held by British individuals. At the end of the fiscal year 1940–41 Britain's deficit with Canada on real trade was approximately $800,000,000. During that year Canada provided London with exchange to the amount of 42.4 percent of the total by the repatriation of Canadian securities held in Britain and to the amount of 26.2 percent of the total by allowing sterling balances to accrue to Canadian account in London. The remainder was met by the transfer of gold. In January 1942 accumulated Canadian sterling credits in London were converted into an interest-free loan. This was followed by a free gift of $1,000,000,000 from Canada to Great Britain. The exhaustion of this gift early in 1943 was marked by the establishment of a Canadian War Supplies Allocation Board to correspond to the United States Lend-Lease Administration in the distribution of Canadian supplies among the United Nations.[25]

Economically and financially Canada has increased steadily her position as a North American country and a dependency of the United States, and this in the very act of asserting her political allegiance to the intercontinental system of the Commonwealth and the unity of her political destiny with that of Britain. Until the Hyde Park Agreement Canada's foreign exchange problem was simply that of obtaining American dollars. It is not that she has an unfavorable balance in all foreign trade, but most of her favorable balance is in sterling and one of the major preoccupations of the war administration has been to find ways and means of financing American imports.

The Foreign Exchange Control Board[26] with its regulatory powers over the issuance of foreign exchange has thus had as its chief object the conservation of American exchange rather than the stabilization of the Canadian dollar, though that has been a secondary and indeed complementary function. Its activities and the effect of the War Exchange Conservation Act have very definitely reduced Canadian civilian spending in the United States, but it is unlikely that the figure for Canadian purchases in the United States of $950,000,000 for the fiscal year 1941–42 can be reduced, because of this amount $428,000,000 is for war pur-

[25] At the same time the Canadian Government purchased $200,000,000 of British Government investments in the Canadian munitions industry.

[26] See Chapter VII, p. 352.

chases and $238,000,000 is for the payment of interest and dividends to United States investors.

V · LABOR POLICY

The war industries were calculated in 1940 to require 200,000 additional skilled workers, and many additional skilled craftsmen were enlisted in the R.C.A.F. and other branches of the armed forces. Unemployment in Canada greatly exceeded this amount in total, but of the unemployed the majority were unskilled or had lost their skills. By the time of the seasonal upswing in late summer when employment figures were at their height, unemployment in all the skilled trades reporting through trades unions had sunk as low as 4 percent, the lowest figure since the boom days of the 'twenties. In certain skilled trades a shortage of labor made its appearance. Obviously in a country with considerable total unemployment, local and trade shortages could be met by training young workers, rehabilitating older workers, and arranging for a transfer of workers both from place to place and from trade to trade. In the successful accomplishment of such a program the enthusiastic support of both labor and management would be essential.

The Government seemed rather slow to realize the growing gravity of the shortage of labor and policy to grapple with this problem was not devised until late in 1940. The Administration took considerable pride in the passage of the Unemployment Insurance Act which, for the first time,[27] guaranteed Canadian workers a certain security in case of unemployment, a forward-looking measure, indeed, but not one conceived to meet the needs of a war economy facing not a scarcity of jobs but a scarcity of workers. To fill this want the Government relied chiefly on the Youth Training Program which it conducted in cooperation with the provinces. For the major part of 1940 this program was operating at a rate of about 24,000 "trainees" a year, and there were some few in training in industry. To the problem of supplementing this admittedly inadequate program by the rehabilitation of older workers and the training of women, the Government's attitude can best be given in the words of the Minister of Labor who said, "I would not want to say that definite representations had been made to industry to

<hr>

27 Labor legislation under the British North American Act was regarded as falling within the jurisdiction of the provinces rather than the Dominion. A constitutional amendment was necessary to obtain the Unemployment Insurance Act. This constitutional difficulty has been one of the obstacles standing in the way of progressive social legislation in Canada.

employ older men. I think that is something which industry will have to take upon itself. As demand increases and supply diminishes industry will almost automatically be required to take on older men and women." [28]

Thus the Government, throughout most of 1940, trusted to the price system, the attraction of higher wages, to provide it with the requisite skilled labor in the defense industries. In spite of the powers enjoyed under the National War Services Act, it did not establish any labor priorities or, until late in the year, develop a policy of planned transfer.

Moreover, the Government's policy raised certain cricitisms in labor circles. There was some labor dilution, and considerable sacrifice was being asked of union standards of hours and conditions of work. The Government made a statement of principle to the effect that these standards should be restored after the war, but the unions, as in Britain,[29] wanted a legislative guarantee. Some labor spokesmen also felt that the Government was less reluctant to issue legislation working in a different way, such as an order-in-council extending the compulsory provisions of the Industrial Disputes Investigation Act to all war industries. The Defense of Canada Regulations in the hands of certain provincial attorneys-general had been used in a manner that aroused resentment and opposition in Labor circles and alarmed the defenders of civil liberties, although the Canadian Trades and Labor Congress approved the Regulations in principle.[30]

All this, coupled with the growing pressure on the available supply of labor, led to a sharp shift in policy in the latter part of 1940. The Youth and Emergency Training Programs were " stepped up " to train 50,000 workers a year, and this was increased in 1941–42 to over 90,000. A national policy of " upgrading " was introduced whereby young workers were taught to perform certain skilled functions, thus relieving the skilled men of all but the most essential and difficult parts of their task. Transfer has been worked out on a national scale through Dominion bureaus spread through the country.

---

[28] Honorable N. A. McLarty, Minister of Labor, House of Commons, *Debates,* Nov. 28, 1940, Vol. LXXIX, No. 15, p. 532. The National Elective Service plan announced March 24, 1942, introduces a more positive program in this respect. See Chapter V, p. 303 and Chapter VII, pp. 346, 347.

[29] See Chapter IV, p. 233.

[30] A new Order-in-Council, P. C. 892, removed one of the most objectionable interpretations of the Defense of Canada regulations, viz.: that which made picketing in defense industries illegal and the Government has declared as a matter of policy that the rights of workers to Trades Union organizations and collective bargaining should be recognized by industry.

Government policy indeed seemed to have been based on the assumption that the industrial unrest which developed throughout Canada in 1941 was chiefly a matter of wages, whereas many authorities on labor problems and indeed the Department of Labor statistics on the causes of strikes, indicated that the question of union recognition was the major issue in many of the important industrial disputes. A firmer stand on the question of union recognition might prove much more effective. In other ways the Government had not been unmindful of the rights and needs of the workingman. Indeed some industrialists felt that the Government leaned backward in its efforts to be fair to labor. When workers went on strike contrary to the provisions of the Industrial Disputes Investigation Act — that is to say, previous to the appointment of a Board of Conciliation — the Department of Labor ordinarily took the attitude that they were unaware that the Act had been extended to cover all defense industries, and handled the workers in a conciliatory spirit. On the other hand, when a prominent corporation engaged in defense work in the city of Hamilton refused to submit a dispute to a Board of Conciliation, the Government promptly stepped in and took over the factory, an episode which occupied the better part of the front page of the *Financial Post* for two weeks.

The Government's initial attempt at wage regulation was set out in Order-in-Council P.C. 7440. The object of this Order was probably twofold: (a) to prevent a wage spiral with inflationary effects, and (b) to safeguard workers against rises in the cost of living and at a minimum level of comfort. The Order provided that wages should not be increased above the 1926–29 level (or any year previous to 1940 where the level was higher than the 1926–29 average) but should be stabilized at that rate and that Boards of Conciliation should not entertain demands for wage increases above that level except in cases where it was shown that the cost of living had increased by 5 percent since August 1939, in which event cost of living bonuses at a flat amount uniform for all workers regardless of earnings should be paid to cover the increase in the cost of living.[31] In October 1941 the Order was extended to constitute a wage ceiling in practically all industries. The effect has been to establish a minimum real wage, but to reduce the differential accruing

---

31 The order made exception for employments in which wages were unduly depressed, but since this phrase was not defined it was not surprising to find a Board of Conciliation established the precedent that wages no matter how low they might be could not be raised above the 1926–29 level.

to the more highly skilled workers. The policy has therefore not commended itself to the trade unions, which for the most part represent such
workers.

By the third year of war Canada had attained full industrial employment; in Mr. King's words, there was " no slack left " in the industrial
economy. The main diversion of resources from civilian to war purposes had been accomplished, and the Government's problem was now
twofold: to continue to drain off excess purchasing power in the hands
of the public so as to prevent inflation; and to provide for war industries
a maximum amount of labor, material, and capital. The second objective could only be attained by limiting supplies of labor, material, and
capital to nonessential industries. In the field of labor the Government
made no attempt to sweep man power into the armed forces or war production by direct conscription, but rather like a monumental vacuum
cleaner proceeded to draw them in by suction. Men of military age and
physically fit were prohibited to enter almost any occupation outside
farming and food production. In addition, a policy of bringing women
into industry was put forward as " the most important single feature of
the program." Discouraged by the drain on their labor supply, the reduction of their market by prohibitive taxation on their products and
the reduction of purchasing power in the hands of the public, and by
the restriction of supplies through various control boards, all nonessential industries were reducing production by 1942. Five hundred of them
had been eliminated, and progressive mortality was to be expected.

Conclusion

Under the pressure of modern war the dominant role of government
in the economy becomes an accomplished and accepted fact. Planning,
at first *ad hoc* and admitted only when necessity drove, promises, before
the war is over, to embrace in its scope the entire economic life of the
nation. What is implied for the future of Canada, the British Commonwealth, and North America remains obscure and must do so until
the issue of the war is decided. But, while none in Canada doubts the
ultimate outcome, most believe that the war will be long drawn out,
and that, during its course, many of the tendencies already well established will become definitely set. Canada's position in finance, vis-à-vis
England, will be permanently changed; she will be the creditor country,
England the debtor. Again Canada will be a much more self-sufficient,

a less exposed, a more industrialized, economy. The internal balance of the economy will be shifted more favorably to the industrial heart in Ontario; the external trading position may well be revolutionized. The extension of government ownership and interference in the free market will both obstruct a reversion to " free capitalism " and complicate the division of jurisdiction as between Dominion and provinces.

Already the regional effects of the war are apparent. Efficient prosecution has precluded any " equitable " provincial distribution of war orders, so that industrial Ontario has been the great beneficiary of the war development, while the prairie wheat economy leans heavily on the Dominion Government's purchase and storage of wheat. The concentration of industry in the central areas and its great development during the war mean the growth of economic power in these central provinces. Only a growth in the powers of the federal government can offset this, can use it for the protection of social welfare throughout the Dominion as a whole. Every month of war intensifies this problem.

Some notion of the problems this will breed when peace comes can be had from a consideration of the opposition of Ontario to the report of the Royal Commission on Dominion-Provincial Relations. This Commission, appointed before the war, was to study the financial and constitutional arrangements obtaining between the Dominion and provinces and to make recommendations for changes which would be in the interest of greater national unity and welfare. The report recommended very moderate increases in the federal power and greater financial aid by the Dominion to the provinces to equalize social welfare standards. When the provincial premiers met in Ottawa in January 1941 to consider the recommendations with the Dominion officials, the Premier of Ontario, Mr. Hepburn, refused even to discuss them.[32] His attitude was responsible for the postponement of the whole matter, much to the confusion of the Dominion Government, which was looking to the recommendations of the report for a consolidation of taxes and an equalization of war tax burdens throughout the country.

In connection with the new tax provisions of 1941 the Dominion Government concluded an agreement with the provinces whereby the latter relinquished their right to impose a provincial or municipal income tax, in consideration of appropriate subventions in lieu from the Dominion Government. The Dominion Government also assumed control of the Succession Duties, previously an exclusively provincial tax field. Thus

---

[32] He received the support of the Premiers of British Columbia and Alberta.

in two important fields the fiscal freedom of the provinces was limited by the federal government, a limitation which constituted a significant change in the British North America Act governing Dominion-provincial relations. This followed along the lines suggested by the Royal Commission on Dominion-Provincial Relations, but whereas the Rowell-Sirois Report had recommended that fiscal changes should be accompanied by an assumption on the part of the federal government of responsibility for a minimum standard of national social services, the actual change made was purely fiscal.[33]

With the economy increasingly dominated by Ontario the political problems of a regional federalism promise to become no less difficult or dangerous. Meantime national unity in the war effort continues. The Dominion Government is increasingly the biggest buyer, the biggest entrepreneur, the biggest investor in the nation, and as long as the war continues the forces which the war releases will be operative to increase the dominant role of government in economic life. We have seen why this must be. Whether it results finally in a greater social democracy, a greater security for the common citizen within a more unified Canada, or whether it leads to regional dominance and the growth of disintegrating centrifugal forces with, perhaps, attempted authoritarianism as a solution, remains for history and the issue of the war to determine.

---

[33] Unfortunately, the subventions made to provincial governments to compensate them for their loss of revenue were based on calculations of revenue for 1940, which were inadequate in 1941 in view of advancing costs and increasing demands on provincial and municipal social services.

CHAPTER VII

The Organization and Work of the Canadian War Administration

by Gwendolen M. Carter

Introduction

The organization of the Canadian war administration demonstrates the ability of the democratic system to add new agencies and controls affecting almost every aspect of life without losing its essence of responsibility to the electorate. This has remained true despite the variety of new functions which have been undertaken, the pragmatic character of the development and the rapidity with which it has been carried through. Marked changes have occurred particularly in the great increase of federal responsibilities. But within the Dominion Government, the concentration of authority in the Cabinet, the politically responsible organ of the parliamentary system, insures control. Despite the greatly increased powers of the executive, Parliament remains ᶠactive, and exercises power of free criticism.

The centralizing tendencies induced by war demands are reversing an earlier constitutional trend. The British North America Act (1867), which provides the constitutional structure for Canada, allots enumerated powers to the provinces in property and civil rights, education, the incorporation of companies whose activity is confined to the province, municipal institutions, control of public works and undertakings, and in general all things of a local nature; to the Dominion it allots regulation of trade, postal service, currency, census and statistics, provisions for military and naval defense, and criminal law and procedure. Concurrent powers exist in immigration and agriculture, the federal government being the superior legislative authority in both. The intention of the Fathers of Confederation was to avoid the weakness exemplified by the American Civil War and by vesting residual powers in the federal government to develop a strong central power. In a curious analogy to American constitutional development, judicial decisions (for Canada, by the Judicial Committee of the Privy Council) reversed somewhat the intended process so that the provinces possess more power than was originally intended. The general power of the Dominion to regulate trade and commerce became restricted by judicial interpretation to cover only regulations for political purposes such as trade in arms. Uniformity in ways of settling industrial disputes, in developing water power, and formulating general company law became virtually impossible.

Such a constitutional development has resulted in less centralized direction in Canada than in any comparably industrialized country. While the size of the provinces and the variety of their problems have given some justification to decentralization, it has raised dangers to national unity and to economic progress which were becoming increasingly obvious during the past decade.

The exigencies of war would have intensified these dangers had not an instrument under which the federal government could assume direction of the life of the country in time of war emergency existed in the War Measures Act of 1914. This was brought into operation on August 2, 1939, by proclamation of the Governor in Council.[1] The Act authorized measures deemed " necessary or advisable for the security, defence, peace, order and welfare of Canada," and in particular extended the powers of the Governor in Council to: " (a) Censorship and the control and suppression of publications, writings, maps, plans, photographs, communications and means of communication; (b) Arrest, detention, exclusion and deportation; (c) Control of the harbours, ports and territorial waters of Canada and the movements of vessels; (d) Transportation by land, air, or water and the control of the transport of

---

[1] That is, by executive act. The Governor-General acts only on the advice of his Canadian ministers. Hence, the executive authority in Canada as in Great Britain is centered in the Cabinet, though executive orders (orders-in-council) are issued in the name of the Governor.

persons and things; (e) Trading, exportation, importation, production and manufacture; (f) Appropriation, control, forfeiture and disposition of property and of the use thereof."

Under this Act and other statutes four new departments of Munitions and Supply, National Defense for Air, National War Services, and National Defense for the Navy have been set up. Besides these, there are numerous specialized agencies, including the Foreign Exchange Control Board, the Wartime Prices and Trade Board, the Agricultural Supplies Board, the Canadian Shipping Board, the Censorship Coordination Committee, and the Bureau of Public Information. Each of the special agencies is responsible to a minister, though it is not part of his department. An elaborate series of Cabinet committees, which will be described in more detail below, provides attention for the fields in which these agencies work, but the major coordination and direction is secured through the War Committee and the Cabinet as a whole.

The Canadian war administration has developed empirically as the strain on a particular aspect of the economy became obvious, or as new needs demanded new controls and direction. It has grown piecemeal with the course of the war and the exhaustion of surpluses. In the first stage of the war it was largely protective in character. The Wartime Prices and Trade Board was set up to protect the civilian consumer against hoarding, profiteering, and curtailment of necessary supplies. The Foreign Exchange Control Board was established to prevent a flight of capital from Canada and to limit uncertainties as to Canada's financial position. Censorship was introduced to prevent harmful dissemination of information. In general the ordinary business mechanism was allowed to function within the limits of foreign exchange control. In industrial supply, the only change before April 1940 was to give wider powers to the purchasing organization. In the supervision of exports and imports, the chief organizational innovation was to appoint special boards and administrators to deal directly with similar bodies or officials in Great Britain. Particular arrangements were necessary from the beginning for transportation because of the scarcity of shipping and because of dangers to it, and the Transport Controller and the Canadian Shipping Board were both active in this period.

The German break-through to the west precipitated the second stage, in which the Department of Munitions and Supply was set up to take over direction of industrial production, and the Department of National Defense separated into three departments, for the Army, Navy, and Air

Force. The Department of National War Services was established to assist in mobilizing the resources of the nation. The third stage, developing throughout 1941, was marked less by the appearance of new organs than by extension of the duties and powers of existing ones. The fourth stage, in which Canada now finds itself, is that of integrating the machinery developed to deal with varied problems which have now become obviously part of a single effort. The instruments responsible for war and civilian supply, the Wartime Industries Control Board and the Wartime Prices and Trade Board, are coordinating their policy through interlocking membership. The comprehensive price control and wage stabilization program adopted in October 1941 brings the closest relation between the price structure, supply, and labor. This program has introduced the most drastic controls yet adopted by a democratic nation.

In wartime the ends of a society become simplified by the singleness of the task at hand. Its facets are many but direction is given by strategic necessities. In contrast the technical organization required is complex, because the compulsion comes from outside and its demands are not limited by the resources easily available. In its fourth year of war, the Canadian Government faces the responsibility of maintaining the smooth working of an elaborate system of control which may be affected by outside forces such as price rises in the United States. How successfully it can be expected to meet future demands may be judged in part by the history of its growth and achievements.

The pattern adopted for detailed analysis of the existing organization and work of the war administration considers first the services of national defense and the organization and problems of wartime supply in the fields of industry and agriculture. Transportation belongs to this as a vital element in linking Canada to the European battle front. Next are examined the agencies of financial control and civilian supply which seek to prevent the concentration upon war needs from disorganizing the life of the country. Finally there is an evaluation of the supervision and coordination of the wartime administration. In describing the organization of the war administration a disproportionate emphasis will inevitably fall upon the special wartime agencies and departments. It must be remembered that they are additions to an existing governmental organization and that the effectiveness of their efforts rests to a considerable extent upon the aid and cooperation extended by the older departments.

Despite the limitation on federal action, very considerable progress had been made since the First World War in building up an efficient federal administration. Perhaps the chief difference between the administrative situation in 1914 and in 1939 lay in the improvement of the caliber and experience of the civil service. It is not too much to say that the achievements of the existing civil service in maintaining ordinary functions, participating in new ones, and providing a large measure of coordination to the whole, have been fundamental to the successful work of the war administration.

1. National Defense

At the outbreak of war, the defense services were consolidated in the Department of National Defense organized under the National Defense Act of 1922 which had brought together the former Department of Militia and Defense, the Department of Naval Service, and the Air Board under one Minister. He was advised by a Defense Council, and in 1936 this was made advisory to a Defense Committee of the Cabinet consisting of the Prime Minister and several senior ministers. Just before war, the Defense Committee was reorganized as the Emergency Council (Committee on General Policy), and subsequently became the War Committee in the Cabinet reorganization of July 1940.

Under the pressure of war, it was decided to set up separate ministries for the Air Service and for the Navy, the former on May 22, 1940, and the latter on July 8, 1940. The work of the Department of National Defense was thus divided between three ministers, each of whom is responsible for the direction of his service and for its administration. The Department of National Defense (for the Army) is divided into four branches, comprising: the General Staff; the Master General of the Ordinance, including the sections of the chief accountant, chief ordnance mechanical engineer, and directors of ordnance services (mechanization, technical stores, general stores, and administration); the Quartermaster-General, under whom are the Director of Engineering Services, responsible for works and buildings, fortifications and equipment, and the Director of Supplies, responsible for supplies and accommodation and transport, on land and sea; and the Director of Organization, who deals with administration and personnel, including enlistments, discharges, administration, and discipline. Each of the three defense services has a somewhat comparable organization and some duplication is inevitable, particularly in auxiliary services such as the medical service and the women's auxiliary services.

There is no organization in Canada comparable to the British Committee of Imperial Defense. Coordination between the three services is maintained through the Minister of National Defense, who is the final authority on any matter involving more than one service. There is also an Associate Minister of National Defense, endowed with the same powers. This latter office is at present held by the Minister of National Defense for Air. These arrangements have made it possible to secure decentralization and at the same time to preserve the essential unity of the services without establishing an outside coordinator.

Working closely with the Department of National Defense is the Department of National War Services set up on July 12, 1940, to assist in carrying out the purposes of the National Resources Mobilization Act of June 21, 1940, for " the mobilization of all the effective resources of the nation, both human and material, for the purpose of the defense and security of Canada." The immediate responsibilities of the new department were to conduct the national registration from which was secured the data for the newly introduced compulsory military training for Canadian youth; to organize and promote different forms of voluntary assistance to the war effort; and to coordinate existing public information services of the government and use them with any necessary additions to secure " the utmost aid from the people of Canada in the national emergency which has arisen." The National War Services Department is also responsible for individual notifications to report for compulsory training. Until the trainees reach camp they are under the Department of National War Services and upon their arrival become the responsibility of the Department of National Defense. The War Services Department has organized the National Salvage Campaign, and supervises all organizations collecting for war charity. It is also responsible for most of the services distributing information. In addition to the Office of the Director of Public Information, the Canadian Broadcasting Corporation, the Travel Bureau, the National Film Board, and the Motion Picture Bureau have been placed under its supervision.[2]

---

[2] The Bureau of Information was originally set up under the Prime Minister's office, then transferred to the Department of Labor, to the Secretary of State, and, in July 1941, to the Department of National War Services.

2. Munitions and Industrial Supply

I · EARLY PURCHASING ORGANIZATION

Arrangements for service purchasing differ in Canada from those used in the United States, where the different services outline their requirements and place their own contracts. The principle of centralized buying was accepted by Canada in July 1939, when the Defense Purchasing Board was set up, following an investigation of the absence of competitive bids for a contract to manufacture Bren machine guns. This central purchasing agency expanded by September 15, 1939, into five buying units directed by experienced purchasing agents drawn from the staff of the Canadian National Railway, and from the Contracts Branch of the Department of National Defense, which was transferred to the Board.

In November the War Supply Board superseded the Defense Purchasing Board. It was empowered to act in Canada on behalf of the British Government as well as for the Canadian Government, and on February 23, 1940, was authorized to act in Canada on behalf of the French Government. The War Supply Board reported to the Minister of Finance at first but was soon made responsible to the Minister of Transport, Mr. C. D. Howe, later Minister of Munitions and Supply.

Increase in the volume of purchases necessitated the reallocation of much of the work to ten purchasing sections,[3] which were united in the General Purchasing Division directed by a general purchasing agent. Final testing was carried on by technical experts in the Department of National Defense. Local purchasing offices were established in Halifax, St. John, Quebec, Montreal, Ottawa, Toronto, Winnipeg, Calgary, and Vancouver for provision of supplies to adjacent military, air force, or naval depots.

Ordinary purchasing routine has not been feasible for the complicated new articles, which since June 1940 have formed an increasingly larger part of production. These are ordered generally on a cost plus fixed fee basis from whatever firm can make them. Various measures have been taken to overcome the objectionable features of the cost plus contract and these include " target " price contracts, " ceiling " price contracts, and management fee contracts. For other goods, requisitions are

---

[3] Clothing, aircraft, machinery, wood products, motor vehicles, fuel and paint, medical supplies, food stuffs, naval and militia stores, and barracks stores.

received from the three branches of the Department of National Defense and distributed to the various sections of the General Purchasing Division. Invitations to tender are either advertised or sent out to firms which might be interested in the order. Final approval for contracts over $5,000 must be given by Order-in-Council. If a contract is placed by agreement instead of tender, the price is investigated by the division expert and subsequently by the head of the purchasing section concerned and the general purchasing agent. In most major contracts and in all contracts awarded without tender, the department reserves the right to examine the books of the contractor in order to insure that the price is fair and reasonable.

In addition to general purchasing, six specialized divisions for Aircraft, Ships, Explosives and Chemicals, Construction, Plant Survey and Production Follow-up, and Overseas Munitions were established in October 1939. The Aircraft Division awarded all contracts on behalf of the Canadian, British, and French Governments, and placed the orders for aircraft and other requirements of the British Commonwealth Air Training Plan. The Construction Division took over from the Department of National Defense all construction work in progress. The Plant Survey and Production Follow-up Division was the continuation of a survey, begun by the Department of National Defense in 1936, which by March 1940 had completed over 2,200 plant inspections. The Overseas Munitions Division handled all purchases made by the British Supply Board in Canada. The work done through these six divisions of the War Supply Board was largely preliminary in character. Much information became available and some small-scale expansion in building was arranged but the general emphasis remained on purchasing.[4]

II · THE DEPARTMENT OF MUNITIONS AND SUPPLY

The establishment of a Department of Munitions and Supply with exclusive authority over the procurement of munitions was provided for by legislation passed in September 1939.[5] But it was not until April 1940

---

[4] During its lifetime the Defense Purchasing Board awarded contracts totalling some $43,000,-000 of which $24,868,498 consisted of purchase of railway equipment for the Canadian National and Canadian Pacific Railways. The War Supply Board placed orders of approximately $133,-350,000. Thus the total for the period from July 14, 1939, to March 31, 1940, was $176,152,714.

[5] Department of Munitions and Supply Act. The Department received wide powers for the organization of industry, including the power to appoint controllers for industrial administration. Supplies could be acquired and holders forced to accept fair and reasonable prices, a wide interpretation being given to the term " supply " to include anything likely to be useful in the prosecution of the war and in the economic life of the country.

that this was brought into effect by proclamation, and the Honorable C. D. Howe was appointed Minister. The establishment of the department on April 9, the day of the invasion of Denmark and Norway, coincided with changes in the war situation which brought a new perspective on what Canada's contribution might be.[6] The Purchasing Branch and the production divisions of the War Supply Board were taken over by the Department of Munitions and Supply, under which they expanded in size and function. Some of their activities have since been undertaken by government-owned companies.

The new department was faced with a much more complex task than that of placing service orders. It became necessary to increase plant capacity to meet the vastly enlarged orders. In consequence, heavy commitments have been made by both the Canadian and the British Governments for capital expenditures for plant extensions.

The government-financed plant construction program is largely concerned with providing additional facilities for the increased production of explosives and chemicals, armaments, ammunition and its components, automotive products, aircraft, machine tools, and base metals.[7] The capital commitments are split three ways, approximately 35 percent being paid by the Canadian Government, 26 percent by the British Government, and 39 percent by joint account. Plants financed by Great Britain sell to Canada its requirements of their output, and plants financed by the Canadian Government similarly sell to Great Britain.

The necessary enlargement of plant facilities was provided under four different arrangements, in two of which the Crown retained title. In some cases, private interests enlarged facilities and paid the cost themselves, a government board determining the sums which they were able to write off for depreciation on any profits which accrued. In other cases, expansion costs were met in the unit price of the first order, subsequent orders being filled at the normal rate. Where the government undertakes the responsibility of financing, it subsequently owns the plant or plant extension and its equipment. In general, private interests operate the plant for a management fee, the government obtaining the output

---

[6] The new situation was reflected in the great increase in the number and value of contracts. During the first quarter of 1940, approximately 1,901 contracts were awarded per month; in the second quarter of 1942, 18,029. By June 1942, the total of contracts placed amounted to $4,877,063,532.

[7] Capital commitments for this construction increased rapidly. By the end of September 1940, they amounted approximately to $235,000,000; by the end of June 1941, to $511,256,321; and by the end of June 1942 to $690,000,000.

at cost. In some special cases, however, the government has set up Crown companies, in which it has retained the management itself.

The Crown companies, now [7a] twenty-two in number, are a novel device for meeting special supply problems where the lowest price can be obtained only by private purchasing or where there are special administrative or manufacturing problems. They are incorporated, but their shares are held by the Minister of Munitions and Supply, and they are subject to Treasury control. Although they are responsible to the Government through the Department of Munitions and Supply, they are organized like private business concerns and each operates as a separate entity under its own president and board.

Four of these companies, the Allied War Supplies Corporation, the Citadel Merchandising Company, Ltd., Wartime Housing, Ltd., and Wartime Merchant Shipping, Ltd., are largely concerned with the administration, supervision, and planning of the programs for explosives and munitions, machine tools, houses to be erected in overcrowded defense areas, and cargo ships respectively. The Citadel Merchandising Company maintains a representative in Washington, attached to the British Purchasing Commission, who centers all orders for machine tools from private manufacturers working on the war program and clears the export licenses.

Five companies undertake specialized tasks in regard to machine tools and ships. Cutting Tools, Ltd., is responsible for salvaging old cutting tools and Machinery Service, Ltd., created on December 22, 1941, employs a group of skilled civilian enemy aliens to repair, rebuild, design and manufacture machinery, machine tools, jigs, and dies. Toronto Shipbuilding Company, Ltd., operates the former Dufferin Shipbuilding Company, which was one of the larger shipbuilding units of Canada and was taken over by the government in order to expand its facilities and output; Trafalgar Shipbuilding, Ltd., arranges priorities for material required in the program being carried on by the Shipbuilding Branch of the department; the Park Steamship Company supervises and controls the operation of newly built Canadian cargo vessels. Five of the Crown companies manufacture along specialized lines: Research Enterprises, Ltd., making optical glass and special instruments; Small Arms, Ltd., manufacturing the Lee-Enfield rifle; Federal Aircraft, Ltd., directing production of the Anson airplanes; National Railway Munitions, Ltd., manufacturing weapons; and Atlas Plant Extension, Ltd.,

[7a] August 1942.

manufacturing special alloy steels. Aero Timber Products, Ltd., which controls the production and use of airplane spruce, was incorporated in June 1942, and Veneer Log Supply, Ltd., in July.

Three companies, the Plateau Company, Ltd., Melbourne Merchandising, Ltd., and Fairmont Company, Ltd., are for the purchase of commodities. Considerable secrecy has been maintained in regard to their purchasing efforts since their function is to acquire certain materials essential to the war effort without allowing it to be apparent that the government is in the market. Fairmont Company, Ltd., did, however, purchase large stocks of rubber in 1940; the Melbourne Company purchases wool; and the Plateau Company administers the Order-in-Council " freezing " all raw silk not required for war purposes. These commodity companies operate on a self-sustaining basis, the cost of operating being added to the selling price of the product. Two companies formed in March 1942 are responsible for the production of scarce materials: the Polymer Corporation, Ltd., to produce synthetic rubber; and Wartime Metals Corporation to produce metallic magnesium and any other emergency projects in the field of war metals.[8]

Still another company, War Supplies, Ltd., was formed to aid the implementation of the Hyde Park Agreement. Through its Washington officers, War Supplies, Ltd., acts as the channel for the transfer of these purchase orders from the various United States Government departments to Canada, where the orders are then handled by the Department of Munitions and Supply.

This use of government corporations by the Department of Munitions and Supply has not gone uncriticized. There is appreciation that the form appeals through its familiarity to the business men who direct it and that it facilitates decentralization, which has been important in a period of rapid growth. It is not clear, however, that the work could not be done as well or, in the case of purchasing, better by a branch of a government department. Whether in view of the independence of action and secrecy of proceedings of the government corporations, a greater degree of responsibility is secured by the use of this form than by giving managerial direction to a private concern is an open question. Whether there is a comparable degree of initiative is also difficult to decide. It must be noted that the presidents of the Crown companies in-

---

[8] It may be noted that the main project of Wartime Metals Corporation arises out of a new method developed at the National Research Council in Ottawa for extracting magnesium metal from dolomite.

clude men of exceptional drive and experience, and the use of this form may make it easier to secure outstanding people.

In addition to supervising production, the Department of Munitions and Supply has had to widen its responsibilities to include control of essential commodities used in production. Controllers have been appointed for steel, lumber, oil, metals other than steel and iron, machine tools and machinery, power and electrical equipment, ship construction and repairs, motor vehicles, chemicals, transit, construction and supplies. This last term has been redefined frequently since the Controller of Supplies was appointed in August 1941, to cover a variety of scarce goods, and since September 1941 covers certain services as well. Each controller has extensive powers to direct the industry by buying, selling, storing, or transporting any commodity in the industry; fixing prices; issuing and cancelling licenses to do business; inspecting premises; and taking possession of any commodity or means of production, storage, or transport used by the industry.

In general it has not been necessary for them to use their coercive powers, and their work has been largely that of advice and adjustment. The controllers are responsible to the Minister of Munitions and Supply. Upon their appointment, they become members of the Wartime Industries Control Board, a clearing house through which points of conflict as to functions may be adjusted and matters affecting the various controls coordinated.

The work of the individual controllers has been far more significant than their published orders suggest. Direction and coordination go on continuously behind the scenes with largely satisfactory results. As with so much of the work of direction, however, the activities of the directors themselves have lacked coordination. To August 1941 the Wartime Industries Control Board had hardly acted even as a clearing house for information. A less indefinite arrangement was secured in August through assigning specific coordinating functions to the Board, and through appointing the Director-General of Priorities as its chairman. Not having the detailed responsibilities of a controller, he can survey the fields administered from a more general standpoint, and with more awareness of the interrelation of actions taken.

In this administrative reorganization the work of the Wartime Industries Control Board was also linked more closely to that of the Wartime Prices and Trade Board, which is responsible for civilian supply and price control. The chairman of each Board was made a member of the other. The simultaneous appointment of a Controller of Supplies provided a channel whereby the Wartime Industries Board may extend its control to other commodities which are not supervised by an administrator, and like rubber and silk are used extensively in war production. Thus a comprehensive integration of the programs for war and civilian supply was secured.

The need for general information on war requirements and for determining priorities gave rise in November 1940 to a new body known as the Wartime Requirements Board, under Mr. H. R. McMillan, formerly Timber Controller. It was empowered to obtain from any source, and more particularly from each of the fighting services, information concerning commitments, and current and future requirements; to coordinate and analyze this information; to formulate plans in relation to priorities; and to supply information to the controllers and departments of the Department of Munitions and Supply. The Board was responsible to the Minister of Munitions and Supply, but reported direct to the War Committee of the Cabinet. Its powers were advisory and investigatory, but an organization with executive powers, the Priorities Branch, was established to work under and in conjunction with it. Due to disagreements between the head of the War Requirements Board, who subsequently resigned, and the Minister of Munitions and Supply, the Board has not played so active a role as was expected.

Its place as arbiter of priorities was taken by the departmental organ, the Priorities Branch, which has two parts: the Priorities Division and the Construction Control Division. Its work is to implement the production and acquisition of war requirements and also to give priority aid, where necessary, to certain important civilian projects. Civilian needs are thus balanced with war requirements in so far as it is possible to do so.

War requirements are primarily a problem for the services, and their relative importance is decided in the first instance by the Army, Navy and Air Force experts, through the Inter-Service Priorities Committee. Their requirements and those of the United Nations are listed in order of importance and urgency. In addition, preferences are established for work on projects closely related to the war program — such as transportation, production of power, and fuel — and on those contributing materially to the export trade, particularly with the United States, such as the mining industry and the pulp and paper industry. Generally speaking, the Priorities Officer in the Priorities Branch of the Department of Munitions and Supply is responsible for the determination of preference ratings on all items, including raw materials, and, subject to the approval of the minister, he has sole authority for issuing priority orders or certificates.

The administration of the priorities system was initially on an informal rather than a formal or automatic basis, and public statements were not made as to classifications or categories. In general it was applied only where it was the sole means of overcoming serious delays in delivery. Since early in 1941, when President Roosevelt authorized a special arrangement extending American priorities to Canadian Government contracts and sub-contracts in the United States, the development of the Canadian priorities system has been closely related to that of the American. Contracts for Canadian war requirements in the United States receive the same ratings as comparable contracts authorized by the United States Army and Navy Munitions Board.

The Civilian Construction Control is part of the priorities organization, since it is a means of controlling civilian activities which may interfere with war requirements. Under its direction new construction, rehabilitation of plants or buildings, and the installation of new equipment not at the moment essential for the war effort are postponed. The stated intention of the control is " to postpone all avoidable non-war expenditures," and one of its additional purposes is to create a backlog for the construction industry after the war.

Unlike ordinary government departments, the Department of Munitions and Supply is not highly centralized. In its early months it was run by an executive committee, in which the heads of the various branches and other senior executives participated with the minister. As the number of branches increased the committee was abandoned. Thereafter the directors-general of the branches have had direct access individually to the minister, who, rather than the deputy minister, is to be regarded as the executive head of the department.[9]

---

[9] The following outline gives the organization of the Department of Munitions and Supply as of July 25, 1942:

Minister, Hon. C. D. Howe
  Executive Assistants
  Special Adviser on Production

ADMINISTRATION

Deputy Minister, G. K. Sheils	Liaison with Department of Trade and Commerce
Executive Assistants (Financial, General, Procurement)	Director of Protection of Petroleum Reserves
General Counsel	United Kingdom Representative (London)
Liaison with Department of Labor	Member War Contracts Depreciation Board

One of the real problems of the department has been that so many of its members, coming often from a background of competitive business, have found it difficult to see their particular part of the work in terms of the whole. This puts heavy responsibilities on the minister and has sometimes made difficult the coordination with other branches of the war administration. Moreover the character of the department's work naturally places the emphasis on completion of construction or production as rapidly as possible rather than on the maintenance of labor standards, and the department policy in the latter regard has been generally unsatisfactory. On the other hand the decentralization of departmental organization limited administrative bottlenecks in a time of rapid growth and drawing upon business experience aided greatly in undertaking at short notice heavy responsibilities in specialized fields.

Wartime Administrator of the Port of Halifax
Representative of Transport Controller

Branches:
Economics and Statistics
Legal
Publicity

PRODUCTION
Coordinator of Production, H. J. Carmichael
Financial Adviser to Department, F. H. Brown
Director of Aluminum Production and Inter-Governmental Distribution
Requisitions and Progress Division

Branches:
Aircraft Production
Ammunition Production
Army Engineering Design
Arsenals and Small Arms Production
Automotive Production
Chemicals and Explosives
Communications and Fire Control Production
Defense Projects Construction
Gauge and Cutting Tool Production

Washington Office

General Purchasing
Gun Production
Industrial Security
Industry and Sub-Contract Coordination
Munitions Contracts
Naval Armament and Equipment
Scrap Disposal
Shipbuilding
Tank Production
United States Purchases

FINANCE
Assistant Deputy Minister, J. P. Pettigrew
Liaison with Land and Expropriations
Liaison with Treasury
  Chief Treasury Officer
  Chief Cost Accountant
Purchase Investigators

Branches:
Comptroller's
Personnel and Organization
Secretary's

III · THE INSPECTION BOARD OF THE UNITED KINGDOM AND CANADA

The need for inspection services has developed in ratio to the increase in production. Beginning with a few inspection officers in the Department of National Defense and one member of the British Purchasing Commission, there has been a steady enlargement until the personnel engaged in this task numbered 7,000 by July 1941. In November 1940 it was decided to join the Canadian and British inspection services and in January 1941 the Inspection Board of the United Kingdom and Canada took over all responsibilities in this regard for both governments. A branch of the Board operated in the United States for the same purpose. The Inspection Board of the United Kingdom and Canada carries out the inspection of all war equipment purchased in Canada for the United Kingdom War Office. Some of the items which they inspect, such as clothing and small arms, are on order for the Air Ministry and the Admiralty as well as for the War Office.[10]

SUPPLY
Priorities Branch
Wartime Industries Control Board
  Chairman, R. C. Berkinshaw
  Controllers:
  Aircraft
  Chemicals
  Construction
  Machine Tools
  Metals
  Motor Vehicles
  Oil
  Power
  Ship Repairs and Salvage
  Steel
  Supplies
  Timber
  Transit
  Transport
  Departmental Production Committee Representative
  Wartime Prices and Trade Board Representatives

CROWN COMPANIES
Aero Timber Products, Ltd.
Allied War Supplies Corp.
Atlas Plant Extension, Ltd.
Citadel Merchandising Co., Ltd.
Cutting Tools and Gauges, Ltd.
Fairmont Co., Ltd.
Federal Aircraft, Ltd.
Machinery Service, Ltd.
Melbourne Merchandising, Ltd.
National Railways Munitions, Ltd.
Park Steamship Co., Ltd.
Plateau Co., Ltd.
Polymer Corp., Ltd.
Research Enterprises, Ltd.
Veneer Log Supply, Ltd.
Small Arms, Ltd.
Toronto Shipbuilding Co., Ltd.
Trafalgar Shipbuilding Co., Ltd.
War Supplies, Ltd.
Wartime Housing, Ltd.
Wartime Merchant Shipping, Ltd.
Wartime Metals Corp.

[10] Admiralty equipment is inspected by the British Admiralty Technical Mission in Ottawa, and all aircraft are inspected by the representative in Montreal of the British Air Commission, Washington.

3. Labor

In the light of the great industrial expansion, major importance accrues to securing a coordinated policy on labor. This is complicated in Canada by the division of authority between the Dominion and the provinces, the understaffing of Dominion and provincial labor departments, the divisions between trade union groups and the general weakness of union organization, the attitude towards labor of employers' organizations such as the Canadian Manufacturers' Association, the lack until recently of a national system of employment offices and the divergent purposes in regard to labor of the Departments of National Defense, Munitions and Supply, Agriculture and Labor. In addition, the absence of labor representation on many government boards and the internment of some labor leaders have led to bitterness which has interfered with smooth relations.

The Labor Department developed a more forward policy during 1941, but it lacked the comprehensive organization needed for increasingly pressing problems. Two organs which had been established to meet special problems were the Interdepartmental Committee on Labor Coordination, an advisory body of senior civil servants set up on October 25, 1940, and the National Labor Supply Council, which was set up in June 1940 to exercise a general supervision over government labor policy, but has become a purely advisory board. The latter reports to the Ministry of Labor and the former to the Committee on Labor Supply of the Cabinet, of which the Minister of Labor is chairman.

Early in the war all disputes in war industries were placed under the Industrial Disputes Investigation Act of 1907, which had been drafted originally to cover disputes in mines and industries connected with public utilities. It requires that every means of mediation and conciliation be exhausted before action is taken. Negotiation between employers and employees is mandatory. Following this, notice must be given of intention to act. Either or both parties then ask the Minister of Labor to appoint a Board of Conciliation and Investigation, which he is supposed to do within fifteen days. The Board of Conciliation and Investigation consists of three members of whom one is recommended by the employees, one by the employer, and the third by the two first chosen. The findings of the Board are not binding on either party, but they must be made public in the *Labor Gazette,* organ of the Labor Department. If the employees reject the board's recommendation, they are free to strike after a majority vote taken under the auspices of the department. In nearly all cases both parties abide voluntarily by the board's opinion. Recently provision has been made for an intermediate stage through the appointment of an investigator to determine whether or not a Board of Conciliation is necessary.

An attempt to regulate wages in war industries by keeping them from going above the levels reached before 1940 was made under Order-in-Council in December 1940.[11] On October 18, 1941, a more comprehensive program of wage stabilization was announced as part of the attempt to secure general stabilization of prices and wages. Under this program all wages and salaries have been stabilized at the rate established before November 7, 1941. Those receiving salaries of more than $3,000 a year are not paid cost-of-living bonuses, but those under that amount may be.[12] Basic wage rates may not be increased or decreased by employers without permission. Restrictions on the movements of workers in war industries have also been introduced, and no application may be accepted from them by any other employers, except in the case of a skilled tradesman not working at his trade. The movement of male labor from agriculture or into a large number of specified services and industries has been prohibited except by special permit from the National Selective Service.

Inspection and enforcement of this program is provided by the joint staffs of the Dominion and provincial departments of labor. They are supervised by a newly created National War Labor Board and nine Regional Labor Boards (one in each province) on which government, labor and employers are represented. Only these boards may authorize changes in wage scales, and permission is given only when the wage level is found to be below that in similar occupations in comparable localities.[13]

On March 24, 1942 an extended National Selective Service plan for mobilizing Canadian labor was announced.[14] The Minister of Labor

---

[11] See Chapter VI, p. 325.

[12] All adult male employees and all other employees employed at basic wage rates of $25 or more a week receive cost-of-living bonuses at the rate of 25 cents a week for each one percent rise in the cost-of-living index. Male employees under twenty-one years of age and female workers employed at basic wage rates of less than $25 a week receive one percent of their basic weekly wage rates. The bonus is paid by the employer, and the rate is adjusted every three months. The first bonus was awarded in July 1942.

[13] Promotion of salaried officials, if it involves a salary increase, must be approved by the Minister of National Revenue.

[14] See Chapter V, p. 303.

and under him the Director and Associate Director of National Selective Service are primarily responsible for the plan. Regional officers were to be appointed and to be advised and assisted by voluntary unpaid citizens' committees.

A central registry has been established in the Department of Labor for the necessary data for the working of the program. This will be based primarily on the records of the 1940 national registration and the unemployment insurance files, and may be supplemented by further surveys. To avoid duplication, administrative responsibility for national registration has been transferred from the Department of National War Services to the Department of Labor, but the calling up of men for compulsory military service continues to be the responsibility of National War Services. The actual mobilization of industrial man power will be effected in the main through the Employment Service of Canada. A record of professional technicians has been compiled by the Wartime Bureau of Technical Personnel set up within the Department of Labor. Under the new regulations employment of engineers, college teachers of engineering science, research scientists, physicists, geologists, mathematicians, and architects is subject to the approval of this Bureau.

4. Food Supply

Canadian agriculture, largely dependent as it is upon exports, suffered severely from the depression and from prewar autarchical policies in Europe, particularly in the totalitarian states. At the outbreak of war, it was far from having recovered the favorable position it held in 1928, nor in general have the demands of war restored this position. Exclusion from continental markets after the German break-through to the west and the need of conserving British shipping have severely limited exports except in a few products, most notably hogs and cheese. Agricultural policy has had to seek expansion in these fields and at the same time plan for reduction in others, particularly wheat.

On September 9, 1939, a special body to supervise Canadian agriculture during the war was set up as the Agricultural Supplies Committee, subsequently renamed the Agricultural Supplies Board. This body is composed of senior members of the Department of Agriculture, and its work is virtually indistinguishable from that of the department. The membership of three special committees — the Seed Supply Committee, the Fertilizer Supply Committee, and the Pesticide Supply Committee — which assist the board [15] is also drawn from the permanent service. Much of the work of the board is carried on in cooperation with provincial committees which are representative of provincial and Dominion field staffs and producer organizations.

The policy of the board, as of the Department of Agriculture, has been conservative. Its purpose is to keep Canadian agriculture functioning to supply the food and fiber needs of Canada and the Allies without unnecessarily complicating the return of the Canadian farmer to a normal program when peace comes. Its work is difficult since British imports are restricted as far as possible to concentrated, storable, and relatively cheap food stuffs that are not difficult to handle and of which sufficient quantities cannot be produced in the United Kingdom. Essential food products in general order of preference are wheat and other cereals, dairy products, bacon and other cured meats, canned and frozen fish, poultry and eggs, canned fruit and canned vegetables.

Canada's surplus production of wheat, despite the fact that the British demand for it is about 160,000,000 bushels a year, places a heavy drain upon dominion resources, since farmers are guaranteed 70 cents a bushel for A-1 quality.[16] Because wheat is such an important item in Canadian agriculture, there has long existed a special statutory organ, the Wheat Board, which gives it exclusive attention. In an effort to reduce the surplus in 1941, farmers were offered bonuses of $2 an acre for the whole or any part of the 1940 wheat acreage transferred to coarse grains, $4 an acre for acreage out of wheat and put in summer fallow, and $2 an acre for placing fiber in the soil to provide a better seed bed for future wheat growing and in the meantime sowing grass on the reduced wheat acreage. Quotas of delivery to the Wheat Board were compulsorily limited to 65 percent of the 1940 deliveries. Through this drastic program, it was hoped that there would be not only reduction of acreage but also a stimulus to dairy products through the increased growing of grass. The cost to the government nevertheless remains very high. For some other surplus products the government has guaranteed from 80 to 85 percent of the prevailing price on about 80 percent of the amount affected by blockade restrictions.

In contrast to the surplus production in many fields there has been

---

[15] The ingredients of fertilizers and pesticides are normally imported into Canada from European sources.

[16] A good crop in 1940 coupled with the loss of continental markets resulted in a carryover of 575,000,000 bushels which necessitated a great expansion of storage space. There were in April 1942 more than 467,000,000 bushels on hand.

steadily increasing demand from Great Britain for specialized products which fitted its particular requirements. One feature of the British agreement in November 1939 to purchase 5,600,000 lbs. of Canadian bacon and ham per week for the next year was that the purchases must be made through a single agency.[17] The Bacon Board was therefore established to insure that regular and sufficient supplies would be available for export as required. It is also responsible for the maintenance of pre-war quality through price differentials as between grades and of a fair relationship between hog and bacon prices. The Bacon Board has power to license packers, to require any packer to give priority to the pricing and delivering of bacon required to fill the export quota and to fix the minimum price to be paid by packers for hogs. A Bacon Advisory Committee reviews the policy of the Board.

A special agreement, administered by the Dairy Products Board, also exists for cheese. There is also a special arrangement for condensed milk, but cheese is preferred.[18] There is no arrangement for butter, lest it interfere with the quantity of cheese delivered. In addition to the Dairy Products Board a Special Products Board was established in the spring of 1941 to deal with egg and poultry export orders and also with orders for any other agricultural product for which handling arrangements had not already been provided.

The British have tried to secure the agricultural agreements at prewar prices f.o.b. (which means that they meet the increased shipping costs), and this has created some difficulty, since agricultural costs vary more than those of raw materials. The department might have pressed for higher prices, but it was difficult to do so in a general situation of surplus, particularly as the period was also one of United States surpluses and low prices. At the time of the passing of the Lend-Lease Act, considerable fear was expressed in Canada that the new arrangement would result in the British taking from the United States the agricultural supplies which until that time had been secured from Canada. Great quantities of food stuffs are taken from the United States, but the United

---

[17] The contract for the period ending October 31, 1940, called for the delivery of 291.2 million lbs. of bacon, and actually 331 million lbs. were delivered. For the next year it was arranged to ship 425.6 million lbs. at a lower price. The agreement for the year ending October 31, 1942 called for the delivery of 600,000,000 lbs., more than was shipped in the ten years between 1927 and 1936.

[18] 90,000,000 lbs. of cheese were delivered in 1939–40. Since then the British have been prepared to take all that can be produced. 115,000,000 lbs. were shipped in the year ending March 31, 1942.

Kingdom has been under political pressure from the Canadian Government to take as much as possible from Canada.

The amount of food and agricultural produce which Canada can provide depends to some extent on the policy adopted by the Department of Agriculture. Demand is high within restricted fields, and there are possibilities of expansion to aid in counterbalancing the potential dangers of existing heavy surpluses. On October 18, 1941, the Prime Minister announced the intention of the Government to apply the principle of the price-ceiling to agricultural prices, as an integral part of the general program of price and wage stabilization. Maximum prices for certain farm products are based on the maximum market prices during the four-week period ending October 11. In March 1942 agricultural workers were forbidden to accept any other occupation without special permission. These efforts to stabilize agricultural employment and prices might well be coupled with a more forward policy of stimulating the production of needed commodities by subsidies so as to meet demand for them when it arises.

5. Transportation. Canadian Shipping Board and Transport Controller

To make available to Great Britain and its Allies the supplies which Canada produces, it has been necessary to keep close supervision over transportation within and outside the country. The Canadian railway transportation system, overdeveloped for peacetime uses, is a distinct asset in the war situation. In contrast, Canadian shipping is comparatively small, though increasing. While the latter is under ultimate Canadian control there is a well-integrated division of responsibility, in accordance with which the Canadian Government has control over the ports while the British direct the movement of ships to and from them. This has worked fairly well, though during most of the war closer cooperation between Canadian and British authorities and more precise recognition of spheres of influence would have been desirable.

In November 1939 a Transport Controller was appointed within the Department of Transport with general power over internal and external transportation arrangements. Applications for priority of transportation for troops, naval forces, materials, and supplies on behalf of the Canadian, British, or Allied Governments, are made through the Department of Transport and determined by the Transport Controller. Before this all vessels of more than 500 gross tons had been licensed by the Minister of Transport, acting through an advisory Ship Licensing Board, which was also empowered to requisition and reroute shipping. The Canadian Shipping Board, which since January 1940 has been associated not with the Ministry of Transport but with the Department of Trade and Commerce, was set up in December 1939 to assist in providing ocean transport for Canadian trade. It maintains close contact with the movements of all Canadian shipping through its own Ship Licensing Committee.

Since Canadian ships have all been placed on "dangerous routes," Canada has been dependent for necessary services in "safe trades" on neutral shipping. The Shipping Board has had great difficulty in procuring neutral shipping space, and since the extension of naval conflict to the Pacific, the shipping problem has become progressively more difficult.

6. Financial Control and Civilian Supply

I · THE FOREIGN EXCHANGE CONTROL BOARD

Foreign exchange control is the most radical of the measures which have been adopted to prevent a dislocation by wartime conditions of Canada's internal structure and external economic relations. Its initial purpose was to prevent a flight of capital from Canada and by curbing the uncertainties of its financial situation to strengthen internal morale. Subsequently, with the new stage following the German break-through, the pressure of heavy government expenditure threatened depreciation, and more rigid restrictions on outflow of capital had to be made.

Canada was in a particularly difficult position because exchange control in the Sterling Area at the outbreak of war made it impossible to convert a favorable sterling balance into dollars to meet an adverse balance of trade with the United States. Britain's increasingly heavy purchases in Canada were, furthermore, financed by the repatriation of Canadian securities held in the United Kingdom and the accumulation of sterling balances in London, or by credits extended by Canada to the United Kingdom.[19] Thus the problem of buying in the United States has become ever more difficult, as Canada has a steadily increasing adverse balance to meet out of capital resources.

---

[19] See Chapter VI, p. 322.

The Foreign Exchange Control Board, set up on September 15, 1939, is not itself a policy-making body but an instrument for carrying out Government policy on exchange matters. It has broad powers to take control over all foreign exchange held or owned by any resident of Canada; it may license all imports and exports and if necessary control or limit their quantities, and it has also the power to fix exchange rates. Its membership, under the chairmanship of the Governor and Deputy Governor of the Bank of Canada (a statutory body with which the Board works closely), is drawn from key members of the civil service.[20]

The regulation of capital exports involves supervision of all transactions between residents of Canada and non-residents.[21] Most of the vast amount of administrative work occasioned by transactions between Canada and the United States is carried on in Ottawa, though a special office has been set up in Vancouver to handle the special exchange problems of the Pacific Coast. Routine work is carried on through five sections: the Foreign Exchange Section, which works with the chartered banks on matters concerning the purchase and sale of foreign exchange; the Securities and Insurance Section, for security questions; the Canadian Payment Section, for exports; the General Section, dealing with trust and loan companies, private problems, and miscellaneous subjects; and the Commercial Section, for relations with corporations and businesses other than financial companies. The latter is subdivided into five divisions: the Examiners Division, with branch offices in Toronto and Montreal, which audits monthly returns of some two thousand companies with permits to operate foreign currency bank accounts and special export-import licenses; the Investigators Division for investigating work in the field, and also the returns to the Examiners Division; the Approvals Division for applications to pay dividends to nonresident shareholders; the Grain Division; and a General Division for miscellaneous problems. Thus a careful check is kept on all aspects of the situation and the effect of the stringent regulations is as far as possible equalized.

The successful working of foreign exchange control is in considerable part due to the secrecy preceding its introduction, the comprehensiveness of the regulations, which paralleled at the time of their introduction

---

20 It includes the Deputy Minister of Finance, the Commissioner of Customs, the Chief Inspector of the Post Office Department, the Director of Commercial Intelligence Service, Department of Trade and Commerce, and the Under-Secretary of State for External Affairs.

21 It should be noted that there are no restrictions on transfers from American holdings of Canadian dollars or on capital payments made under the terms of a contract dated prior to September 16, 1939, where the contract stipulates payment in a foreign currency, as, for example, in the case of maturing Canadian bonds which are payable in United States dollars.

the arrangements arrived at in Great Britain after a year of experimentation, and the possibility of drawing on the facilities of the Bank of Canada in its operations. Such evasions of its rules as have occurred have been in the main from ignorance, and in general the regulations have been accepted cooperatively.

II · THE WARTIME PRICES AND TRADE BOARD

The Wartime Prices and Trade Board was established within a few hours of the British declaration of war, to aid in the transition from a peace to a wartime economy. All civilian " necessaries of life," with the exception of wheat and fish, which were already regulated by statutory bodies,[22] were placed under its supervision. Subject always to the approval of the Governor-in-Council, it was given power to license producers or dealers, fix prices, ration commodities, buy and sell goods, commandeer supplies, and place embargoes on exports. Its function as a supervising agent to prevent hoarding and the charging of exorbitant prices on food, fuel, and other necessities, has loomed large in the public's view of the Board, but is subsidiary to the wider responsibility of securing supplies and arranging their equitable allocation. It has functioned in fact as a civilian board of supply, and its work has been increasingly concerned with planning on a long-range scale.

Members of the Board were drawn from the permanent service, and the policy has been to use where possible the facilities of other organizations such as the Dominion Bureau of Statistics rather than to duplicate their functions. The Board's work has been carried on through investigations into the distribution and sale of a wide range of commodities, through a constant check on retail prices to assure that they are in line with prices of raw materials and wholesale prices, through conferences with representatives of the industries, and through the appointment of administrators who organize and direct supplies in particular fields. The Board has in general relied on investigation and publicity rather than its coercive powers and has been able to depend upon the voluntary cooperation of industry and the public, both of which fear a repetition of the inflation of the last war.

The Board's practice of appointing special administrators in certain fields requiring detailed and continuous attention was early established, and has subsequently been adopted by the Department of Munitions and Supply. The administrators have all been selected from outside the fields

22 The Wheat Board and the Salt Fish Board.

for which they are made responsible, serve on a dollar-a-year basis with their expenses met, and are assisted by technical advisers who are the best experts in the field that could be secured. General lines of policy are worked out by the Board in consultation with the Cabinet on the one hand and the administrator on the other. It is the administrator's responsibility, with the assistance of his technical adviser, and in frequent consultation with the industry, to work out these policies in day-to-day activities. In addition to supervising the distribution and allocation of supplies in Canada, the administrators conduct any necessary negotiations with the United Kingdom controllers for the regular supply of imports.

The work of the administrators, as of the Board as a whole, has a particular interest because it was concerned so early with the organization of supply, and because it met so satisfactorily the initial problems in its field. A good illustration of this is to be found in the handling of wool supplies, about which there was immediate concern. The purchase by the United Kingdom of the entire Australasian wool clip for the duration of the war and subsequent prohibition of export of all wool from Australia, New Zealand, and Great Britain temporarily cut off the normal source of 75 percent of the Canadian wool supply. On September 18, 1939 a Wool Administrator was appointed to coordinate the industry and to allocate the supply and production in accord with need. The Wool Administrator, unlike the Sugar Administrator,[23] does not buy supplies but supervises buying and distribution. On November 24 the Board issued an order temporarily fixing a maximum price for the grades of wool most urgently needed, particularly for uniforms, the only definite price-fixing action the Board undertook in the first months of its existence. Subsequently negotiations with the Wool Control Scheme resulted in increased releases of supplies, and through constant attention satisfactory conditions have been maintained. Other administrators have been appointed for coal, hides and leather, oils, and rentals, the latter in consequence of the extension of the powers of the Board in September 1940 over rent for housing accommodation. This was necessitated by the influx of population and the consequent housing shortage in certain areas in which military or wartime industrial expansion had taken place.

---

[23] Under whom all raw sugar for Canadian use is purchased from the United Kingdom Sugar Control and resold to Canadian refineries, the price for raw sugar being agreed upon each year by the United Kingdom and Canada.

The Wartime Prices and Trade Board was also used by the Government to see that manufacturers did not take advantage of the imposition in June 1940 of a 10 percent War Exchange Tax on imports from non-British countries. The Board has also carried on investigations in regard to the incidence of import prohibitions and excise taxes under the regulations of December 2, 1940, to see that there is no increase in prices of similar goods produced in Canada. But during the first two years of the war the Board used its power sparingly, except in regard to rents. In this respect a definite policy of price-fixing was pursued. The satisfaction it has given depends on the selection of the localities, the time of introduction, and the rate of the ceiling. In general the work has been approved, and no serious restraint appears to have been exercised on private building.[24]

The accomplishments of the Board as described so far comprise the first stage of its activities when it concentrated upon meeting the needs of civilian supply and preventing profiteering. In policing prices it acted on complaints rather than on its own initiative and in general it dealt with cases rather than with broad problems. But the work of the Board and its administrators was an important factor in preventing the cost of living index from rising more than 9.6 percent from the outbreak of war until June 1941, in spite of depreciation of the Canadian dollar, increased taxation on many food stuffs, and the increase of costs on overseas supplies. As scarcities became serious and the United States moved also toward scarcities and price rises, more comprehensive planning and coordination of action became necessary.

Between June and October 1941 the cost of living index rose another 6 percent. Emphasis shifted to the problem of controlling inflation, and the Wartime Prices and Trade Board entered the second stage of its activities with major responsibilities for administering a new program of price stabilization and control. In the middle of August, the Wartime Prices and Trade Board was transferred from the Minister of Labor to the Minister of Finance. At the end of the month, the Board's responsibilities were extended to cover all prices, control being thereby central-

---

24 For certain designated areas the Board fixed rentals at the levels of January 2, 1940, and for others subsequently added, at the level of January 2, 1941. If there was no lease at the given date, maximum rental is determined by the administrator. Hearings to determine a satisfactory policy have been held in a number of places. For the more detailed investigation dependence was had at first on local rentals committees, and subsequently on county or district court judges or other persons appointed by the rentals administrator. Rentals for new housing are fixed only on application of landlord or tenant. The provision of needed housing has been undertaken by a Crown company under the Department of Munitions and Supply, Wartime Housing Ltd.

ized in the Department of Finance with which the Board remains associated. In addition, the Board's responsibilities for supply were extended to "all goods and services" not coming under the jurisdiction of the Wartime Industries Control Board.

Under the new orders the powers of the Wartime Prices and Trade Board included the authority to fix minimum as well as maximum prices and markups, and to prohibit the purchase, sale, or supply of "any goods and services" at variance with such prices. It could also prescribe the terms and conditions under which any goods or services might be sold or supplied. This included regulation of "installment-buying." Complete authority was given to license the suppliers of "any goods or services." To carry out these responsibilities the Board received extensive powers of investigation and regulation. In October the Board instituted a system of licenses for dealers in food and clothing. To curtail purchases it severely restricted consumer credit by making the minimum down payment on a long list of goods 33⅓ percent of the cash price and twelve months the limit within which installments had to be paid.

At the same time that the responsibilities of the Wartime Prices and Trade Board were extended, its organization was coordinated more closely with that of the Wartime Industries Control Board. This made possible more comprehensive planning for and organization of the whole field of supply. A closely integrated organization had thus been secured before fresh responsibilities were laid on the Wartime Prices and Trade Board by the elaborate program for stabilization of prices and wages announced on October 18, 1941 and brought into effect on December 1, 1941.

This program set as a "ceiling" above which prices were not to rise — the highest price of each seller during the four weeks' basic period, September 15 to October 11, 1941. This ceiling covers the prices of all goods except a few which are expressly exempt, and thirteen specified essential services such as electricity and gas. It does not include most professional services. Sales to the Department of Munitions and Supply are exempt, as are exports, sales of personal belongings and of securities. Certain other exceptions take into account normal seasonal fluctuations in price or export of fresh fruit and vegetables, fish, livestock and certain farm products sold by farmers to dealers and processors. These prices are carefully watched, however, and if they rise unreasonably may be put under the ceiling.

The Wartime Prices and Trade Board has the major responsibility for administering the price ceiling. For this purpose it has set up certain additional machinery including administrators and directors from the membership of each industry and trade; and coordinators for textiles, foods, metals, and paper products. In addition it has appointed administrators for the retail and the wholesale trade and for services. The controllers of the Department of Munitions and Supply act as administrators for the Board in respect to the prices of commodities under their jurisdiction. For local supervision of the program regional offices have been established by the Board throughout Canada. It has also set up a Consumers' Branch to watch over the interests of consumers and to coordinate the work of recently established Women's Regional Advisory Committees.

The decision was taken to impose a general price ceiling because it was felt that it could be most quickly imposed, was not discriminatory, involved fewer administrative difficulties, because there would be no uncontrolled group of prices to disturb the program for others, and because it would justify general wage stabilization. Set prices are not imposed for all commodities throughout the country, but individual ceilings determined by the prices charged during the base period are established for every store.

Certain problems inevitably arise, some due to " time lags," others to increased costs due for example to the Pacific war or to future costs-of-living bonuses.[25] In some cases the retail ceiling price will be lower than the price the retailer will have to pay for future supplies. Wholesalers may face similar difficulties in relation to manufacturers' prices, and manufacturers in relation to their costs. The attempt is being made to have all sections of the trade concerned absorb a part of increased cost in accordance with their ability to reduce their profits. Also, unnecessary costs of production and distribution are to be cut out. To supervise this the Wartime Prices and Trade Board established a Division of Simplified Practice to cooperate with their administrators and with the advisory committees which have been set up in each trade. A number of recent orders have provided for conservation of scarce materials, for standardization and for the elimination of competitive practices.

When industries find it impossible to maintain supplies at prices under the ceiling, government assistance may be given, either through a subsidy or through reduction or remission of taxes. Subsidy payments

---

[25] The first cost-of-living bonus was awarded in July 1942. In December, to keep the index steady, subsidies were introduced for several commodities such as milk, tea, coffee, and oranges.

(decided upon by the Wartime Prices and Trade Board) are handled through the Commodity Prices Stabilization Corporation, a government corporation. Recently, temporary subsidies for milk and shoes were provided, but the chief need will be in connection with imports. Thirty classes of unessential goods have been listed as ineligible for subsidy. Consumers' purchases of certain scarce commodities have also been limited.

As in its earlier work, the Wartime Prices and Trade Board is relying extensively upon the voluntary cooperation of business, farmers, labor and consumers. Penalties for violation of its rules may be imposed on both buyers and sellers. There is an Enforcement Administration which cooperates with existing government officials such as the weights and measures inspectors of the Department of Trade and Commerce. So far, however, cooperation on the part of both sellers and consumers has been generously extended. This has been a decisive factor in the successful establishment of the drastic experiment of general price control.

7. Coordination and Control

Coordination and supervision of the new agencies is secured through the Cabinet structure. The new departments are under responsible ministers, and the independent boards are responsible to particular ministers and through them to the Cabinet. Although associated with existing government departments,[26] the agencies are not branches or sections of them and the direct relationship is through the ministers. While the

---

[26] Department of Finance: The Foreign Exchange Control Board, National Loan Committee, National War Savings Committee

Department of Labor: Wartime Prices and Trade Board (transferred, Aug. 1941, to Department of Finance). National Labor Supply Council

Department of Agriculture: Agricultural Supplies Committee (Agricultural Supplies Board) Bacon Board, Advisory Committee to Bacon Board, Dairy Products Board

Department of Fisheries: Wartime Fisheries Advisory Board, Lobster Controller and Advisory Board

Department of Munitions and Supply: The Wartime Industries Control Board

Department of Trade and Commerce: The Canadian Shipping Board, Inventions Board

Department of Transport: Transportation Controller, Advisory Boards recommending compensation for requisitioned boats

Department of Secretary of State: Voluntary Service Registration Bureau, Internment Operations, Custodian of Enemy Property, Censorship Coordination Committee (also with National Defense, Postmaster-General, Transport)

Department of Justice: Registrar-General of Alien Enemies, Advisory Committee on Enemy Aliens, Committee on Emergency Legislation

Department of National Defense: Dependents' Allowance Board

Department of National War Services: Office of the Director of Public Information, War Charities Advisory Board

Prime Minister's Office: Advisory Committee on Economic Policy

detailed programs and the timing of action are decided by the boards themselves, recommendations for action must come before the Cabinet, and some of the powers of the agencies, price-fixing for example, are exercisable only with the approval of the Governor-in-Council in each instance. A recommendation can come before Council only through a minister who must sign and, therefore, make himself responsible for it. While the Cabinet as a whole bears formal responsibility, it operates in part through the War Committee and subcommittees charged with responsibility in special spheres of activity. The War Committee, whose particular functions will be considered below, concentrates on matters of war policy and defense. In the early period, it reviewed decisions of the war agencies, particularly in regard to activities in which more than one department was involved, but subsequently, as the agencies became better established, the review has become more formal.

I · COMMITTEES OF THE CABINET

The subcommittees, ten in number, are designed to provide specialized attention for particular fields of activity. Shortly before the outbreak of war, five subcommittees for supplies, legislation, public information, finance, and internal security were set up. In a reorganization on December 5, 1939, committees were established on War Finance and Supply, Food Production and Marketing, Fuel and Power, Shipping and Transportation, Price Control and Labor, Internal Security, Legislation, and Public Information, in addition to which are the usual standing committee on Wheat and another subsequently set up on Demobilization and Reestablishment. The special war agencies and some statutory bodies with particular war functions are grouped under seven of these committees [27] but report to the minister of the department with

---

[27] Committee on War Finance and Supply: Foreign Exchange Control Board, Inventions Board, Wartime Industries Control Board
Committee on Food Production and Marketing: Agricultural Supplies Board, Bacon Board, Advisory Committee to the Bacon Board, Dairy Products Board, Wartime Fisheries Advisory Board, Lobster Controller, and Advisory Board
Committee on Shipping and Transportation: Canadian Shipping Board, Transport Controller
Committee on Price Control and Labor: Wartime Prices and Trade Board, National Labor Supply Council, Inter-Departmental Committee on Labor Coordination
Committee on Internal Security: Custodian of Enemy Property, Registrar-General of Alien Enemies, Director of Internment Operations, Dependents' Allowance Board, Administrator of War Charities Act, Advisory Committee on Enemy Aliens
Committee on Legislation: Committee on Emergency Legislation
Committee on Public Information: Voluntary Service Registration Bureau, Censorship Coordination Committee, Public Information Office

which they are associated rather than to the chairman of the committee under which they are placed. All committees are organized under the chairmanship of the minister most concerned and include three to five of his colleagues whose departments are particularly interested in the subject.

The extent to which the committees have been used has varied according to the particular minister who acted as its convener. In cases where ministers are also in the War Committee, discussion may be carried on there instead of in the specialized committee. For example, the War Finance and Supply Committee functioned fairly regularly when Mr. Ralston was Minister of Finance, but after he was succeeded by Mr. Ilsley the committee was used very little and matters which would have been discussed there were taken direct to the War Committee. The Food Production and Marketing Committee has been used fairly systematically, and as always the Wheat Committee has been active. The Committee on Fuel and Power has scarcely met and that on Shipping and Transportation not frequently. The Committee on Price Control and Labor meets from time to time to consider recommendations on policy put forward by the Wartime Prices and Trade Board, the National Labor Supply Council and the Inter-Departmental Committee on Labor Coordination. The Committee on Internal Security, concerned with drafting the Defense of the Realm Act, and the Committee on Legislation, which prevents overlapping between new legislation and that already in existence, were more active at the beginning of the war than subsequently. Not very much has been done through the Committee on Public Information. The most recently established committee of the Cabinet, that on Demobilization and Reestablishment, has functioned steadily since the problems with which it is concerned began to attract attention.

II · WAR COMMITTEE OF THE CABINET

The most important of the Cabinet committees and the real center of power in the Government is the War Committee. This body, formally established in July 1940, assumes the major responsibility for directing not only war policy but also general affairs. Matters concerning departments not represented in the War Committee are considered fully in Cabinet Council, and formal action on everything must be taken by the Cabinet through the Privy Council. But the War Committee comprises a quorum in itself if it needs to take instant action. Its decisions pass the larger body with little question and it is accepted as chief coordinator of all activity.

A somewhat similar executive committee has existed since 1936, first as the Defense Committee and after August 1939 as the Emergency Council (Committee on General Policy). The War Committee, however, assumes more general direction of affairs than did either of the other bodies and its control of war policy is virtually complete.

This central position of the War Committee raises two questions which are vital for the successful working of the war administration: its control over the activities of government and the measure of planning and coordination which it is able to undertake. Both are dependent on the effectiveness of the War Committee itself and on the instruments of coordination which it can use.

The size of the War Committee, numbering ten officially,[28] is a handicap in giving concentrated direction and unnecessary for supervision. Reduction of its numbers would run counter to the tradition, which has made the Cabinet so unwieldy, of representing geographical divisions in the executive organ, but would increase its efficiency. As far as functional representation is concerned the War Committee might well be reduced to five members — the Prime Minister, and the Ministers of Justice, Finance, National Defense, and Munitions and Supply. In fact, some such limitation in numbers appears to be evolving empirically. The late leader of the Government in the Senate, M. Dandurand, rarely attended meetings in the months before his death; one of the ministers of National Defense is nearly always abroad; and it does not seem that the new Minister of National War Services is included. This means that usually six or seven attend, making a more manageable number.

The aid of a secretariat is now a regular feature of the War Committee routine. Before the war, some minutes were taken at meetings of the Defense Committee and records are now kept of Cabinet decisions. The most complete minutes are kept of the War Committee, and in addition the clerk of the Privy Council frequently draws up its agenda, circulates

28 War Committee: Prime Minister (Minister of External Affairs)
        Leader of the Government in the Senate
        Minister of Justice
        Minister of Finance
        Minister of National Defense
        Minister of Mines and Resources
        Minister of Munitions and Supply
        Minister of National Defense for Air
        Minister of National Defense for Naval Services
        Minister of National War Services

documents, and sends a record of decisions to the ministers concerned.

Outside of the War Committee and Cabinet responsibilities, each member of the War Committee carries heavy administrative responsibilities (the Prime Minister is also Minister of External Affairs) which entail a serious burden. On the other hand this makes the direct supervision of key departments and agencies possible. The idea of a War Cabinet freed of administrative duties has found little favor in Canada, and it is unlikely that such an expedient will be tried. The burden of parliamentary routine could be somewhat lightened, however, by the use of Parliamentary under-secretaries. This was tried in a modest way during the last war and could lessen the load of overworked ministers for more vital duties of coordination and planning.

While these changes would enable the War Committee to fulfill better its tasks of supervision, coordination and planning, it is clear that it must be able to draw on other coordinating bodies for information and advice. Two bodies of this character have been established of which the second, the Wartime Requirements Board, set up in November 1940 to provide the War Committee with information on current and future requirements, has had little active function. The first, the Advisory Committee on Economic Policy, has had very considerable importance and will be described briefly before a general consideration of the needs of the new situation of growing scarcities is undertaken.

III · THE ADVISORY COMMITTEE ON ECONOMIC POLICY

The Advisory Committee on Economic Policy was set up in September 1939, and is composed of important officials from different departments and boards.[29] It reports direct to the War Committee, particularly

---

[29] Chairman, Dr. W. C. Clark, Deputy Minister of Finance
Assistant to Chairman, Dr. W. A. Mackintosh, Special Assistant to Deputy Minister of Finance
Graham F. Towers, Governor of the Bank of Canada
H. D. Scully, Commissioner of Customs (Steel Controller)
H. B. McKinnon, Chairman of the Tariff Board and of the Wartime Prices and Trade Board
G. S. H. Barton, Deputy Minister of Agriculture
Charles Camsell, Deputy Minister of Mines and Resources
L. D. Wilgress, Deputy Minister of Trade and Commerce
R. H. Coats, Dominion Statistician
Colonel H. DesRosiers, Associate Deputy Minister of National Defense
N. A. M. Robertson, Under-secretary of State for External Affairs
R. A. C. Henry, Economic Adviser, Department of Munitions and Supply
Bryce Stewart, Deputy Minister of Labor
Secretary, R. B. Bryce, Department of Finance

on general economic problems. In the beginning, reports of the special agencies were frequently referred to it, but this became less common as the agencies developed. The almost constant reference of general questions to it during the first fifteen months of war slackened greatly after December 1940 and the Committee met less frequently than was common in the earlier period. It is still important, however, as a clearing house for information and for discussion of general policies, and its work has aided greatly in reducing overlapping and friction.

The reduced importance of the Advisory Committee appeared to be the result of a deliberate policy on the part of the War Committee of preventing other organs from becoming too powerful. By virtue of its membership, however, it will retain a significant position unless superseded by some comparable institution. It is clear that outstanding officers from different branches of the service who have specialized knowledge of departmental work, as well as of the new agencies, can accomplish much through the rather informal meetings of the Committee. When Dr. Mackintosh was brought to Ottawa from Queen's University as a special adviser to the Deputy Minister of Finance, he acted also as assistant to him in his capacity as chairman of the Advisory Committee. With the secretary, he drafted most of its reports as well as carrying a good deal of responsibility for general direction. The fact that his lack of specific administrative duties makes him freer to undertake such important functions suggests the value of including more advisers of similar status.

IV · A MINISTRY OF ECONOMIC AFFAIRS?

Since August 1941, the Canadian war administration has been moving steadily in the direction of greater integration of its technical services. Finance has been used as a coordinating power. The transfer of the Wartime Prices and Trade Board to the Minister of Finance and the greatly extended responsibilities of the board under the price control program are evidence of this. The close working together of the Wartime Prices and Trade Board and the Wartime Industries Control Board has secured a more integrated direction of war and civilian supply.

It may still be asked whether a Ministry of Economic Affairs would not be valuable in aiding the War Committee to make its decisions on general economic policy. The special responsibility of such a ministry would be to study continuously the war activity in all its aspects. It could draw upon the facilities of existing departments but its research workers should not have administrative responsibilities. Such an organ would have two marked advantages over the Advisory Committee: its members could devote their full attention to the specialized work, and it would have a minister participating in the War Committee, who would see that the information collected was made use of in the meetings and that proposals which the investigations had indicated to be valuable were given full consideration.

After three years of war, it is possible to see that the early demands of war gave rise to a multiplicity of new committees, boards, and departments highly diversified in form and function but unified by the dual purposes of furthering the war contribution and of easing the strain upon domestic life and economy. Lack of a general plan resulted in overlapping and a somewhat clumsy organization, but the decentralization permitted the agencies to adapt themselves to circumstances and to new demands. Their flexibility and that of old and new government departments led to some striking individual contributions in complex situations, while supervision and a general coordination was achieved through the unremitting efforts of ministers and key men in the civil service. Close coordination was developed with Great Britain and the United States largely through the personal relations of " opposite numbers," only a small proportion of which were institutionalized in such bodies as the Materials Coordinating Committee, the Joint Economic Committees and the War Production Committee. The resulting structure is firmly integrated both within Canada and as regards Canadian relations with the United States and Great Britain.

CHAPTER VIII

Australia at War

PART ONE

AUSTRALIA'S WAR EFFORT

by Fred Alexander

1. Before the Outbreak

During the first four decades in the life of the Commonwealth of Australia, which was formally inaugurated on January 1, 1901, by the federation of the colonies of New South Wales, Victoria, South Australia, Queensland, Western Australia, and Tasmania, the attitude adopted by the Australian people on issues affecting other parts of the British Commonwealth or foreign countries altered surprisingly little. Differences in emphasis revealed themselves from time to time, before as well as after the First World War; during the second half of the thirties, as will be shown below, these differences became sufficiently marked to suggest the possible emergence of a new Australian nationalism with an autonomous and distinctively Australian foreign policy. The Australian international outlook nevertheless continued to be influenced in September 1939, as it had been in January 1901, by three main factors, geographic, racial, and economic. These three factors, when taken together and passed through the mill of local politics, gave to the Australian people an outlook on world affairs which differed appreciably from that of

Canadians or South Africans on the one hand and that of New Zealanders on the other, and which to some extent determined in advance the Australian attitude to the war against Nazi Germany.

Of the three factors mentioned, geographic situation was the most obviously influential. Isolation in the southwest Pacific encouraged Australians in their preoccupation with the local problems of a partially developed island-continent and prevented the rapid growth of an informed public opinion on international affairs in distant parts of the world. Public interest in foreign affairs outside the southwestern Pacific — in which field Australians have at all times maintained a careful watch upon the activities of foreign nations, whether France in the first half of the nineteenth century, or Germany in the 'eighties or Japan in later times — was at the best spasmodic and as a rule half-hearted. Yet the exposed position of Australia, together with a traditional and uncritical acceptance of the British Navy as the first line of Australian defense, retarded the growth of an avowedly isolationist policy.

In similar fashion, the racial homogeneity of the Australian nation, albeit grossly exaggerated by statistical juggling into the oft-quoted estimate of "98 percent British," made British sentiment a force which acted as a powerful brake upon the autonomist tendencies inherent in dominion nationalism. Even without the small minority of non-British immigrants, the peculiarly Australian amalgam of English, Scotch, Welsh, and Irish tended to create a national viewpoint which was Australian rather than either English or Scotch or Irish, but its political implications were checked by a persistent sentiment for the Mother Country, which was deep-rooted and widespread even if most Australians were not as conscious of its influence as their New Zealand neighbors were said to be. Racial sentiment thus reinforced the prevailing conception of strategic necessity.

During the first four decades after federation, moreover, Australian national sentiment found an outlet in industrial and social progress without the corresponding growth of a strong sense of economic rivalry with Great Britain, which might have made Australian nationalism a more powerful centrifugal force within the British Commonwealth. Foreign observers might talk of the financial domination of London and might cite in confirmation the visit to Australia of Sir Otto Niemeyer of the Bank of England at the beginning of the economic depression. But financial dependence on London did not prevent the growth of Australian manufacturing industries inside a tariff wall which penalized English exporters only less severely than foreign manufacturers. Meanwhile, the United Kingdom remained the most important market for wool, wheat, and meat, staple raw materials upon which Australian prosperity depended.

On the whole, domestic politics in Australia from 1901 to 1939 did little to strengthen the potentially centrifugal tendencies in Australian nationalism. All political parties gave more than lip service to the ideals of Australian nationhood, but none ventured to proclaim distinctively Australian foreign or defense policies which seriously threatened the unity of the British Commonwealth. The fact is clearly evident in the record of the various political groups which were the antecedents of the United Australia Party and the Country Party, the two anti-Labor parties which together controlled the House of Representatives and the Senate in the Federal Parliament of September 1939. Each of these parties still accepted the application to Australia of the view presented by Prime Minister S. M. Bruce in 1923, that "when one part of the Empire is at war, the whole Empire is at war." The statement also holds for the Australian Labor Party, despite occasional indications to the contrary which make a survey of Labor's attitude to foreign relations and defense essential to an understanding of the Party's attitude in September 1939, and after.

It was a Labor Government, the first Fisher administration, which secured the passage, in 1909, of legislation imposing compulsory military training for home defense. Labor also joined with other parties in ·the Federal Parliament in supporting the establishment of an Australian Navy as a mark of Australian nationhood. Confusion regarding Labor's defense and foreign policies began during the First World War, when Prime Minister W. M. Hughes and other leading members of the Labor Party, which had obtained a majority in both the House of Representatives and the Senate at the elections of 1914, favored extension of the compulsory system by advocating conscription for overseas service. The majority of the Labor Party inside and outside Parliament refused to accept this lead; their determined opposition was the chief reason for the defeat of two conscription referenda, in 1917 and 1918 respectively. Throughout the campaigns, Labor spokesmen on anti-conscription platforms vigorously denied charges of disloyalty to the Imperial cause, for which, in fact, 329,000 Australian volunteers (out of a total Australian population which was then only five millions) fought overseas between 1914 and 1918. The charges, however, were repeated; the suspicion and bitterness engendered during the two conscription campaigns carried over into the postwar period and helped to color Labor's attitude on foreign affairs throughout the two decades of peace.

Only one Labor Government held office between November 1918 and September 1939. During their first postwar decade in opposition individual Labor members occasionally gave an isolationist twist to speeches on foreign affairs. The Scullin Labor administration of 1929–32 also drastically reduced the armed forces of Australia. In this, however, the Government's special severity in retrenchment was not without precedent and was largely the result of the demand which came with the economic depression for reduction in government expenditure as well as in wages and in interest, a demand which eventually caused a split in Labor ranks and brought into being the United Australia Party and a coalition Government with the former Labor leader, Mr. Joseph A. Lyons, as Prime Minister.

During its second long postwar period in opposition, the Australian Labor Party gave its critics fresh grounds for charges of isolationist "disloyalty" threatening the unity of the British Commonwealth. In 1935–36, for example, the Labor Party in the Federal Parliament opposed Australia's collaboration in applying League sanctions to Italy in the Ethiopian incident. Uncertainty as to the Party's attitude in the event of a war involving Great Britain was partly responsible for Labor's defeat in the 1937 election campaign and prevented the defense program of the Party, under its new leader, Mr. John Curtin, from receiving the attention it deserved during and after that campaign.

The history of Australian defense policy before and after the establishment of the Commonwealth had been one of vacillation. A well considered policy, consistently applied over a lengthy period, had been lacking; expert opinion had been divided between preparations for resistance to large-scale invasion and short-term protection against more scattered raids, pending the arrival of overseas naval forces; the general public remained uncertain as to the precise objectives to be met by increased expenditure on armaments. The situation was further complicated by the fact that Australia's defenses had suffered severely during the fifteen years following the Armistice of 1918. All branches of the national defense had been affected by postwar economies.

The efficiency of the land forces of Australia had been lowered by a series of changes in periods of training and in methods of recruitment. These began with the advent of war in 1914, three years after the original scheme of compulsory military training had become effective. The period of training was permanently reduced in 1922; compulsory service was suspended in 1929, partly for financial reasons.

Australia's air defenses were also in an unsatisfactory condition in 1937. The Royal Australian Air Force had been constituted as an independent body in 1923, as the successor to the Commonwealth Air Force of 1921 and to the Australian Flying Squadron which had served abroad with distinction during the First World War. Its equipment, training, and administration had, however, been very severely criticized by Sir John Salmond, a British expert who had been commissioned to report on this arm of the services in 1928. The Salmond Plan for additions and improvements which would enable the R.A.A.F. not only to meet military and naval requirements but also to serve as an additional defense against hostile raids and attacks, was accepted by the Bruce-Page Government, but the Air Force shared in the economies suffered by all branches of the defense forces in 1929–30.

The naval forces at the command of the Australian Government in the mid 'thirties had also been weakened. The Australian Navy had shared in the reductions made by all signatories of the Washington Treaties of 1922. Ships in commission had been reduced from twenty-five in 1921 to thirteen in 1928. By January 1929, however, in consequence of a gradual developmental program adopted in 1924, Australia possessed twenty-five vessels of war. As a result of the Scullin Government's retrenchment of 1929–30 only six vessels of this naval unit were retained in commission and the total seagoing strength of the Navy was reduced between 1929 and 1932 from 5,300 to 3,527 men.

Though financial interest rather than a fixed defense policy had been the main cause of the drastic reductions of 1929–30, basic differences in policy, as well as party factiousness, underlay Labor's opposition to the Lyons Government's rearmament program, which began with the breakdown of the Disarmament Conference and the evidence of disturbed political conditions in Europe and the Far East. In September 1933, a three-year plan affecting military, naval, and air forces was announced. In 1934, the defense estimates rose from £A3,500,000 to £A5,270,000; in 1935, a further increase to £A7,350,000 was voted. This rearmament program was accepted without public enthusiasm. To the Australian people war still seemed very remote. Experts also continued to be divided on two main issues: the relation of the naval to the other arms of the national defense and the method of recruitment. On each of these matters the Labor Opposition in the Federal Parliament had decided views.

On the first issue, one school of experts held that Australia's security was so bound up with the maintenance of communications by sea with the outside world that naval expenditure must be a first charge upon Australian defense funds. Protection of trade routes outside Australian waters must needs be left to the British Navy; but it was argued that Australia could make an important contribution by undertaking what might be termed the outward defense of the Empire in the Pacific area. The opposing school admitted the importance of overseas trade routes but discounted the danger of serious and vital interference with all of them. Members of this school placed greater emphasis on the danger of attack upon certain of the vital industrial urban centers of eastern Australia in the event of the Singapore base falling into enemy hands. This second school accordingly favored diversion of funds from naval to military and air expenditure. Its members included some who regarded the resumption of compulsory service as a condition precedent to effective military preparedness.

Advocates of a return to compulsory service were to be found among the Government's supporters in the Federal Parliament as well as among the experts, but any form of conscription was politically impossible in 1937, so strong was the hold which the memory of the conscription referenda of 1917 and 1918 still exercised in Australian politics, and so slight was the public conception of the serious threat to Australia's security. The alignment of political forces did, however, sharpen the divergence of technical opinion on the naval question. When Mr. Lyons led the Australian Delegation to the Imperial Conference of 1937, he took with him the outlines of a new defense program which aimed to spread increased expenditure, which had risen to £A11,500,000, over all three services but which accepted the argument that the Navy was the first line of Australian defense.

On this point, the new defense program was vigorously assailed by the Labor Opposition. Mr. Curtin invited the Government and the people of Australia to face the possibility that a British Government which was hard pressed in Europe would be unable or unwilling to send sufficient reinforcements to the Indian Ocean and Pacific squadrons based on Singapore to give Australia adequate protection from invasion by a first-class naval power in the Pacific. Labor's answer to the Government's defense program was to advocate a mobile and well-equipped mechanized land force and a substantially increased air force, maintained by the output of Australian factories. Thus the issue in the campaign for the triennial elections to the Federal Parliament, which were held in October 1937, concerned the relative merits of naval and air armaments as the first line of Australian defense.

This issue was not squarely faced by the Australian people. The Lyons Government was returned to office, despite serious losses in the Senate, with a reduced but a working majority in the House of Representatives, to which, in accordance with Australian constitutional practice, the Federal Government is responsible. The election was, however, a vote against the Labor Party rather than against Labor's defense policy. The latter suffered from its association with the confused foreign policy pursued by the official leaders of the party in previous years and from the divergent views of certain minority Labor groups, which ranged from support for collective security to extreme forms of isolationism.

Australia thus entered upon the critical year of Munich with its people unprepared for the gravity of the crisis which lay ahead. That the Government was seized of the importance of rearmament was shown by a sharp increase in the 1937–38 defense expenditure and in a new three-year program announced by the Prime Minister in March 1938, for which it was anticipated that a sum of £A43,000,000 would be required. The manner in which the money was to be distributed over the several arms of the national defense continued to receive criticism at the hands of Mr. Curtin, while some of the Labor rank and file went further and questioned the wisdom of entrusting control of increased armaments to a Government whose foreign policy they regarded as virtually directed from Downing Street and subservient to " Fascist " interests at home and abroad.[1] The Prime Minister's declarations on foreign policy were of the vaguest. When the Czech crisis of May brought the threat of war near enough for all to see, the Government did its best to discourage " provocative " comment or discussion, particularly over the radio.

The Government's desire to avoid any provocative action during the mounting tension in Europe was, however, due to more than a desire not to embarrass Mr. Chamberlain. It was, in fact, very largely the result of the Lyons Government's interpretation of the situation in the Far

[1] The Labor Party supported a motion of no confidence on the defense program. In the course of the debate their leader said, " Any increase of defense expenditure after the Munich Pact, so far as Australia is concerned, appears to me to be an utterly unjustifiable and hysterical piece of panic propaganda." (Ed.)

East and its realization of the very grave position in which Australia would be placed, with its existing defenses, if members of the British Commonwealth were brought to war with Germany and Italy, and the Anti-Comintern Pact of 1936 were to become a military alliance involving Japan. In this policy the Lyons Government had the support of some influential Australians outside official circles, who were well-informed on international affairs. Their doubts of the efficacy of collective action against aggression were strengthened by their experience of Japanese aggression in China, and were also combined with a belief that Japan had had genuine economic grievances in the postwar high tariff world and by a recognition that Australia had very recently emerged from an economic brush with Japan following the trade diversion incident of 1936–37, in which neither wisdom nor material advantage had rested with the Australian Government.

Rapid progress in Australian manufactures, accompanied by a high standard of living for industrial workers, had been made possible during the first postwar decade by high world prices for raw materials and by easy borrowing on the London market. Australia's export trade to Japan had also increased until, in 1928–29, the latter country was Australia's third best customer. Hopes of developing markets in the East Indies and elsewhere in the Pacific had led to the appointment of trade commissioners from whose activities some results had been obtained. Nor were the effects of the economic depression in Australia as serious as at one time had seemed likely.

The trouble out of which the trade diversion decision sprang immediately was the intelligible desire of Japanese exporters to offset restrictions on their cheap goods in many foreign (including some British colonial) markets by increased sales in British dominions with which the balance of trade was adverse to Japan. When the Japanese pressed for a trade agreement on these lines the Australian Government refused. With a suddenness, a temerity, and a disregard for some who might well have claimed the right to be consulted, the Government announced a new trade policy, in May 1936. New customs duties and a licensing system were to be introduced, ostensibly to divert imports from countries which were "bad customers," such as the United States, to those with which the balance of trade was less unfavorable to Australia. But the moment chosen for the announcement, immediately after the abortive Japanese trade negotiations, made it seem that the main objective of the new policy was to force the consent of Japan (which, incidentally, was a " good customer ") to a new trade agreement by which she would continue to buy Australian wool and wheat but would accept a limitation upon the sale of cheap Japanese textiles on the Australian market.

It was soon apparent that the trade diversion policy was a grave blunder both economically and politically. The best that can be said is that efforts were made to rectify the policy as soon as possible and to prevent permanent losses resulting from it. Its most damaging economic effect upon Australia was the encouragement it gave to Japanese manufacturers to turn to staple fiber instead of wool to avoid undue dependence on any foreign nation. The Australian Government was given a sharp reminder of the importance to Australia's economic well-being, as well as to its security, of peace and stability in the Pacific. This was a return to the position that had prompted the Government's abortive proposal at the Imperial Conference of 1937 for a Pacific non-aggression pact. Renewed political interest in the Pacific during 1938 also revived earlier suggestions for the establishment of an Australian Legation at Washington and one at Tokyo as a beginning in direct diplomatic representation abroad, in respect to which Australia had failed to follow the lead of her sister dominions, Canada and South Africa.

In all the circumstances of May to September 1938, therefore, it is scarcely surprising that the Chamberlain Government's attitude during the crisis which culminated in the Munich Agreement was generally supported in Australia. How much influence Mr. Lyons and his colleagues exercised upon British policy in the crisis has yet to be fully revealed, but both the Government and the Labor Opposition endorsed the British action at Munich.

The Munich incident may nevertheless be regarded by future writers as the turning point in the history of Australian foreign policy. Hopes persisted that the Munich settlement would produce permanent peace but there was general recognition that no risks should be taken. The Federal Government speeded up and extended its already augmented defense program of March 1938; the cooperation of state premiers was obtained in the establishment of a National Defense Council; the militia was increased; belated provision was made for the strengthening of the Air Force; and a compulsory register of men between the ages of 18 and 64 was taken. In April 1939, a decisive step in economic preparation for effective defense was made by the creation of a new ministerial department of Supply and Development under the former Federal Treasurer, Mr. Richard G. Casey, who was charged with the coordination of industrial and defense activity. In the same month, a Pacific Defense Conference of representatives of Great Britain, Australia, and New Zealand met in the capital of the latter dominion.

By this time, Hitler's invasion of Prague had prepared the Australian people for the worst. The shock of the actual events of September was, however, cushioned in advance for Australians by the isolation of Japan which accompanied the conclusion of the Russo-German Pact of August. In the weeks that preceded the outbreak of war in Europe there was no doubt that the Australian Government would have general support in following the British Government into war, but it was impossible to predict the spirit in which the Australian people would enter the conflict or the extent to which political and strategic conditions, both at home and abroad, would permit a wartime effort comparable with that of 1914–18.

At the beginning of September 1939, a new Prime Minister of only four months' standing, Mr. Robert G. Menzies, faced a Parliament in which his own United Australia Party was in a minority. The Labor Opposition, which might at any moment play upon the personal antipathy to Mr. Menzies of certain Country Party members and thus force a general election, was still accused of harboring elements disloyal to the Empire. Its leaders, moreover, seemed uncertain in their own conception of Australia's wartime role and were, not unnaturally, anxious regarding the social consequences of the conflict. The extent of British naval assistance which would be available in Australian waters in certain eventualities depended upon the outcome of the first real test of air and naval strength in European waters. The efficiency of Australia's own defensive rearmament was yet unproved, the validity of the theory on which it was based was untested. Most important of all, none could tell how the Australian people would respond to a new test of the responsibilities of nationhood after two decades of peace, during which the rank and file of Australians had shown relatively little interest in outside politics.

Such was the state of affairs in Australia when, on the evening of Sunday, September 3, 1939, a meeting of the Federal Executive Council approved the issue of a proclamation declaring the existence of a state of war in Australia — approximately one hour after the British Prime Minister had announced that Great Britain was at war with Germany.[1a]

1a For a discussion of the procedure involved in the declaration of war, see Chapter II, pp. 20 f.

2. *The First Eight Months of War*

In the first few months after the outbreak of war, domestic political complications were much less serious in Australia than might have been expected. The basic reason lay in the fact that the nation at large approved the Government's action in declaring Australia's position at once, without hesitation. The actual declaration of a state of war by Government proclamation without prior parliamentary authorization was, moreover, in keeping with the official Australian interpretation of British Commonwealth unity in vital matters.[2] It was clear that such political differences as were likely to arise regarding the war would concern the manner and not the fact of Australia's participation in it.

Events helped the new Prime Minister. In the early days of the national emergency, firmness rather than finesse was called for. There was no doubt that the Prime Minister proved a steadying influence in the crisis. In his first wartime address in Parliament he coupled an appeal for a united war effort with an avowal of his desire to interfere as little as possible with the machinery of constitutional government and with the democratic way of life:

> However long this conflict may last, I do not seek a muzzled opposition. Our institutions of Parliament, and of liberal thought, free speech and free criticism, must go on. It would be a tragedy if we found that we had fought for freedom and fair play and the value of the individual human soul, and won the war only to lose the things we were fighting for.

In the circumstances, the continuance in office of the Menzies Government, and its effective preparation for the conduct of Australia's war effort without the delay and disorder which would accompany an early appeal to the electors, depended on the attitude adopted by the majority of the Labor Party, with its controlling position in the House of Representatives, and on the skill with which its leader succeeded in serving his Party without endangering the interests of the nation. Mr. Curtin's responsibilities were no less heavy and his difficulties no less acute than those which faced the Prime Minister. A journalist by profession, Mr. Curtin's personal experience as an active anti-conscriptionist in Victoria, during the campaigns of 1917–18, and as editor of the *Westralian Worker,* in the early postwar years, was sufficient to remind him of the

---

[2] Cf. the 1923 declaration of Mr. S. M. Bruce, cited above, p. 367.

havoc which conflicting loyalties may play with the Labor machine in a national emergency.

With the outbreak of war, however, it was clear that very skillful direction would be needed if Labor was to face the electors as one united party in the campaign for the triennial elections to the Federal Parliament, which the Constitution required not later than January 1941. Upon the Labor leader in the Federal Parliament also fell the chief responsibility for seeing that the Party's wartime record was such as to insure Labor reasonable prospects at the polls or, at the worst, to prevent disastrous defeat in a " win-the-war " election. Six months after the outbreak of war, it was apparent that the Federal Labor leader had been unable to maintain the united front he desired; he did, however, succeed in gradually weaning the majority of his Party from the impliedly isolationist policy of 1937, to a position where, if office were thrust upon him by some turn of the political wheel, he and his colleagues would be able to carry on the wartime administration of the country without alienating the nation and without irretrievably splitting the Party as had been done during the First World War of 1914–18, when Mr. William M. Hughes was its leader. Meanwhile, Mr. Curtin maintained a degree of cooperation with the Prime Minister, notwithstanding major differences in the outlook of the two men on both foreign and domestic issues and despite the evident determination of the Labor leader to take no action which could be held disloyal to his Party.

The Prime Minister made little effort to exploit the prevailing sentiment; in the weeks following the outbreak, he refrained from emotional appeals and avoided action likely to provoke an outburst from Labor members of Parliament whose prewar utterances had committed them to opposition to an overseas expeditionary force, and who had not yet adjusted themselves to the facts of the wartime situation. When, on September 15, the Government announced its decision to enlist a volunteer force of 20,000, it was stated that the men would be recruited for service " at home or overseas." Not until November 1 did the Prime Minister indicate that " the second A.I.F." would be sent abroad; even then, the announcement was qualified by the proviso " unless circumstances made such a course impracticable." By the end of November, when it was officially disclosed that the second A.I.F. would go overseas early in 1940, the Prime Minister had completed the initial stages of administrative reform aimed at facilitating the war effort.

The first important administrative change was the formation in mid-

September of a War Cabinet of six members, the Prime Minister, the Attorney-General, the Minister for Supply and Development, the Minister for Defense, the Minister for External Affairs, and the Minister for Commerce, which was to work within the larger Cabinet. The powers of the Executive in its various forms had also been considerably increased by the passage in September of the National Security Act,[3] which authorized the issuing of Government Regulations to secure " the public safety and the defense of the Commonwealth of Australia and the Territories of the Commonwealth," subject to a limiting clause which precluded the use of such a regulation for " the imposition of any form of compulsory naval, military or air force service, or any form of industrial conscription, or the extension of any existing obligation to render compulsory service." On November 11, it was announced that, instead of one Ministry for Defense, three departments of the Army, Navy, and Air Force respectively had been created with separate ministers, but all three, together with the Minister for Supply, to work under the general direction of the Prime Minister in his capacity as Minister for Defense Coordination. What was formerly the Secretariat of the Department of Defense, charged with responsibility for coordinating the three services under the Minister of Defense, became the Department of Defense Coordination. The Secretary of the Department of Defense, who was also Secretary of the War Cabinet, became permanent head of the new Department of Defense Coordination. Extension of the activities of each of the three arms of the national defense was decided upon at the beginning of November. Compulsory military service was reintroduced for home defense, and was calculated to raise the strength of the militia forces to a figure not less than 75,000, out of a total population of 7,000,000. The first trainees, who were to spend three months in camp during 1940, were to consist of unmarried men who would reach the age of 21 during the year ending June 30, 1940.

The Royal Australian Navy, which, as in August 1914, the Commonwealth Government transferred to the control of the British Admiralty on the outbreak of war, then consisted of the following ships in commission, exclusive of survey ships and minesweepers: two 10,000 ton " County " class heavy cruisers, 8 inch guns; three modified " Leander " class cruisers, 6 inch guns; one remodelled cruiser, 5000 tons, 6 inch guns; two sloops; five destroyers including a flotilla leader. These forces were to be strengthened by the construction in Australia of three

---

[3] Act No. 15 of 1939.

"Tribal" class destroyers and four local defense vessels suitable for anti-submarine or mine-sweeping work. The Government chartered other vessels for the latter type of work and a number of ships were converted into armed merchantmen.

Australia's air program had two objectives. The first was to provide sufficient aircraft and trained personnel to insure effective resistance to raids or other action by sea-borne aircraft;[4] the second was to assist the British air effort. The acceptance of the British Commonwealth Air Training Plan led, however, to modifications of the project for a strong expeditionary air force. Instead, Australia accepted responsibility under the plan for what the Prime Minister announced on December 15 as "a first objective" of 26,000 men comprising 10,400 pilots and 15,600 observers and wireless operators and air gunners. A corresponding number of ground personnel were to be provided, the great majority of all men to be fully trained in Australia under a local training scheme which would reach its peak in 1942. It was later announced that, in all, 28,500 men were to be contributed by Australia by June 1941, and 57,473 by March 1943. A small proportion only of these men — two-ninths — would receive the final stages of their advanced training in Canada. At the beginning of November 1939 the air development program was also accelerated so that nineteen squadrons of the Royal Australian Air Force would be in active operation by June 1940.

Provision of airplanes to meet the needs of the R.A.A.F. both in training and in action presented one of the most serious problems before the Australian Government. Experimental prewar production of Wirraways — light planes suitable both for training and for resisting sea-borne aircraft — had reached the point where an output of one Wirraway per day was expected by the end of 1939; 100 privately owned aircraft were acquired; more than 1000 other ships were ordered, some to be built in whole or in part in Australia, some to be obtained elsewhere.

From the first, the Government realized that the war would be won as much in the factory as on the field. The creation in April 1939 of the Ministry of Supply[5] was an indication that an effort would be made to

---

[4] Australia's air transport was developed far beyond that of any country comparable in population and extent of territory. In 1939 there were forty commercial services in operation with a total route mileage of 29,500. There were four well-developed transcontinental air routes. The number of airdromes and emergency landing fields was 500 in 1939, and a great expansion has of course taken place during the war, especially in the northern areas. — Ed.

[5] See above, p. 373.

turn to account the material development of the preceding decade, in the supply not only of personal equipment for individual soldiers but also of munitions and armament of all types. Of the 1939–40 estimated expenditure of £A59,500,000, less than £A8,000,000 [6] was to be spent abroad. This was hailed as an indication of the extent to which Australia had become self-sufficient in the supply of its defense requirements. Additional factories were built for the manufacture of explosives and rifle ammunition, Bren guns and 25 pounder field guns, two pounder anti-tank guns, shells, air bombs, naval mines, and depth charges. The administrative organization rendered necessary by these activities led in November to the creation of an " Economic Cabinet," consisting of the Prime Minister, the Minister for Supply and Development, the Minister and Assistant Minister for Commerce, the Minister for Customs, and the Treasurer.

Economic problems of equal importance arose out of the need to supervise closely the marketing arrangements for Australian exports, which had exceeded £A150,000,000 annually in the years preceding the war. Though only two percent of Australian exports had gone to Germany in the year 1938–39, the extension of German control over other European countries had the effect of cutting off more and more markets for Australian exports until the percentage of the export trade affected had risen to 15 after nine months of hostilities. With this possibility already in view at the beginning of the war it was evident that every effort should be made to retain the valuable United Kingdom market which in peacetime absorbed more than half of the total exports of Australia.

Machinery for this purpose was provided by marketing control boards set up under the National Security Act, which negotiated on behalf of the Australian Government with the Government of Great Britain. Of the contracts agreed upon — which involved sales totalling approximately £A100,000,000 — special publicity was given to the wool agreement. The British Government purchased the entire Australian wool clip for the period of the war and one year thereafter at an average price which represented an increase of approximately one-third on the average price obtained by Australian wool producers in the open market in the previous year. This gave security to producers even if some were

---

[6] When the estimated expenditure rose to £A75,000,000 (March 1940) and again to £A179,-000,000 (September 1940) the amounts to be expended abroad were given as £A14,000,000 and £A33,924,759 respectively.

dissatisfied with the amount of the increase in price, and others doubted whether the provisions for resale by the British Government of supplies in excess of its needs would effectively preserve the Australian market in neutral countries, notably in the United States.

Frozen meat exports, handled after, as before, the outbreak of war by the Australian Meat Board, were maintained. Short-term butter, cheese, and eggs contracts were concluded with the British Government, and no trouble was anticipated in maintaining exports of dried and canned fruits. The unsold portion of the surplus of the 1939 raw sugar crop was also bought by the British Government at a price satisfactory to growers. It was not, however, possible to make equally satisfactory arrangements for the two important exports of wheat and fresh fruit or for wine.

Wheat presented a more difficult problem than wool because of the excess of production over consumption of wheat in the British Empire. The Australian Wheat Board, with some 195,000,000 bushels to be disposed of in 1939–40, had sold 92,500,000 bushels by March 1940 and had reasonable expectations of sales of another 18,000,000, but the board was faced with the certainty of a surplus and also with the problem of storing much of the wheat sold pending removal as shipping space was provided from time to time by an Australian liaison officer working with the British Ministry of Shipping.[7]

The fresh fruit situation was much more serious. In peacetime, the annual export of apples to Great Britain and the European Continent averaged nearly 5,000,000 bushels. Little more than half of the total apple and pear yield was consumed in Australia. Fresh fruit was not included by the British Government among its wartime list of essential commodities. It was recognized, therefore, that the difficulty of securing shipping space would be considerable; it was also feared that the indiscriminate dumping of fresh fruit on the Australian home market would not only depress fruit prices but might also react on the Government's efforts to maintain prices as nearly as possible on their prewar level. As a result of a conference between the Australian Apple and Pear Organization Board and representatives of the state governments, a scheme for orderly marketing of fruit was brought into operation. By zoning of markets and a nationwide " Eat more fruit " campaign it

---

[7] The marketing problem was solved by the fact that owing to dry conditions the 1941 wheat crop was 83,200,000 bushels, the lowest since 1919–20 (the crop for 1940 was a record, 210,-277,000 bushels). The result was a carry-over of only sixteen million bushels, far below the average. (Ed.)

was hoped that fruit growers might receive something from sales in addition to the amount of 2s. per bushel for apples and 3s. per bushel for pears which the Government advanced to growers and which would barely cover costs of production.

Price-fixing plans had been prepared before hostilities broke out. The Prices Commission, with the cooperation of the state and federal governments, sought to achieve the two objectives of preventing wartime profiteering and of permitting such reasonable increases in retail prices as would encourage a continuation of normal peacetime business activities. The cooperation of the business community was obtained, with the result that, after ten months of war, the Commission was able to state that, despite increases of 35 percent in landed costs of imports, 23 percent in the prices of exports and 10 percent in interstate shipping rates, the index of retail prices had risen less than 2 percent. Government control of capital investment was also established. Regulations were promulgated requiring that all projected issues of new or additional capital were to be submitted to the Treasurer, who was provided with special advisory assistance for this purpose.

The immediate problems involved in financing the war effort concerned overseas rather than domestic expenditure, especially expenditure in non-sterling countries. The ordinary peacetime necessity of retaining balances in London to service the interest on Australia's loan indebtedness to Great Britain [8] presented no serious problem in view of the wool purchase and the agreements noted above. It was also decided that purchases by the Australian Government for the equipment and maintenance of expeditionary forces abroad should be met temporarily by loans from the British Government. Even as late as May 2, 1940, when the Federal Treasurer brought down preliminary proposals for the 1940–41 budget, he announced, "with reluctance," that the Government had decided to defer for the present the question for providing funds in Australia to meet any portion of the overseas expenditure in 1940–41.

Provision for expenditure in non-sterling countries, on the other hand, was early recognized as an urgent matter of vital importance. The unfavorable peacetime balance of trade between Australia and the United States [9] was met by drawing on sterling credits in London. The increase in the London demand for dollar exchange, which inevi-

---

[8] The annual interest in 1936–37 was £A18,111,150.
[9] The 1938–39 figures were: Exports £3,614,038; Imports £14,647,305.

tably followed the placing by the British Government of extensive orders for war materials in the United States, had been foreseen in Australia before the outbreak of war. Defense (Monetary Control) Regulations were promulgated by the Governor-General in Council on August 23, 1939, and were subsequently embodied in amended regulations issued in November under the National Security Act. Though the nature and extent of the currency restrictions thus imposed varied from time to time, their purpose throughout was to conserve Australian reserves of foreign currencies and to prevent the importation of commodities not essential to the war effort. Australian owners of certain American stocks were ordered to sell their holdings within six months and to lodge the proceeds with the Commonwealth Bank; arrangements were made with American companies for the retention in Australia of a portion of their Australian profits; the issue of dollar credits by private banks was restricted and was placed in the control of the Commonwealth Bank; importing of certain specified nonessential goods was prohibited and the maximum amount of other imports limited; a system of licensing exports was also introduced on May 1, 1940, to prevent the export of goods required for defense purposes.[10]

The methods adopted by the Government for financing domestic war expenditure also did little to bring home to the Australian taxpayer the actual or potential gravity of the wartime situation. The revised estimates of November 1939 increased the amount for Defense and War Services to £A62,014,000. The Government declared its general financial policy as designed to finance the war effort by a "balanced program of taxation, borrowing from the public and borrowing from the banking system," with a deliberate weighting of the balance towards borrowing with the assistance of the banking system during the early months of the war, so as to add nothing to the temporary dislocation of the economic system due to the passage from a peace to a war economy. The Government was enabled so to weight the balance by the fact that during the years immediately preceding the war the Commonwealth Treasurer had resisted the temptation to accept easy methods of financing federal expenditure without recourse to taxation. Against the estimated expenditure within Australia for the years 1939–40 and 1940–41, which totalled £A125,000,000, provision had yet to be made in

---

[10] For a detailed survey of the restrictions see A. V. Janes, "History of Exchange Control in Australia," *The Economic Record*, Vol. XVI, June 1940. The whole of this issue of *The Economic Record* is worth consulting for the economic side of the Australian war economy in its first nine months.

May 1940 for £A70,000,000. Of this amount, the Treasurer proposed to raise only £A20,000,000 by additional taxation, the balance to be obtained by public loans.[11] Of the £A20,000,000, customs, excise, and sales taxes accounted for £A10,300,000. Less than £A8,000,000 was to be raised by income taxation and of this amount only £A3,000,000 by taxation on individuals, which would be felt mainly by taxpayers in the middle income group. This softening of the impact of the war upon the Australian economy may have been financially sound; together with other influences, however, it helped to create a false sense of security among the Australian people.

Among these influences, geographical situation, as ever, played an important part in conditioning the Australian outlook. The main center of conflict was far removed from Australia; the continued neutrality of the Japanese Government and the evidently anti-Nazi sentiments of the Roosevelt administration emphasized the existing tranquillity of the Pacific scene. Wishful thinking, especially on the subject of American opinion — on which few Australians were well-informed — encouraged the belief that there was slight risk of an extension of the war into Australian waters.

Meanwhile, the political calm which had been maintained on the home front during the first few months of the war had also come to an end. In January a vacancy in the House of Representatives was created by the resignation of the member for Corio, the Rt. Hon. Richard G. Casey, Minister of Supply, who was appointed as Australia's first Minister to the United States.[12] The Labor Party chose to make the issue of the by-election the defense policy of the Government — a challenge which the Prime Minister accepted.

The resulting defeat for the Government, and the election as Labor member for Corio of a former Captain in the first A.I.F. was not as clear an indication of the nation's attitude to the Prime Minister's war and defense policies as might at first sight appear. Other matters entered into the Corio campaign, including a rash decision of the Government to begin the manufacture of motor cars — engines as well as chassis — in Australia.[13]

---

11 The issue of War Savings Certificates by the Government was begun a few months earlier. Certificates were issued in denominations of £1, £5 and £10, bearing 3¼ percent interest and maturing in 7 years, with a maximum of £250 worth to any one person.

12 See below, p. 392.

13 The manner in which a virtual monopoly was granted by the Government during the parliamentary recess to one company, to be formed by the influential Australian Consolidated

Mr. Curtin was not allowed to enjoy his Party's triumph at Corio and to look forward with confidence to the result of the federal elections a few months later. The unity of the Labor movement which he had striven so hard to maintain was seriously threatened by a " Hands off Russia " resolution of the Easter Conference of the Labor movement of New South Wales.[14] The resolution was at once disavowed by Mr. Curtin, who pointed out that only the Federal Labor Conference could direct the Party in matters affecting the federal platform. The damage had, however, been done, and later in the year Labor was to face the electors of New South Wales not as one party, but as three.

The Corio election, moreover, had brought the United Australia Party and the Country Party back into an uneasy alliance against their common opponent of many years. Mr. Menzies, recognizing his weakened position after the by-election, was forced to modify his formal refusal to accept Country Party members of his Cabinet other than those chosen by himself. An agreement was reached whereby the leader of the Country Party (Mr. Archie Cameron) became Deputy Prime Minister, and, in joint consultation, the Prime Minister and Deputy Prime Minister selected six Country Party members, three of whom were to serve as Ministers, three as Assistant Ministers. On March 21, the Prime Minister announced the reconstruction of the War Cabinet and the Economic Cabinet, the former to consist of two Country Party and seven United Australia Party members, the latter of two Country Party and five United Australia Party members. For the time being, the agreement strengthened the Government's position in the Federal Parliament but the Government's future and the future of its wartime program were far from being assured.

Too much still depended on two men, the Prime Minister and the leader of the Opposition, the influence of each of whom had been weakened in recent months. The administrative burdens of the Prime Minister had steadily increased. Moreover, continuance of the satisfactory working results which had emerged from the mutual respect and

Industries, Ltd. provided the Labor opposition with an effective weapon with which to belabor the Government in the Corio campaign. After prolonged public and parliamentary criticism, the chairman of A. C. I. announced, in June 1940, that plans for the production of motor cars in Australia had been deferred " probably until the end of the war."

[14] The war policy adopted by the Conference included the following statements:

" The Conference makes it clear that, while being opposed to Australian participation in oversea conflicts, it is also opposed to any effort of the anti-Labor Government to change the direction of the present war by an aggressive act against any other country with which we are not at war, including the Soviet Union."

restraint which the head of the Government and the leader of the Opposition had displayed towards one another since the outbreak of the war was seriously threatened. Mr. Curtin himself was no longer sure of the support of all members of his Party. And a general election with all its confusion and its conflicting loyalties loomed ahead.

3. From the Blitzkrieg of May to the Elections of September 1940

While none could foresee the rapidity with which the collapse of Belgium and France would follow the German invasion of the Low Countries on May 10, the Australian Government was not slow to realize the gravity of the situation in the middle of that month. Speaking in the House of Representatives at Canberra on May 22, 1940, the Prime Minister bluntly stated that "as British people we have reached a stage of emergency without precedent in the history of the Empire."

The most important administrative measure taken to meet the emergency was the reorganization of the work of munitions supply in Australia by the appointment of a Director-General of Munitions who, the Prime Minister announced, would be "freed from all hampering regulations," and given the utmost authority "not only to get things done with the existing government machinery but to press into service civil factories, or all or any of the mechanical resources of these factories." The Director-General's status was to resemble that of the chiefs of staff and he was to have direct contact with the Prime Minister as the head of the War Cabinet. The Government congratulated itself on obtaining the services as Director-General of Munitions of Mr. Essington Lewis, managing director of the Broken Hill Proprietary Company, Ltd., one of the largest and most powerful concerns in Australia. An Assistant Director-General was appointed and directors (most of them experienced business executives) for each branch of Munitions Supply — Aircraft, Explosives, Ordnance, Gun Ammunition, Materials, Machine Tools, Finance, and Labor Supply and Regulation. Supplementary organizations were set up in each of the States.

The first political test of Labor's attitude to the new war situation following the *Blitzkrieg* in western Europe came on June 20, when the Prime Minister introduced a bill to amend the National Security Act of the previous year to bring it into line with the Emergency Powers Act passed through the British Parliament on May 22 and a similar New

Zealand Act. On the day before the amending bill was brought before Parliament, a special conference of the Federal Labor Party had revised its war policy in terms which permitted the leader of the Opposition to support the amending bill despite the fact that the measure removed all except one of the limitations which had been set up to the 1939 Act, including the safeguard against " industrial conscription." The sole remaining limitation was the proviso to section 13A of the Act " that nothing in the section shall authorize the imposition of any form of compulsory service beyond the limits of Australia," the term " Australia " being defined to include the " Territories of the Commonwealth of Australia." On a division, the amending measure was passed by the House of Representatives by 61 votes for and 9 against.

While the war policy adopted by the special June Conference of the Australian Labor Party revealed considerable changes as the result of the greater emergency, it also made clear that the Party had no intention of sinking its individuality in the national war effort. These changes in policy were made palatable to members of the Labor movement not only by recognition of the emergency. Stress was also laid on the importance which the Labor Party had itself allotted, before and since the outbreak of war, to the strengthening of Australia's air defenses and to the local manufacture of munitions.

The most notable change was the acceptance of compulsion in training for home defense and provision of reinforcements for the expeditionary forces overseas. Mr. Curtin and all Labor spokesmen were, however, adamant in their refusal to participate in a National Government. The matter was considered by the special conference of the Australian Labor Party in the third week of June, but the farthest the conference was prepared to go was to authorize Mr. Curtin and his parliamentary colleagues to participate in a National War Council " to advise the Government in respect to the conduct of the war and in preparing for the postwar reconstruction."

The Labor proposal for a War Council did not appeal to the Government which, in the absence of a partisan opposition, was able to carry on with its fairly comfortable majority of 9 in the House of Representatives. The main political concern of Mr. Menzies arose from the fact that all members of the House of Representatives and half the members of the Senate must face a General Election not later than January 1941. Towards the end of July the Prime Minister confirmed reports that the Government proposed to move for an increase in powers of the federal legislature to enable Parliament, if necessary, to extend its own life. The method of obtaining the desired power, which was fully canvassed in the press, was by resolution, carried by both Houses, requesting the British Parliament to pass legislation amending in this respect the Commonwealth of Australia Constitution Act, the statute which brought the federation of the Australian colonies into being. " The view of the Government," Mr. Menzies said, "is that the next election should occur within its due period, unless circumstances make it impossible or dangerous to Australia's war effort to have an election campaign, but if such circumstances arise and no power to postpone the election exists (as the case now is under the Constitution) Parliament will simply be unable to prevent it, and the consequences may be disastrous."

In his original announcement, Mr. Menzies had intimated that he would not proceed with the matter until after consultation with the leader of the Opposition and with Mr. Beasley, leader of the Australian Labor Party (Non-Communist). On August 6, a discussion between the Prime Minister and the party leaders made it clear that unanimity would not be obtained. The Country Party was favorable in principle, but the opposition of the Labor Party killed the proposal. The Prime Minister announced that polling would take place on September 21; both Houses concluded their sittings on August 22, and members prepared for a whirlwind electioneering campaign.[15]

The policies for which the several parties sought the electors' approval reflected the course of events since the outbreak of war. For the historian of Australia's war effort, the campaign of September 1940 thus serves as a test not merely of the nation's judgment of the Menzies Government's administrative record but also of the considered attitude of the Australian people towards the war and the respective war policies advocated by the five parties [16] which faced the electors. The Prime Minister rested

---

[15] While political negotiations with the Labor Party were hanging fire, the Government had made some progress in associating trade unions with the war effort. As early as April 11 an agreement had been reached with the Amalgamated Union of Engineers for dilution of labor in munitions factories and became effective on May 1. The Prime Minister's negotiations for the formation of a Trade Union Advisory Panel were long drawn out but eventually led to the creation of a Panel representative of the Australian Workers' Union, Amalgamated Engineering Union, Maritime Transport Council, Federated Enginedrivers' and Firemen's Association, Road Transport Union, Textile Workers' Union, Arms Explosives and Munitions Workers' Union with the declared objective of advising and guiding the Government in matters affecting the trades unions engaged in defense work. The Panel as constituted was, however, opposed by the powerful Australian Council of Trade Unions.

[16] United Australia Party, Country Party, Australian Labor Party, Australian Labor Party (Non-Communist) and Australian Labor Party (New South Wales).

the Government's case for return to office on its record in organizing the military, naval, and air forces for overseas and for home service and in directing the economic activities of the nation so that a maximum of assistance should be given to the war effort with the minimum of dislocation of the lives of private citizens. In his policy speech of September 2, Mr. Menzies emphasized the fact that his Government had raised and equipped " the better part of 130,000 men " for the A.I.F. — " and many thousands in addition for the Navy and Air Force." Establishment of a home defense army of nearly 100,000 men made, he declared, " a force immeasurably greater and more efficient than anything we have had before."

The course of events since the German attack on Norway and on the Netherlands had on the whole confirmed, though in some respects it had weakened, the marketing position of the first few months of the war. While some primary producers might not share the satisfaction expressed by the Prime Minister in his policy speech with the results of the Government's system of marketing controls, Mr. Menzies was able to cite the impressive annual figure of £A120,000,000 for contracts concluded for the sale of primary produce. Few, moreover, were likely to challenge his claim that careful attention to retail prices had prevented the rapid increase in the cost of living which had been one of the features of the war of 1914–18 in Australia.

Restrictions on imports were not popular. Some measure of the extent to which the Australian public still failed to appreciate the gravity of the war situation was given by its reluctance to accept serious restrictions on gasoline consumption. Australia's dependence on external supplies of motor fuel was generally recognized. Commendable progress was being made with the distillation of petrol from shale and in the use of producer gas, but the need for storage against possible interference with overseas supplies of gasoline in the event of an extension of active hostilities to the Pacific areas, together with the necessity of conserving dollar exchange, made some restrictions on local consumption of motor fuel inevitable.[17] The proposal was nevertheless fought vigorously and the

---

[17] The Glen Davis Plant in N.S.W. was producing 35,000 gallons of petrol daily by the end of August 1940, but distillation was difficult and expensive. In July 1941 a plan was announced to produce from wheat 10,000,000 gallons of power alcohol, the use of which in automobiles would be made compulsory. In his speech on June 17, 1941, Mr. Menzies announced the cutting of gasoline rations for Australia from 20,000,000 gallons to 12,000,000 gallons a month. The cut as actually introduced a few days later reduced the ration for private cars from 38 miles per week to 20 miles per week. (Ed.)

Government was compelled to amend the rationing schedules which were promulgated on July 11, 1940. Under the amended schedules, the amount of petrol supplied depended on the mileage limit fixed for the class of motor vehicle operated. This limit ranged from 4,000 miles per annum for cars used for non-business purposes to 15,000 miles per annum for cars used for special business, with additional provisions for certain classes of vehicles such as taxicabs and omnibuses.

The Labor Party's policy, on its constructive side, was divisible into two parts: that which concerned the prosecution of the war and that which concerned social standards and peacetime policy. In his war program, Mr. Curtin took his stand on the planks of the platform adopted by the special Federal Labor Conference of June, declaring that "the Australian Labor Party stands inflexible in support of the British cause."

In his immediate social program, the Labor leader sought to outbid the Prime Minister for popular support by promising increases in soldiers' pay, in old-age and in invalid pensions, provision for pensions for widows with dependent children, and a family allowance for families with more than two children under sixteen. Mr. Curtin advocated reconstruction of the Australian Wheat Board and increased rates of payment for the first 3,000 bushels of each farmer's crop. Against the Labor program for social amelioration the Prime Minister set a policy which "means hard times, discomfort, sacrifice, loss, . . . the use of the public and private credit resources of the country to the utmost; much Government control; no profiteering; the forgetting of private interests."

The result of the election was not clear. While the Government had a sweeping victory in the returns for the Senate, its majority in the House of Representatives, on which it depended for continuance in office, was reduced from nine to one (exclusive of the Speaker).

In the circumstances, two, possibly three, inferences should be drawn from the country's verdict on September 21, 1940. The first was that the nation supported the war policy applied in its name by the Menzies Government. On the other hand, the faithful support of the official Labor Party by a very considerable minority of the Australian people indicated that the nation did not desire continued participation in the war to distract attention any more than was absolutely necessary from ideals of social justice, in the attainment of which Australia had already made great progress in the past and of which the Labor Party was the most vigorous advocate. A third inference was permissible: that, while a considerable section of the Australian people expressed at one and the same time its desire for continuation of the war effort and its confidence in Mr. Curtin and his colleagues of the Opposition, the nation as a whole could not be said to have given anyone a mandate for the formation of a national government in which Labor might in course of time lose its identity and weaken itself in the struggle for social reconstruction when the war was over. The problem which Mr. Menzies and Mr. Curtin had to face, therefore, was to effect the greatest possible cooperation in a joint war effort without prejudice to differences in domestic policy on which it was clear that the views of Mr. Curtin's party were widely respected and supported in the country even in the critical wartime situation.

The elections had, if anything, emphasized the significance of personal factors in the political scene. In the first place, the position of Mr. Menzies was greatly strengthened by his overwhelming victory in his own constituency of Kooyong in the State of Victoria. Paradoxically, Mr. Curtin's standing was also improved by the fact that he narrowly escaped defeat — for some days, indeed, was thought to have been defeated — in his electorate of Fremantle, Western Australia. The threatened defeat of Mr. Curtin had the effect of directing attention to his self-effacing services both to his Party and to the nation. His defeat when it was thought to be inevitable was generally deplored; when Mr. Curtin was eventually returned by the results of the soldiers' vote for his electorate, the leader of the Opposition was able to exercise an even greater influence within and without the ranks of his Party than before the elections. The failure of the New South Wales Labor group led by Mr. J. R. Hughes to win a single seat in the new Parliament and the weakening of the representation of the " Non-Communist " group led by Mr. Beasley also strengthened Mr. Curtin's position. Among several new members of the Federal Parliament Mr. Curtin also obtained the support of Dr. H. V. Evatt who had taken the virtually unprecedented course of retiring from the Bench of the High Court of Australia — the highest judicial position open to an Australian lawyer — to contest and win the constituency of Barton, New South Wales.

When the final count of the votes had been made — including the overseas soldiers' vote — and the United Australia and the Country Party Government led by Mr. Menzies was seen to have a majority of two members only in the House of Representatives, from one of whom the Speaker would be taken, it was apparent that two courses were possible for the Prime Minister. He had either to take the risk and the heavy responsibility of preparing to seek another more decisive election at an early date or of coming to some arrangement with the two Labor parties which would insure that his tenuous hold on a majority in the House was not constantly threatened by factious Opposition tactics.

Mr. Curtin had made it a condition precedent to formal negotiations that Mr. Menzies should give an assurance that, in the event of some form of Labor cooperation, the Government would implement some at least of the social, financial, and industrial planks in Labor's electoral program. Mr. Menzies proposed that the Opposition parties should accept " half the seats in a National Government or, failing a National Government, half the seats in some form of National or War Council, with executive functions." The Prime Minister's proposals were submitted to the Official Labor Caucus on October 22. The Labor Party adhered to its pre-election decision not to join a National Government and also rejected the proposal for membership in a War Council with executive powers. Instead, it proposed an Australian War Advisory Council representative of all political parties and " empowered to investigate and to advise and assist the Government in its war efforts," the members of the Council being " sworn to respect all confidences."

In this form the Labor proposal was accepted by the Prime Minister. It was agreed that the Advisory War Council should consist of four members of the existing Government parties, three Official Labor members and one Labor (Non-Communist) member, and that it should sit under the presidency of the Prime Minister or his deputy. Meanwhile, Mr. Menzies rearranged his own Cabinet, one major change being the dropping of Mr. Archie Cameron, who had been replaced as leader of the Country Party by Mr. A. W. Fadden, who therefore became Deputy Prime Minister.[18] Sir Earle Page, the former leader of the Country Party, also rejoined the Government as Minister for Customs. The Prime Minister reduced the size of his War Cabinet in view of the constitution of the Advisory War Council, which was duly set up by the end of October with Mr. Curtin, Mr. F. M. Forde (Deputy Leader of the Labor Party) and Mr. N. J. O. Makin as the three official Labor representatives, and Mr. Beasley as the " Non-Communist " member of the Council. With the machinery of Government thus reorganized, ministers and their semi-official collaborators from the Opposition parties

---

18 Other changes were forced upon the Prime Minister by a tragic air crash of August which had caused the death of the Minister for the Army, the Air Minister, and the Vice-President of the Executive Council, in addition to the Chief of the General Staff.

renewed their attack upon the many problems of the Australian wartime effort.

The weakening of the French position in Indo-China confirmed the immediate prewar trend of Australian thinking towards the Pacific. In the early months after the outbreak of hostilities, there had been a widespread feeling that, whatever the result of the war, it would have the effect of changing appreciably the economic association between Australia and European countries. The emergence of a European politico-economic bloc, while it would not completely destroy Australia's trade relations with Great Britain, would throw Australia more directly upon her own resources and upon the markets of her own geographic hinterland, making closer relations with other Pacific countries highly desirable. When the course of the war increased the threat to Great Britain, and Australian security was seen to be more seriously threatened by the conversion of the anti-Comintern agreement into a military alliance, with Japan likely to seize the first opportunity for a drive to the South, political and strategic rather than economic considerations influenced Australian thinking in regard to the Pacific. In the circumstances, increased attention was given to the future policy of the United States in the Pacific and to the possibility of closer relations between the Australian and the American democracies.

The question of direct Australian diplomatic representation in the leading Pacific countries with which Australia had important political and economic associations had long been the subject of discussion in Canberra. The decision to open the first Australian Legation abroad, in Washington, D.C., had been taken before the outbreak of hostilities. The Menzies Government was not deterred from its purpose by the war, and in March 1940 the first Australian minister arrived in Washington. Corresponding steps were taken to strengthen relations between Australia and Canada by the appointment of high commissioners in Ottawa and Canberra respectively. In April 1939, the Menzies Government had also announced its decision to appoint a minister to Japan. For this important position the Chief Justice of the High Court, Sir John Latham, was given leave from the High Court in August 1940 to establish the first Australian Legation in Tokyo.

By such steps the Menzies Government gave expression to the growing conviction of the Australian people that, whatever the nature of the postwar economic organization of the world, Australia would of necessity find its future linked not only with Great Britain but also with the other countries of the Pacific. In short, the exigencies of the war situation had served at once to strengthen the traditional economic and strategic ties of the British connection and yet to emphasize the significance of Australia's own regional associations, responsibilities, and liabilities.

PART TWO

AUSTRALIA AND THE WAR WITH JAPAN
(1941 TO MARCH 1943)

by H. Duncan Hall

1. The Eve of the War — 1941

In the first eleven months of 1941, ending in war with Japan on December 7, Australia underwent internal political changes which brought the Labor Party into power both in the Commonwealth and in the most important of the states, New South Wales; she expanded greatly her war production; her fighting forces received their first great baptism of fire in this war, in Greece, Crete, North Africa, and Syria. With armed forces entrenched in Malaya, she passed through three periods of suspense in expectation of Japan's drive south that came finally like a typhoon out of the China Sea in the twelfth month of the year.

The Prime Minister, Mr. Menzies, by his great personal qualities, won an outstanding place in Empire councils during his mission to Britain from February to May. When he returned to Australia at the end of May, his personal position seemed stronger than ever and even his political critics paid tribute to the quality of leadership which he displayed. Yet three months after his return he was forced to resign; and his resignation led to the defeat of the Coalition Government and the coming into power of the Labor Party under Mr. John Curtin. The success of the Labor Party in the elections in New South Wales in May had been a warning that the hold of the Ministry over the country was weakening. The crisis came to a head on August 26, and after two days of confused political discussions in which faction fights within the Coalition Government appeared to have played an important part, Mr. Menzies was forced to resign, his place being taken, without other change in the composition of the Ministry, by the leader of the Country Party, Mr. A. W. Fadden.

This political crisis, which had lasted for several weeks during a period of grave tension in Australia's external affairs, discredited the Coalition Government sufficiently to bring about its downfall in a vote of no confidence in the House a few weeks later. The Labor Ministry, announced by the new Prime Minister, Mr. Curtin, on October 6, was composed largely of right-wing members of the Party. It consisted of nineteen ministers, the number to which the Cabinet of Mr. Menzies had been increased in the ministerial reorganization made at the end of June after his return from his visit abroad.

The new Ministry continued the essential elements of the reorganized war program as announced by Mr. Menzies in his important broadcast to the Australian people on June 17. The Government had then proposed " to set up an authority with wide powers to take over factories and plants, or, if necessary, to close factories in whole or in part, with powers like those recently announced in the United Kingdom by the Board of Trade." Among the new authorities created were ministries for tank and armored vehicle production and for aircraft production and a Shipping Commission to requisition and supervise the operation of all Australian shipping, the actual management of the ships remaining with the owners.[19] For the more effective use of internal transport, principally under the control of the State Railway Commissioners and Road Boards, a rail and road transport coordinating authority was set up.[20] " The chairmen of the Shipping Board, the railways authority and the roads authority, will together," Mr. Menzies said, " make up a Commonwealth Transport Authority." A Coal Commission to direct national coal production, consumption, and distribution was also to be established.

---

[19] Sixty-three ships engaged in the coasting trade were requisitioned immediately, to be operated by the Australian Shipping Control Board as a national mercantile marine.

[20] Australian rail communications (although cursed with a break of gauge at a dozen points of strategic importance, which military leaders have sought in vain to remove since before the First World War) are on an extraordinary scale for a country with a population less than that of New York City. In 1939 there were 27,973 miles of track.

A Director-General of Supply with wide powers was also to be appointed together with an authority to control and coordinate the supply of labor. A proposal to prohibit strikes and lockouts and business combinations slowing down war production was also made; but this met with such opposition from Labor that it was not carried into effect until the Labor Government was forced by the Japanese attack on the outer ramparts of Australia to adopt, early in 1942, the drastic policy of complete conscription of labor. In addition, standing parliamentary committees were to be attached to government departments in order to bring the legislature in the fullest possible degree into active contact with the different branches of the war administration. Other steps proposed were a further drastic cutting of nonessential imports, both sterling and non-sterling, as part of an effort to divert private spending to the financing of the war effort.

The magnitude of the Australian effort to make itself an arsenal of democracy was revealed more fully during the year. In the first two years of the war, its munitions expenditure was estimated at £A120,-000,000, compared with a total munitions expenditure in the year before the war of under £A4,000,000. Australian forces abroad were equipped to an important degree with arms of Australian manufacture including armored vehicles, machine guns and light artillery and supplies, and munitions of all kinds.[21]

As a result of a policy of decentralization, a chain of small-arms ammunition factories was being extended right round the Commonwealth. In 1940 some sixty or seventy million rounds of small-arms ammunition were exported to the United Kingdom and were used by the R.A.F. in the Battle of Britain. The complicated 3.7 anti-aircraft gun was produced in 1940 within ten months of the receipt of the blueprints, from which 70,000 tools had to be made before actual production could begin. There were fifty factories making machine tools, compared with three before the war, and eighty-five firms making high precision gauges, compared with five before the war. There has been during the war a great expansion in metallurgical industries; at an earlier stage of the

---

[21] The decision to set up and to equip from Australian factories a complete armored division at a cost of £A30,000,000 was an illustration of the range of Australian arms production. Such a division requires hundreds of tanks, as well as armored vehicles, mobile artillery units, etc., as well as reserves. Part of the equipment was to be Bren guns and carriers, anti-aircraft and anti-tank guns and howitzers (all of which were already being produced), tanks (in mass production early in 1943), mobile anti-aircraft units, sound detector apparatus, of which manufacture had begun or was about to begin at the end of 1941.

war four hundred thousand tons of Australian steel were exported to Great Britain in addition to large quantities supplied to various other parts of the British Empire and the Netherlands Indies. In October 1941 the new Labor Minister announced that Australia was to make available immediately, for British-Soviet use on the trans-Iranian railway, sorely needed standard-gauge locomotives and freight cars.

The Australian airplane industry had its thousandth plane in the air in September 1941, and production of two to three hundred planes a month was predicted for 1942 and 1943. Six-hundred-fifty-horsepower and 1100-horsepower airplane engines are now being manufactured. Beaufort bombers began to come off the production lines, and the first squadron reached Singapore in December some days after Japan struck. The delivery of Australian-built training planes to the Netherlands Indies had begun in 1941. Aluminum sheet production was being expanded and plans were well advanced for the manufacture of aluminum from local bauxite or alunite. Over fifty naval vessels, including three cruisers and several destroyers, were under construction in Australian yards; and a program for the building over a five-year period of sixty merchant ships of 9,200 tons each was under way. Marine engines were being built for them. An optical instrument industry entirely new to Australia and involving the manufacture of practically all types of complicated optical instruments, including about 150 types required in modern war, was established in 1941. All this in a country that at the outbreak of war had only 25,000 skilled engineers.

In November 1941 the total number employed directly and indirectly in the making of arms and munitions was stated to be 210,000 as compared with 5,000 at the time of the fall of France. It was planned to transfer another 160,000 from civil to war industry in 1942. Although the possibilities of the production of armaments and war supplies in Australia far exceeded those of any other country in the Eastern Supply Group,[22] at the end of 1941 it seemed to be approaching its maximum output of munitions; yet in reality it was on the eve of an immensely greater expansion. The consequence for the future of Australia of this immense program of wartime industrial production is incalculable. If Australia escapes actual devastation in war, she will emerge from it one of the highly industrialized small powers of the world, far better able to defend herself than before.

War expenditure for 1941 to 1942 was over £A300,000,000, more than

---

[22] See Chapter XI, p. 467; also Chapter II, p. 72.

Australia's total war expenditure in the five financial years of the First World War, which amounted to £A270,059,000. The personnel of the Royal Australian Air Force, which included less than 500 pilots at the outbreak of the war, had reached 70,000 early in 1942. Air Force pilots and air crews were being turned out at the rate of more than 20,000 per year, being drawn as needed from the pool formed by the more than 200,000 who had applied for enlistment in the R.A.A.F. The total of the Australian armed forces overseas in the three services was put at from 170,000 to 250,000; the Royal Australian Navy, at well over 20,000. The militia and home garrisons totalled 200,000; the Home Guard (A.I.F. veterans), 50,000. The total Australian armed forces at home and abroad were about 450,000 in the fall of 1941.

With 450,000 in the armed forces and 210,000 directly or indirectly in arms and munitions production, even on the limited scale of a war largely confined to one hemisphere with Japan neutral, the problem of man power had become serious. The only important margin of expansion still left seemed to be the employment of women in industry, thus freeing men for new war industry. About 750,000 women were employed, and it was thought this figure might be expanded to an estimated total of 1,000,000 in two years' time. The drawing off into the armed forces and munitions of agricultural and other labor already threatened a decline of production. Group farming was the reply — the collective organization of men and machines to farm a whole district as a unit.[23]

An agreement between Great Britain and Australia regarding the general principles of policy to be pursued in respect of the surplus stocks of Australian produce during and immediately after the war was published in June 1941.[24] In principle, Great Britain agreed to purchase the Australian produce that could be shipped. Reserve stocks of storable foodstuffs were to be created up to a certain quantity to meet probable demand during and after the war; and the cost of acquiring and holding these stocks was to be shared equally between the two governments. This agreement (and the identical agreement between Britain and New Zealand) has an important bearing on postwar world reconstruction on the economic side.

In anticipation of a Japanese drive south, there was intense activity in the fields of defense and diplomacy at Singapore and in London,

[23] Certain classes of agricultural work were made reserved occupations.
[24] Appendix V.

Washington, Manila, and Canberra. The Australian Prime Minister and general staff officers visited London early in the year, attending meetings of the British War Cabinet and its Defense Committee. Important diplomatic discussions between the Australian Minister to the United States, the British Ambassador, and the American Secretary of State took place during the year in Washington, and staff conferences and consultations in Manila. In Singapore and Canberra there were important regional defense conferences in which the British Commander-in-Chief in the Far East conferred with Australian, New Zealand, and Dutch ministers and general staff officers.[25]

In April it was announced that Australia and New Zealand had decided to establish a Permanent Joint Committee, which appeared to resemble the Permanent Joint Canadian American Defense Committee; it was to consist of two ministers from each country, who were to discuss common defense and economic problems and coordinate the interests of the two countries in these fields.[26] In June the New Zealand Minister of National Services stated that Australia had promised to put New Zealand on the same basis for supplies as any Australian state.

Australia also played a leading part in the Eastern Group Conference at Delhi in November 1940 and in the permanent Eastern Group Supply Council and the permanent Central Provision Office, set up early in 1941.[27] Australia's role was to supply equipment and supplies (training planes, naval craft, armored vehicles, shells, small arms and ammunition, boots, woolens, canned meat, etc.) to India, Burma, Malaya, and the armed forces in the area served by the Council.

Australia's war situation from a strategic point of view was quite different from that of the other dominions. Like England, she saw the enemy poised and ready to strike near her frontiers.[28] She alone of the members of the British Commonwealth had her armed forces dispersed over five continents. She felt, thus, more acutely than the others the need of a unified strategy in the higher direction of the war, and

[25] On February 1, 1942, an exchange of ministers with the Netherlands was announced. The Australian High Commissioner in London was accredited to the Dutch Government in London and a consul-general appointed to Java. An exchange of ministers with the U.S.S.R. took place early in 1943.

[26] A joint Australian and New Zealand report on common strategy was made to London in February 1942.

[27] See Chapter XI, p. 467.

[28] On several occasions after the outbreak of war with Japan the Australian Prime Minister and Foreign Minister referred to the failure of two earlier attempts on their part to secure the negotiation between Britain and Russia of a mutual assistance pact whereby they would agree to make war in common against Japan if one of them were attacked by her.

the desirability of an Imperial War Cabinet on which she would be represented by her Prime Minister or his deputy or of an Imperial Conference.[29] That this wish was not realized in 1941 was due not so much to any real opposition in London, where the idea was welcomed, but to the fact that the Canadian Government did not support it.

Without any diminution of the Australian war effort in the matter of men and supplies, directed steadily through Suez, to Egypt, and the Near East, the attention of Australia was focused more and more during the year upon the region between Northern Australia and Singapore. An all-weather strategic highway across the central Australian desert to link the northern port of Darwin with the south and east of Australia was begun in October, 1940, a few days after Japan joined the Axis, and completed to Darwin early in 1941. Steps were taken to double the 2,000-mile telegraph line between Adelaide and Darwin to provide trunk telephone connection for the first time between Darwin and the rest of Australia. A powerful garrison was transported to Darwin, now the base from which Australian planes, munitions, and armies gathered in the more sheltered regions of the south and east of Australia could be launched against any force attacking from the north. Darwin had no docking facilities, but was an oil fueling depot and an air base. Late in January 1942 a second transcontinental roadway was completed to link Adelaide and Perth, thus strengthening the strategically weak "island" of Western Australia, one of the main keys to naval power in the Indian Ocean.

Though dependent for its ultimate safety on the British Navy and the security of Britain, Australia was fast becoming a powerful fortress in its own right. It was garrisoned by a trained army equipped by its own factories, and rapidly becoming mechanized. A ring of radio-location stations gradually being built round its shores began to give it eyes far out at sea to warn against surprise attack. But better than new mechanical inventions against such surprises was reputation. The legend spread throughout the entire world of the valor and fighting skill of the Anzacs, renewed in this generation by their sons in Greece and Crete, in Libya and at Tobruk, warned would-be enemies to think twice before committing themselves to the conquest of the thinly populated island continent. But the country had been stripped of equipment to make good the heavy losses of the A.E.F. in these campaigns and faced Japan without military planes — either fighters or bombers.

[29] See Chapter II, p. 35.

2. *Australia as United Nations Base*

The first four months of Australia's war with Japan were the most critical in her history. The sea-walls had cracked. In four months of war, Japan took Singapore and Java, crashed through the barrier of the Netherlands Indies into the Indian Ocean, the Timor Sea, and the Coral Sea.[30] Australia's outer ramparts were invaded on January 23, 1942, with the occupation of Rabaul and attacks on New Guinea. The bombing of Darwin on February 19 brought war at last to the only continent that had never known it.

But, as the Japanese struck at the North, with repeated bombings of Port Moresby, Thursday Island, Darwin, and other points along the northern coast of Australia, the vanguard of an American army arrived in the South. An American General, who had already become a world figure, arrived dramatically in Australia to take over command, at the request of the Australian Government, of the United Nations forces in the Southwest Pacific, including Australia but not New Zealand. Time alone will show the full significance of these events. They are incidents in the general strategy of an indivisible war extending to all continents.

The fact that an American and not a British army went to Australia was not due to any greater will on America's part to come to the aid of Australia. Britain's contribution to the defense of Australia in the period before December 7, and even more before June 22, 1941, when she faced the Axis alone, had been immense. The defense of Malaya was the defense of Australia. Britain had in, Malaya an army several times greater than the Australian forces. Before America's entry into the war, Britain dispatched to Singapore several of the most powerful units of the British Navy. The defense of Suez and the Near East was part of the defense of Australia. The main body of the Australian Imperial Force stationed in Syria, alongside a British and Indian army, was playing almost as vital a part in the defense of Australia as the Australian and American troops were later to play on the beaches of Northern Australia. The entry of the United States made possible a sharing of this great burden.

The arrangement whereby an American army went to Australia resulted from the decisions on the grand strategy of the war taken by

---

[30] The Australian casualties in the Malayan campaign were announced on March 13, 1942, as 17,301, the great majority taken prisoners at the fall of Singapore.

Mr. Churchill and President Roosevelt, in consultation with the dominions, in December 1941 and early January 1942. Then it was agreed to put aside political considerations, and to distribute forces in the common war in such a way as to secure the maximum result in the shortest time. Britain was to concentrate on the defense of the northwestern, and the United States, of the southern end of the common battle line. This decision was dictated primarily by two facts. The first was that Britain was already heavily engaged in the northern areas and could not divert forces from them without risking an Axis break-through. The withdrawal of the Australian garrison at Tobruk seriously delayed the British Libyan offensive and perhaps spoiled the chance of getting through to Tripoli before the Japanese struck at Pearl Harbor on December 7.[31] The second fact was that the distance of Britain from Australia is almost twice that of the United States of America; so that the transport of an American army involves only about half the amount of shipping. As it was the lack of ships that was most likely to lose the war for the United Nations, this factor was of capital importance.

A corresponding arrangement was made at the same time in the matter of the naval forces in the Southern Hemisphere. As Mr. Churchill stated on January 27, the British Navy was to be primarily responsible for the Indian Ocean, and therefore for the west coast of Australia, while " the eastward approaches to Australia and New Zealand have been called the Anzac area and are under United States command " and responsibility. New Caledonia, a vital strategic point midway between New Guinea and New Zealand, received an American garrison, and by the middle of March 1942 substantial American forces had arrived in Australia. By the end of April and in May the air reinforcements were sufficient to gain mastery of the air over New Guinea, and by midsummer the American Navy had fought the great battles of the Coral Sea, the Solomons, and Midway.

All this movement of forces to Australia and New Zealand was planned and supervised day by day by the Anglo-American Combined Chiefs of Staff Group in Washington, with the assistance of other joint Anglo-American boards, including the Munitions Assignments Board, the Combined Shipping Adjustment Board, and the Combined Raw Materials Board. The Australian Government was kept informed of

[31] Further withdrawal then became necessary to reinforce Singapore and Burma. Substantial forces were brought back from the Near East at the end of March 1942. The Ninth Division, which had formed the British spearhead at El Alamein, returned to Australia early in 1943 for action against Japan.

these developments through its service liaison officers and its Minister in Washington.

The Government left no stone unturned, as was its duty to its people, to make certain that Australia's need of aid was fully understood in London and Washington. The decision to allow the United States to give sole aid on land without even token British forces and planes was bad political psychology. "We are Britain's sons," Mr. Curtin said in a broadcast to America. British aid to her sons in the Near East, Singapore, India, and the Indian Ocean was immense, but invisible and unknown to the public; the eleven precious destroyers lent by the Royal Navy were unseen; so were the British Beaufighters in the skies over New Guinea and the British Spitfires over Darwin. There was no visible aid and comfort. And the absence of such aid from the Mother Country could not fail to create in many people an uneasy sense of being let down. The result was in some cases a deep psychological disturbance, out of all proportion to the real facts.

The second point on which the Australian Government concentrated was a demand, many times repeated, for full and equal participation of Australia in any councils in London, Washington, or Singapore which might be set up to decide the political and strategical war policy. The formation of the short-lived War Council under Mr. Duff Cooper at Singapore was proposed by the Australian Government. In January 1942 repeated requests were made to the British Government for full representation of Australia in an Imperial War Cabinet in London, for the setting up of an inter-allied Pacific War Council, and for full Australian participation in the Combined Chiefs of Staff Group in Washington dealing with the broad strategy of the Pacific war.

Divergence of views, and sharp discussion before agreement is reached, do not necessarily mean that a family is divided against itself. Such situations have been frequent in the family life of the British Commonwealth even in time of war. The personality of the leaders, above all the individual and characteristic reaction of each to the family relationship of the Empire, may play an important part in such a situation. The tendency on the part of some dominion statesmen to combine devotion to the Mother Country with opposition to the existing British Government is as old as British colonization.[32] Such ambivalence is all the more likely to flourish if there are no direct personal relationships. Unlike the Labor Cabinet in New Zealand, the Australian

---

[32] See Chapter II, p. 75.

Labor Cabinet, in power after long years in opposition, had no personal relations with the British Cabinet. This fact was in itself a sufficient justification for the request which Australia made for representation in an Imperial War Cabinet.[33]

In January 1942 Mr. Churchill announced the agreement between himself and President Roosevelt for the "setting up of a Pacific War Council in London on a ministerial plane comprising Great Britain, Australia, New Zealand, and the Dutch East Indies, assisted by the British Chiefs of Staff and the great staff organizations beneath them." "The united view of the British Commonwealth and the Dutch," he continued, "would be transmitted on the Chiefs of Staff level to the Combined Chiefs of Staff sitting in Washington." The first meeting of the Council, with Mr. Churchill as chairman, was attended by the Dutch Prime Minister, the Australian and New Zealand High Commissioners in London, the British Foreign Secretary, the Secretary of State for India, the British Deputy Prime Minister, and the three British Chiefs of Staff. China became a member of the Council shortly after. The function of the Council was formally that of advice rather than executive decision.

The arrangement whereby the Pacific War Council met in London without American representation, while the Combined Chiefs of Staff Group dealing with strategy met in Washington without direct dominion participation was open to criticism, and as a result of pressure from Australia and New Zealand the United States and British Governments agreed to the setting up of a Pacific War Council in Washington. It met on April 1, with President Roosevelt as chairman, and was attended by representatives of the United States, the United Kingdom, Canada, Australia, New Zealand, China, and the Netherlands Indies. The Council was to be parallel to the Pacific War Council in London, with provision for liaison between the two. But the latter had still no representative of the United States or Canada, while the Washington Council had no representative of India. It was described by President Roosevelt as a consultative body dealing with broad questions of policy and not with fighting strategy and the immediate allocation of supplies.

The Australian and New Zealand plea for direct representation on

---

[33] The misunderstandings that arose regarding the appointment on March 19, 1942 of Mr. R. G. Casey, the Australian Minister to Washington, as British Minister of State at Cairo to coordinate the British Commonwealth war effort in the Near and Middle East offer a clear illustration of the kind of difficulty which might easily have been avoided by the setting up of an Imperial War Cabinet.

the Combined Chiefs of Staff Group and its three subsidiary Anglo-American bodies dealing with munitions, shipping, and raw materials was thus rejected. But Australia and New Zealand (like Canada) sent joint staff missions, with officers from the three services, to act as liaison with the Chiefs of Staff Group and as advisers to their representatives on the Pacific War Council. What were to be the ultimate consequences for the British Empire of the defense of Australia by an American army could not be foreseen. But it was clear that this dramatic entry of America into Australia's history was the beginning of far closer bonds between Australia, New Zealand, and the United States of America. These two dominions seemed likely in future to serve, like Canada, as bonds of union between Britain and the United States. But Australia's ties with Britain show no signs of diminishing. As Mr. Menzies put it on February 7, 1942, " the overwhelming bulk of Australians are utterly and soundly British, and nothing is further from their thoughts than to appear to be reproaching Great Britain at this critical time."

On February 19, 1942, sweeping government regulations to regiment the man power and material resources of the country were issued. The sale or transfer of capital without government authorization, except for obvious war purposes, was prohibited. (Government bonds and notes were excepted.) Prices and wages were pegged at their existing levels, provision being made for the continuance of cost of living adjustments in wage rates at the discretion of the Commonwealth Court of Conciliation and Arbitration. All transfers of labor were placed directly under the Minister of Labor. Profits in all enterprises with capital above $5,000 were limited to 4 percent of capital employed,[34] though this limitation has subsequently been repealed as impossible of uniform application, and the direct control of individual costs has proved more effective. The Commonwealth Bank, subject to the Federal Treasurer, was to determine interest rates for different classes of investment in relation to the bond rate.

The Defense Coordination Minister could direct any person to perform any duty in relation to his trade, business, or profession deemed necessary. It became illegal for employers and employees to be absent from their work. This was equivalent to a prohibition of strikes and lockouts. Industrial tribunals were to continue to settle disputes and to deal with hours and conditions of labor. The system involved the compulsory registration of all persons. As a Government spokesman put

---

[34] As defined by the War-Time (Company) Tax Assessment Act.

it on February 18, " the government has now assumed supreme power over the private life and property of every individual Australian." It now possessed full power to close nonessential industries and to transfer labor to war industries. Total mobilization of man power for service in the army and industry, a *levée en masse,* has probably been carried as far in Australia as in any other belligerent country.

Several new pieces of machinery were added to the war organization. An Industrial Relations Council, presided over by an Arbitration Court Judge and comprising eight employer and eight labor members, was set up at the beginning of January to advise with a view to securing the maximum war production. An Allied Works Council with Mr. E. G. Theodore as Director General was set up to deal with defense works other than munitions production. The Director was armed with wide powers for the compulsory recruitment through the army of the man power needed to construct urgent defense works such as airdromes and strategic roads. Civilians up to the age of sixty could be called up for such work at award rates of pay. A mobile labor army of over 50,-000 constructed in a year 5,000 miles of strategic roads and hundreds of full-scale airdromes and flight strips. Production for civil needs was cut so ruthlessly that by August 1942 two-thirds (511,000 out of 705,000) of the factory workers were on government or private defense work. In addition there was the labor army mentioned above, and the fighting forces had been expanded to about 650,000. A United Nations Supply Council was also set up. Its function was to coordinate Australian supplies required by the United Nations (especially the United States). A large-scale supply agreement with the United States — involving a two-way Lend-Lease arrangement — was negotiated at meetings of the Council in the latter part of March 1942.

The constitutional relation of the Commonwealth Government and the state governments was vitally affected by the Commonwealth Government's assumption, in the summer of 1942, of the exclusive right to levy income tax for the period of the war. It was argued that as the burden of taxation increased it should be more equitably distributed than could be the case with varying state rates of taxation. The state governments are reimbursed from the proceeds of the uniform tax amounts equal to the average of their income tax receipts for the two years before.

Meanwhile the Opposition had become more and more closely associated with the conduct of the war through the increased importance of the Advisory War Council of five Labor leaders and five Opposition party leaders. The Council met frequently, and dealt with important issues of policy. The Government adopted the policy of implementing all unanimous decisions of the Council. Out of this there may be developing a new mechanism for maintaining continuity of foreign policy despite changes of Government.

The invasion of Australia involved for Japan a greater and more risky effort than any she had undertaken.[35] Australia's coastline of 12,000 miles was open at a thousand points to invasion; but if the enemy were to invade any part of the thousands of miles of virtually undefended coastline in the North and Northwest he would have against him the continental distances and appalling difficulties of communications through arid country under heavy attack by enemy bombers. The country accepted the threat of invasion without flinching and in a resolute and aggressive spirit. The early plan of falling back on a defense line north of Brisbane, emptying the North of food for any Japanese invading army by vast cattle drives southwards, was soon abandoned. By March 1943 an offensive movement had carried the United Nations armies, with Australians making up 80 percent of the ground troops, a thousand miles forward, across the Owen Stanley Range, to the northern coasts of New Guinea. The insular stronghold of democracy had been held. Protected on the left flank by the armed force of Britain and on the right by the United States, it was being organized by the United Nations as the southern anchor of their power, the base from which the task of pushing the enemy back out of his island conquests could later be undertaken.

---

[35] For a study of this problem see H. Duncan Hall, "The Invasion of Australia," *Atlantic Monthly*, April 1942 and *New York Times*, January 11 and May 3rd.

CHAPTER IX

The Dominion of New Zealand at War*

by F. L. W. Wood

1. Domestic Politics and Relations with Britain

In 1939 as in 1914 New Zealand proudly claimed to have been the first dominion to declare itself at war by Britain's side; and this alacrity fitly epitomized her century of political and economic evolution. She has always lacked some of the most potent of those factors which helped to foster nationalism in her fellow dominions by giving a sense of difference from England. Unlike Canada and South Africa, she has a population which is homogeneous. Her Maori race — now some 90,000 — has never lacked grievances, but it has long exercised equality of citizenship, and European immigrants rapidly became assimilated to a self-consciously British stock. Nor did New Zealand's early colonists include any coherent group which brought to the new world a traditional sense of grievance. Their memories were not of Irish distresses and evicted crofters but of a solid and potentially pleasant life which could be recreated, free from old-world stresses, amid colonial abundance. New Zealand's climate, soil and scenery were ideal for those determined to live like Englishmen. Games, books, educational methods and social traditions all came straight from Home, and so did the voluminous news printed by numerous journals modeled on the format of the *Times.* A steady

* Events from January 1941 to early 1943 have been dealt with by the editor, H. D. H.

stream of immigrants kept personal bonds numerous and strong, while in later years habits of travel refreshed the affection of the well-to-do for a Mother Country whom they had learnt to regard with sentimental optimism as the source of all good things, whether cultural or material.

During the past seventy years, indeed, and particularly since the development of refrigeration in the 1880's, economic self-interest powerfully reinforced sentiment. New Zealand became one of the great exporting countries of the world: lately she has exported goods worth £70,000,000 per year (about £40 per head of the population), or not far short of half her total production. Four-fifths of these exports went to England, and most of them had no alternative market. New Zealand had in fact organized herself to produce butter, cheese, wool, and meat on the assumption that Britain's appetite for these things was insatiable. Organization to meet this visionary demand depended not only on technical efficiency in farming, but on capital; and capital was provided without stint or forethought by a London market eager for investments. To this day, therefore, New Zealand's production, commerce, shipping, and insurance are very largely financed, but not controlled, by British capital. Large-scale "borrowing for development" by the state began seventy years ago. Since then it has been carried on with enthusiasm by Governments of all political complexions, so that by 1932 New Zealand had, with London's benevolent approval, accumulated a public debt in England of nearly £160,000,000 — more than £100 per head of the population.

Commercial and financial dependence on a kindly Mother Country was not, on nineteenth and early twentieth century assumptions, undesirable; for with dependence went security. Between 1919 and 1939, however, it became evident to experts if not to public opinion that the rigidity of the economic bond with Britain had disadvantages. For example, it was seen to transmit depressions to New Zealand with exaggerated effect; hence some experiments in price control to give her some protection from fluctuations on the English market, leading to Labor's scheme of guaranteed prices for dairy products, and its ambition to "insulate" the country, as far as possible, from overseas depressions. Again, it became clear that British demand for New Zealand's exports would not be unlimited after all. The falling birth rate and attempts to revive British agriculture gave plain warning, and, even after the depression, New Zealand faced the possibility of quotas and falling prices. Consequently there was talk (so far fruitless) of exploring new markets, and of developing local industries to give New Zealand's economy a better balance. Here again, though the ground was prepared by the collection of information, not much had been achieved by 1939 save a certain expansion due to local prosperity. Finally, in 1938–39 New Zealand was read a sharp lesson in the disadvantages of being a large-scale debtor who is unwilling or unable to repudiate.

During the Labor Government's first term, suspicion of its domestic policy felt (rightly or wrongly) by British and New Zealand investors led to a big withdrawal of capital, which some estimates put at over £20,000,000 during four or five years. In 1938 withdrawal became a flight of capital, ten to fifteen million pounds being sent out of the country in the second half of the year. This made necessary exchange control and drastic restriction of imports. Next year the moral was· pressed home, for a large loan had to be converted in London. Times were in any case bad for such operations, but London's particular suspicions of New Zealand led to the demand that £17,000,000 of capital should be repaid in five years. Repayment at this rate involved further drastic cuts in New Zealand's imports (which are also British exports) and so reacted on her domestic situation. It can be argued that the crisis would have been avoided if the Government had realized the inevitable consequences of its financial policy and imposed exchange control in good time; and it is easy enough to understand the grounds for London's action. All the same, it was plain to those interested that New Zealand's indebtedness made the reactions of British investors, who presumably knew little about New Zealand issues, vitally important for her domestic policy. Significantly enough, however, this aspect was not greatly stressed, for the two political parties agreed in blaming each other for what had happened. With time, however, this difficulty was overcome. Government control of imports was designed to cut down imports to absolutely essential requirements. During the war the restrictions have been extended to imports from all parts of the British Commonwealth, not merely to conserve New Zealand's sterling funds but also to lessen the demands made upon the productive capacity of Great Britain.

In short, the checkered economic history of the years 1919–39 did nothing to weaken New Zealand's sentimental and economic link with Britain. Commercial agreements were negotiated directly with some foreign countries, beginning with Japan in 1928, but did not lessen her fundamental dependence on the British market. Again, the Government acquired great power over overseas trade and the financial system through the guaranteed prices scheme, the establishment of the Reserve Bank (1934), and the enforcement of exchange-control; but these powers were deliberately used to buttress existing trade with Britain rather than to pursue business in new and unlikely places. In this the Government undoubtedly reflected the country's instinct, and showed that, right up to the present time, the forces of sentiment and economic interest have acted in harmony to bind New Zealand closely to the British system.

It is notable, however, that these forces operated slowly, if surely, and did not produce their consummation till the sense of dangerous isolation became their ally in the twentieth century. In the early days of colonization New Zealand had her own views on Imperial and foreign affairs, and was not notable for loyalty to British leadership. On the contrary, instinctive belief in the permanence of *pax Britannica* permitted a turbulent independence of spirit which could frankly contemplate separation from an ungrateful motherland, and even, in hostility to Britain, junction with the United States. However, confidence was shaken by the Russian scares of the 1880's, and it died away in the tension that preceded the First World War. Nor was there any powerful neighbor on whom an isolated dominion could rely. She had lost touch with the United States, and cooperation with Australia became less and less attractive. The Australian colonies, with whom New Zealand had once ranked as equal, combined in 1900 to form a federal commonwealth. To suspicious eyes this looked big and close enough to crush New Zealand's individuality if she should be foolish enough to enter into too close an association. Australia was, moreover, a trade competitor, and after all lacked the power to guarantee security in the Pacific. Therefore, reacting against Australian nationalism, New Zealand clung all the more earnestly to the Mother Country, whose navy gave security, and whose cultural and political attraction was exercised across 12,000 miles of friendly ocean. Thus was the way prepared for enthusiastic participation in the First World War, and for that following period when New Zealand's sense of her own insignificance and of the wisdom and goodness of Britain reached a climax. This was the period of so-called "Mother-complex." While Canada, South Africa, and Ireland fought successfully for dominion status, and the right to independence in foreign affairs, New Zealand strove passionately to preserve the Imperial connection as an organic reality.

The appearance of exaggerated subservience to British leadership in foreign affairs provoked reaction, and the Labor Party became spokesman of that minority which urged New Zealand to form views in such matters, and which championed the cause of collective security. Taking power at last at the end of 1935, the Party proceeded, in foreign as in domestic affairs, to carry out a policy based on conditions during its previous long years of opposition. For the first time New Zealand formed vigorously expressed views on foreign policy which were out of harmony with those of the British Government, and, until checked by the chilly atmosphere of crisis in 1938, she was an acknowledged crusader for collective security and other unpopular policies.[1] In 1938, however, it became clear that war and peace hung in the balance, and that in the first instance at least war would be waged in Europe. Facing this fact, the New Zealand ·Government apparently concluded that it would be unfair to clamor for a policy the drawbacks of which would be borne by others. Thus, though there is no reason to think that New Zealand changed her mind on collective security, or ceased to advocate it in Imperial discussions, she no longer crusaded in public. Nor was this evolution rejected by public opinion. In September 1938, for example, New Zealand was in the middle of a general-election campaign. Though the Czech crisis raised in an acute form the whole question of collective security, the Government gave no lead to public opinion beyond making it clear that New Zealand would in any event stand by Britain. And the public was content. The issues were not discussed in the press or on the platform, and election propaganda went on undisturbed. New Zealand seemed to have returned to her traditional attitude towards foreign affairs: frank loyalty to British leadership, tempered by confidential comment. In the following year no one asked whether the guarantee to Poland had been given with dominion approval, and though it was noted with uneasiness that the " Tokyo Agreement " of July 1939 had apparently been concluded without full consultation with all the Pacific dominions, no public protest was made.

Thus by 1939 the cycle in New Zealand's foreign policy was complete, and with the outbreak of war she associated herself with Britain instantly and without question. The Prime Minister's words, " Where Britain goes we go. Where she stands we stand," summed up the feeling

---

[1] See for example the remarkable memorandum forwarded to the League of Nations in 1937 by the New Zealand Government containing observations on the amendment of the Covenant. New Zealand also refused to fall into line with the rest of the Empire in recognizing the Italian conquest of Ethiopia. (Ed.)

of the country. The decision was made by her own Cabinet, for the British declaration of war was apparently not held to involve New Zealand automatically.[2] Some argued that the responsibility should have been thrown on Parliament, which in fact unanimously endorsed Cabinet's action; but prompt and wholehearted support of Britain was clearly in accord with the wish of the great majority of citizens and with recent pronouncements by Government spokesmen. Even those ministers who had opposed the " Imperialist " war of 1914 showed no hesitation. In 1938 and 1939 they had gone very close to saying that Britain's wars were of necessity New Zealand's, and with the declaration of war they threw themselves into the work of war organization. In particular, they vigorously denounced those small elements in the population which questioned the majority view that New Zealand's fate was inextricably bound up with that of Britain. The Communist paper was suppressed, pacifist speakers were disciplined through the courts, and there was something like a purge in the civil service, all on the ground that, since New Zealand was at war, she must prevent any action which would weaken her military efficiency.

In supporting Britain to the limit the Government undoubtedly commanded the widest support not only from the conservative Opposition, but from the great majority of the Labor Party, which is traditionally anti-Imperialist, and which remembers bitterly the appeasement phase of British policy. At Easter 1940, for example, the annual conferences of the Federation of Labor and of the Labor Party adopted an interesting statement on the war position. According to this statement, the British Government had at length adopted the policy urged for years by the Labor movements throughout the British Commonwealth, so that to support even Mr. Chamberlain in his belated resistance to Hitlerism was an elementary act of good faith — and of self-preservation.

General agreement on the basic war issue, however, did not clarify the obscurity of domestic politics, which arose primarily from a struggle for power within the Government party. Labor won a sweeping victory in the election of 1938, partly because of the unique command over public opinion of its leader, Mr. Savage. He stood for a humanitarian and undoctrinaire socialism which was strictly in line with New Zealand tradition, and which his confident and kindly personality was ideally fitted to present from the platform and over the radio. However, the very size of Labor's majority made possible some vocal criticism against

[2] See Chapter II, p. 21.

his leadership. His Cabinet, virtually unchanged since Labor took office in 1935, was composed of the Party's elderly stalwarts, and no steps had been taken to introduce younger blood into high places. Thus there was persistent criticism in Labor's ranks. This was partly personal, claiming changes in the Cabinet and greater control over the Cabinet by caucus (the Parliamentary Party as a whole).

This conflict arose before the war and was undisturbed by it, for there was no disagreement on the need to resist Hitlerism; but it was greatly confused by the illness of Mr. Savage. He underwent a serious operation just before the war and died at Easter 1940. During the intervening months passions rose, and for a time it seemed that the Party might split asunder in personal wrangles. In the end Mr. Fraser, Mr. Savage's able and moderate Deputy, became Prime Minister, and the older group remained in charge.

Even so, clear political stability was not reached. On the one hand, the new Prime Minister had not yet found that ready access to public confidence that would make him an obvious wartime leader. On the other hand, some of the criticisms brought against his predecessor, which were backed by a strong and active minority, had not yet been met. For example, many who agreed that Hitlerism must be fought complained that in their eagerness to support Britain the Government had not sufficiently safeguarded the dominion's independence of judgment in matters of high policy, and that they were too sensitive to local criticisms of their war effort. The demand was accordingly made for more democratic frankness both as between members of the Commonwealth and on the home front: a demand in line with the Party's caucus's apparent intention to exercise a greater control over policy in general. In November Mr. Fraser was re-elected leader for three years. In December, as promised, the composition of the Cabinet was submitted to caucus and some changes made in its membership.

The war, in its earlier stages, did not solve the problem of leadership in the Labor Party; nor did it lead to suspension of party politics. The opposition, while eager to fight Hitler or any other enemy of Britain, complained that Labor was pushing its private policy of socialism under the thin disguise of war-emergency measures, and it demanded things which the Government was pledged to refuse: notably conscription of man power and a coalition national government. Parliament had been prorogued since the early days of the war but with the German breakthrough in the West it was called together again, and in June passed what was popularly known as the " all-in " legislation. This followed Mr. Churchill's similar Act in Britain and gave the Government potentially absolute control over men, money, and industry.

Finally, in July, a curious compromise War Cabinet was set up. The existing Cabinet continued intact for the ordinary functions of government, but there was superimposed upon it a War Cabinet of five: three key ministers — Messrs. Fraser (Prime Minister), Nash (Deputy Prime Minister and Minister of Finance), and Jones (Minister of Defense), and two leaders of the Opposition, Messrs. Hamilton and Coates. The War Cabinet was given full charge of the war effort.[3] While it apparently worked smoothly and usefully, on the political side it gave an additional weapon to those leftists who accused the Labor Government of undue truckling to conservatism. It was assisted by an advisory war council made up of representatives of political, commercial, and workers' organizations.

In November 1940 the Opposition changed its leadership, and it has been suggested that one object was to regain some of the freedom of opposition criticism which was lost when the former leader of the Opposition joined the War Cabinet; the Prime Minister said that in his view the leader of the Opposition must be a member of the War Cabinet, if it was to have a national character.[4]

2. The War Organization and the War Effort

The war effort thus elaborately supervised was in part military and in part economic. On the military side, the understanding before the outbreak of the war was that the primary duty of the Pacific dominions would be to protect themselves, and presumably detailed plans were discussed at the Pacific Defense Conference between the representatives of Britain, Australia, and New Zealand who met in Wellington on New Zealand's initiative in April 1939. But in the upshot the whole war situation was altered for a time by the abstention of Japan and Italy, and popular sentiment, governed by memories of the First

---

[3] Though it contains leading members of the opposition the War Cabinet has full executive authority in all war matters. It is not an advisory body like the Australian Defense Council. Although policy is left to the War Cabinet, administration remains in the hands of the Labor ministers. An attempt to expand the War Cabinet into a war administration with seven Labor and six National Party members failed in October 1942.

[4] On October 15, 1941, the Prime Minister announced the postponement for a year of the General Election which was due in the normal course in 1941. In October 1942 the Government decided to hold an election twelve months later. (Ed.)

World War, thought of war efforts in terms of trained man power sent overseas. The natural result was that an expeditionary force was rapidly organized, and New Zealand undertook to maintain a division abroad, which has for long been stationed in the Middle East. Any damage to Territorial organization resulting from the drawing off of this expeditionary force was energetically repaired in 1940, when, following the military disasters in France, the whole Territorial Force was called up for intensive training. From July 1940 onwards the men needed for home or overseas service were found by ballot under the conscription law. Service in the Home Guard is compulsory. It provides static defense in home districts, the members giving army service on a shift basis which does not interfere with their civil occupations.

By the first half of 1942 New Zealand had become an armed camp. Her total man power and woman power was organized in the armed forces, in the civil defense organizations and the emergency services. She had some 60,000 men abroad in the three services — army, navy, and air force.[5] Over 5,000 of her airmen were serving abroad in separate New Zealand fighter, bomber, or torpedo-bomber squadrons, or with the R.A.F. in the various combat zones. R.N.Z.A.F. patrols kept watch over the Pacific islands, five widely scattered groups of which (including Fiji and Samoa) were garrisoned by New Zealand forces. Her air force at home was over 12,000 airmen. It was based on over 200 airdromes, most of them constructed since 1936. Her annual air quota to the British Commonwealth Air Training Plan was 5,000 airmen. Her naval personnel was over 4,500 men. Units of her small navy (containing two cruisers, the *Achilles* and the *Leander,* and a number of auxiliary vessels) distinguished themselves in the battle of the River Plate with the *Admiral Graf Spee,* and in the Mediterranean and the Indian Ocean; and throughout the war they did silent service in convoy work and minesweeping.

Her armed forces in New Zealand were well over 150,000 men. These included over 50,000 men in the Home Guard. How far total mobilization had gone is shown by the fact that in June 1942 one out of every six males of military age was in the actual battle line; that nearly one in three of the total male population of New Zealand was trained and equipped for combat duties or was being trained; that over half of the

---

[5] New Zealand casualties in the Eastern Mediterranean area were given in May 1942 as 13,000. Only a limited number of officers were brought back to New Zealand for training purposes after the outbreak of war with Japan.

total males aged 20 to 60 years were mobilized in the armed forces. Those that were not in the armed forces were in the Civilian Defense Organization or organized in the Emergency Services. There were 60,000 in the Women's War Service Auxiliary.

In the matter of munitions and war supplies New Zealand's contribution was necessarily small. She was mainly a primary producing country without an iron and steel industry. In the early months of the war she continued to look to Britain for military supplies.[6] But when France collapsed, and Britain, besieged, was in desperate need of supplies to replace the losses at Dunkirk, New Zealand's light engineering industry was swiftly and successfully geared to war production. With the railway workshops as a basis nearly sixty firms were turned over to the manufacture of some seventy different types of munitions. These included trench mortars and mortar bombs, high explosive bombs, Bren-gun carriers, light-armored cars, hand grenades, small arms ammunition, steel helmets. Minesweepers and parts of training aircraft were also built. For some supplies, particularly steel, New Zealand was able to turn to Australia, but even in 1942 the main source of supplies for her essential requirements in steel and armaments was still Great Britain and the United States.

A small country, which even before the war had a more centralized form of government than the other dominions, New Zealand gave far-reaching powers to its Government for the conduct of the war without hesitation. At the outbreak of war a number of domestic economic controls were set up along lines previously planned. Each important branch of supply and production was placed under the supervision of a Controller with wide powers. There were also set up two advisory councils, with ministerial chairmen, to provide an effective link between the Government and those actually operating industry. The National Council of Primary Production represented farming interests and workers and had numerous local branches to keep in touch with farming problems and farmers' grievances. The Industrial Emergency Council was nominated equally by the Employers' Federation and the Federation of Labor, and considered all cases where modification of labor conditions, such as the extension of hours of work, seemed necessary in the public interest. Parallel with these economic controls, the state took wide cen-

---

[6] But as a result of the early wartime expansion of exports to Great Britain, New Zealand's favorable annual balance of trade was £24.7 in June 1940, an improvement of £16 over the position a year before.

sorship powers, together with the right virtually to govern by regulation; and these wide powers were made wider still during 1940.

On the whole the Government made sparing use of its potential dictatorship. It had already a firm grip on the country's economy before the war, so in most cases the new powers were not needed; moreover, its deliberate wartime policy was to cooperate with industry rather than bludgeon it. Consequently the new controls were little before the public eye, except where inescapable circumstances forced the Government into action. For example, shortage of non-sterling exchange led to severe gasoline rationing, at Britain's urgent request, while lack of structural steel threw power into the hands of the Building Controller. For similar reasons the importance of the Factory Controller proved to be considerable. His main function was at first to apportion government contracts among private firms. But the importance of government orders in some trades became very great. Moreover, it was natural for those officials controlling the importation and rationing of industrial raw materials to act to some extent in consultation with the Factory Controller. Thus quietly, and without apparent friction, steadily increasing influence fell to the Controller and to those officials with whom he was in constant if sometimes informal contact. Even this modest development took place in the second year of war rather than in the first, and for the most part life proceeded much as usual. A considerable change-over from butter to cheese production, following a request from Britain, was organized almost entirely by persuasion and provision of the necessary financial assistance.

As the armaments manufacture of Britain and the United States increased and the strain on overseas shipping became greater, the problem of supply grew more and more serious. To insure continuity of production, arrangements were made by the Government for the accumulation by manufacturers of stocks of some of the basic materials. In some cases the Government made bulk purchases to put in stock. The practice of issuing certificates of essentiality was begun for some commodities; import licenses covering as much as a year were issued. A Supply Council was set up in 1941 with powers to operate under the general control of the War Cabinet and the Minister of Supply, mainly with the object of planning production on a long-term basis and obtaining supplies for the armed forces. By this means manufacturers could be given longer-term contracts, and could be assured of the necessary materials for carrying them out. These arrangements were of special importance to a country with so few of the raw materials required by defense industry.

The emergency powers of the Government were not fully used until the entry of Japan brought war close to the shores of New Zealand. The first of a number of farreaching orders issued then declared certain industries essential to the war effort, placing on all employers and employees an obligation to maintain production. No employee in such industries could terminate his engagement or transfer to another employment. Nor could he be discharged without the consent of the Government working through its man power officials. The obligation to serve in the armed forces if called of course remains. A further order restricts the flow of workers into nonessential industries. Retail shops, other than those engaged in the distribution of food, drugs, and fuel, fall into this category. By this and other measures (enrollment in the Emergency Corps, registration of all those with engineering experience, etc.), the whole of the male population was brought within the scope of the National Service Department. In marshaling the man power and woman power of the dominion the Government acted on the principle of " a post for everyone and everyone trained for his post."

Over 160,000 men were drawn off from production into the armed forces. This was more than one-third of the total number of males gainfully employed in normal times. Despite this decrease in the labor force, harder work, longer hours, and the employment of women in industry pushed up production in farm and factory continuously to points never before attained in the history of the country. A further step was the appointment of a Director of Production. He was given wide powers to insure the most effective use of material and machines for the production of munitions and war supplies. He himself was an executive officer of the Supply Council, and one of his principal tasks was the coordination of the work of the eleven controllers attached to the Ministry of Supply.

The Japanese threat to the shores of New Zealand greatly increased the importance of local defense works. A Commissioner of Defense Construction was appointed with the role of commander-in-chief of the building and construction trade. He was empowered to move workers from any part of the country to particular jobs; to take over material and equipment for urgent defense works; to take over the management of concerns; to set the price at which contract work was to be done.

To facilitate the working of this plan labor awards were set aside. A flat rate of £5/5s. a week was guaranteed with allowances for traveling and board. Hours of work were extended from forty to fifty-four per week. Similar extensions took place in all war industries. Award conditions were varied, statutory holidays suspended. With a non-party national War Cabinet pledged to the principle of equality of sacrifice and service, and with employers and employees fully represented in war advisory councils, it was possible to carry through these changes in the social structure without friction.

Though her military contribution has been considerable for a small country, it was generally agreed in the earlier stages of the war that New Zealand could best help the British Commonwealth through her characteristic exports of wool and food. In September 1939 she offered to Britain her whole surplus of these goods, and after lengthy negotiations agreements were concluded in which a fine balance between good business and Imperial sentiment concealed from the public eye a real threat to the dominion's economy. The British Government promised to buy all surplus wool for the duration of the war and one year after, together with fixed quantities of butter, cheese, and meat: quantities which were subject to revision from year to year. The details were fair enough in the first instance. The quantities fixed practically covered the season's surplus, and the prices were above the figures for 1939. However, no satisfactory arrangements were made for revision. New Zealand suggested that if the price-level of Britain's exports to New Zealand rose by 10 percent, then the prices paid for New Zealand's exports should be correspondingly revised; but nothing was promised. Other dangers for New Zealand lurked in the background. It was possible that war conditions might do much to persuade overseas manufacturers that staple fiber was just as good as wool, and housewives that vitaminized margarine at 8d. per lb. was better than butter at 1s. 7d. If these things should happen, the prewar nightmare of falling markets might become real with sudden and devastating effect. Indeed, the only one of New Zealand's normal exports for which the demand seemed likely to increase was cheese, which offers cheap and concentrated nourishment for low-paid workers. The catastrophe of Denmark and Holland did indeed postpone the economic threat to New Zealand. For the year ending September 1941 the British Government agreed " to purchase, shipped or unshipped, 248,000 tons of meat, 120,000 tons of butter, and all the cheese available." The meat contract for the first year of the war was 300,000 tons. For the first two full years of the war New Zealand shipped to the United Kingdom 254,000 tons of butter, 210,000 tons of cheese, 598,000 tons of meat and 1,600,000 bales of wool. On making this agreement the British Government promised that the general arrangement would be continued throughout the war, and that every effort would be made to provide ships: a vital point, since all British shipping was centrally controlled. However, in spite of this more generous treatment, it was clear that New Zealand's trading position in the long view was entirely dependent on the fortunes of the war. As witness the British Government's announcement in January 1941, that for the time being meat imports from the dominion must be cut down drastically, owing to shipping difficulties. The vastly increased cold-storage space, which was provided locally, could not be more than a temporary remedy for such a stoppage.

On June 27, 1941, the texts of identical agreements between the governments of the United Kingdom, and Australia and New Zealand, were issued in London.[7] The agreements set out the principles governing the cooperation between the governments in the matter of the surplus produce of Australia and New Zealand for the period of the war. The United Kingdom Government agrees to purchase produce of each country that can be shipped in any one season. Reserve stocks of storeable foodstuffs are to be created to meet demand during or after the war, the costs being shared equally between the governments.

As the Honorable Walter Nash, the Minister of Finance, explained to Parliament in his budget speech, this agreement " provides a definite basis on which the future financial obligations of our export trade with the United Kingdom will be determined. Secondly it creates a broad framework within which our future primary production must be organized and directed." Having promised to sell in bulk to Britain, the New Zealand government had to buy from its own producers. This meant applying to wool and meat a procedure roughly similar to that already evolved for butter and cheese, and virtually completed the government's control over the whole of the country's overseas trade. Dairy produce had for some years been bought by the Marketing Department at the point of shipment; the only change was that it was now resold to the British Government instead of to trading interests. Wool, previously sold at auction, was appraised under the wartime arrangement by the men formerly employed as wool buyers by private firms but now acting as government valuers. Meat was still handled by the normal agencies such as freezing works, which now acted for the government in buying from farmers and delivering·frozen meat ready for shipment. These arrangements worked extremely well, the main point of friction

---

[7] See Appendix V.

being the vociferous discontent of the dairy farmers' organizations in the earlier phase of the war with the prices for butter and cheese. As regards wool and meat the Marketing Department simply paid out on the basis of prices to be collected from Britain, but dairy farmers claimed that under the guaranteed price procedure they should be paid according to local costs irrespective of prices received.

Nevertheless in a world full of grim uncertainties the policy of the Government gave the dairy industry stability. As Mr. Nash pointed out, it protected the farmers against " the major risks " and gave them financial security to carry on their operations with confidence. A number of other steps announced by him in his budget speech were aimed at protecting the pastoral industries from " the major economic shocks arising from the war "; these included fertilizer subsidies and railway rebates. Owing to increasing shipping difficulties, especially in the third year of the war, the Government made arrangements to facilitate the change-over from butter to cheese. The goal set in 1942 was 153,000 tons — more than the total cheese imports of the United Kingdom in peace years. A special war costs allowance was also made to the dairy industry to compensate for increased manufacturing costs. This was to be accompanied by a corresponding increase in the wages of dairy farm workers.

New agreements with Great Britain made in accordance with the surpluses agreement of June 1941, in respect of meat, butter, and cheese, were announced in February 1942. The general effect of the agreements was to stabilize or reduce the quantities of meat and butter produced. To offset the need for less production of meat and butter the Minister of Marketing called for " a greater production of wheat, linen-flax, cheese and possibly other milk products such as whole milk powder."

If the Government's first principle was to help Britain to the limit, its second was to preserve New Zealand's social experiment with as little change as possible. This fact, together with the Government's view on war finance, was made clear in the Budget of June 1940. About £20,-000,000 was to be borrowed from the British Government for overseas war expenses in 1940–41, but for the rest, the war should be paid for out of revenue so as to avoid leaving a deadweight burden to posterity. The Government had previously turned its face against the suggestion that the war should be financed by cutting down ordinary expenditure. It was willing in principle to economize to the bone where this could be done without injury to the social structure, but it had already shown clearly that in practice it found the field for socially desirable economy narrow indeed. The result was that ordinary expenditure increased slightly to stand at £37,000,000. This, with total war expenditure of £37,500,000 and public works at £20,589,000, makes a total expenditure of nearly £100,000,000. To meet this large total, taxation rates were increased again on every section of the community, and it was estimated that special taxes would provide £14,120,000 towards war expenditure in New Zealand. The remainder would apparently be borrowed, together with about £15,000,000 for public works; this last being a reduction of about £4,000,000 on the amount borrowed for this purpose in 1939.

The Budget showed the gap separating the ideas of the Cabinet from those of the Opposition on the one hand and of its own leftist critics on the other. For the Opposition the basic principle of war finance should be economy in all other directions. Any other course, in its view, led to straight-out inflation, and it pointed to alarming danger signals in the size of the state's overdraft with the Reserve Bank and in the increasing note circulation. To the leftists, on the other hand, war taxation on lower incomes and borrowing were alike evil, for they both sacrificed the happiness of human beings to the shibboleths of discredited financial orthodoxy. Their solution was, therefore, " debt free money " to be issued by the Reserve Bank. Talk of inflation, said a spokesman of this group, was a capitalist dodge; it could not happen under a socialist government. And apart from such theorists a powerful trade union movement was unfailingly vocal in defense of working conditions and real wages.

Between such conflicting advice the Government steered the difficult course of moderation in a sea of trouble. On the one hand, they refused to cut social services. The 40-hour week remained intact, except where a few carefully safeguarded extensions for war purposes seemed unavoidable. Wage rates were maintained, and in August 1940 the Arbitration Court gave an all round 5 percent increase in award wages, based on increased cost of living since 1937. On the other hand, the possibility of inflation was for the Government no bogey to be exorcised by bland nonrecognition. Mr. Nash, Minister of Finance, had always argued that new bank credit is not inflationary when matched by increased consumer's goods on which credit could be spent. But in 1940, he argued, import restrictions and war stringencies were actually cutting down the goods available to the people at a time when heavy war spending must increase their purchasing power. Therefore, the duty of the wise administrator was plain. Secondary industry should be stimulated to supply as many as possible of the missing consumer-goods; and, indeed, in spite of the absorption of men into the Army, all important industries except motor assembly reported substantial increases in production in 1940. However, in the official view, there were technical limits to the pace of such expansion, while the supply of industrial equipment was limited by sterling funds, and in any case a considerable proportion of the increased production was absorbed by the Army. In these circumstances the Government's case was that bank credit should be used sparingly; and purchasing power must be cut down to safe levels by taxation and by loans, which might be made compulsory for the well-to-do, at nominal rates of interest. This must have been a distasteful policy to a Government elected to raise purchasing power; but wars produce odd necessities in dependent communities.

Eighteen months later, in June 1942, the full effects of the war had become more manifest. Mr. Nash, now New Zealand Minister in Washington, estimated the total war expenditure for the year at £NZ133,-000,000, three times the war expenditure in 1941. Of this sum £46,000,-000 was to be expended on war account overseas. Of the total war expenditure approximately £40,000,000 was expected to be obtained from revenue, £8,000,000 from national savings and departmental funds, and £28,000,000 by war loans. "The total national expenditure for this year under all headings," he said, "amounts to the enormous sum, for New Zealand, of £188,000,000, an amount in excess of New Zealand's total national income only a few years ago." Despite heavy taxation, war loans, and large contributions to patriotic funds, savings continued at a fair level. Net savings registered in bank deposits for the year ending in March 1942 were £32,000,000. While food supplies remained adequate, luxuries had almost disappeared; many goods formerly imported were no longer available or were severely rationed. As in Australia, only enough gasoline was allowed for 40 miles a month, just sufficient to keep cars in running order — as a strategic reserve. As a result of the decrease of imports and the heavy demands of the armed forces, the supply of goods available for civilian consumption in 1942 was estimated by Mr. Nash as 30 percent less than usual, while the spending power of the community was 10 percent higher. Taxation had reached a maximum rate of 90 cents in the dollar on incomes equivalent to $12,000. In accordance with the principle of "pay as you go" more than half of the war cost had been met up to that date out of revenue.

As a result of price control and other measures, retail price increases from September 1939 to June 1942 were kept down to an average of less than 10 percent above the prewar level — only about a third of the retail price increases in the United Kingdom. Rents as well as prices were rigidly controlled. Prices for a range of 38 items of food, clothing, footwear, light, and public utilities were stabilized. In order to keep prices at this level, subsidies were paid for bread, sugar, and coal, commodities for which New Zealand had been in part dependent on imports. To meet the rise in cost of living the 5 percent increase of wages in October 1940 was repeated in April 1942. On each occasion a cost of living bonus at a flat rate of £13 per year was granted to government employees on the low income levels.[8] Regulations issued on December 15, 1942, marked an important further step to secure stabilization. The freezing of rents was made complete; wages and all other forms of remuneration including salaries and fees were frozen at existing levels. A new quarterly cost-of-living index was set up. The Arbitration Court was empowered to adjust wages in the event of a rise or fall in the index beyond a fixed percentage. The list of stabilized prices was extended to cover 110 commodities which go into the average family budget. Prices of the major items entering into farm costs, such as power, transport, fertilizers, etc., were also fixed.

Even in the third year of the war, Mr. Nash claimed that " in spite of the heavy added burden of war expenditure there has been no wholesale retrenchment in the field of social services. . . . No general retreat . . . in fact some notable advances." These included the widening of the scope of family allowances to cover the first child instead of the third, and an increase of the allowance payable for each child from 4s. to 6s. per week; and the provision of free medical (general practitioner) and pharmaceutical benefits irrespective of income.[9]

The immediate effect of the war was, of course, to tighten considerably New Zealand's already intimate bonds with the Mother Country. On the economic side she embraced the inevitable with enthusiasm, and willingly gave her whole export trade into Britain's keeping. On the political side, again, it may be doubted whether the situation left New Zealand much freedom of choice. After all, Britain had taken up arms

---

[8] In judging the significance of figures given here (or in Chapter VIII), it should be remembered that, measured in terms of purchasing power, the New Zealand (or Australian) pound is worth two or three times its nominal fixed dollar exchange value. (H. D. H.)

[9] The shortage of doctors due to the war delayed the full application of this scheme.

in the name of principles unanimously approved by New Zealanders, however much some of them might question whether those principles had really guided British policy in the past, and anything like a desertion of Britain in these circumstances would have been a denial of all New Zealand's history.

This attitude was criticized by radicals, but the Cabinet may have preserved a greater degree of independence in judgment than appeared on the surface. If so, it probably represented "average opinion," in so far, that is, as a conflict of undigested individual wills may ever be represented. The "general will" has in fact matured somewhat during the last twenty-five years. It is still dominated by loyalty to the British connection, but alongside of that loyalty there has grown up an increasing appreciation of the facts of world politics. There was an increasing minority which realized, even before Japan's final plunge into the war, that New Zealand, though bound to Europe by trade and tradition, was a Pacific country; and that the Pacific was no more likely than Europe itself to keep forever its nineteenth century framework.[10]

---

[10] Japan's southward drive in the spring and summer of 1942 opened a new phase in the political and military history of New Zealand, linking her far more closely than ever before with the United States of America. Her old instinctive friendship for the United States had become more conscious as the war developed. The first diplomatic appointment in New Zealand's history was the naming of a minister to Washington early in 1942 in the person of Mr. Walter Nash. As a result of the Roosevelt-Churchill decisions of January 1942, New Zealand was placed in the American operational sphere. American armed forces were stationed in the country and an American naval force under Vice-Admiral Ghormley was based on Auckland. The aid of the United States was enthusiastically welcomed by New Zealanders, but without any feeling that Britain had "let them down." Already in May 1942 British military equipment was reaching the country in unprecedented quantities. With the double aid of Great Britain and the United States New Zealand faced her future with confidence and resolution — with much of her armed power abroad, with her coasts blacked out, her beaches guarded, and trenches dug in her cities. (Ed.)

CHAPTER X

The Union of South Africa in the War

by Lucretia Ilsley

1. Party Politics, 1932–41

This chapter deals first with the background of the political crisis which was occasioned by South Africa's entry into the war, then with the crisis itself and the political realignments resulting from it. The Union's war effort is next considered from the military and economic viewpoints. At the beginning of the war the United Party Fusion, led by Prime Minister Hertzog and General Smuts, was shattered on the issue of neutrality. To appreciate the significance of the Fusion and its breakdown, it is essential to recall the struggle of 1932 over the abandonment of the gold standard, which led ultimately to the formation of the United Party.

From 1924 until February 1933, General Hertzog, head of the Afrikaans-speaking Nationalist Party, was Prime Minister of the Nationalist-Laborite Pact Government, while the South African Party, composed of both Afrikaans- and English-speaking elements under the leadership of General Smuts, formed the Opposition. As the effects of the depression became apparent in South Africa, the Pact Government was confronted with increasingly serious problems. Prices for diamonds, wool, and other agricultural products fell, and the hardships of the farmers were intensified by a severe drought. The gold industry, by contrast,

426

remained prosperous and contributed to the financial stability of the country.

In the fall of 1931 came the Central European banking crisis and the resulting departure of Great Britain from the gold standard, events which inevitably caused repercussions in South Africa. During the next fifteen months the question of whether South Africa should remain on gold became the outstanding political issue which was debated with increasing vehemence in Parliament and outside. The Hertzog Government stood firm for gold, while the South African Party, after some initial hesitancy, advocated action similar to that taken in Great Britain. Among the Government's supporters were Afrikaans-speaking farmers who, in spite of their economic plight, hesitated for political reasons to denounce the gold standard. At first the gold mining interests approved the Government's policy. Within a few months, however, leaders of this group reversed their position on the ground that abandonment of the gold standard would make it profitable to work low-grade ores and thus prolong the life of the mines by 50 percent. The Government's tenacity in clinging to gold in the face of growing opposition was probably motivated in considerable part by its Nationalist aspirations to demonstrate that South Africa was not merely an economic satellite of Great Britain. Speculation on probable devaluation caused a flight from the South African pound; but the Government, in the face of its outspoken commitments for gold, seemed unable to take decisive action to remedy the situation.

Finally, in December a *deus ex machina* appeared in the person of Tielman Roos, former Minister of Justice in the Pact Government. Roos suddenly announced his resignation from the Appellate Division of the Supreme Court, together with his intention of leading a movement for a national government on non-racial lines which would devalue the currency. This dramatic incident gave such impetus to the flight from the pound that between two and three million pounds of foreign exchange had to be supplied by the South African Reserve Bank within three days. In the face of this crisis the Government, on December 28, decided to go off gold.

Aside from bringing to a head the issue of the gold standard, the Roos movement had important political repercussions. While the Government was denouncing Roos for betrayal of the Nationalist cause, General Smuts was trying to effect a coalition between the Roosites and the South African Party, but negotiations broke down because Smuts could not accept Roos as Prime Minister. Smuts thereupon tried to render the Roos movement harmless by introducing in the House of Assembly a motion for the formation of a national government. The Prime Minister at first rejected the idea and with the support of the Roosites brought about the defeat of General Smuts's motion. Private negotiations between Hertzog and Smuts continued, however, and culminated in the announcement on February 28, 1933, of a Coalition between the Nationalist and South African Parties under the premiership of General Hertzog. The principles on which the Coalition was based included maintenance of the Union as a national unit on the basis of the sovereign independence guaranteeed by the Statute of Westminster and protection of the Union's capital assets.

At the general election on May 17, the Coalition won 138 out of 150 seats in the House, while the Roosites, who had made the Coalition possible, secured only 2. Thus the economic depression and the monetary problems arising from it had as a significant consequence the reconciliation of two political enemies of long standing and the inauguration of a period of greater cooperation between the two European races in South Africa.

As a step toward welding the Coalition into Fusion, the Government in 1934 found it expedient to appease Nationalist sentiment by the passage of legislation which defined more explicitly South Africa's status in the British Commonwealth. The Status of the Union Act declares that all sovereign legislative power for the Union is vested in the Union Parliament alone. It further states that all executive power over internal and external affairs is vested in the King, acting on the advice of his South African ministers, but administration of this power may be carried on either by the King or by the Governor-General, as his representative, upon the advice of Union ministers.[1]

During lengthy parliamentary debates the Government took the position that the Status Bill did not go beyond the constitutional resolutions of 1926–30 and the Statute of Westminster. There was, however, a divergence of opinion between Prime Minister Hertzog and his deputy, General Smuts, regarding interpretation of the aforesaid constitutional measures. Throughout the debates the Prime Minister remained silent, but shortly before the introduction of the Status Bill he had written to

---

[1] The Royal Executive Function and Seals Act, 1934, provides further that if the signature of the King to a measure cannot be obtained, the Governor-General may execute and sign on behalf of the King.

a leader of the Nationalist Party that since 1926 he had never doubted the reality for South Africa of sovereign independence, divisibility of the Crown, and the twin rights of neutrality and secession, although, he added, too close definition of these rights might be confusing. General Smuts asserted in the House that the pending legislation did not touch these contentious points, on which he held views less advanced than those of the Prime Minister, but merely affirmed the existing constitutional position. The group of extreme Nationalists led by Dr. D. F. Malan voted for the status legislation because they professed to see in it divisibility of the Crown and sovereign international status. A small faction of the South African Party with strong British sympathies, headed by Col. C. F. Stallard, unsuccessfully fought the bills as an attempt to impair the prerogative of the Crown.

In December 1934, a few months after the adoption of the Status and Seals Acts, the Coalition was transformed into Fusion by the formation, under the leadership of Prime Minister Hertzog and General Smuts, of the United South African National Party. Dr. Malan and his followers decided to reject the Fusion, and taking up the cause of Afrikanderism with the slogan, " A republic, not necessarily in our time," became the Nationalist Opposition. At the opposite pole, Col. Stallard organized as the Dominion Party that group which opposed the trend away from the Commonwealth which they saw in the adoption of the legislation on status. At the general election of May 1938, the Fusion Government appealed for a further mandate on the grounds of national unity, and its record of achievement as shown by general recovery and increasing revenue. Election results showed that the United Party was still in a strong position, as it won 111 out of 150 seats, losing only 6 seats to the two extreme groups.

Before the political crisis which immediately preceded South Africa's entry into hostilities with Germany is discussed, a brief survey of Union foreign policy in the latter part of the decade prior to the conflict may contribute to an understanding of the disintegration of the Fusion on the neutrality issue. After the collapse of the Disarmament Conference in 1934, the South African Government continued to uphold collective security despite Nationalist insistence on South Africa's right to neutrality. Italy's Ethiopian adventure aroused fears in South Africa that the attack on a native state might have unfavorable repercussions among Union natives and might encourage Germany to future action. The Government and a large section of public opinion gave strong support to League sanctions against Italy, although protests were heard from the Nationalist Opposition. It may be noted that the Italian shipping subsidy [2] remained in force despite the imposition of sanctions by the Union. When the League Assembly voted to recommend abandonment of sanctions, the South African delegate, Mr. ter Water, abstained from voting after an emphatic protest. General Hertzog officially upheld the League system to the extent that in April 1939 he opposed a Nationalist demand for South African withdrawal. In the fall of 1939 South Africa was elected to membership on the League Council.

When Germany's remilitarization of the Rhineland in 1936 demonstrated that collective security had failed to preserve the *status quo* of Versailles, public sentiment in the Union was divided with regard to German colonial claims. The Fusion Government's official position with regard to Southwest Africa, expressed in a communiqué of December 1936, was that transfer of the mandate to another power would not be considered. Notwithstanding this declaration, which enjoyed widespread support in United and Dominion Party circles, in March 1937, the Prime Minister asserted in Parliament that the psychological aspect of Germany's case should not be overlooked, and that while in favor of retaining Southwest Africa for the Union, he was prepared to take Germany's legal claim into account.

A tour of European capitals undertaken by the Minister of Defense, Mr. O. Pirow, during the post-Munich era, aroused suspicion that he was promoting a scheme for appeasing Germany with a colonial area in West Africa to be carved from the possessions of Great Britain, France, Belgium, and Portugal. Although disavowing that he had ever negotiated with any government or individual about such a transfer of territory, Mr. Pirow in June 1939 declared that the problem of compensating Germany must be faced. Dr. Malan announced in May 1939 that the Nationalist Party would resist any attempt to use the connection between the Union and the mandate as a pretext for dragging South Africa into war.

If there was divided opinion in South Africa over the question of German colonial demands, the issue of neutrality revealed a deeper cleavage, which antedated the Fusion. In organizing the Coalition of 1933, Prime Minister Hertzog and General Smuts had reached a compromise

---

[2] A subsidy of £150,000 per annum was granted to Italian shipping lines in 1934 for a five-year period. Since the grant failed to effect any marked expansion of Union trade in West Africa and the Mediterranean, it was not renewed upon its expiration in February 1939.

on this controversial point. It was then agreed that the Union was not automatically bound to enter into a war involving the Commonwealth, but would participate only if Parliament should so decide when the occasion arose. Since the South African Government, under the Smuts-Churchill Agreement of 1922, had assumed responsibility for the land defenses of the British naval base at Simonstown, there was a question as to the compatibility of the Coalition's attitude on neutrality with this Agreement. Asserting that Union neutrality was possible despite the Agreement, General Hertzog in 1935 compared Simonstown with Gibraltar. Later he took the rather questionable position that South African neutrality would not be contravened by granting military assistance to a belligerent in accord with a previous agreement.

As European political tension increased in the summer of 1938, the issue of neutrality came to the fore in South Africa. Prime Minister Hertzog steadfastly refused to make any public commitments regarding the Union's attitude in a hypothetical European struggle, but from subsequent disclosures by Generals Hertzog and Smuts, it now appears that the inner Cabinet favored neutrality during the Czech crisis which culminated in the Munich Agreement. European political developments after Munich failed to deflect Prime Minister Hertzog and several of his colleagues from their neutral policy. But with the Nazi attack on Poland a public decision could no longer be avoided.[3]

Prime Minister Hertzog announced his stand for neutrality at a Cabinet meeting called only on September 3, after Parliament had been summoned in special session. General Smuts and other Cabinet members who advocated Imperial cooperation tried vainly to persuade General Hertzog at least to bring the issue before the caucus of the United Party. On September 4 the Prime Minister introduced into the House of Assembly a motion favoring neutrality, without impairment of Union obligations resulting from the Simonstown Agreement, membership in the League of Nations, and free association in the British Commonwealth. At the close of the debate, in which the two leaders of the Cabinet eloquently set forth their conflicting views, General Smuts and his supporters brought about the defeat of the motion by a margin of 13 votes.[4] By the same majority, the House adopted the

---

[3] On August 25, 1938, General Smuts had stated in the House that if England were attacked, he could not imagine South Africa's withdrawal from the friendly bonds uniting the two countries, but that the Union Parliament would decide whether South Africa would go to war.

[4] It may be recalled that when on September 9, 1914, the Botha Government introduced into the House of Assembly an address assuring His Majesty of the Union's cooperation in maintain-

Smuts amendment, calling for the severance of relations with Germany and continued cooperation with the British Commonwealth.[5]

South Africa's subsequent entry into the war was achieved at the cost of a change of political leadership and a rupture of the United Party. General Hertzog, supported by Dr. Malan, leader of the Nationalist Opposition, recommended a dissolution of Parliament and upon the Governor-General's rejection of his advice resigned the premiership with an appeal to his followers to confine their activities within constitutional limits. The question of the constitutionality of Sir Patrick Duncan's action in refusing a dissolution to General Hertzog has become something of a political issue in South Africa. Although General Hertzog at first admitted that the Governor-General had acted constitutionally, several months later he joined with Dr. Malan in criticizing General Smuts for having accepted office without a mandate from the people. Constitutionality aside, it appears from the political viewpoint that dissolution would probably have increased factional bitterness and would have placed the Union in the uncertain position of remaining neutral during an election campaign in which the German Minister and his friends would undoubtedly have aided the Nationalist cause.

The new Government, formed by General Smuts on September 6, included both English and Afrikaans-speaking leaders of the United Party who were loyal to Smuts and also the heads of the Dominion and Labor Parties. Its first act was to advise the Governor-General to issue a proclamation of a state of war with Germany.[6]

In the months after the opening of the war, there occurred a disintegration of the United Party Fusion, which left General Smuts in control of the party machinery, and subsequently, a realignment of opposition groups. Protracted negotiations between the more extreme Nationalists under Dr. Malan and the Hertzogites finally culminated at the end of January 1940 in the formation of the Reunited Nationalist or People's Party (commonly known as the " or " Party), a title which reflected the unwillingness of the two factions to merge their identity.

---

ing the integrity of the Empire, General Hertzog, then leader of a Nationalist minority group, proposed an amendment to the effect that while the House favored measures to defend Union territory, " any act in the nature of an attack on German territory in South Africa would be in conflict with the interests of the Union and of the Empire." The House voted favorably upon the address, rejecting General Hertzog's amendment by a vote of 92 to 12. Hertzog accepted the position of the majority in that he refrained from supporting the subsequent Nationalist rebellion.

[5] See Chapter II, p. 25, notes 17 and 18.
[6] See Chapter II, p. 23.

One obstacle to agreement was the Malanite Nationalists' demand that republicanism be made a tenet of the new party, which while acceptable to some Hertzogites, including Mr. Pirow, aroused opposition from the moderates, among whom were General Hertzog himself and his chief deputy, Mr. Havenga. In taking the position that "a republican form of government separated from the British Crown is best suited to the traditions and aspirations of the South African people," the " or " Party apparently accepted the Nationalist view. As a sop to the moderates, it was conceded that a republic should be achieved not merely by a parliamentary majority, but by a special mandate from the voters.

This reluctant union proved to be short-lived. The issue of republicanism was brought into the open by Dr. N. J. van der Merwe who, shortly before his death in the summer of 1940, organized a mass meeting at Bloemfontein "to consider active constitutional steps to establish a republic." General Hertzog thereupon issued a statement in which he expressed the strongest possible disapproval of the meeting. The former Premier characterized the republican movement as extremely unwise under the existing circumstances and warned the public against irresponsibility. Internal discord within the Opposition was further intensified by the personal antagonism between General Hertzog and Mr. C. R. Swart, successor of Dr. van der Merwe as Nationalist leader in the Orange Free State, which had long been General Hertzog's political stronghold.

Rupture of the " or " Party occurred in November 1940, when the party congress of the Free State adopted principles which would give the English section only language and cultural rights in the future republic. This was interpreted by General Hertzog as a manifestation of lack of confidence in his leadership, and he thereupon resigned from the leadership of the party, subsequently advising his own supporters not to vote for Mr. Swart's candidacy in a forthcoming local election. These events were followed by the announcement in December that General Hertzog and Mr. Havenga, who had followed him out of the Reunited Nationalist Party, were resigning from Parliament with the intention of retiring to private life.[7] In January 1941, however, the Afrikaner Party came into existence with ten Hertzogite members of the House and four Senators as its nucleus. This organization subscribes

---

[7] Mr. Swart defeated his opponent of the United Party in the Winberg by-election in January 1941. Nationalist candidates were elected over opponents of the Afrikaner Party to the seats vacated by General Hertzog and Mr. Havenga.

to the principle of equality between Afrikaner and English elements and to General Hertzog's anti-war policy as well. General Hertzog accepted the position of honorary chief of the new party, which is not as yet an important political element in the country.[7a]

General Hertzog's retirement and the withdrawal of the moderate Hertzogites from the " or " Party did not result in unanimity among the left-wing Nationalists. Dr. Malan's leadership seemed to be facing keen competition both from Mr. Pirow and from the Ossewa Brandwag (Oxwagon Fire Watch). Mr. Pirow's brand of republicanism was advertised as " South African Christian National Socialist " in character. While declaring himself against dictatorship in South Africa, the former Minister for Defense has said that the present constitution must go and that the franchise should be restricted to persons with " a certain degree of Afrikaner sentiment." [8]

Probably more significant politically than Mr. Pirow's " new order " is the Ossewa Brandwag, which originated in 1938 ostensibly as a non-political, cultural association of Afrikaners dedicated to Voortrekker ideals. Since October 1940, when it entered into an agreement with the Reunited Nationalist Party, the Ossewa Brandwag has assumed an increasingly important role in South African politics.[9] According to compact, the two organizations were to cooperate but to refrain from interference in each other's affairs. As the Ossewa Brandwag has a secret military organization on Nazi lines, its professed republicanism is obviously not democratic in character. Its Commandant-General, Dr. J. F. J. van Rensburg, who assumed leadership in January, 1941 (after resigning the post of Administrator of the Free State), is known to be an admirer of Nazism.

It is apparent that for some time prior to the opening of the present war, the Nazis were developing a " fifth column " in South Africa and its mandated territory.[10] Nazi propaganda was spread by broadcasting from Zeesen, by diplomatic and trade agents, as well as by the activities of German colonists who, at the close of World War I, remained in

---

[7a] Mr. Havenga was unanimously elected to succeed General Hertzog as head of the party after the latter's death in November 1942.

[8] Early in 1942 Dr. Malan issued a draft constitution based on racial ascendancy and restricting the franchise to those who might be " expected to assist in building up the nation." (Ed.)

[9] In February 1941 Dr. Malan asserted that the Ossewa Brandwag numbered between 300,000 and 400,000 members. Opponents of the organization claim these figures include women and children.

[10] General Smuts has revealed that in the spring of 1939 a contemplated *Putsch* by Nazi agents and South African Black Shirts in Southwest Africa was thwarted by official precautions.

Southwest Africa. Shortly after the beginning of hostilities, the South African authorities interned over a thousand Nazi agents and Nazi sympathizers. At the end of June 1940, it was reported that in the past few weeks more than 3,000 persons, including all Germans not previously arrested, as well as 200 Italians, had been interned in South Africa and Southwest Africa. Among Union nationals taken into custody were a number of men who had been holding responsible positions in the government service and in business.

Convinced that the Ossewa Brandwag's activities were subversive in character, the Smuts Government in November 1940 forbade the police to be members of the society.[11] After serious riots occurred in Johannesburg between Union soldiers and Brandwagian sympathizers, the Government, in February 1941, further prohibited all public servants from joining the Ossewa Brandwag. In February 1941 a more stringent National Security Code was issued.

In view of the lack of unanimity for South African participation in the war, it is of interest to review the trend of public opinion towards the Smuts Government and its war policy. With regard to the attitude of the general public at the outbreak of the war, it has been estimated by Colonel Reitz (who, as Minister of Native Affairs, may be considered as an *ex parte* authority) that 50 percent of the Afrikaans-speaking population favored participation in the war. Since the Afrikaans element constitutes roughly 60 percent of the European population and the British 40 percent, Colonel Reitz's statement would imply that 70 percent of the people favored entering the war. This proportion may be contrasted with the vote of 80 to 67 by which the Smuts amendment for belligerency was carried in the House.

General Hertzog brought about a trial of the Government's strength when Parliament met in January 1940 by a motion to restore peaceful relations with Germany. This was defeated by an increased Government majority of twenty-two votes, which was due in part to Nationalist abstentions. In August 1940, although he had thrown cold water on the Nationalist outburst of republicanism in July, General Hertzog introduced a second motion favoring immediate peace negotiations with Germany and Italy,[12] and this was rejected by a majority of eighteen

---

11 The Minister of Justice informed the House of Assembly on January 26, 1942, that over 300 Johannesburg policemen had been arrested as members of the organization. An outbreak of sabotage in Johannesburg and elsewhere early in 1942 was ascribed mainly to enemy agents working from Portuguese East Africa. (Ed.)

12 War with Italy was brought about by a proclamation of the Governor-General issued

votes. The Prime Minister had received shortly before from United
Party supporters a "Peace Through Victory" petition bearing over
600,000 signatures. A Nationalist motion to secede from the British
Empire in January 1942 was rejected by a majority of forty-two votes in
the House of Assembly, and by twenty votes to five in the Senate.

It is unsafe to prophesy how soon the broken ranks of the Opposition
will coalesce. The Nationalist Party in August 1941 condemned both the
"new order" of Mr. Pirow and the Ossewa Brandwag. General Hertzog's sensational statement in October 1941 that Nazism was in keeping
with Afrikaner tradition was immediately repudiated by Mr. Havenga,
the leader of the Afrikaner Party. It seems likely that the several Nationalist and Hertzogite elements will ultimately have to choose between the United Party of General Smuts and the authoritarianism of
the Ossewa Brandwag.

It is not too much to say that the political future of South Africa
depends on Britain's military success. If British resistance seems to
weaken, it is likely that defeatists of the Opposition will press the issues
of republicanism and secession, as well as peace. With regard to the
legal aspect of secession, Keith in 1934 expressed the opinion that in
strict law there seemed to be no obstacle to passage of a Union act of
secession.[13] From the external viewpoint, it is fairly safe to predict that
in case of a German victory, the Union would have been the first dominion (if exception is made for Eire) over which Hitler attempted to extend his sway. The principal gold-producing country in the world, with
its mandated territory of Southwest Africa, a strategic gateway to the
Indian Ocean — South Africa would have been a major prize for the
Nazis. And the Fuehrer would have found a welcome in the Union
from that minority of whom General Smuts has said, "They dream of
a republic and would welcome it even from the hands of a Hitler."[14]
On the other hand, if England is victorious, General Smuts's war policy
will undoubtedly appear as justified in the eyes of many South Africans
who have favored neutrality.[15]

June 12, and dating belligerency from June 11. The Opposition condemned this declaration of
war without parliamentary sanction in their peace campaign during the summer of 1940. (Ed.)

[13] A. B. Keith, "Notes on Imperial Constitutional Law," *Journal of Comparative Legislation
& International Law*, Vol. XVI, November 1934, p. 291.

[14] Speech on Empire Day, May 24, 1940.

[15] In 1942 and 1943 the German attack on Soviet Russia, the belligerency of the United States,
and United Nations successes helped to consolidate public opinion in South Africa behind the war
effort, though a considerable section of the Afrikaans-speaking population held aloof. (H. D. H.)

2. The Union's War Effort in Its Military Aspects

Turning from party politics to the Union's war effort, we find that for at least two cogent reasons the Smuts Government adopted a policy of limited participation, which, in contrast to the Union's policy of 1914, excluded military action in the European theatre of the war.[16] In the first place, the Government's pledge not to send troops overseas undoubtedly made the status of belligerency acceptable to many South Africans who would otherwise have favored neutrality. Furthermore, as a result of Mr. Pirow's inactivity as Minister of Defense in the Fusion Cabinet, Prime Minister Smuts, who also holds the Defense portfolio, found the Union in a state of military unpreparedness in September 1939. After the Smuts Cabinet took office, the defense forces had to be equipped not only to assume responsibility for the land and air defense of the Union, but also to cooperate with British troops on the East African and Egyptian fronts.

Although disavowing any idea of a Monroe Doctrine for Africa, the new Prime Minister immediately pledged assistance to British colonies in southern Africa — " northern outposts of the Union " — and further stated that Mozambique should be able to rely on South African aid. Since there was opposition, particularly among the Nationalists, to the idea of ordering troops to serve outside the Union, General Smuts in November 1939 stated that only volunteers would be sent beyond the frontiers to protect African colonies. At the end of March 1940, however, in accordance with an invitation issued by the Government a voluntary oath was taken by nearly the whole of the defense forces to serve " anywhere in Africa." Many of the members of the forces in taking the oath crossed out the words " in Africa," leaving only the word " anywhere." A few weeks later it was officially announced that no new volunteers would be accepted for the defense forces unless they were prepared to give a similar pledge. In May the few members of the defense forces who had refused to sign the new oath, binding them to serve outside the Union, were given permission to terminate their service with the forces. Some 40 percent of the forces raised in South Africa by voluntary recruitment have been of Afrikaner stock.

South Africa's war effort may be better understood if the framework

---

[16] This was based upon a resolution of Parliament under which troops would not be sent " overseas," which was interpreted to mean outside the African continent. General Smuts assured Parliament on March 26, 1941, that troops would not be sent farther without Parliament's consent. In February 1943 Parliament agreed to overseas service for South African forces. (Ed.)

of her defense organization is recalled. Defense legislation (Union acts of 1912 and 1922) provides for compulsory registration of all youths between the ages of 17 and 25, who are liable for peacetime training over a period of four years. A minimum of 50 percent of those liable are required by law to take this training with the defense forces, while the remaining number must enroll as members of Defense Rifle Associations for four years' training. Lack of training facilities and a shortage of modern equipment meant that the total number of registrants in any year were never called up for training. A five-year plan for building up the South African land and air forces was inaugurated in 1934, and in 1936 another five-year plan, calling for larger forces and more modern equipment, was superimposed upon it. Rearmament was not taken very seriously until the Munich crisis aroused Parliament to authorize larger defense expenditures.

At the outbreak of the war, when Mr. Pirow followed General Hertzog into opposition, and the Defense portfolio was assumed by Prime Minister Smuts, it became apparent that the defense plans in most respects had not advanced beyond the paper stage. According to statements by General Smuts, the Active Citizen Force in training at the opening of the war totalled 18,700 men, one-third the number reported by Mr. Pirow. Reserves and rifle associations were unorganized and modern equipment for all services was woefully lacking. The Air Force was in possession of only a very few modern training planes, and the planes turned over to the Air Force in September 1939 by South African Airways were mostly German Junkers. For the defense expansion program £3,000,000 had been provided by the 1939–40 budget in addition to the defense vote. When Mr. Pirow left office not more than £290,000 had been spent on the expansion program.

A War Measures Act passed early in 1940 validated a number of emergency actions taken by the Smuts Government at the outbreak of the war. Strong objections in Parliament prevented the inclusion of a proposed omnibus clause giving the Government practically unlimited power in the war sphere. Several months later, when the legality of General Smuts's order commandeering rifles of private individuals was contested, the Government found itself hampered by lack of power which the omnibus clause would have conferred, and the War Measures Act had to be amended to include such a clause with retroactive effect. Owing to the neglect in recent years of the machinery of the Defense Act, the Defense Department relied upon volunteers until

May 24, 1940, when a system of selection was instituted. By November 1941 the total strength of the armed forces of the Union was 163,400 men of all ranks. This does not include 10,000 in women's auxiliary defense corps nor 57,000 non-Europeans in the labor and pioneer corps.[17]

The strength of the S.A.A.F. stood at about 22,000 in August 1941 and was expected by General Smuts to reach in time 50,000. Although it decided not to participate in the British Commonwealth Air Training Plan in Canada, the Union Government offered to train air personnel from Great Britain and British African colonies. Owing to the fall of France, the British Air Ministry was forced to delay acceptance of this proposal, but by October 1940 British airmen were in training in the Union.

As for coastal and naval defense, the Smuts Government is honoring South Africa's obligations under the Smuts-Churchill Agreement of 1922 to provide for the land defense of the Simonstown naval base. Coastal defenses are considered adequate except in case of attack by a battle fleet. A South African Seaward Defense Force for mine sweeping and patrol service has been organized. Early in 1941, when German reinforcements greatly strengthened the position of the Axis in North Africa, it was announced that units of the South African Seaward Defense Force were cooperating with the Royal Navy in the Mediterranean off the northern shores of Africa and in the Red Sea. As in the past, however, the burden of Union naval defense rests upon the Africa station of the British Navy.

3. The Economic Structure and the War Effort

From the economic viewpoint the period from 1933 to 1939 was one of recovery for South Africa, and so far as the gold mining industry was concerned, an era of growing prosperity. Gold mining has long occupied a predominant position in the South African economy. The main attraction for foreign capital,[18] it accounts ordinarily for about 70 percent of the Union exports and provides employment for about one-half of the total working population occupied in mining and manufacturing. The industry, it is estimated, contributes £140,000,000 in

---

[17] Editor.

[18] S. H. Frankel, *Capital Investment in Africa*, 1938, pp. 102–105. Of the £200,000,000 new capital invested in the Rand mines between 1887 and 1932, roughly £120,000,000 came from overseas. By comparison £20,000,000 of overseas capital was invested in the diamond industry during those years.

earning and spending power in a year, equaling 33 to 40 percent of the national income.[19] In addition, heavy taxation of the gold mining industry is the backbone of the Union's economic policy for fostering other industries, and especially agriculture.

Gold mining held its own during the depression, and, in fact, improved its position when the gold standard was abandoned. The industry then experienced the greatest boom in its history; more capital was invested in new mines between 1932 and 1936 [20] than in any other four-year period. The rise in the price of gold, with unit working costs remaining relatively unchanged, made it profitable to crush low-grade ores and the Government encouraged this by increasing the rate of surtax with the increase in profit per ton of ore crushed.

The annual volume of gold production on the Rand increased by 21.5 percent between 1932 and 1940, when the output totalled more than 14,000,000 fine ounces valued at £117,900,000, a figure more than double that of 1932, due to the steady rise in the sterling price per ounce. The Government income from gold mining taxation rose from £4,-265,000 in the fiscal year 1932–33 to approximately £26,500,000 in 1940–41, accounting for about one-sixth of the total revenue in the former period and two-fifths in the latter.

Wartime conditions brought an added tax burden to the gold mining industry in the form of a levy on profits derived from the rise in the price of gold. It was immediately announced on August 30, 1939, that the Union Government would appropriate all proceeds arising from the sale of gold in excess of 150s. per ounce. The London price of gold was within a short time fixed by the British Government at 168s. per ounce. In preparing its budget for 1940–41, the Government yielded to protests of the mining industry, thus relieving producers of low-grade ore, and substituted for the levy a special war contribution from the mines of 9 percent of their taxable income. This contribution was raised to 11 percent later in the fiscal year and to 16 percent for the year 1941–42.

Among the problems which have confronted the gold mining industry has been the shortage of native labor. The industry, presently employing more than 300,000 native workers, has found difficulty in recruiting adequate native labor within the Union, and has been regu-

---

[19] Professor Reedman estimates the national income at present as between £360,000,000 and £420,000,000. Quoted in *Commercial Opinion*, March 1941, p. 294.
[20] Frankel, *op. cit.*, p. 98.

larly compelled to secure natives from other African territories. Employment of natives increased during the last decade from 203,473 on December 1930 to 346,726 on December 31, 1940. While it was possible to increase the number of Union and adjoining protectorate natives employed from 131,000 to 244,000 during that period, east coast natives and natives from tropical areas had to be secured in ever larger numbers. It is here that the largest reservoir of native labor may be found in the future.[21]

In comparison with gold, diamond mining has been a declining industry for many years, and though the 1938 production of 1,200,000 carats showed an increase in volume of 181.3 percent above the low point of 1934, it was still only about a third of the production of 1929. A new stimulus has been given by the war demand for industrial diamonds, but they account normally only for about one-fifth of the value of diamond sales. The general outlook for the industry was considerably darkened when, through the invasion of the Low Countries, cutting and polishing transactions were practically stopped.

Agriculture, which was severely depressed in the period immediately preceding departure from the gold standard, experienced only a measure of recovery. Largely because of unfavorable natural conditions, South African agriculture suffers from excess costs to the extent that in the years preceding the outbreak of the present war there was no important agricultural commodity except wool which was not dependent on the maintenance of an artificial internal price structure or some form of protection.[22] A White Paper issued on March 15, 1939, stated that in the preceding eight years Government expenditure for agricultural subsidies amounted to approximately £20,000,000, of which about one-eighth would be repaid. Half the total had been expended on export subsidies and one-fifth on interest subsidies.

At the beginning of the war, marketing schemes [23] were in force for maize, wheat, dried fruit, and tobacco in addition to dairy products and livestock and meat, while several new schemes were under consideration. Export bounties have been granted to individual products, as for example, dark tobacco, butter, and maize. Maize is produced mainly

21 There were over 22,000 natives from those areas employed at the end of 1940. An agreement of 1940 with the Portuguese Government increased the number of Mozambique natives contracted for 12 or maximal 18 months' employment in Union mines from 80,000 to 100,000.
22 Wool production in 1938–39 was still one-fifth below the production of 1932–33.
23 Under the Marketing Act of 1937 (Amended 1938) which established general conditions for the operation of control boards.

for domestic consumption. The export of its surplus is made possible by a levy on the internal price. Wheat production has been stimulated by a subsidization scheme which guarantees the producer a fixed price well above the world market level, while at the same time imports have been restricted by a licensing system. But in normal years the production still falls short of domestic requirements.[24] The war stimulated exports of cane sugar,[25] which reached a high of 340,000 tons and an increase in value of around £1,000,000 in 1940.

Prior to the present war, the outlook of secondary industries in the Union for future expansion appeared restricted on several grounds, among which the question of an adequate labor supply has been of main importance. The characteristic feature of the South African labor markets is the wide spread in the wages of the skilled or European group, the semiskilled group composed of poor whites and Asiatics, and the unskilled or native group. The wages of the second group vary from 30 to 75 percent and of the third group from 15 to 30 percent of the skilled rate. Though the unemployed European farmers come to the cities to seek employment, they cannot maintain anything like a European standard of living at the low rates paid for unskilled labor. On the other hand, there is not sufficient cheap native labor available to form the necessary base of the labor force. Furthermore, development of an extensive local market has been restricted by the lack of purchasing power of the unskilled poor whites and natives; while due to excessive costs and the remoteness of potential markets, the prospects for promoting the export of South African manufactured goods in peacetime were slight.

The war, however, has changed the whole outlook considerably, although the question of a sufficient labor supply remains precarious and the shortage of skilled labor has been keenly felt in an industrially undeveloped country, suddenly faced with a tremendous expansion. A special Controller of Industrial Man Power was appointed in February 1941. The cost problem is of lesser importance for defense production and for the production of goods no longer obtainable through imports. New enterprises have opened up in many manufactures, quite a number of which will be established on a permanent basis. By the establishment of the Industrial Development Corporation which began to

---

[24] Since the outbreak of the war, export of wheat and wheat products, which was of some importance in only one year, 1937, has been prohibited except under permit.

[25] The Agreement limits output to 476,488 tons per annum, while the Union's annual export quota under the International Sugar Agreement of 1937 was set at 230,000 tons.

function in October 1940 with a capital of £5,000,000, the Government has created an instrument for the advancement of loans to heavy industries.

The Union has been in the rather fortunate position of amassing budget surpluses, even though in peacetime the population enjoyed a relatively small income tax (2s. in the pound maximum) and a rebate of 30 percent on the income tax. That the individual taxpayer's burden

TABLE I

UNION REVENUES AND EXPENDITURES *

Fiscal Year (Ending March 31)	REVENUES				EXPENDITURES			
	Total	† From Gold Mining in 'ooo £	In percent of total revenues	Total	Land and Agriculture in 'ooo £	Assistance to Farmers	Total Agriculture	In percent of total expenditures
1933	28,442	2,338	8.2	22,714	1,302	2,759	4,061	17.9
1934	37,625	10,648	28.3	27,282	1,603	3,731	5,334	19.5
1935	38,730	9,205	23.8	29,551	2,951	2,969	5,920	20.0
1936	39,676	10,594	26.7	30,136	2,082	3,036	5,118	17.0
1937	43,087	13,921	32.3	30,796	2,162	2,348	4,510	14.6
1938	43,611	9,456	21.7	32,629	2,294	1,610	3,904	12.0
1939	44,076	9,204	20.9	35,095	2,752	1,506	4,258	12.1

* *Official Yearbook of the Union of South Africa.*

† From income tax, state ownership credited to income tax (1933-37), excess profits duty (1934-36), gold profits surtax (1936-37). The larger part of the income from state ownership is credited to the loan account.

was comparatively light was mainly due to heavy reliance on the gold mines as a large contributor to the revenue of the state. This financial consideration has been responsible for the reluctance of the Smuts Government to reduce gold mining in favor of strategic minerals. By keeping the tax load of the individual income taxpayer relatively low and by paying large sums as assistance to the struggling farmers, the Government distributed the wealth accruing to the mines over the whole of the population.[26]

With regard to public debt, the significant development since 1933 has been the constant trend toward substituting internal debt for external debt. While in 1933 61 percent of the total gross debt was external, the relationship was more than reversed in 1940, when 64 percent of the

[26] See Table I.

total indebtedness was internal.[27] The successful internal flotation of two Union defense loans in October and November 1940 illustrates the Union's growing economic independence.

TABLE II

UNION OF SOUTH AFRICA PUBLIC DEBT
In 'ooo £ *

31st of March	GROSS DEBT					SINKING FUND	NET DEBT
	Total	External Debt	In per-cent of of Total Gross Debt	Internal Debt	In per-cent of Total Gross Debt		
1933	272,134	165,656	60.87	106,478	39.13	21,789	250,345
1934	274,311	165,037	60.17	109,274	39.83	23,277	251,034
1935	274,115	156,676	57.16	117,439	42.84	24,064	250,052
1936	251,087	122,654	48.85	128,433	51.15	4,680	246,407
1937	254,937	103,973	40.78	150,964	59.22	5,710	249,227
1938	262,618	101,123	38.51	161,495	61.49	6,780	255,838
1939	278,876	101,123	36.26	177,753	63.74	7,885	270,991
1940	291,449	106,103	36.41	185,346	63.59	6,426	285,023
1941	335,997	98,142	29.21	237,856	70.79	7,638	328,359

* *Official Yearbook of the Union of South Africa.*

Foreign trade plays the most prominent role in South African economic life; the Union maintained a favorable trade balance even in the black year of 1932. At present South Africa's exports of manganese, chromite, coal, iron ore, asbestos, and other essential materials are of great strategic value both to Great Britain and to the United States.

South Africa has sent by far the greater part of her exports to the United Kingdom and imports far more from her than from any other country. During recent years Britain supplied over 40 percent of the Union's imports and received about 80 percent of the Union's exports including specie.[28] The Ottawa Agreement of 1932 failed to increase the latter very high percentage.[29] South Africans in general have not been enthusiastic about intra-Commonwealth preferences. It has been charged that the Agreements have led to sharp competition between Empire

---

[27] See Table II.
[28] See Table III.
[29] In 1936 about 50 percent of Union nongold exports to the United Kingdom were on a preferential footing. In 1937–38 the preference given by the United Kingdom on Union merchandise was valued at £2,374,000. This preference, calculated in relation to the *total* of South African merchandise exports to the United Kingdom, amounts to about 16 percent.

TABLE III

VALUE OF SOUTH AFRICAN EXPORTS *
(including ship stores and specie)

Year	Total	Percentage of total exports going to			
	(£'000)	U.K.	Other Br. Countries	Germany	U.S.A.
1932	68,938	81.42	5.59	2.12	.49
1933	95,275	82.10	4.67	2.15	.80
1934	82,074	80.16	5.98	2.46	.70
1935	102,293	81.42	5.07	3.71	.63
1936	113,770	82.75	4.23	2.06	.93
1937	125,380	78.26	5.60	3.97	1.07
1938	105,885	79.52	5.94	4.67	.71

VALUE OF SOUTH AFRICAN IMPORTS *
(including Government stores, excl. specie)

Year	Total	Percentage of total imported from			
	(£'000)	U.K.	Other Br. Countries	Germany	U.S.A.
1932	32,673	46.27	11.17	7.62	12.99
1933	49,121	50.32	9.6	6.60	12.28
1934	66,259	48.75	9.87	5.04	16.33
1935	75,301	48.64	9.69	5.17	16.93
1936	86,282	46.30	9.40	5.71	18.72
1937	103,368	42.56	9.36	6.56	19.57
1938	95,859	43.25	10.08	8.00	17.41

* Official Yearbook of the Union of South Africa.

producers in the United Kingdom market and to a lesser degree in Canada. A larger proportion of total Union imports has been brought within the scope of tariff preferences.[30] Trade between the Union and the rest of the Commonwealth has been comparatively small. The possibilities of colonial markets for South African exports have as yet hardly been explored.

Germany was South Africa's second best customer from December 1934 (when the first clearing agreement between the Union and Germany was signed) through 1939, except in 1936 when France occupied

---

[30] In 1936 39 percent of British and 15 percent of colonial imports into the Union enjoyed preferential margins compared with 34 and 9 percent in 1932. British and colonial suppliers increased their share in the preferential sector of the Union market from 53 to 59 percent and from 7 to 40 percent respectively, but the British share in the nonpreferential category declined from 44 to 40 percent between 1932 and 1936. Van Biljon, *State Interference in South Africa,* 1938, pp. 202, 203. In 1938 the preference given by the Union to the United Kingdom was valued at £ 1,377,677. This preference, calculated in relation to *total* British exports to the Union works out at about 4 percent.

that position. Following Great Britain and the United States, Germany has ranked third as a source of South African imports since 1932 and maintained that position in 1939, even though trade relations were severed in September. Under successive clearing agreements the debits and credits were made to balance at the ratio of 1:1, but at the outbreak of the war there was a substantial balance in favor of the Union. As regards trade with the United States, South Africa has had a large adverse balance. Since the opening of the war, however, increased American purchases of South African wool, manganese, and chrome ore have improved the Union's position. The United States held third place as a buyer of Union produce before the war and second place as a source of Union imports.

The war has made governmental regulation of foreign trade necessary. The Government immediately assumed control of the purchase, sale, and holdings of foreign currency, foreign securities, and gold, and at the end of June 1940, of the foreign exchange proceeds of all exports. Provision for the prohibition of imports and exports of any specified goods were part of the National Emergency Regulations of September 14, 1939.[31] The entire economy of the Union is dependent upon the exchange of the Union's production for manufactured products used in domestic consumption and raw materials and semi-manufactured goods essential to the Union's own industry. Every effort has been made to maintain her foreign trade. Loss of Germany as a buyer and a supplier was a serious disruption. Other difficulties were the lack of shipping space and the increasing freight and insurance rates.

Wool formed by far the largest share of exports to Germany, which had taken more than a third of all wool exports. This loss was for the most part compensated for by large sales to the United States and Japan, which could no longer obtain Australian wool. To protect the wool market, the United Kingdom in October 1939 agreed to purchase an undisclosed quantity at the same basic price guaranteed to Australia of

---

31 A system of permits for the control of imports and exports was brought into operation on September 11, 1941. Permits had to be obtained for all imports, with a few minor exceptions, from countries outside the Commonwealth. The issue of the permit was dependent on the importance of the imports from the point of view of the prosecution of the war. Private purchases of certain classes of commodities from the United States would no longer be possible under this arrangement, but arrangements were being made whereby the Government itself in conjunction with other countries in the Commonwealth could obtain supplies of such commodities for essential purposes under the Lend Lease Act. A system of permits was also to be introduced for the export of goods to destinations outside the British Commonwealth, and in the case of a number of specific commodities within the Commonwealth itself. (Ed.)

10.75d. per pound, which was 30 percent above the average price realized for the Union clip of the previous season. For the season 1940–41 an agreement with the United Kingdom was announced in August 1940 according to which for the duration of the war and one year afterward, Britain will buy and market the entire clip, as she did the Australian clip of the preceding season. The price guarantee remains the same as in the first agreement. As wool exports in 1940 were valued at £2,219,000, the farming population of the Union is thus assured of a considerable money income.[32]

All gold exports are purchased by the Bank of England, which also bears the insurance cost. This arrangement gives the Union treasury an additional revenue of roughly £2,000,000 a year. The war may have a stimulating effect upon Union coal trade. There is a possibility of developing new markets in South American countries which find it difficult to buy coal in Europe. Shipments have already been made to the Argentine. Furthermore, the diversion of shipping from the Suez Canal to the route around the Cape has increased sales of bunker coal.

Serious difficulties have arisen for the deciduous fruit export. Britain licensed imports during the first war months, and lack of refrigerated shipping space has forced a ban on almost all imports of fruit to Great Britain. An experimental shipment to the United States proved unsuccessful, as the price realized did not cover the expenses. The Union Government has granted a special subsidy to the deciduous fruit growers and is attempting to assist the farmers by encouraging a canning industry.

The Union's rich resources in gold, diamonds, copper, manganese, chrome, and tin are of high wartime value. So is her surplus wool and foodstuff production. Her rich deposits of iron are not sufficiently developed to satisfy more than her own needs. The steel ingot capacity of the government-controlled South African Iron and Steel Corporation (ISCOR), and three smaller companies, accounted in the summer 1940 for 42 percent of the domestic requirements. Efforts are being made to increase the steel production. A new branch plant of ISCOR and expansion of the existing works will bring the total production to two-thirds of the domestic consumption.

Production of ammunition began in 1936, when a government ammunition factory was opened. Educational orders for armament equip-

---

[32] The entire sugar export and three-quarters of the 1940 citrus crop were also taken by Britain.

ment were advocated by the Chief of Staff in 1937, but apparently not much was done in that direction. General Smuts stated that in September 1939 there was not sufficient artillery ammunition for one day's fighting. In November 1939 a War Supplies Directorate was formed with the function of organizing the procurement and manufacture of war materials. Wide powers were conferred on the Director-General of this body for the purchase and production of goods and the establishment of factories.

The South African boot industry has been able to meet the Union's needs and to fill large orders for the British Army. But the clothing industry was unable, in April 1940, to supply the army with 250,000 uniforms, and orders for cloth had to be placed in the United States and India, the uniforms to be made up, however, in Union factories.

It is evident that the Union's industrial rearmament got a rather late start. But it must be remembered that other parts of the defense program fared no better. For each of the fiscal years 1937–38, 1938–39, and 1939–40, the regular defense vote was only £1,800,000. At the time of the Munich crisis an additional £6,000,000 was appropriated, to be expended over a period of three years. £1,000,000 was appropriated from the loan account in 1938–39, the first authorization for defense expenditure from loan funds during the period of rearmament. The budget of 1939–40 provided, in addition to the defense vote, £3,000,000 for the defense expansion program.

The total defense expenditure in 1939–40 amounted to £5,600,000 while the February budget for 1940–41 contained a total defense appropriation of £14,000,000. To meet the increased expenditure, heavier taxes were introduced. As a special war contribution, the gold mining industry was to pay on its taxable income an additional 9 percent from which £3,500,000 was expected. The diamond mines were to contribute £30,000. Furthermore, withdrawal of the 30 percent rebate on the income tax accounted for £1,800,000 revenue. An excess profit tax of 10s. in the pound on profits (except in gold and in diamond mining) in excess of the average of the three years prior to the war was expected to bring in £8,000,000.

Italy's entrance into the war necessitated far larger defense expenditure by the Union than had been provided in the main budget for 1940–41. A first supplementary budget, presented at the special session of Parliament in August 1940, called for an additional defense expenditure of £32,000,000, of which £4,800,000 was to be obtained from increased revenue, £23,600,000 from loan account, while the remainder was taken care of by saving on other votes and higher than estimated revenue under the main budget. To provide the needed revenue, the war contribution of the gold mining companies was raised from 9 to 11 percent while the normal income tax which had been 1s. in the pound and the supertax operating on incomes exceeding £2,500 a year were increased by 20 percent. Postal charges were advanced and heavier taxes placed on gasoline, tires, cigarettes, and liquor. The Government intended borrowing from the public £18,000,000. When the lists were closed ahead of the anticipated time, this amount was oversubscribed by £10,000,000.

A second supplementary budget of January 1941 brought the total defense expenditure for the fiscal year to £60,000,000; the additional £14,000,000 was debited to the loan account but could be financed in part by further savings on other votes. In the fiscal year 1941–42 defense expenditures were £72,000,000. Income and excess profit taxes were again raised, as were customs duties and excises, while the special contribution from the gold mines was fixed at 16 percent of their taxable income. This was increased to 20 percent for the year 1942–43, when defense expenditures were estimated at £80,000,000.

Since 1941 the Union has produced small-arms ammunition and TNT for export to Great Britain and the Middle East as well as for her own needs. The defense equipment now being manufactured in South Africa includes certain types of light artillery, shells, bombs, cordite, anti-tank armor-piercing ammunition, infantry mortars and ammunition, steel helmets, steel airplane hangars, armored car bodies made of South African armor plate, and portable bridges. Airplane frames and airplane engines, automobile engines and chassis, and more complicated forms of artillery have to be imported. Under the Eastern Group supply arrangements spare parts for the repair of damaged tanks and planes are transported from South Africa to the Middle East by air. There are also naval and mercantile marine repair bases at Simonstown, Capetown, and Durban.

The attempt since the outbreak of the war to build up an efficient secondary industry may change the whole economic structure of South Africa. This development is still in its infancy, and it is highly uncertain which industries will be strong enough at the close of the war to fulfill civilian requirements for which goods have hitherto been imported. It seems probable, however, that after the war the Union will no longer be classed with countries primarily producing raw materials for export. The fact which General Smuts recognized in the first year of the war, that the decision to declare war had been " a turning point in the history of South Africa," has become increasingly plain with the progress of events.[33]

[33] South Africa's future in Africa and her place in the British Commonwealth and in world affairs are all involved. That South Africa is likely to play a positive role in these events more important than that which a small state might normally expect to play, is indicated by several factors. The first is her strategic position as one of the pivotal points of world sea and air power — not only in this war but in any postwar international security system set up by the United Nations. Powerful British and American forces for the defense of India, the Near East, and Egypt making the passage of the Cape of Good Hope have brought South Africa more closely than ever into contact with Britain and the United States. The second factor is the important part played by South African armed forces in the liberation of Ethiopia and the battles of Libya and Tunisia. This reinforces her claim to a voice in the common affairs of the African continent, in which she has taken a constantly increasing interest. The third factor is the quality of her leadership — her possession in General Smuts of one of the three or four men who have achieved the stature of world statesmen. His visit to London in the fall of 1942 to sit in and confer with the War Cabinet, his famous speech before the unique joint meeting of both Houses of the British Parliament held in his honor, his pronouncements on the place of the British Commonwealth in world affairs, all pointed to his playing once more, as in 1918–19, a leading role in a new world settlement. The strengthening of his position in his own country was shown when, in February 1943, Parliament carried his motion to free South African forces for service overseas by a majority twice as great as that which brought South Africa into the war in 1939. The lengthening arm of air power from the north, the Japanese threat to Madagascar on the east, the vicious U-boat wolf-packs off Capetown pointed unmistakably to South Africa's entry into the full stream of world politics and to the need of redoubling, to a point beyond the power of her small population, of the guard over the world's richest gold fields and its most important cape. (H. D. H.)

CHAPTER XI

India and the War

Introduction

India's central geographic position, her wealth of natural resources, her expanding industries, and her large reserves of man power go to make up her great strategic importance. " India is the pivotal defence center of the mid-East," said Sir Girja Shankar Bajpai, India's first envoy to the United States, on his arrival in New York.

About two-thirds of the British Commonwealth lies in a huge semicircle around the Indian Ocean, a semicircle which curves from South Africa up through the East African colonies, across the southern coasts of Asia and down to Australia and New Zealand. Midway on the arc of the semicircle lies the subcontinent of India. From around the Cape of Good Hope, from the Red Sea and from the Persian Gulf, up from New Zealand and Australia, ships converge on India's ports, and from her ports they put out again laden with Indian produce and manufactures. India's airports are relatively short flights from Egypt, Iraq, or Darwin.

India is thus the natural collecting and distributing center for all the Allied territories in the Eastern Hemisphere. India is the central base for operations in the Middle or Far East. From India troops and supplies can readily be dispatched around the Mediterranean, to East or South Africa, or through Iraq and Iran.

The ships that put out from India's ports are laden with varied cargos. There are convoys of supply ships for the armed forces. America's defense program calls for manganese ore and mica from India's mines. The black sea sands of Travancore yield the rarer industrial minerals, ilmenite and monazite. Indian kyanite, sillimanite, and magnesite provide furnace linings in many of the world's great industrial plants. India has a virtual monopoly of jute — her most important raw material contribution to the United Nations — of the burlap made from jute, and of lac, and she is the world's major source of hides and skins. Vegetable oils, raw drugs, and timber are among her other products.

Nor does India export only raw materials. Ranked by the International Labor Office as one of the eight leading industrial countries of the world, she manufactures annually thousands of millions of yards of textiles: cotton, jute, and woolens. The Tata Iron and Steel plant at Jamshedpur is the largest in the British Commonwealth. By far India's greatest resource is of course her immense man power. About one-fifth of the peoples of the world live in India. The 1941 census estimates the population at 389,000,000.

There is no political party or group in India which has not publicly proclaimed its abhorrence of Nazi, Fascist, and Japanese aggression, and no group or party has shown the least desire to pin their hopes for the realization of their political aspirations to an Axis victory.[1] The communal rivalries and differences of religion, race, and culture in India at first glance appear to offer an ideal field for the favorite preliminary technique of Nazi propagandists, the exploitation of minority grievances, nor has this possibility been overlooked by the Nazis or the Japanese. In the summer of 1940, however, when a bitter opponent might have seized the chance to administer a *coup de grâce* to Britain, the political deadlock in India came nearer to a settlement than ever before. This does not mean, of course, that all elements in India are democratic in their political conceptions; the Hindu caste system is based on a hierarchical principle which has no close parallel in Western or in Moslem traditions.

India's unique contribution to world politics has been the development of the technique of passive resistance as a political weapon. *Satyagraha,* or nonviolence, first employed by Mr. Gandhi in his struggle for the rights of Indians in South Africa, has long been the official policy of the National Congress Party,[1a] the largest and best organized party in India. At times Mr. Gandhi has restricted the practice of pas-

---

[1] Mahatma Gandhi's statement after his interview with the Viceroy at the outbreak of war in September 1939 — "I told His Excellency that my own sympathies were with England and France from the purely humanitarian standpoint." — is often quoted in this connection.

[1a] Some popular misunderstanding has arisen from the name of the "Indian National Congress," which is not a legislative body but a political party.

sive resistance to specified individuals or even to himself, when he felt that the movement was degenerating or when, as earlier in the present war, he did not wish to embarrass the British Government by a mass civil disobedience program. His own faith in the efficacy of nonviolence, which is based on his experience of a regime guaranteeing personal freedom and equality before the law, has never been shaken. So strong is Mr. Gandhi's hold on the Congress Party that nonviolence has remained its official policy through the third year of the war.

1. India's Relations with Britain and the British Commonwealth

At the outbreak of war, the new constitution provided by the Government of India Act, 1935, had been in effect in British India for almost two and a half years. In eight of the eleven self-governing provinces, ministers of the National Congress Party controlled the administration, and had inaugurated numerous social and economic reforms. More than one Congress premier has testified to the sympathetic and loyal cooperation he received from the Governor of his Province and the members of the Indian Civil Service, although only a few years earlier the Congress Party had been an illegal organization. Negotiations between the Viceroy and the Indian States, comprising about one-fourth of India's population, with a view to bringing into operation the provisions of the constitution for the federation of the provinces of British India and the Indian States were in progress.

Not only were the States reluctant to surrender the powers sought for the central administration, but both the Congress Party and the Moslem League, the second largest party in India, were also opposed to the scheme of federation. Under the federal provisions of the 1935 Act a proportion of seats in the Central Legislature had been reserved for Moslems, Sikhs, and other minorities. The Congress Party strongly objected to these reservations, maintaining that all seats should be open to the election of any candidate whatever his creed. The All-India Moslem League, whose leader is Mr. Jinnah, retorted that the reason for this attitude was obvious: Hindus with a population of approximately 256,000,000 would form the vast majority of the electorate and the Moslems and other minorities would form a permanent minority. While the Moslems also considered their own interests insufficiently safeguarded by the reservation of seats for minorities provided for in the 1935 Act, it would at least have rendered government by coalition essential, and it is arguable that this would have provided the basis for a solution of India's communal problem.

When Britain declared war, the Viceroy, Lord Linlithgow, immediately proclaimed that, " A state of war exists between his Majesty and Germany." India was thus at war. This was constitutionally correct, but nationalist sentiment was deeply offended that the consent of India's political leaders had not first been obtained, and the Legislature not consulted. The majority of the Congress Party leaders adopted a resolution, drafted by Pandit Jawaharlal Nehru, condemning both Nazi aggression and British " imperialism," and making cooperation in the war conditional on a statement of war and peace aims by the British Government and an immediate grant of independence to India. The Moslem League, too, expressed sympathy for Poland, England and France, but asked for " an assurance that no declaration regarding the question of constitutional advance for India should be made without the consent and approval of the All-India Moslem League."

Meanwhile the Viceroy was holding a series of interviews with the leaders of every political party and representatives of every shade of opinion, and as a result he made two offers on behalf of Britain. The first was a promise to reconsider the whole question of the constitution at the end of the war; the second was a proposal to form a consultative committee representing all parties, to cooperate with him in the conduct of the war.[2]

The Viceroy's proposal was rejected by the Congress Party, and as a sign of protest the Working Committee of the Party ordered the eight provincial Congress ministries to resign. In one province, Assam, a coalition government was soon formed; Orissa formed an alternative ministry in November 1941; the administration of the other provinces was undertaken by the Governors with advisory councils, in accordance with the Act of 1935. In no case were reforms instituted by the Congress Party ministries interrupted.

A conciliatory statement by Mr. Gandhi early in 1940 aroused hopes that an agreement might be reached, but in March 1940, at the annual party conference, the Congress Party reiterated its demand for complete independence and for a constituent assembly to draft a new constitution elected on a basis of adult suffrage. This would of course result in preponderant Hindu representation. The resolution added that the with-

---

[2] Cmd. 6121, 1939.

drawal of Congress ministries from the provinces "must naturally be followed by civil disobedience." At the same time the Moslem League, meeting at Lahore, widened the breach by demanding that any new constitution should divide India and create independent Moslem states in the northwest and east where Moslems are in a majority.

The suggestion for the partition of India and the creation of a Moslem state, Pakistan,[3] was not new, but it had never before been put forward as a serious political demand. Since its adoption in March 1940, Mr. M. A. Jinnah, the president of the Moslem League, has been increasingly insistent that it is the only solution of the constitutional problem the Moslem League will accept. The growth of political consciousness among the Moslems of India is due to a variety of causes. From the time of the Government of India Act of 1935 it has been apparent that great powers were to be transferred in the near future to Indians, and it was a natural corollary that the Moslems, like other parties, should seek to muster their electoral strength.[3a] Again, the conviction that Moslem interests suffered in provinces where popular Congress ministries held office served to mobilize a mass of "floating" Moslem opinion into the ranks of the All-India Moslem League.

In July the Congress passed a resolution demanding complete independence for India and the establishment of a provisional nationalist government as measures which would "enable the Congress to throw in its full weight in the efforts for the effective organization of the defense of the country." Although Pandit Nehru in an explanatory statement made it perfectly clear that the resolution envisaged only defense measures for an independent India, and did not imply active participation in the war effort, it was the closest approach to cooperation yet made by the Congress.

The British Government found it impossible at that time to meet the Congress Party demand.[4] But on August 8, 1940 the Viceroy issued a statement reaffirming that the British Government's objective for India was dominion status, and announcing that the Government was ready to replace the Act of 1935 immediately after the war by a new constitution to be drafted by Indians, which "should originate from Indian con-

---

[3] Pakistan is said to be derived from the initial letters of the territories affected, i.e., Punjab, Afghanistan (North West Frontier Province), Kashmir, and Sind.

[3a] From one point of view, the increased tension of communal relations in recent years and the constant jockeying for position may be taken as evidence of faith in British promises of Indian independence.

[4] 364 H. C. Deb. 5s., c. 875.

ceptions of the social, economic, and political structure of Indian life," the only condition being that it must not be unacceptable to large and powerful elements in India's national life.[5]

At the same time, the Viceroy was authorized to enlarge his Executive Council by inviting a number of representative Indians to join, and to create a new, representative War Advisory Council. The response to this offer was not encouraging. The Moslem League approved in principle, but hedged its acceptance with so many conditions that no agreement could be reached. The Congress Party rejected the Viceroy's proposal and, apparently repenting its temporary defection, returned to its old attitude. On September 17, 1940, the All-India Congress Committee reaffirmed the party's faith in nonviolence and requested Mr. Gandhi to assume its leadership. The Viceroy announced in November 1940 that, failing to obtain the cooperation of the chief parties, he would not proceed with the proposals, but that the offer remained open.

Mr. Gandhi had meanwhile been informed that he and his followers would be accorded the rights of conscientious objectors in Britain, that is, absolved from the duty of fighting but not permitted to dissuade soldiers from fighting or war workers from working. Since the Congress Party insisted on the right to urge Indians not to enlist or to work in munitions factories, a campaign of civil disobedience was opened. Mr. Gandhi, who had repeatedly declared that he had no desire to embarrass the British Government, directed the campaign, which he designated individual civil disobedience, as distinct from the mass movement advocated by some of his supporters.

The plan of campaign showed Mr. Gandhi's desire to avoid embarrassing India's war effort while registering his protest against the conditions in which that war effort was being carried out. Mr. Gandhi nominated a Congress Party member, who thereupon sent word to the local authorities that at a stated time and place he proposed to offer satyagraha, i.e., to preach nonviolence and urge noncooperation in the war effort. At the time and place appointed, Mr. Gandhi's nominee arrived to find the police waiting for him; he began his speech or shouted a few satyagraha slogans, and was arrested. Nevertheless, the arrest, however deliberately courted, of such prominent Nationalists as Pandit Jawaharlal Nehru, Maulana Abdul Kalam Azad, the President of the Congress Party, and former provincial premiers and presidents of

---

[5] Cmd. 6219, 1940. The Secretary of State for India on April 22, 1942, referred to this as " recognition in advance of India's status as a dominion."

the party could not fail to be an acute embarrassment. Failure to act would have implied one law for obscure individuals and another for well-known leaders.

Among moderate elements in the country there was a sense of frustration at the twofold political deadlock. Under the chairmanship of Sir Tej Bahadur Sapru a conference of moderates met in Bombay in March 1941 and submitted a series of suggestions to the Government. These included recommendations that for the duration of the war the Viceroy's Council should be composed exclusively of Indians, acting on a basis of collective responsibility, and that this government should occupy the same position in intra-Imperial and international affairs as the governments of the dominions. In rejecting the Sapru proposals as impracticable, the Secretary of State for India emphasized that they had been repudiated by the president of the Moslem League, while the secretary of the Hindu Mahasabha Party had declared that his party would not cooperate in any scheme in which the numerical majority of Hindus was not reflected in the composition of the council.

The Viceroy then returned to his proposals of August 8, 1940, and even though the major parties held aloof it was announced on July 22, 1941 that a number of Indian statesmen had consented regardless of party affiliations to serve on the Executive Council, which was enlarged from seven to twelve members. Eight of the twelve portfolios were held by nonofficial Indians, who thus for the first time outnumbered Europeans on the Council. At the same time a National Defense Council was set up, an advisory body of about thirty members, all of them Indians except for one representative of the European commercial community and one Anglo-Indian. A Defense Committee of the legislature had already been formed to keep the members of the legislature in touch with the work of the Defense Department. Sir Gurunath Bewoor, a distinguished Indian civil servant, was appointed additional secretary of the Defense Department, hitherto regarded as "a European preserve."

The new administrative measures encountered a good deal of criticism, chiefly because the portfolios of Defense and Finance were not entrusted to Indians. The Sikh community protested that it was given no representation. The Moslem League ordered the Premiers of Bengal, the Punjab, and Assam to resign from the National Defense Council, on the ground that they had been appointed not *ex officio* but as members of the Moslem League, without the consent of that body. They did resign, the Premier of Bengal resigning simultaneously from the Moslem League in protest. The only woman member of the Defense Council and the new Law Member of the Executive Council defied Mr. Jinnah by refusing to resign, and were expelled from the Moslem League for five years. The Member for Indians Overseas anticipated similar disciplinary action by resigning from the National Congress Party.

It should be noted that the nonofficial Indian majority of the Executive Council exercises decisive control over the Government of India's policy as a whole. It is true that the Viceroy could under certain circumstances overrule his Council, but to this the nonofficial majority would have a simple and extremely effective retort: resignation, accompanied by publication of the reasons which led them to do so. Such a crisis would be acutely embarrassing to the Viceroy as a public confession of the imposition of Britain's will against Indian wishes and he would naturally strive to the utmost to avoid such an outcome. All the nonofficial members of the Viceroy's Council were distinguished in Indian business and political life, and some of them had been closely associated at different stages in their careers with the Congress Party. The inclusion of nine representatives of the Indian States in the National Defense Council was another significant step, which was expected to make it easier for representatives of the States and of British India to cooperate in peace as well.

Till December 1941, the political deadlock remained unchanged. The Moslem League rested upon its demand for a separate Moslem state. The Congress Party had not officially deserted its policy of nonviolence, but the number of prisoners dwindled, and those who had been released showed no desire to court rearrest. On December 3, the Government announced the release of Pandit Nehru, of Maulana Azad, the President of the Congress Party, and of those " whose offences have been formal or symbolic in character." The dramatic sequel of Sir Stafford Cripps' mission is told in the final section of this chapter.

2. Indian Defense

For many years before the outbreak of war in 1939 India differed in no way from the rest of the British Commonwealth in being unprepared for defense in comparison with the potential enemy. In 1938,[6] however,

---

[6] In November 1937 a grant of £600,000 was made, to be spread over three years beginning April 1938. In September 1938 a further capital grant up to £500,000 was voted, as well as an increase by £500,000 of the annual grant of £1,500,000 in aid of military expenditure.

a grant was made by the British Parliament for the mechanization of the Indian Army, and an expert committee under Lord Chatfield was sent from Britain to India to investigate both the military and the financial aspects of the modernization of the Indian Army.

Hitherto responsibility for the defense of India had been divided between India and Great Britain. India had been responsible for the " minor danger " of the maintenance of internal security and the protection of her frontiers, while Britain assumed responsibility for the " major danger " of an attack by a great power upon India or upon the Commonwealth through India. The Chatfield Committee in its report departed from this principle, on the grounds that India was now more vulnerable to attack in forms not envisaged when the principle was formulated, and that India was therefore directly interested in defense measures extending beyond her local frontiers. The Committee recommended that the forces maintained by India should not only be adequate for purely local defense but should include what were termed " external defense troops."

It was for the purpose, therefore, of the defense of India's external " bastions " that on the outbreak of war Indian troops were dispatched to Egypt and Malaya to guard those vital approaches to India, the Suez Canal, and Singapore, while smaller units were sent to Hong Kong, Aden, and Burma. In December 1939 a small Indian contingent landed in France, a self-contained unit consisting almost entirely of pack transport companies. For Indian forces the main theater, however, was the Middle East, and General Wavell stated in August 1941 that " for more than a year after the outbreak of war the Fourth Indian Division and the Seventh Armored Division (of the British Army) formed the main, almost the only, bulwark of the defense of Egypt on the west." [7]

India entered the war with an army of about 170,000 Indian soldiers.[8] By the beginning of 1942 more than a million had volunteered, for in India conscription for military service is applied only to men from the United Kingdom. It had long been a grievance in some parts of India that the Army was recruited from the so-called " martial races " of Northern India, but thanks to the understanding of Sir Claude

[7] Indian Information, Vol. IX, p. 236. " After the Battle of Sidi Barrani was won, two Indian Divisions, supported by Sudanese troops, carried out that brilliant campaign in Eritrea and Abyssinia. . . . In Cyrenaica, and at Tobruk, an Indian Motor Brigade was of very great value, doing most gallant work. In East Africa, the Western Desert, and in Syria, the 4th Indian Division contributed greatly to success and enhanced the reputation of Indian troops. Indian troops helped restore our position in Iraq and assisted our occupation of Syria."

[8] There were about 50,000 British troops in India.

Auchinleck, during his term as Commander-in-Chief, the basis of recruitment was widened and new regiments formed. At the same time facilities for the training of Indian officers were increased. In the course of 1941, the intake of Indian officers was 600 and it was expected that this would be raised to 2,000 a year.

The Royal Indian Navy at the outbreak of war consisted of eight vessels, intended primarily for patrolling India's long coastline. This small force has been expanded by the addition of many sloops and patrol craft and of anti-submarine vessels and mine sweepers. Italy's entry into the war meant arduous and continuous naval work in escort and patrol duty in the Indian Ocean, the Red Sea, and the Persian Gulf. During the East African campaign Indian naval units cooperated with conspicuous efficiency in landing troops and supplies on the hostile coast of Eritrea, and at the recapture of Berbera in British Somaliland the first troops to land were carried by Indian warships. Ships of the Royal Indian Navy, manned by Indian officers and ratings, have taken part in the Battle of the Atlantic. They have played an important part in the patrol of the Indian Ocean, and participated in the battle off Java. Nor should India's 40,000 merchant seamen be forgotten.

The Indian Air Force on the outbreak of war consisted of headquarters and two flights, with a complement of sixteen officers and 152 air ratings.[9] Within a year the first squadron, an Army Cooperation Squadron, had been fully equipped and a second squadron was being trained. Ten civil flying clubs were transformed into training schools, and the Directorate of Civil Aviation undertook the training of 300 pilots and 2,000 mechanics a year. An Indian Air Force Volunteer Reserve was formed for defense duties mainly on coastal patrol, and was immediately overwhelmed with recruits. With the exception of a few technical experts, the personnel of the Indian Air Force Volunteer Reserve is entirely Indian.

The size of the Indian forces in future depends essentially upon the amount of equipment and material becoming available from Indian industry and from British and American sources. By the middle of 1942 recruits were being accepted by the Indian Army at the rate of 70,000 a month, while many volunteers were refused for lack of equipment. India's effort during the first two years of the present war exceeded by astronomical figures in every direction the whole of her effort between 1914 and 1918.

---

[9] Units of the Royal Air Force were also stationed in India.

3. Economic and Financial Mobilization

Even with aid from the British Exchequer,[10] the war has meant a heavy increase in the Indian budget, an increase which has been met by additional taxation, defense loans, and a defense savings movement. An excess profits tax of 66 2/3 percent has been imposed, and a surcharge of 25 percent on income tax and surtax introduced in a supplementary budget in November 1940 was increased to 33 1/3 percent in the 1941–42 budget. Two 3 percent defense loans have been floated as well as a three-year interest-free loan for those persons anxious to assist the war effort without receiving interest. There are many such in India, including some with religious scruples against interest. For the small investor, Post Office ten-year defense savings certificates were introduced, giving a tax-free yield of 3 1/8 percent.[11]

The calling in of sterling securities by the British Treasury enabled the Government of India to undertake a great program of debt repatriation, i.e., the cancellation of sterling debt and its replacement by rupee loans. By the beginning of 1943, out of a total sterling debt (inclusive of railway stock, debentures, and annuities) amounting in 1936–37 to £360,000,000, £294,000,000 had been repatriated.

At the beginning of the war the control of foreign exchange was put in the hands of the Reserve Bank of India. All dealings in foreign exchange were required to be transacted through authorized dealers, comprising the exchange banks and a few joint stock banks. No restrictions were placed on transactions in Empire currencies, except Cana-

---

10 It was announced in the House of Commons on February 29, 1940, that the "Indian budget should provide during the war for:

" (a) the normal cost of India's prewar Forces whether they are employed within or outside India, adjusted from time to time in accordance with the trend of prices, etc.; and

" (b) the cost of special defense measures undertaken by India in Indian interests during the war.

"In addition a contribution as recommended by the Chatfield Committee will be made towards the extra costs of certain troops while employed outside India. All defense expenditure over this amount incurred by the Government of India will be met by the British Exchequer. This arrangement will be made retrospective to 1st April, 1939, and will take account of sums issued from grants-in-aid provided for re-equipment in the Estimates of the current year." 357 H. C. Deb. 5s., c. 2255–6.

11 Reckoning the rupee as 30 cents, total subscriptions to Indian Defense Loans up to February 7, 1942 were $370,116,000. This should be compared with the average prewar budgets of the Government of India and eleven provincial governments combined of $480,000,000.

dian, Newfoundland, and Hong Kong dollars, but sales of non-Empire currencies were restricted to genuine trade purposes. In March 1940 a scheme was introduced to control the foreign exchange proceeds of exports to countries on hard currencies (i.e., countries nominally on the gold standard). Originally relating only to jute and rubber, the scheme was later extended to all commodities. The licensing of imports for the conservation of foreign exchange was also introduced in March 1940. An ordinance of July 1940, in conformity with practice in other parts of the Commonwealth, called for the registration of dollar securities held by Indian nationals, and certain specified American securities were acquired by the Government of India in the spring of 1941.

In general the monetary authorities have kept money as cheap as possible through the expansion of currency to meet the increased requirements of trade and industry and through the purchase of securities in the open market to avoid the dangers of inflation of the last war.[12] With an abrupt rise in prices in September 1939 the Government of India gave the provincial governments power to fix the extent of the rise in prices of necessary commodities at each stage of production and distribution. Price control conferences at which certain guiding principles were formulated were later held in Delhi under the chairmanship of the Commerce Member of the Executive Council, Sir A. Ramaswami Mudaliar.

It was found undesirable to control any tendency for agricultural products to rise, and the primary stage of production was therefore left uncontrolled. In the secondary stage of distribution, the conferences decided that control of the wholesale markets ought to be left to the central government, while profits in the retail market could be controlled by the provincial authorities. The central control did not mean that wholesale prices would be uniform throughout the country; the action of the Government would be to regulate the price in each area according to the circumstances prevailing there. Where price control on any large scale is necessary in a province, a controller of prices is appointed at the headquarters of the province. With him is associated an advisory board representing producers, commercial bodies, traders, consumers, and other interests affected.

In view of shortages created by the demands of the fighting services

---

[12] After a steady advance for the first four months of the war, prices have gradually declined. The peak was reached in the first week of January, 1940, when prices rose to 39 percent above the prewar level.

and war industries and by restrictions on trade, an Economic Resources Board, also under the presidency of Sir A. Ramaswami Mudaliar, was established in October 1939. The Board has no executive functions, but acts as a clearing house of economic and statistical information, discussion and advice, and coordinates the work of all departments concerned with the development and conservation of India's resources. Various trades and industries affected by the loss of European markets, or otherwise concerned with the development of India's potentialities as a supply center, were represented on an Export Advisory Council, which met regularly under Sir A. Ramaswami Mudaliar to plan the expansion of export trade and to seek alternative markets.

4. War Industries

Since the First World War the growth of manufacturing in India, thanks to protective tariffs and the stimulus exerted on domestic industries by the Indian Stores Department, has assumed the proportions of an industrial revolution. The Indian Stores Department took every opportunity to assist Indian manufacturers to improve the quality of their products, and preference was invariably given to supplies of indigenous manufacture. Thus in September 1939 the Army could turn not only to the Ordnance Factories, which play a much greater role than government arsenals in most countries and provide an example for private undertakings, but also to a flourishing steel industry built up over many years by Indian capital and enterprise, and great cotton and woolen mills. All the armies of the Middle East march on India-made boots, and Indian timber provides railway ties, piles, and telegraph poles as well as packing cases and hutting. By July 1942 India was manufacturing 80 percent of her total war requirement. She had also sent overseas large quantities of ammunition and had undertaken the manufacture of armored fighting vehicles, while aircraft assembly plants had been established, and Indian shipyards were producing various types of small craft. Lack of machine tools, the simpler types of which are now being manufactured in India, has been one of the chief obstacles to the development of new industries, as formerly almost all machine tools were imported.

On April 1, 1940, the Board of Scientific and Industrial Research was set up to advise the Government on the coordinated development of India's industries, particularly potential new enterprises related to the war effort. It has not only been able to suggest improved methods in existing industries, but has insured the production in India of such wartime articles as anti-gas fabrics, solid fuel for a portable cooking outfit, and an unbreakable container for dropping gasoline or water supplies from the air without parachutes.

The Indian workman adapts himself readily to the use of precision tools, but technical experience as well as natural aptitude is required. Thus in June 1940 the first compulsory war service in India was introduced for skilled labor and accepted throughout the continent without difficulty. National Service Labor Tribunals were set up in specified areas to administer the calling up for work in munitions factories of technicians not already engaged in work of national importance. For munitions work 10,000 men were thereby made available. Indian technicians have also been sent in small parties of fifty to Great Britain for intensive training over periods of six months. One of the purposes of the British Minister of Labor in this arrangement was obviously to send the workmen back to India with some knowledge of trade unionism and other labor organizations in Britain.

To consider the postwar readjustment of industry and labor the Government of India appointed in the middle of 1941 a Reconstruction Coordination Committee. The committee began its work through four sub-committees for labor and demobilization, disposals and contracts, public works and government purchases, and international trade policy.

5. Supply

For some years before the war the Government of India had maintained an organization known as " The Principal Supply Officers' Committee." Its chief functions were to investigate wartime requirements and the resources available to meet them, taking into consideration the needs not only of the defense services but of communications, public utilities, essential industries, and civilian supplies. During 1938 special consideration had been given to the needs of the iron and steel industry, oil refinery, textiles, government workshops, and shipping.

The way was thus paved for the creation on August 26, 1939 of a Department of Supply, which was added to the portfolio of the Law Member of the Executive Council. At the same time a Director-General of Supply was appointed and a War Supply Board established. The function of the Board was to ensure an adequate supply of war materials. At first largely an advisory body, it was reconstituted in November 1939 and given executive powers.

The Department of Supply and the War Supply Board were not concerned with supplies for normal trading purposes, but procured the essential materials for firms engaged on war contracts, for utility services, and for concerns of national importance. Priority arrangements were made for essential imports, and close liaison was maintained with Indian industrial interests. The actual procurement of armaments and ammunition, army clothing, and saddlery for the armed forces was not at first the responsibility of the Supply Department, but of the Master-General of Ordnance.

By the summer of 1940 the new demands upon India's productive capacity had so increased that it was thought best to put all the supply organizations under unified control. A new War Supply Board was formed in July 1940, with the Supply Member of the Executive Council as president and the former Director-General of Supply as vice-president. The Board worked through two branches, for munitions production and supply. The Director-General of Munitions Production was responsible for armaments and ammunition, steel production and all metals; the Director-General of Supply had charge of all other war supplies: foodstuffs, textiles, leather, lumber, and miscellaneous stores. The two directors-general were stationed, respectively, at Calcutta and New Delhi. The Indian Stores Department and the Contracts Directorate at New Delhi remained responsible for the actual purchase of all stores. In the provinces there were provincial purchase branches, industrial planning officers, and the agents of the controllers appointed for particular commodities, such as steel and machine tools. Since a great part of India's industry is situated in Bengal and Bihar, it was found that these arrangements resulted in excessive centralization at Delhi and the organization was therefore modified in December 1940. Responsibility was decentralized by converting the two Directorates-General into self-contained units, one of them at Calcutta, and empowering the directors-general to take decisions, with the concurrence of their financial advisers, without financial restrictions on all matters within their jurisdiction.

A War Transport Board was constituted on September 8, 1939, to control and coordinate transport by rail, road, and sea. Constant supervision is maintained on the movements of both civil supplies and essential war material. The Communications Member of the Executive Council originally presided over the Board, on which the Commerce, Finance, Defense, and Supply departments were also represented. In the middle of 1942 the Board was reconstituted as a separate "portfolio" in the Executive Council.

To meet some of the intricate problems arising in the course of letting and adjusting war supply contracts, an Advisory Panel of Accountants was established by the Government of India in June 1941. The Panel's duties were to advise on general accountancy questions relating to the terms of contracts for war supplies, such as those terms bearing on system of payments, elements of costs, profit percentages, the extent of check to be applied on the accounts of contractors, and similar problems. Six Indians and four Europeans were nominated to the Panel, which held its first meeting in Delhi in July 1941.

The collapse of France and the entry of Italy into the war meant the diversion of shipping from the Mediterranean to the Cape of Good Hope route. The British Commonwealth countries east and south of Suez were thereby cut off to a certain extent from the Mother Country and had to place more reliance on their own resources. In order to coordinate their war effort, the Viceroy, Lord Linlithgow, invited representatives of the various parts of the British Commonwealth in the Eastern Hemisphere to a conference at Delhi. The Eastern Group Supply Conference which met from October 25 to November 25, 1940, under the chairmanship of an Indian, Sir Muhammad Zafrullah Khan, was an event of capital importance in the development of the British Commonwealth and a landmark in the war. It promised a new solidarity between all the parts of the Commonwealth round the shores of the Indian Ocean out of which a permanent regional organization might develop. It was attended by delegates from Australia, New Zealand, South Africa, India, Southern Rhodesia, Kenya, Uganda, Tanganyika, Northern Rhodesia, Nyasaland, Zanzibar, Burma, Ceylon, Malaya, Hong Kong, and Palestine. Great Britain was represented by a special mission, which had been sent to India to discuss the production of munitions and other war stores both for Indian needs and for the forces in the Middle East. Delegates from the Netherlands East Indies also attended the Conference as observers.

The interchange of information at the Conference revealed opportunities hitherto unsuspected by many of the delegates, and from the "plus" and "minus" items in each country's capacity it was possible to map the actual and potential war resources of the entire Eastern Group.

While the Conference was still in session it had been possible, by correlating surpluses in equipment with existing requirements, to supply important deficiencies without waste of time or undue call on shipping space.

To continue the work of coordinating supply and planning production on a permanent basis the Eastern Group Supply Council was established, with headquarters at Delhi, on February 14, 1941. The chairman of the Council represents the United Kingdom and the colonies, and the other five members include representatives of India, Australia, South Africa, and New Zealand and an army officer, the controller-general of army provision (Eastern Group).

Side by side with the Eastern Group Supply Council, which is a civil organization, there has been set up in Delhi a Central Provision Office under military control. The military member of the Supply Council is in charge of the office and is the link between the two organizations. His staff consists of about forty to fifty officers drawn from the forces of Great Britain, India, and the dominions concerned. Delhi is thus the seat of two councils, one civilian and one military, through which the industrial activities and military equipment of two-thirds of the British Commonwealth are coordinated.

The Central Provision Office acts as an agency for the armed forces, and also maintains contact with the countries participating through local provision offices. Its functions are to estimate the immediate and future needs of the armed forces in the Middle and Far East that cannot be met locally and to inform the Supply Council of them. The Provision Office also assumes responsibility for the holding and distribution of military stores, which includes the coordination of all shipping requirements for the conveyance of supplies throughout the Eastern Group. The Supply Council in its turn meets the demands of the Provision Office by drawing on available resources in the group countries, maintains information about the actual and potential productive capacity of each member, and arranges for new production through the supply departments of the cooperating countries.

Thus, if the army of the Middle East, for example, or one of the local provision offices, requires supplies which cannot be obtained locally, a demand is made on the Central Provision Office. The Central Provision Office informs the Eastern Group Supply Council, which determines from what country it will be best to obtain the supplies, and asks the government of that country to place the necessary contracts. Delivery of supplies is arranged by the Central Provision Office. By the close collaboration between the two organizations in Delhi, the forces of the Eastern Group are provisioned through a system which makes the fullest use of the industrial capacity of each unit, conserves shipping space, and makes due allowance for the general strategic position.

An American Technical Supply Mission visited India in the spring of 1942, the first United States Minister to India having been appointed in July 1941.[12a] As a result of its recommendations the executive direction of India's economic war effort was placed with a committee of the Viceroy's Executive Council known as the War Resources Committee. This committee was to be responsible for implementing the production program of the government. Its decisions were made binding on all authorities.

6. The Indian States

The foregoing survey has dealt almost exclusively with the war effort of British India. But there is another India, comprising two-fifths of the area and one-fourth of the population, the India of the Indian States. At the outbreak of war the different Princes published loyal messages placing their services and resources at the disposal of the Crown.

Since 1888 certain of the states have maintained Indian States' Forces, troops trained by their own officers, in consultation with the Indian Army authorities, and armed by the British Government, ready to take their place beside units of the Indian Army. By 1938 the Indian States' Forces numbered over 45,000. The Bikaner Camel Corps and some other units from the states are serving overseas; a Jammu and Kashmir Mountain Battery distinguished itself in the East African campaign; units from Jaipur, Patiala, Udsipur, Bhopal, Travancore, Jodhpur, and Indore, are serving outside their own states, thereby releasing units of the Indian Army for overseas. The states are collaborating with British India to recruit and train for the Indian Army new motor transport and signalling units, labor companies are being raised in Kapurthala and Tehri-Garwhal, and among the flying clubs that are training pilots for the Indian Air Force are those of Jodhpur and Hyderabad.

Many states are equipped to take part in the industrial war effort. Railway workshops in Bikaner and Jodhpur have undertaken the mak-

---

[12a] In April 1942 India and China exchanged diplomatic representatives. The Indian Agent-General in China was to stand in the same relation to the British Ambassador in China as any dominion Minister.

ing of munitions, surveys have been made of the industrial resources of
several states, and the output of the factories of Mysore has greatly
increased. States' subjects are eligible for technical training under various schemes of the British Indian authorities. The Indian member of
the Eastern Group Supply Council speaks for the Indian States as well
as for British India. Very large individual money gifts have been made
to the government by the rulers and by the people of the states, usually
for a definite object, such as a fighter squadron or a naval vessel, and
large contributions are also made to the Viceroy's War Purposes Fund,
which is applied to relief as well as armament.

When restrictions on finance and trade were imposed in British India,
some apprehension was felt that unscrupulous traders might evade them
by transferring their activities to the Indian States. But the princes have
cooperated with the Government of India by adopting in their territories the same financial, import and export regulations as in British
India, thereby ensuring uniformity of policy throughout India.

7. The Mission of Sir Stafford Cripps

With the crisis in Indian affairs arising out of the Japanese advance early
in 1942, it was announced that Sir Stafford Cripps, who had recently
accepted a seat in the Churchill Cabinet, enjoying " the full confidence
of His Majesty's Government," would undertake a mission to India.
He arrived in New Delhi on March 23. Invitations had been issued
previously to the Indian political parties and other groups to select
representatives to discuss draft proposals unitedly agreed upon by the
British War Cabinet. Sir Stafford first met the members of the Executive
Council, the Commander-in-Chief, the governors of the provinces, and
then began negotiations with representative political leaders.[18]

The stated purpose of the draft proposals issued by Sir Stafford was
" the creation of a new Indian Union which shall constitute a dominion
associated with the United Kingdom and the other dominions by a
common allegiance to the Crown, but equal to them in any respect, in

---

[18] Pandit Jawaharlal Nehru, Maulana Abul Kalan Azad, for the Congress Party, Mr. M. A.
Jinnah for the Moslem League, Mr. V. D. Savarkar, president of the Hindu Mahasabha, Sir Tej
Bahadur and the Rt. Hon. M. R. Jayakar as spokesmen for the nonparty group, Sir Jogendra
Singh, speaking for the Sikhs, Dr. Ambedkar and Mr. Rajah for the scheduled castes, Mr. N. M.
Joshi for Labor; Mr. Fazl-ul-Huq, premier of Bengal, Khan Bahadur Allah Baksh, premier of
Sind, a committee representative of the Chamber of Princes, and Mr. Gandhi, who came espe-
cially from Wardha, were among those with whom Sir Stafford consulted.

no way subordinate in any aspect of its domestic or external affairs." Since these proposals have continued to form the basis of much discussion, they are here given in full:

(a) Immediately upon the cessation of hostilities, steps shall be taken to set up in India, in the manner described hereafter, an elected body charged with the task of framing a new Constitution for India.

(b) Provision shall be made, as set out below, for the participation of the Indian States in the constitution-making body.

(c) His Majesty's Government undertake to accept and implement forthwith the Constitution so framed subject only to: —

(i) the right of any Province of British India that is not prepared to accept the new Constitution to retain its present constitutional position, provision being made for its subsequent accession if it so decides.

With such nonacceding Provinces, should they so desire, His Majesty's Government will be prepared to agree upon a new Constitution, giving them the same full status as the Indian Union, and arrived at by a procedure analogous to that here laid down.

(ii) the signing of a Treaty which shall be negotiated between His Majesty's Government and the constitution-making body. This Treaty will cover all necessary matters arising out of the complete transfer of responsibility from British to Indian hands; it will make provision, in accordance with the undertakings given by His Majesty's Government, for the protection of racial and religious minorities; but will not impose any restriction on the power of the Indian Union to decide in the future its relationship to the other Member States of the British Commonwealth.

Whether or not an Indian State elects to adhere to the Constitution, it will be necessary to negotiate a revision of its Treaty arrangements, so far as this may be required in the new situation.

(d) The constitution-making body shall be composed as follows, unless the leaders of Indian opinion in the principal communities agree upon some other form before the end of hostilities: —

Immediately upon the result being known of the provincial elections which will be necessary at the end of hostilities, the entire membership of the lower houses of the Provincial legislatures shall, as a single electoral college, proceed to the election of the constitution-making body by the system of proportional representation. This new body shall be in number about one-tenth of the number of the electoral college.

Indian States shall be invited to appoint representatives in the same proportion to their total population as in the case of the representatives of British India as a whole, and with the same powers as the British Indian members.

(e) During the critical period which now faces India and until the new Constitution can be framed His Majesty's Government must inevitably bear the responsibility for and retain control and direction of the defense of India as part of their world war effort, but the task of organizing to the full the military, moral, and material resources of India must be the responsibility of the Government of India with the cooperation of the peoples of India. His Majesty's Government desire and invite the immediate and effective participation of the leaders of the principal sections of the Indian people in the counsels of their country, of the Commonwealth and of the United Nations. Thus they will be enabled to give their active and constructive help in the discharge of a task which is vital and essential for the future freedom of India.

Mr. Amery's previous offer to accept any constitution drawn up by Indians which was not rejected by some substantial and powerful section of Indian opinion had been criticized in India on the ground that it enabled the Moslem minority to impede India's independence for ever; the first aim of the Cripps plan was to meet this objection by providing that rejection of the constitution by any province need not impede India's independence because it could have separate autonomy. On the other hand, in order not to stimulate the formation of separate states but to promote the unity of India, it was essential to offer some strong inducement to the minorities in general, and to the Moslems in particular, to partake in the work of the constitution making body. Hence the provision allowing for separate autonomy was inserted to allow the minorities a margin of bargaining power.

The first practical difficulty encountered was over defense, and this occupied most of the discussions with the Congress Party. The demand from the Congress Party stated that the defense of India should be placed in Indian hands. No suggestion was made that the Commander-in-Chief of the armed forces should be an Indian, but the party asked that his functions as Defense Member should be transferred to an Indian. This would have entailed " a long and difficult reorganization " of the Defense Secretariat, and it was countered with a proposal to create a new department under the Commander-in-Chief as war member for the governmental relations of general headquarters and naval and air head-quarters, leaving the other functions of the existing Defense Department to an Indian member.

The Congress objections appeared to take no account of an offer of nominations by the nationalist parties for the Pacific War Council or of the fact that all the departments of government would have been in Indian hands, so that, through the Departments of Supply and Finance particularly, they could have exercised a powerful brake on any policy of the Commander-in-Chief of which they disapproved.

The nationalized Executive Council, representing the great political parties, would have had positive power, and if the Viceroy had attempted to oppose it he would have faced the risk of a major political crisis, uniting against him all or some of the most powerful political forces in India. While such a nationalized Viceroy's Council would not of course have meant responsible government, the measure of power in fact transferred would have been very real and very great. Until the very last night of the negotiations the Congress Party raised no general issues or discussions on " responsible government "; until then all negotiations were attempts to find a new formula for clause (e) — defense — of the draft.

Sir Stafford Cripps' own explanation of the rejection of his proposals was that " the plan broke down on the question of to whom the proposed interim Indian National Government was to be responsible," the Congress Party reiterating in their final statement that they could not accept the British Government's contention that any interim Indian Government must remain responsible either to the Viceroy or to the British Government.[14] The Congress, the Hindu Mahasabha, the Sikhs, the Moslem League, and the depressed classes were agreed in rejecting, for varying reasons, the suggestion to allow provincial independence. The Secretary of State for India, however, after Sir Stafford Cripps had reported to the House of Commons the failure of his mission, made a concluding statement that the Viceroy would welcome any " practical suggestions " from Indian leaders to implement the War Cabinet's proposals for independence.

Significant administrative changes followed in July 1942. The Viceroy's Executive Council was enlarged to fifteen members, with separate departments for War and for Defense. The Commander-in-Chief, Sir Archibald Wavell, remained War Member. Coordination between the

[14] Cf. dispatch by Mallory Brown, *Christian Science Monitor*, April 23, 1942.

defense forces and other departments of the government, defense legislation, the recruitment of man power, the administration of cantonment areas, the acquisition of land for defense purposes, the provision of oil supplies, and the care of prisoners of war were, however, vested in the new Indian Defense Member, Sir Firoz Khan Noon, who had been High Commissioner for India in London from 1936 to 1941.[15] At the same time two Indian members, Sir A. Ramaswami Mudaliar, who remained a member of the Viceroy's Council without portfolio, and the Maharaja Jam Saheb of Nawanagar, Chancellor of the Chamber of Princes, were appointed to the War Cabinet in London and the Pacific War Council. Their status in the British War Cabinet has apparently been exactly comparable to that of the representatives of any of the dominions.[16]

The foregoing chapter on India was the product of many mishaps, including the going astray of material prepared in the winter of 1941–42 by Mr. Pargat Singh Muhar which never reached the editors, possibly through loss in the mails or through censorship. His earlier contributions to the chapter had become too far out of date to be useful except for background. As it has now been written the chapter represents on the whole a non-official British view of India, which closely reflects the official view and is interesting for that reason.

To an American editor two things become of major interest. One is that a situation of the complexity of the Indian one does not lend itself to solution in the forum of American public opinion. Our national interest is at stake in seeing that a secure base is maintained for operations for the relief of China and for a counterattack through Burma and for the holding of Ceylon and of India proper. It is therefore to our interest that no government antipathetic to the war effort should be set up in India, and some doubt has been raised by Mahatma Gandhi's statements as to his own attitude in this respect.[17]

On the other hand, it is clear that India is far larger even than the much publicized figure of Gandhi, and that a growing nationalism has now touched nearly all elements of the population, even those which are, from the point of view of literacy, hardly comparable with modern electorates elsewhere. It has reached even the groups which formerly inclined to support the British raj as a matter of self-interest. To speak of democracy in India is perhaps to anticipate, but to speak of nationalism in India is certainly to deal with a fact.

The second point for an American is that our own interest lies in convincing the Asiatic peoples that this war is a genuine war for freedom. It is obvious that China views the solution of the Indian problem as a measure of the sincerity of the professions of the United Nations. It is to our interest to see that this problem does not go by default merely because of the breakdown of Sir

---

[15] At the beginning of 1943 a new Food Department was added to the Government of India. Because of the cutting off of supplies of rice from Burma, the demands of the armed forces, and unfavorable weather conditions in several provinces it was necessary to concentrate various functions of food purchase and distribution which had formerly been scattered in several departments in this one.

[16] The Maharaja of Nawanagar, on a trip to India in February 1943 described his position in the War Cabinet to the Indian press. He had received no instructions from the Secretary of State for India, and his only instructions from the Viceroy had been to do what he thought best "in the interest of the Indian States, India as a whole, and the Empire. . . . Political questions did not come before the War Cabinet, whose business was the conduct of the war." *The Times*, London, February 19, 1943.

[17] See Appendix VI.

Stafford Cripps' efforts to work out a solution along the lines of Churchill's willingness to concede dominion status after the war.

Without attempting to indicate the outlines of British policy at this time, it would seem an act of statesmanship to offer India self-government on any terms that could be arrived at by substantially unanimous agreement among conflicting communal and other interests in India, subject always to the retention of military and, if necessary, police control in areas of military importance. The psychological effects of such an offer at this time would be enormous. If, as has often been averred, Indians cannot get together, there would at least be no harm in an examination of the reasons why. If Indians are capable of finding a formula for the setting up of a constitution, or for the constructive combination of their efforts until the formation of a constitution can be undertaken, there can be no doubt of the effect upon morale, not only in India but among the other peoples of the East.

There is a natural reluctance on the part of the British at a time of great danger to concede military control or civil control that might endanger military success. There is also, however, such a thing as political warfare, and it is in this light that the independence of India presents problems of immediate and pressing importance. — W. Y. E.

The dominions, like the United States, rarely make official public reference to India. But knowing the Empire as "a school of government that inevitably leads to self-government," they have no doubt that Britain will carry out her pledge to India when Japan is defeated. They feel that swapping the horses of government in mid-stream, in face of enemy fire from the banks, would be all too likely to break down India's internal peace and undermine the fine discipline of the Indian Army of 2,000,000 volunteers, destined to play a vital part in Japan's defeat.

From experience the dominions know that national unity and federation are not easy to achieve. These cost the dominions decades of hard effort, and success was due to a positive nationalism — not mere negative opposition to Britain, but a substantial agreement and identity of purpose among the peoples, parties, and creeds of the newly emerging states. Of this they see little sign in India. They see instead a baffling maze of races, languages, states, and principalities, in population equal to Europe and three times the remainder of the British Commonwealth of Nations, and cleft to the roots by ancient incompatibilities of caste, creed, and different levels of domestication. Their liberal sympathies call for quick action; but their reason tells them that more haste is less speed. — H. D. H.

CHAPTER XII

Fighting Ulster and Neutral Eire

by H. Duncan Hall

The scope of this book does not admit of more than a short note upon the role either of Neutral Eire or of that part of Ireland which is not neutral in the common war of all the democracies for the preservation of their liberties. The story of Ulster's contributions, if it could be told in detail, would show that with her population of about 1,280,000 she has played a part in the common war effort hardly less than that of the smaller dominions.

It would be hard to imagine a greater contrast than that between the mental atmosphere of Belfast and Dublin during the war. To the people of Belfast the war was the one thing that mattered; the issues were crystal-clear; everything they held dear was at stake; they stood or fell with Britain and the Empire. But from Dublin the war looked strangely different — remote and confused; political neutrality was accompanied by a curious mental paralysis, a neutralism which blurred the sharp edges of facts as well as of moral and political principles. It was not easy to deduce from the speeches of political or even of spiritual leaders in Dublin that most of the people of Erie shared the general detestation of Nazi tyranny and its attack upon the foundations of the common Christian civilization of the West. Tens of thousands of them had indeed enlisted as individuals in the armed forces of the British Commonwealth;[1] they were no doubt glad that they could serve in a common

---

[1] Reports said some 100,000 with another 180,000 in war work in Britain.

cause with fellow Irishmen from Ulster in some of the famous old Irish regiments whose very names summoned up so much of the military history of the British army. Many of them had already given their lives; nearly one-fifth of those lost on H.M.S. *Courageous* at the beginning of the war bore Irish names.

But the people of Eire as a whole were war-weary people, for whom the First World War was followed by a civil war that lasted years after the Armistice. The preoccupation of some was to avoid war at almost all cost, in order to save, as they thought, the remnant of four million people which constitutes the Mother Country of the Irish race. To many of them it seemed possible to answer in the affirmative the incredulous question asked by President Roosevelt on December 30, 1940: If the Nazis won, " would Irish freedom be permitted as an amazing pet exception in an unfree world? "

The debate on external affairs in the Dail on April 23, 1941, showed something of this mood. It seemed to show that the representatives of Eire gathered together in the Dail hardly shared the tremendous preoccupations and anxieties of Northern Ireland, of Britain, of the British overseas dominions, and of the United States. The debate left no doubt of the almost unanimous acceptance in the Dail of the policy of neutrality, not of the active American type, but of a type which in many cases went so far as to wash its hands of the deeper issues of the war, denying through its principal leaders that any clear-cut religious or moral issues were involved. Thus the plea made by Mr. J. M. Dillon, deputy leader of the opposition party — the United Ireland Party — in the debate on July 17, 1941, fell on deaf ears. The Parliament of Eire, he said, " should ascertain precisely what cooperation Great Britain and the United States of America may require to insure success against the Nazi attempt at world conquest and, as expeditiously as possible, to afford to the United States and Great Britain that cooperation to the limit of our resources. . . . The Atlantic life line joining these two champions of democracy and civilization is no stronger than its weakest link. . . . A gap is opening in that life line. . . . We can close that gap." His suggestion was repudiated by most of the other speakers in the debate, including the leaders of all parties; and he was forced some six months later to resign on this issue from his own party.

This and other debates on external affairs revealed that the division was not one between Catholic Ireland and Protestant Ulster, but rather one between the chief leaders of Catholic Ireland and the colonies of

Irish Catholics in England and all parts of the British Commonwealth. The contrast between the views of the leaders of the Irish Catholic community was revealed in two declarations made some five months later — one by the head of the Catholic Church in Dublin, and the other from across the narrow waters in the war-torn city of Liverpool. From the head of the Catholic Church in Dublin came the demand for a negotiated peace. From Liverpool the Irish Catholic Archbishop Downey spoke of the intrepid flock standing amidst the debris of one of his churches crying, " We shall build it again." " They had seen," he said, " their sanctuary reduced to ruins that the sanctuary of their souls might not be defiled." And he called for a relentless prosecution of the war " against the oppressors of humanity." Time alone could show what the real view of Catholic Ireland was upon these grave issues. In the debate referred to, a private member gave a warning that " if a vote came before the House on the moral issue, even the Prime Minister might be surprised at the result."

On the economic side both parts of Ireland have made an important contribution to the war. With the swallowing up by the Axis of Denmark, the value of the contribution of Eire as the nearest important supplier of food to Britain was greatly enhanced. Even before the war nearly the whole of Eire's external trade was with Britain. During the war she continued to export to Britain virtually the whole of her exportable surplus of foodstuffs. Her secondary industries, patiently fostered over the past decade by de Valera's Government, suffered from a shortage of raw materials. Virtually without a mercantile marine (her few ships having been freely sunk, with apologies, by German submarines), she was dependent on what supplies Britain could afford from those fought through the U-boat wolf-packs by British and American convoys. In the matter of supplies of vital raw materials, Eire received from Britain at least as favorable treatment as other neutrals.

Of Ulster's contribution on the material side not much needs to be said. It has been of considerable importance in the matter of war industries, particularly the shipbuilding of Belfast, and of man power for the armed forces of the United Kingdom of which Ulster forms a part. All controls, such as the rationing of gasoline, food, and clothing, operating in the United Kingdom extend to Northern Ireland, and are carried out through the departments of the Government of Northern Ireland. Though service in the defense forces and in civil defense had to remain on a voluntary basis, a number of men volunteered for service in the army, particularly in such Irish regiments as the Royal Inniskilling Fusiliers, the Royal Ulster Rifles, the Royal Irish Fusiliers, the North Irish Horse, and the Irish Guards. In addition, numbers of men served in all branches of the Royal Navy and the R.A.F., as well as in the Merchant Marine. The Home Guard, set up in the summer of 1940, was about 30,000 strong a year later.

Virtually the whole of industry in Ulster served directly or indirectly the needs of war production. In the matter of shipbuilding, hundreds of thousands of tons of shipping were launched annually from the yards of Messrs. Harland and Wolff. The Belfast shipyards made a very important contribution in the matter of naval vessels, including the aircraft carrier, H.M.S. *Formidable,* and the heavy cruiser, H.M.S. *Belfast.* Other spheres in which the industry of Belfast contributed to war production were in the manufacture of various types of aircraft, tanks, iron and steel, shells, artillery, gun mounts, etc. The linen industry constituted an important element in the wartime export trade of the United Kingdom.

But the most important contribution of Ulster has been strategic. The intense loyalty of at least two-thirds of her citizens, and the good will of some at least of the remaining third, have rendered fully available to the British Commonwealth Ulster's vital strategic situation. So important is this contribution that the loss of Northern Ireland might well have meant the loss of the war. The strategic position has been well put by a writer in the *Round Table* of March 1941: " Throughout the centuries one continuous thread can be detected running through the variegated web of British military and naval policy; it is the strategical indivisibility of the British Isles. The defense of Ireland is the defense of Britain. Elizabeth knew it; Cromwell knew it; William of Orange . . . knew it; and so did Pitt and Castlereagh; so, too, in our time did Mr. Lloyd George. . . ." It was the unvarying view of Britain that the latter expressed in 1921 in these words: " The security of this country depends on what happens on this breakwater, this advance post, this front trench of England." [1a]

Britain's enemies also knew it at each critical epoch in her history — Philip of Spain, Napoleon, the German General Staff in 1916; and again in 1939, when on August 31 the German minister in Dublin called hopefully upon Mr. de Valera to assure him that the German Government would respect Eire's neutrality. Britain depends for its life upon the sea lanes to the Atlantic, running north and south of Ireland. The sur-

---

[1a] H. C. Deb. 14 Dec. 1921.

render in 1938 of the two Southern British bases, Cobh and Berehaven, followed by the neutrality of Eire and the German occupation of France, cut the southern lane — and halved the problem of the German submarine commanders. " It is, therefore," as the writer cited above pointed out, " through the narrow waters of the North Channel that the bulk of our shipping must make the western ports of Britain under the protection of the Royal Navy and the Royal Air Force, only because and only as long as six of the thirty-two counties of Ireland still render allegiance to the British Crown." How great was the cumulative effect of the loss of the three Irish bases was shown when Japan's entrance into the war threw a sudden enormous strain on the shipping resources of the United Nations. The loss of Ulster, whether by enemy action or a policy of appeasing Eire, might have meant the loss of the Battle of the Atlantic. It might also have made Ireland into a second Crete, whereby she would have become the classical example of how a small neutral country can destroy a great power by leaving its flank wide open to the enemy.

It was to prevent such a catastrophe, involving perhaps the destruction of England and certainly of ill-defended Eire, that a fully-equipped British mechanized army stood poised for many months upon the Ulster boundary, ready to sweep down the entire length of Eire to destroy an enemy force landed on its southern coast. It was joined by an American force in January 1942.

The policy of appeasement in 1938 renounced naval and air bases in Eire which were essential to the defense of the British Isles. But for the passionate loyalty of less than a million Ulstermen, that policy might well have had a fatal sequel. It might have bowed to the insistence of the Government of Eire and sacrificed Ulster and with it the port of Belfast. The leaders of Ulster steadfastly opposed any step involving, as the present Prime Minister, Mr. J. M. Andrews, said on July 7, 1940, the " further dismemberment of the United Kingdom," and the giving-up by the people of Northern Ireland of their British citizenship " to become citizens of Eire, which was really a republic standing neutral in the war and harbouring the Empire's enemies." The heavily overstaffed legations and consulates which neutral Eire permitted the enemies of the Empire and the United Nations to maintain in Dublin proved invaluable to the intelligence services of the Axis. The war offered no stranger contrast than that between the stream of enemy messages pouring out of these legations to Berlin, Rome and Tokyo, and the messages going from Belfast to London and the whole British Commonwealth. The burden of them was the message of Ulster's veteran Prime Minister, the late Lord Craigavon, "We are King's men. We will be with you to the end."

There were not wanting in the Dublin Parliament voices which recognized these facts and the impossibility of taking any step that would run counter to the deep feeling of loyalty binding the majority of the people of Ulster to the rest of the British Commonwealth.[2] But Mr. de Valera himself had never wavered in peace or in war in his relentless opposition to what, in his letter to the Secretary of State for Dominion Affairs on April 5, 1932, immediately after coming into power, he called " the outrage of Partition and the alienation of the most sacred part of our national territory." In that letter partition was coupled (as always in his mind) with the British naval bases established in the three Irish ports which he declared gave Britain the power " to make our neutrality a mockery."

The only terms on which apparently he felt he could accept the ending of partition were the withdrawal of Ulster, like the three ports, into the neutral zone of Eire, thus removing her from the common defense system of the British Commonwealth. Thus he stated in an interview on July 5, 1940, in the darkest hour of the war, a little more than a fortnight after Dunkirk: " In face of the present emergency Ireland should be whole and undivided," the Northern Parliament becoming " subject to the Parliament of All Ireland instead of to the British Parliament. . . . The determination of policy and defense measures were possible only on such a basis, and such measures must be founded on neutrality."[3]

In the face of this policy the possibility of a joint defense scheme between Northern Ireland and Eire, which at that time had been under discussion, fell to the ground. In the judgment of the leaders of Ulster acceptance of Mr. de Valera's proposals must mean the withdrawal of Ulster, as Lord Craigavon put it, from " full partnership in the United Kingdom and the British Empire," as well as, in the words of one of his colleagues, from " the fight for liberty, justice, and civilization." Nevertheless, because of the opposition of Eire, the Ulster leaders were forced nine months later to abandon a proposal for conscription, which the Northern Ireland Cabinet regarded as the only means whereby it could

---

[2] E.g., J. M. Dillon, then Deputy Leader of the United Ireland Party in the Dail, February 15, 1939, and July 16, 1941, and Senator MacDermot in the Seanad on January 26, 1939.
[3] As reported in *The Times*, London, July 9, 1940.

play its full part in the war as an integral part of the Empire. They repudiated strongly the claim which Mr. de Valera made in the Dail May 26, 1941, to speak, as the Prime Minister of Northern Ireland put it, " in the name of the people of this area. . . . All matters connected with Northern Ireland are completely outside the jurisdiction of the Eire Government and so they shall remain." [4]

The entry of the United States into the war, as a result of the direct attack of the Axis upon her, made no difference in Dublin's determination to remain neutral — " Irish neutrality is unchanged; our policy of state remains unchanged," Mr. de Valera said on December 14, 1941. The landing of the American armed force in Ulster at the end of January 1942 led on January 27 to a protest by Mr. de Valera in the sharpest terms against this violation of the national sovereignty and the neutral status of Ireland. In defiance of President Wilson's principle of self-determination and a 3-to-1 vote of the Irish people, Britain, Mr. de Valera said, had partitioned Ireland: " The partition of Ireland was no different from the partition of Poland. Nor are the events that flow from it less than those Abraham Lincoln foresaw from the projected partition of the United States. . . . Maintenance of the partition of Ireland is as indefensible as aggression against all nations, which it is the avowed purpose of Britain and the United States to bring to an end." At the same time Dublin once more repeated the warning often given before that any attempt to seize ports, no matter by whom, would be resisted by force. The Premier of Northern Ireland replied on January 28, welcoming the American Army, and repudiating Mr. de Valera's claim to sovereignty over Ulster. " Northern Ireland," he said, " is in the fight for freedom and intends to see it through." That he did not speak for an important part of the Catholic minority in Ulster was shown by the statement of Cardinal MacRory, Archbishop of Armagh and Primate of Ireland, on September 26, 1942. The Cardinal referred to partition as a " flagrant and intolerable injustice against Catholics doomed to live under the narrow and unjust domination of the Belfast Parliament and Executive." " When I read," he continued, " day after day, that this war is being fought for the rights and liberties of small nations and then think of my own corner of my country overrun by British and United States soldiers against the will of the nation, I confess I sometimes find it hard to be patient." [5]

---

[4] *J. P. E.*, Vol. XXII, p. 367.
[5] As reported in the *New York Times*, September 28, 1942.

It would hardly be fair to deduce from such words that only a matter of patience and tactics separated the Cardinal and Mr. de Valera from the Irish Republican Army, which continued to wage its underground war by violence against the Government of Northern Ireland and the invader — both American and British. The I.R.A.'s program of violence was generally frowned on by the hierarchy, and Mr. de Valera's government waged war ceaselessly upon it.

Such statements were, indeed, a striking example of the tragedy of Anglo-Irish relations. Some Irishmen, brooding over the past, went on living in a private world quite different in its proportions and scale of values from the normal world. Thus the setting up in 1920 of the Parliament of Northern Ireland in accordance with the freely-expressed will of two-thirds of the people of the area, though against the will of the other third, became equivalent in the minds of some of Eire's leaders to the partition of Poland, the American Civil War, and the violent rape by the Axis of fifteen free nations.

In the dire hour of common need ghosts of the past rose up before the eyes of official Dublin, obscuring all the clear lines of reality, Britain's fight for freedom, America's peril, even the fate of all the colonies of Mother Ireland. Nation after nation, including all Overseas Ireland, became members of the United Nations. But Eire remained outside brooding over the past. It was a theme for the epic and saga; it recalled an incident in the Burnt Njal Saga. The hero, Gunnar of Lithend, in his death-fight held off a great band of enemies that besieged his house, and had slain many of the attackers. But one of them climbed up unnoticed and slashed his bowstring. Gunnar then turned to his wife, Hallgerda, "'Give me two locks of thy hair, and ye two, my mother and thou, twist them together into a bowstring for me.' 'Does aught lie upon it?' she said, 'My life lies on it,' he said; 'for they will never come to close quarters with me if I can keep them off with my bow.' 'Well!' she said, 'now I will call to thy mind that slap on the face which thou gavest me; and I care never a whit whether thou holdest out a long while or a short.'"

The end of the story of Eire and Britain was not yet revealed. In the early months of 1942 neutral Eire was reported to be receiving weapons sorely needed by those fighting to the death for their liberties in Russia, at Singapore, in Java and Burma. Ships of war and transports that might have saved Singapore were tied up in the Atlantic because of the neutrality of Eire. But Dublin was still haunted by ghosts. From it came hints of a possible settlement that had little relation to reality — the ending of partition by American pressure on Ulster and Britain. It was a settlement that could hardly be bought except at the cost of civil war in Ireland and a crisis in Anglo-American relations. It ignored the deep gulf of distrust dug already between Ulster and Eire by the policy of neutrality. Union with an Eire which had already shown that it was capable of insisting on neutrality in a life and death struggle involving the whole British Commonwealth, could only mean permanently removing Ulster from the mutual security system of the British Commonwealth, and so undermining the central citadel of the British Isles and jeopardizing all the United Nations.

In December 1921 Mr. Lloyd George commended the Irish Treaty to the House of Commons. Speaking to a House still under the shadow of the First World War, he expressed the faith in which the whole of the British Commonwealth had welcomed this charter of Irish freedom: " There are still dangers lurking in the mists. Whence will they come? . . . Who knows? But when they do come I feel glad to know that Ireland will be there by our side, and that the old motto that ' England's danger is Ireland's opportunity' will have a new meaning." In the Second World War — which was the thing lurking not far ahead in the mists — many thousands of individual Irishmen justified this faith; but into the fourth year of the war the Irish Government had given no sign. One minister, Dr. James Ryan, on January 10, 1942, had hinted at forces seething underneath: " When the position becomes acute there will be some who will favour departing from neutrality. . . . There may possibly be a stampede." When would the position become acute . . . ? — Malaya and the Netherlands Indies gone; Japan at the gates of India; two million Irishmen in Australia standing guard to prevent the Japanese from bursting over the northern boundary; the German Army on the Volga; and the transport of American armies and supplies for the United Nations still held up for lack of facilities that Eire, if it had been a member of the United Nations, could have furnished. Or was Eire's choice already final — to remain in its backwater, watching in uneasy silence the tide flooding back to the ocean, bearing on its crest all the ships of the United Nations to their appointed tasks of founding the new world of tomorrow?

Appendix I

EMERGENCY POWERS (DEFENCE) ACT, 1939

An Act to confer on His Majesty certain powers which it is expedient that His Majesty should be enabled to exercise in the present emergency; and to make further provision for purposes connected with the defence of the realm. (24th August 1939.)

BE it enacted by the King's most Excellent Majesty, by and with the advice and consent of the Lords Spiritual and Temporal, and Commons, in this present Parliament assembled, and by the authority of the same, as follows:

1. (1) Subject to the provisions of this section, His Majesty may by Order in Council make such Regulations (in this Act referred to as " Defence Regulations ") as appear to him to be necessary or expedient for securing the public safety, the defence of the realm, the maintenance of public order and the efficient prosecution of any war in which His Majesty may be engaged, and for maintaining supplies and services essential to the life of the community.

(2) Without prejudice to the generality of the powers conferred by the preceding subsection, Defence Regulations may, so far as appears to His Majesty in Council to be necessary or expedient for any of the purposes mentioned in that subsection,

(a) make provision for the apprehension, trial and punishment of persons offending against the Regulations, and for the detention of persons whose detention appears to the Secretary of State to be expedient in the interest of the public safety or the defence of the realm;

(b) authorise

(i) the taking of possession or control, on behalf of His Majesty, of any property or undertaking; (ii) the acquisition, on behalf of His Majesty, of any property other than land;

(c) authorise the entering and search of any premises; and

(d) provide for amending any enactment, for suspending the operation of any enactment, and for applying any enactment with or without modification.

(3) Defence Regulations may provide for empowering such authorities, persons or classes of persons as may be specified in the Regulations to make orders,

rules and byelaws for any of the purposes for which such Regulations are authorised by this Act to be made, and may contain such incidental and supplementary
provisions as appear to His Majesty in Council to be necessary or expedient for the
purposes of the Regulations.

(4) A Defence Regulation, and any order, rule or byelaw duly made in pursuance of such a Regulation, shall have effect notwithstanding anything inconsistent
therewith contained in any enactment other than this Act or in any instrument
having effect by virtue of any enactment other than this Act.

(5) Nothing in this section shall authorise the imposition of any form of
compulsory naval, military or air force service or any form of industrial conscription, or the making of provision for the trial by courts martial of persons not being
persons subject to the Naval Discipline Act, to military law or to the Air Force Act.

(6) In this section the expression " enactment " includes any enactment of the
Parliament of Northern Ireland.

2. (1) The Treasury may by order provide for imposing and recovering, in
connection with any scheme of control contained in or authorised by Defence Regulations, such charges as may be specified in the order; and any such order may be
varied or revoked by a subsequent order of the Treasury.

(2) Any charges recovered by virtue of such an order as aforesaid shall be
paid into the Exchequer of the United Kingdom or, if the order so directs, be paid
into such public fund or account as may be specified in the order.

(3) Any such order as aforesaid shall be laid before the Commons House of
Parliament as soon as may be after it is made, but, notwithstanding anything in
subsection (4) of section one of the Rules Publication Act, 1893, shall be deemed
not to be a statutory rule to which that section applies.

(4) Any such order as aforesaid imposing or increasing a charge shall cease
to have effect on the expiration of the period of twenty-eight days beginning with
the day on which the order is made, unless at some time before the expiration of
that period it has been approved by a resolution of the Commons House of Parliament, without prejudice, however, to the validity of anything previously done
under the order or to the making of a new order.

In reckoning any period of twenty-eight days for the purposes of this subsection, no account shall be taken of any time during which Parliament is dissolved or
prorogued, or during which the Commons House is adjourned for more than four
days.

(5) Without prejudice to the preceding provisions of this section, any Defence Regulations may provide —

(a) for charging, in respect of the grant or issue of any license, permit,
certificate or other document for the purposes of the Regulations, such
fee not exceeding five pounds as may be prescribed under the Regulations with the approval of the Treasury; and

(b) for imposing and recovering such charges as may be so prescribed
in respect of any services which, in pursuance of such Regulations, are
provided on behalf of His Majesty, or under arrangements made on
behalf of His Majesty, other than services necessary for the performance of duties imposed by law upon the Crown;

and all sums received by way of such fees or charges as aforesaid shall be paid into the Exchequer of the United Kingdom or, if the Treasury so direct, be paid into such public fund or account as they may determine.

3. (1) Unless the contrary intention appears therefrom, any provisions contained in, or having effect under, any Defence Regulation shall —

    (a) in so far as they specifically impose prohibitions, restrictions or obligations in relation to ships, vessels or aircraft, or specifically authorise the doing of anything in relation to ships, vessels or aircraft, apply to all ships, vessels or aircraft in or over the United Kingdom and to all British ships or aircraft, not being Dominion ships or aircraft, wherever they may be; and

    (b) in so far as they impose prohibitions, restrictions or obligations on persons, apply (subject to the preceding provisions of this subsection) to all persons in the United Kingdom and all persons on board any British ship or aircraft, not being a Dominion ship or aircraft, and to all other persons being British subjects except persons in any of the following countries or territories, that is to say, —

    (i) a Dominion,

    (ii) India, Burma and Southern Rhodesia,

    (iii) any country or territory to which any provisions of this Act can be extended by Order in Council, and

    (iv) any other country or territory, being a country or territory under His Majesty's protection or suzerainty:

Provided that Defence Regulations may make provision whereby the owner, manager or charterer of any British ship or aircraft, being a person resident in the United Kingdom or a corporation incorporated under the law of any part of the United Kingdom, is subjected to restrictions in respect of the employment of persons in any foreign country or territory in connection with the management of the ship or aircraft.

(2) In this section the expression "Dominion ship or aircraft" means a British ship or aircraft registered in a Dominion, not being a ship or aircraft for the time being placed at the disposal of, or chartered by or on behalf of, His Majesty's Government in the United Kingdom; and, for the purposes of subsection (1) of this section, any ship or aircraft registered in India, Burma or Southern Rhodesia, not being a ship or aircraft for the time being placed at the disposal of, or chartered by or on behalf of, His Majesty's Government in the United Kingdom, shall be treated as if it were a Dominion ship or aircraft.

(3) Subsection (1) of this section shall apply in relation to British protected persons, as that subsection applies in relation to British subjects.

4. (1) His Majesty may by Order in Council direct that the provisions of this Act other than this section shall extend, with such exceptions, adaptations and modifications, if any, as may be specified in the Order,

    (a) to the Isle of Man or any of the Channel Islands,

    (b) to Newfoundland or any colony,

    (c) to any British protectorate,

    (d) to any territory in respect of which a mandate on behalf of the League of Nations has been accepted by His Majesty, and is being exercised by His Majesty's Government in the United Kingdom, and

(e) (to the extent of His Majesty's jurisdiction therein) to any other country or territory being a foreign country or territory in which for the time being His Majesty has jurisdiction;

and, in particular, but without prejudice to the generality of the preceding provisions of this section, such an Order in Council may direct that any such authority as may be specified in the Order shall be substituted for His Majesty in Council as the authority empowered to make Defence Regulations for the country or territory in respect of which the Order is made.

(2) His Majesty may by Order in Council make, or authorise the making of, provision whereby persons offending against any Defence Regulations may be apprehended, tried and punished in the United Kingdom, or any of the countries or territories specified in the preceding subsection, whether section one of this Act extends to that country or territory or not.

5. (1) If and so far as the provisions of any Act for purposes of defence passed by the Parliament of the Commonwealth of Australia or by the Parliament of the Dominion of New Zealand purport to have extra-territorial operation as respects —

(a) ships or aircraft registered in the said Commonwealth or Dominion, or

(b) the employment of persons in relation to British ships or aircraft by owners, managers or charterers of such ships or aircraft who are persons resident in the said Commonwealth or Dominion or corporations incorporated under the law of the said Commonwealth or Dominion or any part thereof,

the said provisions shall be deemed to have such operation.

(2) No law made for purposes of defence by the Indian Legislature or the Federal Legislature of India or by the Legislature of Burma shall, on the ground that it would have extra-territorial operation, be deemed to be invalid in so far as it makes provision whereby any owner, manager or charterer of a British ship or aircraft who is a person resident in India or Burma or a corporation incorporated under the law of India or Burma or any part thereof, is subjected to restrictions in respect of the employment of persons in relation to the ship or aircraft.

Nothing in this subsection shall be taken to prejudice the effect of section ninety-nine of the Government of India Act 1935, or section thirty-three of the Government of Burma Act, 1935.

(3) If and so far as the provisions of any law for purposes of defence made by the Legislature of Southern Rhodesia purport to have extra-territorial operation as respects

(a) aircraft registered in Southern Rhodesia, or

(b) the employment of persons in relation to British aircraft by owners, managers or charterers of such aircraft who are persons resident in Southern Rhodesia or corporations incorporated under the law of Southern Rhodesia,

the said provisions shall be deemed to have such operation.

6. (1) If, as respects any proceedings before a court (whether instituted before or after the commencement of this Act), the court is satisfied that it is expedient,

in the interests of the public safety or the defence of the realm so to do, the court

(a) may give directions that, throughout, or during any part of, the proceedings, such persons or classes of persons as the court may determine shall be excluded;

(b) may give directions prohibiting or restricting the disclosure of information with respect to the proceedings.

The powers conferred by this subsection shall be in addition to, and not in derogation of, any other powers which a court may have to give such directions as aforesaid.

(2) If any person contravenes any directions given by a court under the preceding subsection, then, without prejudice to the law relating to contempt of court, he shall be liable, on summary conviction, to imprisonment for a term not exceeding three months or to a fine not exceeding one hundred pounds or to both such imprisonment and such fine, or, on conviction on indictment, to imprisonment for a term not exceeding two years or to a fine not exceeding five hundred pounds or to both such imprisonment and such fine.

(3) The operation of subsection (4) of section eight of the Official Secrets Act, 1920, shall be suspended during the continuance in force of this Act.

7. Every document purporting to be an instrument made or issued by any Minister or other authority or person in pursuance of any provision contained in, or having effect under, Defence Regulations, and to be signed by or on behalf of the said Minister, authority or person shall be received in evidence, and shall, until the contrary is proved, be deemed to be an instrument made or issued by that Minister, authority or person; and *prima facie* evidence of any such instrument as aforesaid may, in any legal proceedings (including arbitrations), be given by the production of a document purporting to be certified to be a true copy of the instrument by, or on behalf of, the Minister or other authority or person having power to make or issue the instrument.

8. (1) Every Order in Council containing Defence Regulations shall be laid before Parliament as soon as may be after it is made; but, notwithstanding anything in subsection (4) of section one of the Rules Publication Act, 1893, such an Order shall be deemed not to be a statutory rule to which that section applies.

(2) If either House of Parliament, within the next twenty-eight days on which that House has sat after such an Order in Council as aforesaid is laid before it, resolves that the Order be annulled, the Order shall thereupon cease to have effect except as respects things previously done or omitted to be done, without prejudice, however, to the making of a new Order.

(3) Any power conferred by the preceding provisions of this Act to make an Order in Council shall be constructed as including a power to vary or revoke the Order.

9. The powers conferred by or under this Act shall be in addition to, and not in derogation of, the powers exercisable by virtue of the prerogative of the Crown.

10. (1) In this Act the expression " Dominion " means any Dominion within the meaning of the Statute of Westminster, 1931, except Newfoundland, and includes any territory administered by His Majesty's Government in such a Dominion.

(2) References in this Act to British aircraft shall be constructed as references to aircraft registered in any part of His Majesty's dominions, in any British protectorate or in any territory in respect of which a mandate on behalf of the League of Nations has been accepted by His Majesty and is being exercised by the Government of any part of His Majesty's dominions.

(3) For the avoidance of doubt it is hereby declared that any reference in this Act to Defence Regulations includes a reference to regulations made under any provision of this Act, as extended to any country or territory by an Order in Council under this Act, and that any reference in this Act to any country or territory includes a reference to the territorial waters, if any, adjacent to that country or territory.

11. (1) Subject to the provisions of this section, this Act shall continue in force for the period of one year beginning with the date of the passing of this Act, and shall then expire:

Provided that, if at any time while this Act is in force, an address is presented to His Majesty by each House of Parliament praying that this Act should be continued in force for a further period of one year from the time at which it would otherwise expire, His Majesty may by Order in Council direct that this Act shall continue in force for that further period.

(2) Notwithstanding anything in the preceding subsection, if His Majesty by Order in Council declares that the emergency that was the occasion of the passing of this Act has come to an end, this Act shall expire at the end of the day on which the Order is expressed to come into operation.

(3) The expiry of this Act shall not affect the operation thereof as respects things previously done or omitted to be done.

EMERGENCY POWERS (DEFENCE) ACT,
1940

An Act to extend the powers which may be exercised by His Majesty under the Emergency Powers (Defence) Act, 1939. (22nd May 1940.)

WHEREAS by the Emergency Powers (Defence) Act, 1939, His Majesty was enabled to exercise certain powers for the purpose of meeting the emergency existing at the date of the passing of that Act:

And whereas by reason of the development of hostilities since that date it has become necessary to extend the said powers in order to secure that the whole resources of the community may be rendered immediately available when required for purposes connected with the defence of the Realm:

Now therefore be it enacted by the King's most Excellent Majesty, by and with the advice and consent of the Lords Spiritual and Temporal, and Commons, in this present Parliament assembled, and by the authority of the same, as follows:

490

APPENDIX

1. (1) The powers conferred on His Majesty by the Emergency Powers (Defence) Act, 1939, (hereinafter referred to as the " principal Act ") shall, notwithstanding anything in that Act, include power by Order-in-Council to make such Defense Regulations making provision for requiring persons to place themselves, their services, and their property at the disposal of His Majesty, as appear to him to be necessary or expedient for securing the public safety, the defence of the Realm, the maintenance of public order, or the efficient prosecution of any war in which His Majesty may be engaged, or for maintaining supplies or services essential to the life of the community.

(2) In paragraph (d) of subsection (2) of section one of the principal Act and in subsection (4) of that section the expression " enactment " shall mean any enactment passed before the commencement of this Act.

(3) Subsection (1) of section eleven of the principal Act (which relates to the duration of that Act) shall have effect as if for the words " one year," where those words first occur, there were substituted the words " two years."

2. This Act may be cited as the Emergency Powers (Defence) Act, 1940, and this Act and the Emergency Powers (Defence) Act, 1939, may be cited together as the Emergency Powers (Defence) Acts, 1939 and 1940.

EMERGENCY POWERS (DEFENCE) (NO. 2) ACT, 1940

An Act to remove doubts as to the extent of the powers which may be exercised by His Majesty under the Emergency Powers (Defence) Act, 1939. (1st August 1940.)

WHEREAS by the Emergency Powers (Defence) Act, 1939, His Majesty was enabled to exercise certain powers for the purpose of meeting the emergency existing at the date of the passing of that Act, but the said powers did not enable provision to be made for the trial by courts martial of persons not being subject to the Naval Discipline Act, to military law, or to the Air Force Act:

And whereas by reason of the development of hostilities since that date it has become expedient to remove doubts as to the extent of the said powers in order to secure that provision for the trial of such persons by special courts may be made where necessary:

Now, therefore, be it enacted by the King's most Excellent Majesty, by and with the advice and consent of the Lords Spiritual and Temporal, and Commons, in this present Parliament assembled, and by the authority of the same, as follows:

1. (1) It is hereby declared that the powers conferred on His Majesty by the Emergency Powers (Defence) Act, 1939 (hereinafter referred to as " the principal Act ") to make by Order in Council such Defence Regulations as appear to him to

be necessary or expedient for securing the public safety, the defence of the realm, the maintenance of public order, and the efficient prosecution of any war in which His Majesty may be engaged, include power to make provision for securing that, where by reason of recent or immediately apprehended enemy action the military situation is such as to require that criminal justice should be administered more speedily than would be practicable by the ordinary courts, persons, whether or not subject to the Naval Discipline Act, to military law, or to the Air Force Act, may, in such circumstances as may be provided by the Regulations, be tried by such special courts, not being courts martial, as may be so provided.

(2) After paragraph (a) of subsection (2) of section one of the principal Act there shall be inserted the following paragraph —

" (aa) make provision for the apprehension and punishment of offenders and for their trial by such courts, not being courts martial, and in accordance with such procedure as may be provided for by the Regulations, and for the proceedings of such courts being subject to such review as may be so provided for, so, however, that provision shall be made for such proceedings being reviewed by not less than three persons who hold or have held high judicial office, in all cases in which sentence of death is passed, and in such other circumstances as may be provided by the Regulations: "

and in the said paragraph (a) the words " for the apprehension " trial and punishment of persons offending against the Regulations " and " are hereby repealed.

Appendix II

THE ATLANTIC CHARTER

The President of the United States of America and the Prime Minister, Mr. Churchill, representing His Majesty's Government in the United Kingdom, being met together, deem it right to make known certain common principles in the national policies of their respective countries on which they base their hopes for a better future for the world.

FIRST, Their countries seek no aggrandizement, territorial or other;

SECOND, They desire to see no territorial changes that do not accord with the freely expressed wishes of the peoples concerned;

THIRD, They respect the right of all peoples to choose the form of government under which they will live; and they wish to see sovereign rights and self-government restored to those who have been forcibly deprived of them;

FOURTH, They will endeavour, with due respect for their existing obligations, to further the enjoyment by all States, great or small, victor or vanquished, of access, on equal terms, to the trade and to the raw materials of the world which are needed for their economic prosperity;

FIFTH, They desire to bring about the fullest collaboration between all nations in the economic field with the object of securing, for all, improved labor standards, economic advancement and social security;

SIXTH, After the final destruction of the Nazi tyranny, they hope to see established a peace which will afford to all nations the means of dwelling in safety within their own boundaries, and which will afford assurance that all the men in all the lands may live out their lives in freedom from fear and want;

SEVENTH, Such a peace should enable all men to traverse the high seas and oceans without hindrance.

EIGHTH, They believe that all of the nations of the world, for realistic as well as spiritual reasons, must come to the abandonment of the use of force. Since no future peace can be maintained if land, sea or air armaments continue to be employed by nations which threaten, or may threaten, aggression outside of their frontiers, they believe, pending the establishment of a wider and permanent system of general security, that the disarmament of such nations is essential. They will likewise aid and encourage all other practicable measures which will lighten for peace-loving peoples the crushing burden of armaments.

Franklin D. Roosevelt
Winston S. Churchill

Dated August 14, 1941.

DECLARATION BY UNITED NATIONS

A joint declaration by the United States of America, the United Kingdom of Great Britain and Northern Ireland, the Union of Soviet Socialist Republics, China, Australia, Belgium, Canada, Costa Rica, Cuba, Czechoslovakia, Dominican Republic, El Salvador, Greece, Guatemala, Haiti, Honduras, India, Luxembourg, Netherlands, New Zealand, Nicaragua, Norway, Panama, Poland, South Africa, Yugoslavia.

The governments signatory hereto,

Having subscribed to a common program of purpose and principles embodied in the joint declaration of the President of the United States of America and the Prime Minister of the United Kingdom of Great Britain and Northern Ireland dated August 14, 1941, known as the Atlantic Charter, being convinced that complete victory over their enemies is essential to defend life, liberty, independence and religious freedom, and to preserve human rights and justice in their own lands as well as in other lands, and that they are now engaged in a common struggle against savage and brutal forces seeking to subjugate the world, *Declare:*

1. Each government pledges itself to employ its full resources, military or economic, against those members of the tripartite pact and its adherents with which such government is at war.

2. Each government pledges itself to co-operate with the governments signatory hereto and not to make a separate armistice or peace with the enemies.

The foregoing declaration may be adhered to by other nations which are, or which may be, rendering material assistance and contributions in the struggle for victory over Hitlerism.

Done at Washington, January first, 1942.

TREATY OF ALLIANCE IN THE WAR AGAINST HITLERITE GERMANY AND HER ASSOCIATES IN EUROPE

and of Collaboration and Mutual Assistance Thereafter Concluded between the Union of Soviet Socialist Republics and the United Kingdom of Great Britain and Northern Ireland.

His Majesty the King of Great Britain, Ireland and British Dominions beyond the Seas, Emperor of India, and the Presidium of the Supreme Council of the Union of Soviet Socialist Republics;

Desiring to confirm the stipulations of the agreement between His Majesty's Government in the United Kingdom and the Government of the Union of Soviet

Socialist Republics for joint action in the war against Germany signed at Moscow, July 12, 1941, and to replace them by a formal treaty;

Desiring to contribute after the war to the maintenance of peace and to the prevention of further aggression by Germany or the States associated with her in acts of aggression in Europe;

Desiring, moreover, to give expression to their intention to collaborate closely with one another as well as with the other United Nations at the peace settlement and during the ensuing period of reconstruction on a basis of the principles enunciated in the declaration made Aug. 14, 1941, by the President of the United States of America and the Prime Minister of Great Britain, to which the Government of the Union of Soviet Socialist Republics has adhered;

Desiring finally to provide for mutual assistance in the event of attack upon either high contracting party by Germany or any of the States associated with her in acts of aggression in Europe;

Have decided to conclude a treaty for that purpose and have appointed as their plenipotentiaries;

His Majesty the King of Great Britain, Ireland and the British Dominions Beyond the Seas, Emperor of India, for the United Kingdom of Great Britain and Northern Ireland:

The Right Hon. Anthony Eden, M. P., His Majesty's Principal Secretary of State for Foreign Affairs;

The Presidium of the Supreme Council of the Union of Soviet Socialist Republics:

M. Vyacheslav Mikhailovich Molotov, People's Commissar for Foreign Affairs.

Who, having communicated their full powers, found in good and due form, have agreed as follows:

PART ONE

Article I

In virtue of the alliance established between the Union of Soviet Socialist Republics, the high contracting parties mutually undertake to afford one another military and other assistance and support of all kinds in the war against Germany and all those States which are associated with her in acts of aggression in Europe.

Article II

The high contracting parties undertake not to enter into any negotiations with the Hitlerite Government or any other government in Germany that does not clearly renounce all aggressive intentions, and not to negotiate or conclude, except by mutual consent, any armistice or peace treaty with Germany or any other State associated with her in acts of aggression in Europe.

PART TWO

Article III

1. The high contracting parties declare their desire to unite with other like-minded States in adopting proposals for common action to preserve peace and resist aggression in the post-war period.

2. Pending adoption of such proposals, they will after the termination of hostilities take all the measures in their power to render impossible a repetition of aggression and violation of the peace by Germany or any of the States associated with her in acts of aggression in Europe.

Article IV

Should one of the high contracting parties during the post-war period become involved in hostilities with Germany or any of the States mentioned in Article III, Section 2, in consequence of an attack by that State against that party, the other high contracting party will at once give to the contracting party so involved in hostilities all the military and other support and assistance in his power.

This article shall remain in force until the high contracting parties, by mutual agreement, shall recognize that it is superseded by the adoption of the proposals contemplated in Article III, Section 1. In default of the adoption of such proposals, it shall remain in force for a period of twenty years and thereafter until terminated by either high contracting party as provided in Article VIII.

Article V

The high contracting parties, having regard to the interests of the security of each of them, agree to work together in close and friendly collaboration after the reestablishment of peace for the organization of security and economic prosperity in Europe.

They will take into account the interests of the United Nations in these objects and they will act in accordance with the two principles of not seeking territorial aggrandizement for themselves and of non-interference in the internal affairs of other States.

Article VI

The high contracting parties agree to render one another all possible economic assistance after the war.

Article VII

Each high contracting party undertakes not to conclude any alliance and not to take part in any coalition directed against the other high contracting party.

Article VIII

The present treaty is subject to ratification in the shortest possible time and the instruments of ratification shall be exchanged in Moscow as soon as possible.

It comes into force immediately on the exchange of the instruments of ratification and shall thereupon replace the agreement between the Government of the Union of Soviet Socialist Republics and His Majesty's Government in the United Kingdom signed at Moscow July 12, 1941.

Part One of the present treaty shall remain in force until the re-establishment of peace between the high contracting parties and Germany and the powers associated with her in acts of aggression in Europe.

Part Two of the present treaty shall remain in force for a period of twenty years. Thereafter, unless twelve months' notice has been given by either party to terminate the treaty at the end of the said period of twenty years, it shall continue in force until twelve months after either high contracting party shall have given notice to the other in writing of his intention to terminate it.

In witness whereof the above-named plenipotentiaries have signed the present treaty and have affixed thereto their seals.

Done in duplicate in London on the twenty-sixth day of May, 1942, in the English and Russian languages, both texts being equally authentic.

Anthony Eden
V. Molotov

Appendix III

☼

AGREEMENT BETWEEN THE GOVERNMENTS OF THE UNITED STATES OF AMERICA AND OF THE UNITED KINGDOM OF GREAT BRITAIN AND NORTHERN IRELAND

on the Principles Applying to Mutual Aid in the Prosecution of the War Against Aggression, Authorized and Provided for by the Act of March 11, 1941.

WHEREAS the Governments of the United States of America and the United Kingdom of Great Britain and Northern Ireland declare that they are engaged in a cooperative undertaking, together with every other nation or people of like mind, to the end of laying the bases of a just and enduring world peace securing order under law to themselves and all nations;

And whereas the President of the United States of America has determined, pursuant to the Act of Congress of March 11, 1941, that the defense of the United Kingdom against aggression is vital to the defense of the United States of America;

And whereas the United States of America has extended and is continuing to extend to the United Kingdom aid in resisting aggression;

And whereas it is expedient that the final determination of the terms and conditions upon which the Government of the United Kingdom receives such aid and of the benefits to be received by the United States of America in return therefor should be deferred until the extent of the defense aid is known and until the progress of events makes clearer the final terms and conditions and benefits which will be in the mutual interest of the United States of America and the United Kingdom and will promote the establishment and maintenance of world peace;

And whereas the Governments of the United States of America and the United Kingdom are mutually desirous of concluding now a preliminary agreement in regard to the provision of defense aid and in regard to certain considerations which shall be taken into account in determining such terms and conditions and the making of such an agreement has been in all respects duly authorized, and all acts, conditions and formalities which it may have been necessary to perform, fulfill or execute prior to the making of such an agreement in conformity with the laws either of the United States of America or of the United Kingdom have been performed, fulfilled or executed as required;

The undersigned, being duly authorized by their respective Governments for that purpose, have agreed as follows:

497

Article I

This Government of the United States of America will continue to supply the Government of the United Kingdom with such defense articles, defense services, and defense information as the President shall authorize to be transferred or provided.

Article II

The Government of the United Kingdom will continue to contribute to the defense of the United States of America and the strengthening thereof and will provide such articles, services, facilities or information as it may be in a position to supply.

Article III

The Government of the United Kingdom will not without the consent of the President of the United States of America transfer title to, or possession of, any defense article or defense information transferred to it under the Act or permit the use thereof by anyone not an officer, employee, or agent of the Government of the United Kingdom.

Article IV

If, as a result of the transfer to the Government of the United Kingdom of any defense article or defense information, it becomes necessary for that Government to take any action or make any payment in order fully to protect any of the rights of a citizen of the United States of America who has patent rights in and to any such defense article or information, the Government of the United Kingdom will take such action or make such payment when requested to do so by the President of the United States of America.

Article V

The Government of the United Kingdom will return to the United States of America at the end of the present emergency, as determined by the President, such defense articles transferred under this Agreement as shall not have been destroyed, lost or consumed and as shall be determined by the President to be useful in the defense of the United States of America or of the Western Hemisphere or to be otherwise of use to the United States of America.

Article VI

In the final determination of the benefits to be provided to the United States of America by the Government of the United Kingdom full cognizance shall be taken of all property, services, information, facilities, or other benefits or considerations provided by the Government of the United Kingdom subsequent to March 11, 1941, and accepted or acknowledged by the President on behalf of the United States of America.

Article VII

In the final determination of the benefits to be provided to the United States of America by the Government of the United Kingdom in return for aid furnished under the Act of Congress of March 11, 1941, the terms and conditions thereof shall be such as not to burden commerce between the two countries, but to promote mutually advantageous economic relations between them and the betterment of world-wide economic relations. To that end, they shall include provision for agreed action by the United States of America and the United Kingdom, open to participation by all other countries of like mind, directed to the expansion, by appropriate international and domestic measures, of production, employment, and the exchange and consumption of goods, which are the material foundations of the liberty and welfare of all people; to the elimination of all forms of discriminatory treatment in international commerce, and to the reduction of tariffs and other trade barriers; and, in general, to the attainment of all the economic objectives set forth in the Joint Declaration made on August 12, 1941, by the President of the United States of America and the Prime Minister of the United Kingdom.

At an early convenient date, conversations shall be begun between the two Governments with a view to determining, in the light of governing economic conditions, the best means of attaining the above-stated objectives by their own agreed action and of seeking the agreed action of other like-minded Governments.

Article VIII

This Agreement shall take effect as from this day's date. It shall continue in force until a date to be agreed upon by the two Governments.

Signed and sealed at Washington in duplicate this 23ª day of February 1942.

For the Government of the United States of America:

Sumner Welles,
Acting Secretary of State of the
United States of America.

For the Government of the United Kingdom
of Great Britain and Northern Ireland:

Halifax
His Majesty's Ambassador Extraordinary
and Plenipotentiary at Washington

Appendix IV

MEMORANDUM OF AGREEMENT REGARDING INTERNATIONAL TRADE IN WHEAT

1. Officials of Argentina, Australia, Canada and the United States, wheat exporting countries, and of the United Kingdom, a wheat importing country, met in Washington on July 10, 1941 to resume the wheat discussions which were interrupted in London by the outbreak of war in September 1939 and to consider what steps might be taken towards a solution of the international wheat problem.

2. The discussions at Washington, which extended over a period of many months, have made it clear that a satisfactory solution of the problem requires an international wheat agreement and that such an agreement requires a conference of the nations willing to participate which have a substantial interest in international trade in wheat. It was also recognized that pending the holding of such a conference the situation should not be allowed to deteriorate. The Washington Wheat Meeting has recorded the results of its deliberations in the attached Draft Convention in order to facilitate further international consideration of the subject at such time as may be possible and to provide a basis for such interim measures as may be found necessary.

3. The Washington Wheat Meeting has recognized that it is impracticable to convene at the present time the international wheat conference referred to above. Accordingly, the five countries present at that Meeting have agreed that the United States, so soon as after consultation with other countries it deems the time propitious, should convene a wheat conference of the nations having a substantial interest in international trade in wheat which are willing to participate, and that the Draft Convention above mentioned should be submitted to that conference for consideration.

4. In the meantime there should be no delay in the provision of wheat for relief in war-stricken and other necessitous areas so soon as in the view of the five countries circumstances permit. Likewise it is imperative that the absence of control measures over the accumulation of stocks in the four countries now producing large quantities of wheat for markets no longer available should not create insoluble problems for a future conference. Accordingly, the five countries have agreed to regard as in effect among themselves, pending the conclusions of the conference

referred to above, those arrangements described in the attached Draft Convention which are necessary to the administration and distribution of the relief pool of wheat and to the control of production of wheat other than those involving the control of exports.

5. If the conference contemplated above shall have met and concluded an agreement prior to the cessation of hostilities, no further action will be needed by the countries represented at the Washington Meeting. However, if this is not the case, it will be necessary, in order to prevent disorganization and confusion in international trade in wheat, to institute temporary controls pending the conclusions of the conference. Accordingly the five countries agree that in the period following the cessation of hostilities and pending the conclusion of a wheat agreement at the conference referred to the arrangements described in the attached Draft Convention which relate to the control of production, stocks and exports of wheat and to the administration thereof will be brought into effect among themselves. Those arrangements will come into effect on such date as may be unanimously agreed. Announcement of that date will be made within six months after the cessation of hostilities.

6. Pending the conclusions of the conference contemplated above, the five countries, on the cessation of hostilities or such earlier date as they may agree, will regard as in effect among themselves the arrangements described in the attached Draft Convention for the control of the prices of wheat. The determination of prices required to be made in accordance with those arrangements will be made by unanimous consent. If no determination of prices has been made on the cessation of hostilities, the five countries will, pending such determination but for a period not exceeding six months, maintain as the export price of wheat the last price negotiated by the United Kingdom for a bulk purchase of wheat from the principal country of supply; equivalent f.o.b. prices will be calculated for wheats of the other exporting countries and will be adjusted from time to time to meet substantial changes in freight and exchange rates.

7. In taking any decisions under this Memorandum and the arrangements of the Draft Convention which it brings into operation each of the five countries will have one vote, and a two-thirds majority will be required for decision except as otherwise provided herein.

8. The provisions of this Memorandum will be superseded by any agreement reached at the proposed wheat conference or by any arrangements which the five countries and other interested countries may make to deal with the period pending such a conference. In any event they are to terminate two years from the cessation of hostilities.

ARGENTINA
AUSTRALIA
CANADA
THE UNITED KINGDOM
THE UNITED STATES

Washington,
April 22, 1942.

Appendix V

STATEMENT OF POLICY IN REGARD TO AUSTRALIAN SURPLUSES[1]

His Majesty's Governments in the United Kingdom and the Commonwealth of Australia, in consultation, have agreed upon the following statement of principles for dealing, on a basis of co-operation, with the surplus produce of the Commonwealth for the period of the war.

His Majesty's Government in the United Kingdom fully recognise the grave difficulties created for Australian industries by the shortage of shipping. They are anxious to continue taking all the Australian produce that can be shipped. They also appreciate the serious effect upon Australia's economic and financial structure which these difficulties are causing. With a view to minimizing these effects and preventing the impairment of Australia's war effort, the United Kingdom Government are prepared to join with the Commonwealth Government in co-operative arrangements to ease the burden falling on Australia during the war, framed on lines that will not prejudice the post-war position.

The Governments have agreed that the following principles should be applied as a basis for such co-operation:

1. The United Kingdom Government to purchase the Australian produce that can be shipped and to pay for such produce at the price and upon such terms and conditions as are from time to time agreed with the Ministry of Food.
2. The Australian industries to make every effort to adapt their production to shipping possibilities, e.g., deboning, canning or pressing meat.
3. Alternative markets to be developed wherever possible.
4. Reserve stocks of storable foodstuffs to be created up to certain quantities to be agreed.
5. The quantities to be stored to be determined in relation
   (a) to probable demand during or after the war;
   (b) to the importance of the industry to Australia.
6. The financial burden of acquiring and holding these reserve stocks, pending their disposal, to be shared equally between the two Governments.
7. The payments to be made for produce acquired for the reserve stocks to be

[1] Cmd. 6287, 1941.

agreed between the two Governments. While it will be necessary to take due account of such matters as costs of storage, depreciation, etc., it is intended that the payments shall be fixed on such a basis as will so far as practicable achieve the objective of keeping the industry operating efficiently, avoiding the creation of unmanageable surpluses.

8. The detailed application of the above principles to be referred to competent representatives from the two countries.

The Commonwealth Government will be ready to collaborate in any discussions which may be convened within the British Commonwealth or internationally to consider marketing or related problems.

Appendix VI

✿

CHRONOLOGICAL EXCERPTS FROM SPEECHES AND DOCUMENTS ILLUSTRATING THE INDIAN POLITICAL CRISIS FROM APRIL TO OCTOBER, 1942

April 28. — Sir Stafford Cripps in describing the course of his mission in the House of Commons:

"But do not let the House or the people of this country imagine that all the results of the War Cabinet's action and my mission are on the debit side . . . the content of the scheme has put beyond all possibility of doubt or question that we desire to give India self-government at the earliest practicable moment and that we wish her to determine for herself the form which that government shall take . . . no responsible Indian leader has challenged our sincerity upon that point. I think it would be accurate to say that this is the first time that such an assertion could be truly made, and it is a most important and significant fact for our future relationships. . . .

". . . It is in fact the past exercising its influence upon all parties that has proved too strong for us, and we must now leave the leaven of better understanding to work quietly toward an ultimate and satisfactory solution of the political problem. . . ." [1]

April 30. — Resignation from Working Committee of All-India Congress Party of Chakravarthi Rajagopalachari, former Premier of Madras, to work for agreement between the Moslem League and the Congress Party on the basis of the acceptance of "Pakistan."

May 2. — Resolution passed by Committee of All-India Congress Party at Allahabad meeting:

"The present crisis, as well as the experience of negotiations with Sir Stafford Cripps, make it impossible for Congress to consider any schemes or proposals which retain even a partial measure of British control and authority in India. . . . It is on the basis of independence alone that India can deal with Britain or other nations.

"The committee repudiates the idea that freedom can come to India through interference or invasion by any foreign nation. . . . In case invasion

---

[1] As reported in *The Times,* London, April 29, 1942.

504

takes place, it must be resisted. Such resistance can only take the form of non-violent non-cooperation. . . ." [2]

July 2. — Appointment of Indian members of British War Cabinet and Pacific War Council and increase of Viceroy's Council to fifteen members.

July 14. — Resolution passed by Working Committee of All-India Congress Party at Wardha meeting:

"Events . . . confirm the opinion of Congressmen that British rule in India must end immediately, not merely because foreign domination, even at its best, is evil in itself and a continuing injury to the subject people, but because India in bondage can play no effective part in defending herself and in affecting the fortunes of war that are desolating humanity. . . .

" This frustration (Cripps negotiations) resulted in a rapid and widespread increase of ill-will against Britain, and a growing satisfaction at the success of Japanese arms.

" The Working Committee view this development with grave apprehension, as this, unless checked, will inevitably lead to the passive acceptance of aggression. The Committee hold that all aggression must be resisted. . . .

" Congress representatives have tried their utmost to bring about a solution of the communal tangle. But this is made impossible by the presence of a foreign Power, and only after ending foreign domination and intervention can . . . the people of India, belonging to all groups and parties, face India's problems and solve them on a mutually agreed basis.

" The present political parties, formed chiefly with a view to attracting the attention of and influencing British power, will then probably cease to function. . . .

" On the withdrawal of British rule from India responsible men and women of the country will come together to form a provisional Government, representative of all important sections of the people of India, which will later evolve a scheme whereby a constituent Assembly can be convened in order to prepare a constitution for the Government of India acceptable to all sections of the people.

" The representatives of free India and Great Britain will confer together for the adjustment of future relations and for the cooperation of the two countries as allies for a common cause in meeting aggression. . . .

" Congress is . . . agreeable to the stationing of the armed forces of the allies in India should they so desire in order to ward off and resist Japanese or other aggression and to protect and help China.

" The proposal for the withdrawal of British power from India was never intended to mean the physical withdrawal of all Britons from India, and certainly not those who would make India their home and live there as citizens and as equals with others. If such a withdrawal takes place with good will, it would result in establishing a stable provisional Government in India, and cooperation between this Government and the United Nations in resisting aggression and helping China. . . .

---

[2] As reported in *The Times*, London, May 4, 1942.

"Should . . . this appeal fail . . . Congress will then reluctantly be compelled to utilize all the non-violent strength it has gathered since 1920, when it adopted non-violence as part of its policy. . . . Such a widespread struggle would inevitably be under the leadership of Mr. Ghandi. . . ." [3]

Resolution referred to meeting of Committee of All-India Congress Party in August.

July 19. — Statement by Pandit Nehru that Congress Party demands not limited to British India.

July 20 — August 4. — Opposition to Wardha resolution expressed by United Provinces Liberal Federation, All-India Scheduled Castes Conference, Radical Democratic Party, Hindu Mahasabha, and Nationalist League (member of National Democratic Union). Opinion of the *Hindu* (Madras) and the *Indian Social Reformer* that Congress Party should have waited for assured support of whole country and for agreement with Moslem community.

July 30. — Statement by Mr. L. S. Amery, Secretary of State for India, in House of Commons in reply to question concerning future protection of British commercial interests in India:

"His Majesty's Government made it clear in connection with the recent offer that a guarantee of special protection for British commercial interests in India would not be a condition for the acceptance of whatever constitution India might evolve after the war, and that any such provisions would more properly be a matter for negotiation with the future Government of India." [4]

Statement by M. A. Jinnah, President of the Moslem League:

"The program of Gandhi and his Hindu Congress has been to blackmail the British and coerce them into establishing a system of government and transfer of power which would establish a Hindu Raj immediately under the aegis of a British bayonet, thereby throwing the Moslems and other minorities and interests at the mercy of the Congress Raj. . . . Gandhi asked for an immediate declaration of independence and freedom for India, with the right for the people to frame their own constitution by a constituent assembly elected by adult franchise — which meant a 75 percent Hindu majority. . . . In 1939 Gandhi asked the Congress Ministries to resign, thereby making the working of a constitution impossible. Then he set upon another method based on the same line of coercion. Under the guise and slogan of ' freedom of speech,' he launched his individual civil disobedience after the August declaration of 1940. . . .

"It was the policy of the British Government that clearly encouraged Gandhi. The British Government had concentrated its attention on the Congress view. . . .

"It was quite obvious for two reasons the British Government dare not surrender to Gandhi's demands. Firstly, because it would be going against the solemn resolve of 100,000,000 Moslems that they stand for ' Pakistan ' and will never submit to a Hindu Raj or any unitary central government with a

[3] As reported in *The Times*, London, July 16, 1942.
[4] As reported in *The Times*, London, July 31, 1942.

Hindu majority; and secondly, it would be the grossest breach of faith with the Moslems if the British Government disregarded all its declarations that it could not contemplate the transfer of its present responsibilities to any system of government whose authority was directly denied by large and powerful elements of India's national life.

"Gandhi cannot believe that immediately the British withdraw, the representatives of various parties and interests would at once agree and set up a provisional government for this subcontinent. What is there to prevent them from agreeing now? . . .

"Moslems of India have not the slightest objection to the British withdrawing from India today. But what Moslems fear is that in their dire distress and shaken condition the British may commit the blunder of appeasing the Congress at the cost of Moslem and other minorities. . . ." [4a]

August 4 — Appeal by Sir Tej Bahadur Sapru (Liberal) to leaders of all parties to call joint conference to avert civil disobedience.

Publication by Government of India after raid on Congress Party headquarters of text of resolution originally proposed by Gandhi at Allahabad meeting of Working Committee of Party:

"India's participation in the war has not been with the consent of the representatives of the Indian people. It was purely a British act. If India were freed her first step would probably be to negotiate with Japan. The Congress is of opinion that if the British withdrew from India, India would be able to defend herself in the event of Japanese or any aggressor attacking India.

". . . The Princes need have no fear from unarmed India.

"The question of majority and minority is a creation of the British Government, and would disappear on their withdrawal. . . .

"This committee desires to assure the Japanese Government and people that India bears no enmity either towards Japan or towards any other nation. India only desires freedom from all alien domination. But in this fight for freedom the committee is of opinion that India, while welcoming universal sympathy, does not stand in need of foreign military aid . . . the committee hopes that Japan will not have any designs on India. But if Japan attacks India and Britain makes no response to its appeal the committee would expect all those who look to Congress for guidance to offer complete non-violent non-cooperation to the Japanese forces and not render any assistance to them. . . .

". . . At present our non-cooperation with the British Government is limited. Were we to offer them complete non-cooperation when they are actually fighting it would be tantamount to placing our country deliberately in Japanese hands. Therefore not to put any obstacle in the way of the British forces will often be the only way of demonstrating our non-cooperation with the Japanese. Neither may we assist the British in any active manner. . . .

"It is not necessary for the committee to make a clear declaration in regard to the scorched earth policy . . . it can never be the Congress policy to destroy what belongs to or is of use to the masses.

[4a] As reported by Reuter.

". . . Whether the British remain or not it is our duty always to wipe out unemployment, to bridge the gulf between rich and poor, to banish communal strife, to exorcise the demon of untouchability, to reform dacoits and save the people from them. If crores of people do not take a living interest in this nation-building work, freedom must remain a dream and unattainable by either non-violence or violence.

" The All-India Congress Committee is of opinion that it is harmful to India's interests and dangerous to the cause of India's freedom to introduce foreign soldiers in India. . . .

". . . Japan's quarrel is not with India. She is warring against the British Empire." [5]

August 5. — Statement by Chakravarthi Rajagopalachari:

". . . the only way to save India is to form an interim popular government at once. All suspicions and legalities should be scrapped and full power transferred to such an interim government, subject only to the maintenance of the present war policy and international relations.

". . . I am sure the statesmen of Britain have knowledge of the present feeling of the people of India and also of the peril inherent in the situation. They have imagination and experience enough to see whom the people would trust and whom they would not. . . ." [6]

August 7. — Introduction of civil disobedience resolution to meeting of Committee of Congress Party at Bombay. Statement by Maulana Azad, president of the party:

". . . It is absurd to suggest that we want anarchy and the complete absence of government in the country. What we want is a change of administration. It is also wrong to say that we want the British and American armies to leave India. . . . The slogan " Quit India " means nothing more and nothing less than the complete transfer of power to Indian hands. . . ." [7]

Statement by Gandhi:

". . . We shall get our freedom by fighting. It cannot fall from the skies. I know full well that the British will have to give us our freedom when we have made sufficient sacrifices and proved our strength. . . .

" There is one principle in the fight which you must adopt. Never believe — as I have never believed — that the British are going to fail. . . .

" Sardar Patel is reported to have said that the (civil disobedience) campaign may be over in a week. . . . If it ends in a week it would be a miracle. . . .

" Once independence is obtained, whoever is capable of taking power will do so. . . ." [8]

Order by Government of India prohibiting the closing of food shops and restaurants between specified hours.

[5] As reported in *The Times,* London, August 5, 1942.
[6] As reported in *The Times,* London, August 6, 1942.
[7] As reported in *The Times,* London, August 8, 1942.
[8] Ibid.

August 8. — Resolution adopted by Committee of Congress Party:

". . . The committee has viewed with dismay the deterioration in the situation on the Russian and Chinese fronts. . . . This increasing peril makes it incumbent on all those who strive for freedom and who sympathize with the victims of aggression to examine the foundations of the policy so far pursued by the allied nations which have led to repeated and disastrous failures. . . .

"A free India will assure this success (of freedom and democracy) by throwing all her great resources into the struggle for freedom and against the aggression of Nazism, Fascism, and Imperialism. This will not only affect materially the fortunes of the war but bring all subject and oppressed humanity to the side of the United Nations. . . .

". . . Only the glow of freedom now can release that energy and enthusiasm in millions of people which will immediately transform the nature of the war. The All-India Congress Committee therefore repeats with all emphasis its demand for the withdrawal of British power from India.

" On the declaration of India's independence, a provisional Government will be formed, and free India will become the ally of the United Nations. . . . A provisional Government can only be formed by the cooperation of the principal parties and groups in the country. . . .

" Its primary functions must be to defend India and resist aggression with all the armed as well as the non-violent forces at its command, together with its allied Powers, and to promote the well-being and progress of workers in the fields and factories and elsewhere to whom essentially all power and authority must belong.

" The provisional Government will evolve a scheme for a constituent assembly. . . . This constitution, according to the Congress view, should be a federal one with the largest measure of autonomy for federating units, and with residuary powers vesting in these units.

". . . Freedom for India must be a symbol of, and prelude to, the freedom of all other Asiatic nations under foreign domination.

" Burma, Malaya, Indo-China, the Dutch East Indies, Persia, and Iraq must also attain their complete freedom. It must be clearly understood that such of these countries as are under Japanese control now, must not subsequently be placed under the rule or control of any other colonial Power.

". . . the committee is of opinion that the future peace and security and ordered progress of the world demand a world federation of free nations. . . .

" In view of the war, however, a federation to begin with must inevitably be confined to the United Nations. . . .

" The earnest appeal by the Working Committee to Great Britain and the United Nations has so far met with no response. . . .

" But the committee feels that it is no longer justified in holding the nation back from endeavoring to assert its will against the imperialist and authoritarian Government which dominates it. . . . The committee resolves therefore to sanction . . . the starting of a mass struggle on non-violent lines on the widest possible scale. . . .

" Such a struggle must inevitably be under the leadership of Gandhi, and the committee requests him to take the lead and guide the nation in the steps to be taken. . . ." [9]

Statement by Gandhi:

" We shall make every effort to see the Viceroy before starting the movement." [10]

Statement by Governor-General of India in Council:

". . . The Governor-General in Council has been aware . . . for some days past of the dangerous preparations by the Congress Party for unlawful, and in some cases violent, activities directed, among other things, to interruption of communications and public utility services, the organization of strikes, tampering with the loyalty of Government servants, and interference with defence measures, including recruitment.

". . . To a challenge such as the present there can be only one answer. The Government of India would regard it as wholly incompatible with their responsibilities to the people of India, and their obligations to the allies, that a demand should be discussed the acceptance of which would plunge India into confusion and anarchy internally and would paralyse her effort in the common cause of human freedom. . . .

". . . The Congress Party is not India's mouthpiece, yet, in the interests of securing their own dominance, and in pursuit of a totalitarian policy, its leaders have consistently impeded efforts made to bring India to full nationhood. But for the resistance of the Congress Party to constructive endeavors, India might even now be enjoying self-government.

". . . They (the Government of India) urge the people of India to unite with them in resistance to the present challenge of a party. . . ." [11]

Orders by Government (1) prohibiting publication of " factual news " about civil disobedience movement not obtained from official or authorized sources and (2) empowering provincial governments to supersede local authorities.

August 9. — Arrest of Gandhi and all members of Working Committee of Congress Party who took part in the Bombay meeting. Committee of Congress Party and provincial committees declared illegal associations by Government.

, Broadcast statement by Mr. L. S. Amery, Secretary of State for India:

". . . What we are really concerned with is not a demand which no one can take seriously, but the action which Congress has resolved upon. . . .

" There was abundant ground for punitive action, but the Government of India have confined themselves to action which is essentially preventive. What they have in fact done is to disconnect Mr. Gandhi and his confederates, to cut out the fuse leading from the arch-saboteurs to all the inflammable and explosive material which they hoped to set alight all over India.

[9] As reported in *The Times,* London, August 7, 1942.
[10] As reported in *The New York Times,* August 9, 1942.
[11] As reported in *The Times,* London, August 10, 1942.

"By their prompt and resolute action the Government of India have saved India and the allied cause from a grave disaster. . . ."[12]

Beginning of rioting.

August 19. — Appeal by president of Hindu Mahasabha for:

"(1) Immediate declaration by the British Parliament that India is raised to the position of a completely free and equal partnership — as equal and free as Britain herself in the Commonwealth. (2) During wartime this declaration of India's independence should be implemented by complete Indianization of the Viceroy's Executive Council, the decisions of which should be binding on the Viceroy; the only exceptions being those of military and strategical matters and the suppression of any internal anarchy. (3) Indianization of the Army as rapidly as possible. (4) Provincial governors to have executive councils similar to that of the Viceroy. (5) A conference to be called immediately at the end of the war to frame a national constitution for India and to give full effect to the declaration of independence."[13]

August 20. — Resolution passed by Working Committee of Moslem League making acceptance of Pakistan the condition of participation in any national government.

August 21. — Resignation from Viceroy's Council of Sir Ramaswami Aiyar in order to oppose with complete freedom the Congress Party's "mass action that if unchecked was bound to hamper India's progress and war effort and those of the Indian States in whose well-being and fortune he was vitally interested."[14]

August 24. — Statement by Sir Stafford Cripps for *New York Times:*

". . . The action against Mr. Gandhi and his followers was a decision of the Government of India, supported fully by, but not proposed or initiated by, the British Government."[15]

Statement by Sir Firoz Khan Noon, Defense Member of Viceroy's Council at Aligarh Moslem University:

". . . During his term of office the Viceroy had not on a single occasion overruled him or rejected his advice. . . . On many occasions controversial questions had come before the Executive Council. In no case had the Viceroy vetoed the decision of the majority. . . .

"The political unity of India was the great aim which every Indian ought to have in view. . . . His suggestions were that British India should be divided into five Dominions consisting of 1. Bengal and Assam; 2. the Central Provinces, the United Provinces, and Bihar; 3. Madras; 4. Bombay; and 5. the Punjab, Baluchistan, Sind, and the North-West Frontier.

". . . for certain matters central authority and united effort by the Dominions were essential. These were defense, customs, foreign relations, and

---

[12] Ibid.
[13] As reported in *The Times,* London, August 19, 1942.
[14] As reported in *The Times,* London, August 22, 1942.
[15] As reported in *The Times,* London, August 24, 1942.

currency. For the administration of these four subjects only there should be a central authority, consisting of delegates nominated by the five Dominion Governments. If at any time any Dominion were dissatisfied with the working of the central authority, it should be entitled to secede, but there should also be provision for the seceding Dominion to return to the centre when the point of difference was removed. . . ." [16]

September 12. — Statement by Mr. Churchill in the House of Commons:

". . . The broad principles of the declaration made by His Majesty's Government, which formed the basis of the Lord Privy Seal's mission to India, must be taken as representing the settled policy of the British Crown and Parliament. . . .

" The good offices of the Lord Privy Seal were rejected by the India Congress Party, but that does not end the matter. The Congress Party does not represent all India. It does not represent the majority of the people of India. It does not represent the Hindu masses. It is a political organization, part of a party machine sustained by certain manufacturing and financial interests. Outside that party, and fundamentally opposed to it, are 90,000,000 Moslems, who have their rights of self-expression, 50,000,000 depressed classes . . . and 95,000,000 subjects of the Indian Princes, to whom we are bound by treaty. In all there are 235,000,000 in these three groups out of a total of about 390,000,000 in India. This takes no account of large elements among the Hindus, Sikhs, and Christians who deplore the present policy of the Congress Party.

". . . The Congress Party has now abandoned, in many respects, the policy of non-violence Mr. Gandhi has inculcated in them. It has come into the open as a revolutionary movement designed to paralyse communications by rail and telegraph, and generally to promote disorder, the looting of shops, sporadic attacks on the Indian police, accompanied from time to time by revolting atrocities — the whole having the intention or, at any rate, the effect of hampering the defense of India against the Japanese invader. . . .

" It may well be that these activities of Congress have been aided by Japanese ' Fifth Column ' work on a widely extended scale and with special direction to the strategic points. . . .

" It is fortunate indeed that the Congress Party has no influence with the martial races on whom the defence of India, apart from the British forces, largely depends. Many of these are divided by unbridgable religious gulfs from Hindu Congress and would never consent to be ruled by them. Nor shall they ever be against their will so subjugated. . . .

". . . I may add that large reinforcements have reached India, and the number of white soldiers now in the country, although very small compared with its size and population, is larger than at any time in the British connection. I therefore feel entitled to report to the House that the situation in India at this moment gives no occasion for undue despondency or alarm." [17]

---

[16] As reported in *The Times*, London, August 27, 1942.
[17] As reported in *The Times*, London, September 11, 1942.

September 13. — Statement by M. A. Jinnah that " Congress Party's civil disobedience movement not merely a declaration of war against the British Government, but also a war against the Moslem League, which had not been consulted. . . . Mr. Churchill's reference to the Moslem League as opposing the Congress Party did not mean that the League supported the Government."

September 15. — Statement by Sir Reginald Maxwell, Home Member of Viceroy's Council, in Legislative Assembly:

" The extent of the damage caused and the extreme seriousness at one time of the situation in the whole of Bihar except the most southern districts and the eastern part of the United Provinces had perhaps not been generally appreciated. . . . A large part of the railway systems in this area was put out of action. For a considerable period Bengal was almost completely cut off from northern India, while communications with Madras were interrupted by damage done to the railways in that Presidency. . . .

" There were some aspects of the disturbances which in his view negatived the idea that they were spontaneous. Attacks on railways and communications had started simultaneously in various parts of India. Special implements were used. . . . There was evidence also that the saboteurs had technical knowledge . . . strategic importance of the areas affected and the objects of attack. . . . On the other hand, the ordinary characteristics of spontaneous disturbances were largely absent — looting was less than expected, hartals were not observed to the extent that seemed likely, and the selective nature of the acts of sabotage was brought into relief by the fact that there had been little or no sabotage of industrial plant or machinery. . . .

". . . The police had been through a very trying ordeal. They had been compelled on many occasions to fire on riotous mobs and gangs of saboteurs, and often in defense of their lives. Thirty-one policemen so far had been reported killed. . . . British and Indian troops had been called out in not less than 60 places, and on a number of occasions they stood by. . . ." [18]

His preliminary figures indicated that in $5\frac{1}{2}$ weeks of rioting 340 persons had been killed and 850 wounded by police, and 318 killed and 153 wounded by British Indian troops, and that 49 police, civil servants, and soldiers had been killed by mobs.[19]

September 16. — Statement by Sir T. B. Sapru (Liberal) and M. R. Jayaker (non-party group) urging attempt to form an Indian national government.

September 23. — Statement in Indian Council of State by the Leader of the House in reply to the question whether the Government of India were prepared to reopen negotiations for the formation of a composite Government:

" That was primarily a question for the Governor-General and the British Government, rather than for the Government of India. . . . Constitutional questions did not come within the purview of the Executive Council." [20]

---

[18] As reported in *The Times,* London, September 16, 1942.
[19] As reported in *The Times,* London, September 17, 1942.
[20] As reported in *The Times,* London, September 24, 1942.

September 28. — Allah Baksh, Premier of Sind (subsequently dismissed) and President of All-India Independent Moslem Conference renounced British title and honors.

October 9. — Statement by Mr. L. S. Amery, Secretary of State for India in the House of Commons:

". . . Indian nationalism, the desire to see India's destiny directed by Indian hands free from all external control, is not confined to any one party in India. It is shared by all. To that aim we in this country have solemnly pledged ourselves before India and before the world. In the name of his Majesty's Government I repeat that pledge today. . . .

". . . We have . . . come to the conclusion that no constitution imposed from without can meet the case. It is for those who have to live under the constitution to find the compromises and concessions which will enable them to work it. It is those who frame the constitution for themselves who will bring to it the good will without which it can never succeed. It is on that principle that his Majesty's Government based the draft declaration of policy which Sir S. Cripps took out to India to discuss with Indian political leaders. . . .

". . . The limitation of any interim Government to the framework of the existing constitution was in any case a necessity so long as the final responsibility for waging the war rested with his Majesty's Government, for it is upon the whole machinery of Government, and not merely upon the Commander-in-Chief's department, that India's war effort depends. . . .

" To understand why the Congress Party executive under Mr. Gandhi's influence was determined to wreck any settlement however generous to India, I must ask the House to go back for a moment to the whole course of Congress policy in recent years. Originally a constitutional party with a programme of evolution towards complete self-government, Congress had in the last generation, and especially since it had come under Mr. Gandhi's autocratic influence, become a party of revolution. . . .

" What I wish to make clear to the House is that . . . this rebellion, to use Gandhi's own words . . . was deliberately resolved upon in order to defeat the generous policy put forward by his Majesty's Government. . . .

" It is idle to suggest that anything could possibly have resulted from negotiations after the passing of the All-India Congress Committee's resolution except the more complete organization of plans for dislocating communications and making rebellion effective. . . .

" The firmness of the Government, loyally supported by the civil service, the police, and when it became necessary, the army, has broken the back of the movement. . . . The forces of law and order will for months to come have to be unceasingly vigilant, and will need all the support that the Government of India and this House can give them. . . .

" For all this tragic business the responsibility and the whole responsibility must rest with Mr. Gandhi and the Congress leaders. . . .

". . . So far as Congress is concerned, its leaders have by their action put themselves out of court. There can be no question of the Government of India entering upon negotiations with them or allowing others to do so so long as there is any danger of a recrudescence of the troubles for which they have been responsible, or until they have made it clear to the authorities that they have abandoned the whole policy of securing control of India by illegal and revolutionary methods and are prepared to come to an agreed settlement with the rest of their fellow-countrymen. . . ." [21]

October 21. — Statement to the press by Chakravarthi Rajagopalachari:

". . . The Viceroy should immediately invite the most popular and responsible Indian leaders to form a Government. Thereafter the Viceroy should arrange for direct elections to the provincial Legislatures and indirect elections to the Central Legislature from provincial Legislatures. . . .

". . . it was a calumny to say that Mr. Jinnah and the League wanted partition of the country today. What Mr. Jinnah wanted was that in a postwar decision that issue should not be prejudged. It would be open to the provisional Government which he proposed to give such an assurance in the clearest possible terms. . . . The Viceroy should select for the Government five Congress men whom the Viceroy thought would be likely to head the poll at the election — including persons now in prison — and ask Mr. Jinnah to join the Government with as many men of his choice as he liked. . . . The Congress Party and Moslem League nominees should add to themselves, say, three persons representative of any important interests left out. . . .

". . . The Viceroy could easily envisage the kind of Legislature that the Government would have to face, and could make his selection accordingly. If the Government did not get the confidence of the Legislature, the Viceroy, acting for the Crown, could dismiss the one or dissolve the other.

". . . Britain's temporary hold on India today was, by its own admission, only for the purpose of the war, and should therefore be exercised in such a way as to help the war. . . ." [22]

April 2, 1943. — Letter to American Defense, Harvard Group, by Sumner Welles, Under Secretary of State:

" You also mention our ' failure to mediate in Indian affairs ' as a criticism of the Department of State. The present military situation in the Far East is one in which all of us, including the people of India, face grave perils. The future constitutional status of India is a tremendously complicated and delicate problem. The United States Government is, of course, anxious to give full assistance to its solution. The people of India have been most solemnly assured that as soon as the necessities of war permit they will be given the opportunity to choose freely the form of government they desire. Wise men, vitally concerned both with the welfare of the people of India and with the defeat of our enemies, may differ as to the possibility of fighting the war and solving India's historic problems at the same time. But to make active intervention in the Indian situation a test of liberalism, as some have done, presupposes a definition of liberalism which, I must confess, is beyond my comprehension." [23]

[21] As reported in *The Times*, London, October 9, 1942.
[22] As reported in *The Times*, London, October 22, 1942.
[23] U. S. State Department *Bulletin*, Vol. VIII, No. 199, April 17, 1943.

Index